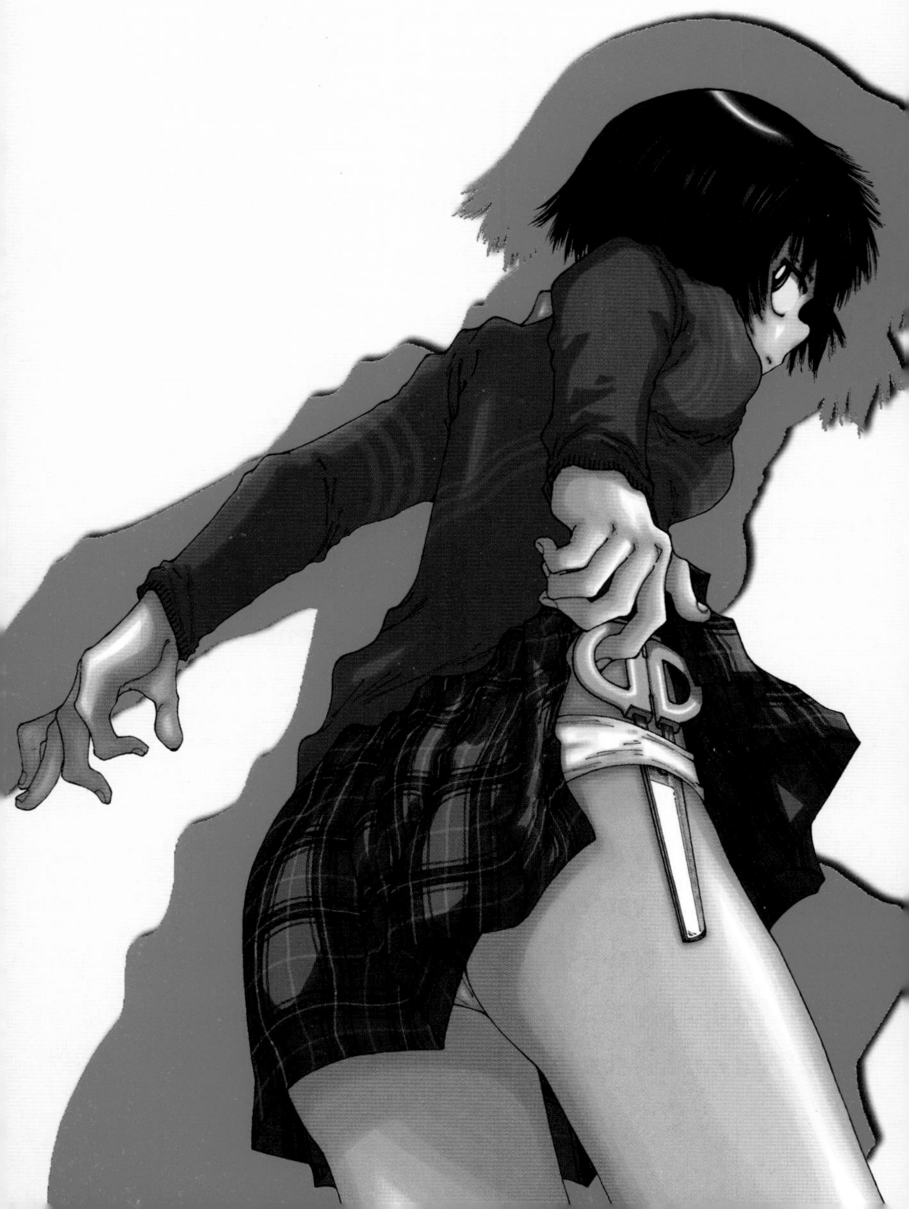

CONTENTS

VERTICAL COMICS

MYSTERIOUS GIRLFRIEND X
3

RIICHI UESHIBA

MYSTERIOUS GIRLFRIEND X

Characters

Akira Tsubaki (17)

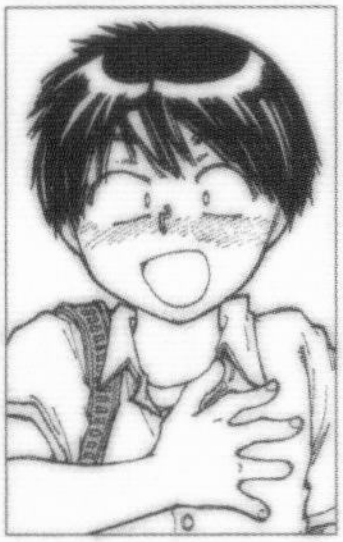

The protagonist of the story. His bizarre relationship with Urabe began after he licked her drool one day. He is as interested in girls as any boy his age, but Urabe takes the lead in their relationship and Tsubaki can't seem to initiate any progress between them.

Mikoto Urabe (17)

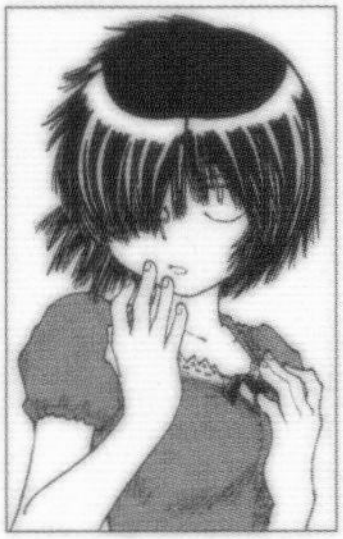

A transfer student who joined Tsubaki's class. She can convey her own feelings through her drool, as well as pick up on Tsubaki's feelings through his. She's antisocial and everything she says and does is mysterious, but her ideas about love are very pure. Her hobby is using scissors, which she can use to cut up anything.

Ayuko Oka (17)

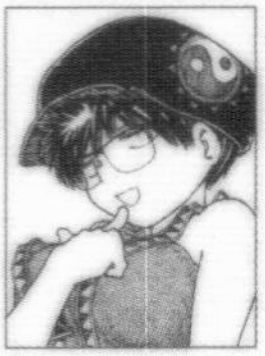

At 4'8", she's very small, but her figure is well-developed and quite gorgeous. Tsubaki spotted her kissing Ueno in the classroom after school, but she's not too bothered by it. Like Tsubaki, she is responsive to Urabe's drool.

Kouhei Ueno (17)

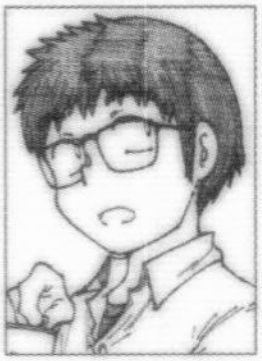

Tsubaki's best friend.
He's been going out with their classmate, Oka, since they were sophomores. Ueno's fond way of talking about Oka frequently influences Tsubaki's ideas about relationships.

Aika Hayakawa (17)

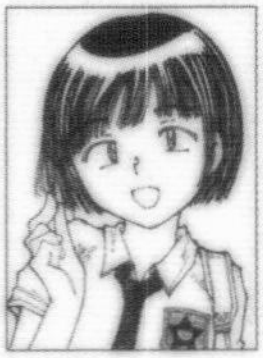

Tsubaki's former classmate, whom he had a crush on in middle school. She now attends the prestigious Hoshinome Girls' Academy. Though she is a typical young beauty, her sense of values is slightly off.

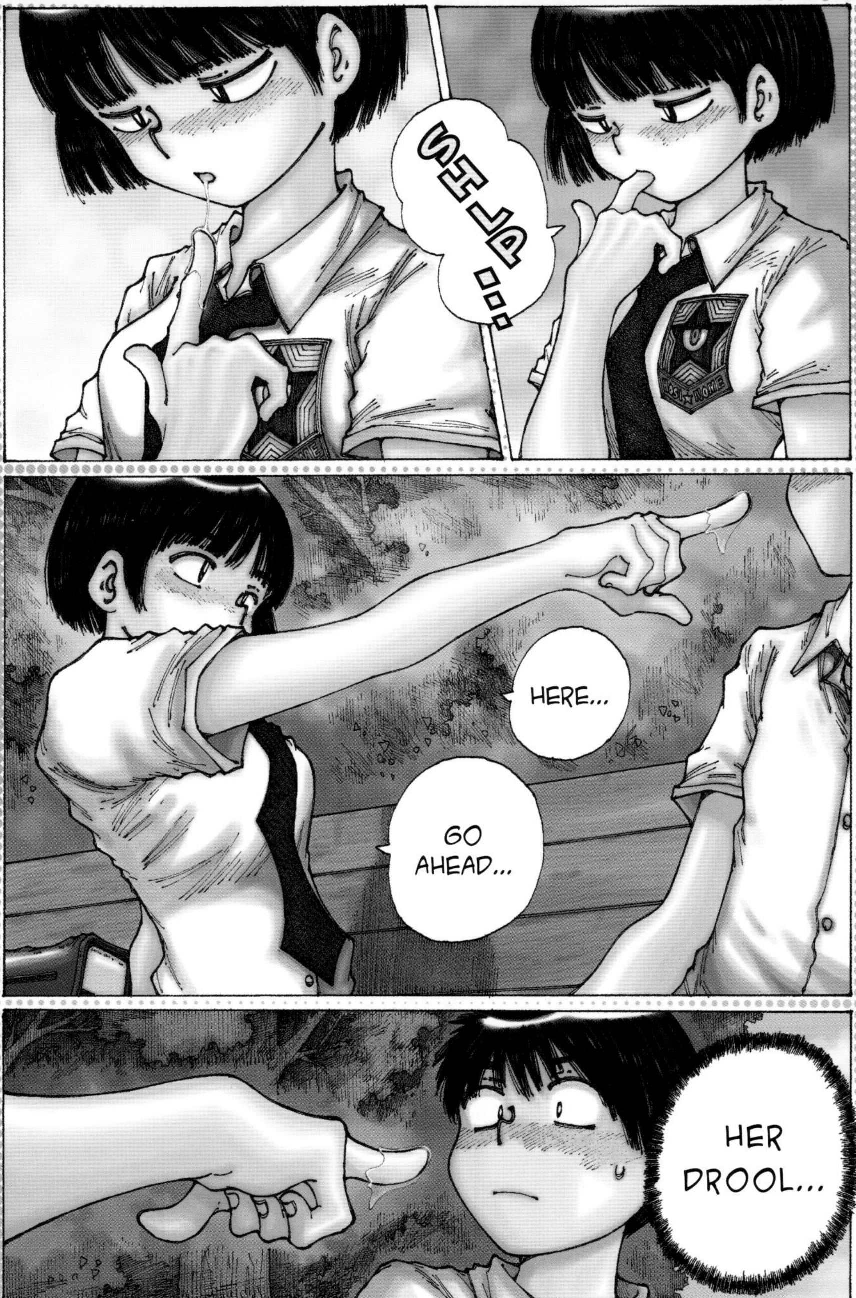
SHLP...
HERE...
GO AHEAD...
HER DROOL...

CHAPTER 29: MYSTERIOUS LETTER OF CHALLENGE

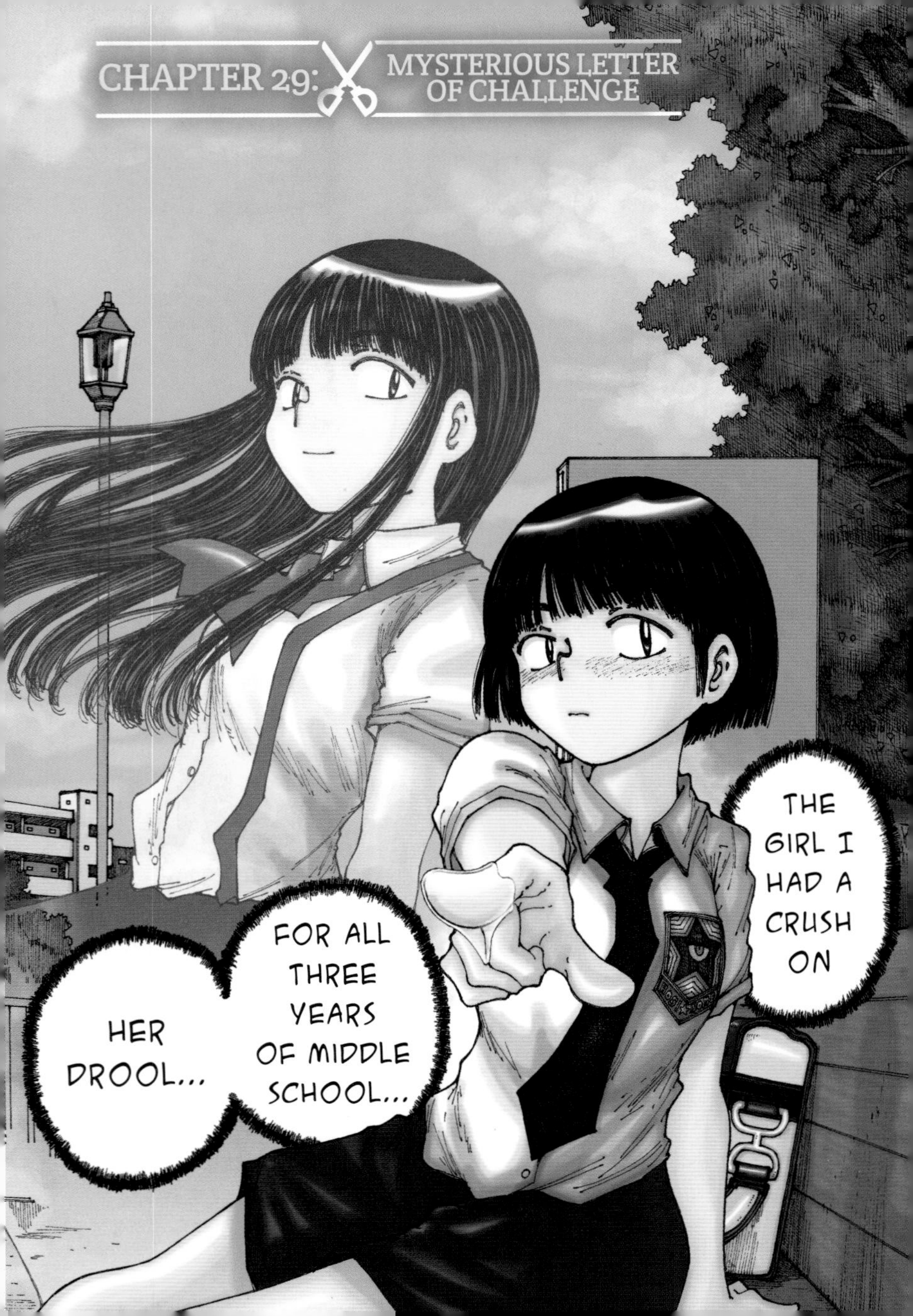
THE GIRL I HAD A CRUSH ON
FOR ALL THREE YEARS OF MIDDLE SCHOOL...
HER DROOL...

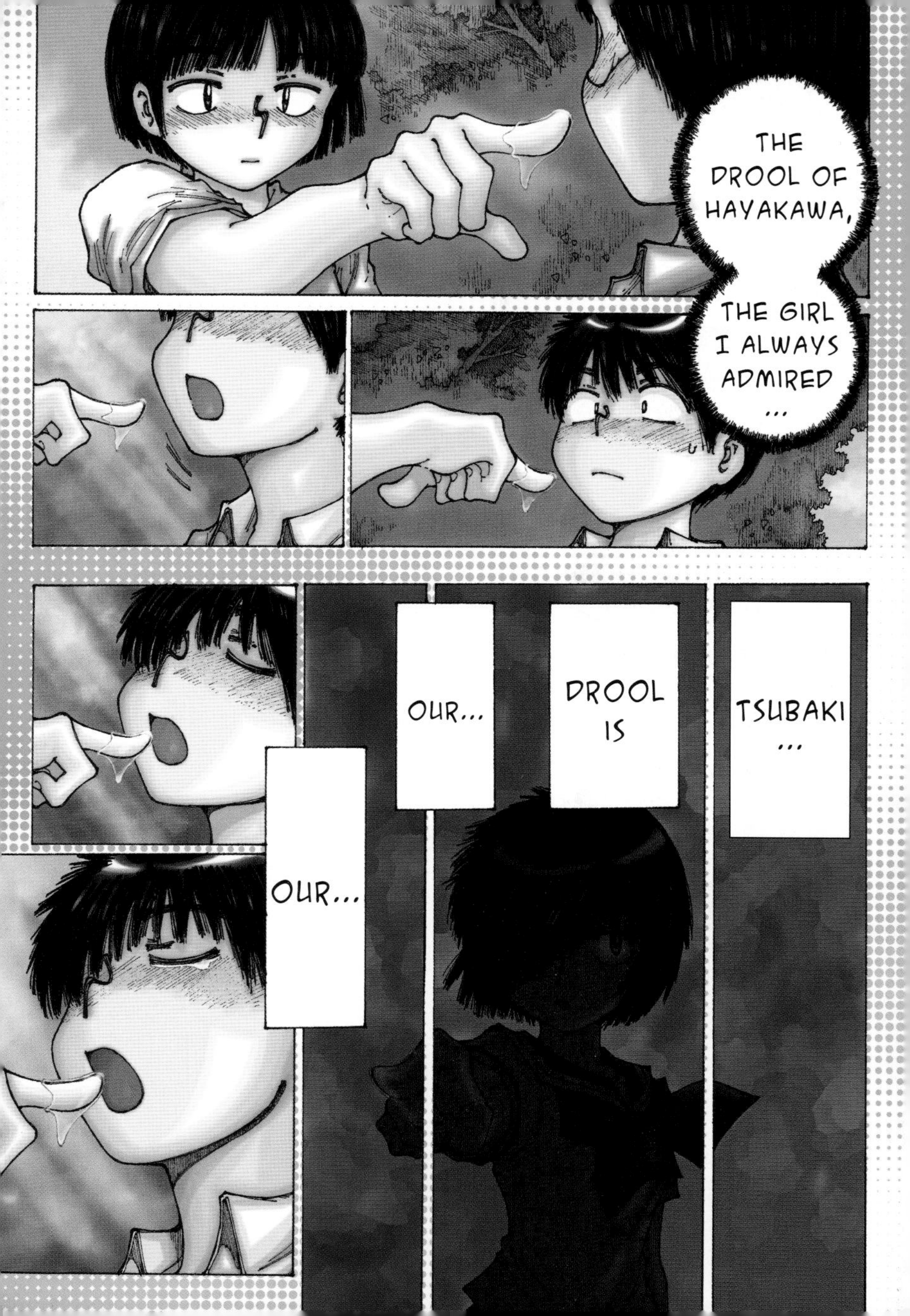
THE DROOL OF HAYAKAWA,
THE GIRL I ALWAYS ADMIRED ...
TSUBAKI ...
DROOL IS
OUR...
OUR...

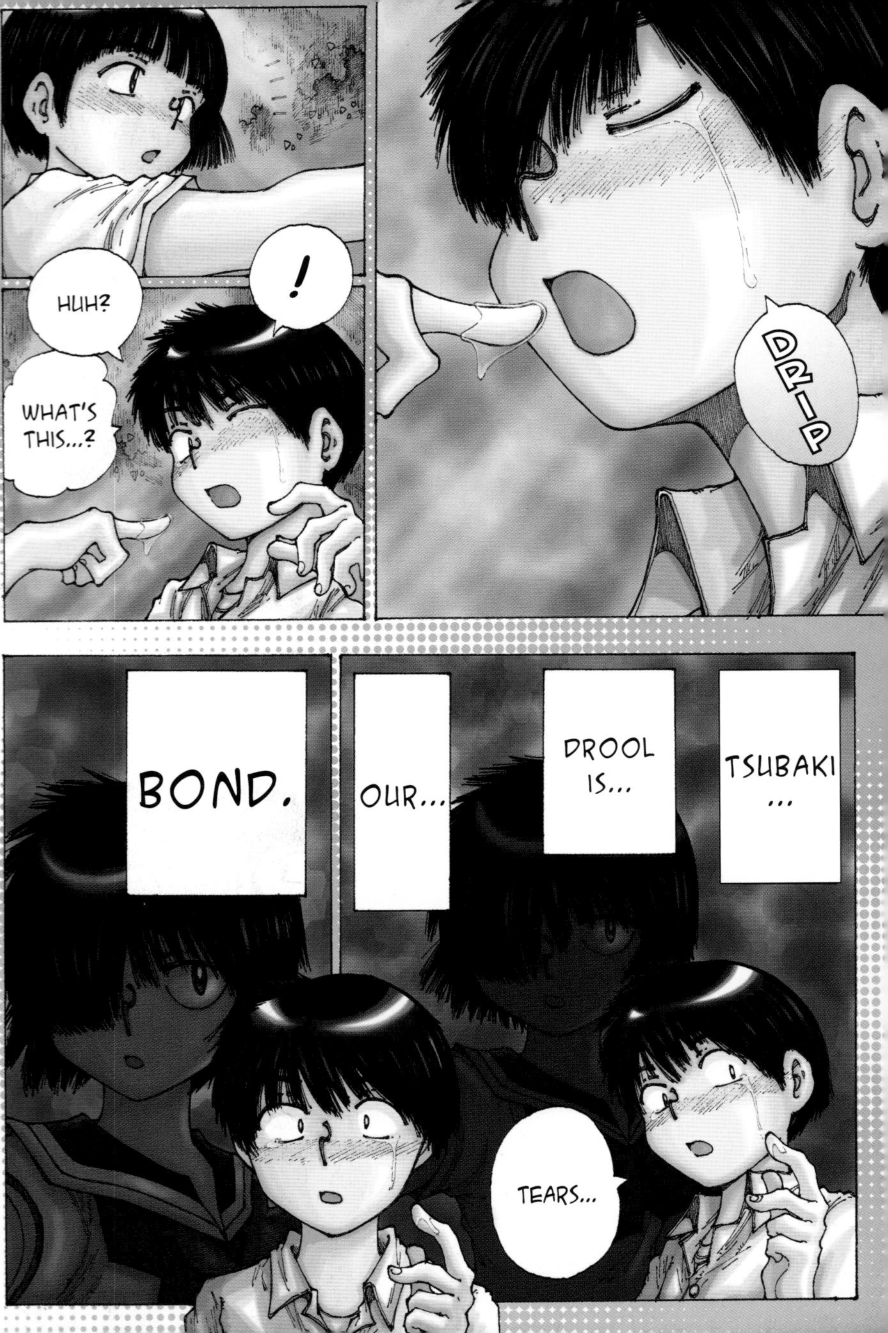
DRIP
!
HUH?
WHAT'S THIS...?
TSUBAKI...
DROOL IS...
OUR...
TEARS...
BOND.

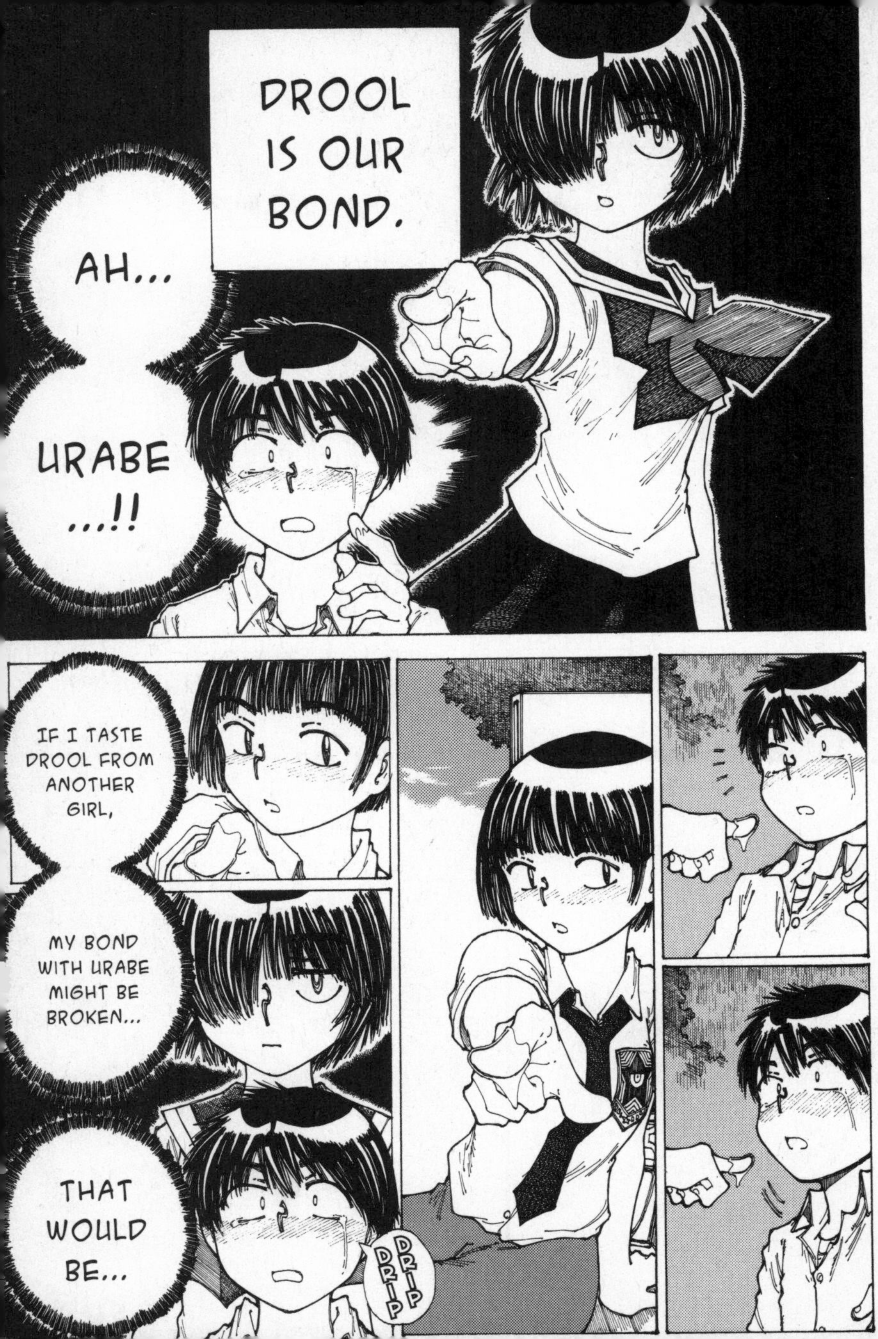
DROOL IS OUR BOND.
AH... URABE ...!!
IF I TASTE DROOL FROM ANOTHER GIRL,
MY BOND WITH URABE MIGHT BE BROKEN...
THAT WOULD BE...
DRIP DRIP

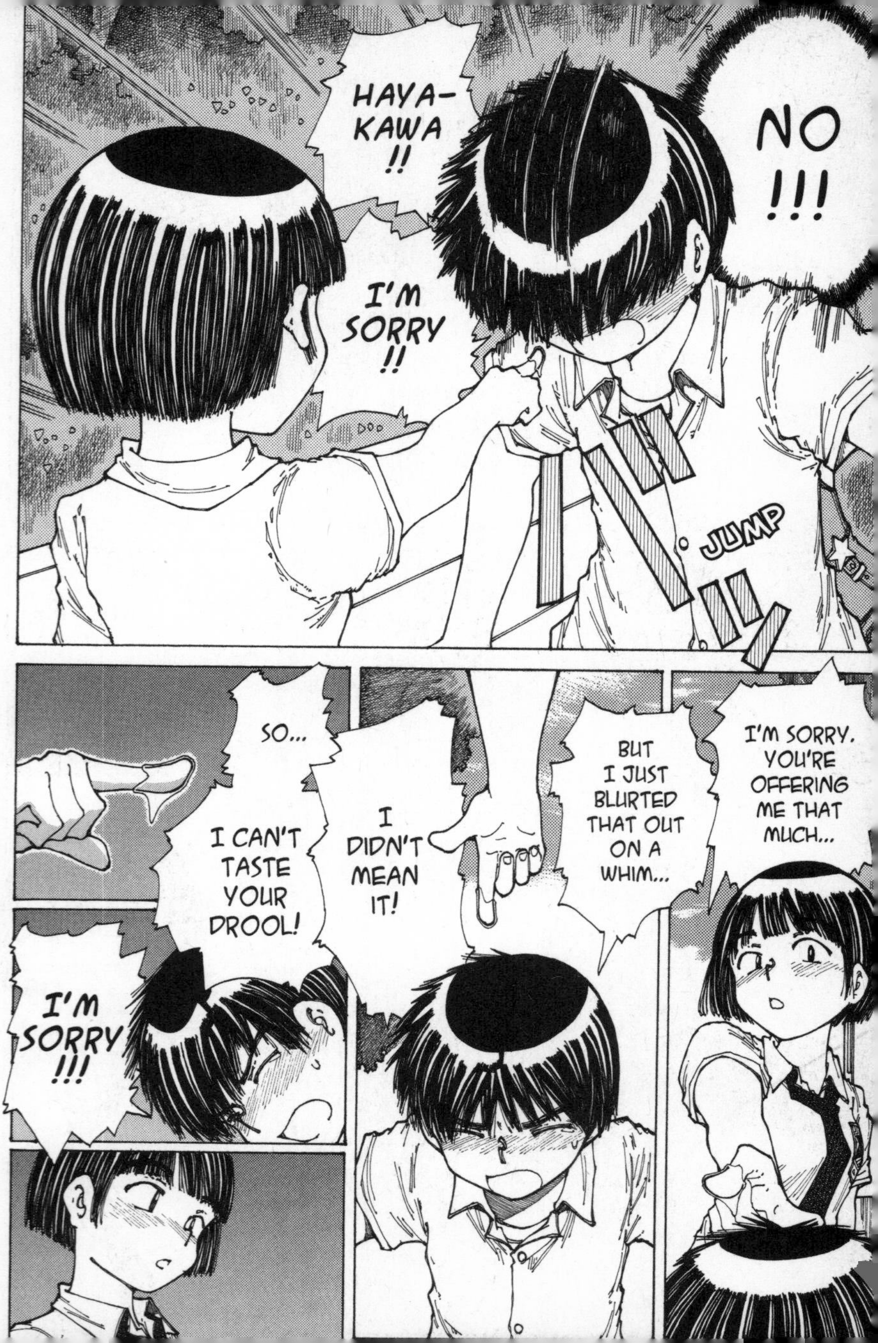
NO!!!
HAYA-KAWA!!
I'M SORRY!!
JUMP
I'M SORRY. YOU'RE OFFERING ME THAT MUCH...
BUT I JUST BLURTED THAT OUT ON A WHIM...
I DIDN'T MEAN IT!
SO...
I CAN'T TASTE YOUR DROOL!
I'M SORRY!!!

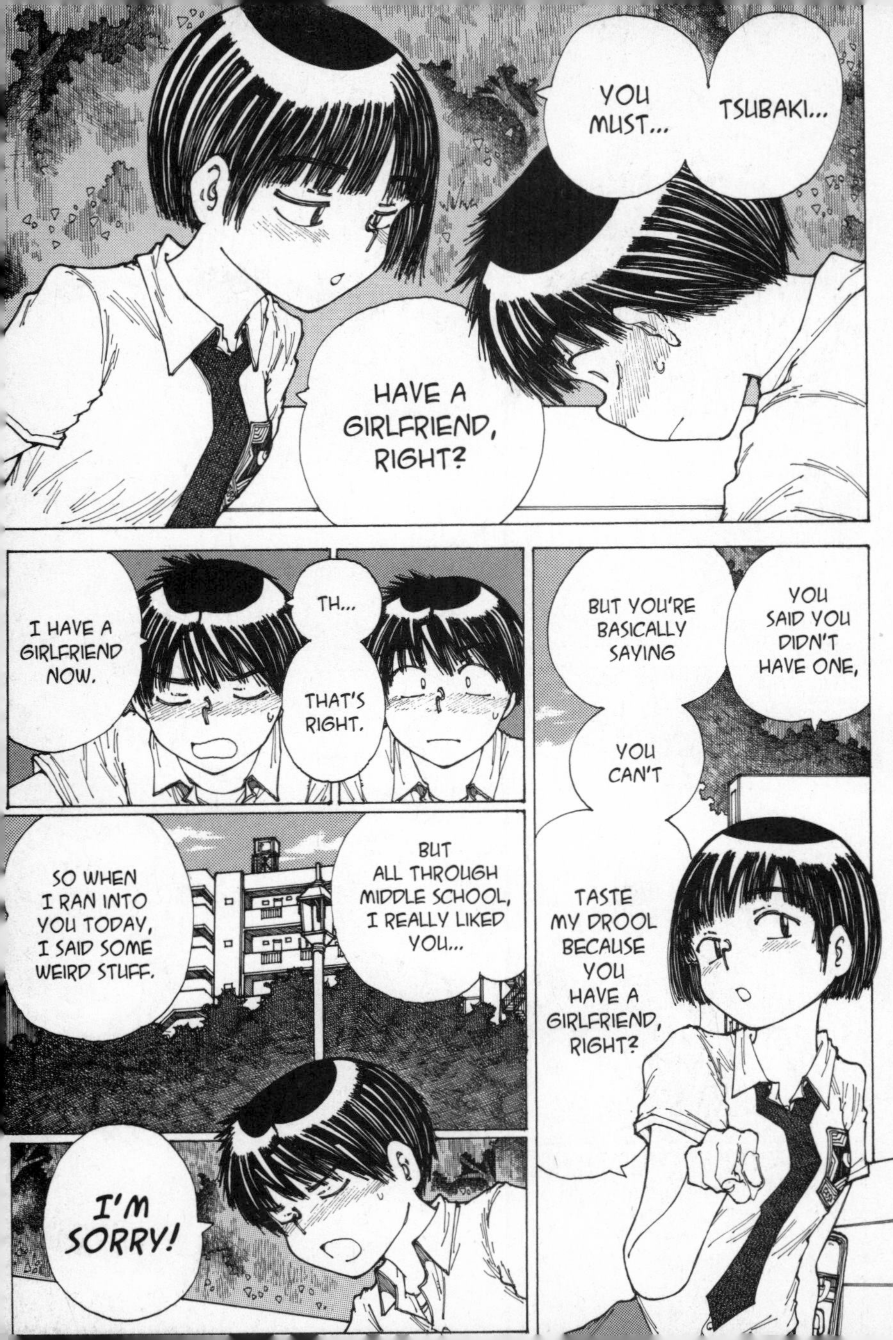
TSUBAKI...
YOU MUST...
HAVE A GIRLFRIEND, RIGHT?
YOU SAID YOU DIDN'T HAVE ONE,
BUT YOU'RE BASICALLY SAYING
YOU CAN'T
TASTE MY DROOL BECAUSE YOU HAVE A GIRLFRIEND, RIGHT?
TH...
THAT'S RIGHT.
I HAVE A GIRLFRIEND NOW.
BUT ALL THROUGH MIDDLE SCHOOL, I REALLY LIKED YOU...
SO WHEN I RAN INTO YOU TODAY, I SAID SOME WEIRD STUFF.
I'M SORRY!

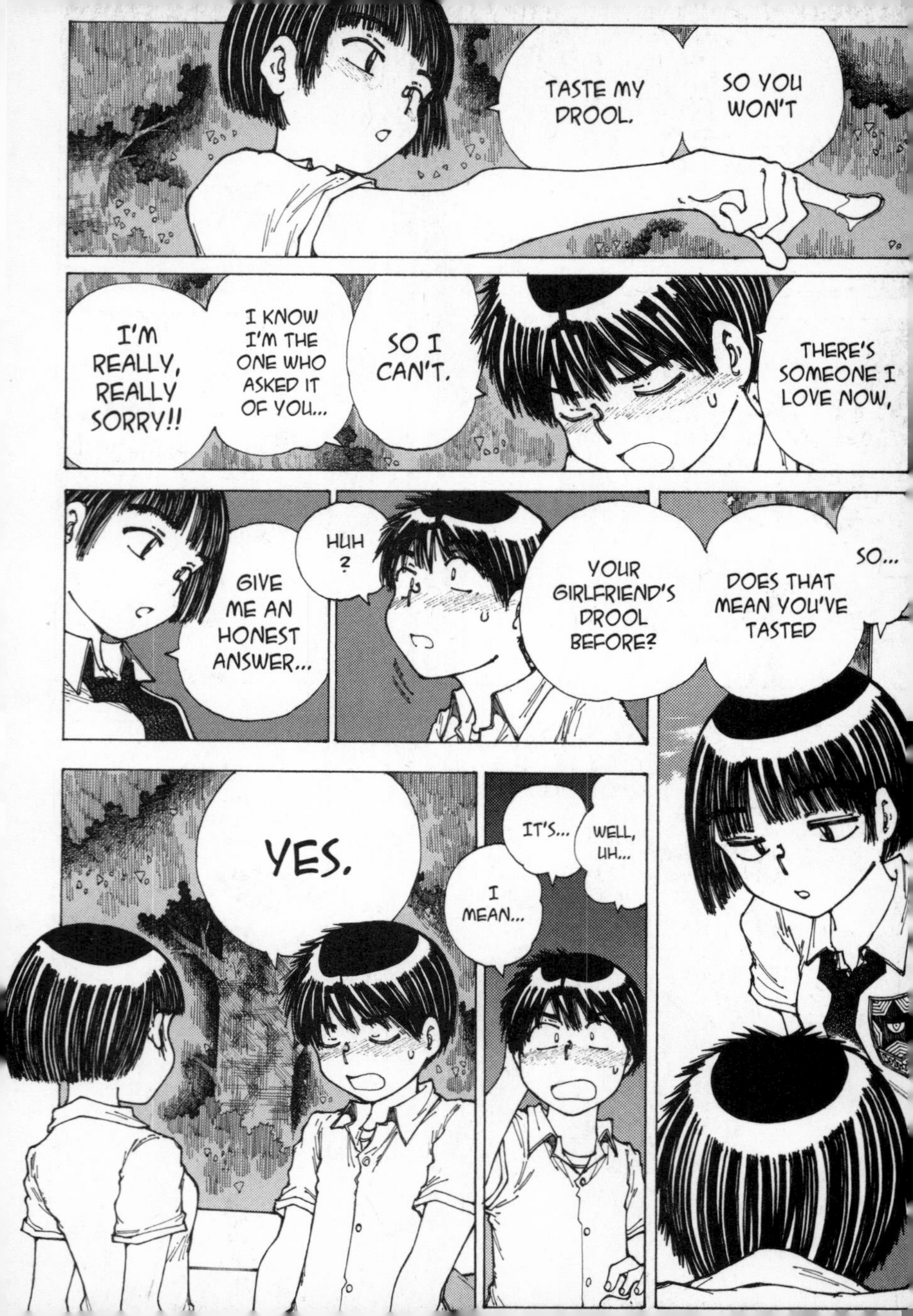
SO YOU WON'T
TASTE MY DROOL.
THERE'S SOMEONE I LOVE NOW,
SO I CAN'T.
I KNOW I'M THE ONE WHO ASKED IT OF YOU...
I'M REALLY, REALLY SORRY!!
SO...
DOES THAT MEAN YOU'VE TASTED
YOUR GIRLFRIEND'S DROOL BEFORE?
HUH?
GIVE ME AN HONEST ANSWER...
IT'S...
WELL, UH...
I MEAN...
YES.

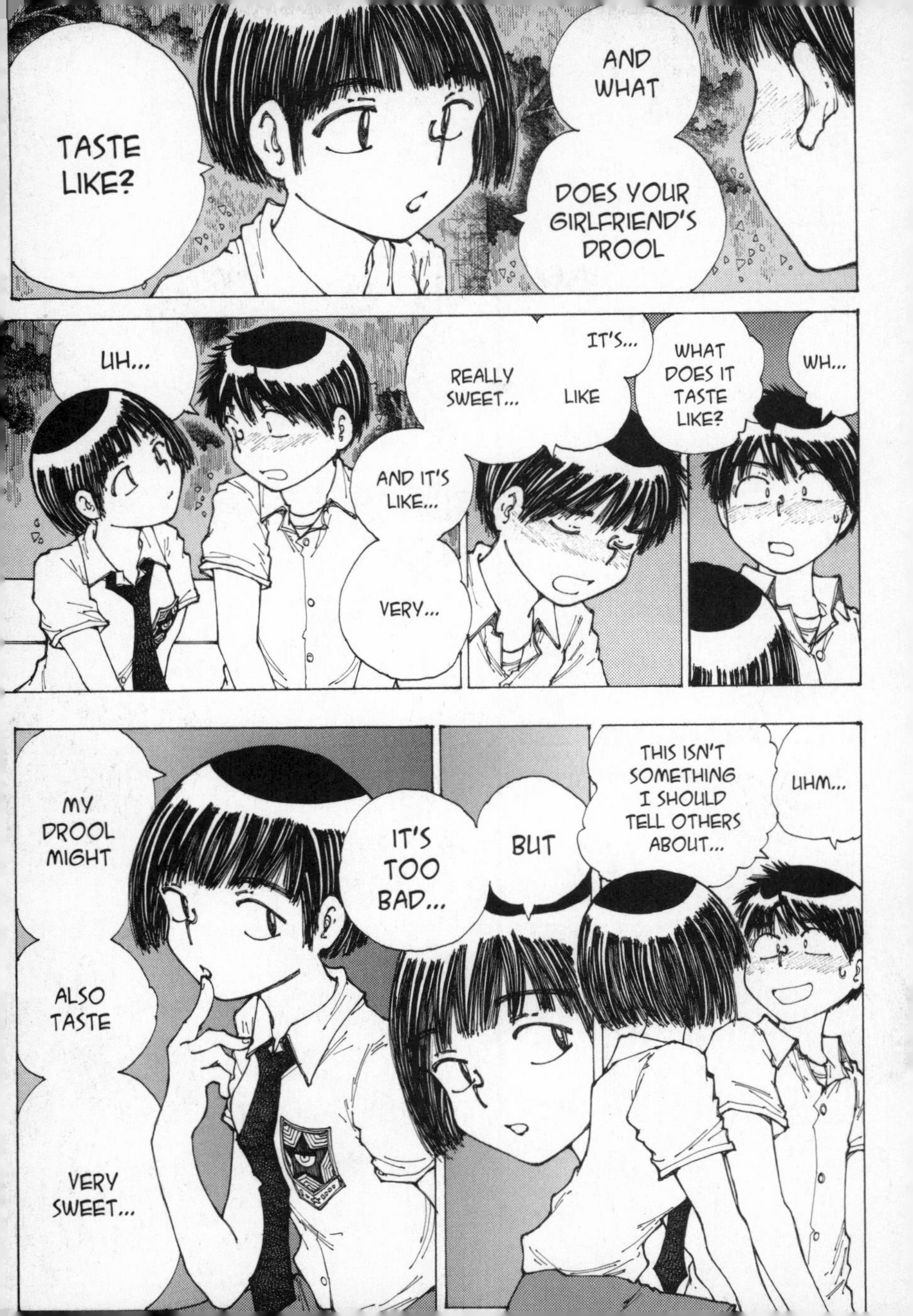
AND WHAT
DOES YOUR GIRLFRIEND'S DROOL
TASTE LIKE?
WH...
WHAT DOES IT TASTE LIKE?
IT'S...
LIKE
REALLY SWEET...
AND IT'S LIKE...
VERY...
UH...
UHM...
THIS ISN'T SOMETHING I SHOULD TELL OTHERS ABOUT...
BUT
IT'S TOO BAD...
MY DROOL MIGHT
ALSO TASTE
VERY SWEET...

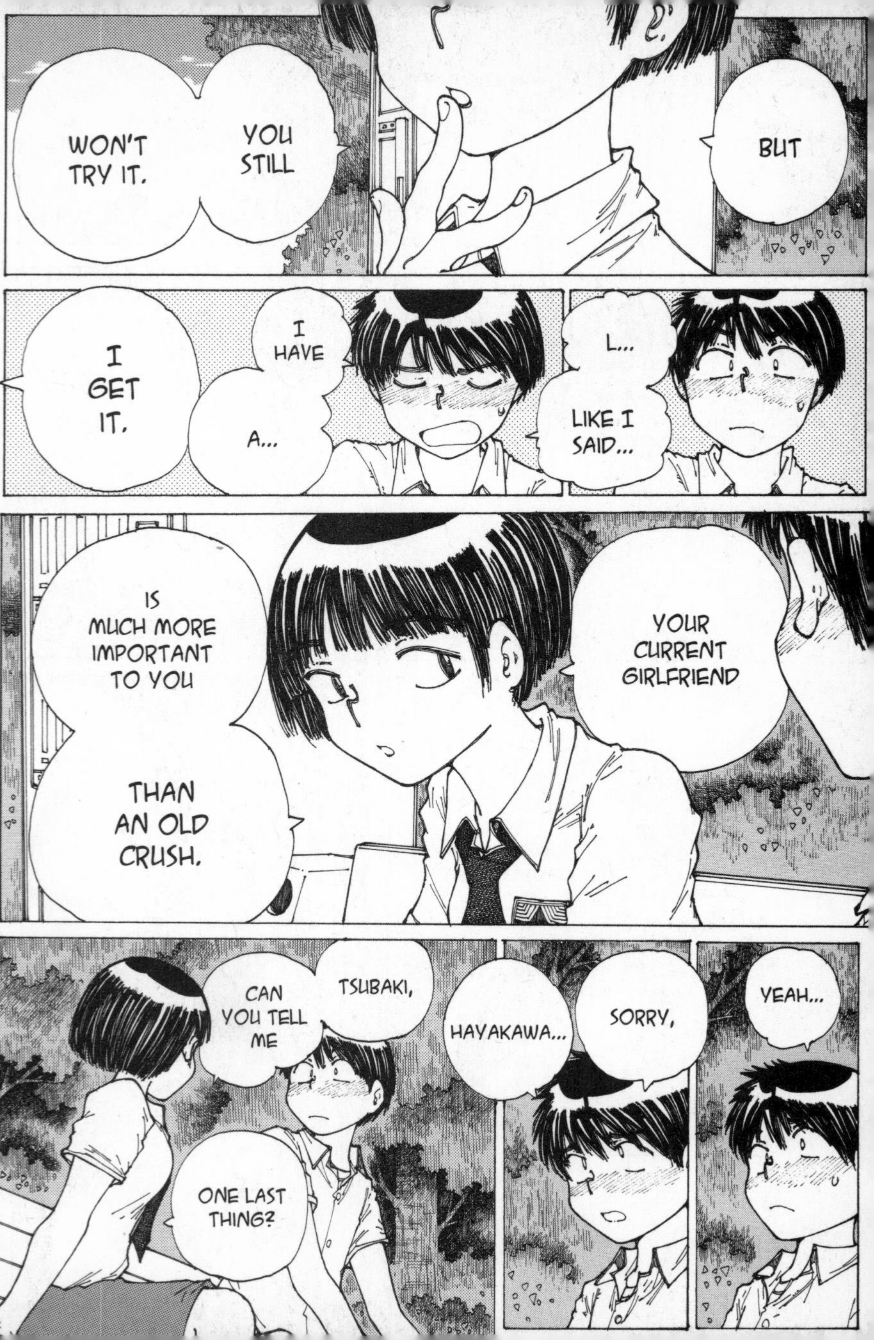
BUT
YOU STILL
WON'T TRY IT.
L...
LIKE I SAID...
I HAVE
A...
I GET IT.
YOUR CURRENT GIRLFRIEND
IS MUCH MORE IMPORTANT TO YOU
THAN AN OLD CRUSH.
YEAH...
SORRY,
HAYAKAWA...
TSUBAKI,
CAN YOU TELL ME
ONE LAST THING?

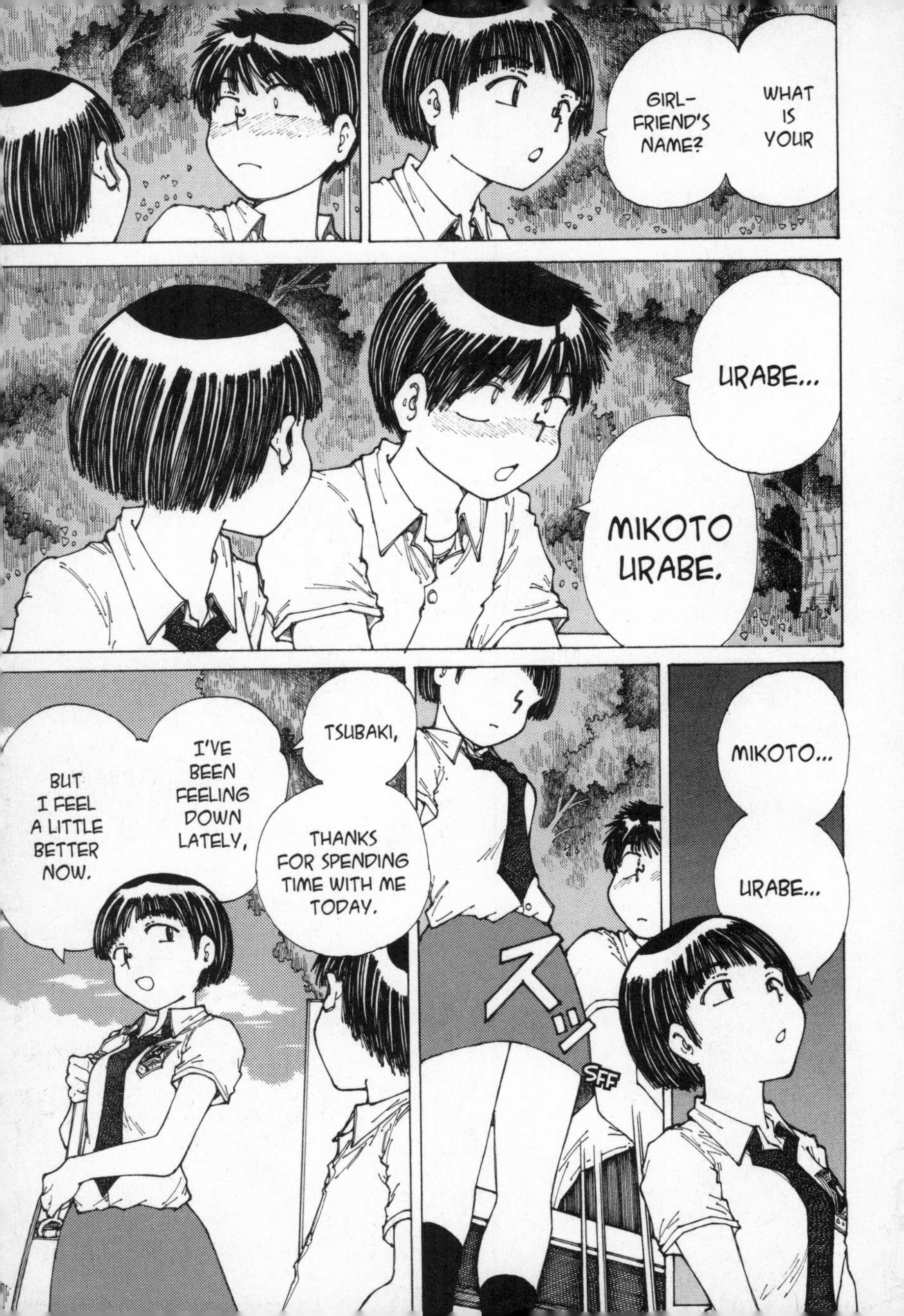
WHAT IS YOUR GIRL-FRIEND'S NAME?
URABE...
MIKOTO URABE.
MIKOTO...
URABE...
スッ
SFF
TSUBAKI,
THANKS FOR SPENDING TIME WITH ME TODAY.
I'VE BEEN FEELING DOWN LATELY,
BUT I FEEL A LITTLE BETTER NOW.

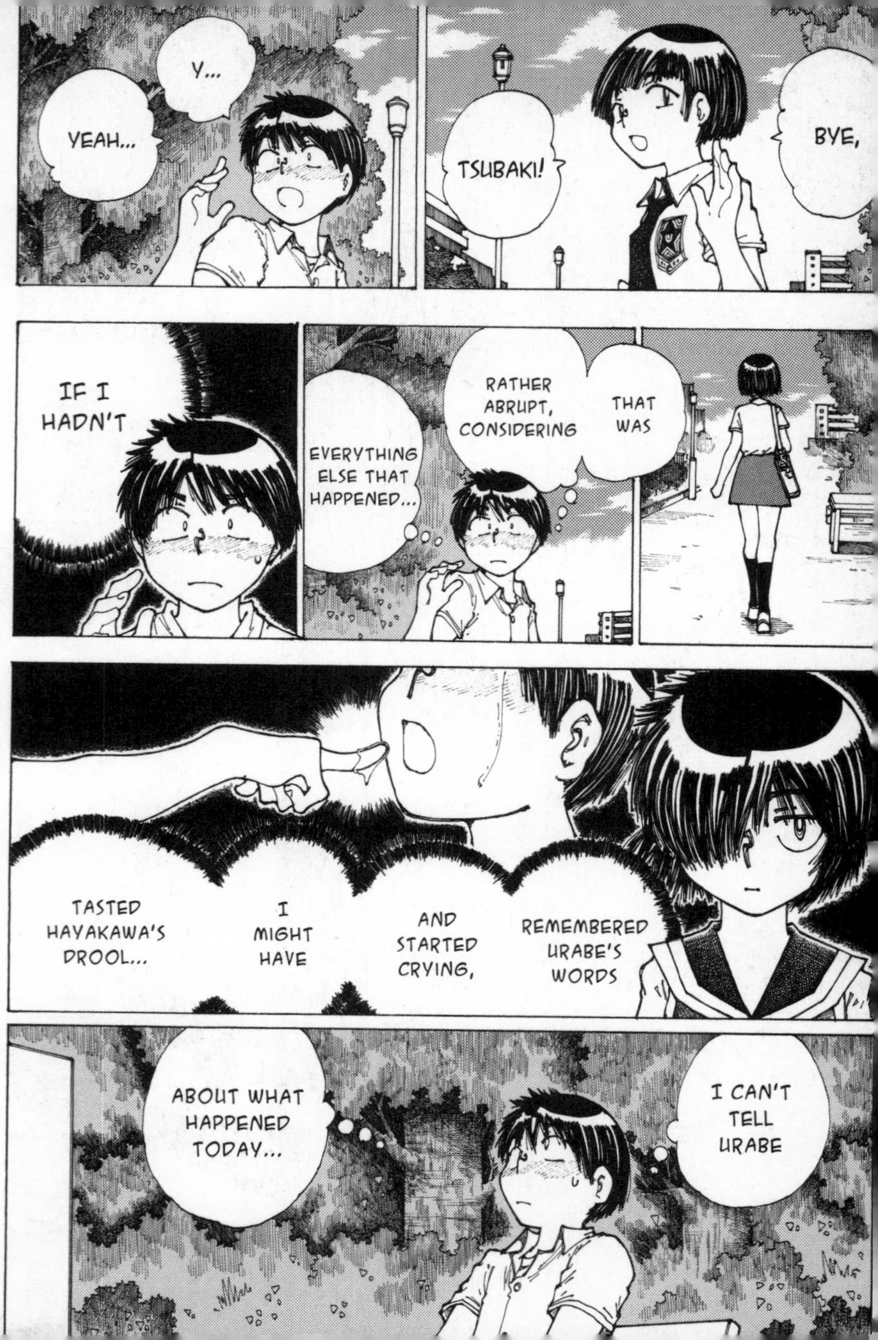
BYE,
TSUBAKI!
Y...
YEAH...
THAT WAS
RATHER ABRUPT, CONSIDERING
EVERYTHING ELSE THAT HAPPENED...
IF I HADN'T
REMEMBERED URABE'S WORDS
AND STARTED CRYING,
I MIGHT HAVE
TASTED HAYAKAWA'S DROOL...
I CAN'T TELL URABE
ABOUT WHAT HAPPENED TODAY...

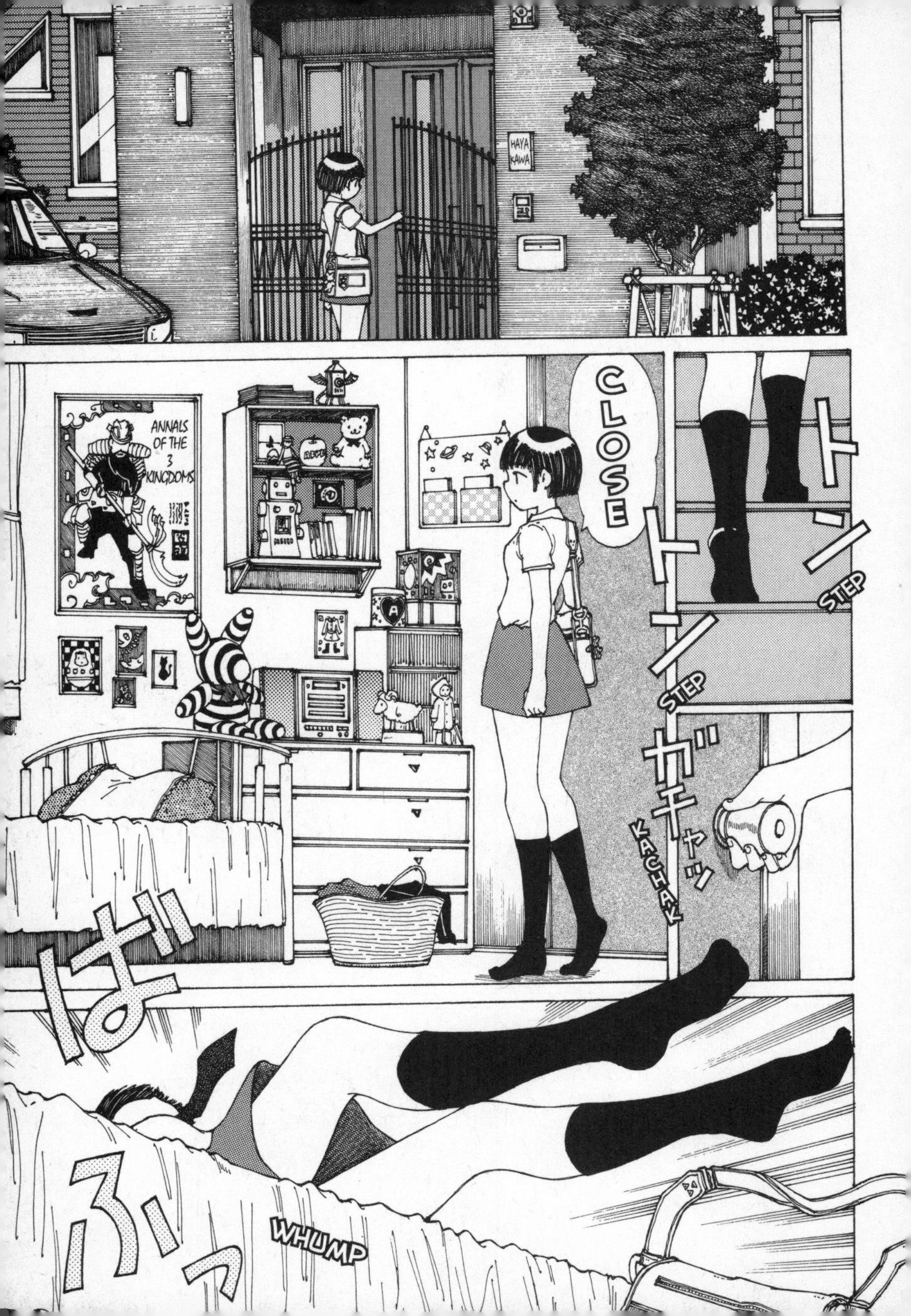
HAYA KAWA
トン
STEP
トン
STEP
ガチャッ
KACHAK
CLOSE
ANNALS OF THE 3 KINGDOMS
ばふっ
WHUMP

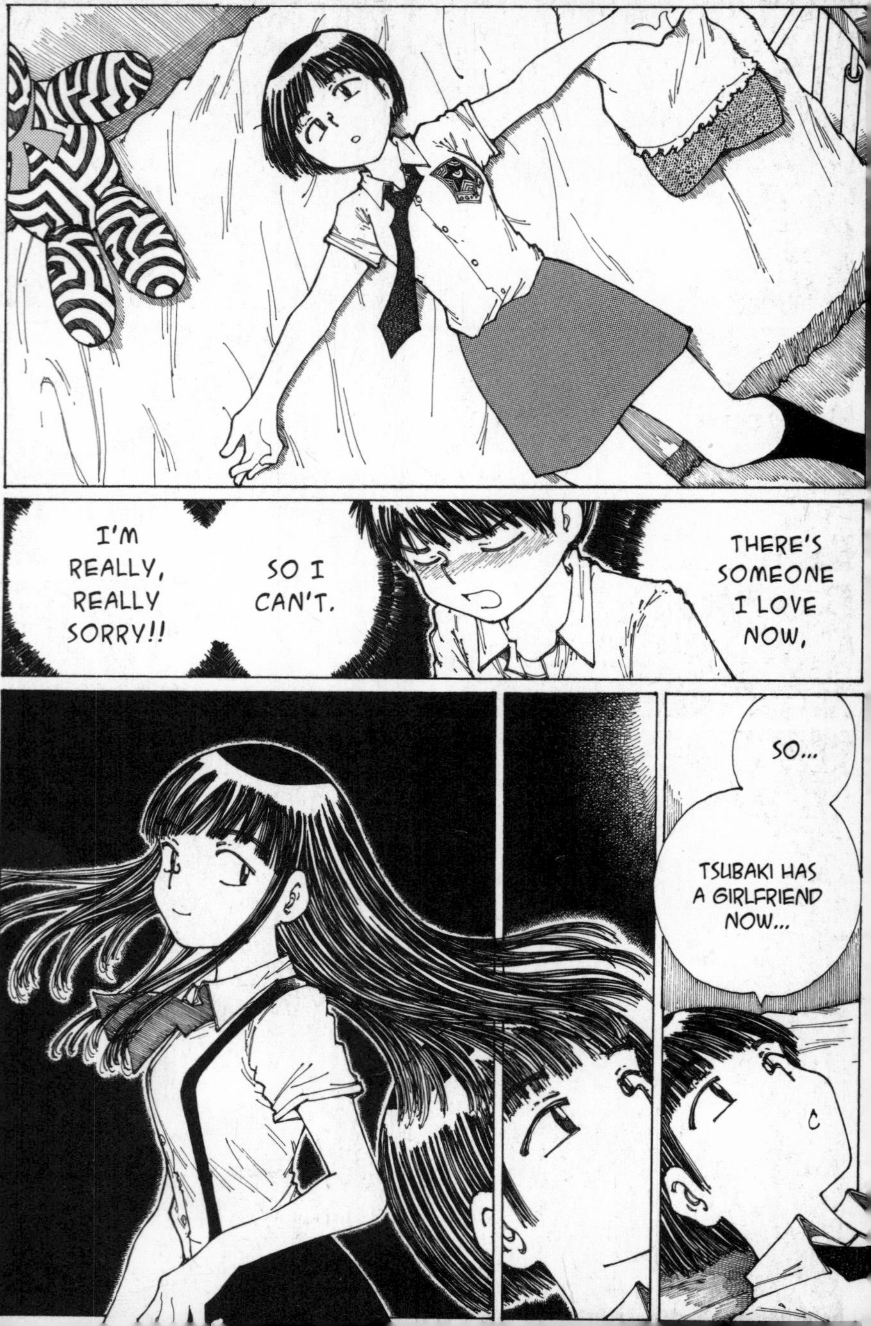
THERE'S SOMEONE I LOVE NOW,
SO I CAN'T.
I'M REALLY, REALLY SORRY!!
SO...
TSUBAKI HAS A GIRLFRIEND NOW...

SHLP

TASTE THIS...

TSUBAKI,

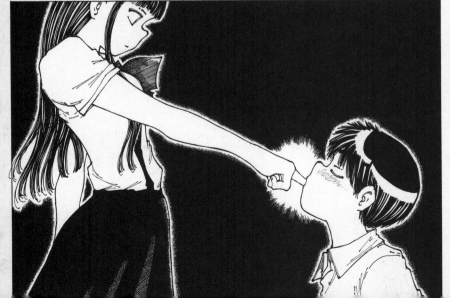

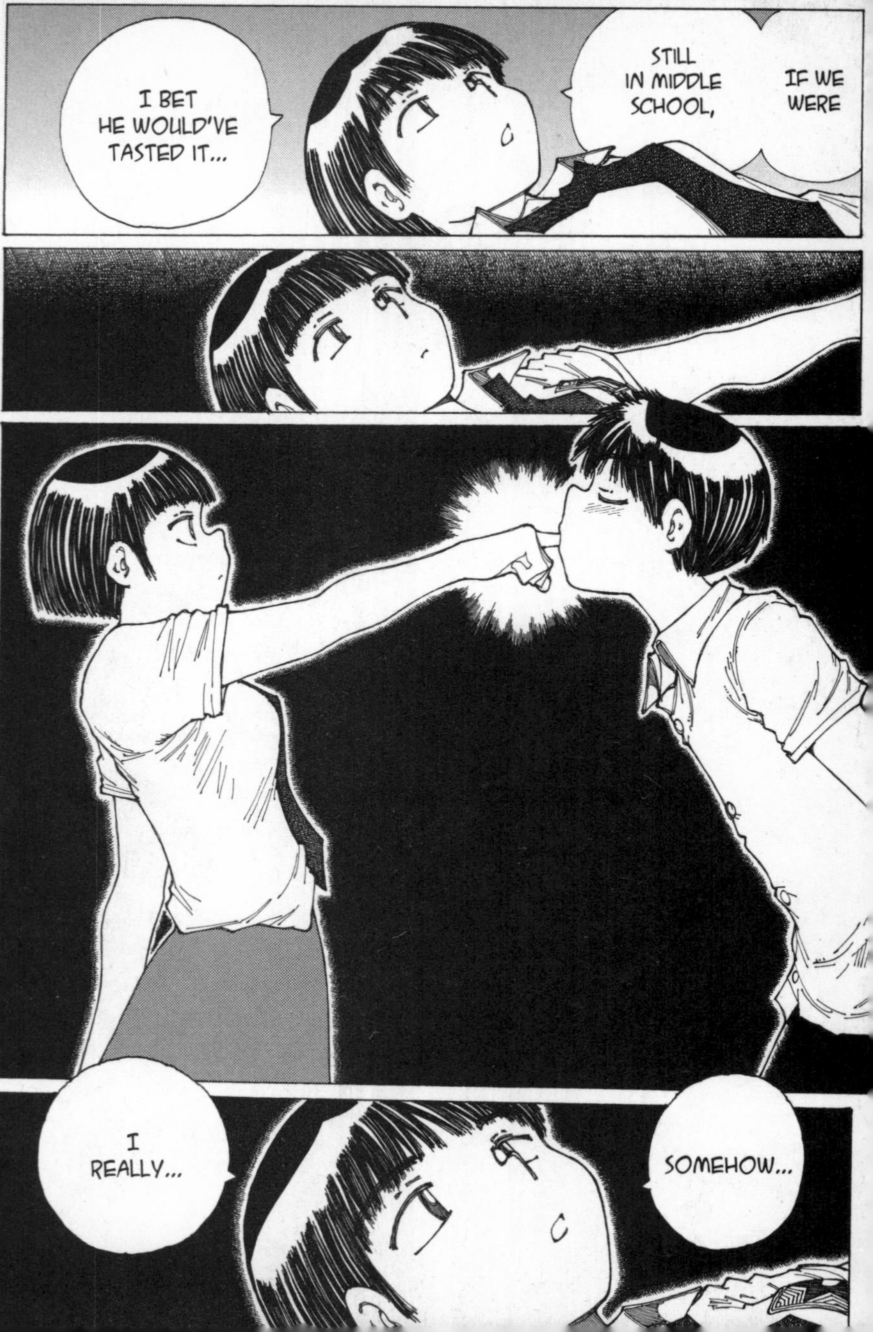
IF WE WERE STILL IN MIDDLE SCHOOL,
I BET HE WOULD'VE TASTED IT...
SOMEHOW...
I REALLY...

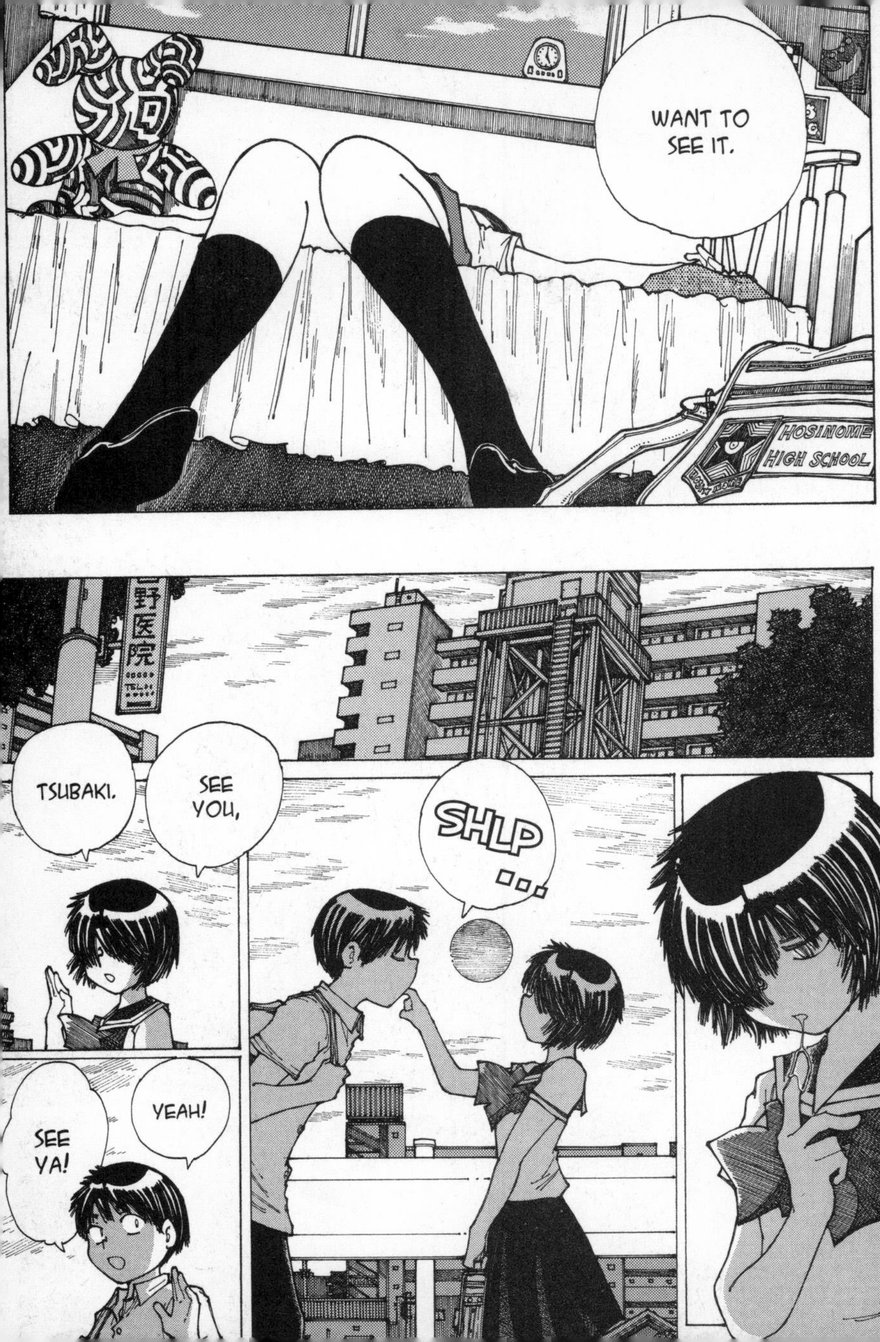
WANT TO SEE IT.
HOSINOME HIGH SCHOOL
野医院
SHLP ...
SEE YOU,
TSUBAKI.
YEAH!
SEE YA!

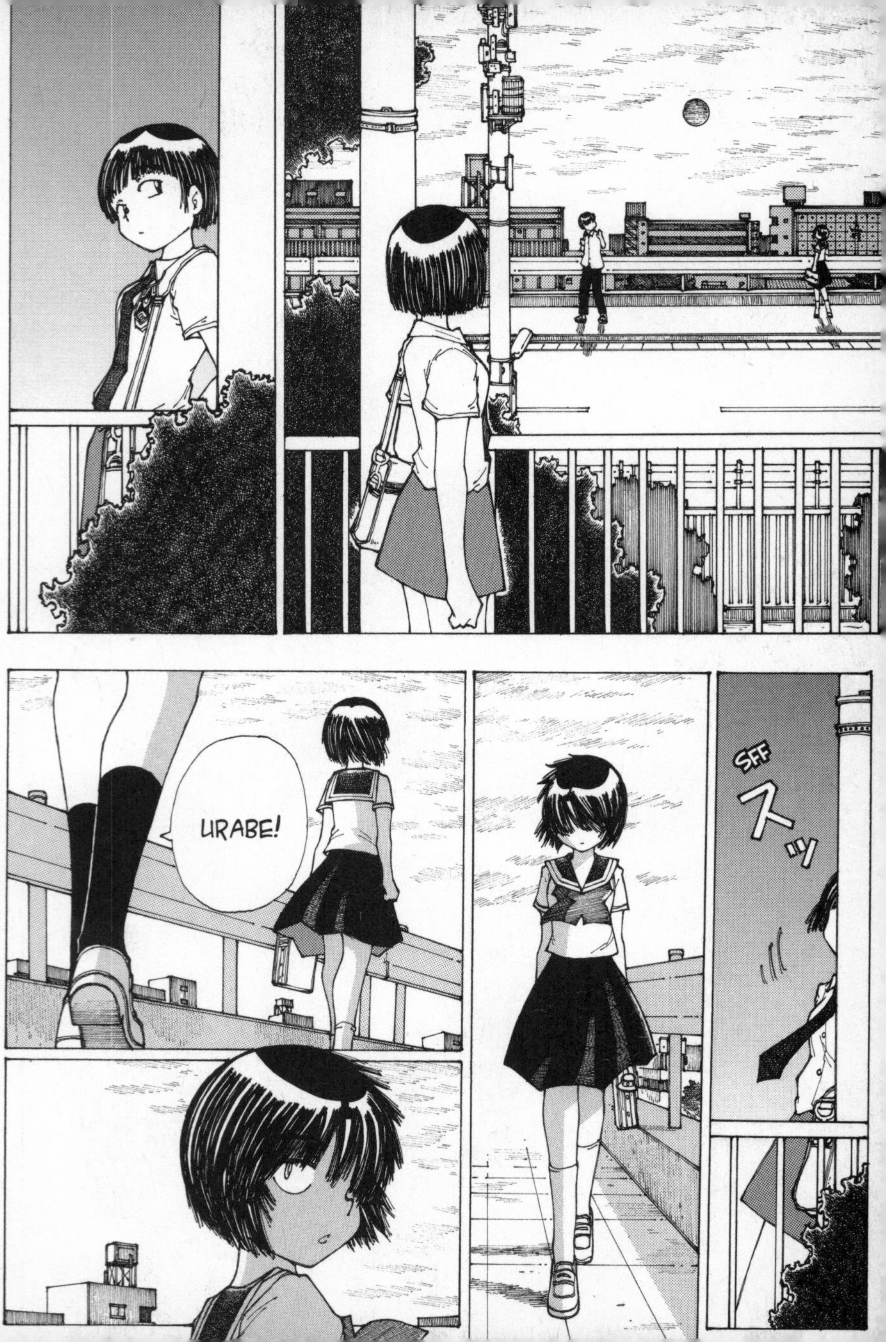
SFF
スッ
URABE!

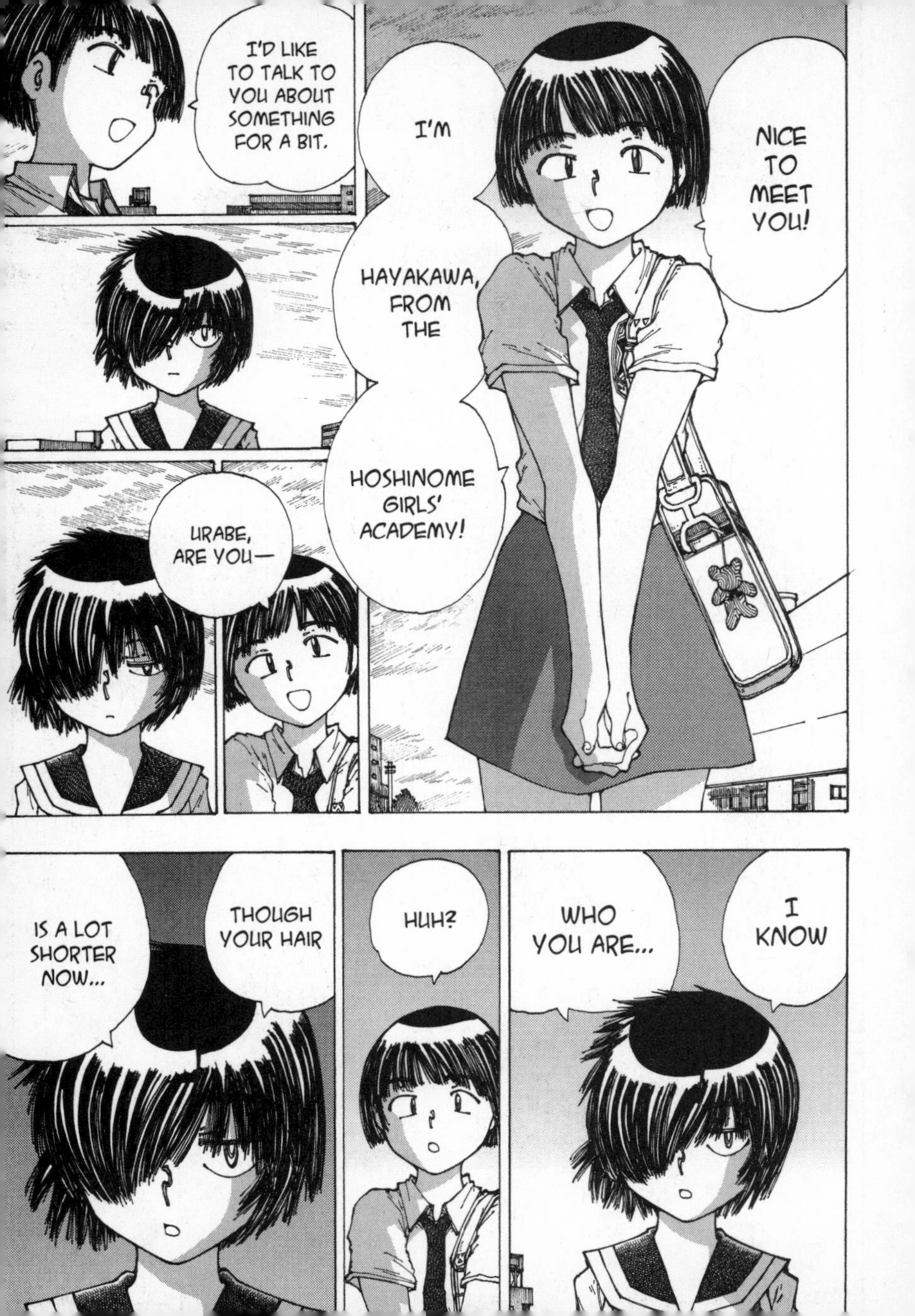
NICE TO MEET YOU!
I'M
HAYAKAWA, FROM THE
HOSHINOME GIRLS' ACADEMY!
I'D LIKE TO TALK TO YOU ABOUT SOMETHING FOR A BIT.
URABE, ARE YOU—
I KNOW
WHO YOU ARE...
HUH?
THOUGH YOUR HAIR
IS A LOT SHORTER NOW...

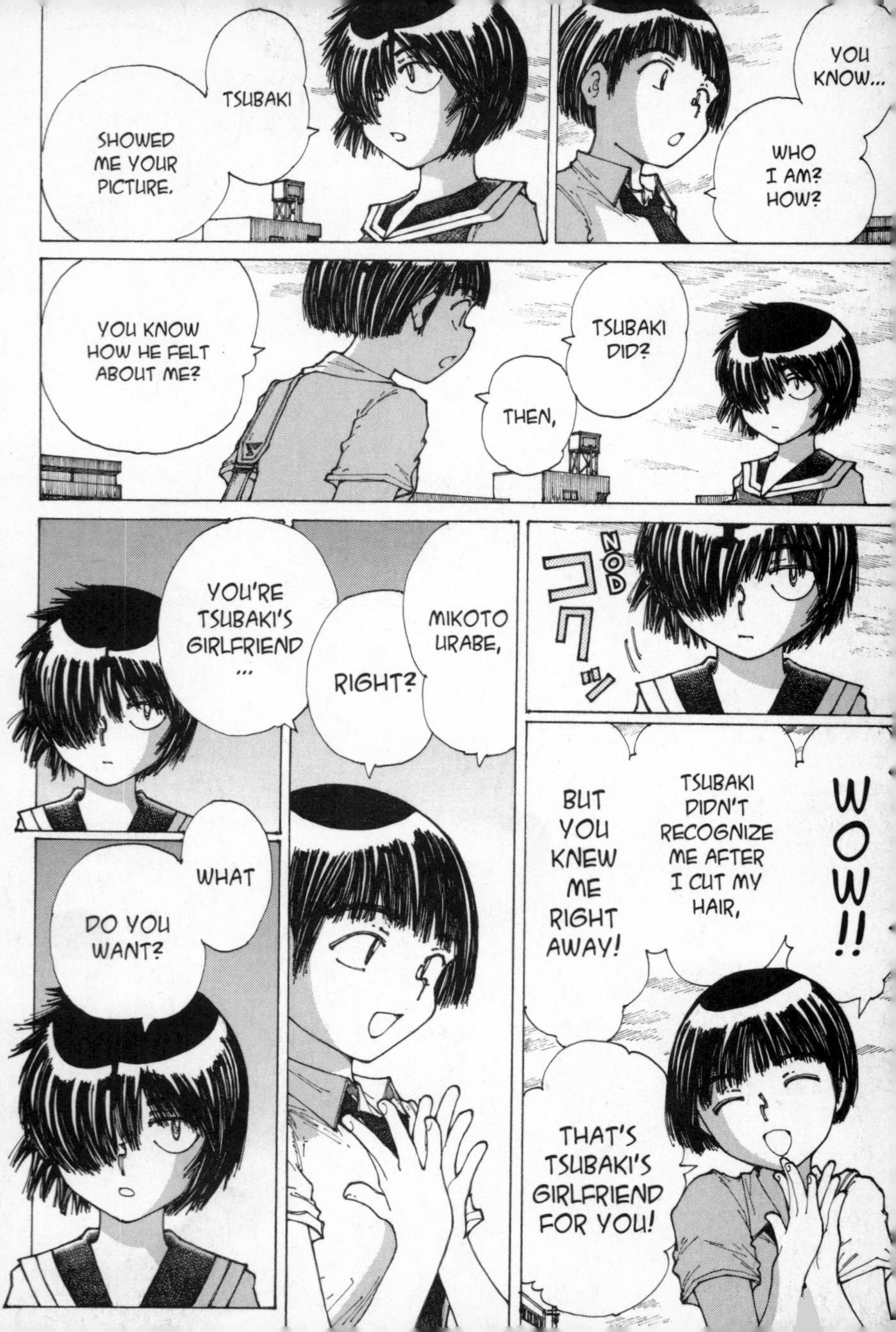
YOU KNOW...
WHO I AM? HOW?
TSUBAKI
SHOWED ME YOUR PICTURE.
TSUBAKI DID?
THEN,
YOU KNOW HOW HE FELT ABOUT ME?
NOD
WOW!!
TSUBAKI DIDN'T RECOGNIZE ME AFTER I CUT MY HAIR,
BUT YOU KNEW ME RIGHT AWAY!
THAT'S TSUBAKI'S GIRLFRIEND FOR YOU!
MIKOTO URABE,
RIGHT?
YOU'RE TSUBAKI'S GIRLFRIEND ...
WHAT
DO YOU WANT?

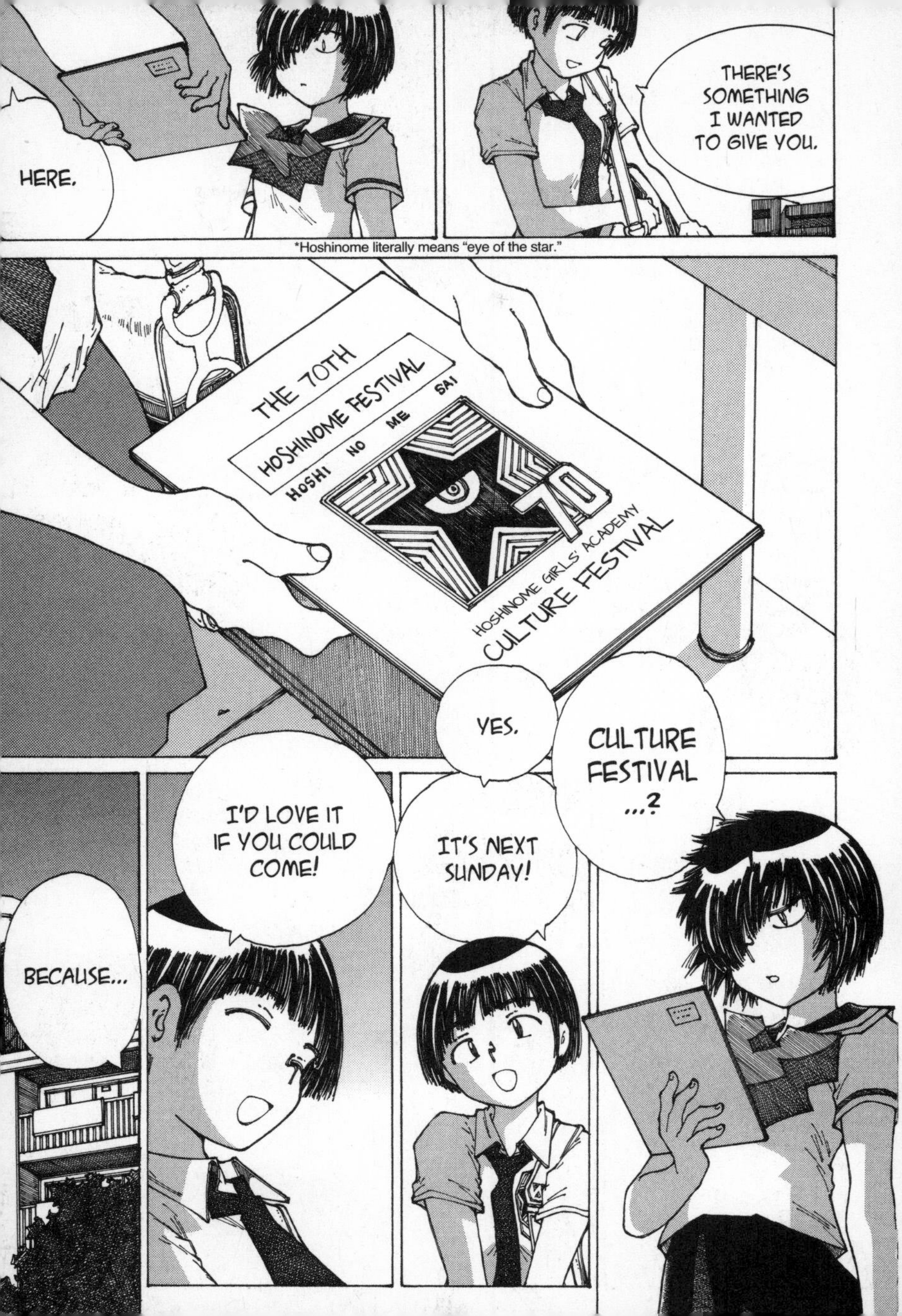
THERE'S SOMETHING I WANTED TO GIVE YOU.
HERE.
THE 70TH
HOSHINOME FESTIVAL
HOSHI NO ME SAI
70
HOSHINOME GIRLS' ACADEMY
CULTURE FESTIVAL
CULTURE FESTIVAL ...?
YES.
IT'S NEXT SUNDAY!
I'D LOVE IT IF YOU COULD COME!
BECAUSE...
*Hoshinome literally means "eye of the star."

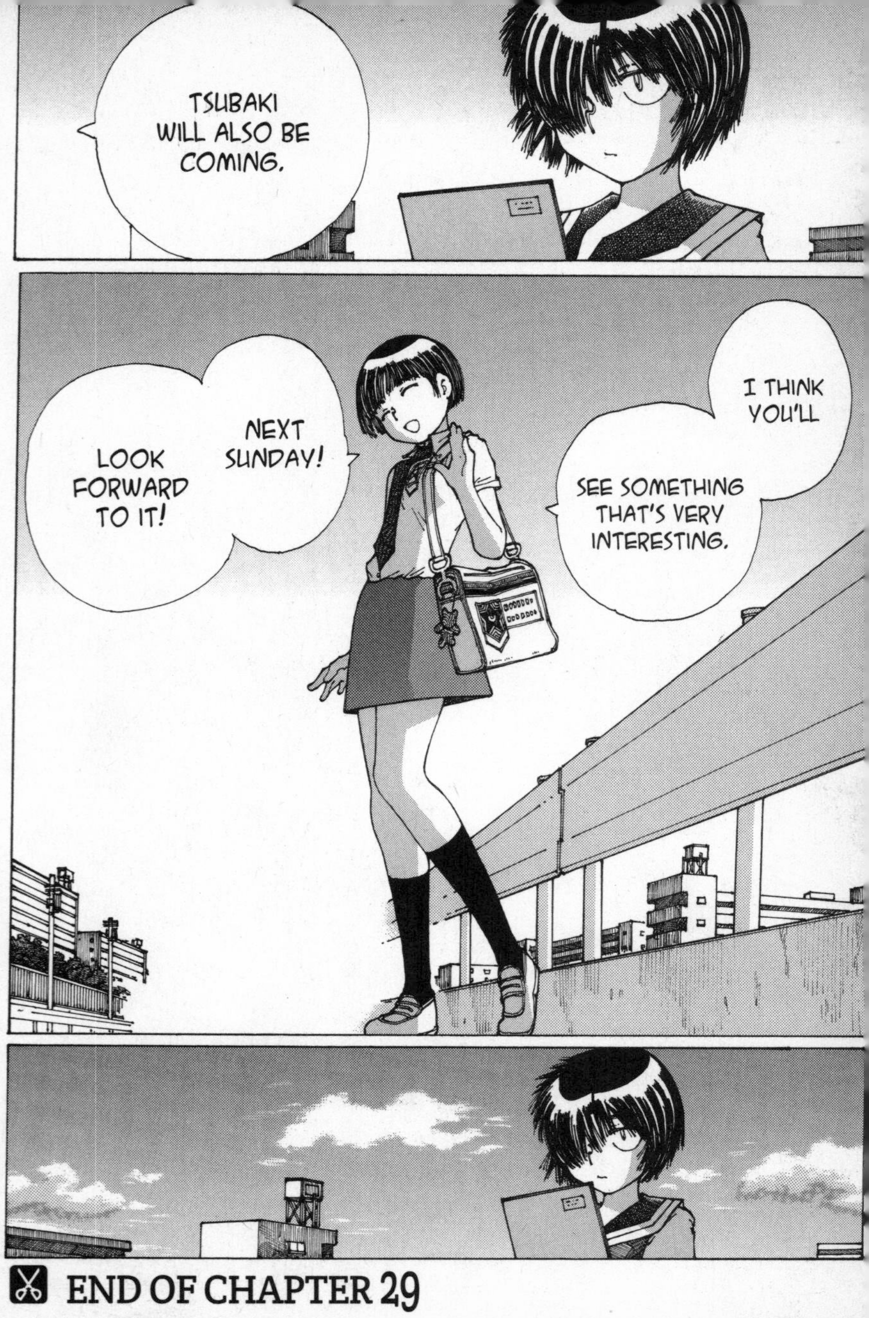
TSUBAKI WILL ALSO BE COMING.
I THINK YOU'LL
SEE SOMETHING THAT'S VERY INTERESTING.
NEXT SUNDAY!
LOOK FORWARD TO IT!

END OF CHAPTER 29

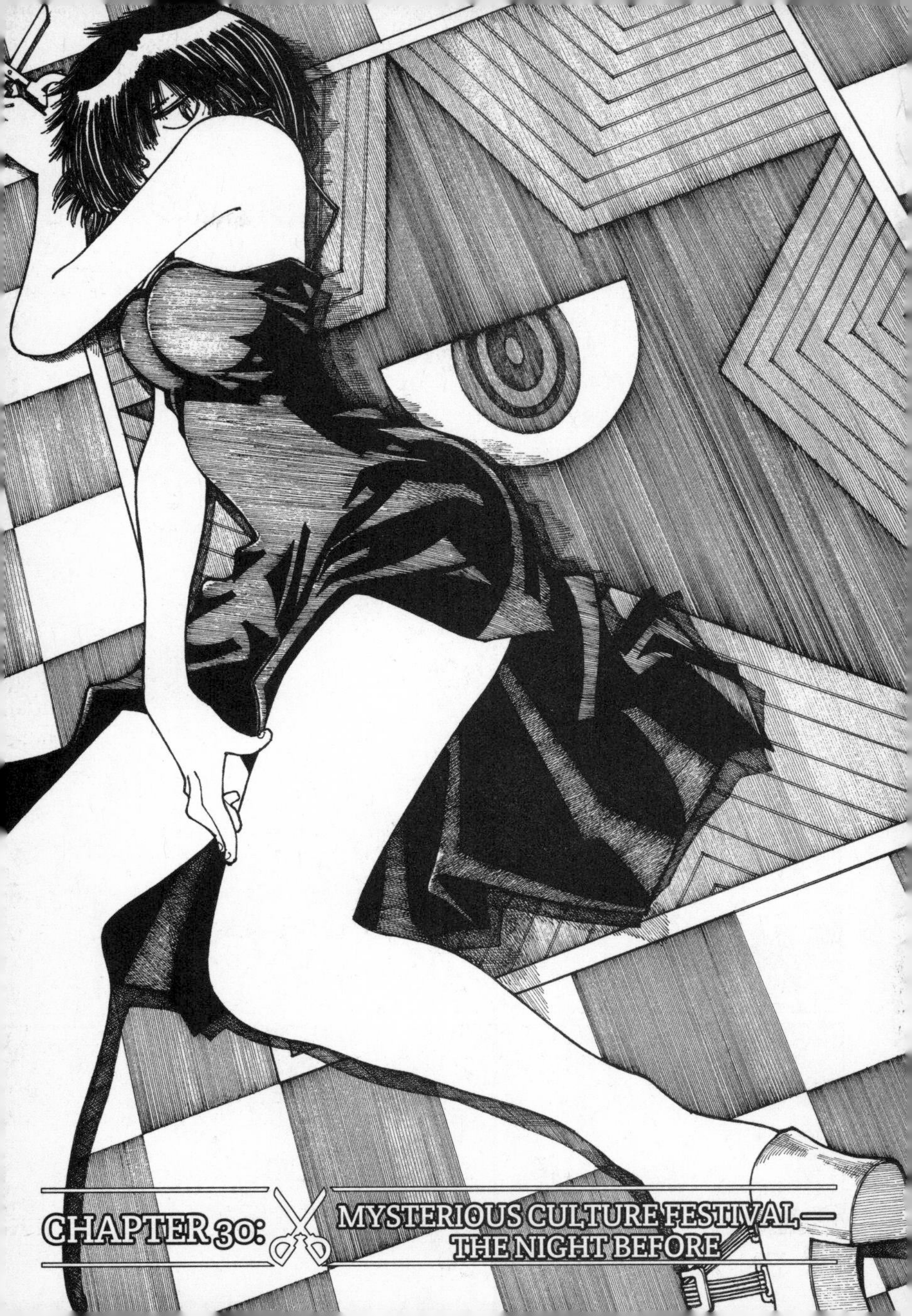
CHAPTER 30:
MYSTERIOUS CULTURE FESTIVAL—
THE NIGHT BEFORE

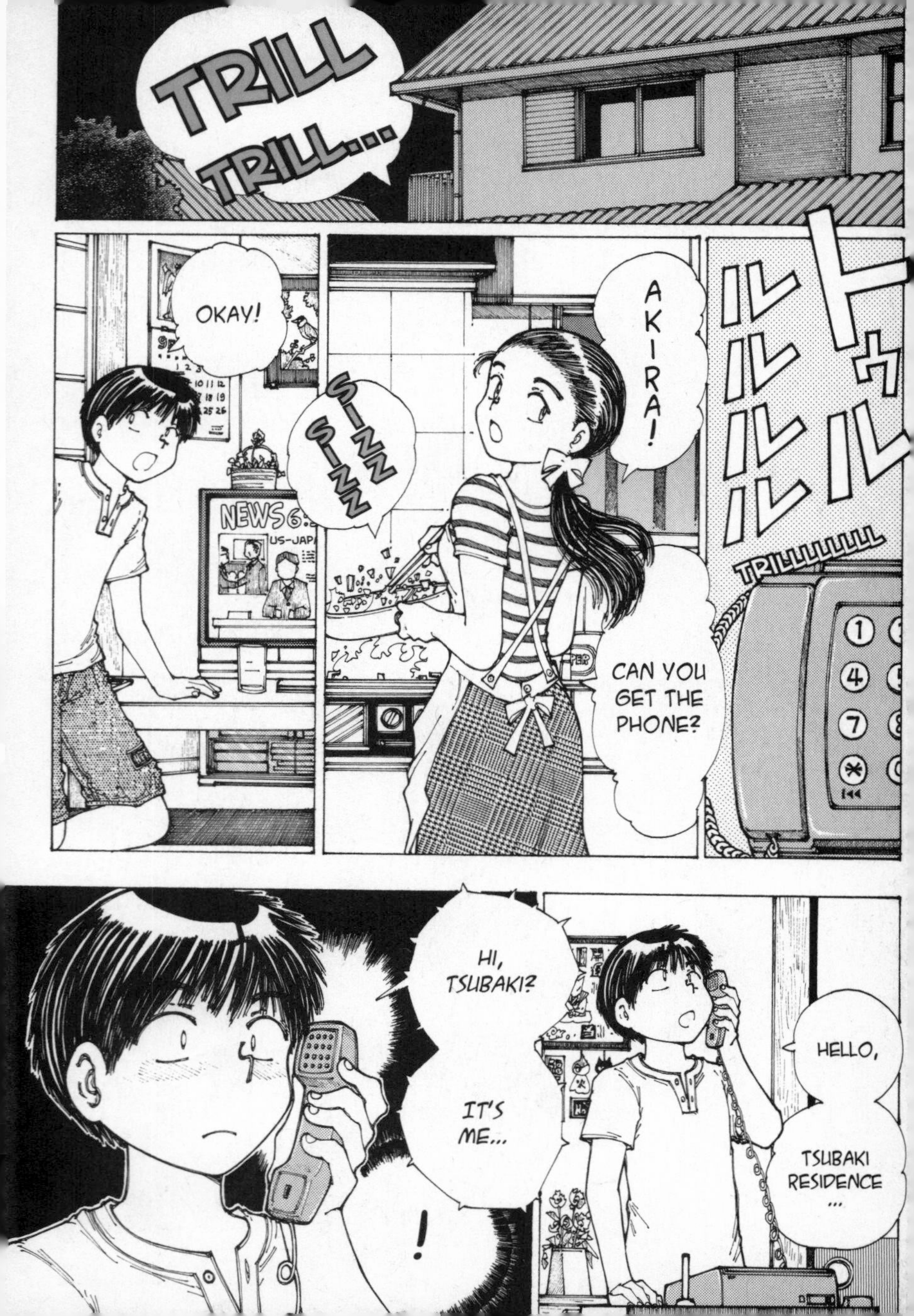
TRILL TRILL...
トゥルルルルル
TRILLLLLLLLL
AKIRA!
CAN YOU GET THE PHONE?
SIZZ SIZZ
OKAY!
HELLO,
TSUBAKI RESIDENCE ...
HI, TSUBAKI?
IT'S ME...
!

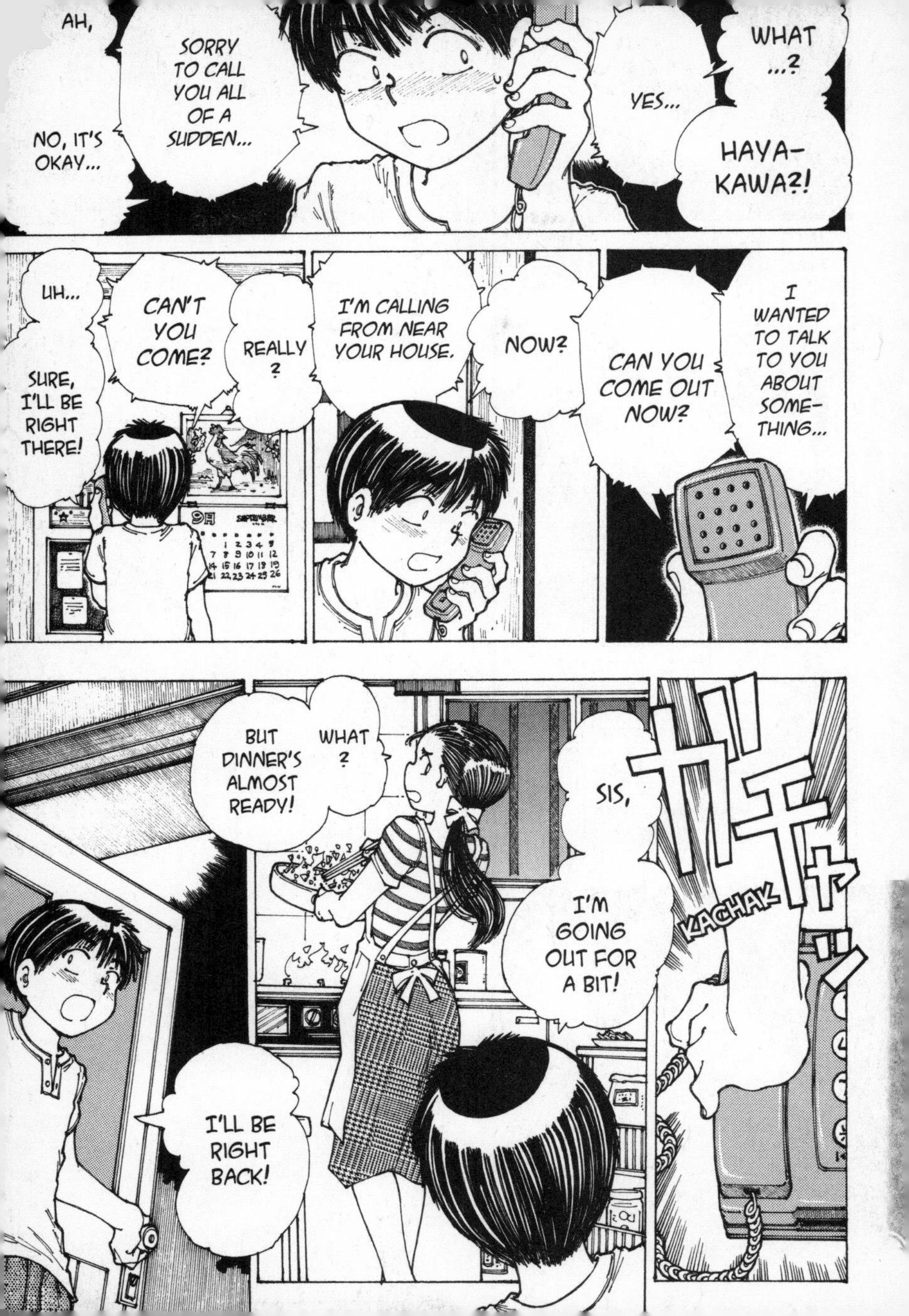
WHAT ...?
YES...
HAYA-KAWA?!
SORRY TO CALL YOU ALL OF A SUDDEN...
AH,
NO, IT'S OKAY...
I WANTED TO TALK TO YOU ABOUT SOME-THING...
CAN YOU COME OUT NOW?
NOW?
I'M CALLING FROM NEAR YOUR HOUSE.
REALLY?
CAN'T YOU COME?
UH...
SURE, I'LL BE RIGHT THERE!
ガチャ
KACHAK
SIS,
I'M GOING OUT FOR A BIT!
WHAT?
BUT DINNER'S ALMOST READY!
I'LL BE RIGHT BACK!

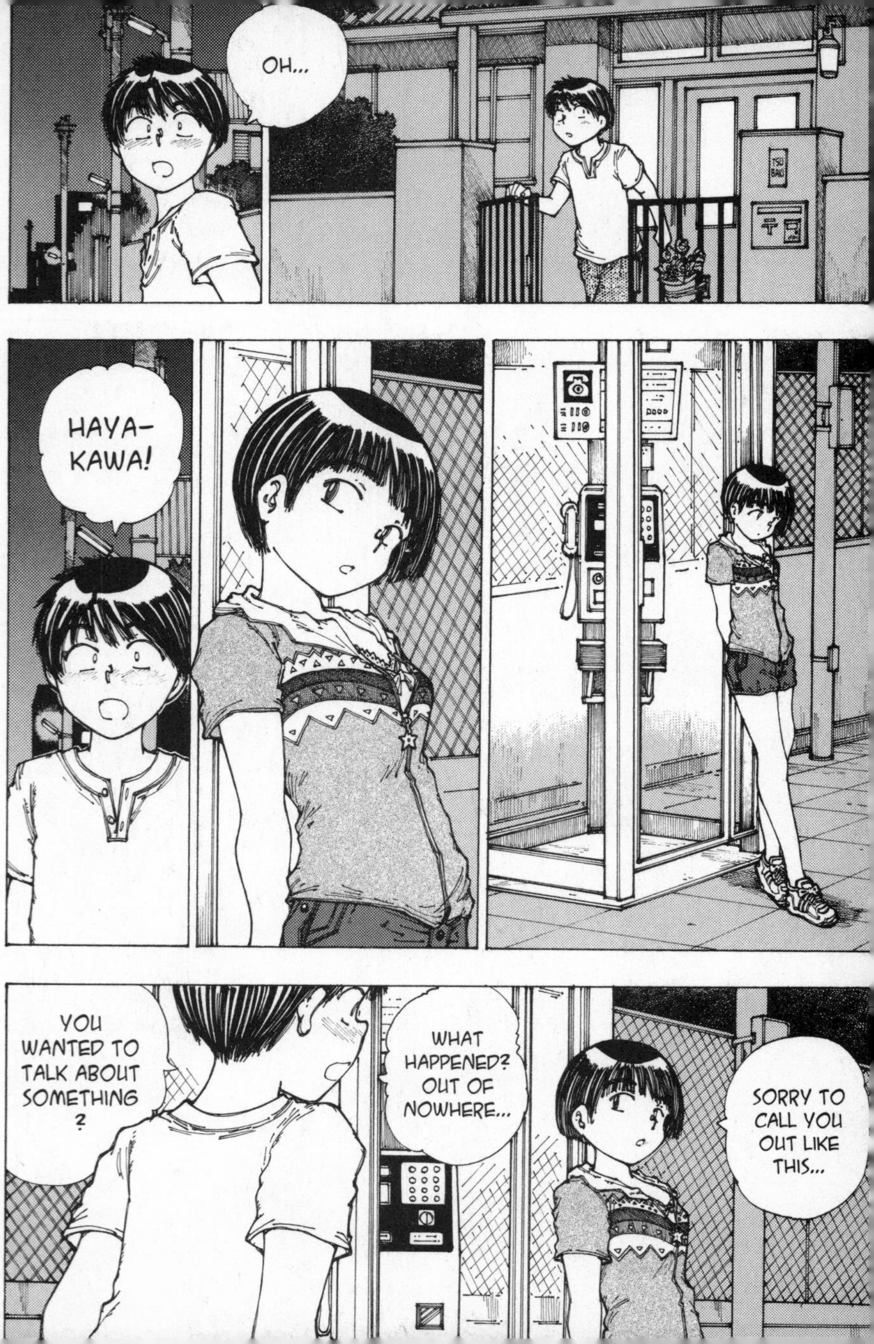
TSU BAKI
OH...
HAYA-KAWA!
SORRY TO CALL YOU OUT LIKE THIS...
WHAT HAPPENED? OUT OF NOWHERE...
YOU WANTED TO TALK ABOUT SOMETHING?

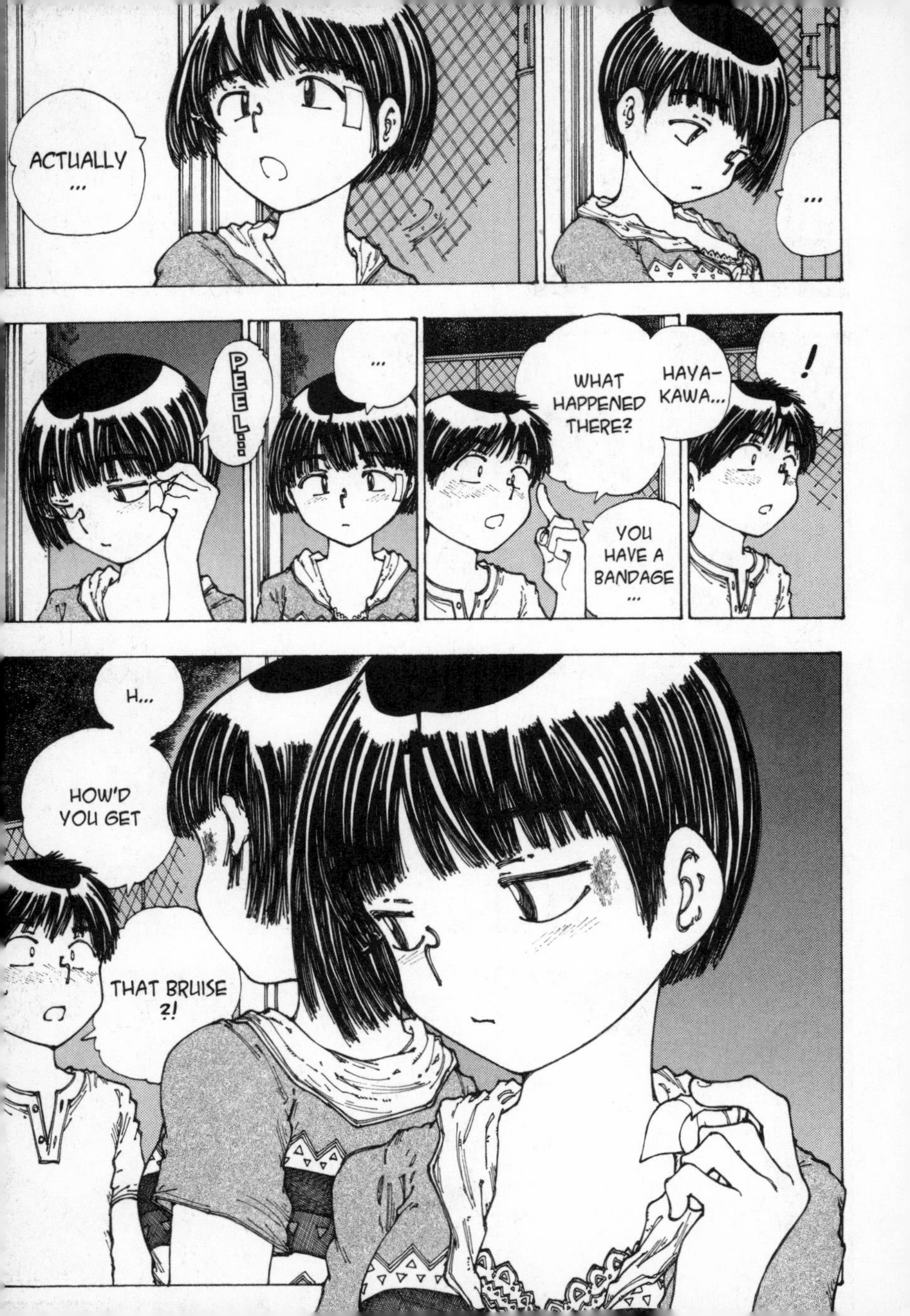
...
ACTUALLY ...
!
HAYA-KAWA...
WHAT HAPPENED THERE?
YOU HAVE A BANDAGE ...
...
PEEL...
H...
HOW'D YOU GET
THAT BRUISE ?!

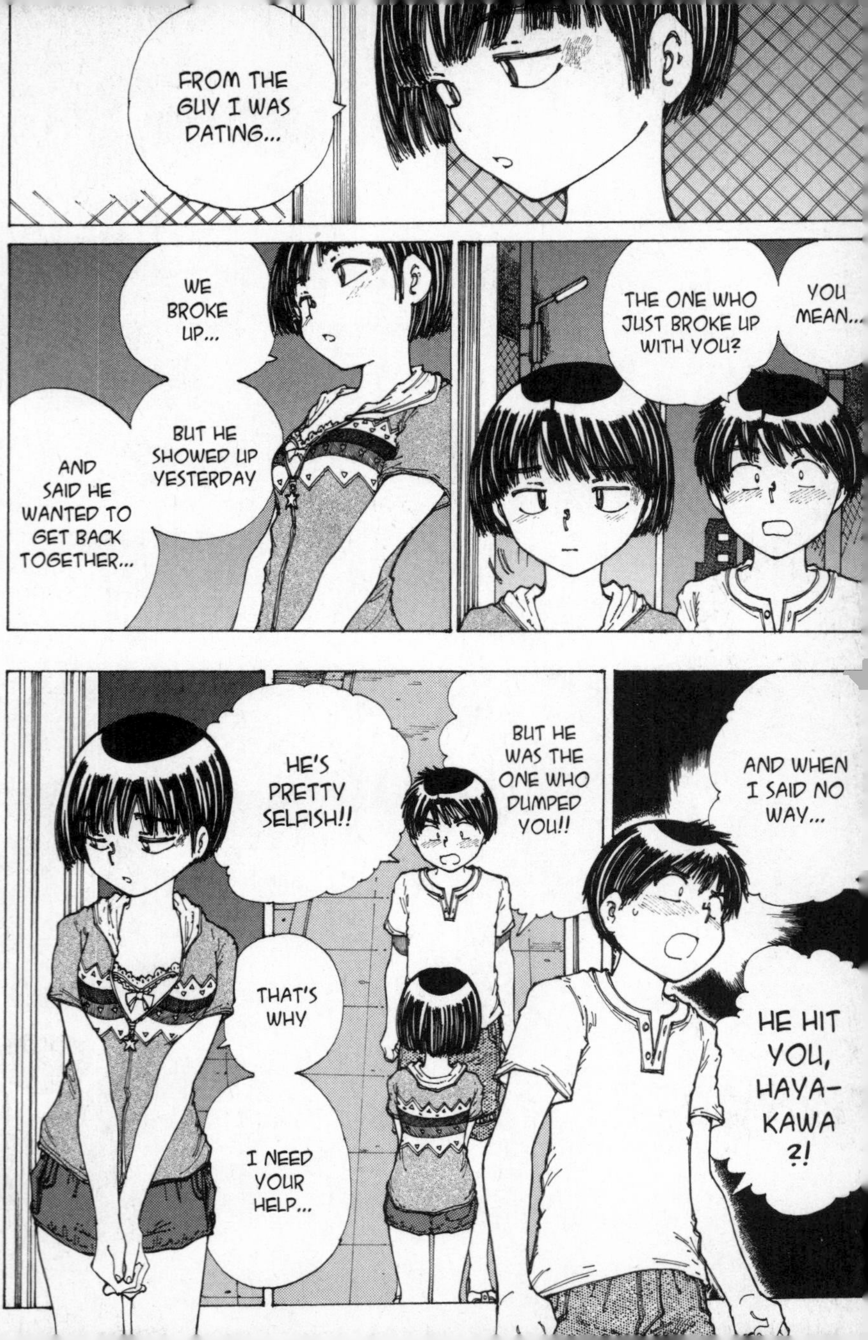
FROM THE GUY I WAS DATING...
YOU MEAN...
THE ONE WHO JUST BROKE UP WITH YOU?
WE BROKE UP...
BUT HE SHOWED UP YESTERDAY
AND SAID HE WANTED TO GET BACK TOGETHER...
AND WHEN I SAID NO WAY...
HE HIT YOU, HAYA-KAWA?!
BUT HE WAS THE ONE WHO DUMPED YOU!!
HE'S PRETTY SELFISH!!
THAT'S WHY
I NEED YOUR HELP...

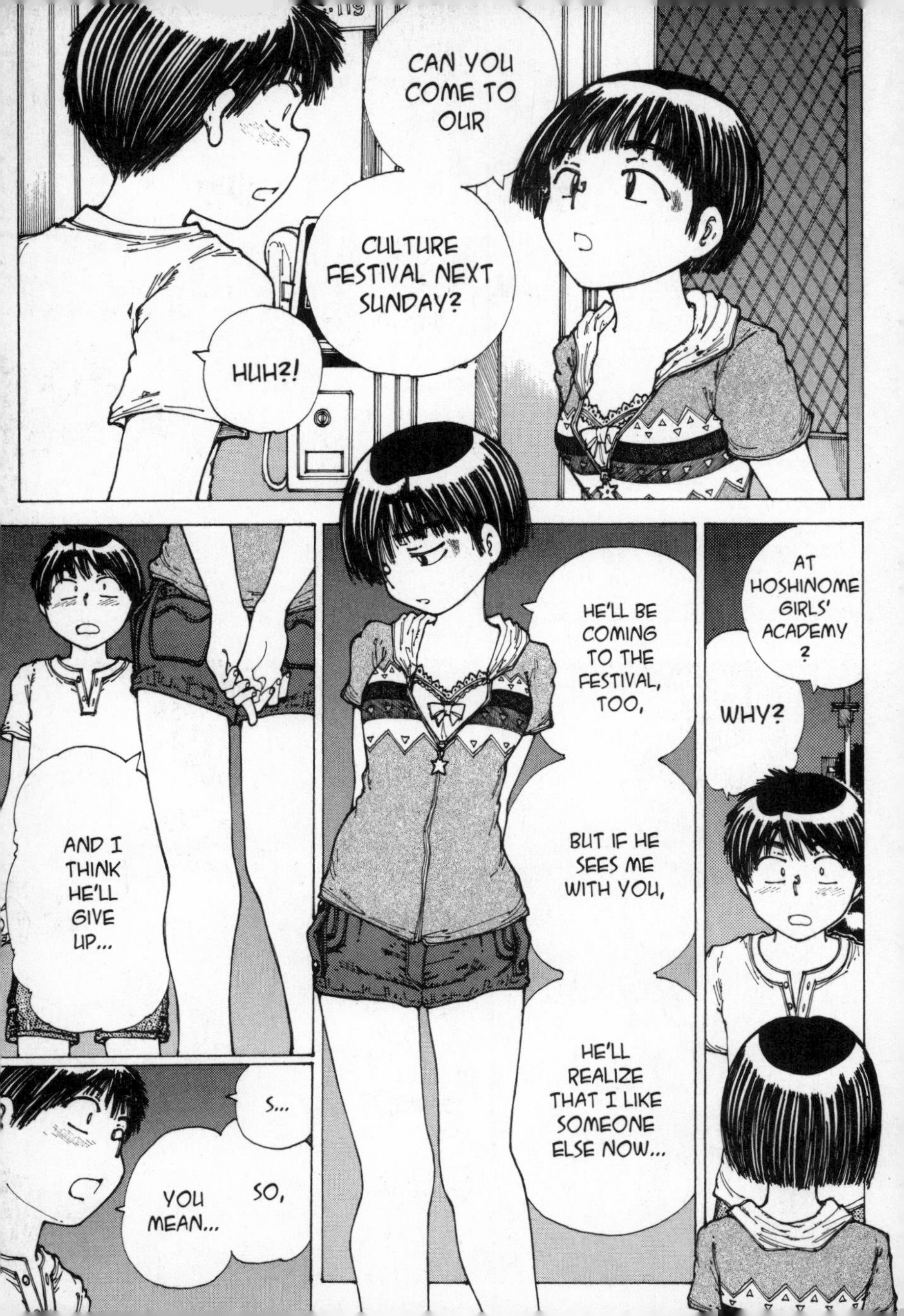
CAN YOU COME TO OUR
CULTURE FESTIVAL NEXT SUNDAY?
HUH?!
AT HOSHINOME GIRLS' ACADEMY?
WHY?
HE'LL BE COMING TO THE FESTIVAL, TOO,
BUT IF HE SEES ME WITH YOU,
HE'LL REALIZE THAT I LIKE SOMEONE ELSE NOW...
AND I THINK HE'LL GIVE UP...
S...
SO,
YOU MEAN...

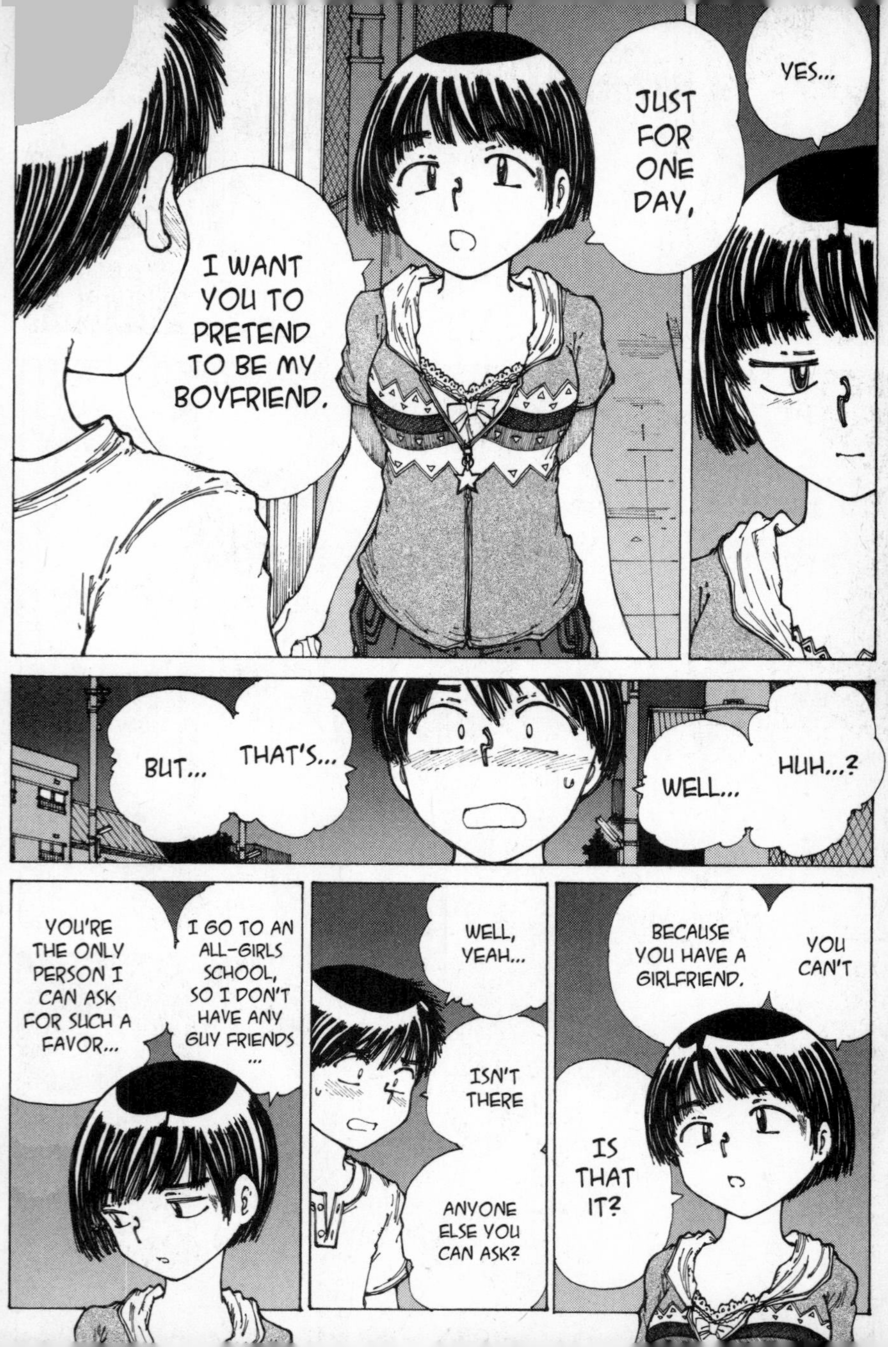
YES...
JUST FOR ONE DAY,
I WANT YOU TO PRETEND TO BE MY BOYFRIEND.
HUH...?
WELL...
THAT'S...
BUT...
YOU CAN'T
BECAUSE YOU HAVE A GIRLFRIEND.
IS THAT IT?
WELL, YEAH...
ISN'T THERE
ANYONE ELSE YOU CAN ASK?
I GO TO AN ALL-GIRLS SCHOOL, SO I DON'T HAVE ANY GUY FRIENDS ...
YOU'RE THE ONLY PERSON I CAN ASK FOR SUCH A FAVOR...

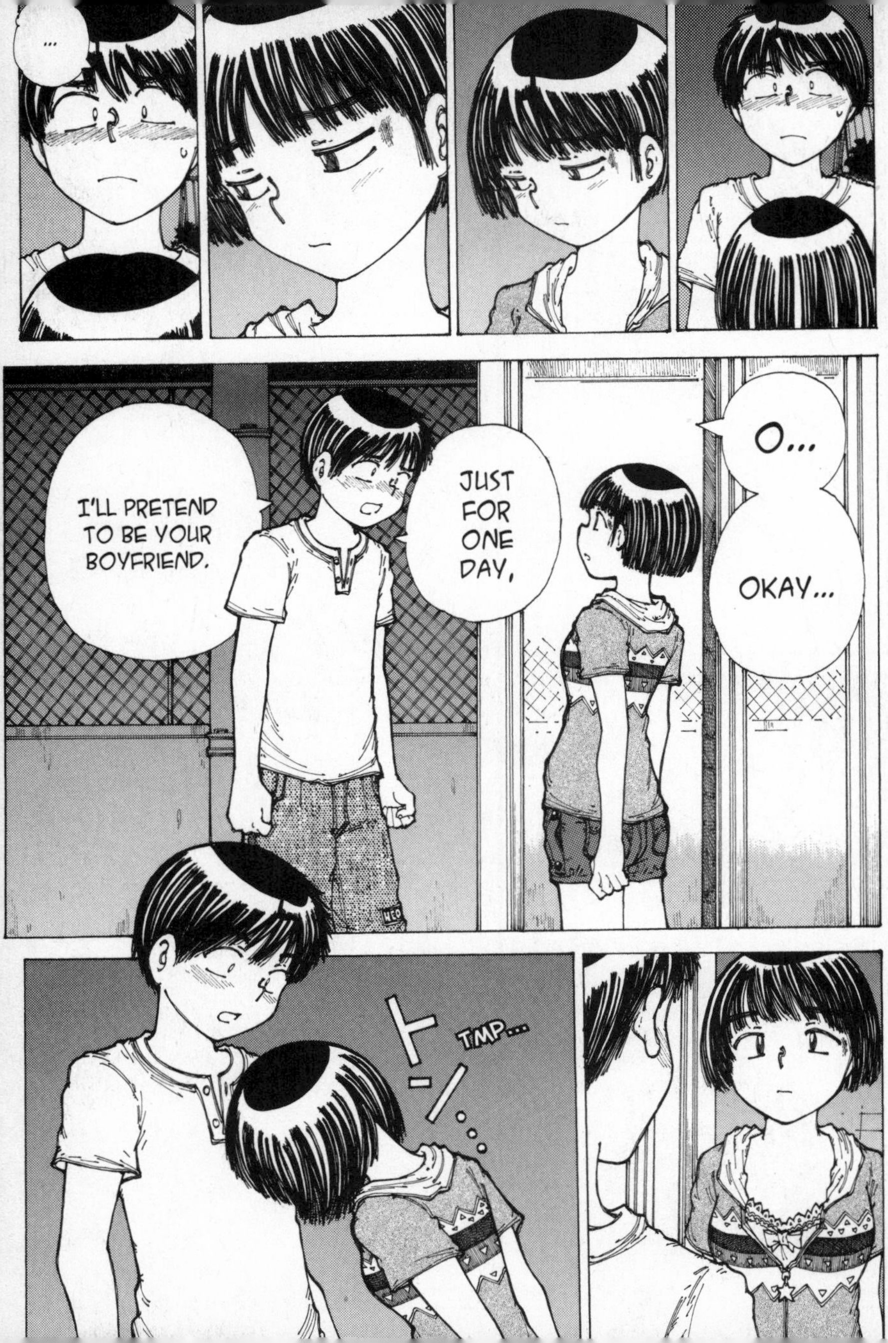
...
O...
OKAY...
JUST FOR ONE DAY,
I'LL PRETEND TO BE YOUR BOYFRIEND.
TMP...

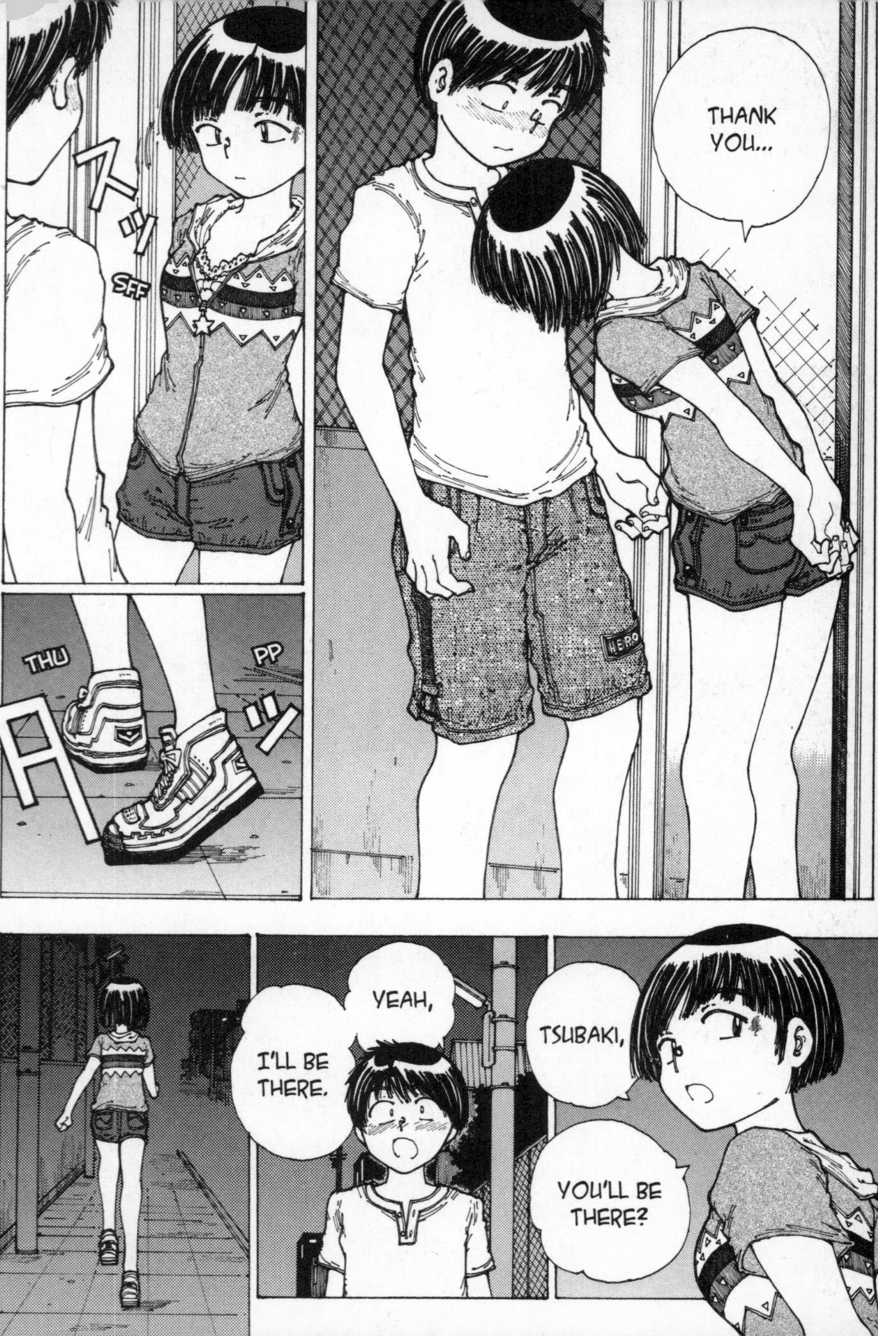
THANK YOU...
SFF
THU
PP
TSUBAKI,
YOU'LL BE THERE?
YEAH,
I'LL BE THERE.

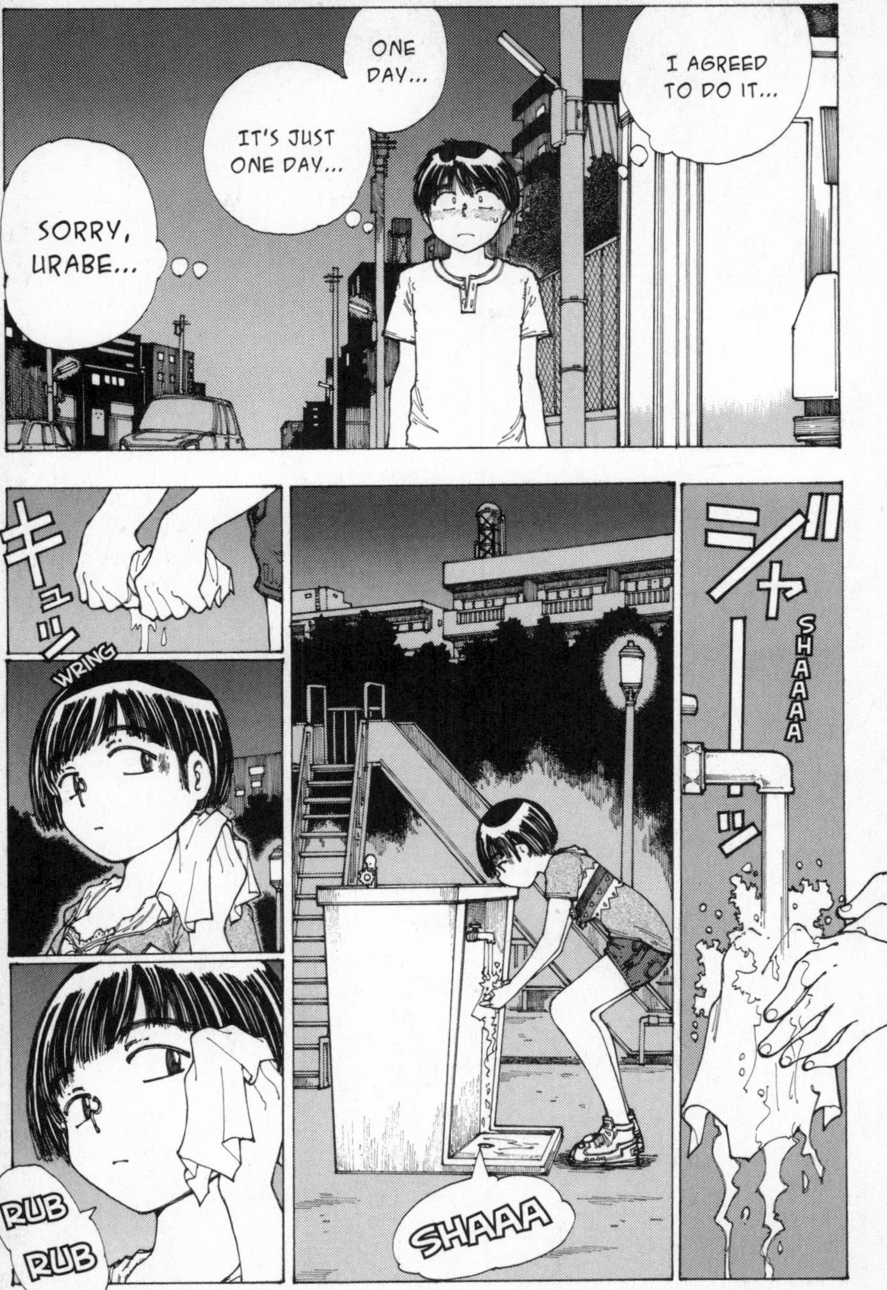
I AGREED TO DO IT...
ONE DAY...
IT'S JUST ONE DAY...
SORRY, URABE...
ジャーッ
SHAAAAA
SHAAA
キュッ
WRING
RUB RUB

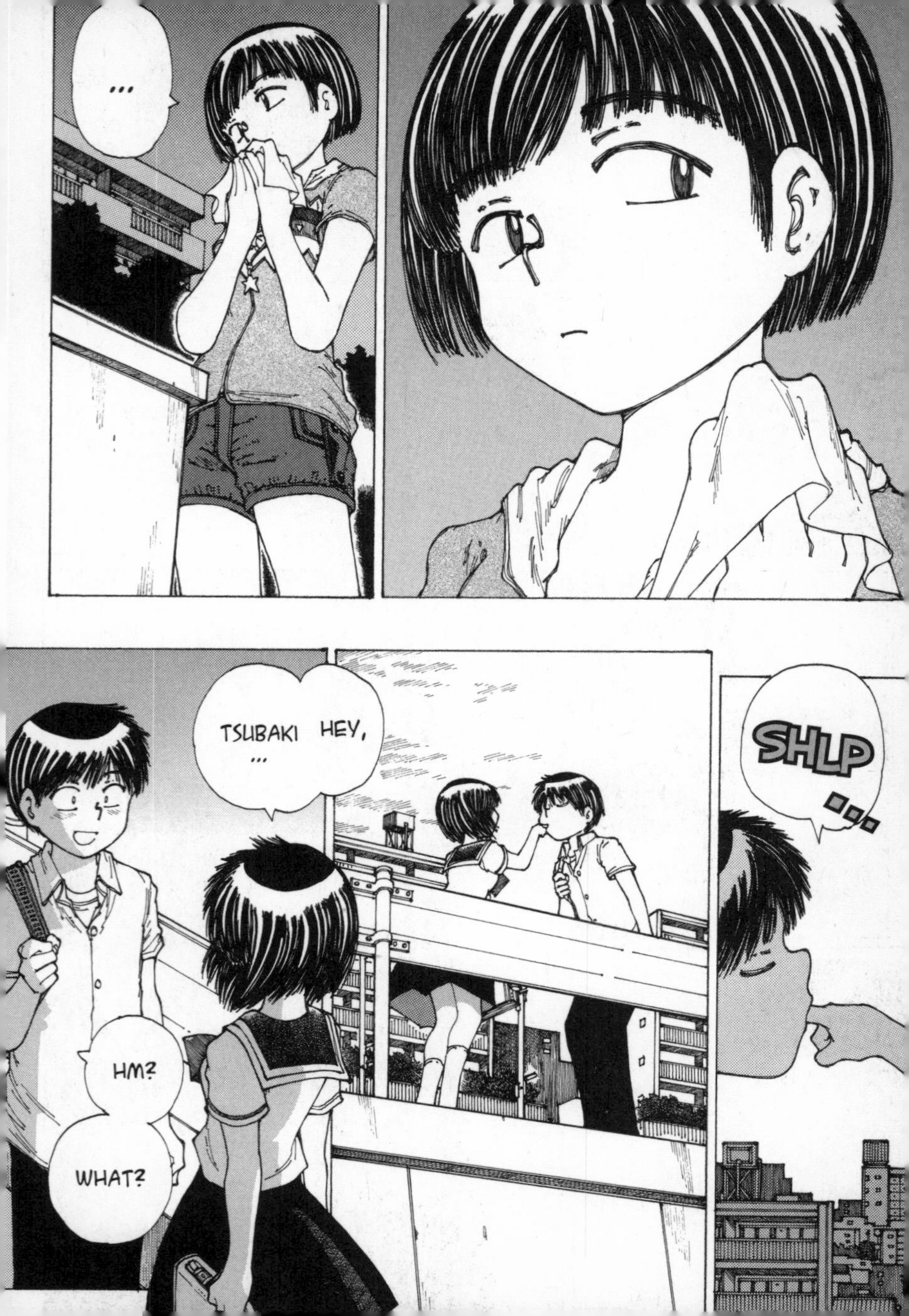
...
SHLP
...
HEY, TSUBAKI ...
HM?
WHAT?

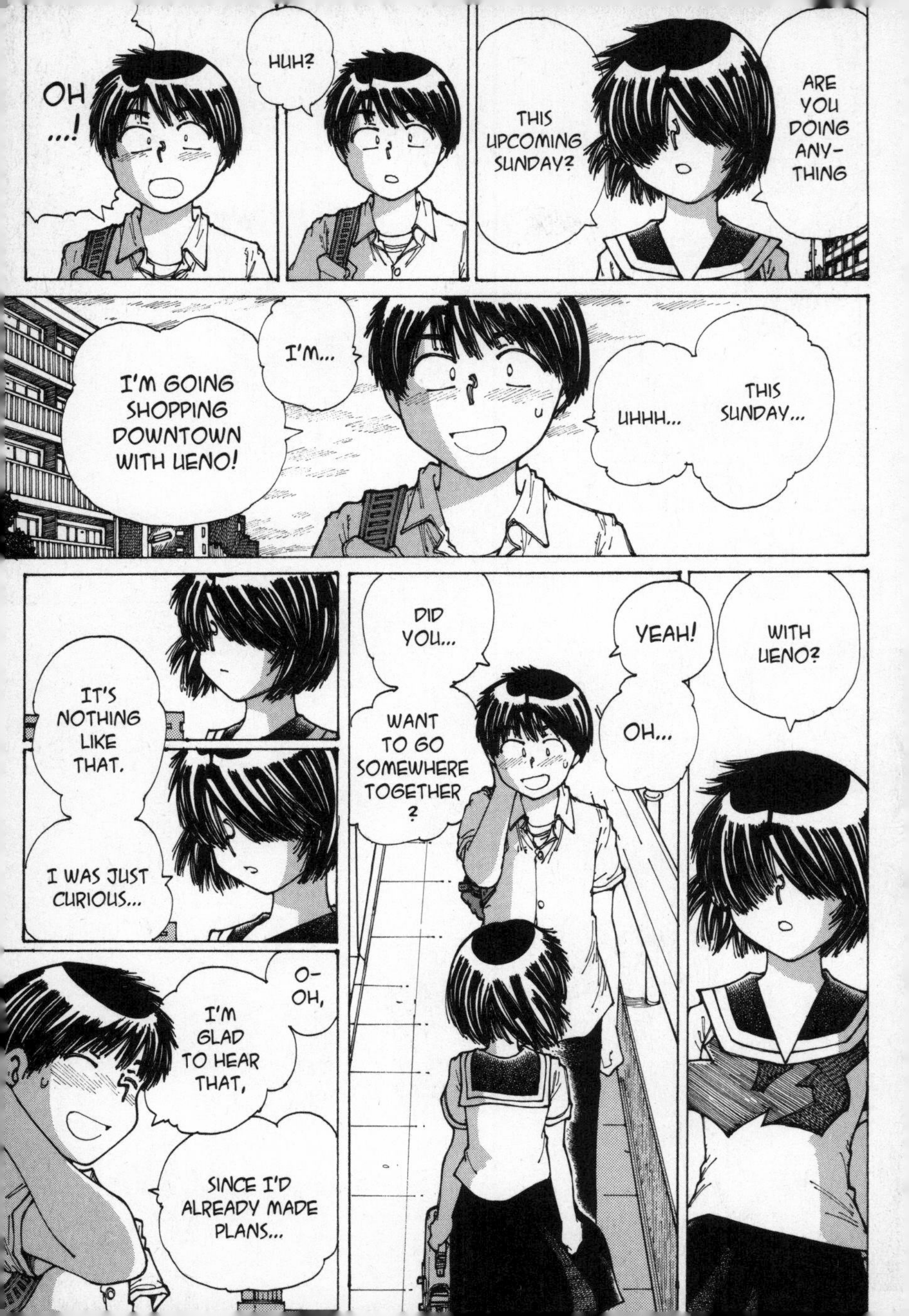
ARE YOU DOING ANYTHING
THIS UPCOMING SUNDAY?
HUH?
OH ...!
THIS SUNDAY...
UHHH...
I'M...
I'M GOING SHOPPING DOWNTOWN WITH UENO!
WITH UENO?
YEAH!
OH...
DID YOU...
WANT TO GO SOMEWHERE TOGETHER?
IT'S NOTHING LIKE THAT.
I WAS JUST CURIOUS...
O-OH,
I'M GLAD TO HEAR THAT,
SINCE I'D ALREADY MADE PLANS...

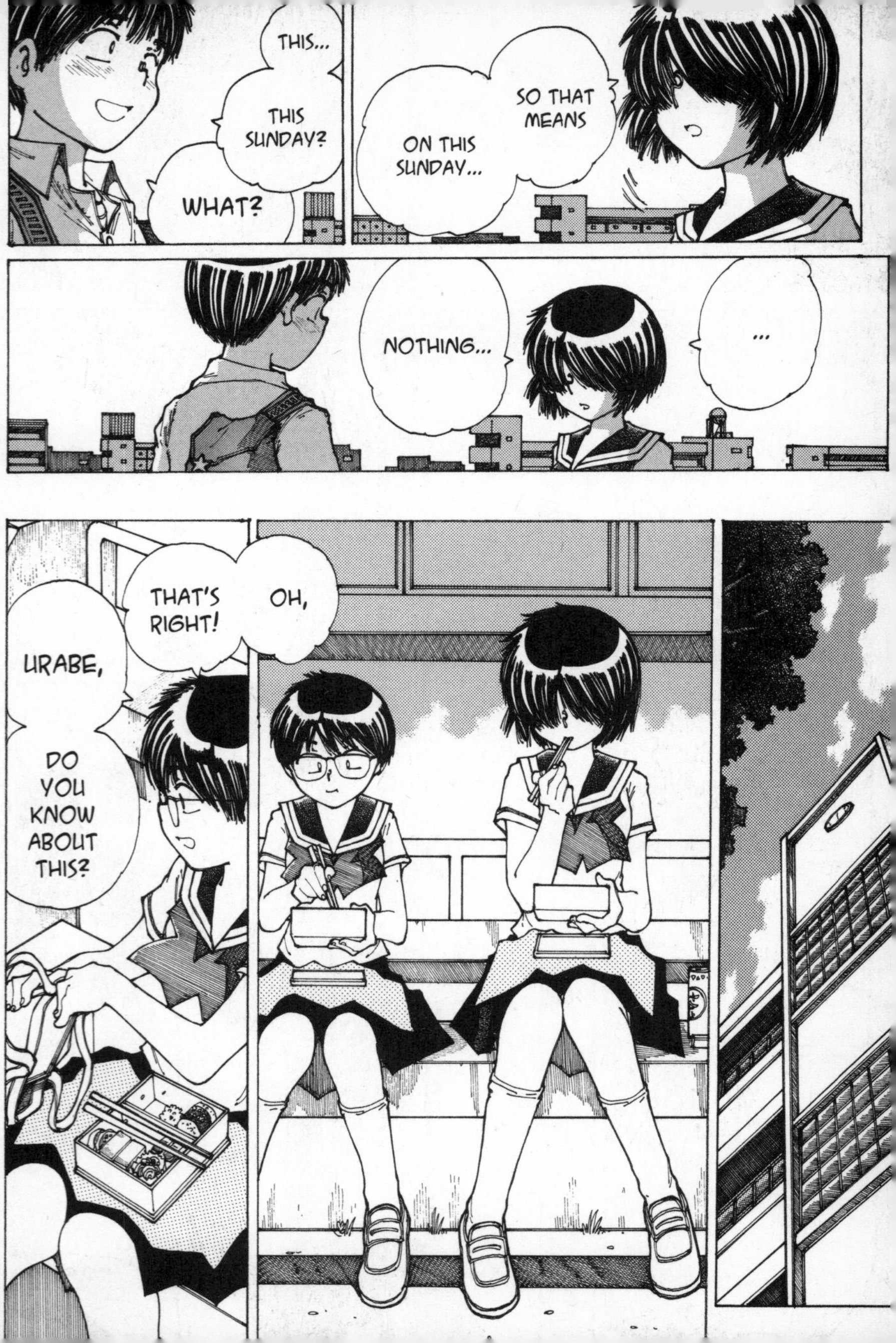
SO THAT MEANS
ON THIS SUNDAY...
THIS...
THIS SUNDAY?
WHAT?
...
NOTHING...
OH,
THAT'S RIGHT!
URABE,
DO YOU KNOW ABOUT THIS?

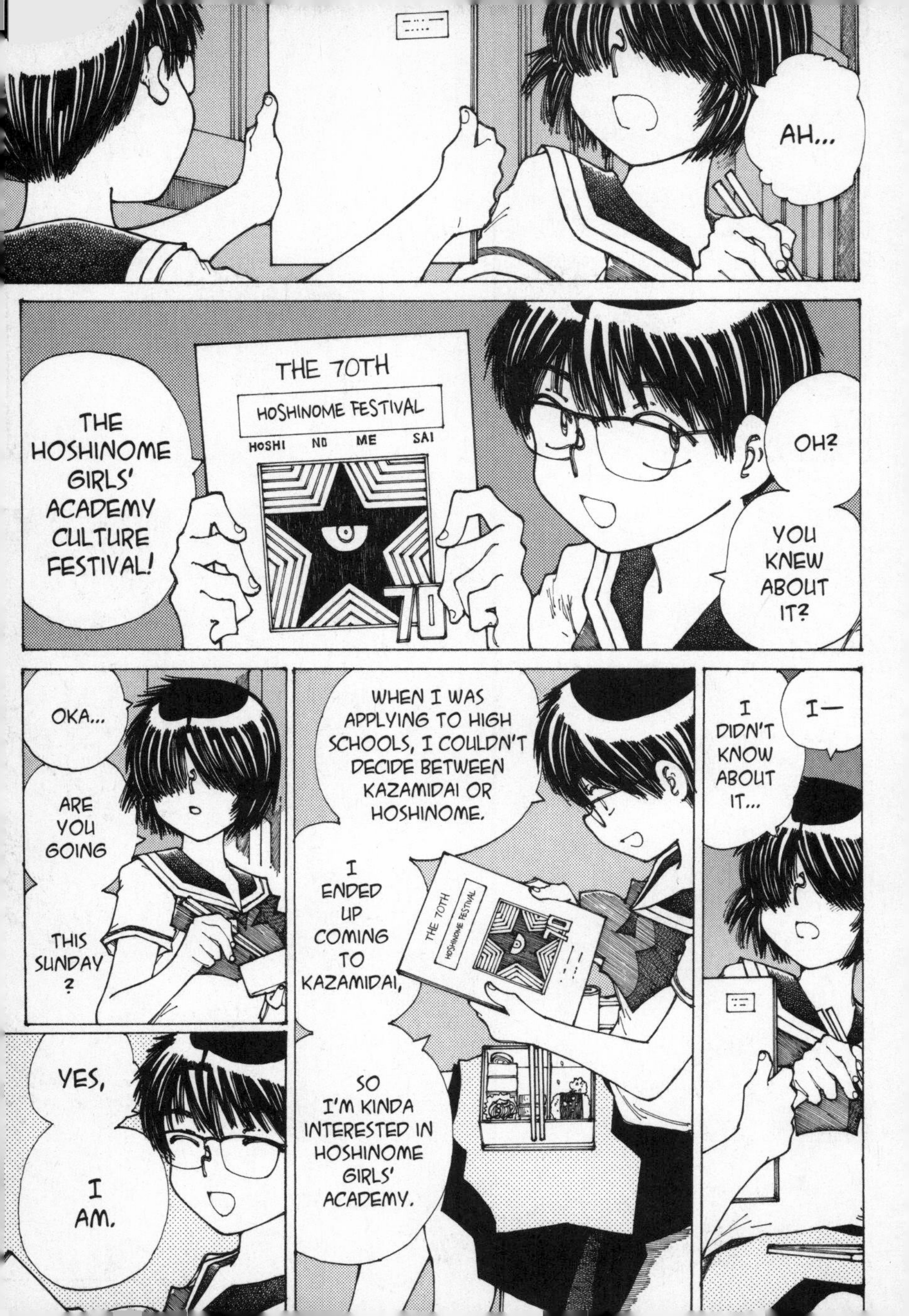
AH...
OH?
YOU KNEW ABOUT IT?
THE 70TH
HOSHINOME FESTIVAL
HOSHI NO ME SAI
70
THE HOSHINOME GIRLS' ACADEMY CULTURE FESTIVAL!
I—
I DIDN'T KNOW ABOUT IT...
WHEN I WAS APPLYING TO HIGH SCHOOLS, I COULDN'T DECIDE BETWEEN KAZAMIDAI OR HOSHINOME.
I ENDED UP COMING TO KAZAMIDAI,
THE 70TH
HOSHINOME FESTIVAL
SO I'M KINDA INTERESTED IN HOSHINOME GIRLS' ACADEMY.
OKA...
ARE YOU GOING THIS SUNDAY?
YES, I AM.

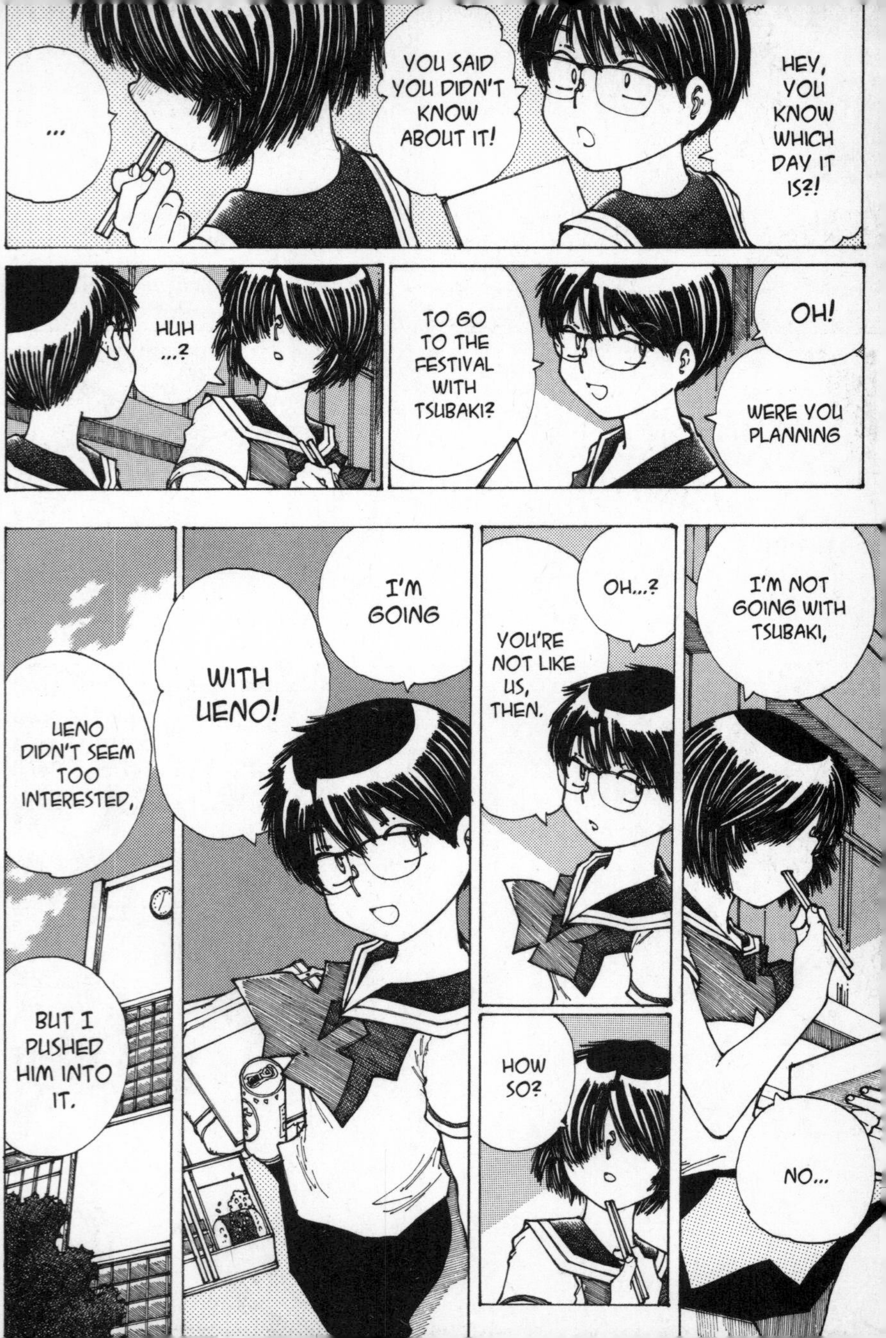
HEY, YOU KNOW WHICH DAY IT IS?!
YOU SAID YOU DIDN'T KNOW ABOUT IT!
...
OH!
WERE YOU PLANNING
TO GO TO THE FESTIVAL WITH TSUBAKI?
HUH ...?
I'M NOT GOING WITH TSUBAKI,
NO...
OH...?
YOU'RE NOT LIKE US, THEN.
HOW SO?
I'M GOING
WITH UENO!
UENO DIDN'T SEEM TOO INTERESTED,
BUT I PUSHED HIM INTO IT.

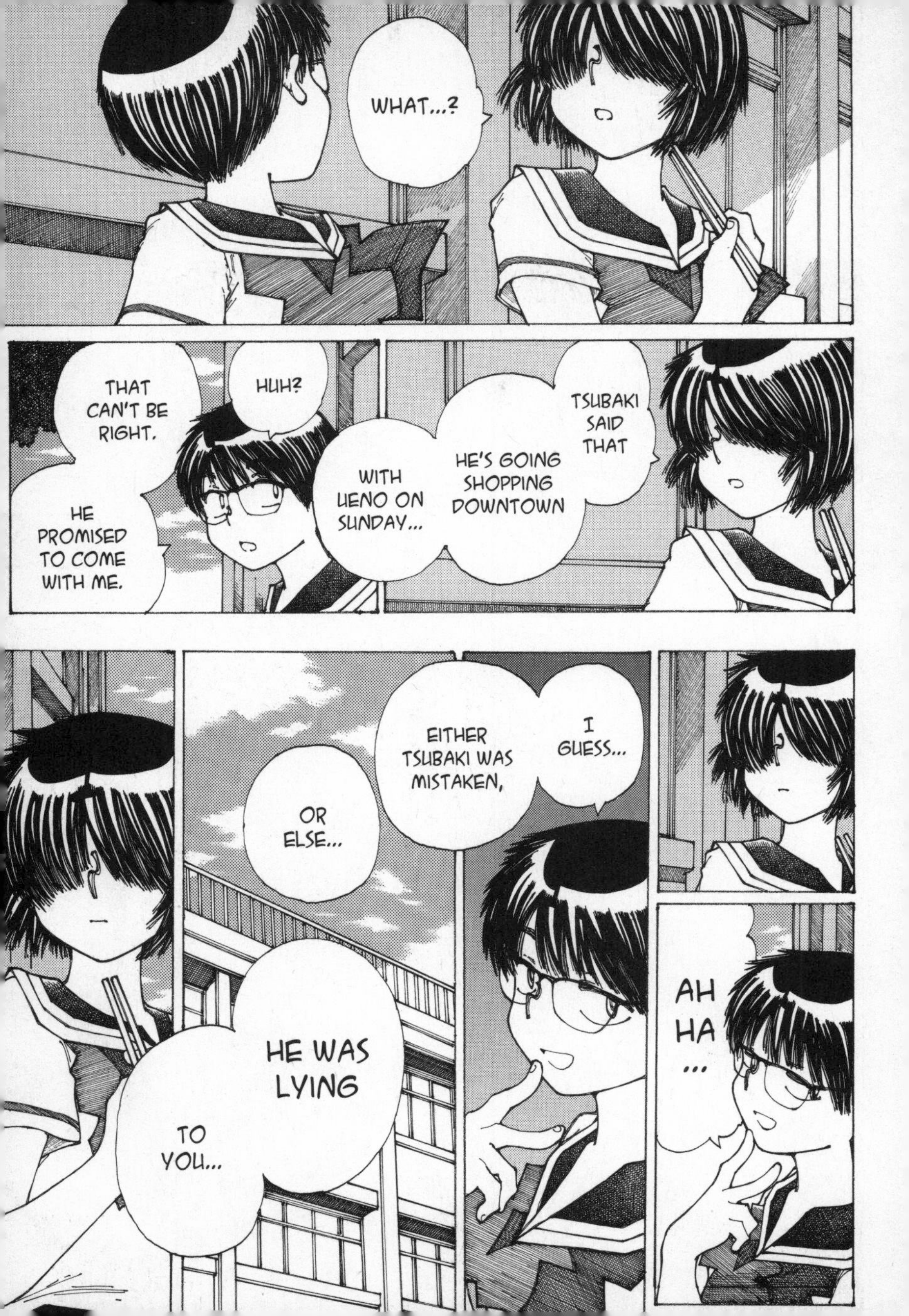
WHAT...?
TSUBAKI SAID THAT
HE'S GOING SHOPPING DOWNTOWN
WITH UENO ON SUNDAY...
HUH?
THAT CAN'T BE RIGHT.
HE PROMISED TO COME WITH ME.
AH HA ...
I GUESS...
EITHER TSUBAKI WAS MISTAKEN,
OR ELSE...
HE WAS LYING
TO YOU...

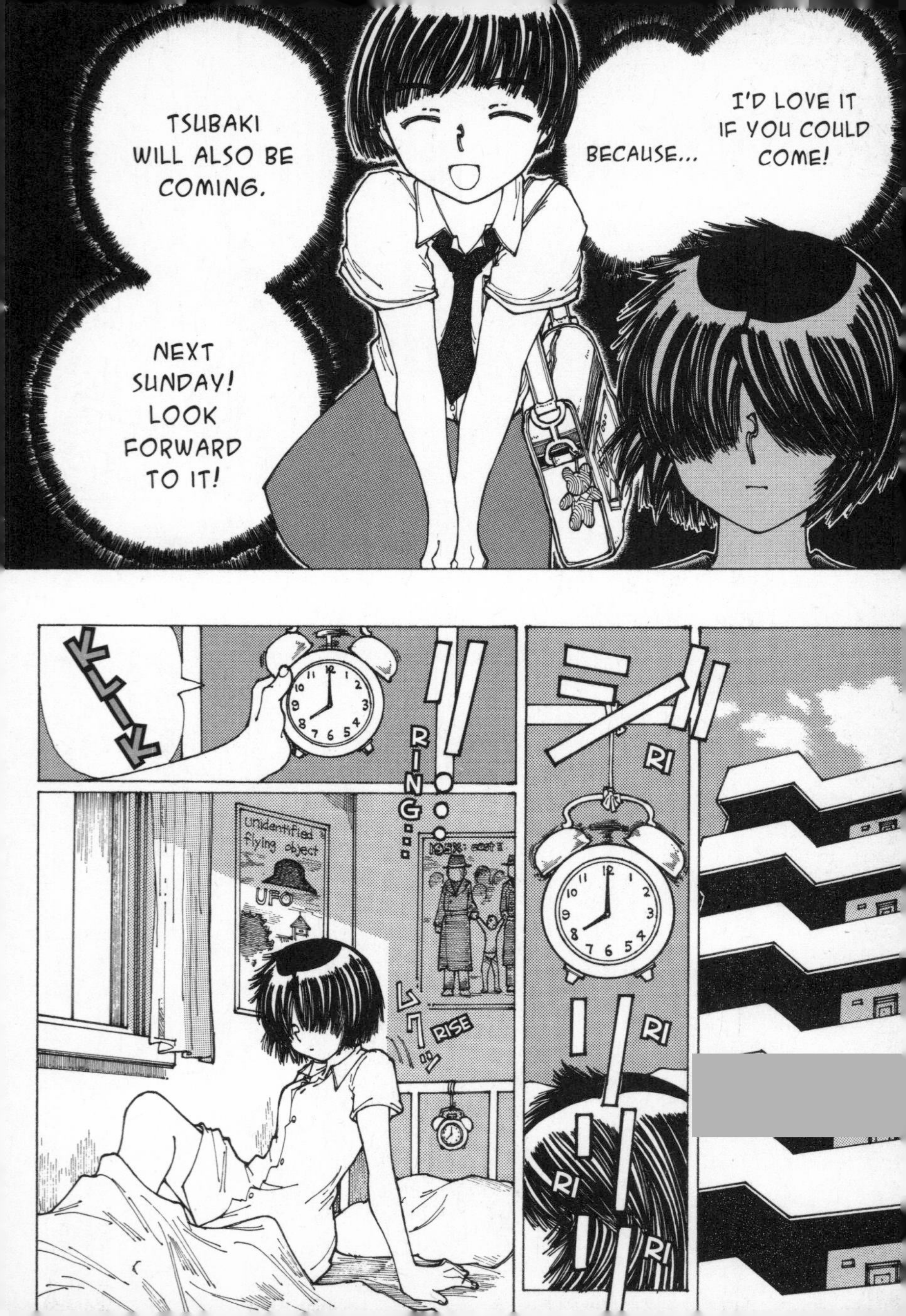
I'D LOVE IT IF YOU COULD COME!
BECAUSE...
TSUBAKI WILL ALSO BE COMING.
NEXT SUNDAY! LOOK FORWARD TO IT!
RI
RI
RI
RI
KLIK
RING...
Unidentified flying object
UFO
RISE

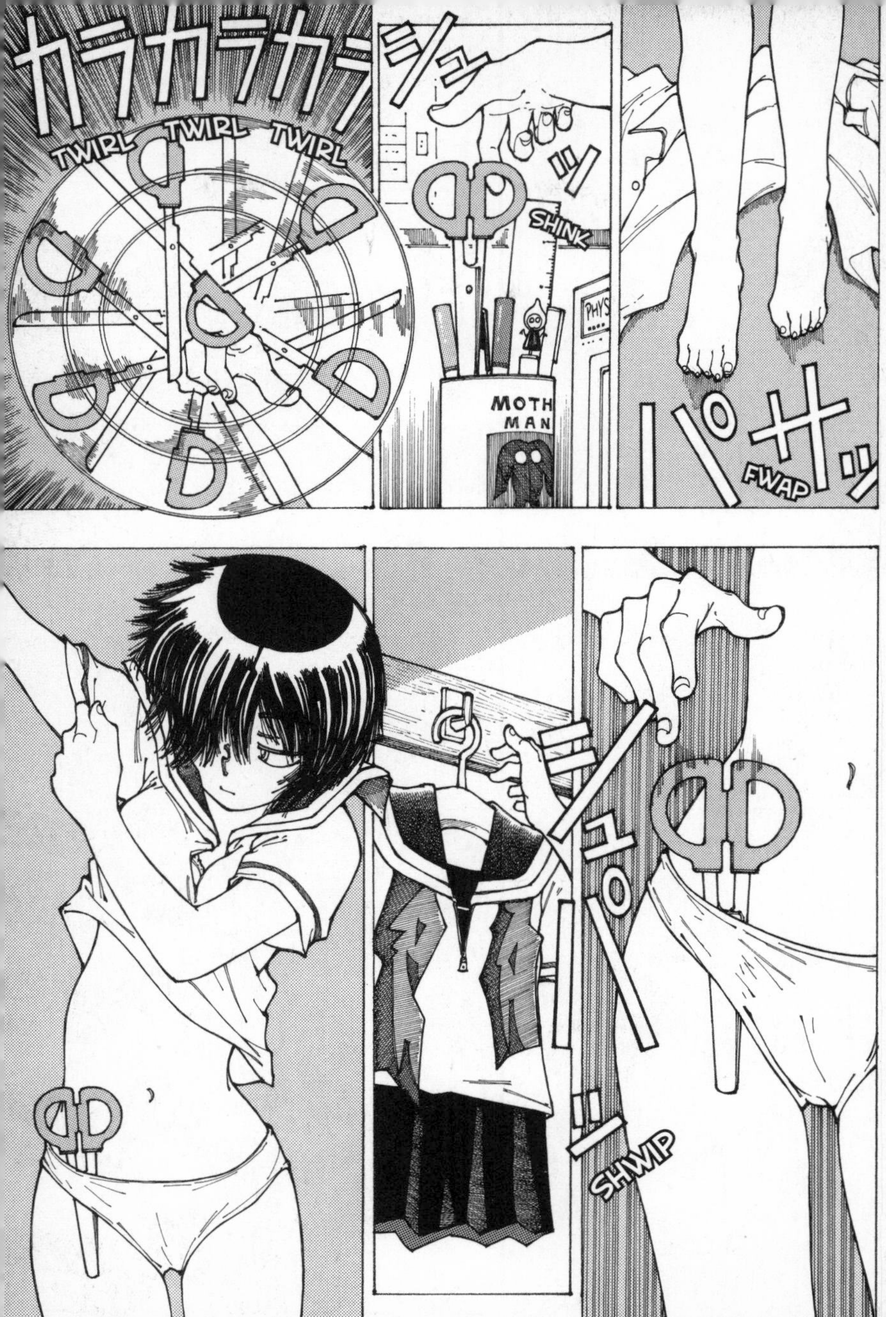

パサッ
FWAP
シュッ
SHINK
カラカラカラ
TWIRL TWIRL TWIRL
シュパ
SHWIP

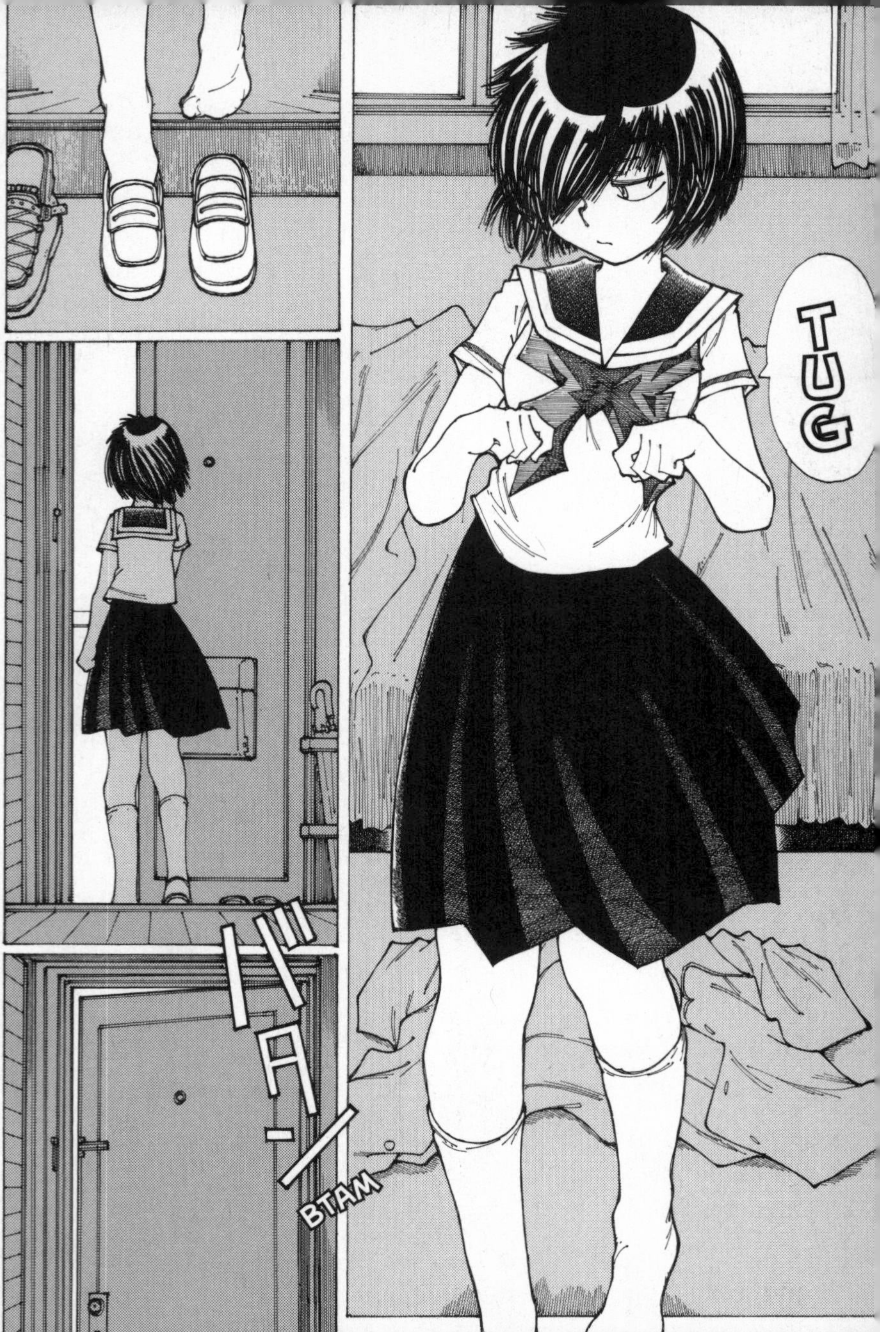
TUG
BTAM

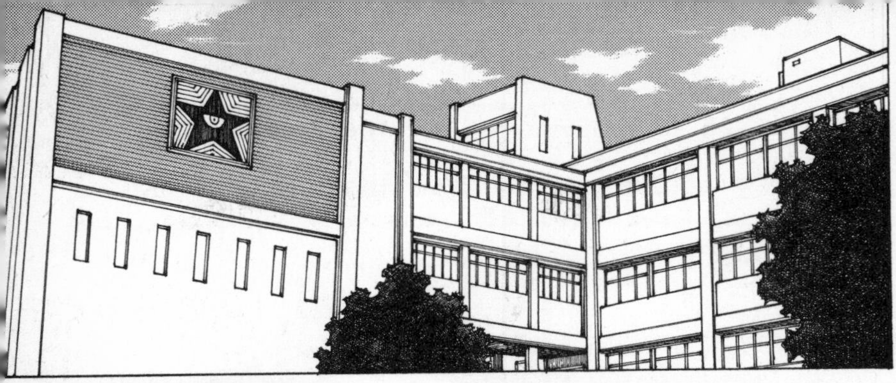

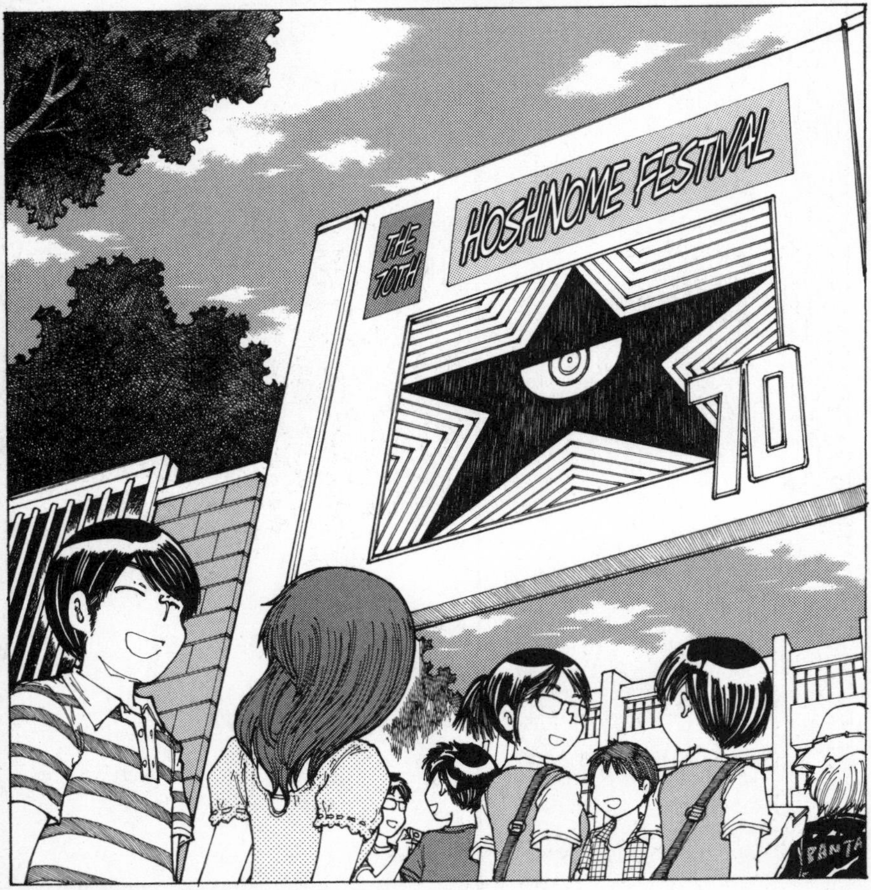
HOSHINOME FESTIVAL
THE 70TH
70
PANTA

END OF CHAPTER 30

"Mysterious Girlfriend X" School Uniform Guide, Part 1

The Prestigious Girls' School with a 70-Year History

HOSHINOME GIRLS' ACADEMY HIGH SCHOOL

LOCATION: A town in Tokyo **POPULATION:** 900 students

REMARKS: Known for the unusual nature of its culture festival.

By the way, this is the uniform of Urabe's school, Kazamidai Municipal High School.

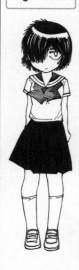

Red tie, navy blue skirt. Two white lines on collar. A very orthodox sailor-style uniform.

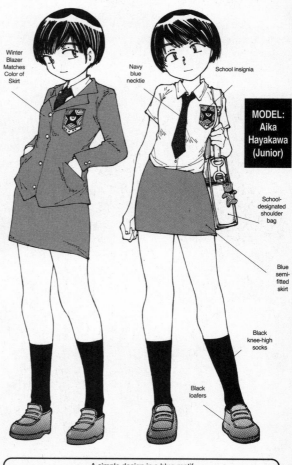

Winter Blazer Matches Color of Skirt
Navy blue necktie
School insignia
MODEL: Aika Hayakawa (Junior)
School-designated shoulder bag
Blue semi-fitted skirt
Black knee-high socks
Black loafers

A simple design in a blue motif.

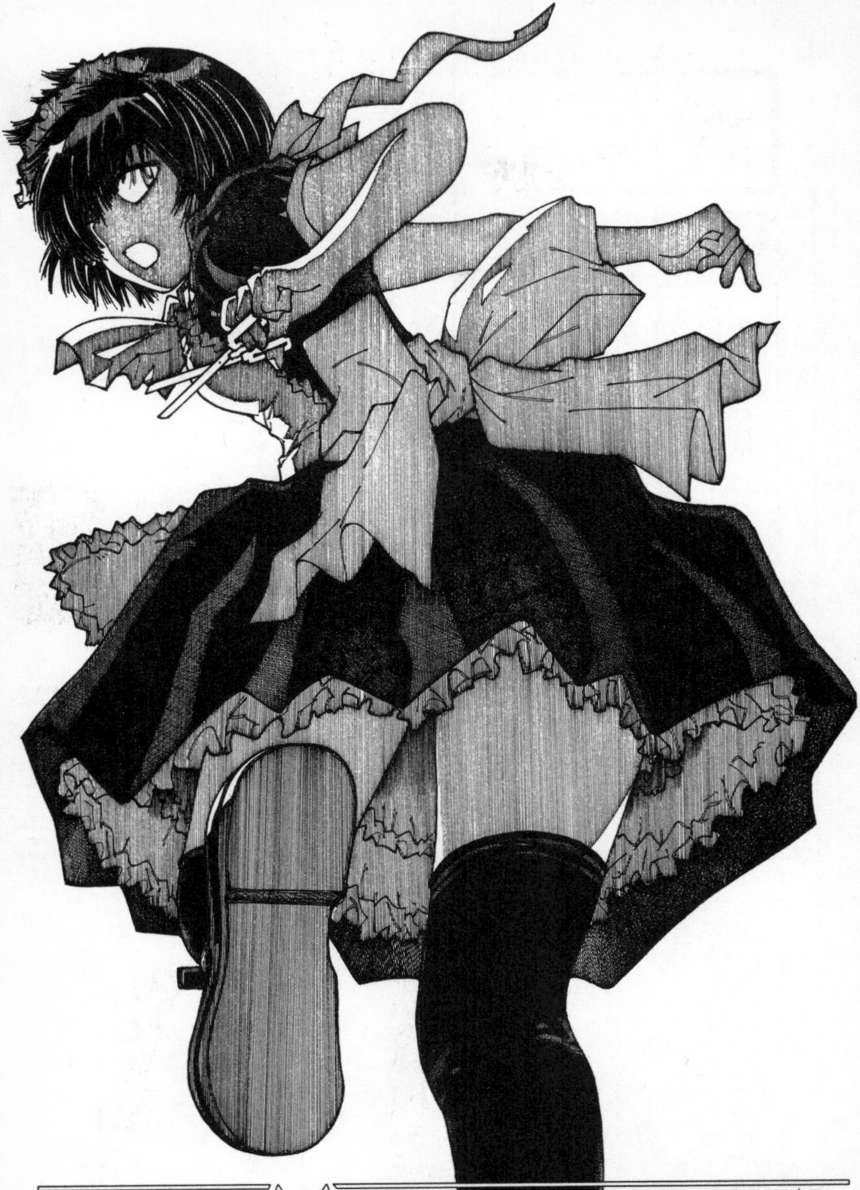

CHAPTER 31: MYSTERIOUS CULTURE FESTIVAL (PART 1)

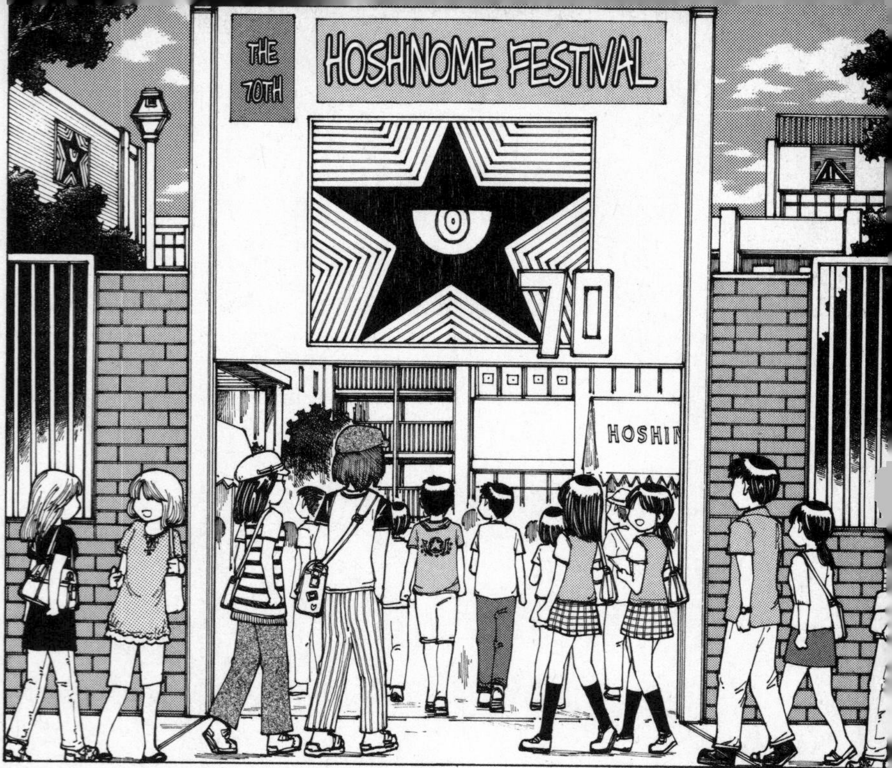
THE 70TH
HOSHINOME FESTIVAL
70
HOSHIN

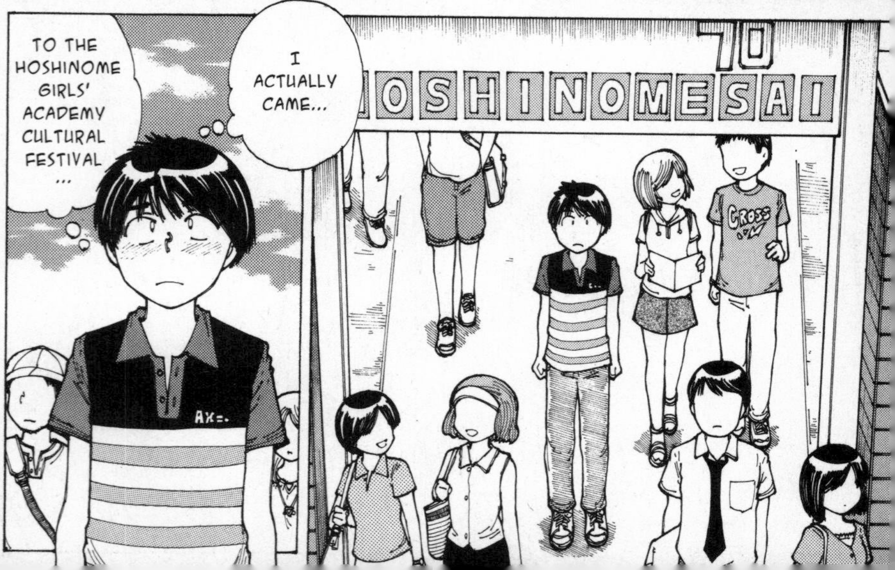
I ACTUALLY CAME...
TO THE HOSHINOME GIRLS' ACADEMY CULTURAL FESTIVAL ...
70
OSHINOMESAI
CROSS

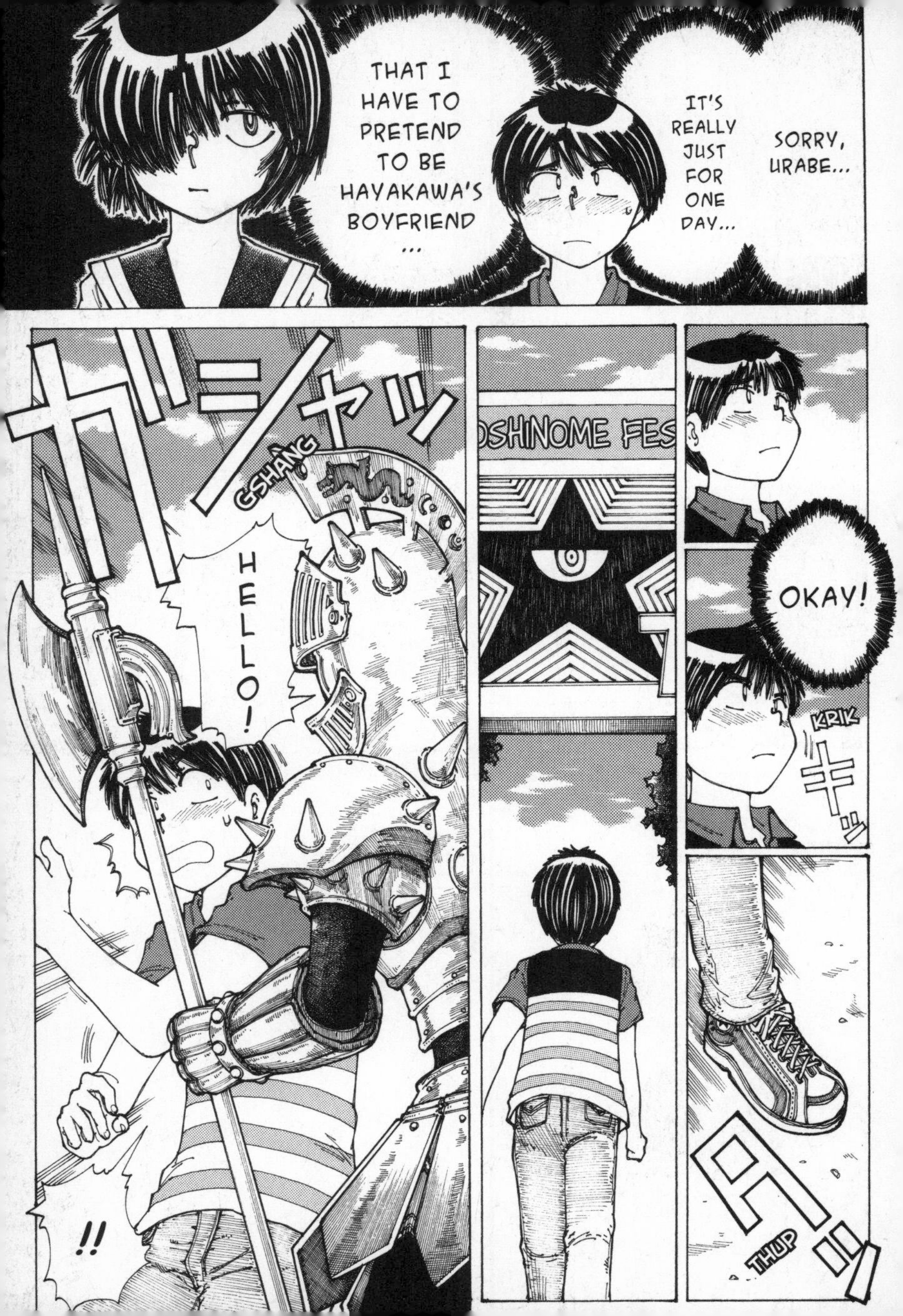
SORRY, URABE...
IT'S REALLY JUST FOR ONE DAY...
THAT I HAVE TO PRETEND TO BE HAYAKAWA'S BOYFRIEND ...
OKAY!
KRIK
キッ
THUP
OSHINOME FES
ガシャッ
GSHANG
HELLO!
!!

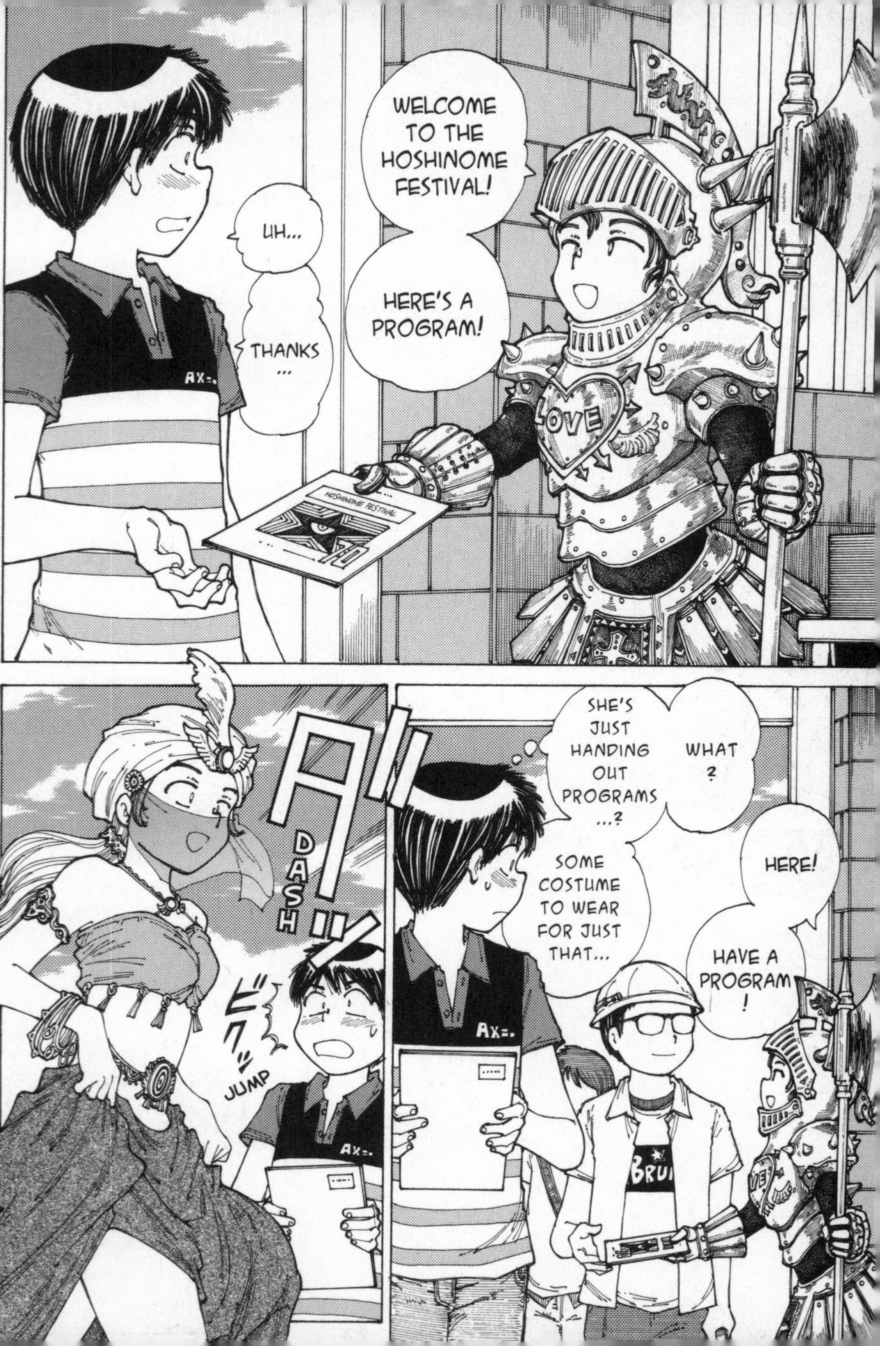
WELCOME TO THE HOSHINOME FESTIVAL!
HERE'S A PROGRAM!
UH...
THANKS ...
HOSHINOME FESTIVAL
WHAT ?
SHE'S JUST HANDING OUT PROGRAMS ...?
SOME COSTUME TO WEAR FOR JUST THAT...
HERE!
HAVE A PROGRAM !
DASH
JUMP

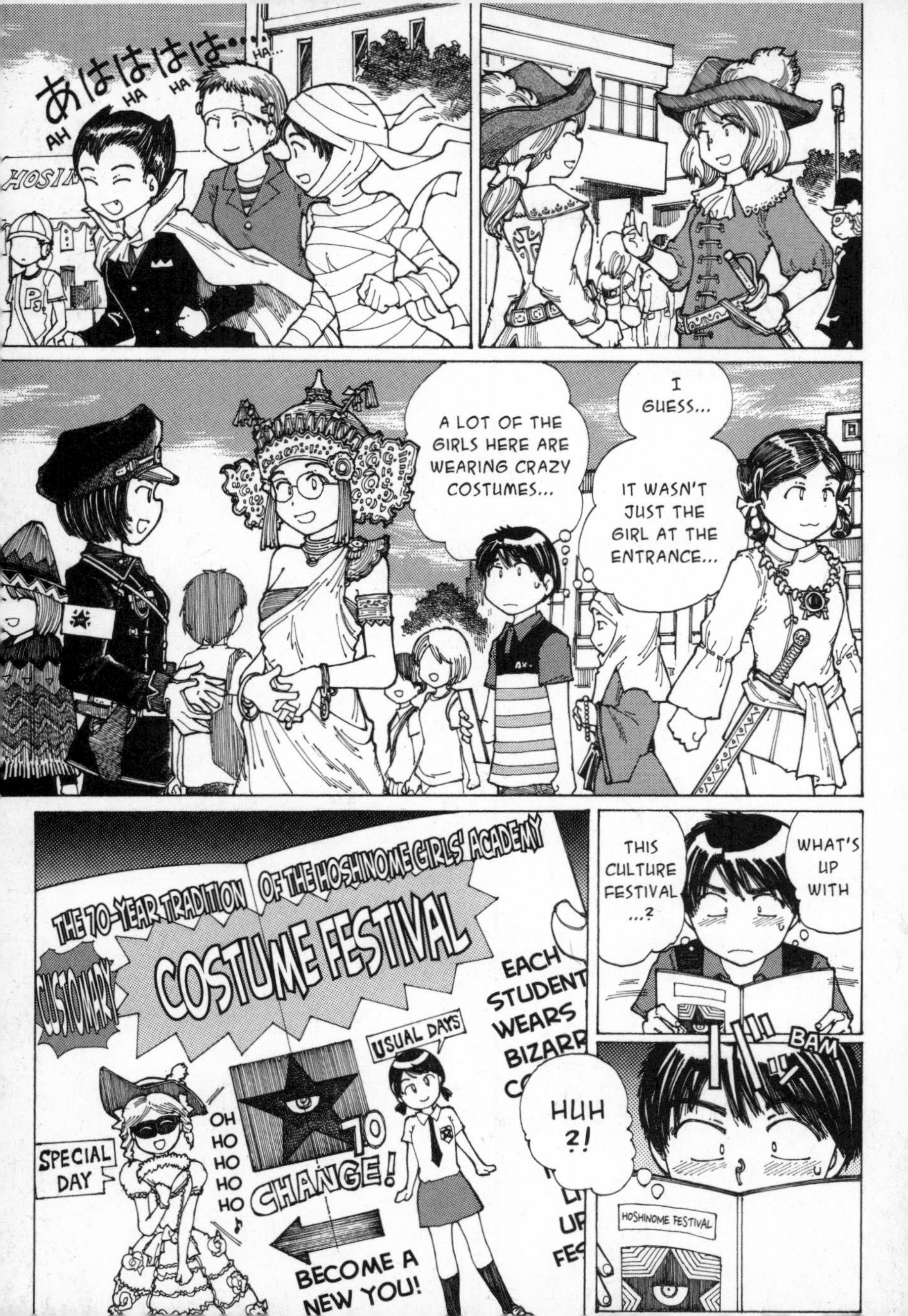
あははは…
AH HA HA HA...
HOSIN
I GUESS...
IT WASN'T JUST THE GIRL AT THE ENTRANCE...
A LOT OF THE GIRLS HERE ARE WEARING CRAZY COSTUMES...
WHAT'S UP WITH
THIS CULTURE FESTIVAL ...?
BAM
HUH ?!
HOSHINOME FESTIVAL
THE 70-YEAR TRADITION OF THE HOSHINOME GIRLS' ACADEMY
CUSTOMARY
COSTUME FESTIVAL
EACH STUDENT WEARS BIZARR
USUAL DAYS
SPECIAL DAY
OH HO HO HO HO HO ♪
70
CHANGE!
BECOME A NEW YOU!

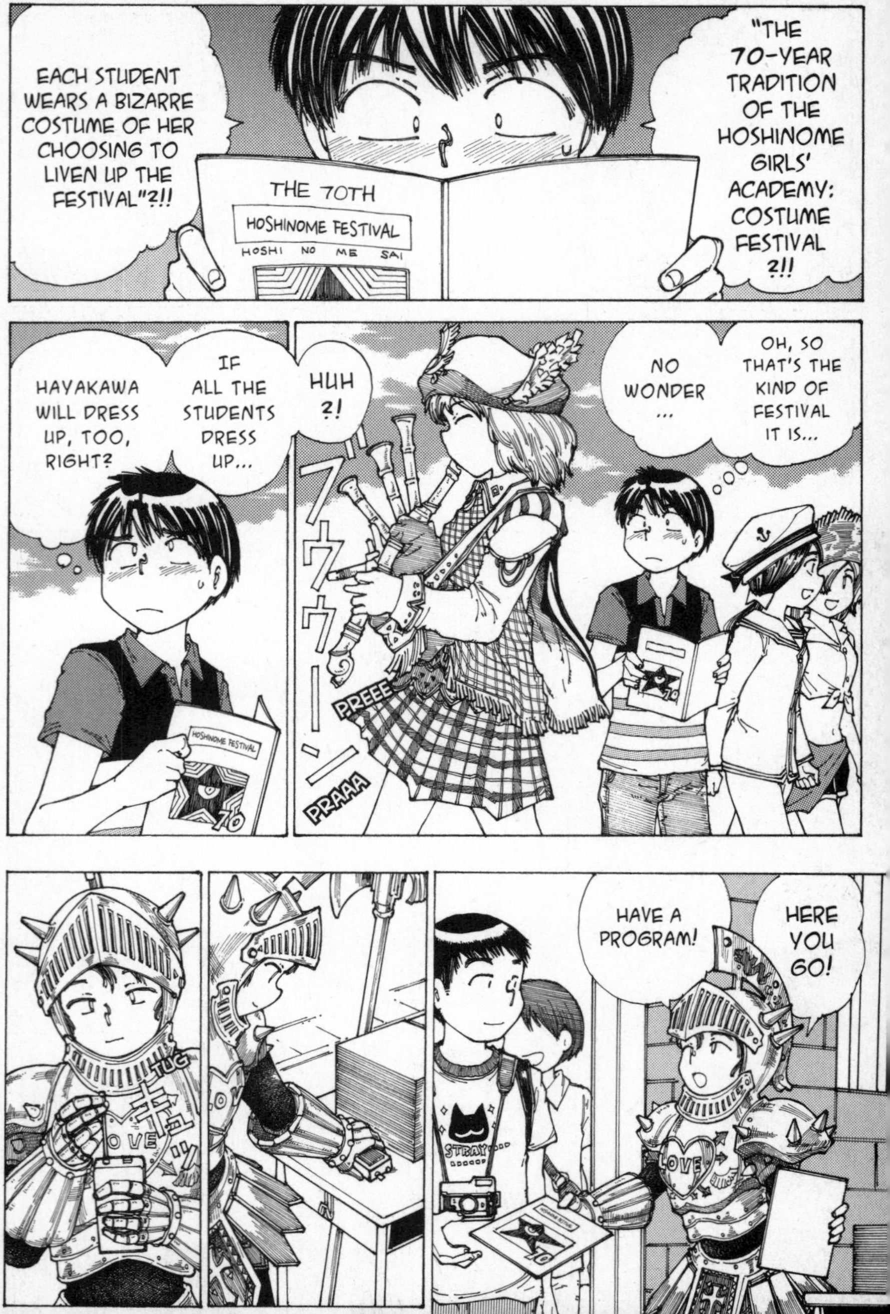
"THE 70-YEAR TRADITION OF THE HOSHINOME GIRLS' ACADEMY: COSTUME FESTIVAL ?!!
EACH STUDENT WEARS A BIZARRE COSTUME OF HER CHOOSING TO LIVEN UP THE FESTIVAL"?!!
THE 70TH
HOSHINOME FESTIVAL
HOSHI NO ME SAI
OH, SO THAT'S THE KIND OF FESTIVAL IT IS...
NO WONDER ...
HUH ?!
PREEE
PRAAA
IF ALL THE STUDENTS DRESS UP...
HAYAKAWA WILL DRESS UP, TOO, RIGHT?
HOSHINOME FESTIVAL
HERE YOU GO!
HAVE A PROGRAM!
STRAY
TUG
LOVE

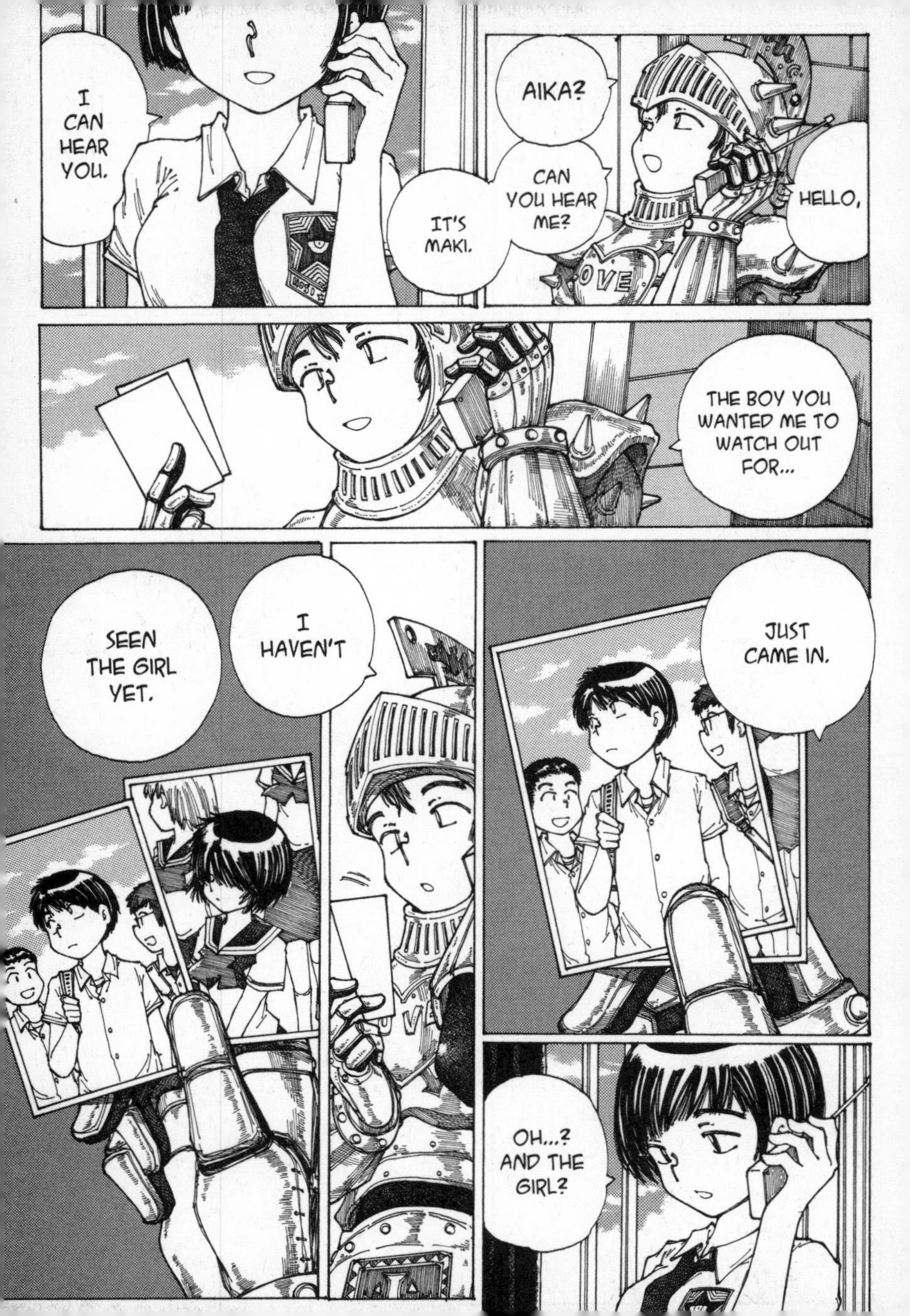
HELLO,
AIKA?
CAN YOU HEAR ME?
IT'S MAKI.
I CAN HEAR YOU.
THE BOY YOU WANTED ME TO WATCH OUT FOR...
JUST CAME IN.
OH...? AND THE GIRL?
I HAVEN'T
SEEN THE GIRL YET.

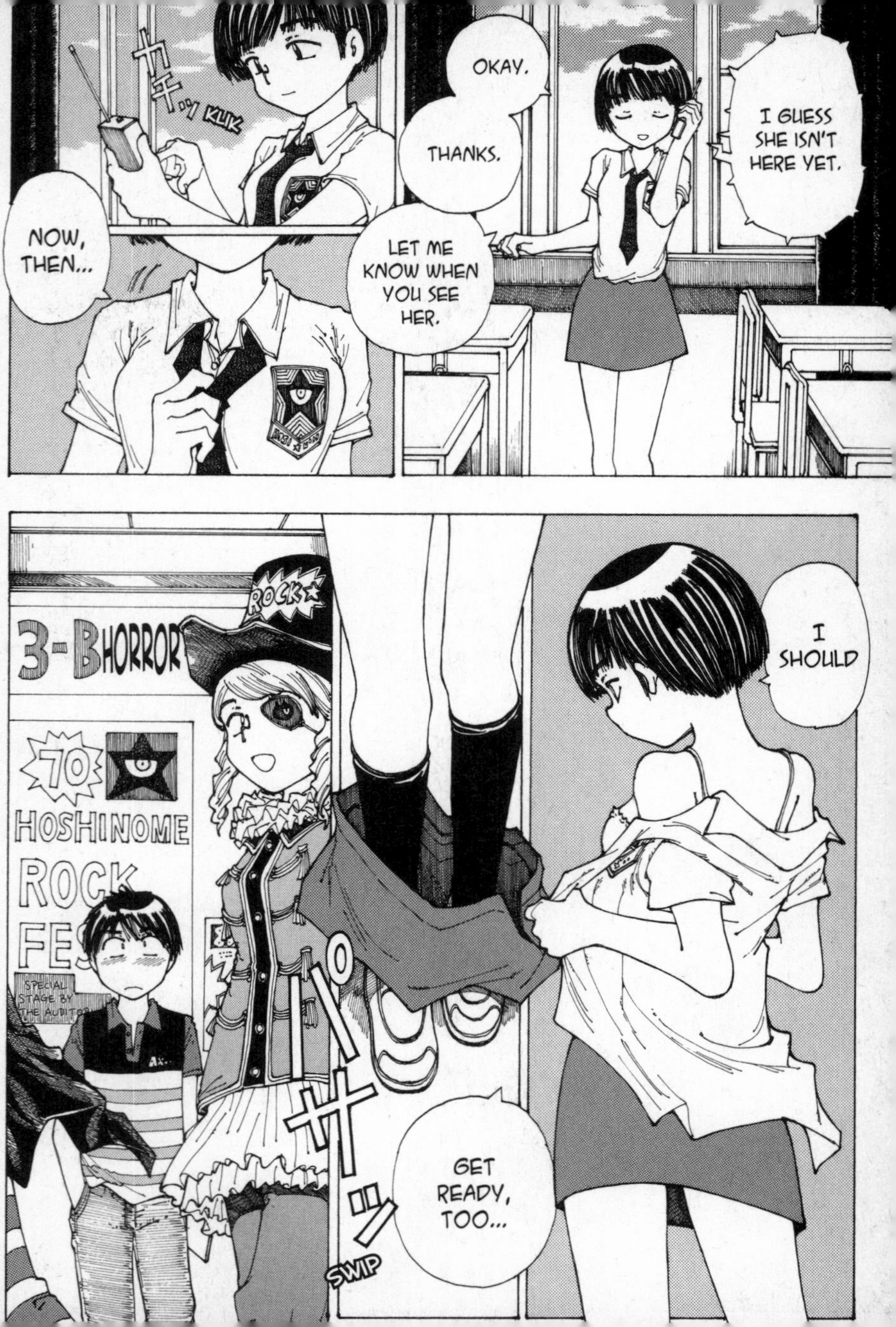
I GUESS SHE ISN'T HERE YET.
OKAY.
THANKS.
LET ME KNOW WHEN YOU SEE HER.
KLIK
NOW, THEN...
I SHOULD
ROCK
3-B HORROR
70
HOSHINOME
ROCK
FES
SPECIAL STAGE BY THE AUDITO
GET READY, TOO...
SWIP

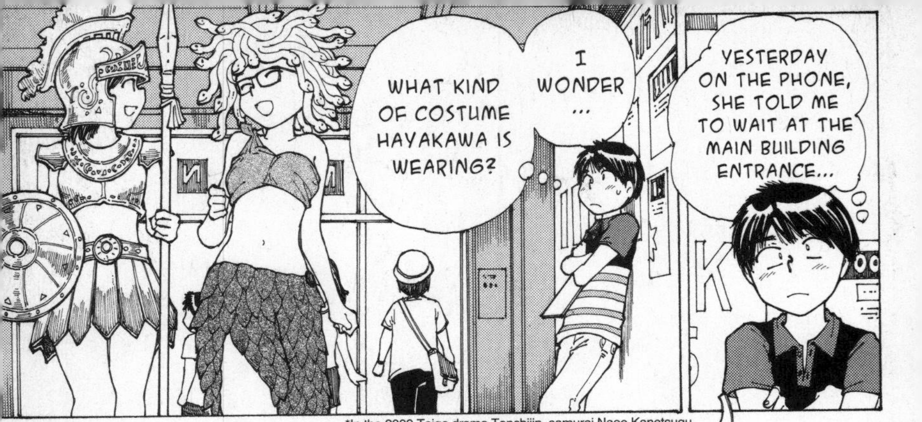
YESTERDAY ON THE PHONE, SHE TOLD ME TO WAIT AT THE MAIN BUILDING ENTRANCE...
WHAT KIND OF COSTUME HAYAKAWA IS WEARING?
I WONDER ...

*In the 2009 Taiga drama Tenchijin, samurai Naoe Kanetsugu wore a helmet with the character "*ai*," meaning love.

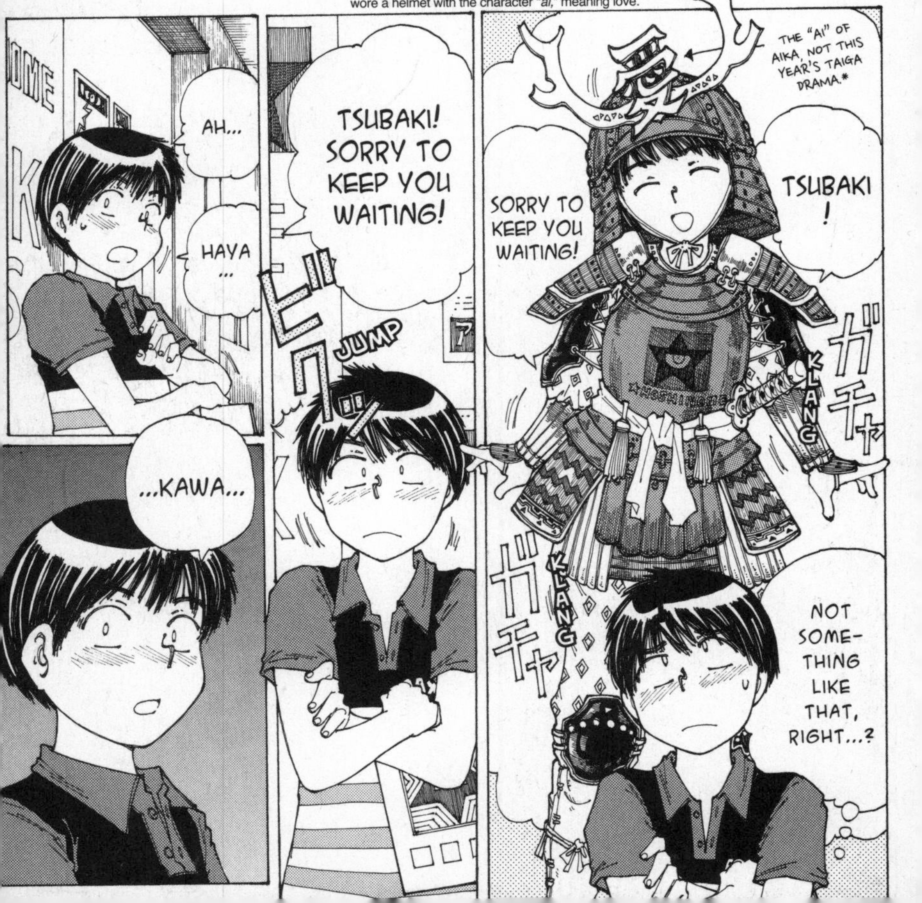
TSUBAKI !
THE "AI" OF AIKA, NOT THIS YEAR'S TAIGA DRAMA.*
SORRY TO KEEP YOU WAITING!
KLANG
ガチャ
KLANG
ガチャ
NOT SOME-THING LIKE THAT, RIGHT...?
TSUBAKI! SORRY TO KEEP YOU WAITING!
ビクッ
JUMP
AH...
HAYA ...
...KAWA...

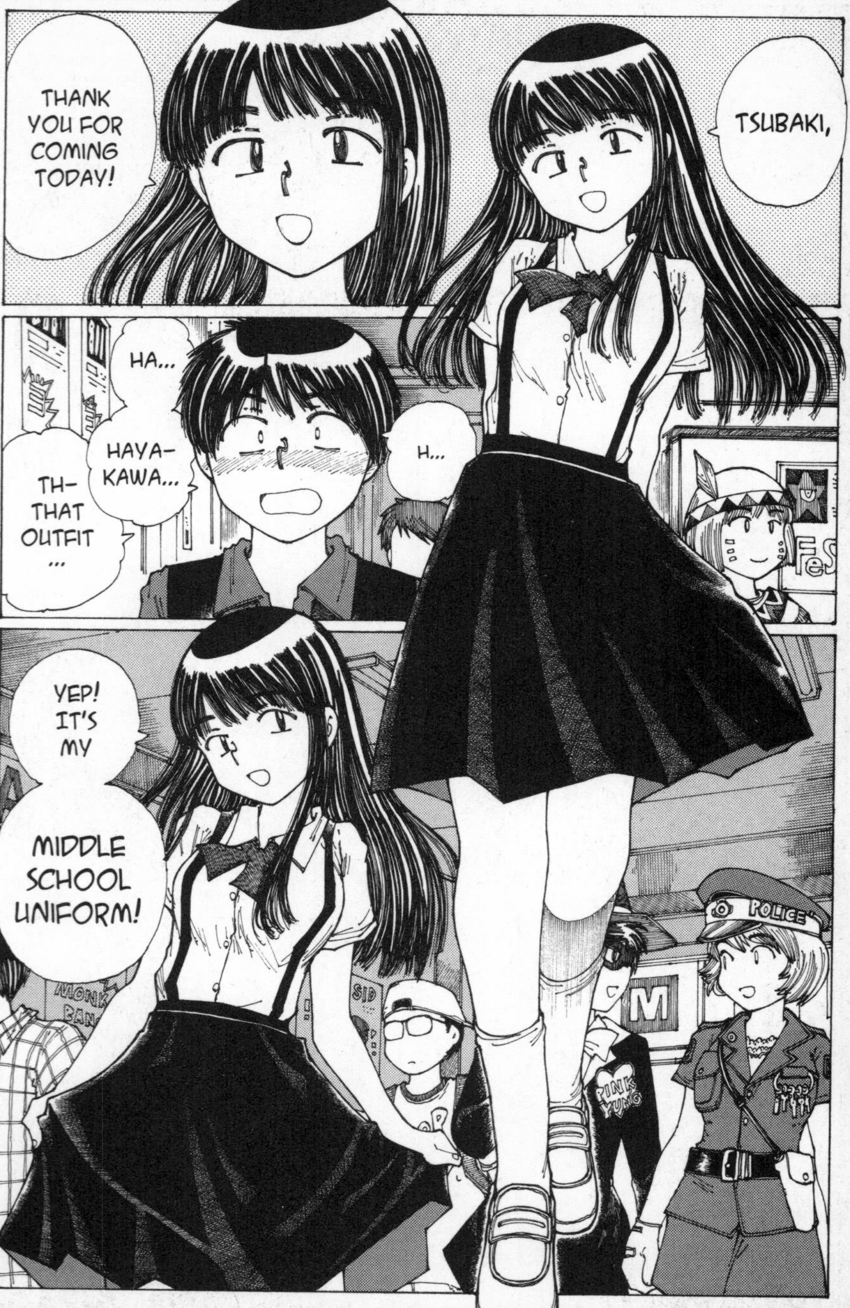
TSUBAKI,
THANK YOU FOR COMING TODAY!
H...
HA...
HAYA-KAWA...
TH-THAT OUTFIT ...
YEP! IT'S MY
MIDDLE SCHOOL UNIFORM!
POLICE
PINK YUNG

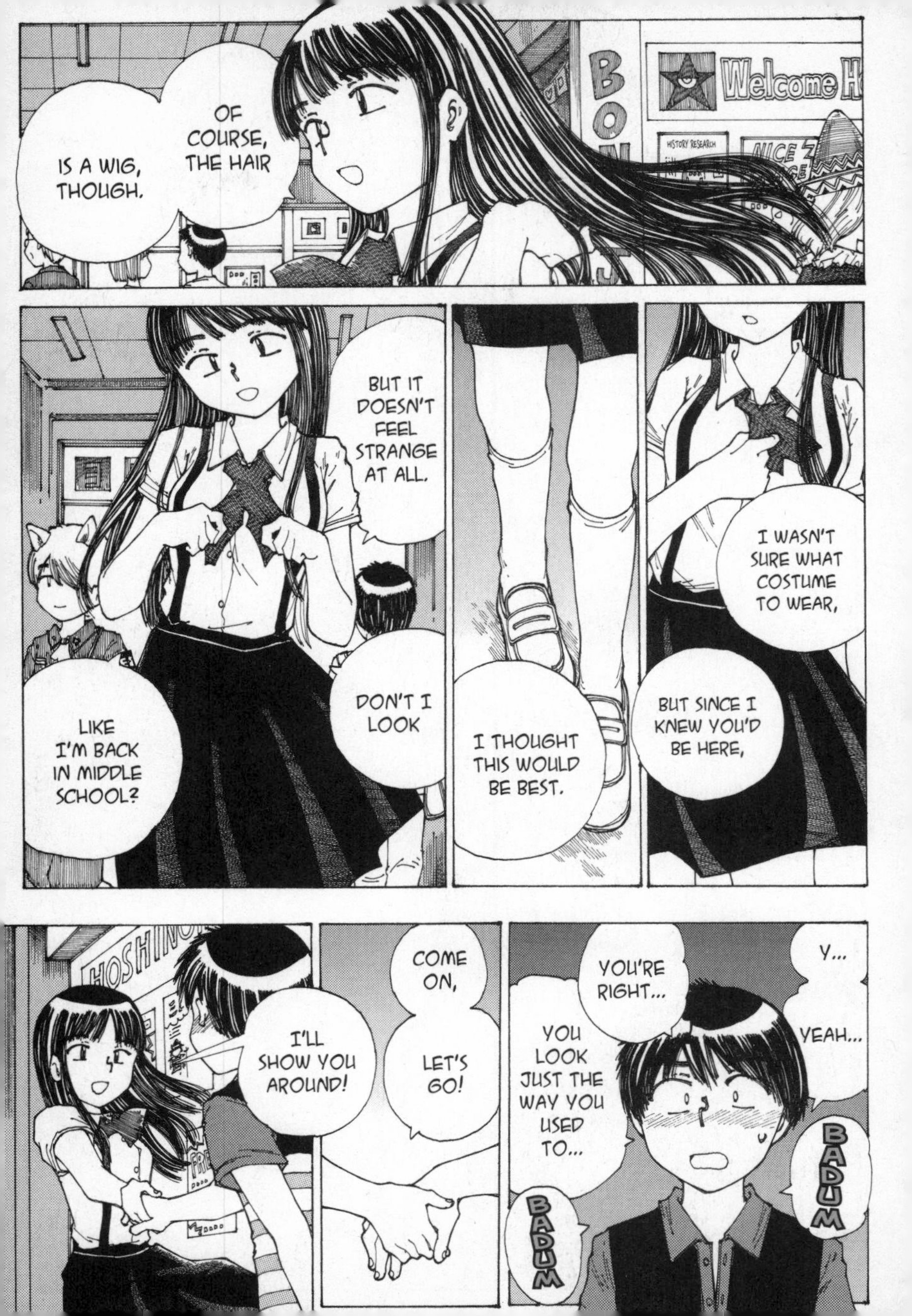
Welcome
HISTORY RESEARCH
OF COURSE, THE HAIR
IS A WIG, THOUGH.
I WASN'T SURE WHAT COSTUME TO WEAR,
BUT SINCE I KNEW YOU'D BE HERE,
I THOUGHT THIS WOULD BE BEST.
BUT IT DOESN'T FEEL STRANGE AT ALL.
DON'T I LOOK
LIKE I'M BACK IN MIDDLE SCHOOL?
Y...
YEAH...
YOU'RE RIGHT...
YOU LOOK JUST THE WAY YOU USED TO...
BADUM
BADUM
COME ON,
LET'S GO!
I'LL SHOW YOU AROUND!

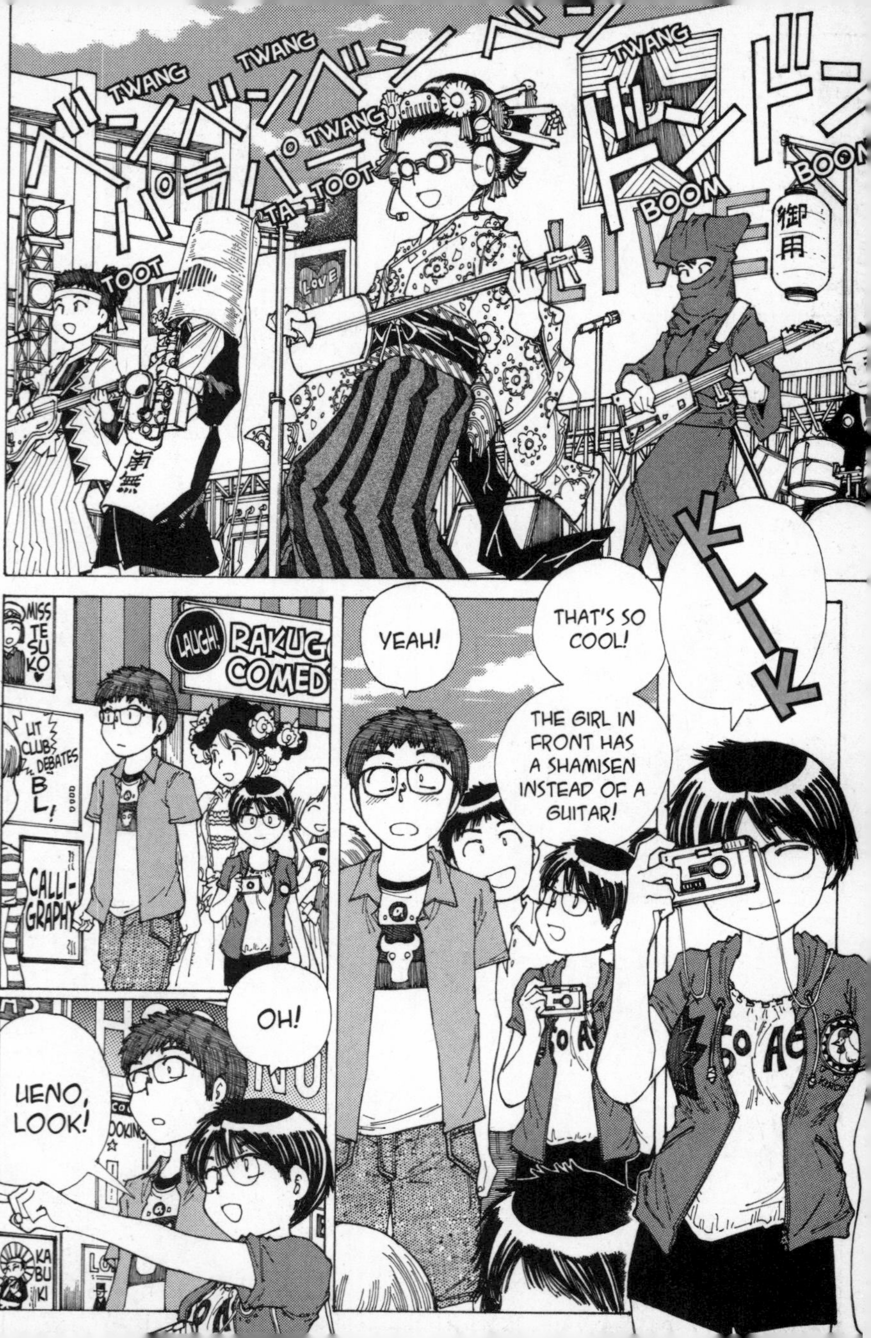
TWANG
TWANG
TWANG
TWANG
TA TOOT
TA
TOOT
BOOM
BOOM
LOVE
御用
KLIK
THAT'S SO COOL!
THE GIRL IN FRONT HAS A SHAMISEN INSTEAD OF A GUITAR!
YEAH!
MISS TESUKO
LAUGH! RAKUG COMED
LIT CLUB DEBATES BL!
CALLI-GRAPHY
OH!
UENO, LOOK!
KABUKI

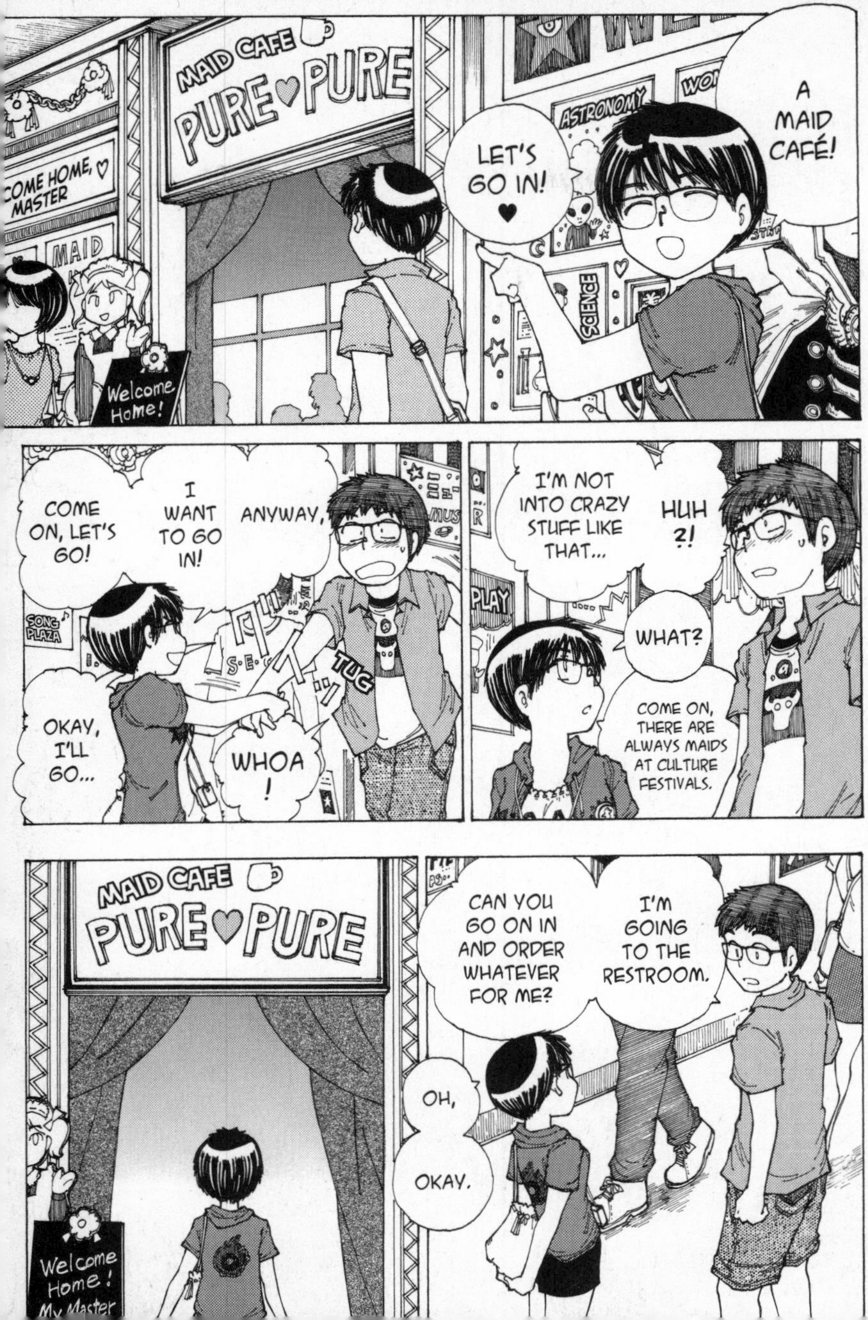
A MAID CAFÉ!
LET'S GO IN! ♥
MAID CAFE
PURE♥PURE
COME HOME, MASTER ♡
Welcome Home!
ASTRONOMY
SCIENCE
HUH ?!
I'M NOT INTO CRAZY STUFF LIKE THAT...
WHAT?
COME ON, THERE ARE ALWAYS MAIDS AT CULTURE FESTIVALS.
ANYWAY,
I WANT TO GO IN!
COME ON, LET'S GO!
SONG PLAZA
TUG
WHOA!
OKAY, I'LL GO...
I'M GOING TO THE RESTROOM.
CAN YOU GO ON IN AND ORDER WHATEVER FOR ME?
OH,
OKAY.
MAID CAFE
PURE♥PURE
Welcome Home! My Master

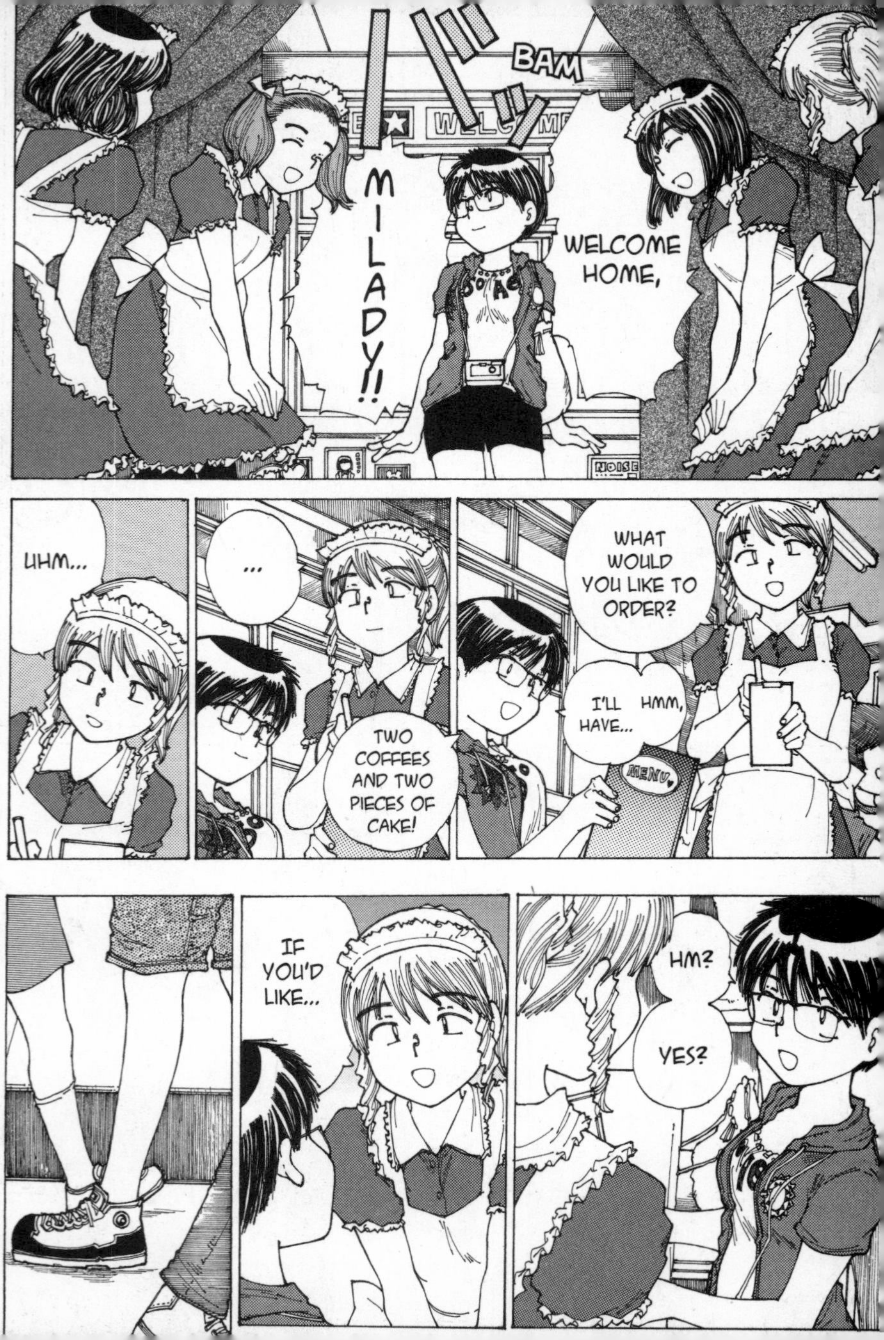
BAM
WELCOME HOME,
MILADY!!
NOISE
WHAT WOULD YOU LIKE TO ORDER?
HMM, I'LL HAVE...
MENU
...
TWO COFFEES AND TWO PIECES OF CAKE!
UHM...
HM?
YES?
IF YOU'D LIKE...

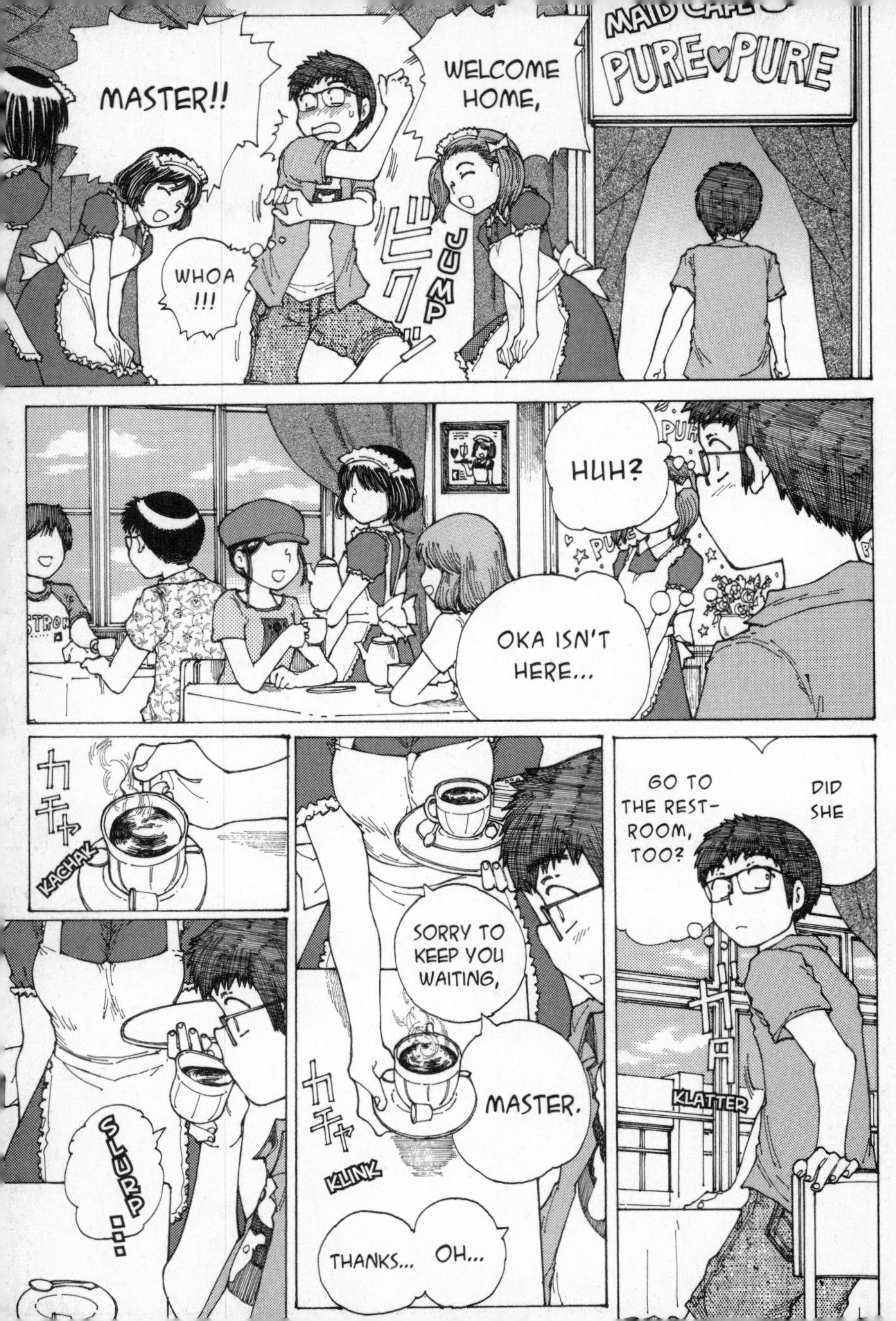
MAID CAFE'S
PURE♥PURE
WELCOME HOME,
MASTER!!
ビクッ
JUMP
WHOA !!!
HUH?
OKA ISN'T HERE...
DID SHE
GO TO THE REST-ROOM, TOO?
ガタ
KLATTER
SORRY TO KEEP YOU WAITING,
MASTER.
カチャ
KLINK
THANKS... OH...
カチャ
KACHAK
SLURP ...

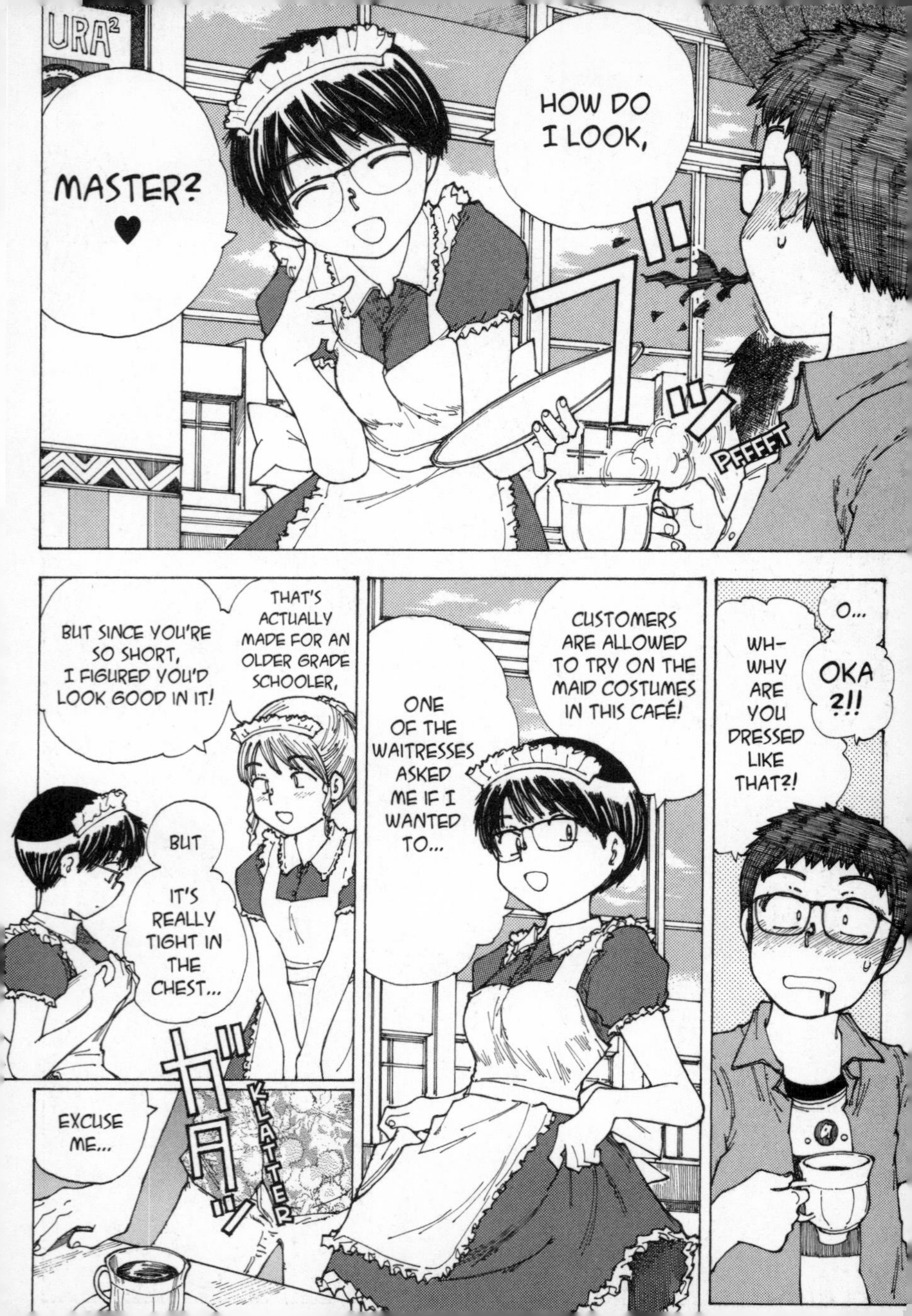
URA²
HOW DO I LOOK,
MASTER? ♥
PFFFT
O...
OKA?!!
WH-WHY ARE YOU DRESSED LIKE THAT?!
CUSTOMERS ARE ALLOWED TO TRY ON THE MAID COSTUMES IN THIS CAFÉ!
ONE OF THE WAITRESSES ASKED ME IF I WANTED TO...
THAT'S ACTUALLY MADE FOR AN OLDER GRADE SCHOOLER,
BUT SINCE YOU'RE SO SHORT, I FIGURED YOU'D LOOK GOOD IN IT!
BUT IT'S REALLY TIGHT IN THE CHEST...
KLATTER
EXCUSE ME...

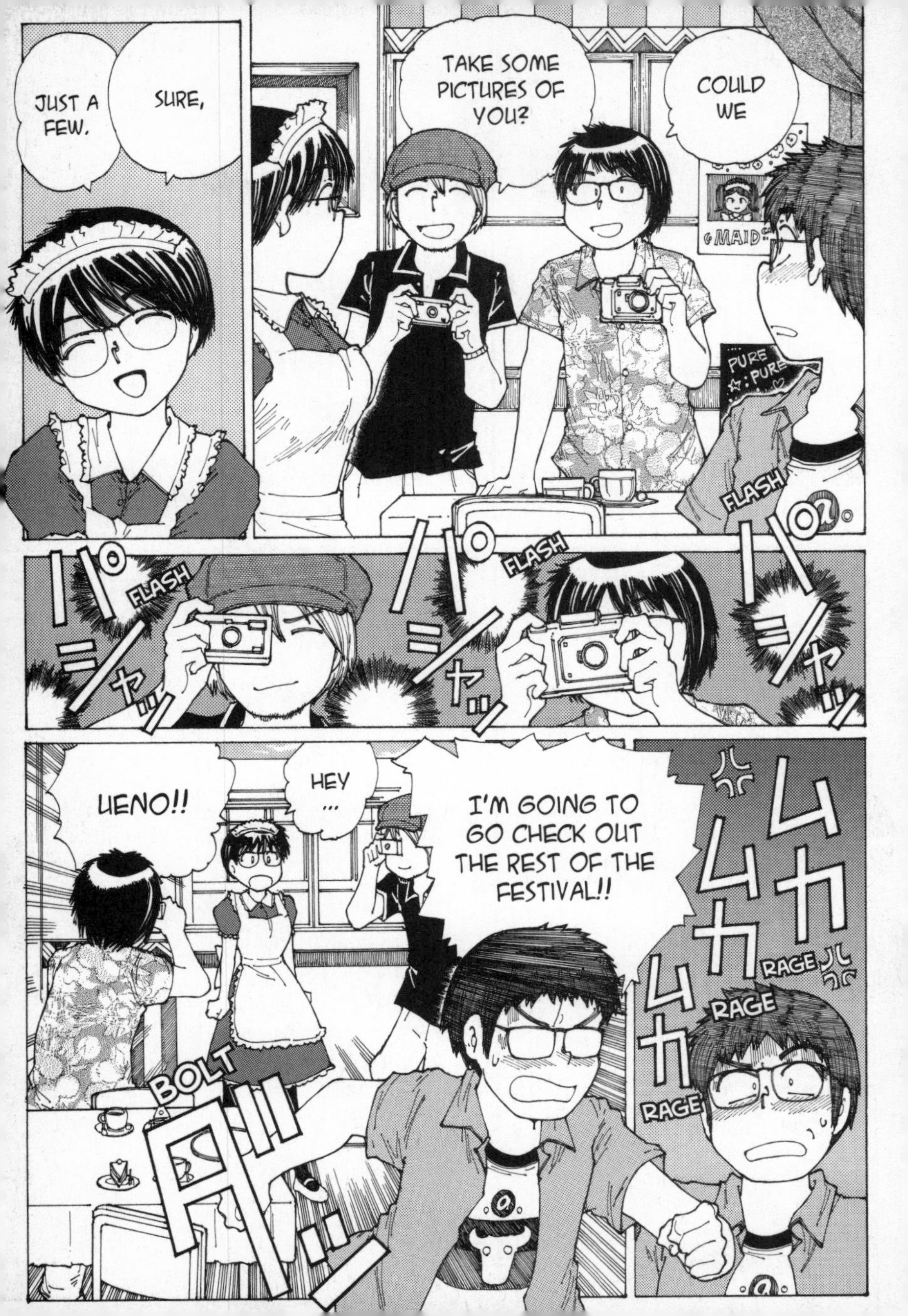
COULD WE
TAKE SOME PICTURES OF YOU?
SURE,
JUST A FEW.
MAID
PURE☆PURE
FLASH
FLASH
FLASH
FLASH
RAGE
RAGE
RAGE
I'M GOING TO GO CHECK OUT THE REST OF THE FESTIVAL!!
HEY ...
UENO!!
BOLT

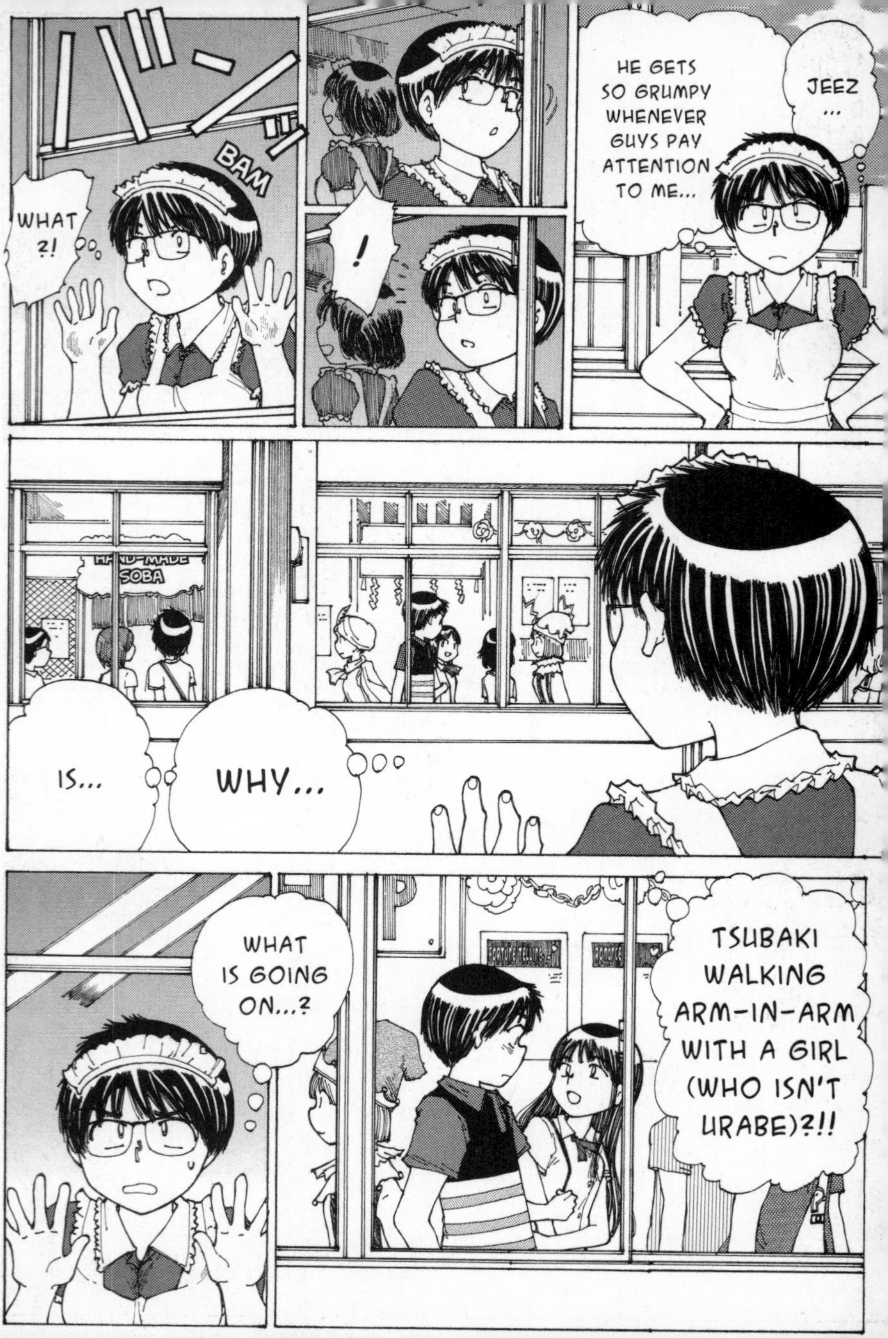
JEEZ ...
HE GETS SO GRUMPY WHENEVER GUYS PAY ATTENTION TO ME...
!
BAM
WHAT ?!
HAND-MADE SOBA
WHY...
IS...
TSUBAKI WALKING ARM-IN-ARM WITH A GIRL (WHO ISN'T URABE)?!!
WHAT IS GOING ON...?

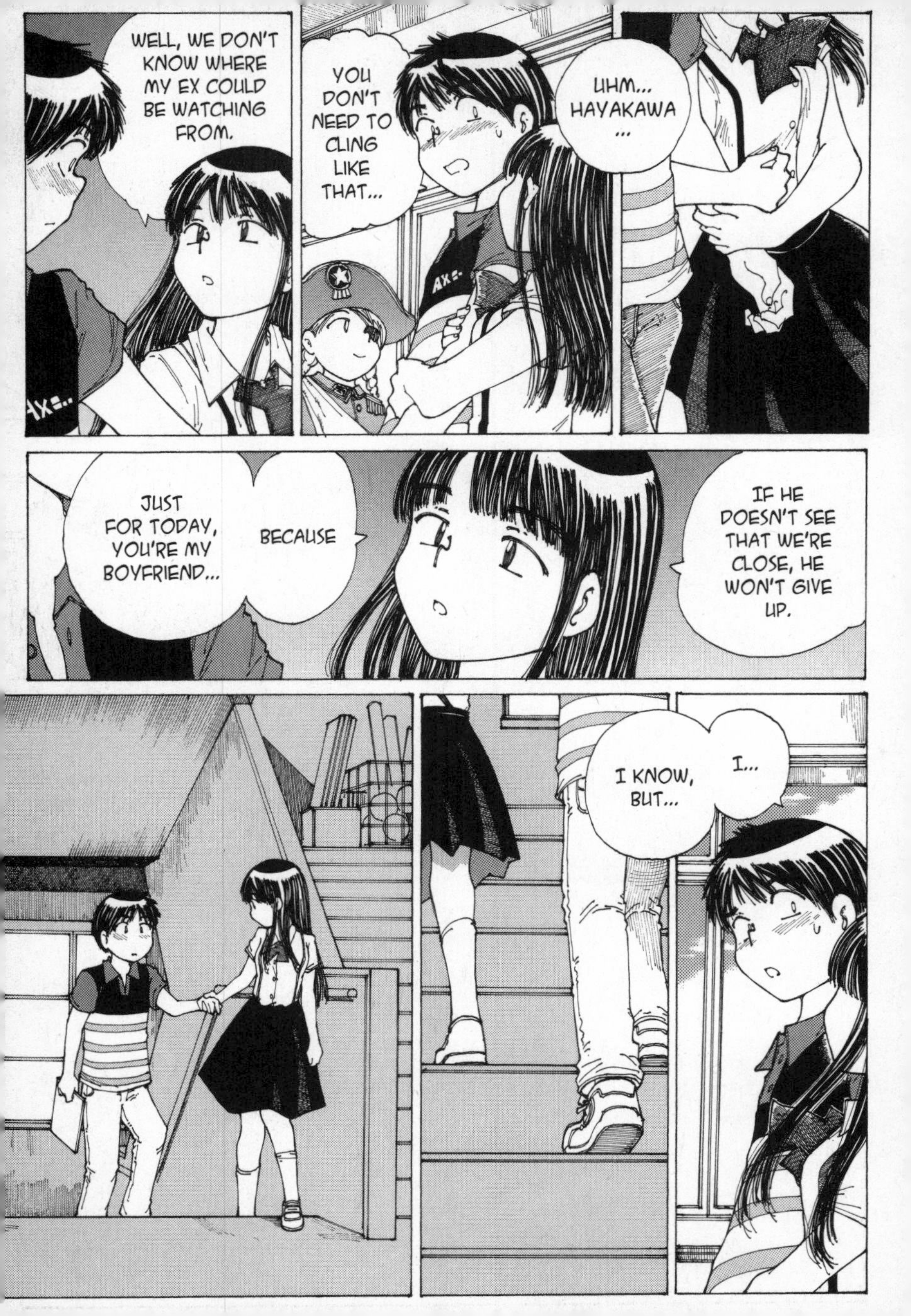
UHM... HAYAKAWA ...
YOU DON'T NEED TO CLING LIKE THAT...
WELL, WE DON'T KNOW WHERE MY EX COULD BE WATCHING FROM.
IF HE DOESN'T SEE THAT WE'RE CLOSE, HE WON'T GIVE UP.
BECAUSE
JUST FOR TODAY, YOU'RE MY BOYFRIEND...
I...
I KNOW, BUT...

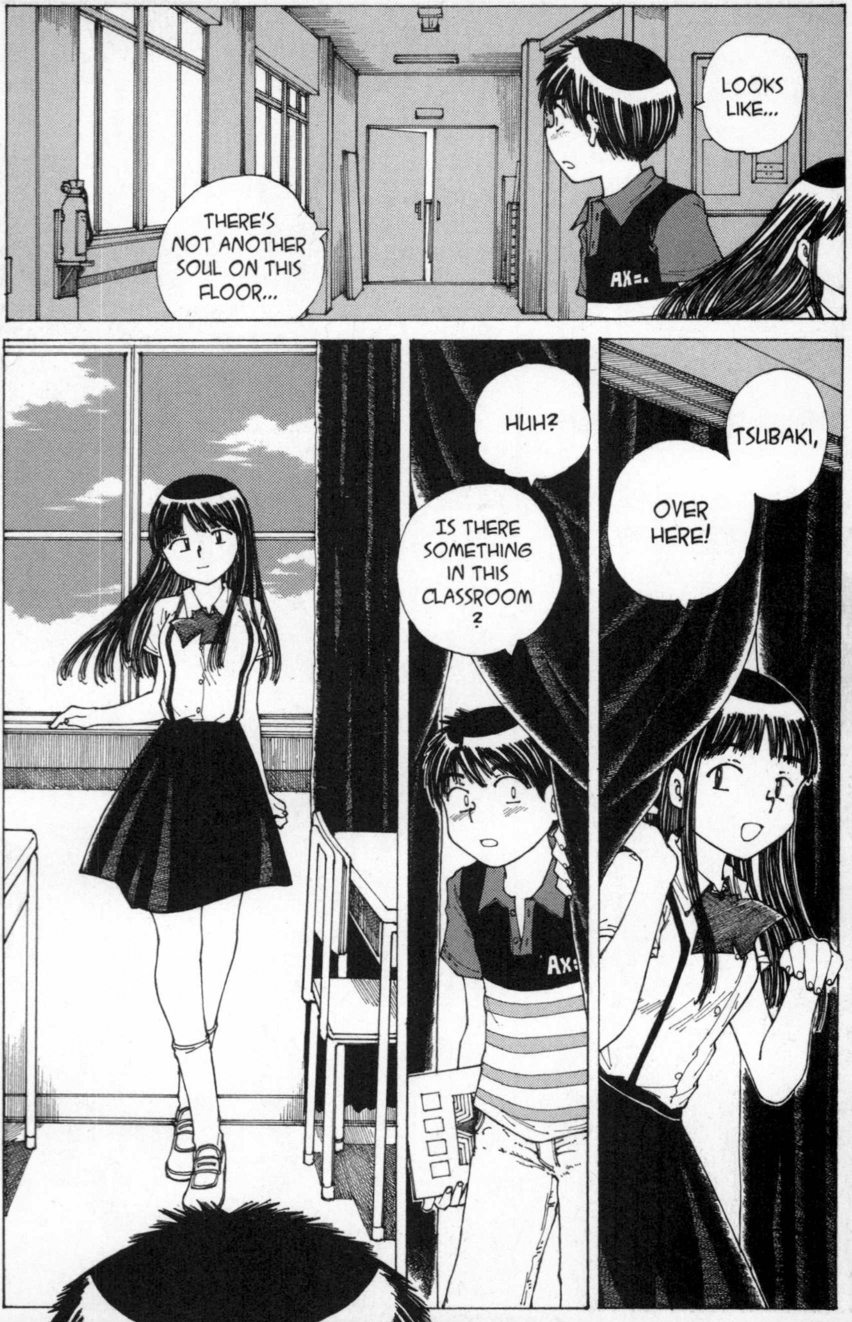
LOOKS LIKE...
THERE'S NOT ANOTHER SOUL ON THIS FLOOR...
TSUBAKI,
OVER HERE!
HUH?
IS THERE SOMETHING IN THIS CLASSROOM?

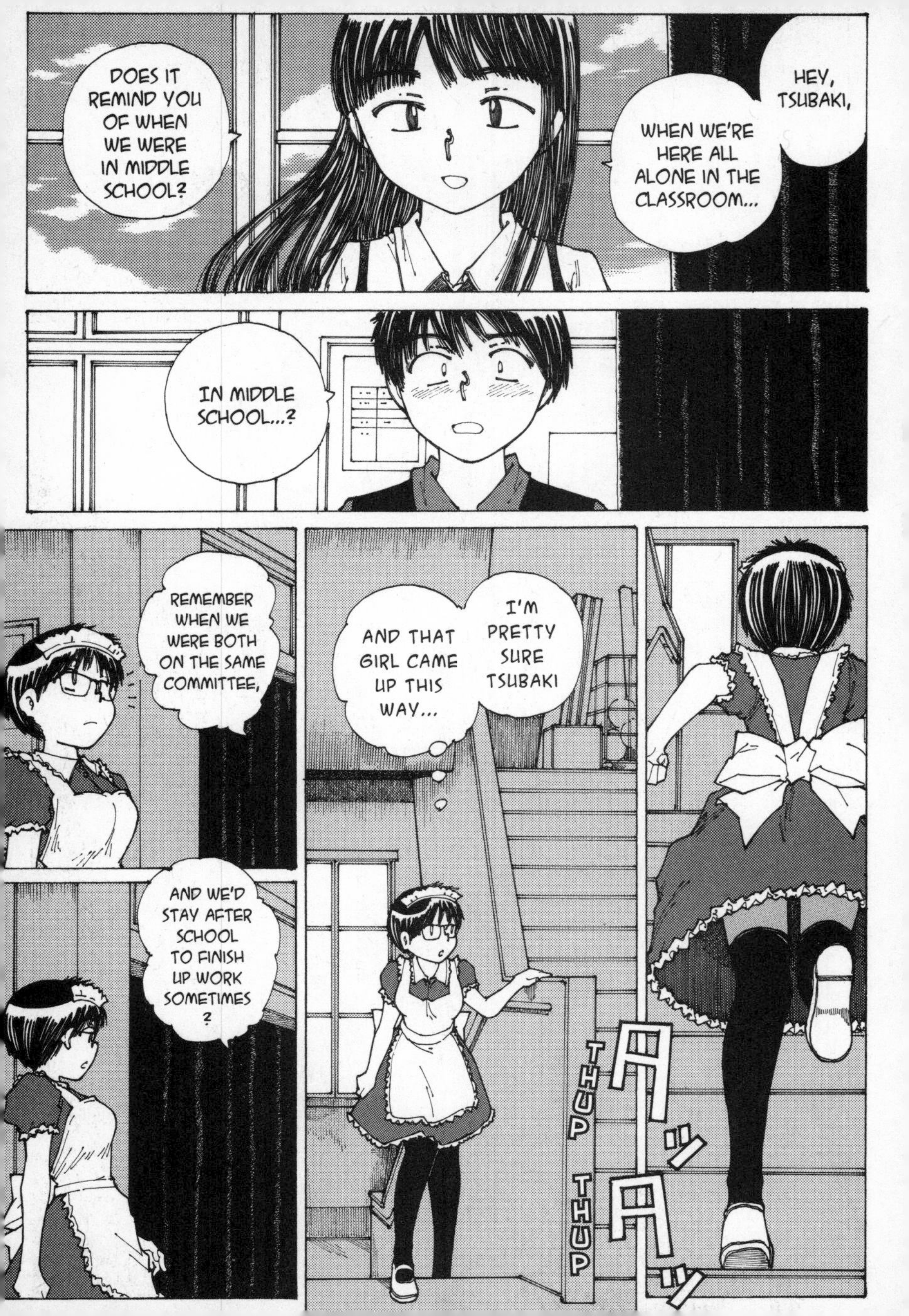
HEY, TSUBAKI,
WHEN WE'RE HERE ALL ALONE IN THE CLASSROOM...
DOES IT REMIND YOU OF WHEN WE WERE IN MIDDLE SCHOOL?
IN MIDDLE SCHOOL...?
THUP THUP
I'M PRETTY SURE TSUBAKI
AND THAT GIRL CAME UP THIS WAY...
REMEMBER WHEN WE WERE BOTH ON THE SAME COMMITTEE,
AND WE'D STAY AFTER SCHOOL TO FINISH UP WORK SOMETIMES?

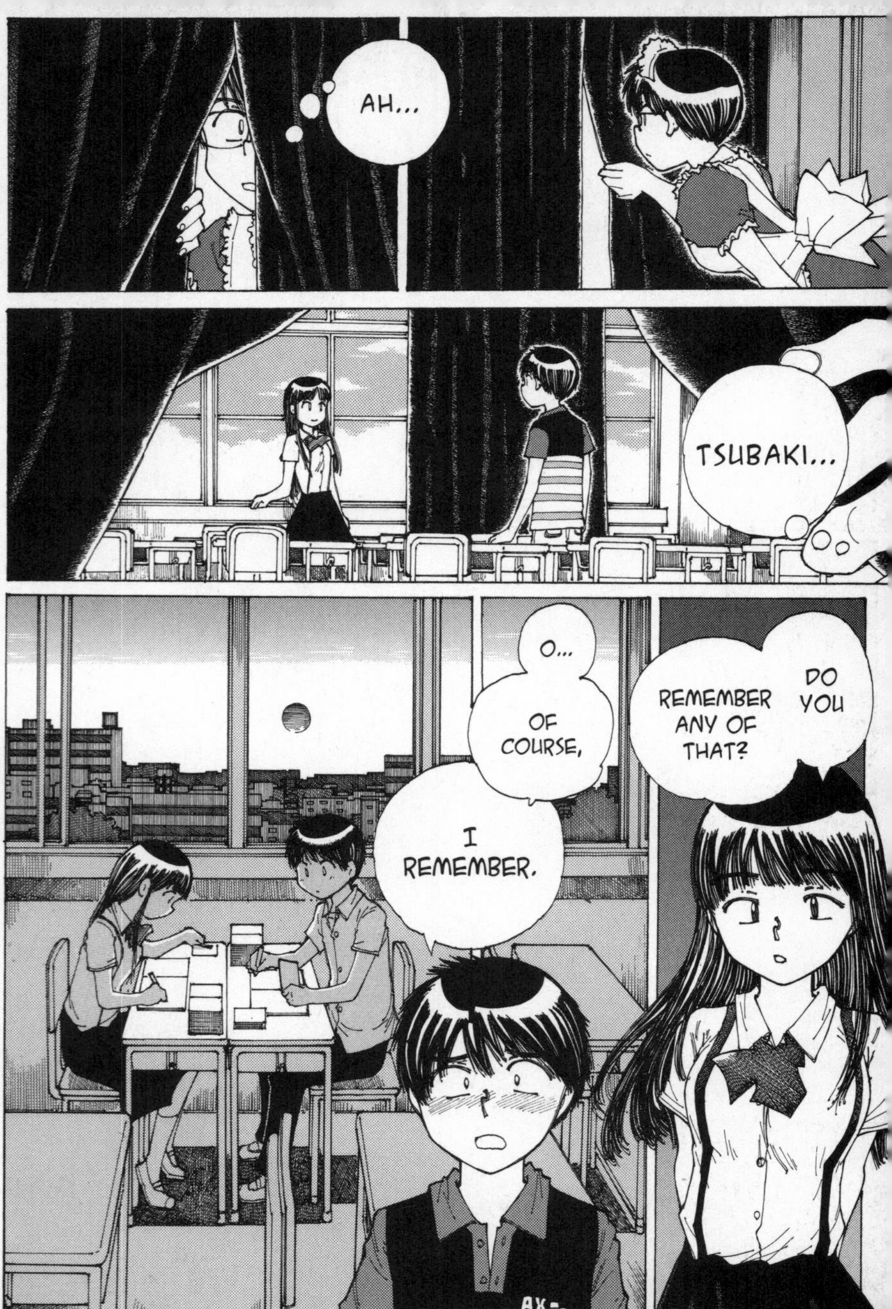
AH...
TSUBAKI...
DO YOU REMEMBER ANY OF THAT?
O... OF COURSE, I REMEMBER.
AX=.

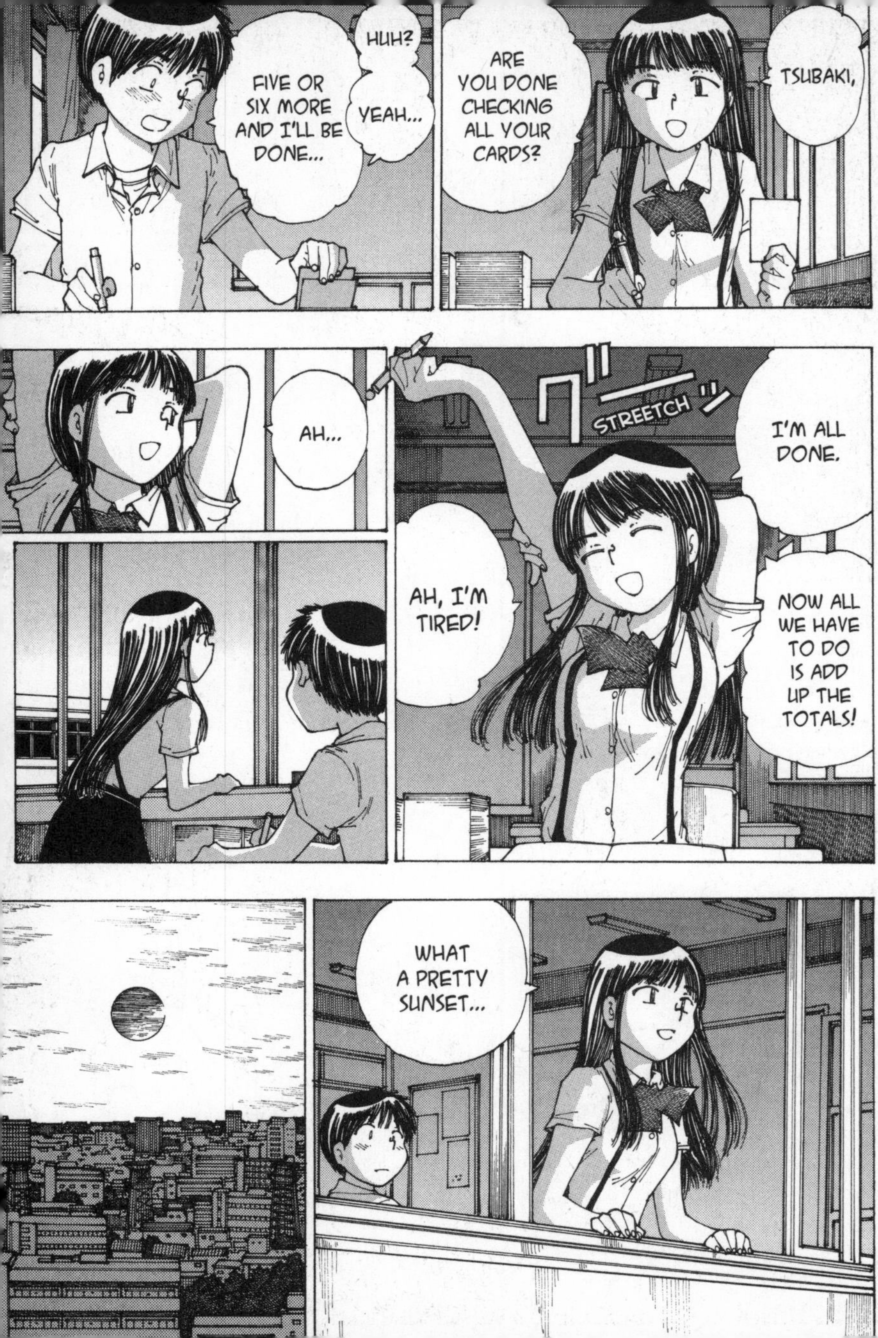
TSUBAKI,
ARE YOU DONE CHECKING ALL YOUR CARDS?
HUH?
YEAH...
FIVE OR SIX MORE AND I'LL BE DONE...
ヴーッ
STREETCH
I'M ALL DONE.
NOW ALL WE HAVE TO DO IS ADD UP THE TOTALS!
AH, I'M TIRED!
AH...
WHAT A PRETTY SUNSET...

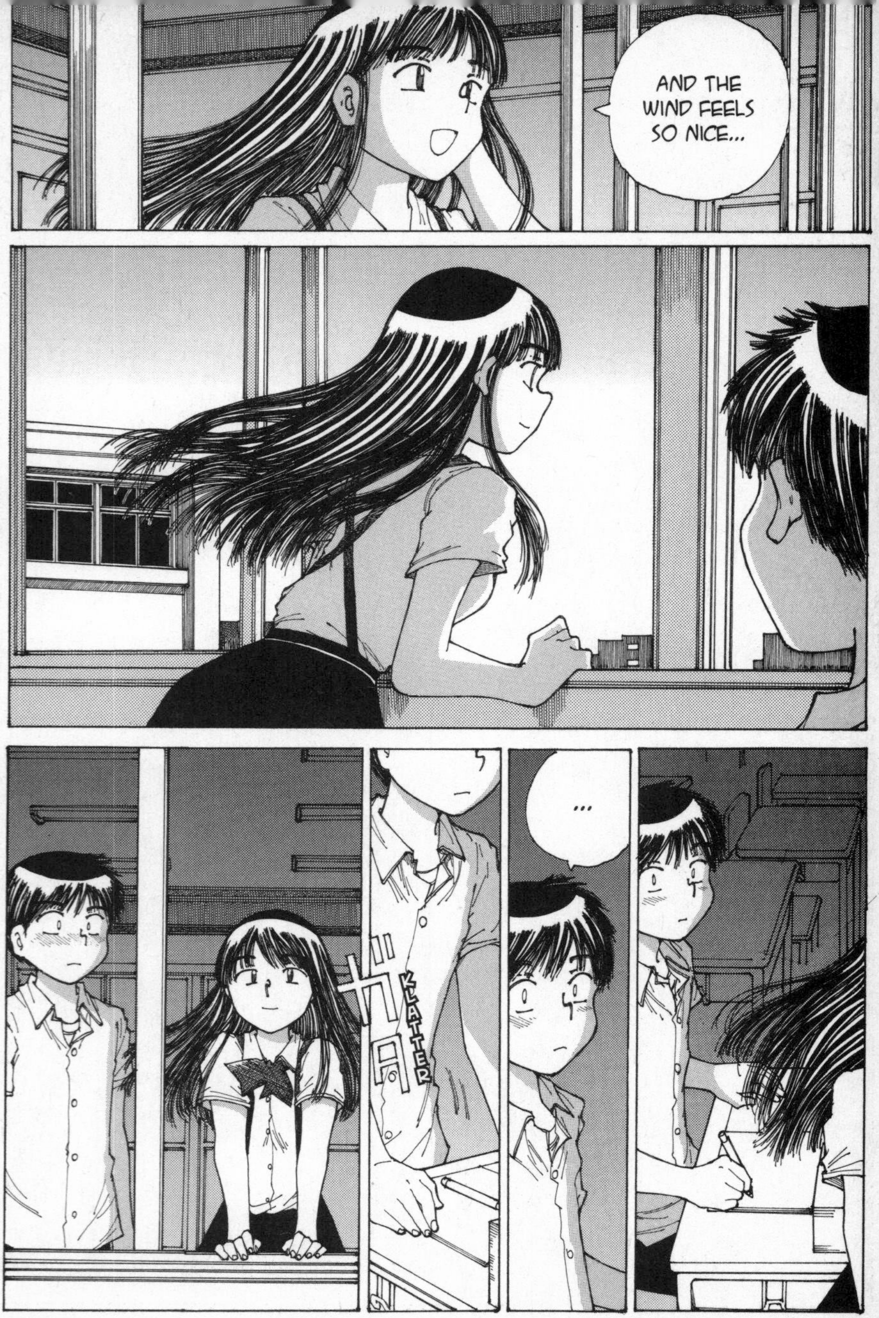
AND THE WIND FEELS SO NICE...
...
KLATTER
ガタ

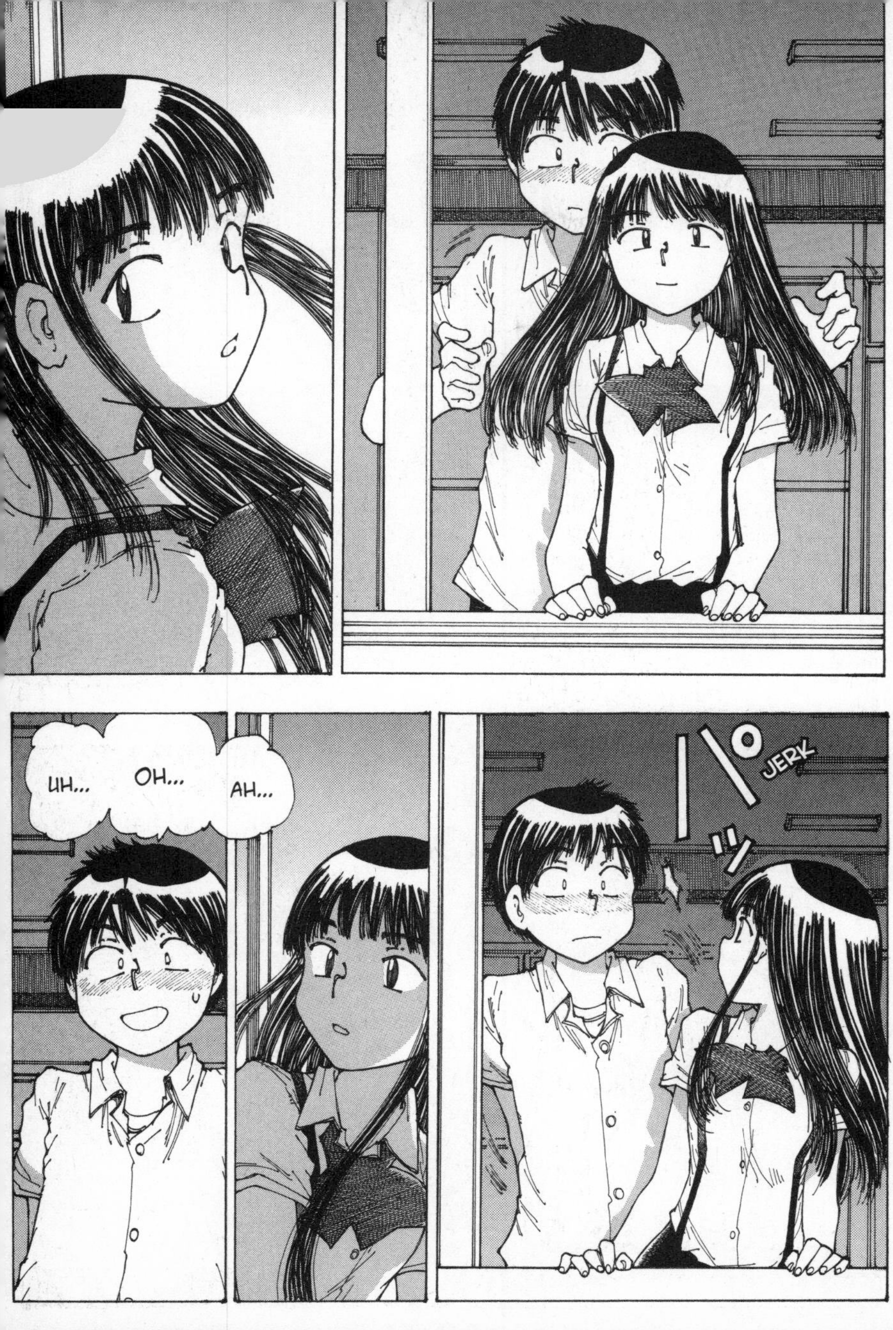
パッ
JERK
UH... OH... AH...

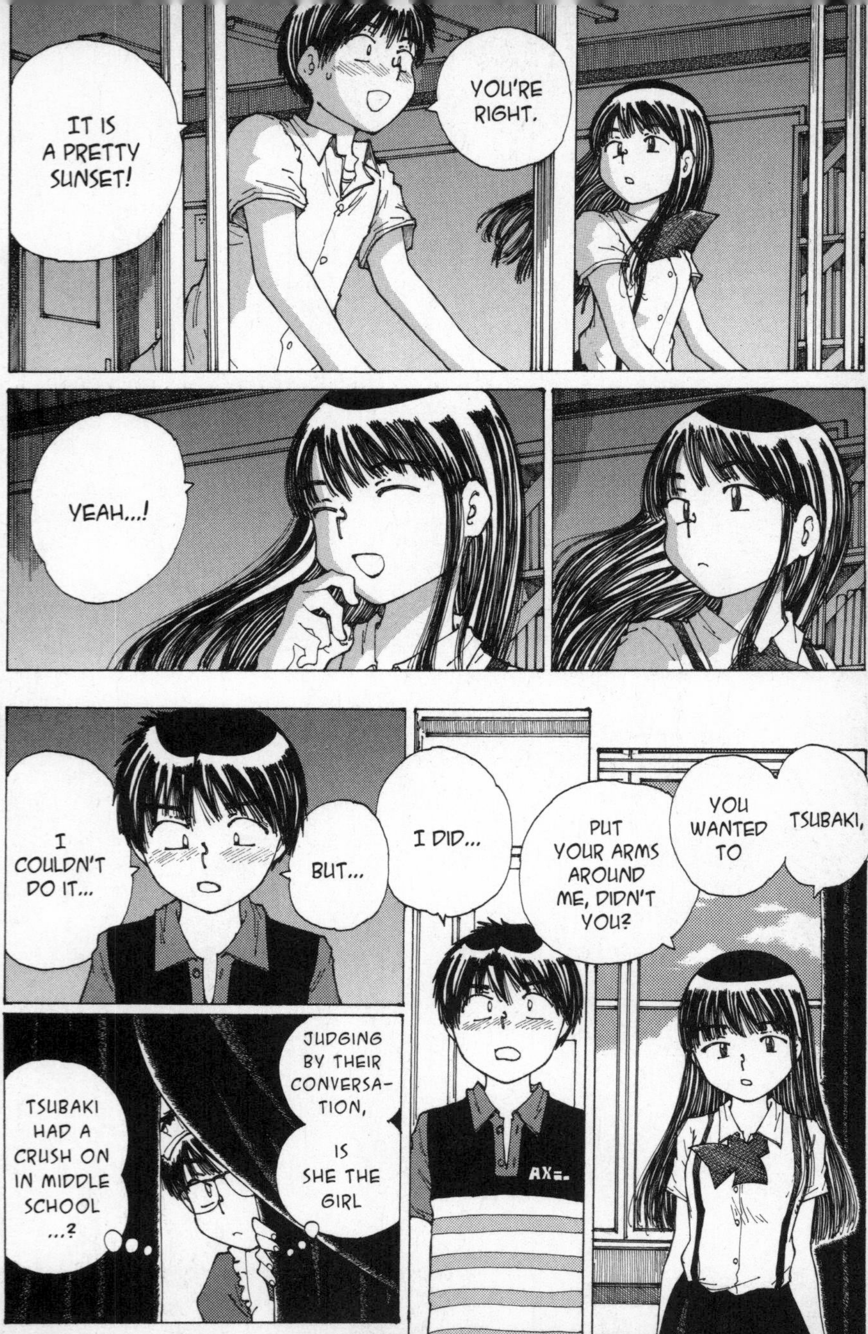
YOU'RE RIGHT.
IT IS A PRETTY SUNSET!
YEAH...!
TSUBAKI,
YOU WANTED TO
PUT YOUR ARMS AROUND ME, DIDN'T YOU?
I DID...
BUT...
I COULDN'T DO IT...
JUDGING BY THEIR CONVERSA-TION,
IS SHE THE GIRL
TSUBAKI HAD A CRUSH ON IN MIDDLE SCHOOL ...?
AX=.

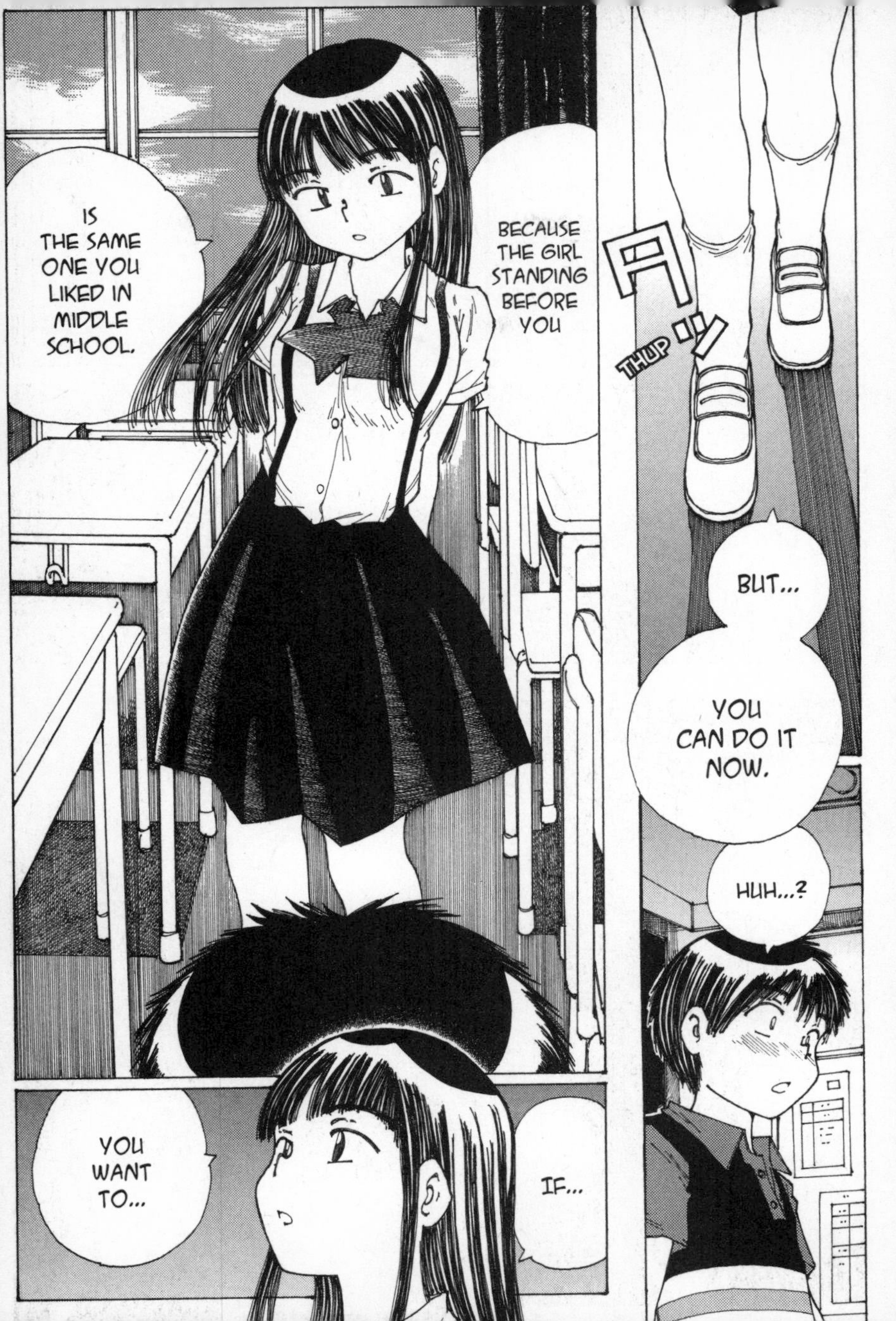
THUP
BUT...
YOU CAN DO IT NOW.
HUH...?
BECAUSE THE GIRL STANDING BEFORE YOU
IS THE SAME ONE YOU LIKED IN MIDDLE SCHOOL.
IF...
YOU WANT TO...

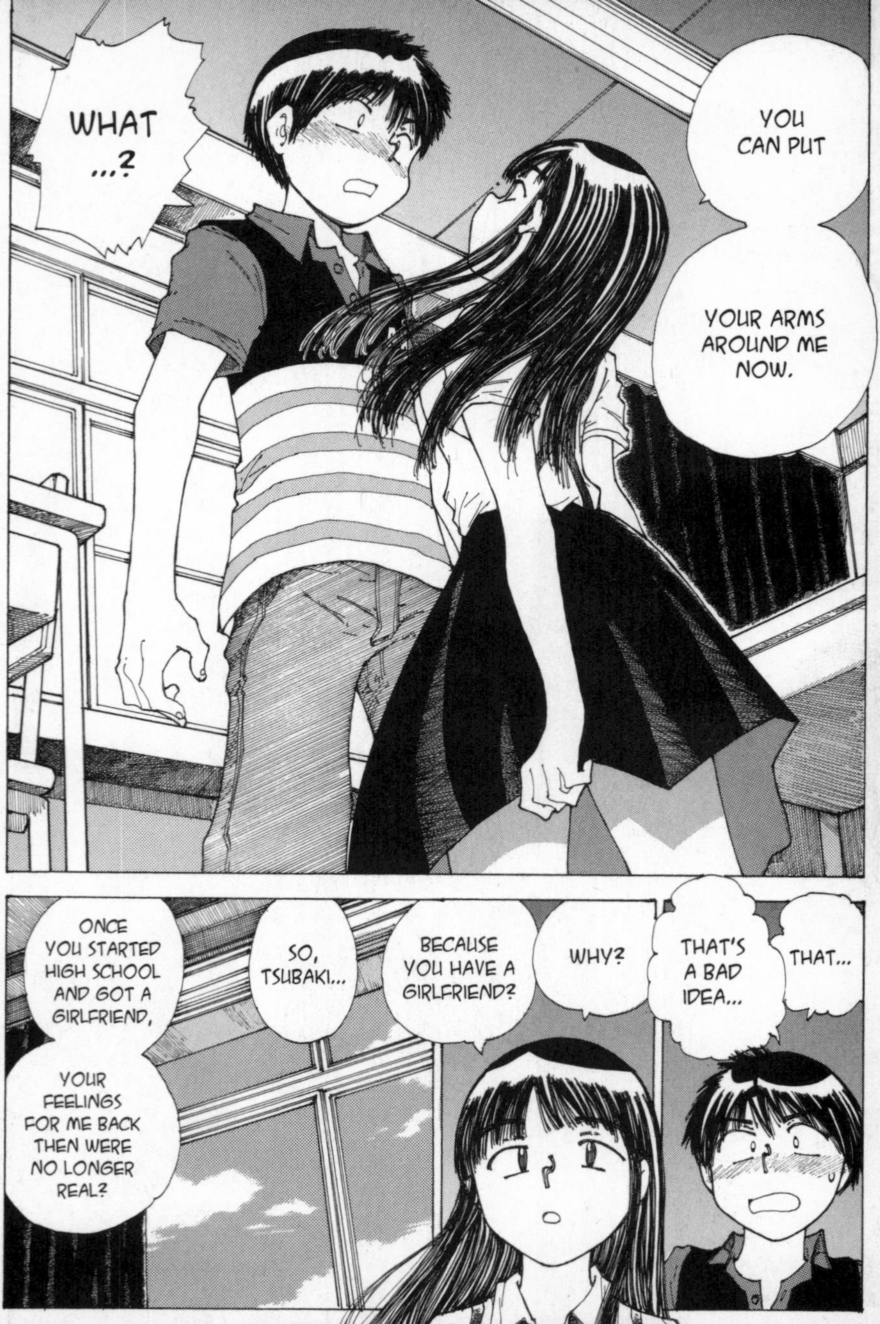
YOU CAN PUT
YOUR ARMS AROUND ME NOW.
WHAT ...?
THAT...
THAT'S A BAD IDEA...
WHY?
BECAUSE YOU HAVE A GIRLFRIEND?
SO, TSUBAKI...
ONCE YOU STARTED HIGH SCHOOL AND GOT A GIRLFRIEND,
YOUR FEELINGS FOR ME BACK THEN WERE NO LONGER REAL?

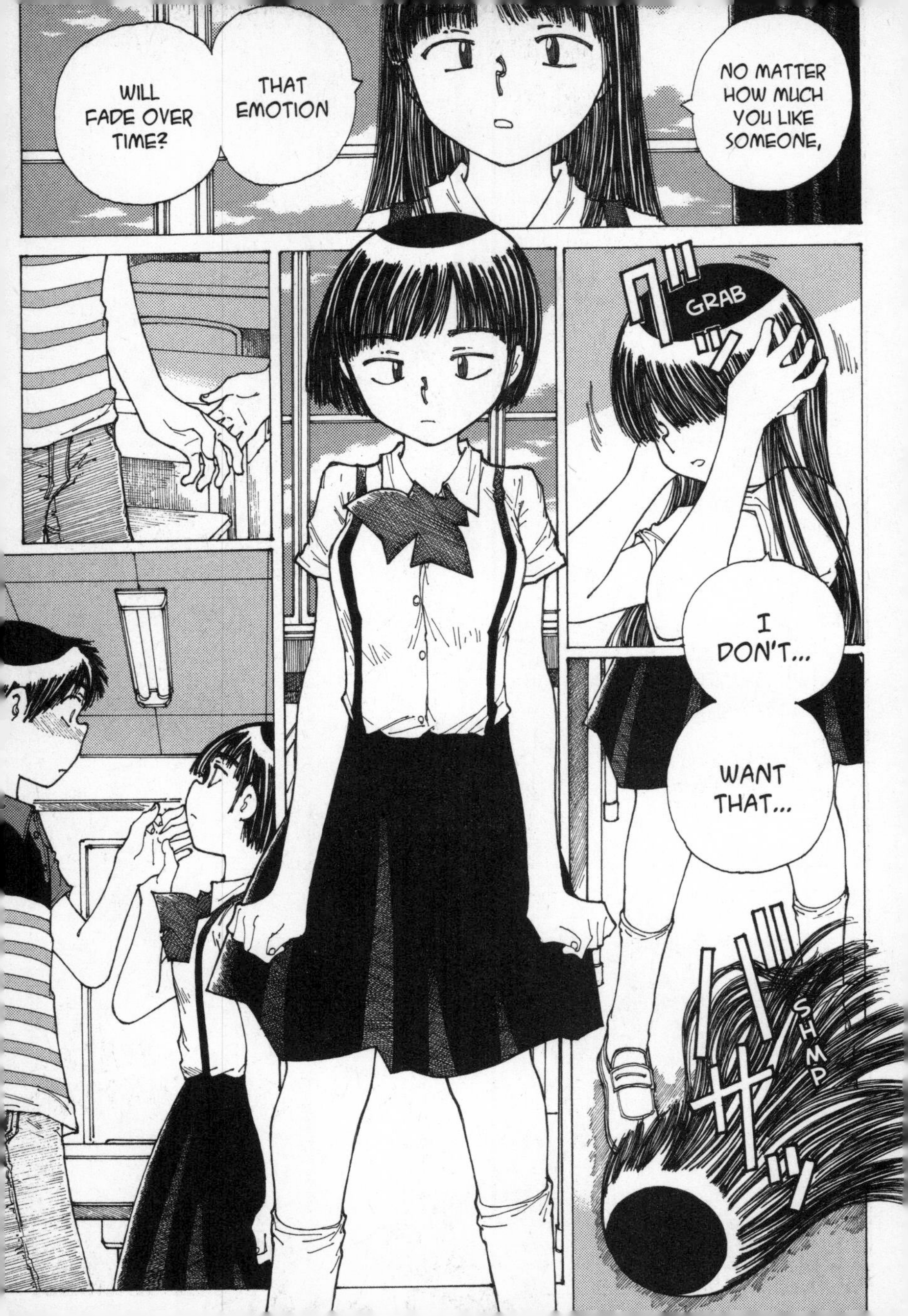
NO MATTER HOW MUCH YOU LIKE SOMEONE,
THAT EMOTION
WILL FADE OVER TIME?
GRAB
I DON'T...
WANT THAT...
SHMP

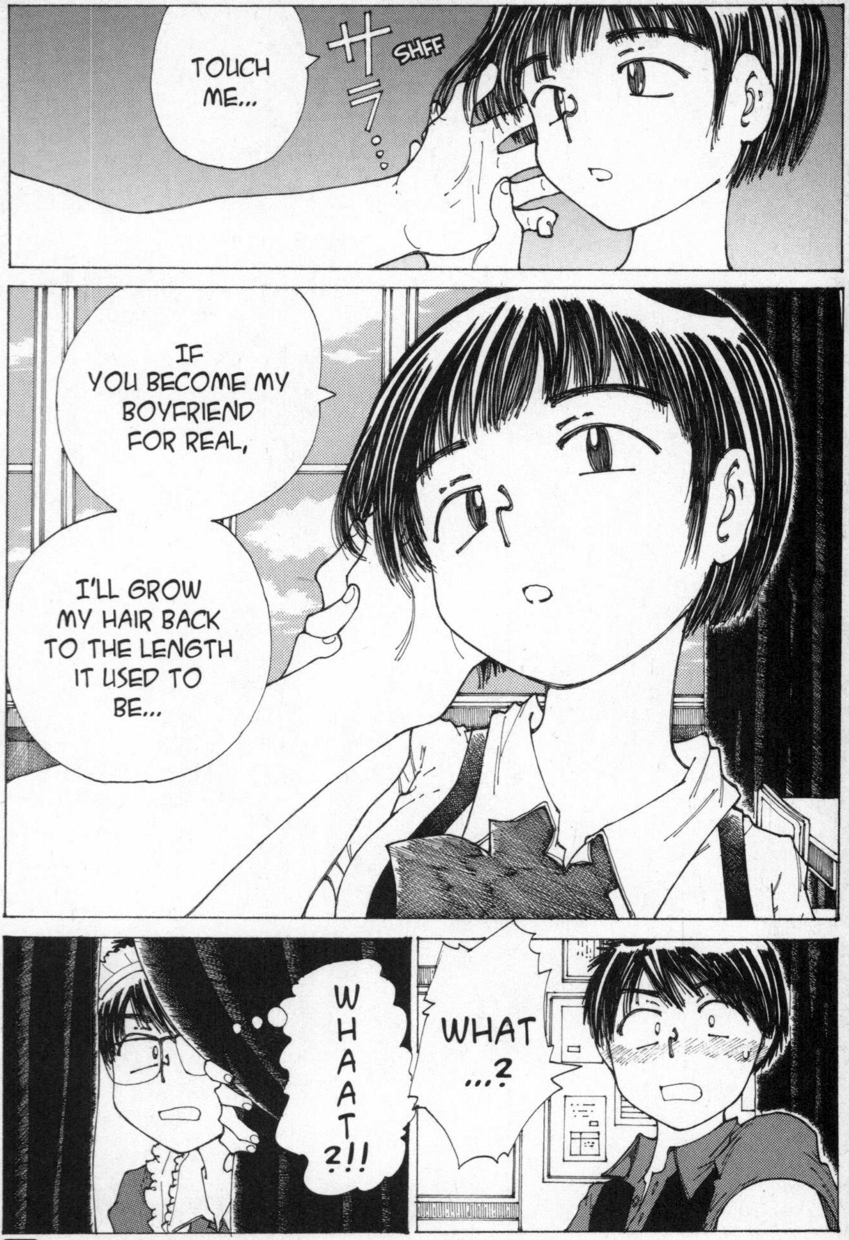
TOUCH ME...
サラ
SHFF
IF YOU BECOME MY BOYFRIEND FOR REAL,
I'LL GROW MY HAIR BACK TO THE LENGTH IT USED TO BE...
WHAT ...?
WHAAT?!!

END OF CHAPTER 31

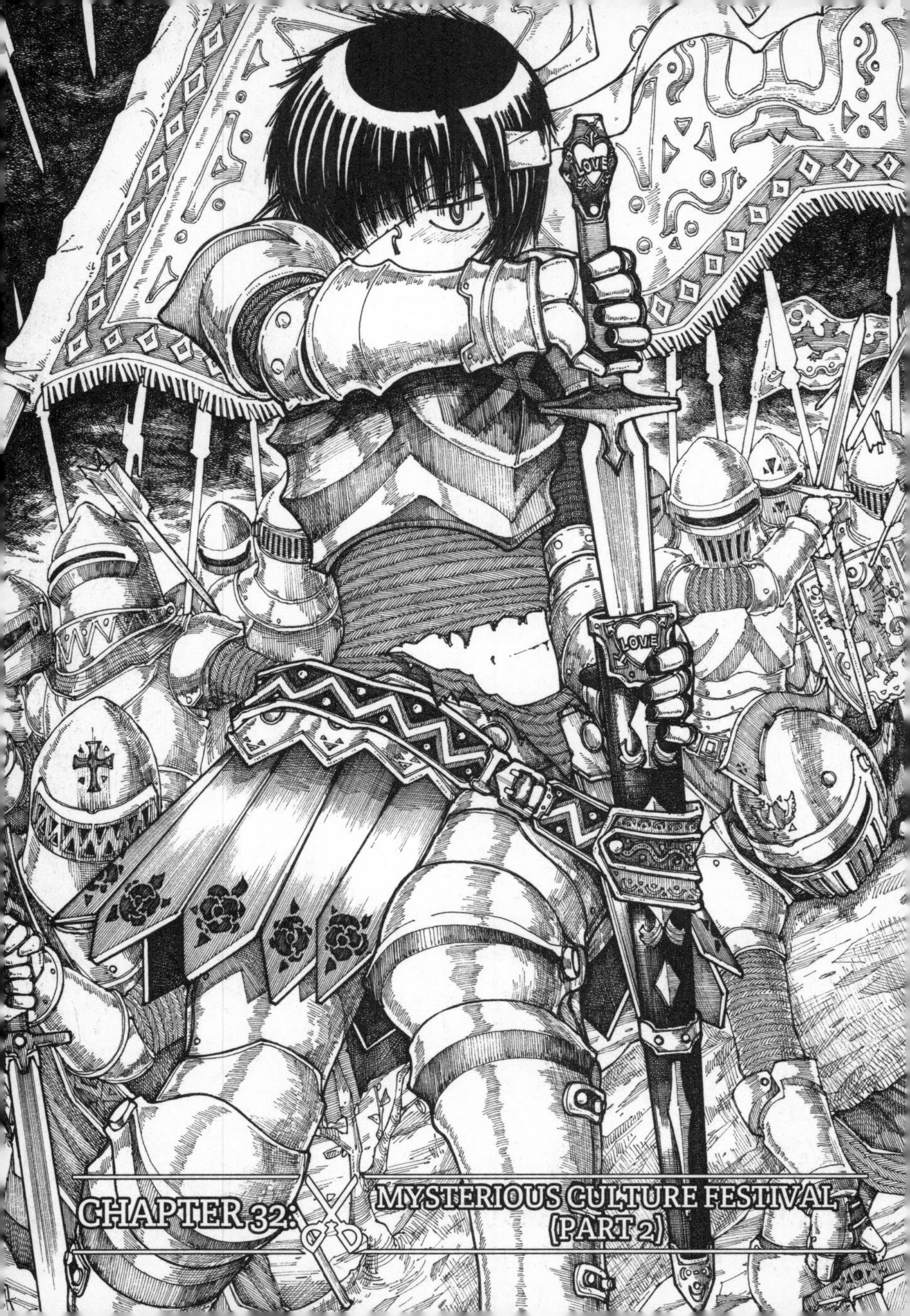
LOVE
LOVE
CHAPTER 32: MYSTERIOUS CULTURE FESTIVAL (PART 2)

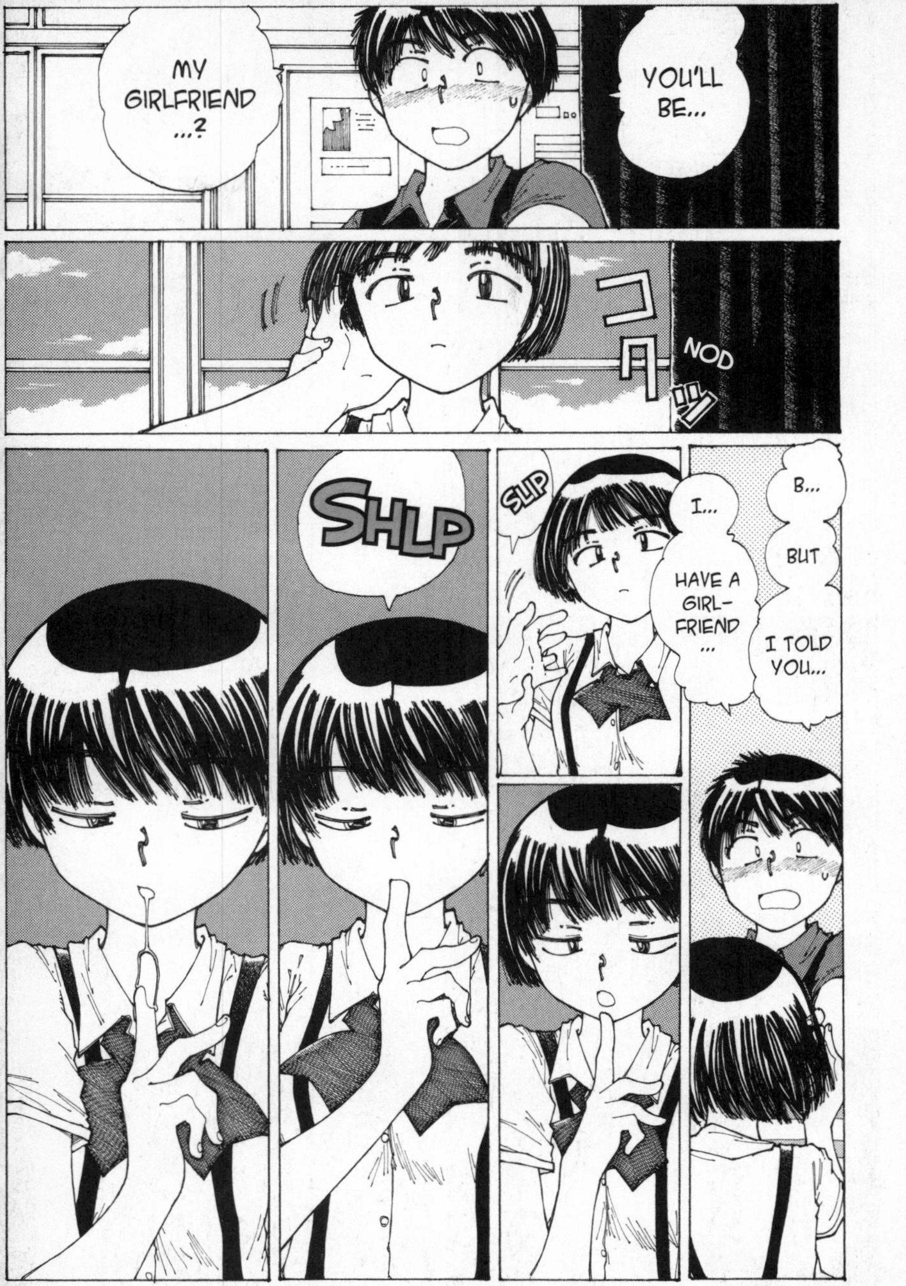
YOU'LL BE...
MY GIRLFRIEND ...?
コクッ
NOD
B... BUT I TOLD YOU...
I... HAVE A GIRL-FRIEND ...
SLIP
SHLP

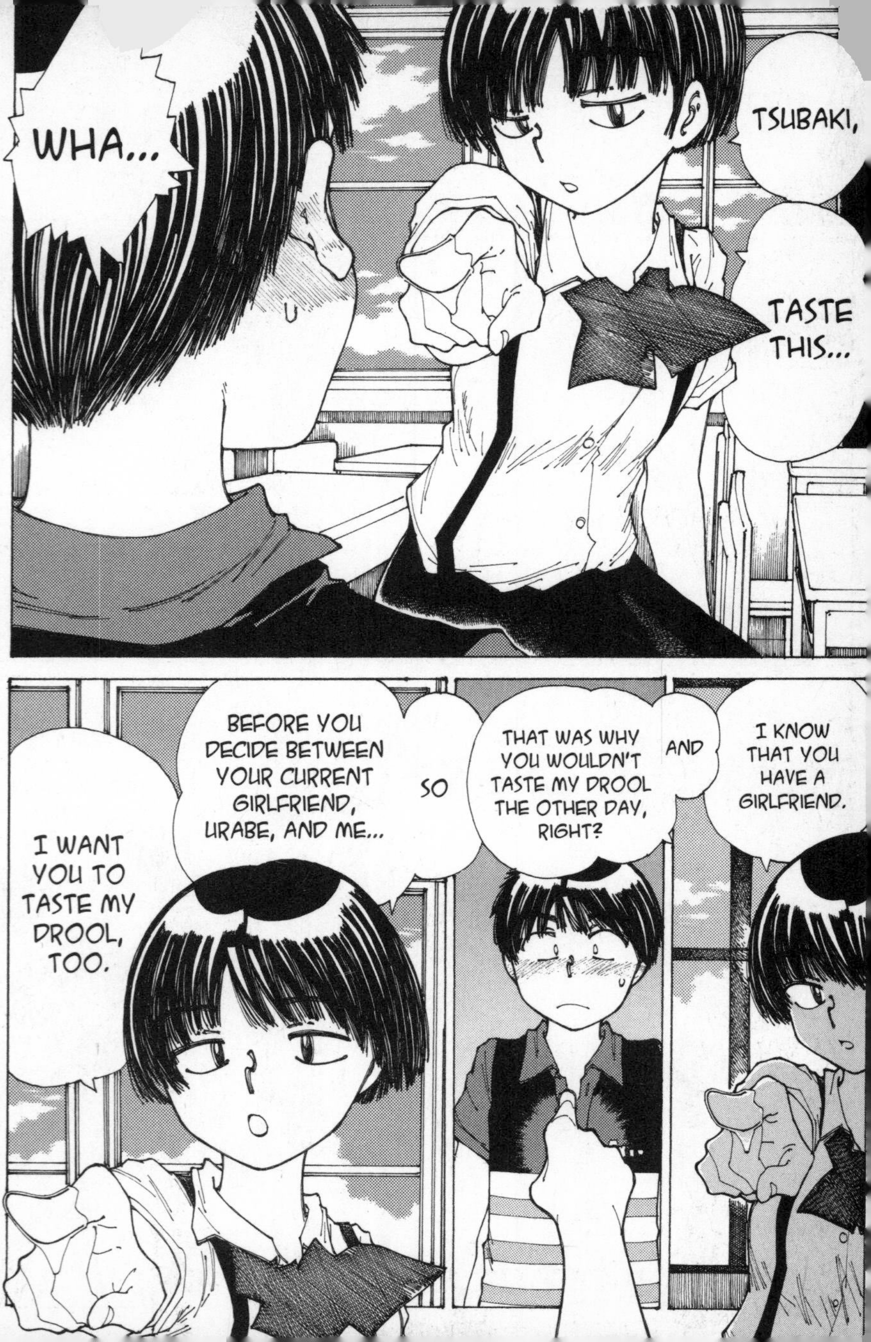
TSUBAKI,
TASTE THIS...
WHA...
I KNOW THAT YOU HAVE A GIRLFRIEND.
AND
THAT WAS WHY YOU WOULDN'T TASTE MY DROOL THE OTHER DAY, RIGHT?
SO
BEFORE YOU DECIDE BETWEEN YOUR CURRENT GIRLFRIEND, URABE, AND ME...
I WANT YOU TO TASTE MY DROOL, TOO.

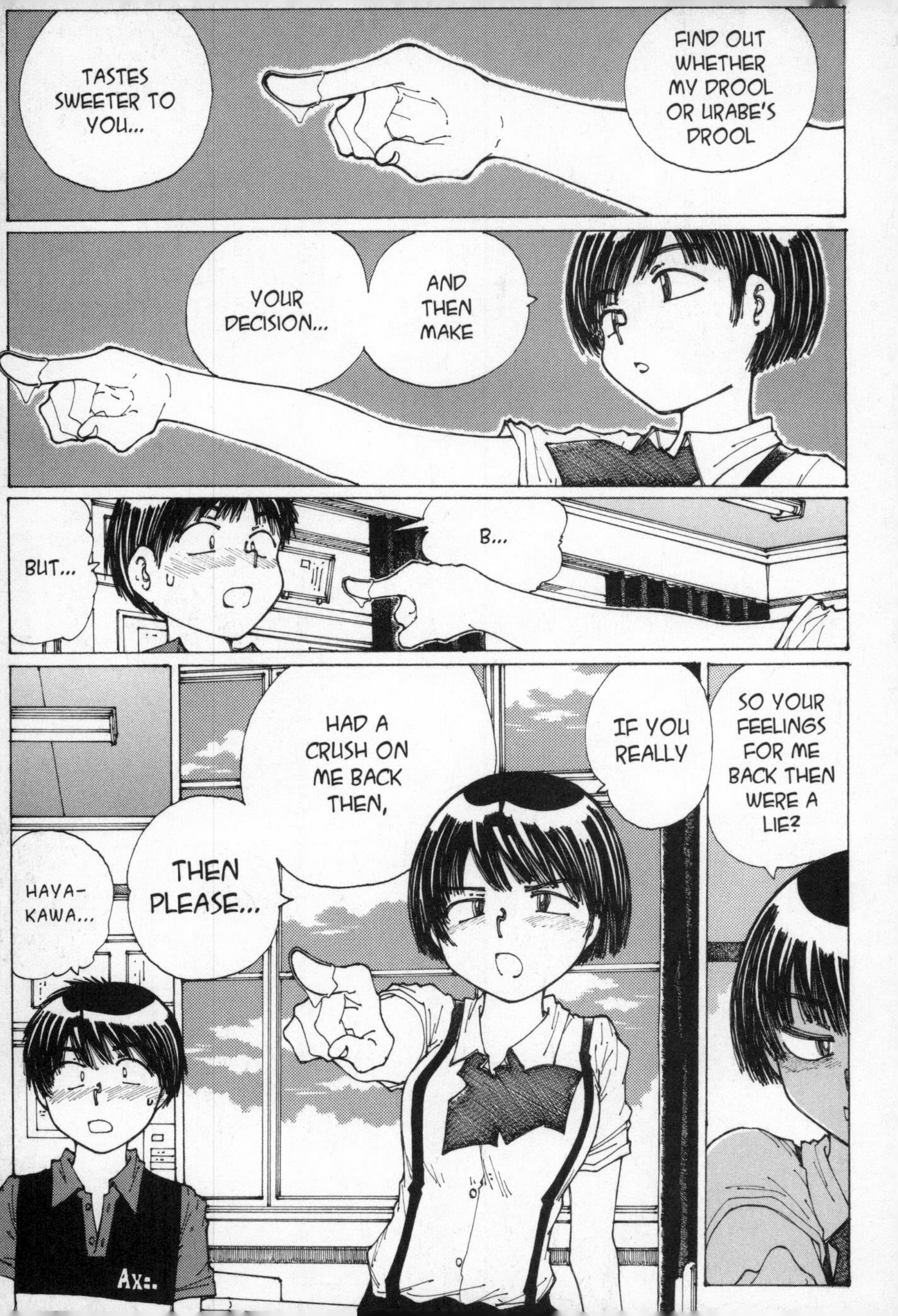
FIND OUT WHETHER MY DROOL OR URABE'S DROOL
TASTES SWEETER TO YOU...
AND THEN MAKE
YOUR DECISION...
B...
BUT...
SO YOUR FEELINGS FOR ME BACK THEN WERE A LIE?
IF YOU REALLY
HAD A CRUSH ON ME BACK THEN,
THEN PLEASE...
HAYA-
KAWA...

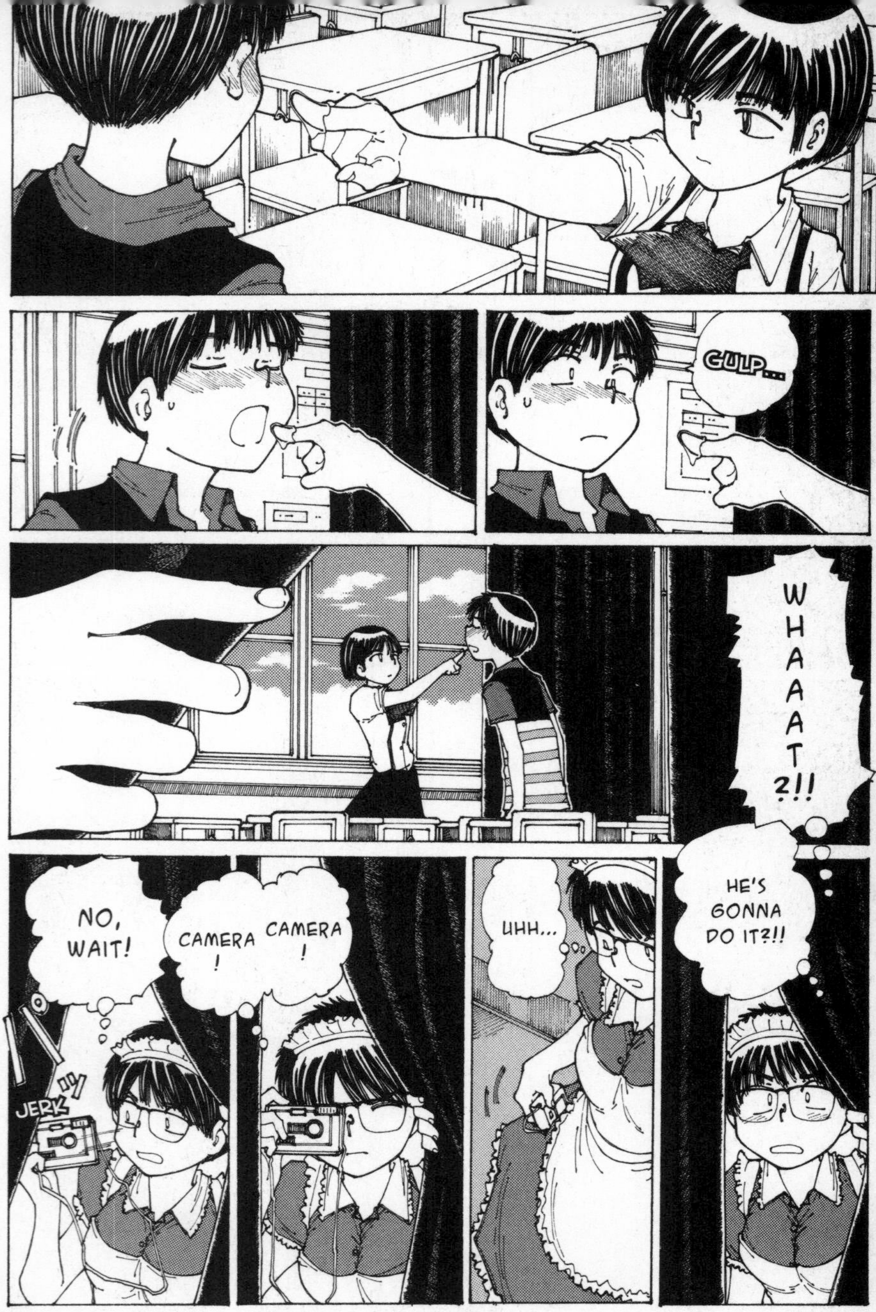
GULP...
WHAAAAT?!!
HE'S GONNA DO IT?!!
UHH...
CAMERA! CAMERA!
NO, WAIT!
JERK

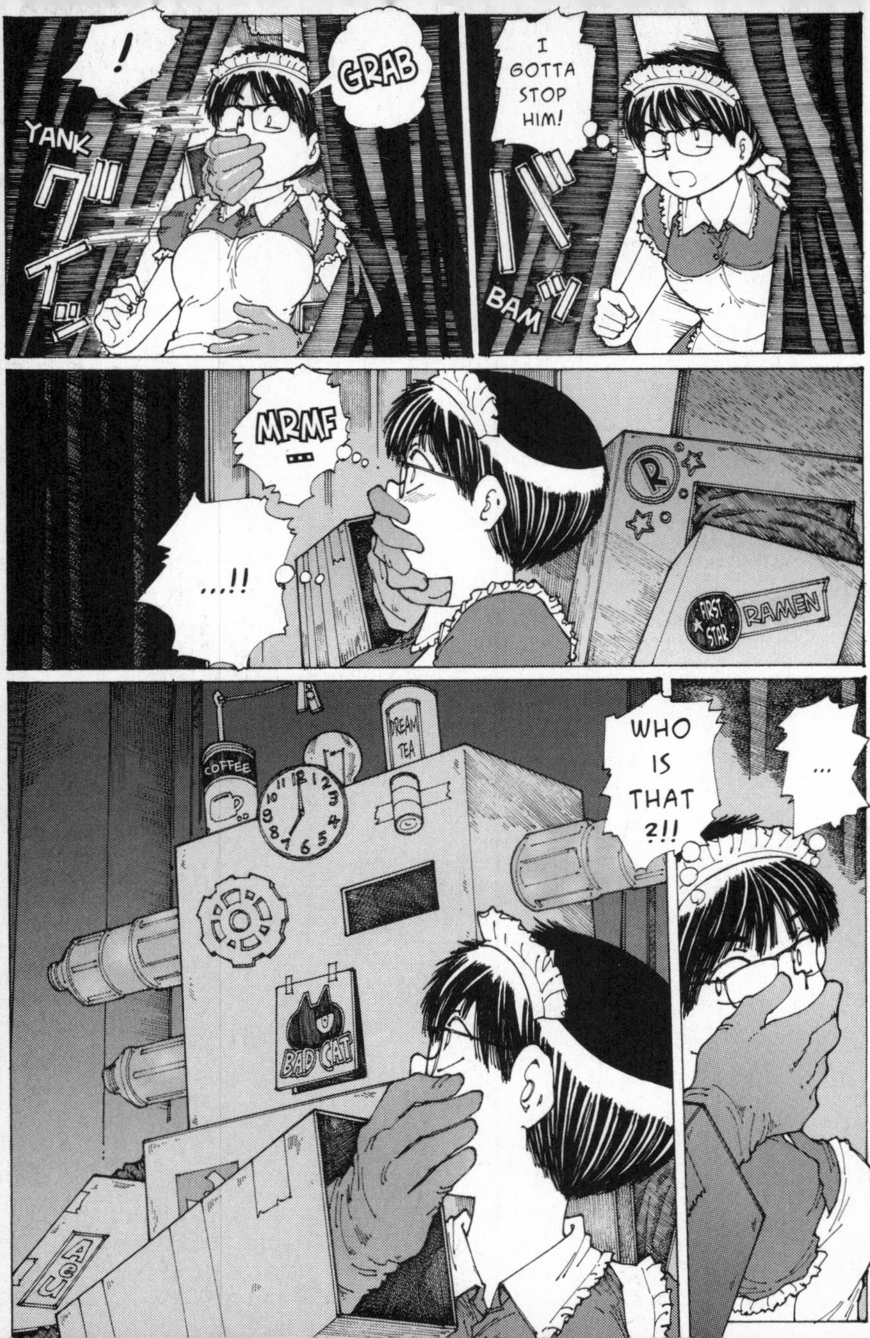
I GOTTA STOP HIM!
BAM
!
GRAB
YANK
MRMF ...
...!!
R
FIRST STAR
RAMEN
WHO IS THAT ?!!
...
DREAM TEA
COFFEE
BAD CAT
AGU

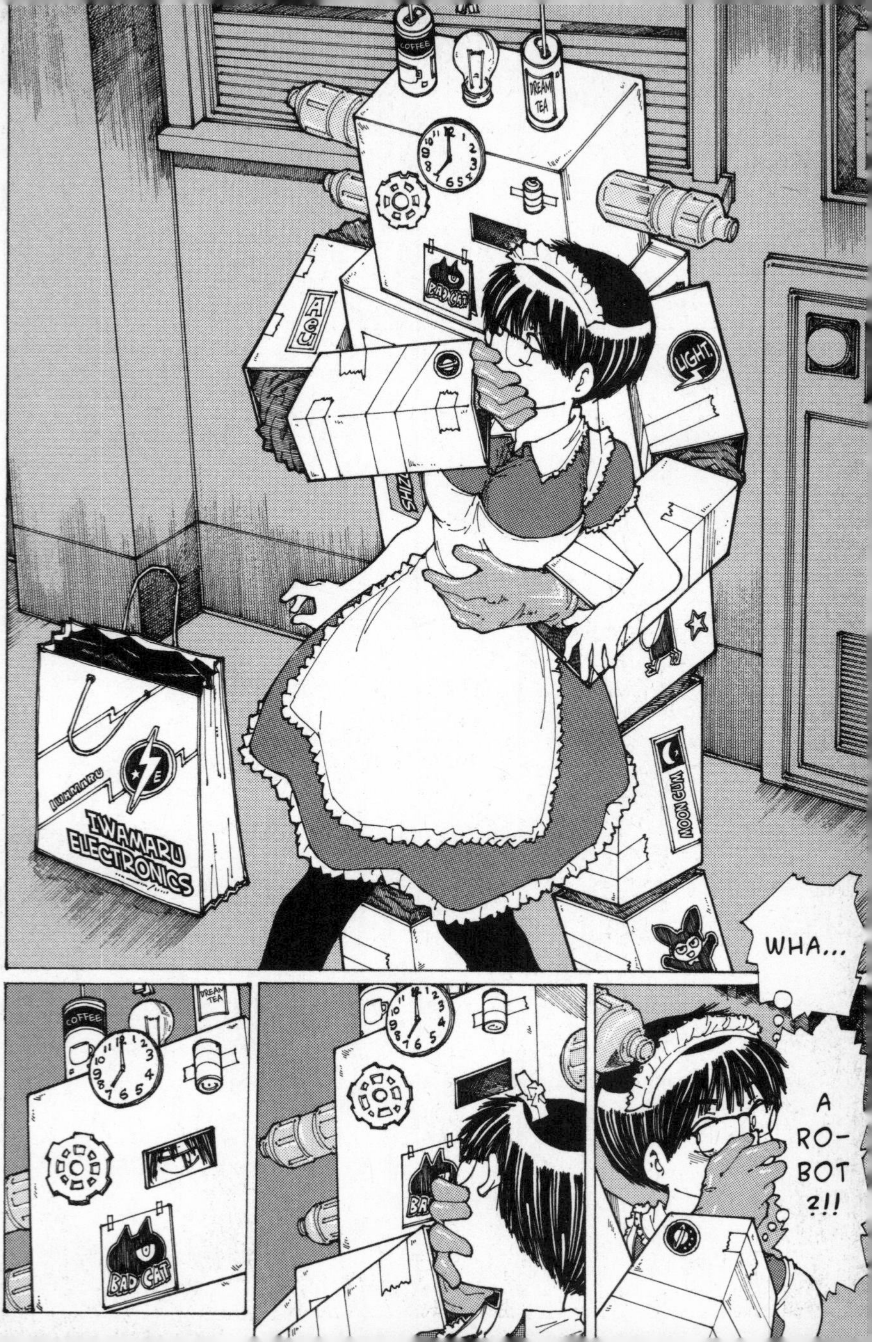

COFFEE
DREAM TEA
BAD CAT
LIGHT
MOON GUM
IWAMARU
IWAMARU ELECTRONICS
WHA...
A RO-BOT ?!!
COFFEE
DREAM TEA
BAD CAT

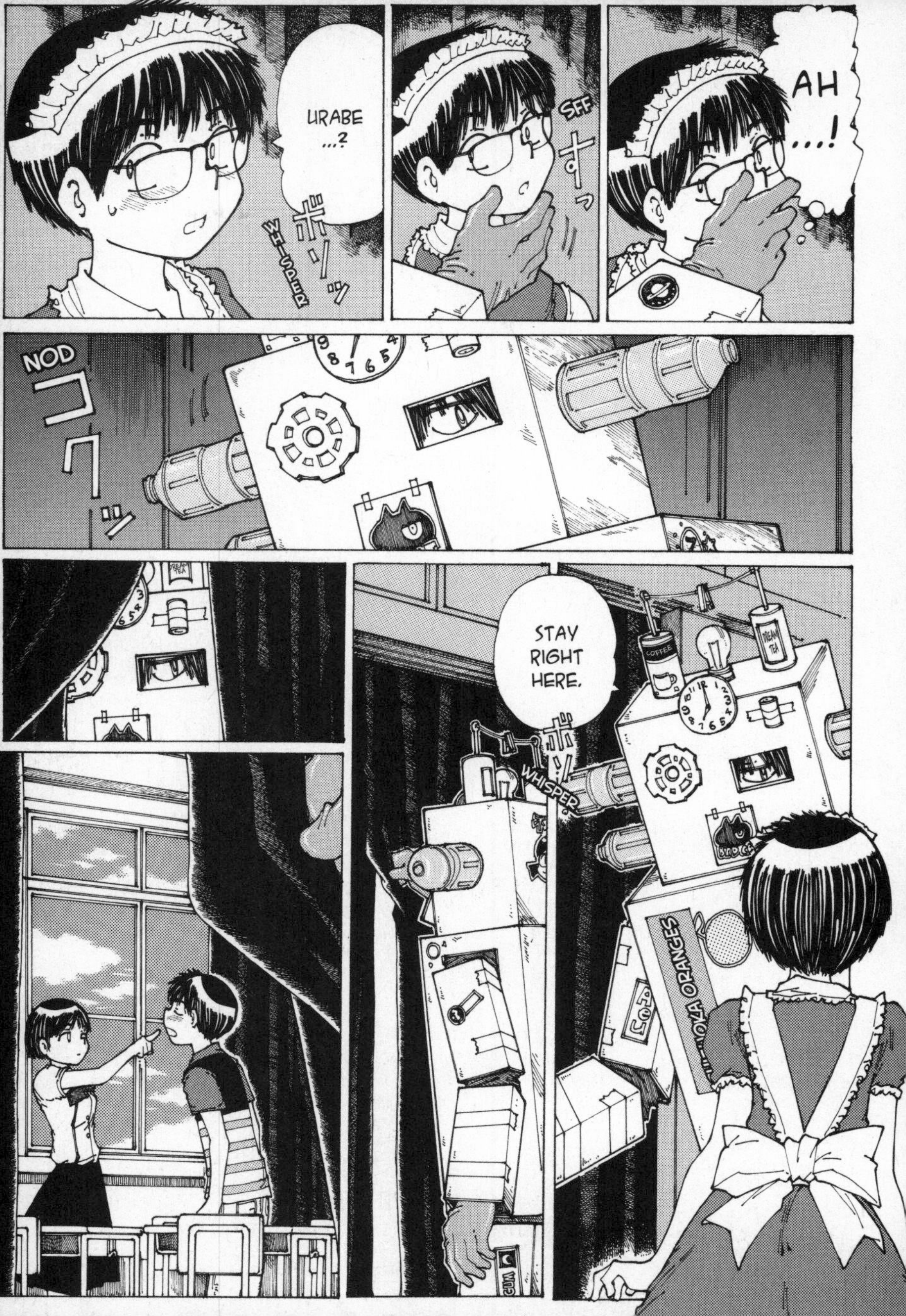
AH
...!
SFF
すっ
URABE
...?
ボソッ
WHISPER
NOD
コクッ
STAY RIGHT HERE.
ボソ
WHISPER.
COFFEE
DREAM TEA

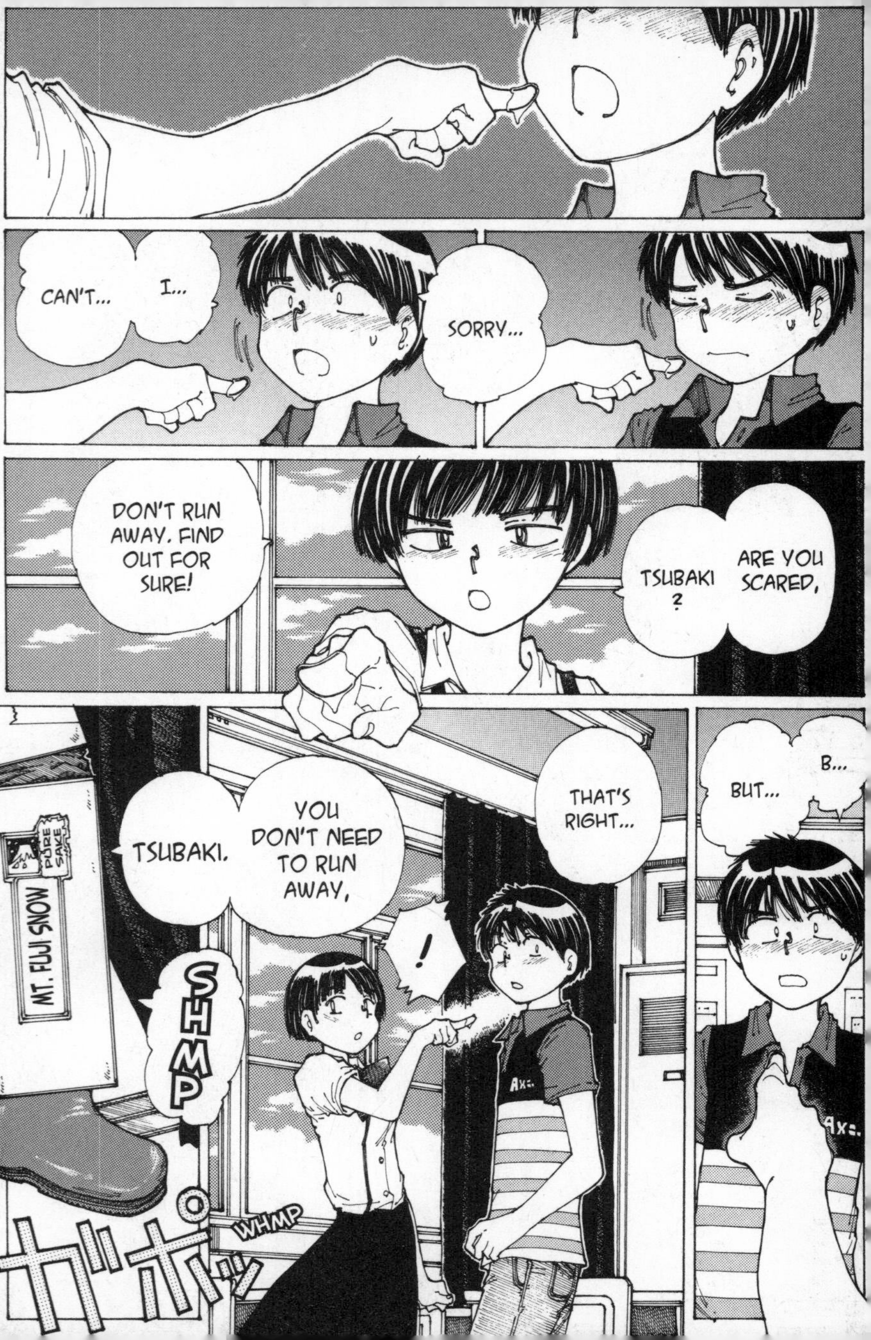

SORRY...
I...
CAN'T...
ARE YOU SCARED, TSUBAKI?
DON'T RUN AWAY. FIND OUT FOR SURE!
B...
BUT...
THAT'S RIGHT...
YOU DON'T NEED TO RUN AWAY,
TSUBAKI.
!
PURE SAKE
MT. FUJI SNOW
SHMP
ガポッ
WHMP

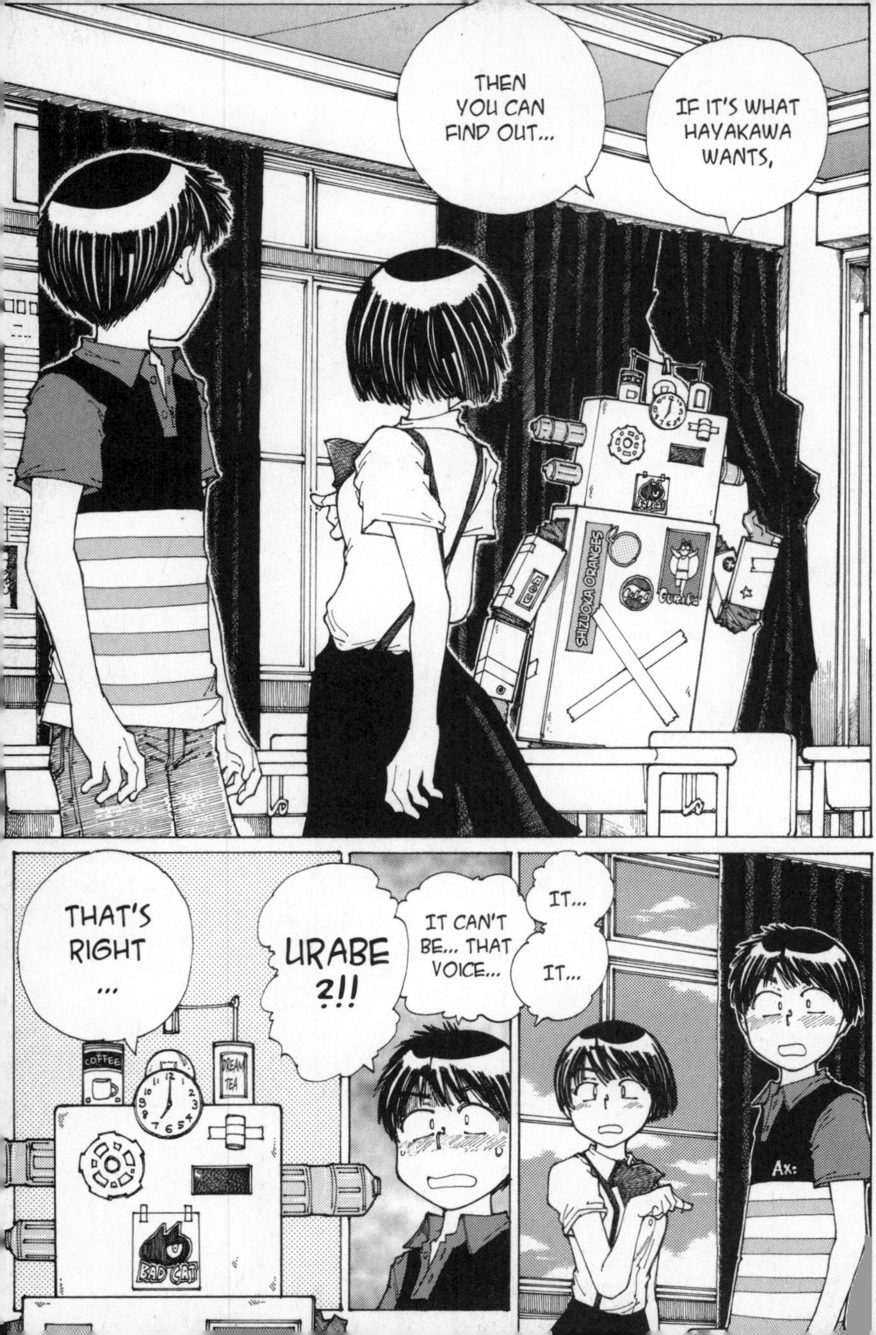
IF IT'S WHAT HAYAKAWA WANTS,
THEN YOU CAN FIND OUT...
SHIZUOKA ORANGES
IT...
IT...
Ax:
IT CAN'T BE... THAT VOICE...
URABE ?!!
THAT'S RIGHT ...
COFFEE
DREAM TEA
BAD CAT

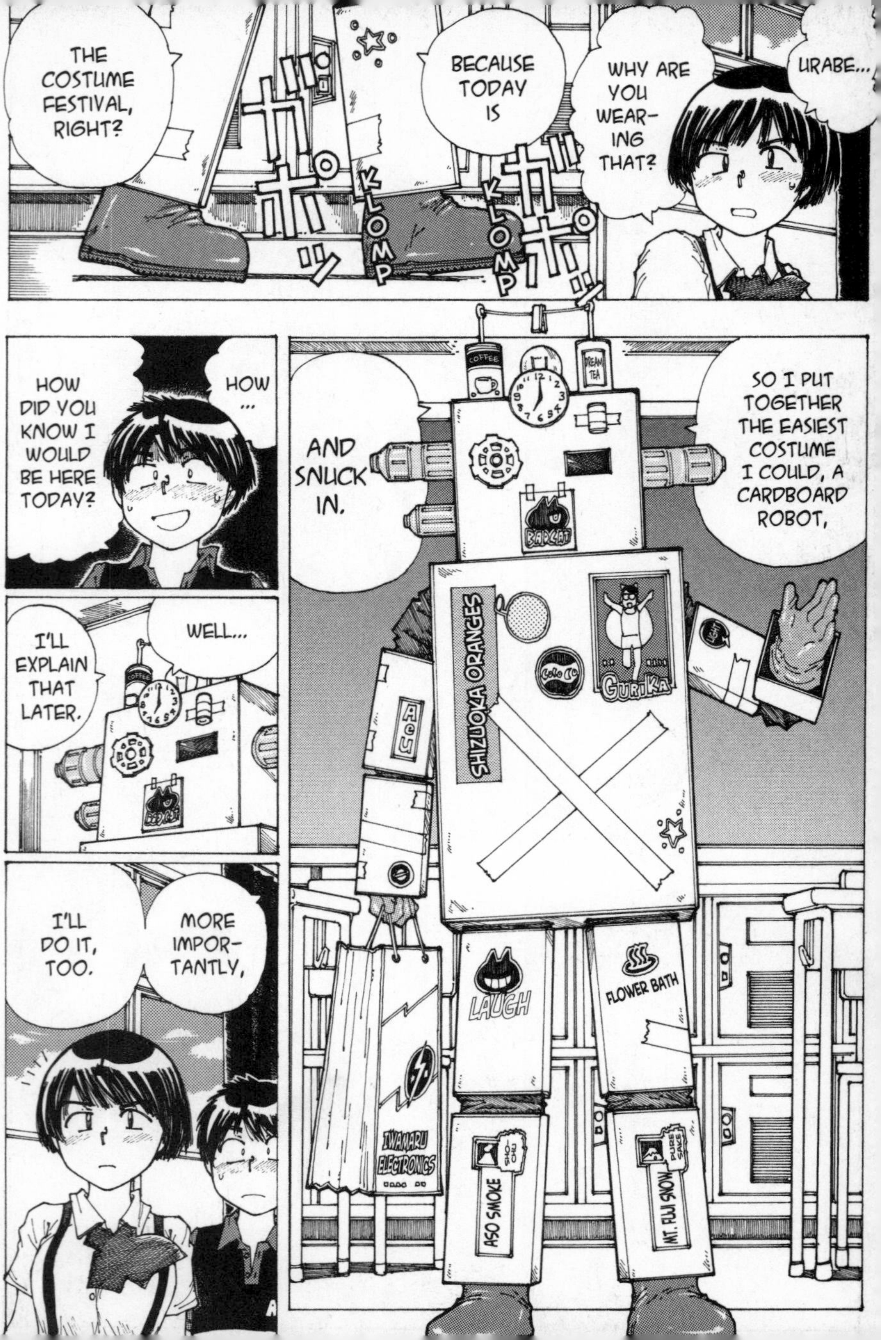
URABE...
WHY ARE YOU WEARING THAT?
KLOMP
BECAUSE TODAY IS
KLOMP
THE COSTUME FESTIVAL, RIGHT?
SO I PUT TOGETHER THE EASIEST COSTUME I COULD, A CARDBOARD ROBOT,
AND SNUCK IN.
COFFEE
DREAM TEA
BADCAT
SHIZUOKA ORANGES
GURIKA
AeU
LAUGH
FLOWER BATH
IWAMARU ELECTRONICS
ASO SMOKE
SHO-CHU
MT. FUJI SNOW
PURE SAKE
HOW...
HOW DID YOU KNOW I WOULD BE HERE TODAY?
WELL...
I'LL EXPLAIN THAT LATER.
MORE IMPORTANTLY,
I'LL DO IT, TOO.

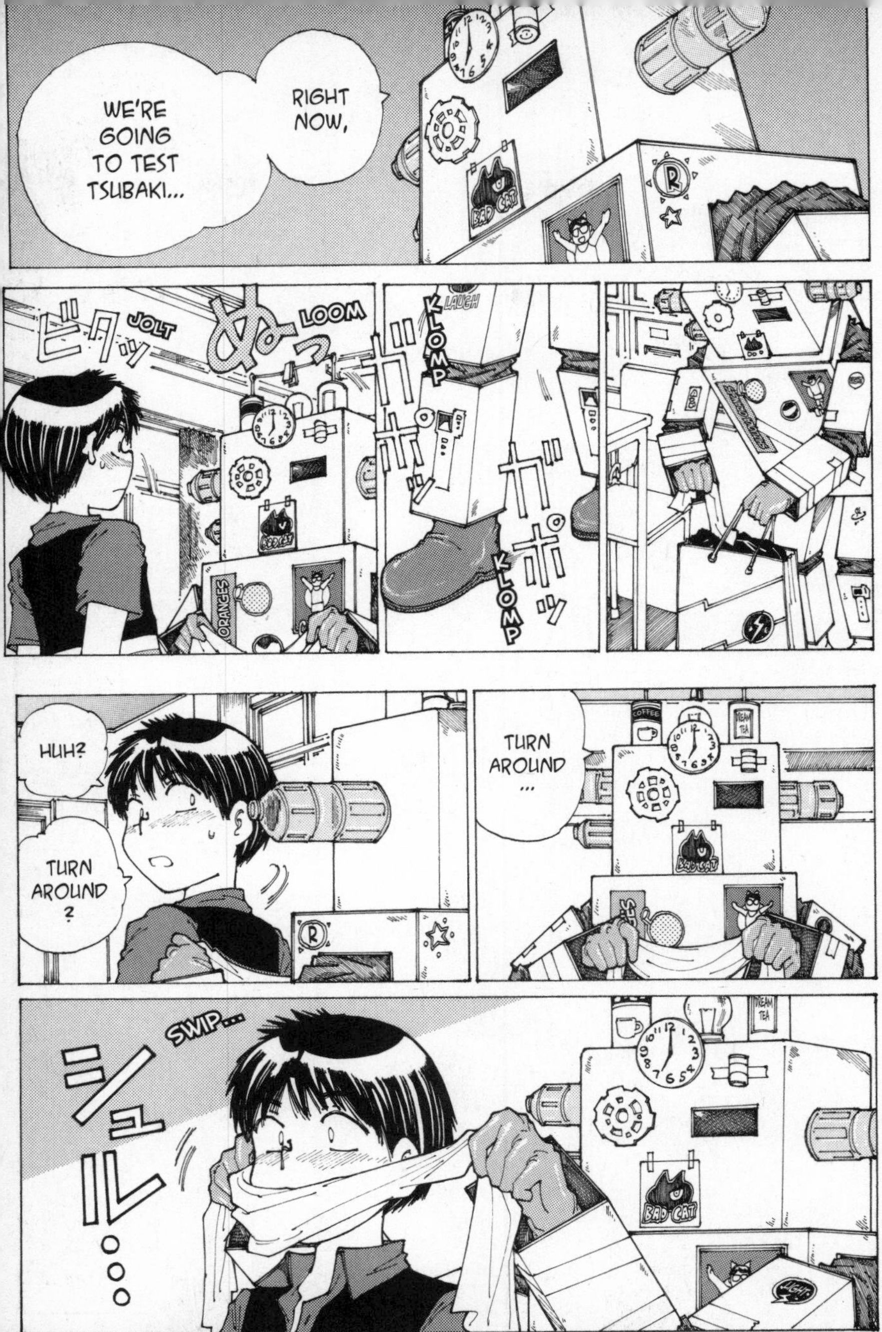

RIGHT NOW,
WE'RE GOING TO TEST TSUBAKI...
KLOMP
KLOMP
ビクッ
JOLT
ぬっ
LOOM
TURN AROUND ...
HUH?
TURN AROUND ?
SWIP...
シュル

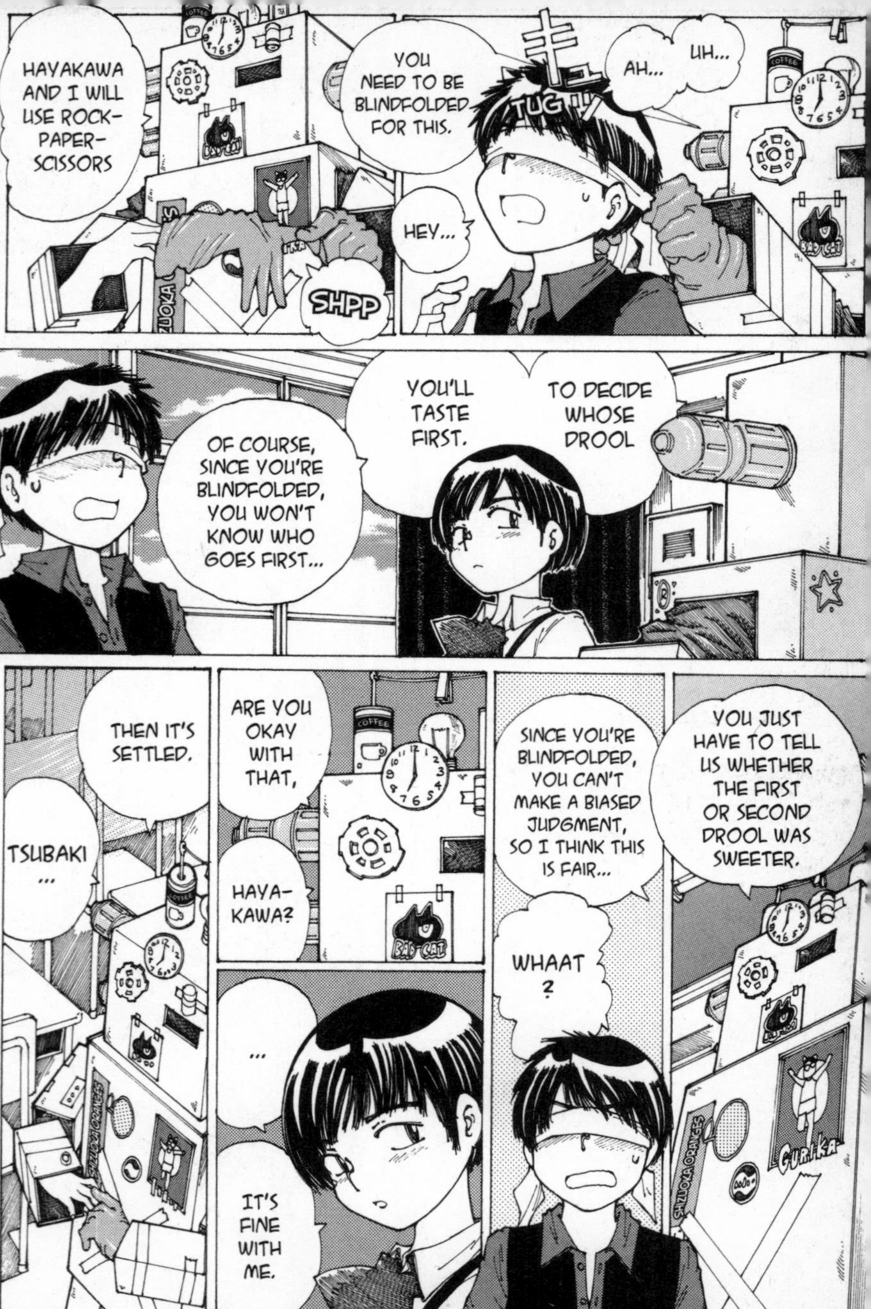
UH...
AH...
YOU NEED TO BE BLINDFOLDED FOR THIS.
TUG
HEY...
HAYAKAWA AND I WILL USE ROCK-PAPER-SCISSORS
SHPP
TO DECIDE WHOSE DROOL
YOU'LL TASTE FIRST.
OF COURSE, SINCE YOU'RE BLINDFOLDED, YOU WON'T KNOW WHO GOES FIRST...
YOU JUST HAVE TO TELL US WHETHER THE FIRST OR SECOND DROOL WAS SWEETER.
SINCE YOU'RE BLINDFOLDED, YOU CAN'T MAKE A BIASED JUDGMENT, SO I THINK THIS IS FAIR...
WHAAT?
ARE YOU OKAY WITH THAT,
HAYA-KAWA?
...
IT'S FINE WITH ME.
THEN IT'S SETTLED.
TSUBAKI...

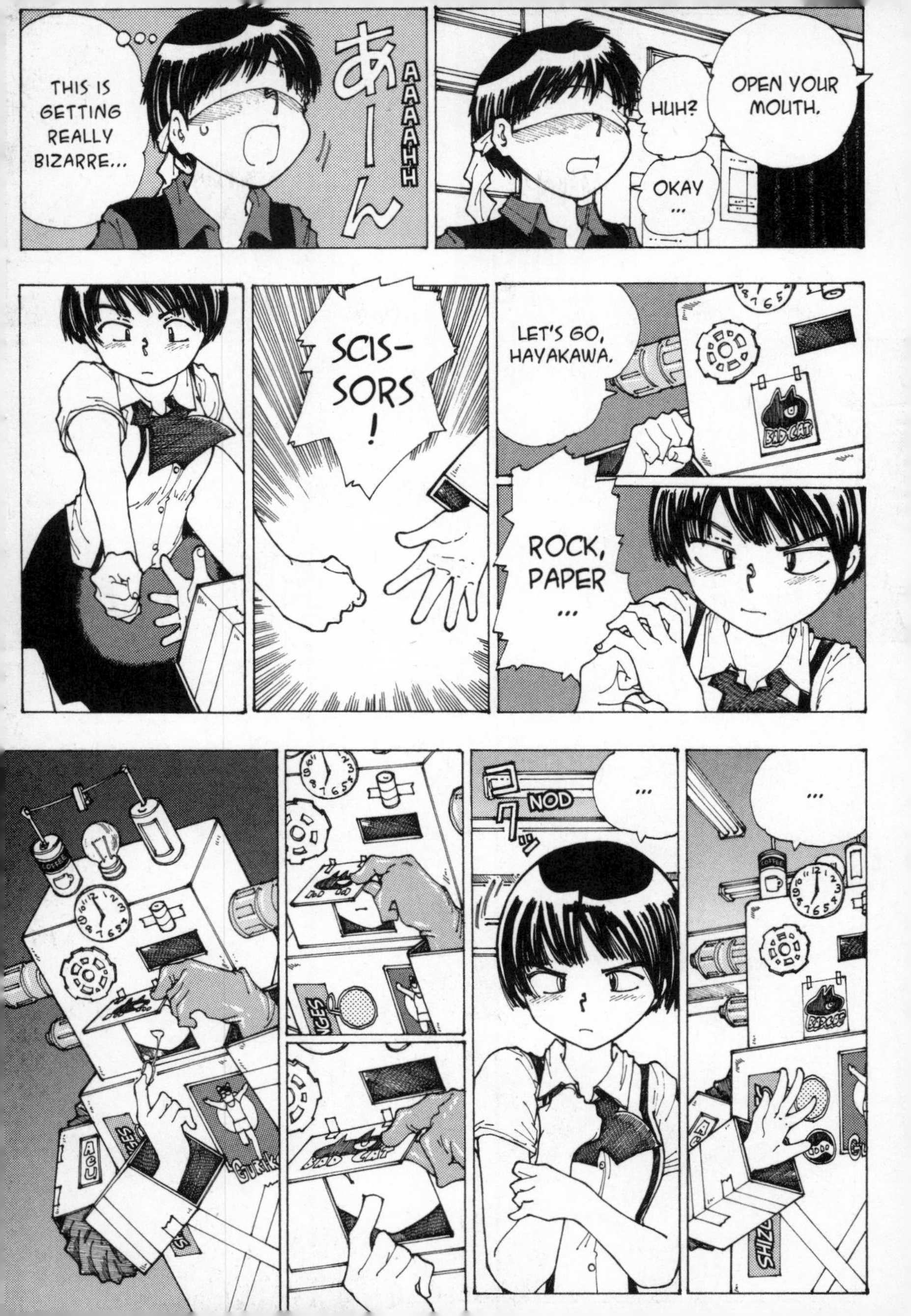
OPEN YOUR MOUTH.
HUH?
OKAY ...
あーん
AAAAAHH
THIS IS GETTING REALLY BIZARRE...
LET'S GO, HAYAKAWA.
BAD CAT
ROCK, PAPER ...
SCIS-SORS!
...
BAD CAT
...
NOD

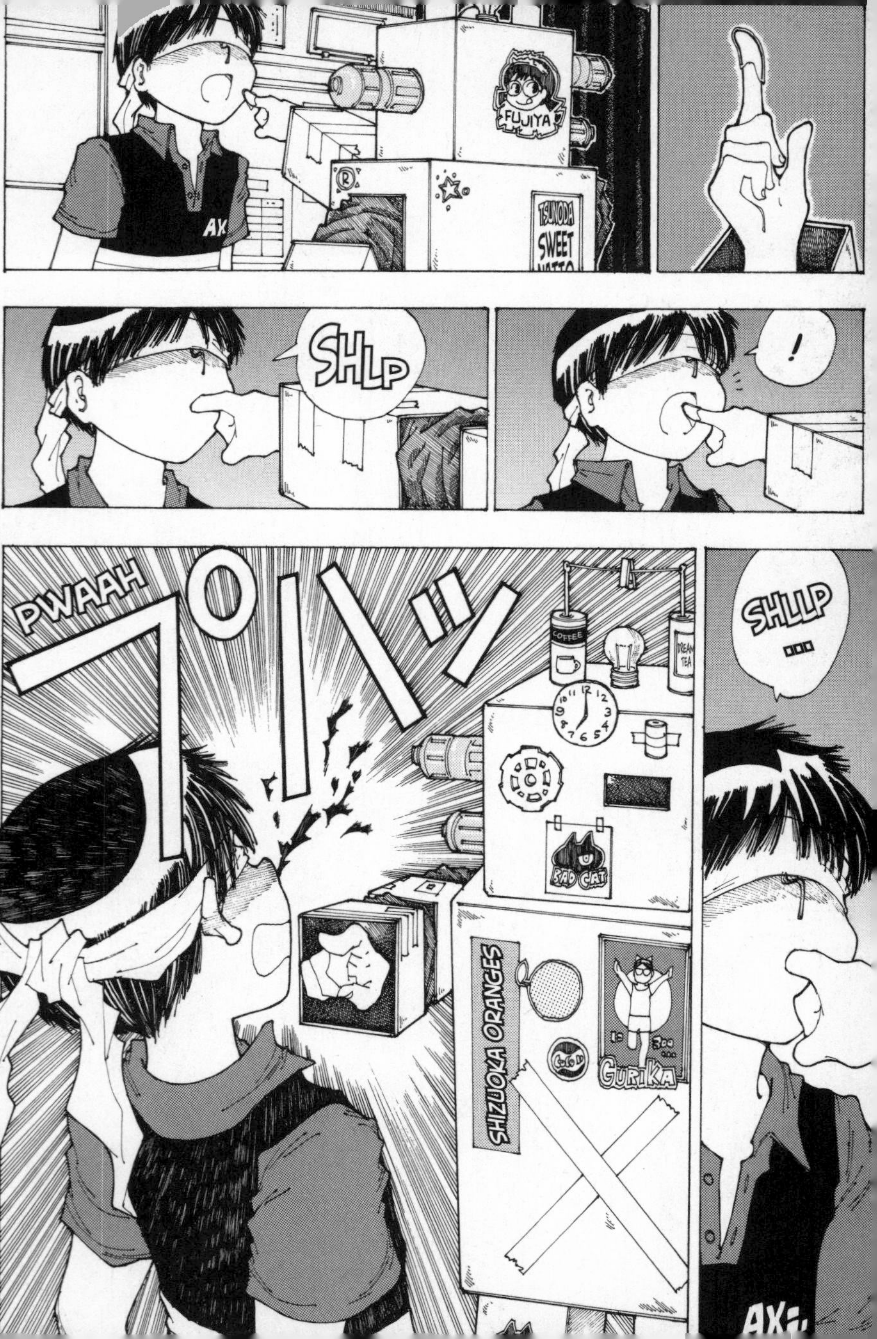

FUJIYA
TSUNODA
SWEET
!
SHLP
SHLP ...
PWAAH
COFFEE
DREAM TEA
BAD CAT
SHIZUOKA ORANGES
GURIKA

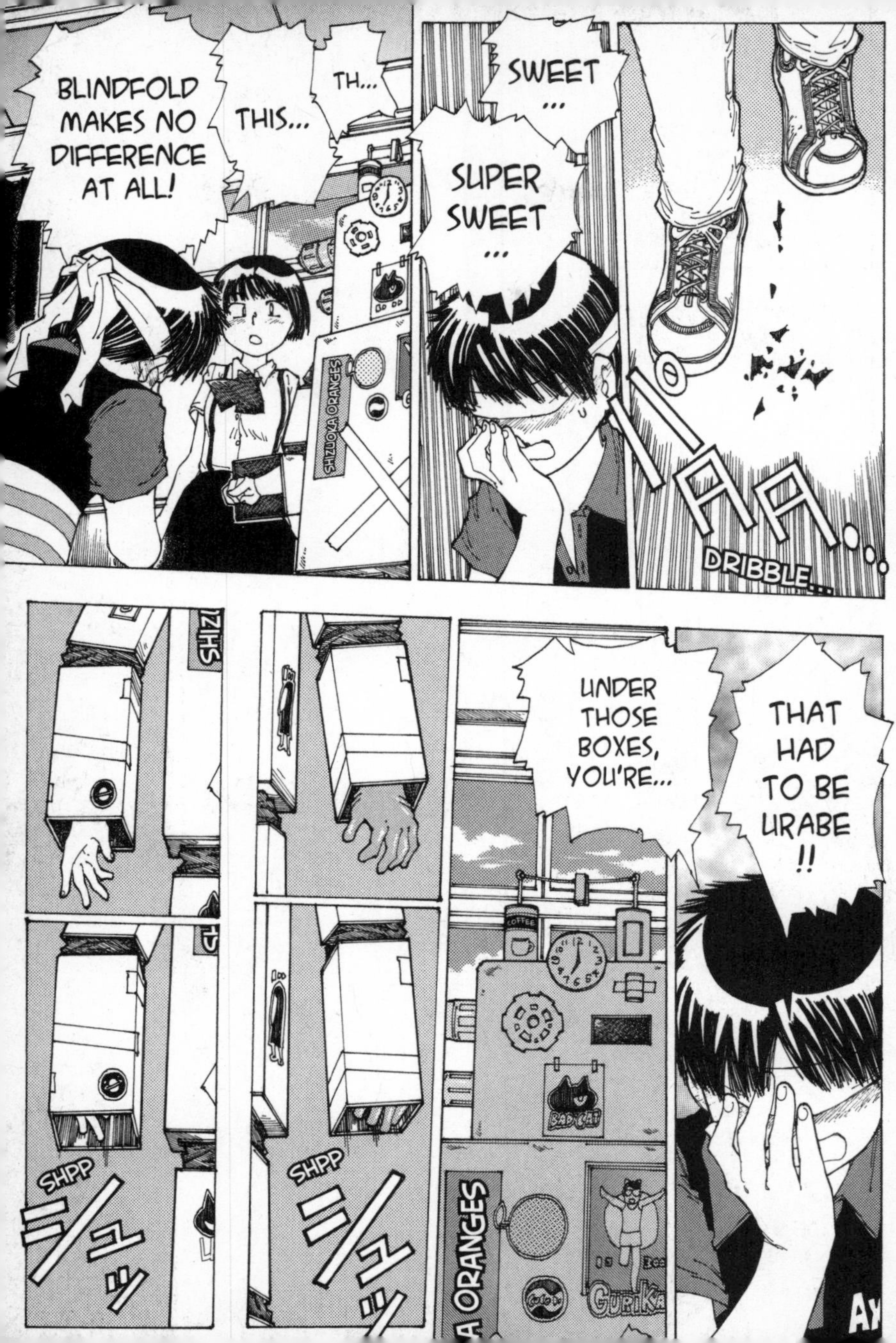

SWEET ...
SUPER SWEET ...
IAA...
DRIBBLE...
TH...
THIS...
BLINDFOLD MAKES NO DIFFERENCE AT ALL!
SHIZUOKA ORANGES
THAT HAD TO BE URABE !!
UNDER THOSE BOXES, YOU'RE...
COFFEE
BAD CAT
ORANGES
SHPP
シュッ
SHPP
シュッ

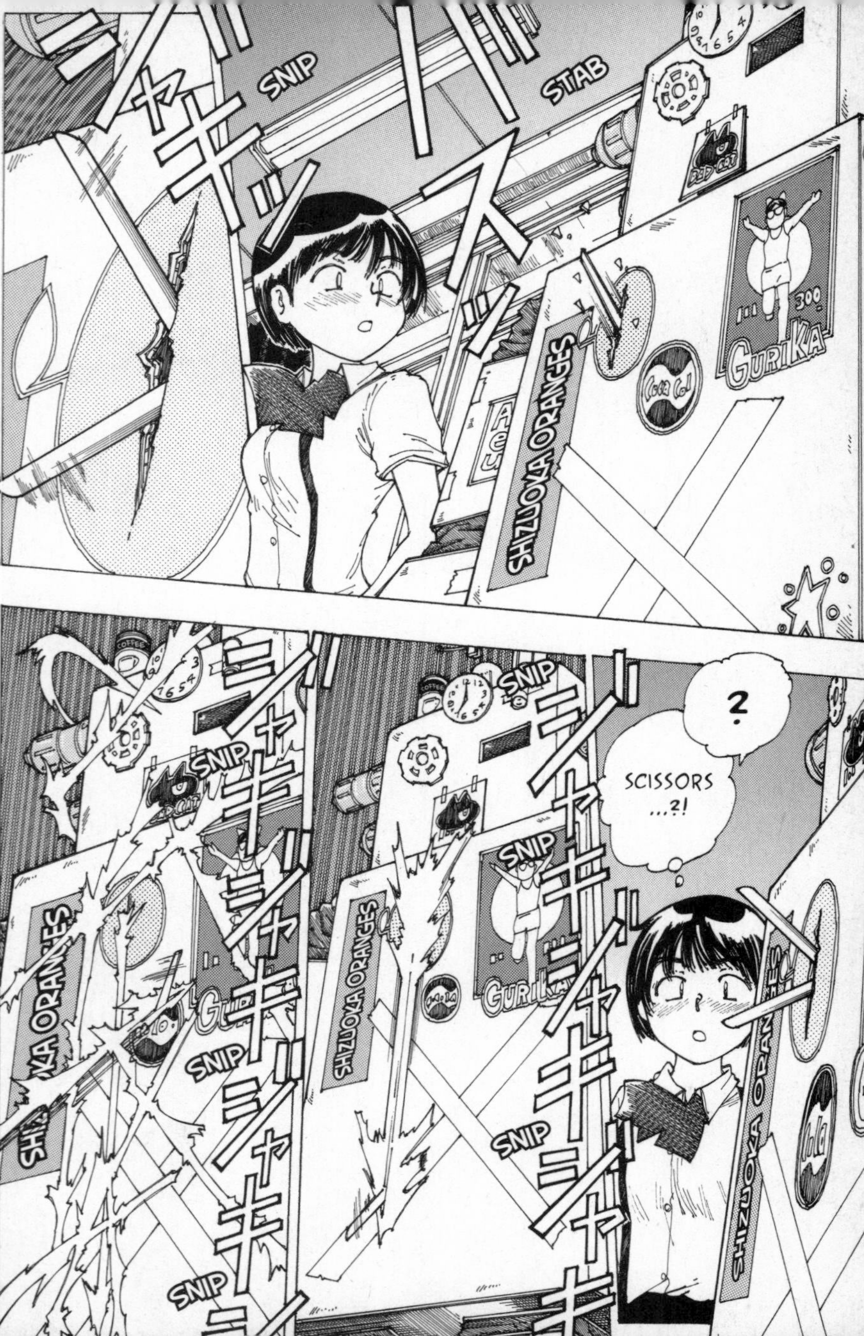
STAB
SNIP
SHIZUOKA ORANGES
GURIKA
?
SCISSORS ...?!
SNIP
SNIP
SNIP
SHIZUOKA ORANGES
SNIP
SNIP
SHIZUOKA ORANGES
SNIP

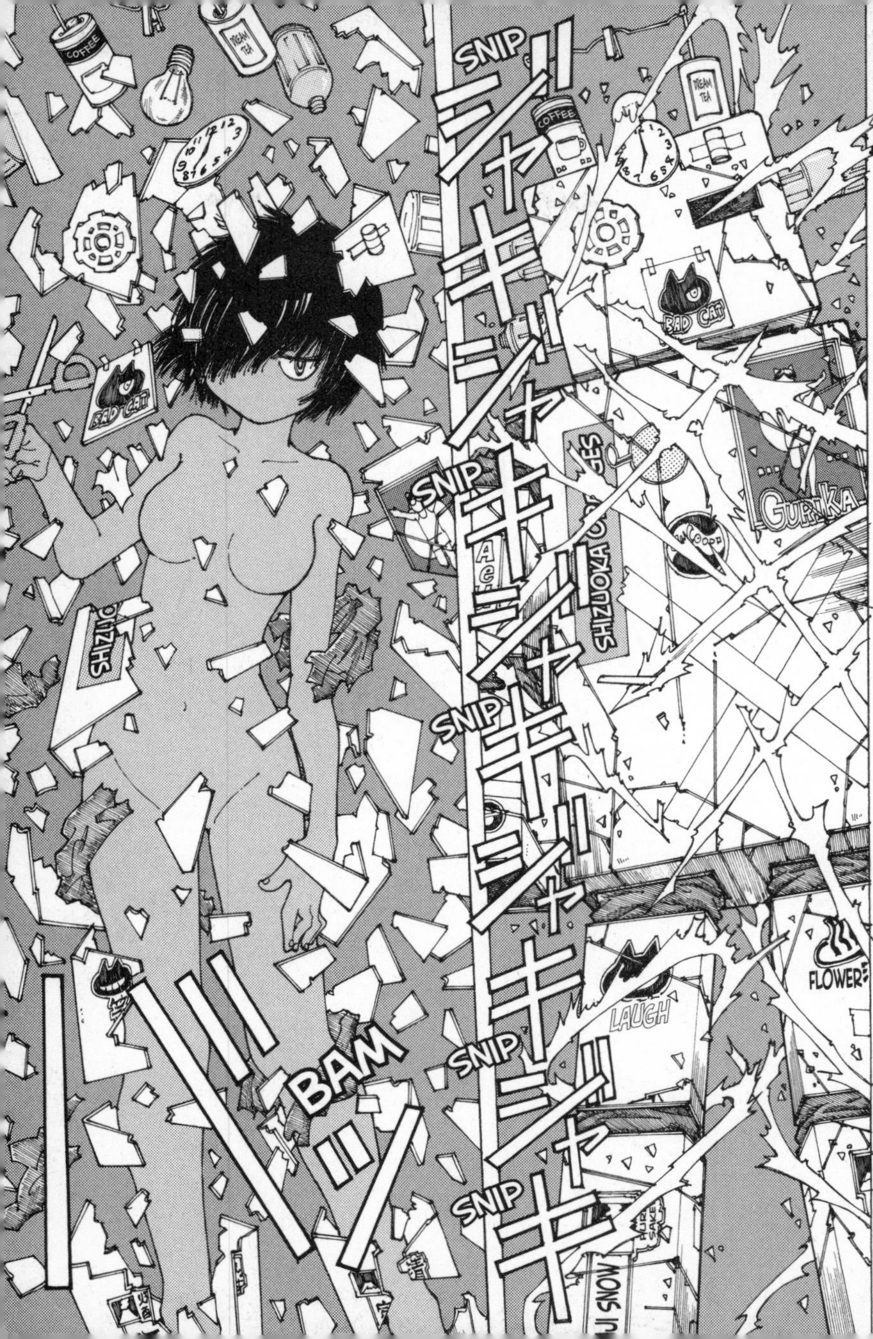
SNIP
ジャキ
ジャキ
SNIP
ジャキ
SNIP
ジャキ
SNIP
ジャキ
SNIP
ジャキ
DREAM TEA
COFFEE
BAD CAT
SHIZUOKA
GURIKA
LAUGH
FLOWER
SAKE
SNOW
COFFEE
DREAM TEA
BAD CAT
SHIZUO
BAM

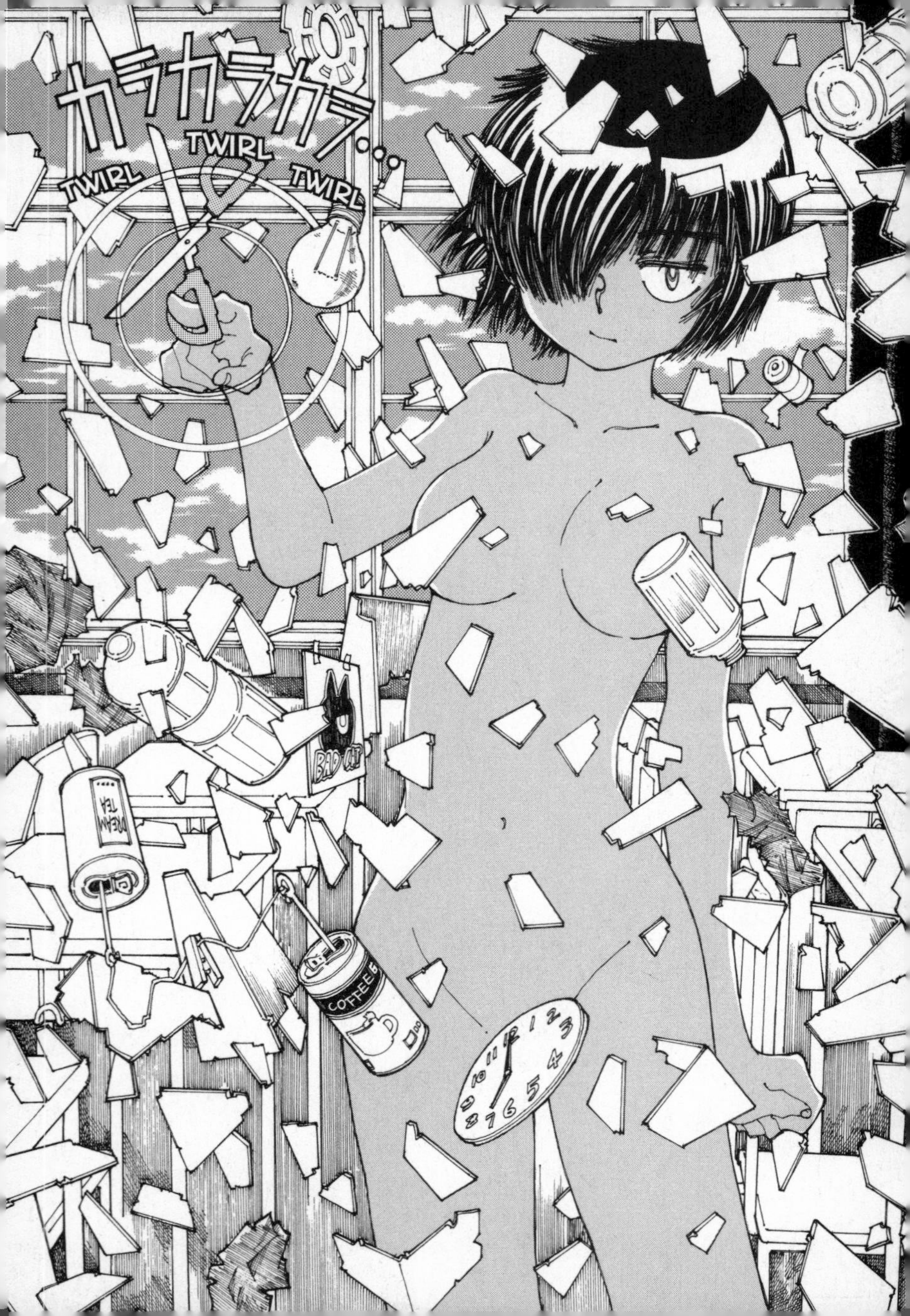
カラカラカラ…
TWIRL
TWIRL
TWIRL
BAD CAT
DREAM TEA
COFFEE

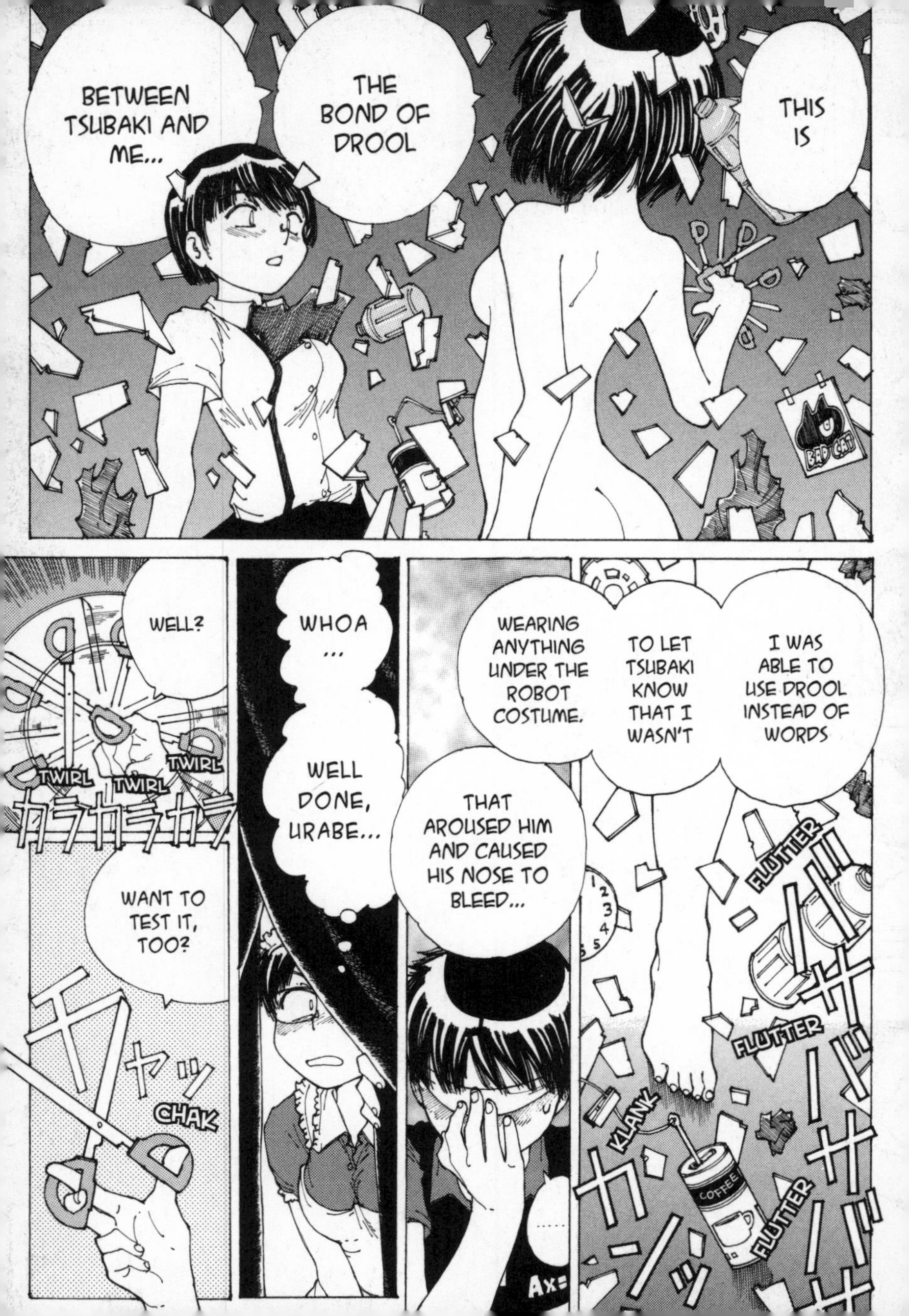
THIS IS
THE BOND OF DROOL
BETWEEN TSUBAKI AND ME...
BAD CAT
I WAS ABLE TO USE DROOL INSTEAD OF WORDS
TO LET TSUBAKI KNOW THAT I WASN'T
WEARING ANYTHING UNDER THE ROBOT COSTUME.
FLUTTER
FLUTTER
KLANK
COFFEE
FLUTTER
THAT AROUSED HIM AND CAUSED HIS NOSE TO BLEED...
......
WHOA ...
WELL DONE, URABE...
WELL?
TWIRL
TWIRL
TWIRL
カラカラカラ
WANT TO TEST IT, TOO?
チャッ
CHAK

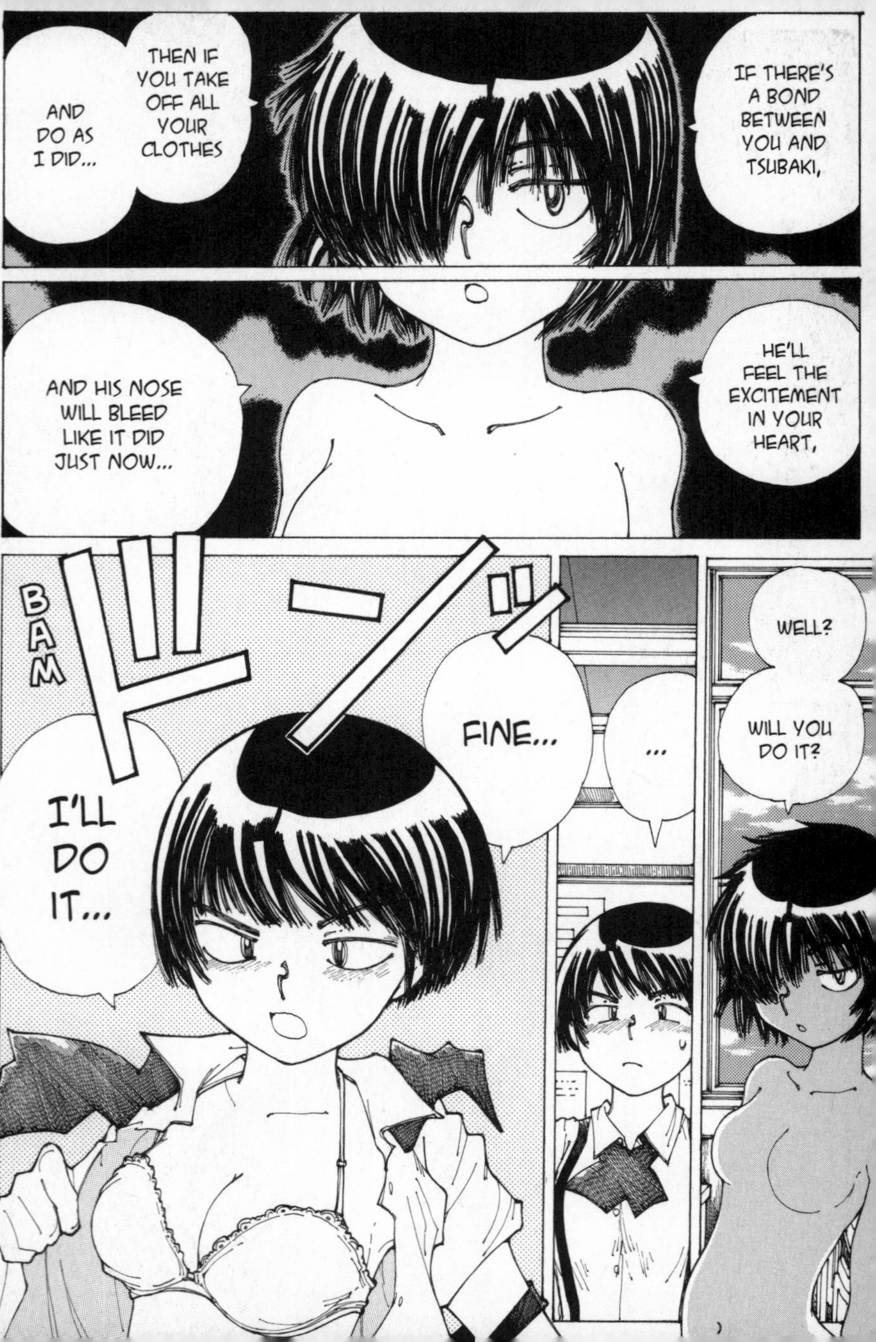
IF THERE'S A BOND BETWEEN YOU AND TSUBAKI,
THEN IF YOU TAKE OFF ALL YOUR CLOTHES
AND DO AS I DID...
HE'LL FEEL THE EXCITEMENT IN YOUR HEART,
AND HIS NOSE WILL BLEED LIKE IT DID JUST NOW...
WELL?
WILL YOU DO IT?
...
FINE...
BAM
I'LL DO IT...

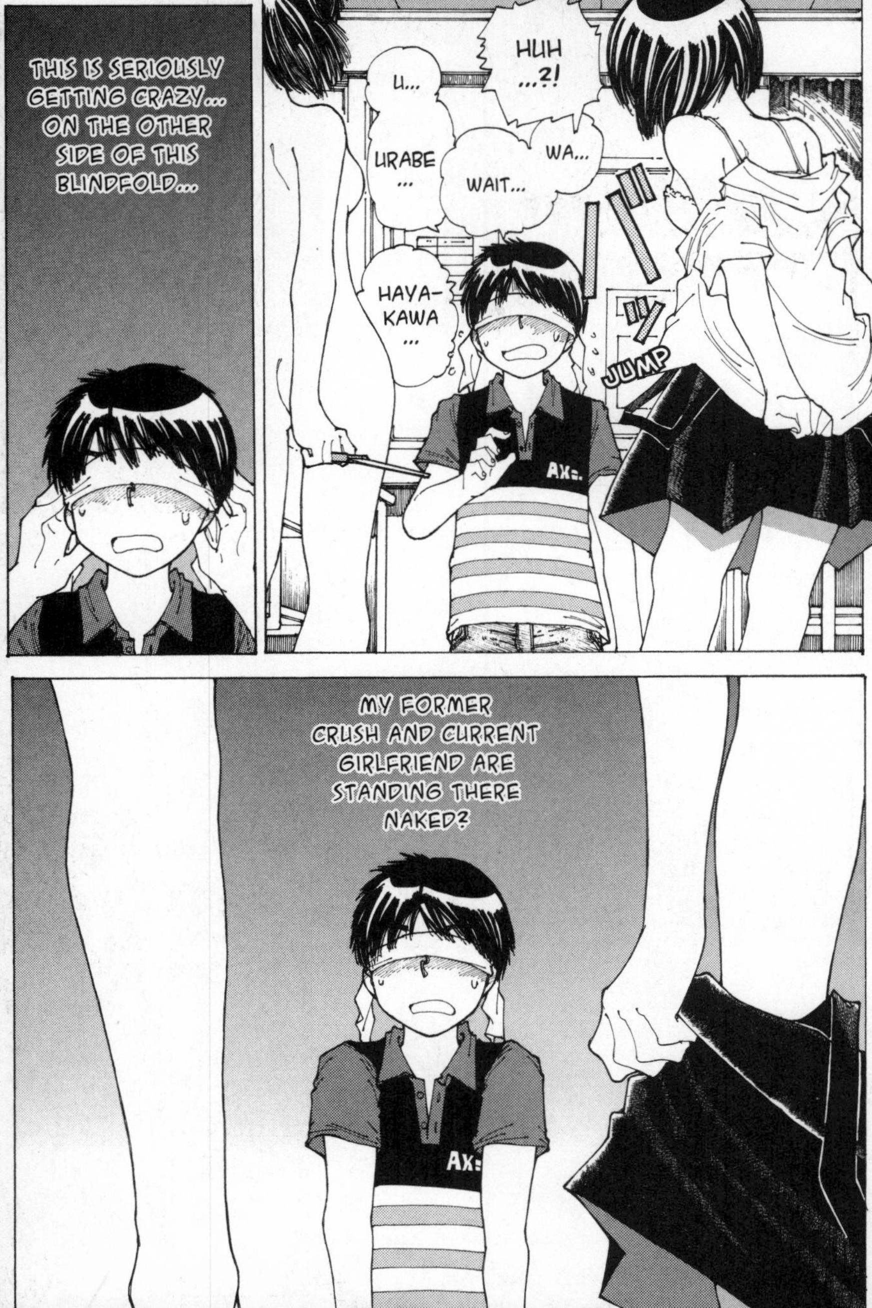
HUH ...?!
WA... WAIT...
U... URABE ...
HAYA-KAWA ...
JUMP
THIS IS SERIOUSLY GETTING CRAZY... ON THE OTHER SIDE OF THIS BLINDFOLD...
MY FORMER CRUSH AND CURRENT GIRLFRIEND ARE STANDING THERE NAKED?

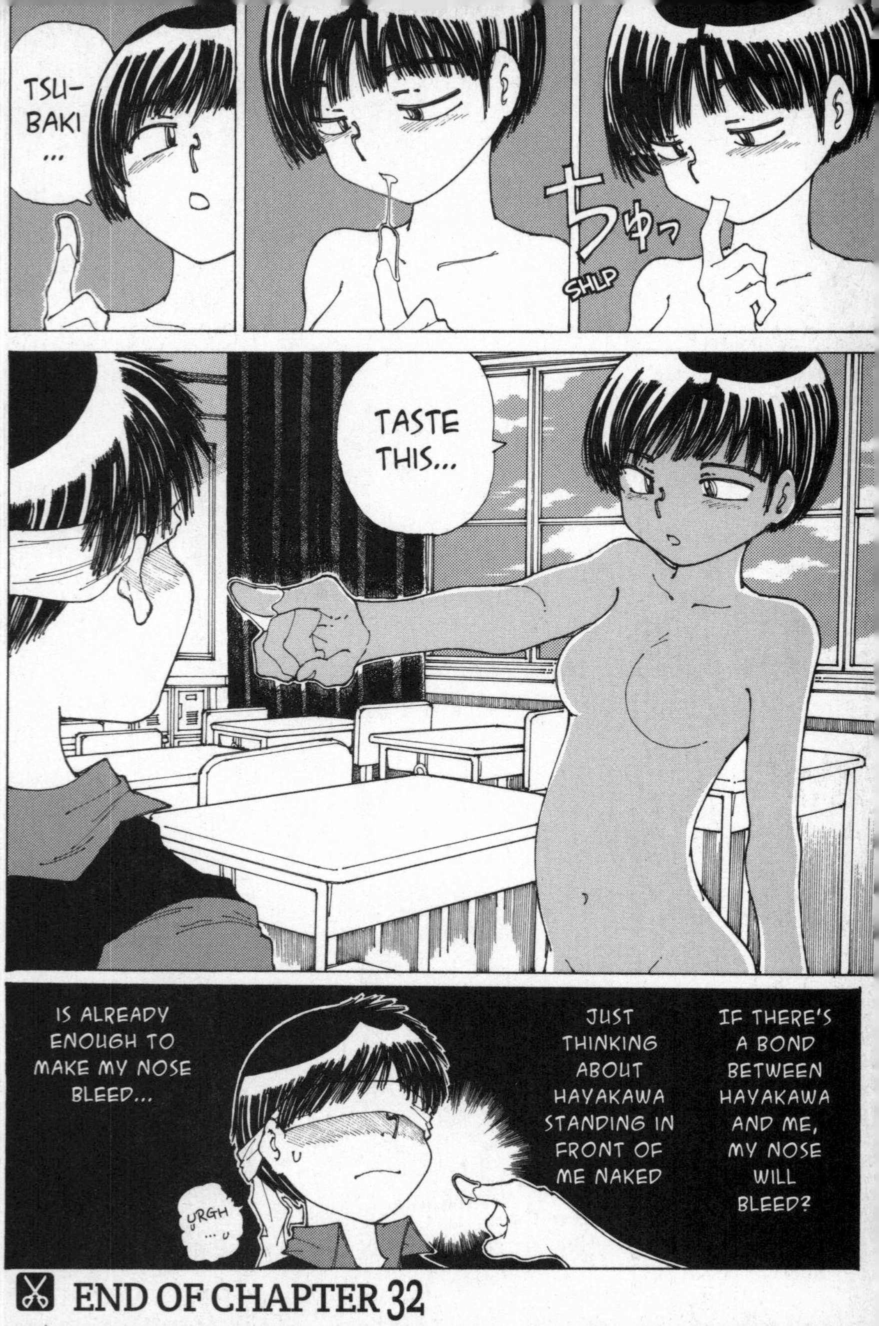
ちゅっ
SHLP
TSU-BAKI ...
TASTE THIS...
IF THERE'S A BOND BETWEEN HAYAKAWA AND ME, MY NOSE WILL BLEED?
JUST THINKING ABOUT HAYAKAWA STANDING IN FRONT OF ME NAKED
IS ALREADY ENOUGH TO MAKE MY NOSE BLEED...
URGH ...

END OF CHAPTER 32

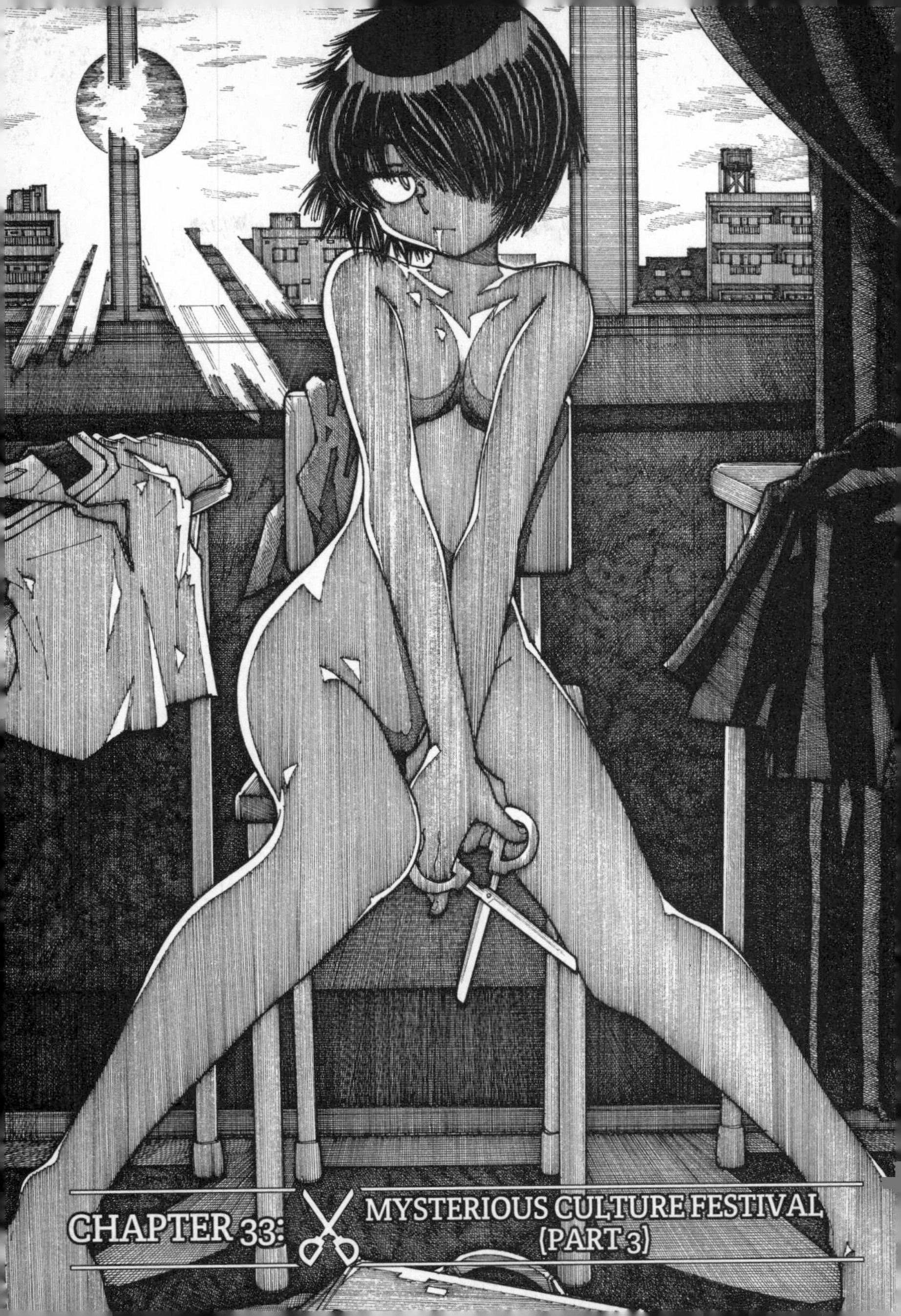
CHAPTER 33:
MYSTERIOUS CULTURE FESTIVAL
(PART 3)

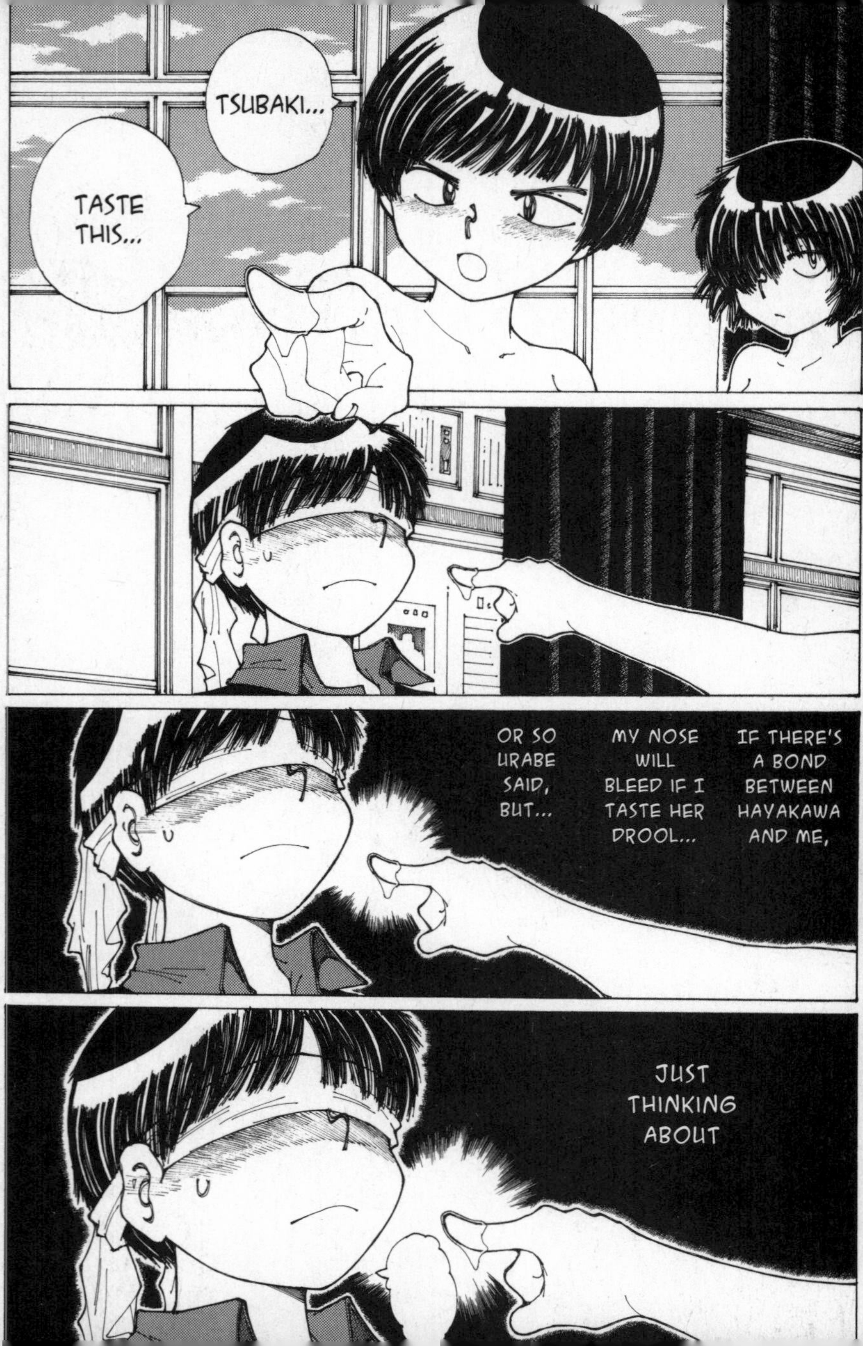
TSUBAKI...
TASTE THIS...
IF THERE'S A BOND BETWEEN HAYAKAWA AND ME,
MY NOSE WILL BLEED IF I TASTE HER DROOL...
OR SO URABE SAID, BUT...
JUST THINKING ABOUT

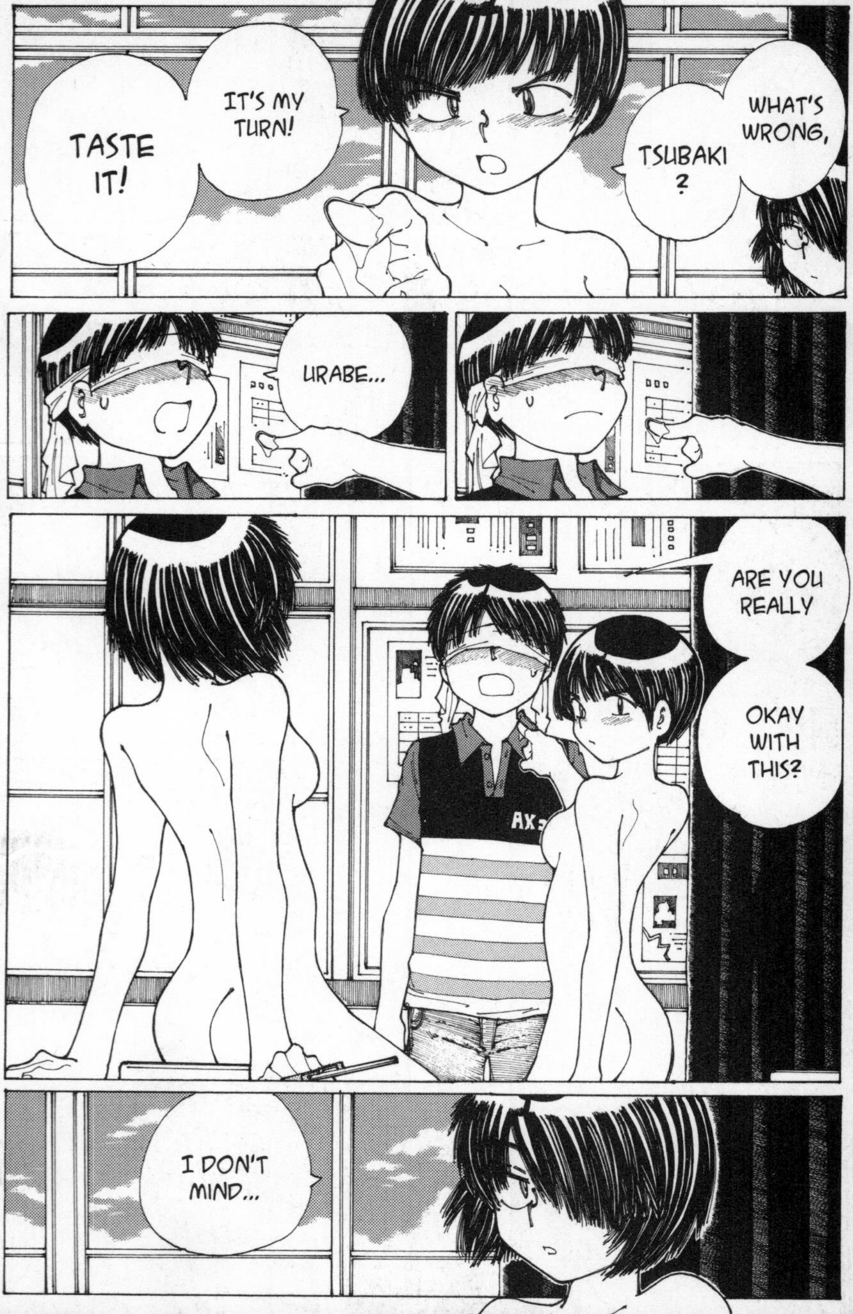
WHAT'S WRONG, TSUBAKI?
IT'S MY TURN!
TASTE IT!
URABE...
ARE YOU REALLY
OKAY WITH THIS?
I DON'T MIND...

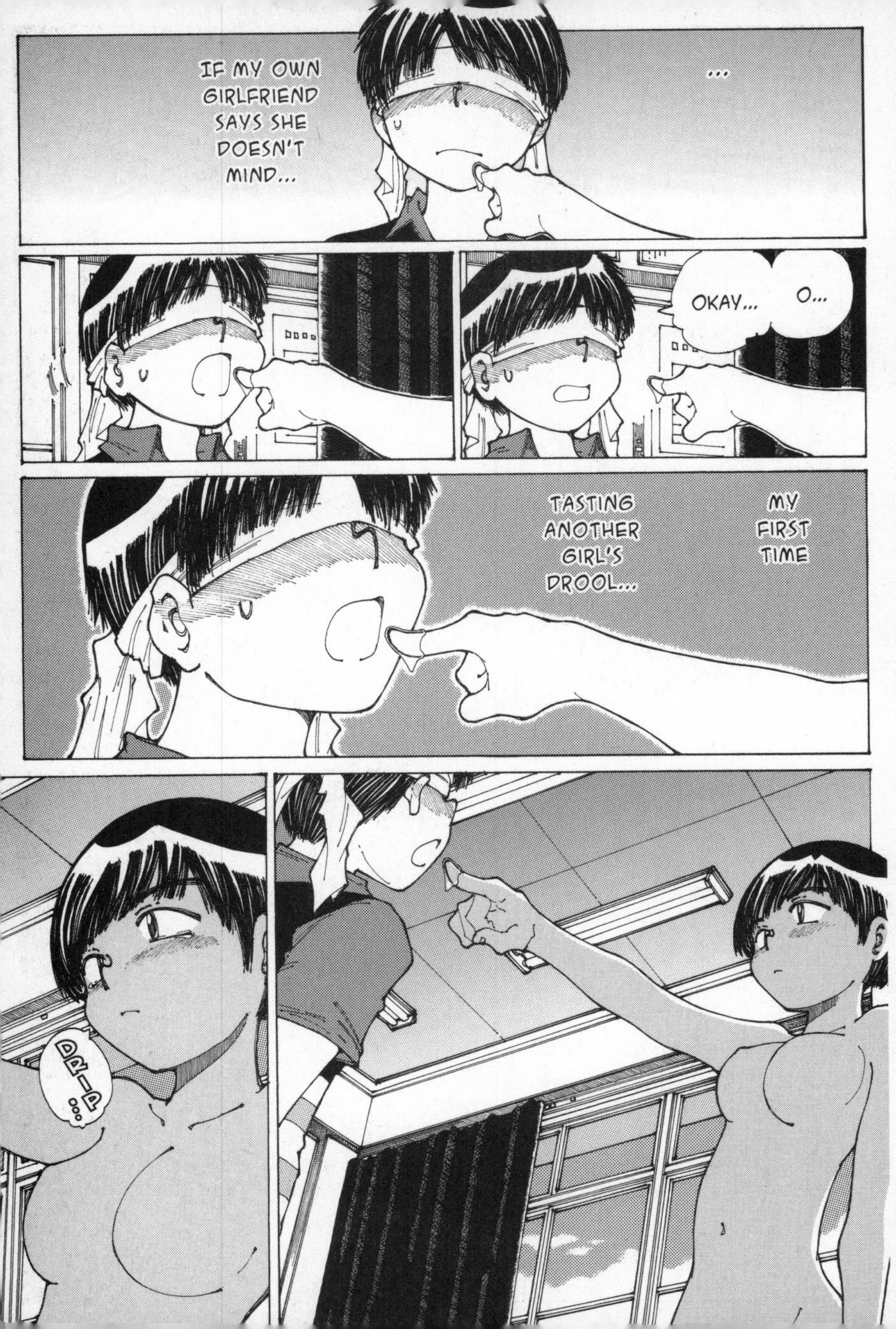
...
IF MY OWN GIRLFRIEND SAYS SHE DOESN'T MIND...
O...
OKAY...
MY FIRST TIME
TASTING ANOTHER GIRL'S DROOL...
DRIP...

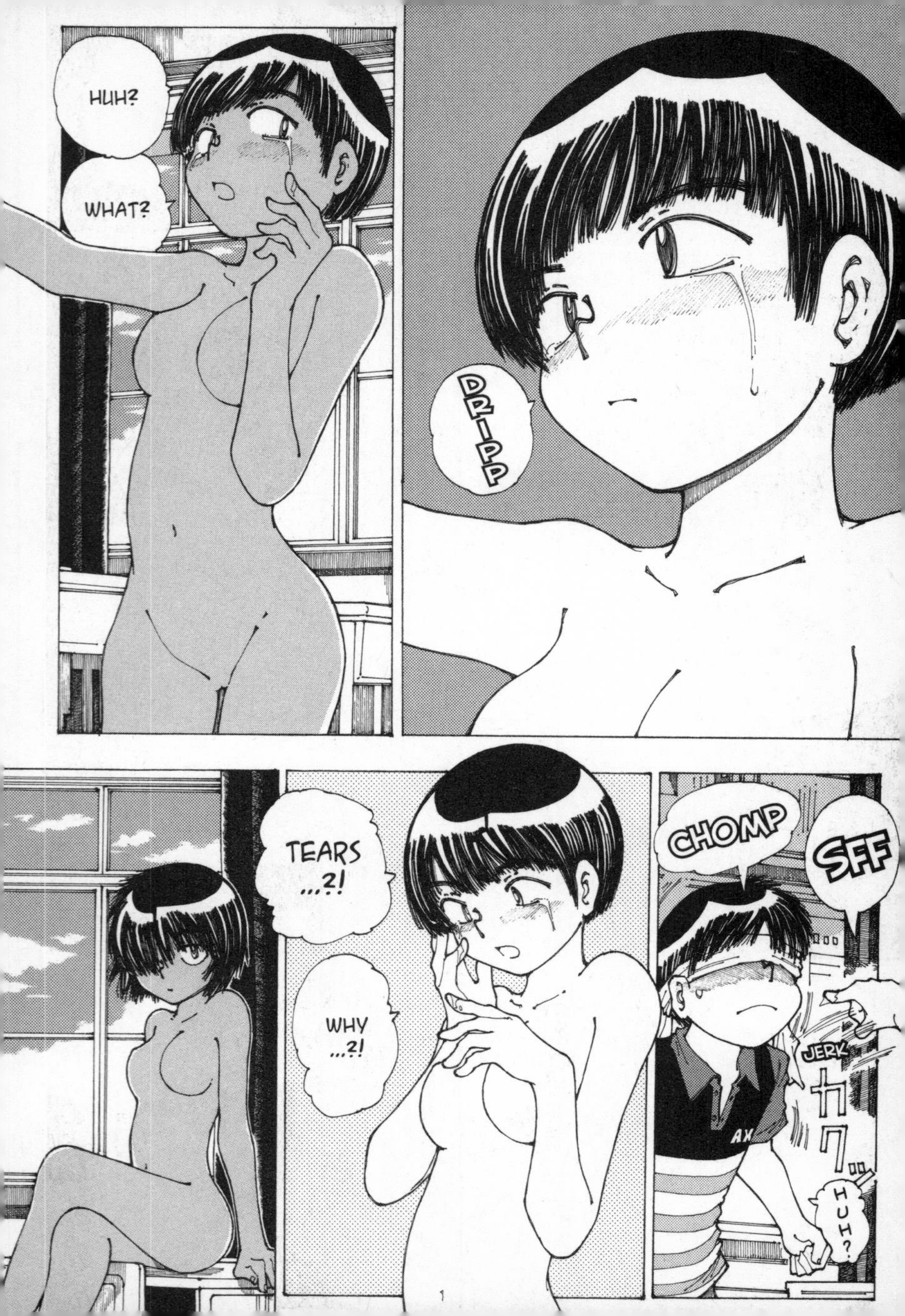
DRIPP
HUH?
WHAT?
CHOMP
SFF
JERK
カク
HUH?
TEARS ...?!
WHY ...?!

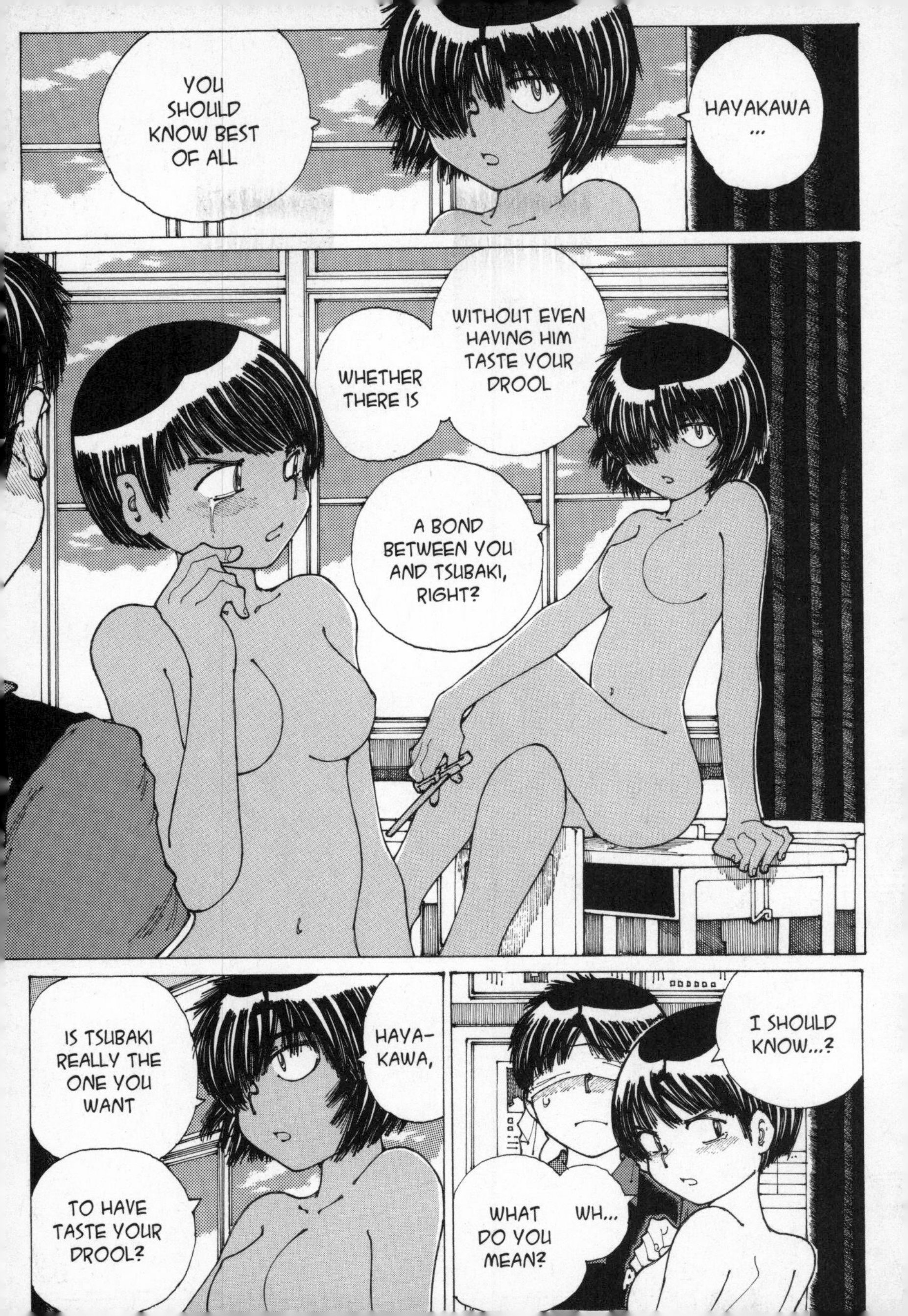
HAYAKAWA ...
YOU SHOULD KNOW BEST OF ALL
WITHOUT EVEN HAVING HIM TASTE YOUR DROOL
WHETHER THERE IS
A BOND BETWEEN YOU AND TSUBAKI, RIGHT?
I SHOULD KNOW...?
WH...
WHAT DO YOU MEAN?
HAYA-KAWA,
IS TSUBAKI REALLY THE ONE YOU WANT
TO HAVE TASTE YOUR DROOL?

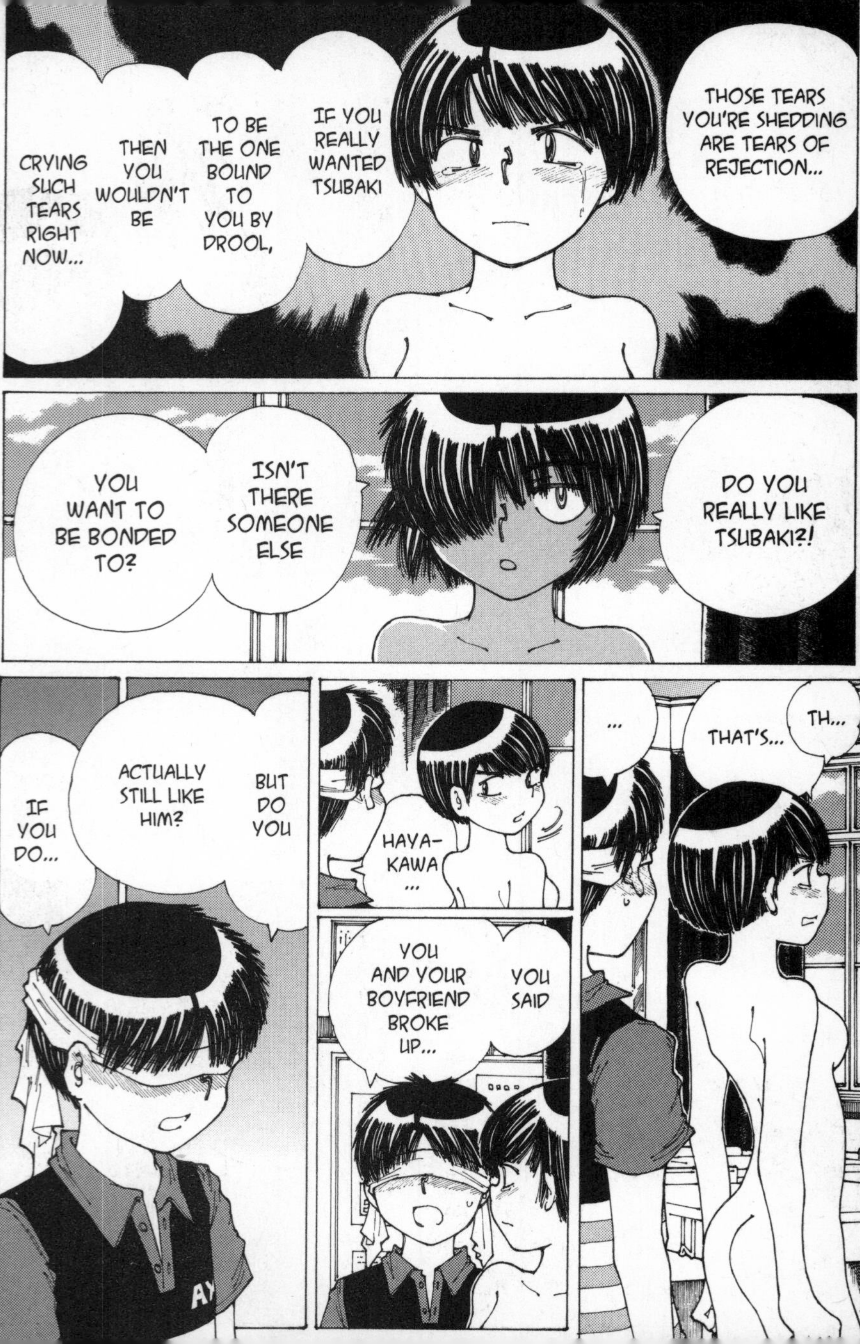
THOSE TEARS YOU'RE SHEDDING ARE TEARS OF REJECTION...
IF YOU REALLY WANTED TSUBAKI
TO BE THE ONE BOUND TO YOU BY DROOL,
THEN YOU WOULDN'T BE
CRYING SUCH TEARS RIGHT NOW...
DO YOU REALLY LIKE TSUBAKI?!
ISN'T THERE SOMEONE ELSE
YOU WANT TO BE BONDED TO?
TH...
THAT'S...
...
HAYA-KAWA ...
YOU SAID
YOU AND YOUR BOYFRIEND BROKE UP...
BUT DO YOU
ACTUALLY STILL LIKE HIM?
IF YOU DO...

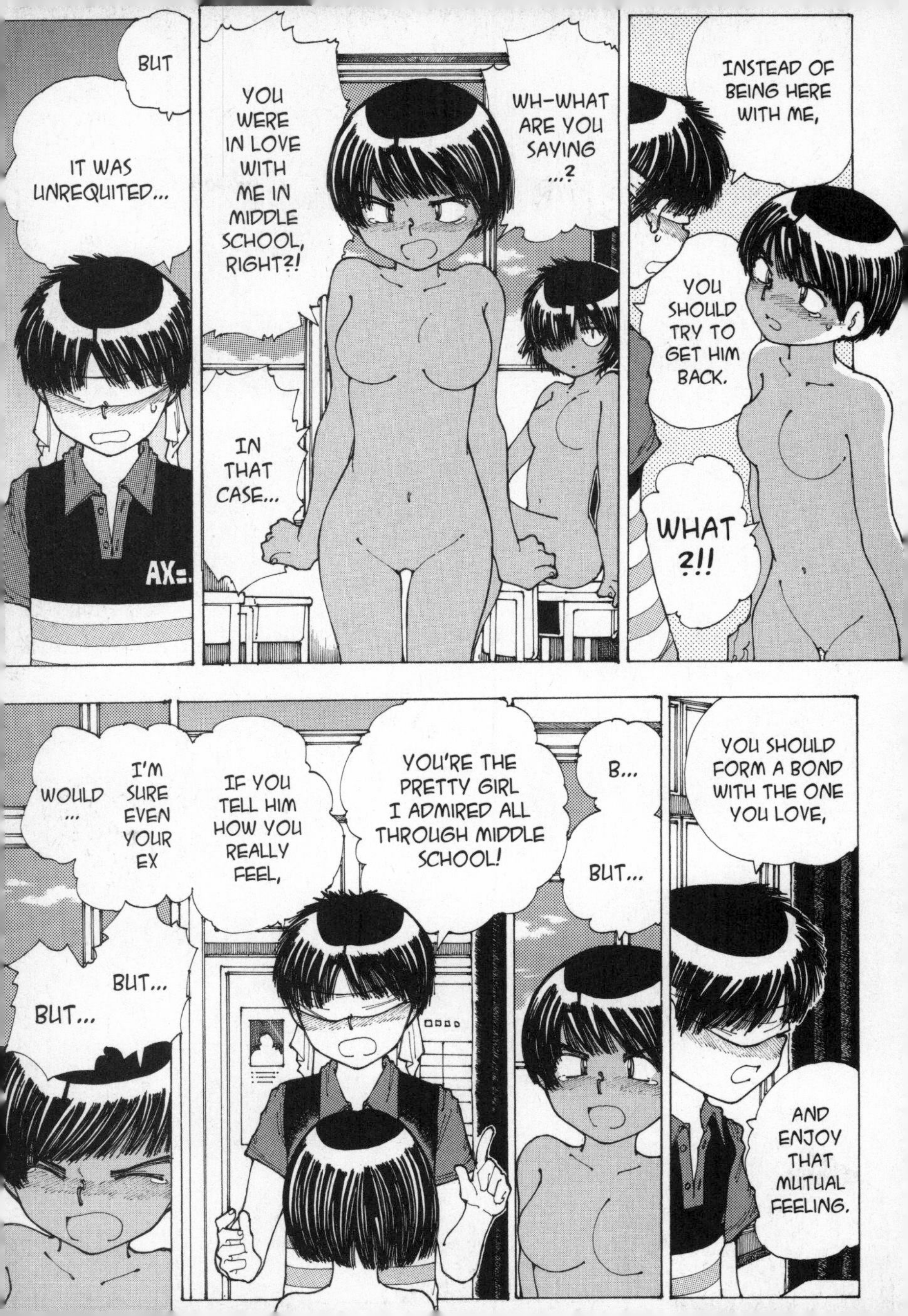

INSTEAD OF BEING HERE WITH ME,
YOU SHOULD TRY TO GET HIM BACK.
WHAT ?!!
WH-WHAT ARE YOU SAYING ...?
YOU WERE IN LOVE WITH ME IN MIDDLE SCHOOL, RIGHT?!
IN THAT CASE...
BUT
IT WAS UNREQUITED...
YOU SHOULD FORM A BOND WITH THE ONE YOU LOVE,
AND ENJOY THAT MUTUAL FEELING.
B...
BUT...
YOU'RE THE PRETTY GIRL I ADMIRED ALL THROUGH MIDDLE SCHOOL!
IF YOU TELL HIM HOW YOU REALLY FEEL,
I'M SURE EVEN YOUR EX
WOULD ...
BUT...
BUT...

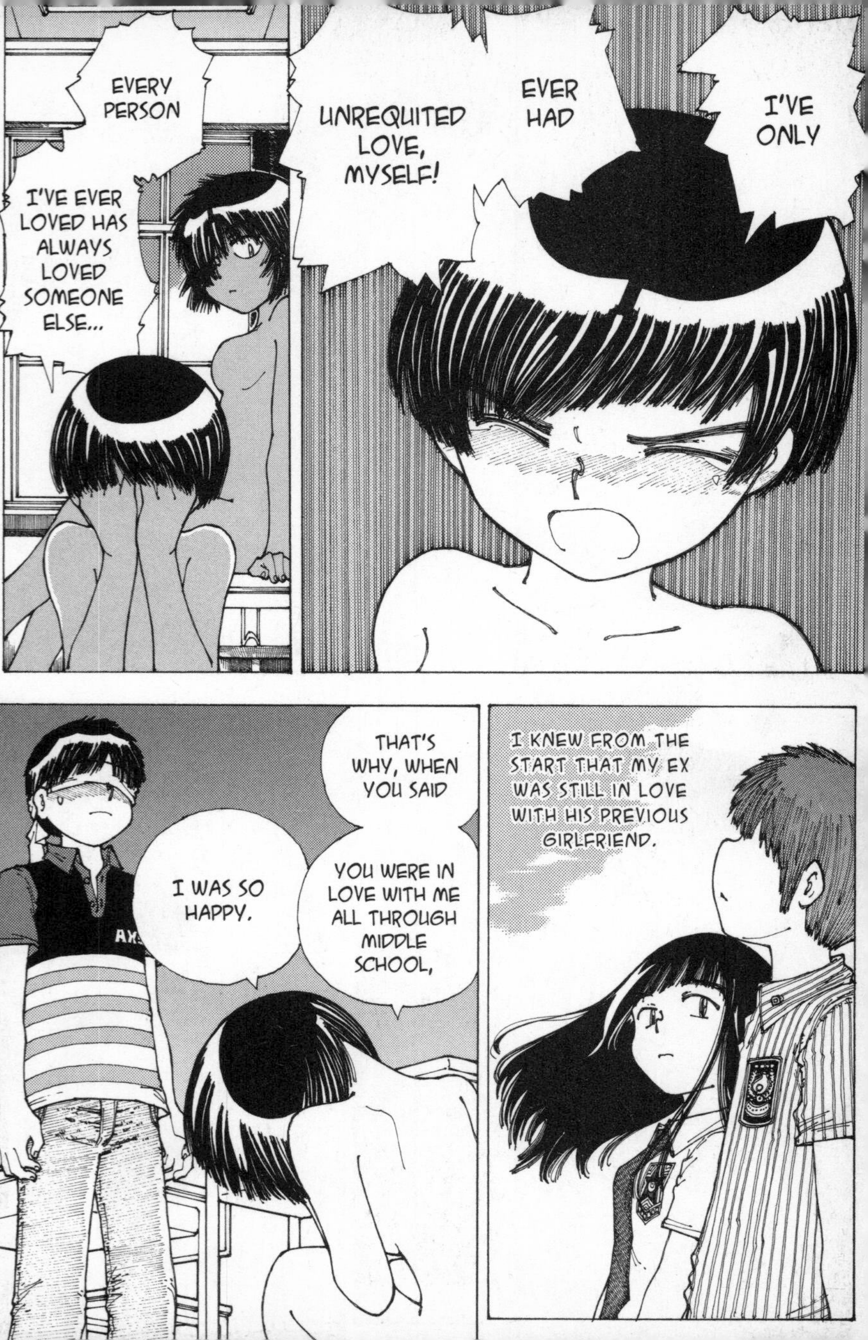
I'VE ONLY
EVER HAD
UNREQUITED LOVE, MYSELF!
EVERY PERSON
I'VE EVER LOVED HAS ALWAYS LOVED SOMEONE ELSE...
I KNEW FROM THE START THAT MY EX WAS STILL IN LOVE WITH HIS PREVIOUS GIRLFRIEND.
THAT'S WHY, WHEN YOU SAID
YOU WERE IN LOVE WITH ME ALL THROUGH MIDDLE SCHOOL,
I WAS SO HAPPY.

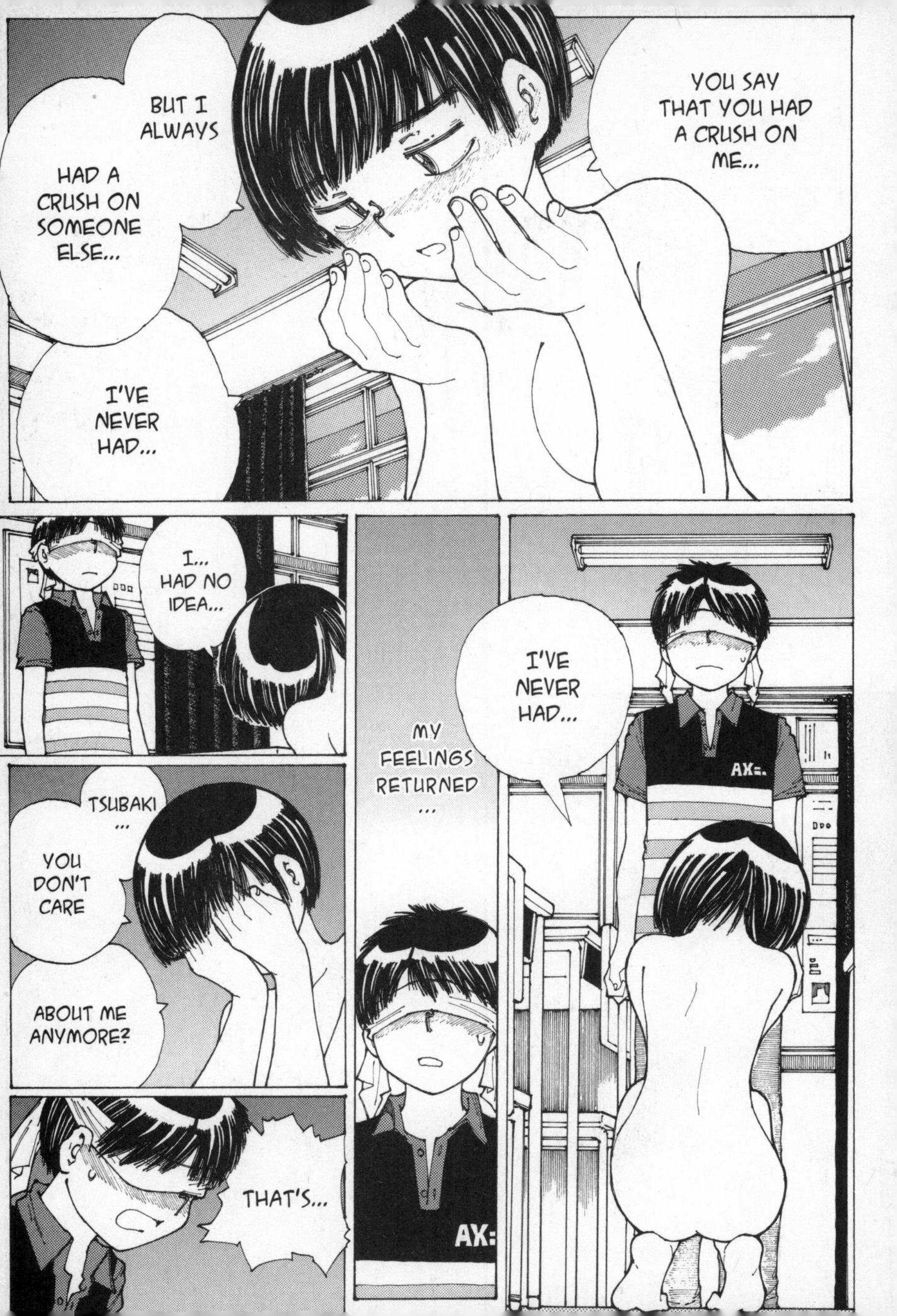
YOU SAY THAT YOU HAD A CRUSH ON ME...
BUT I ALWAYS
HAD A CRUSH ON SOMEONE ELSE...
I'VE NEVER HAD...
I'VE NEVER HAD...
MY FEELINGS RETURNED ...
I... HAD NO IDEA...
TSUBAKI ...
YOU DON'T CARE
ABOUT ME ANYMORE?
THAT'S...

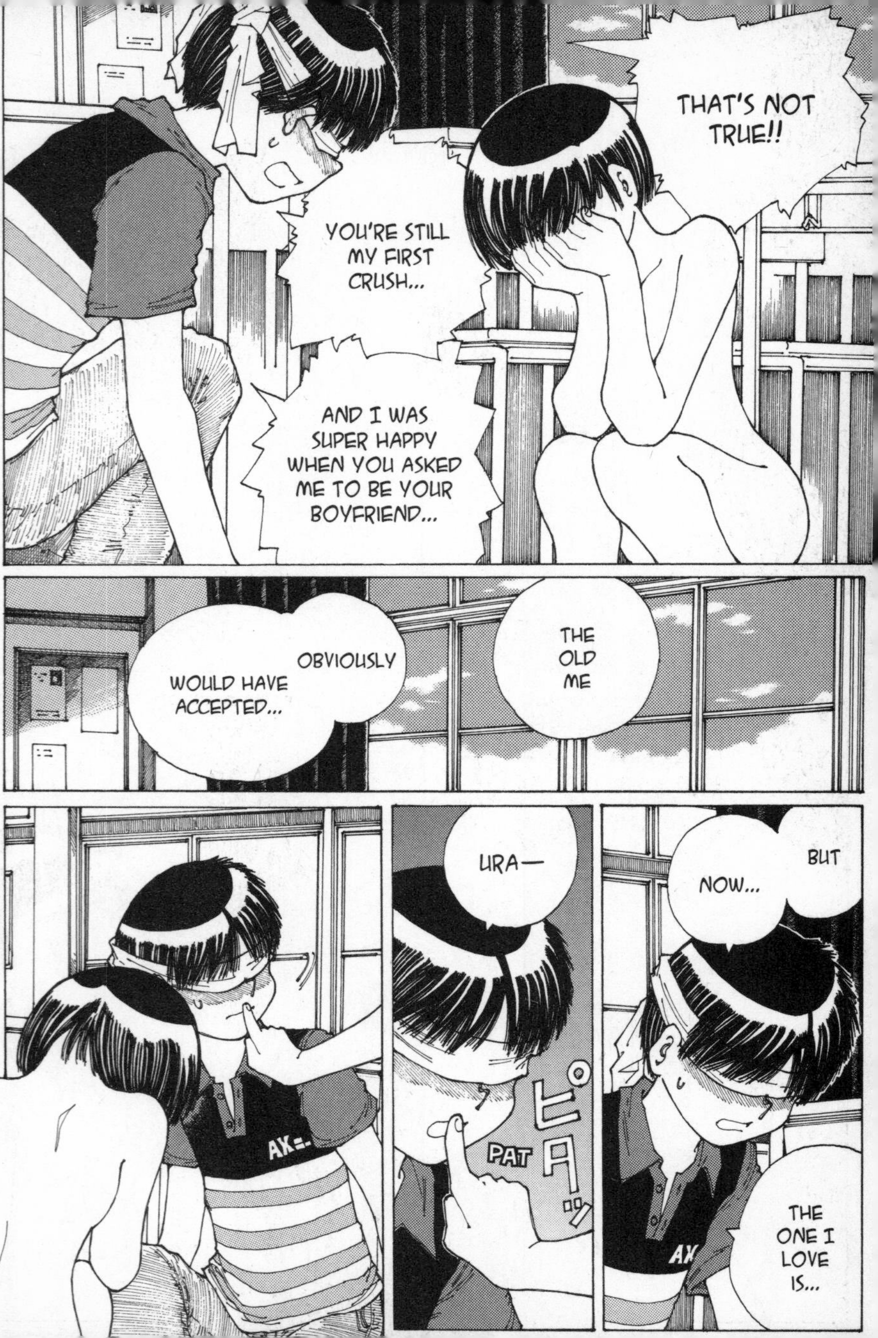
THAT'S NOT TRUE!!
YOU'RE STILL MY FIRST CRUSH...
AND I WAS SUPER HAPPY WHEN YOU ASKED ME TO BE YOUR BOYFRIEND...
THE OLD ME
OBVIOUSLY
WOULD HAVE ACCEPTED...
BUT
NOW...
THE ONE I LOVE IS...
URA—
ピタッ
PAT

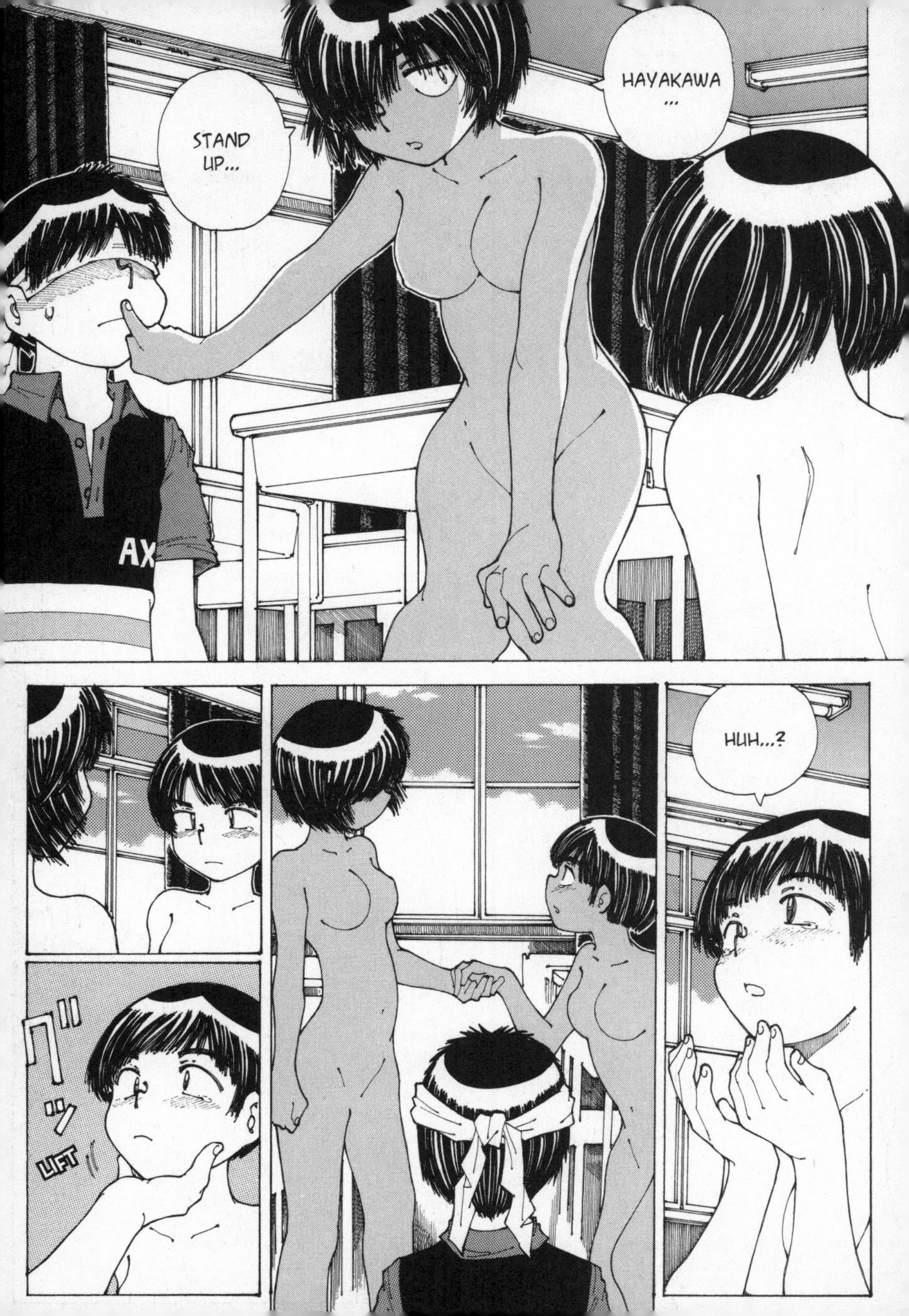
HAYAKAWA ...
STAND UP...
HUH...?
グッ
LIFT

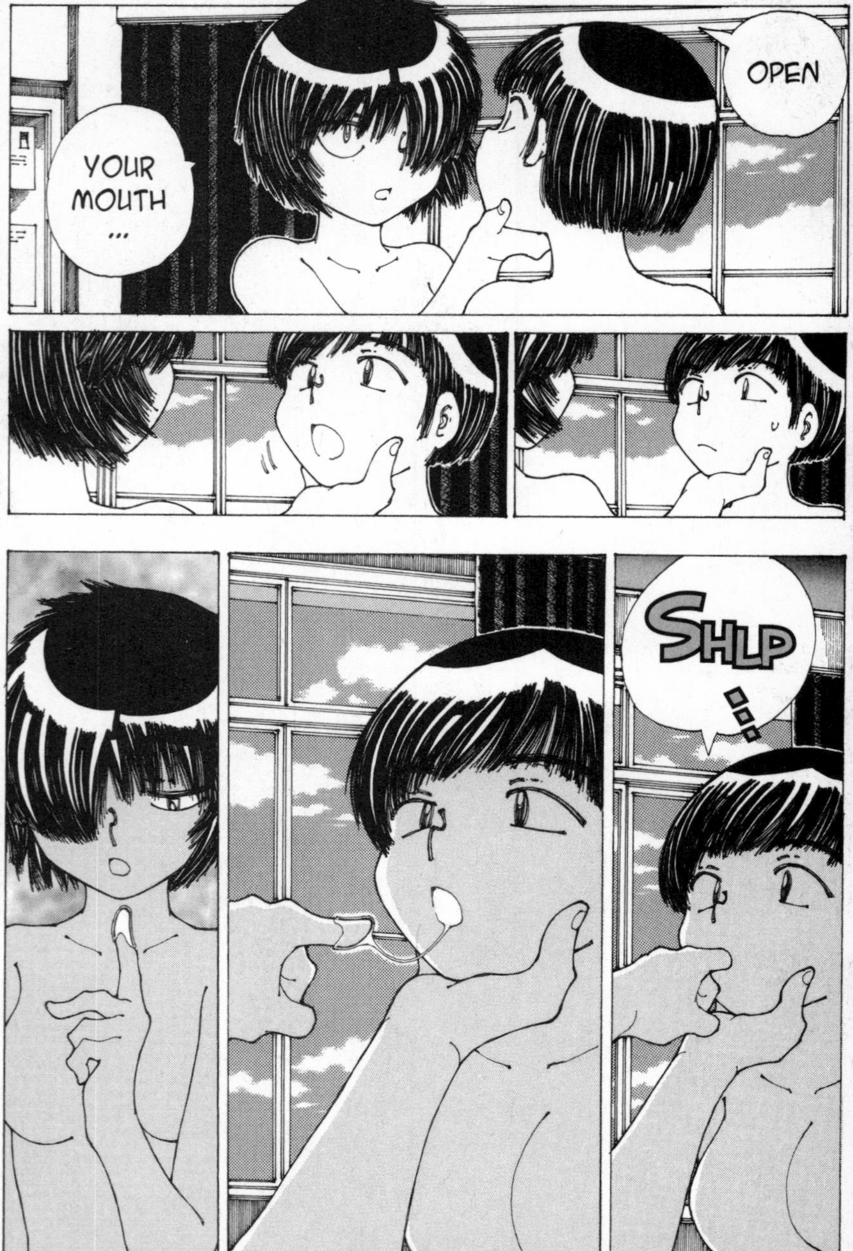
OPEN
YOUR MOUTH ...
SHLP ...

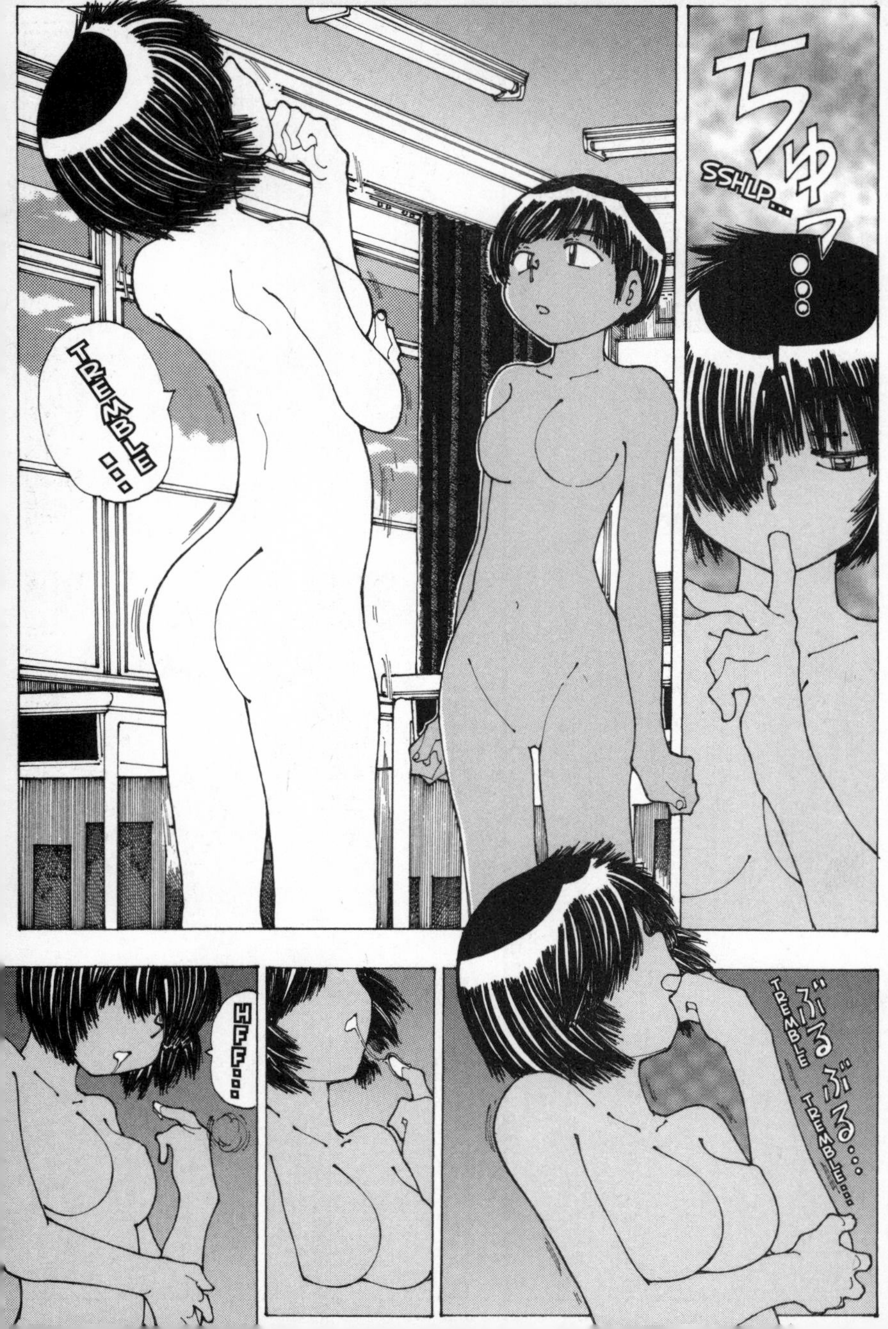
ちゅっ
SSHLP...
...
TREMBLE...
ぶるぶる...
TREMBLE TREMBLE...
HFF...

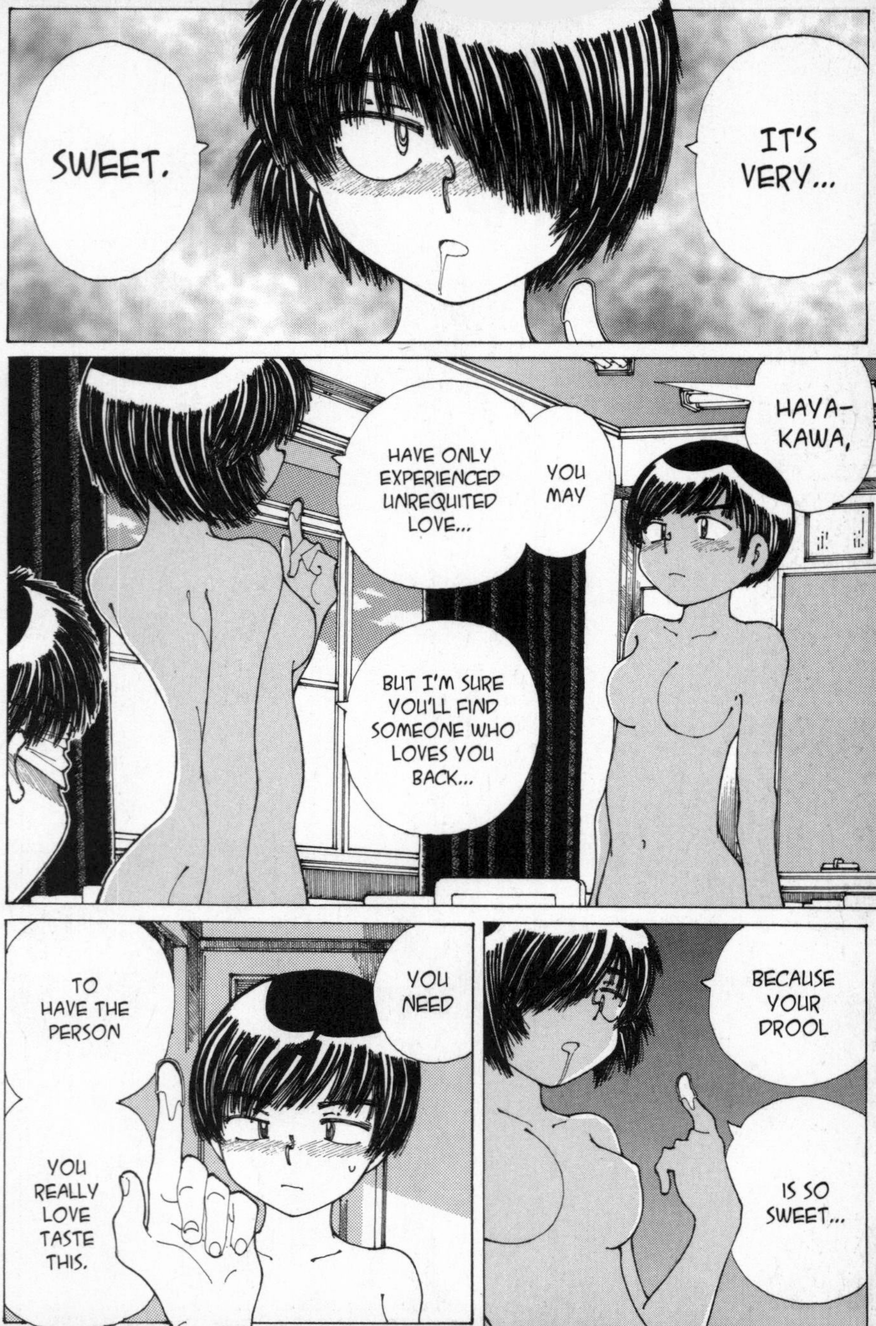
IT'S VERY...
SWEET.
HAYA-KAWA,
YOU MAY
HAVE ONLY EXPERIENCED UNREQUITED LOVE...
BUT I'M SURE YOU'LL FIND SOMEONE WHO LOVES YOU BACK...
BECAUSE YOUR DROOL
IS SO SWEET...
YOU NEED
TO HAVE THE PERSON
YOU REALLY LOVE TASTE THIS.

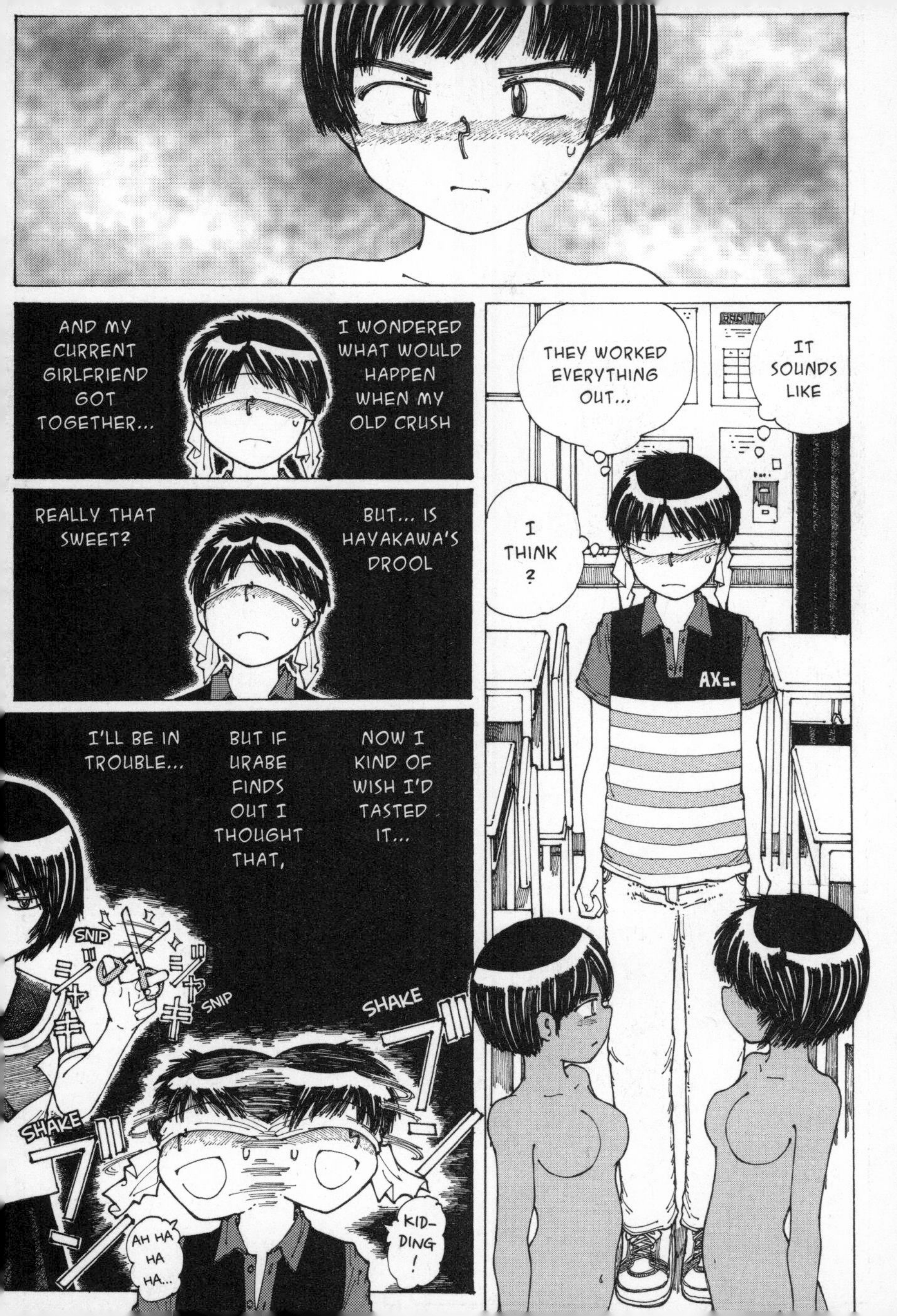
IT SOUNDS LIKE
THEY WORKED EVERYTHING OUT...
I THINK?
I WONDERED WHAT WOULD HAPPEN WHEN MY OLD CRUSH
AND MY CURRENT GIRLFRIEND GOT TOGETHER...
BUT... IS HAYAKAWA'S DROOL
REALLY THAT SWEET?
NOW I KIND OF WISH I'D TASTED IT...
BUT IF URABE FINDS OUT I THOUGHT THAT,
I'LL BE IN TROUBLE...
SNIP
SNIP
SHAKE
SHAKE
KID-DING!
AH HA HA HA...

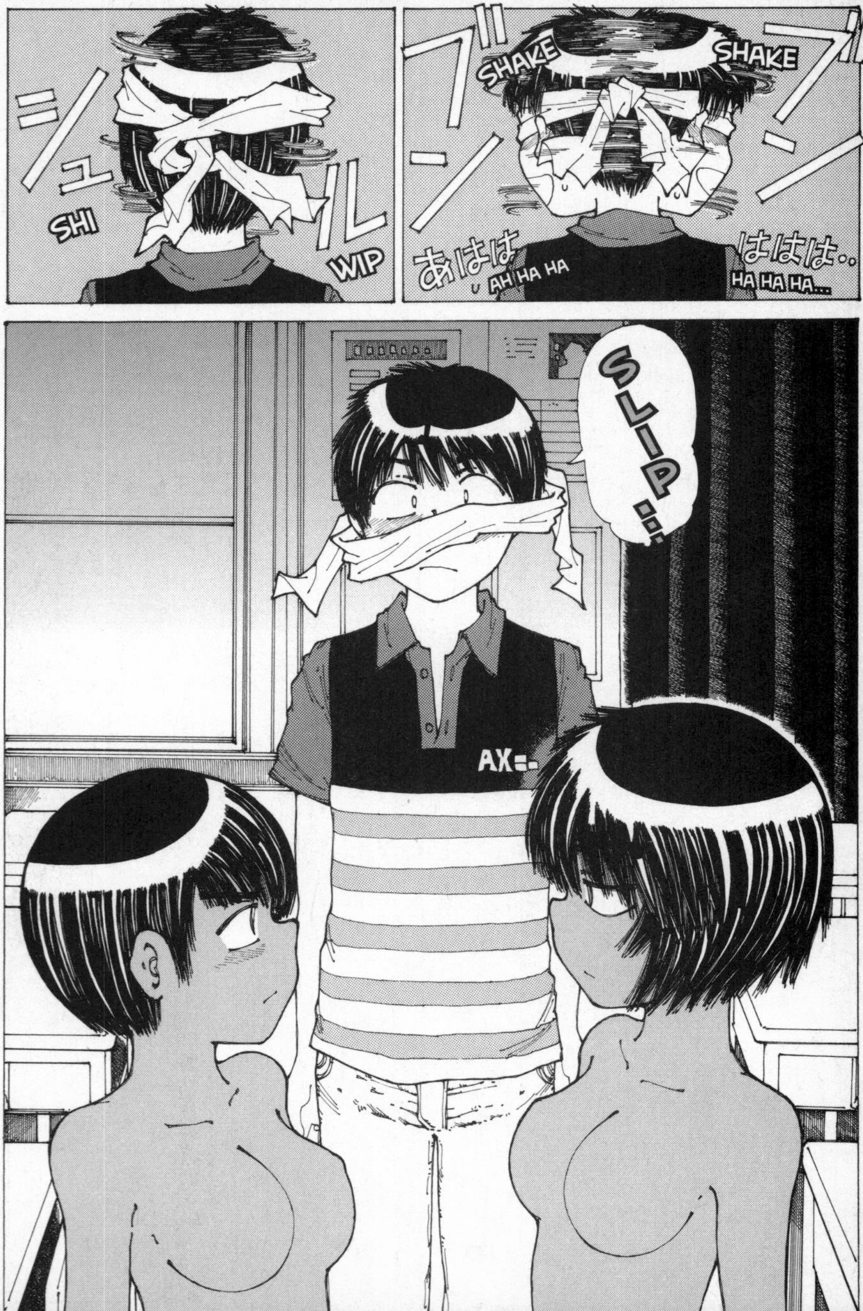

ブーン
SHAKE
ブーン
SHAKE
ははは..
HA HA HA...
あはは
AH HA HA
シュル
SHI
WIP
SLIP...

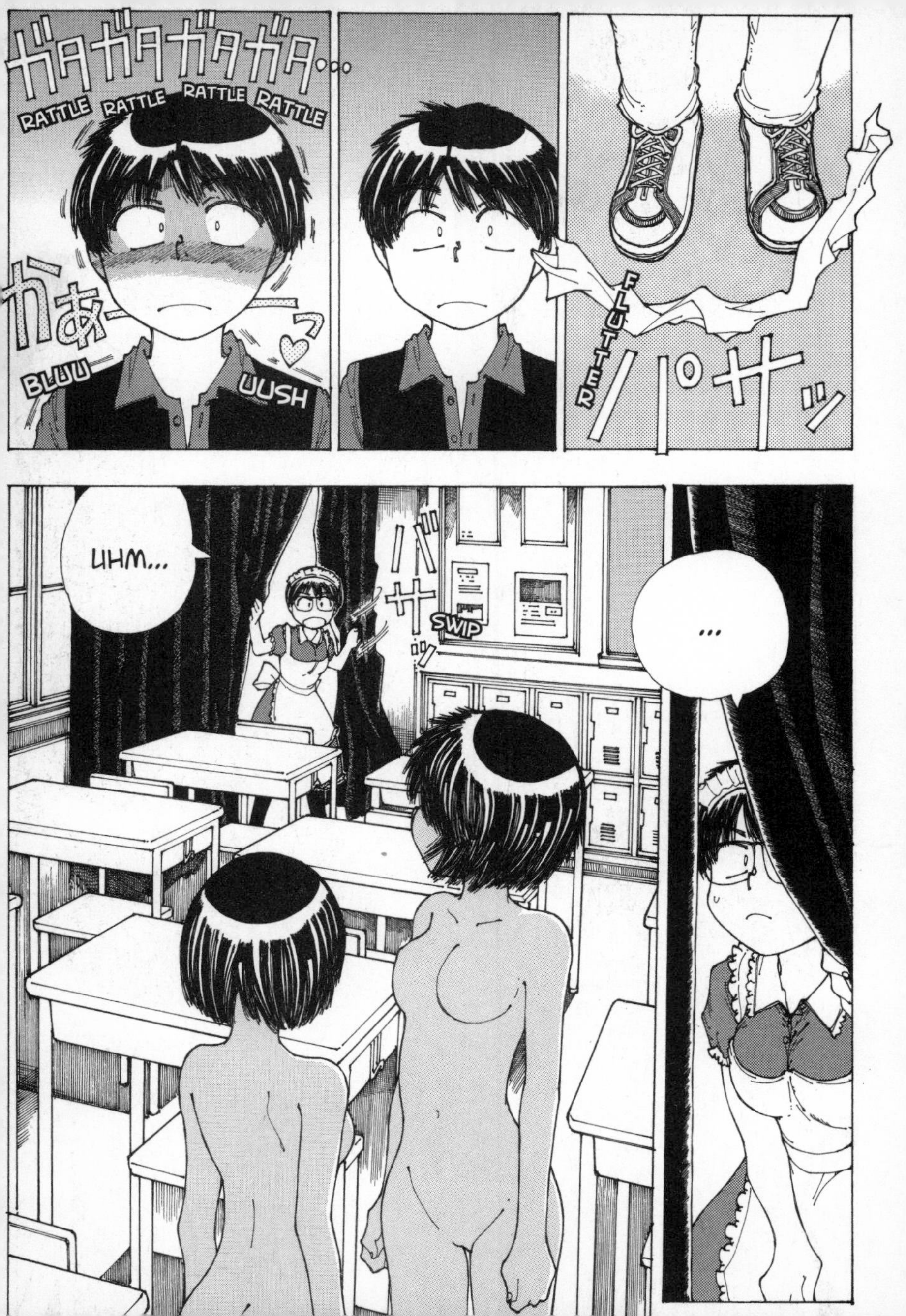

パサッ
FLUTTER
ガタガタガタガタ...
RATTLE RATTLE RATTLE RATTLE
がぁーっ
BLUU UUSH
...
UHM...
バサッ
SWIP

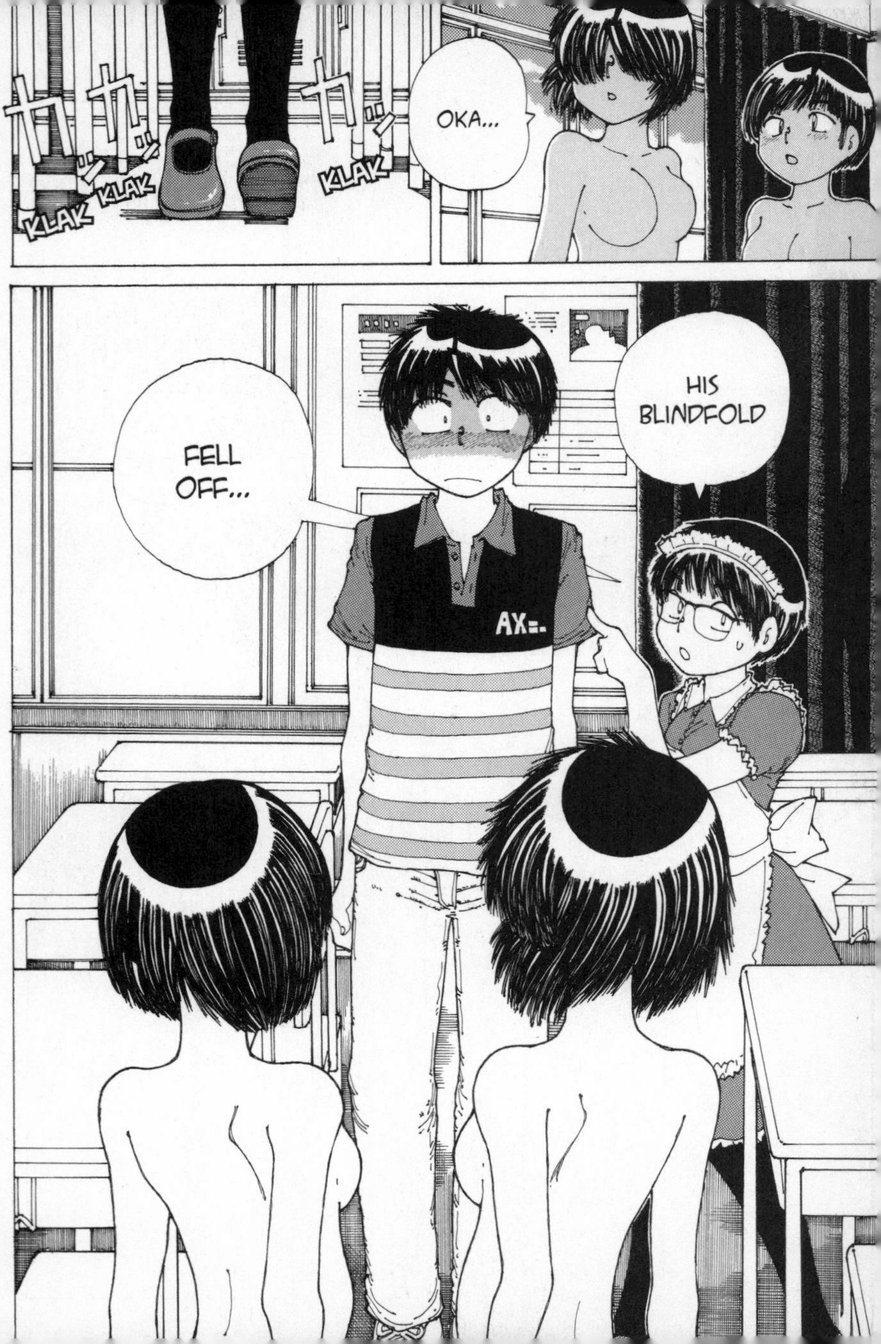
OKA...
KLAK
KLAK
KLAK
HIS BLINDFOLD
FELL OFF...

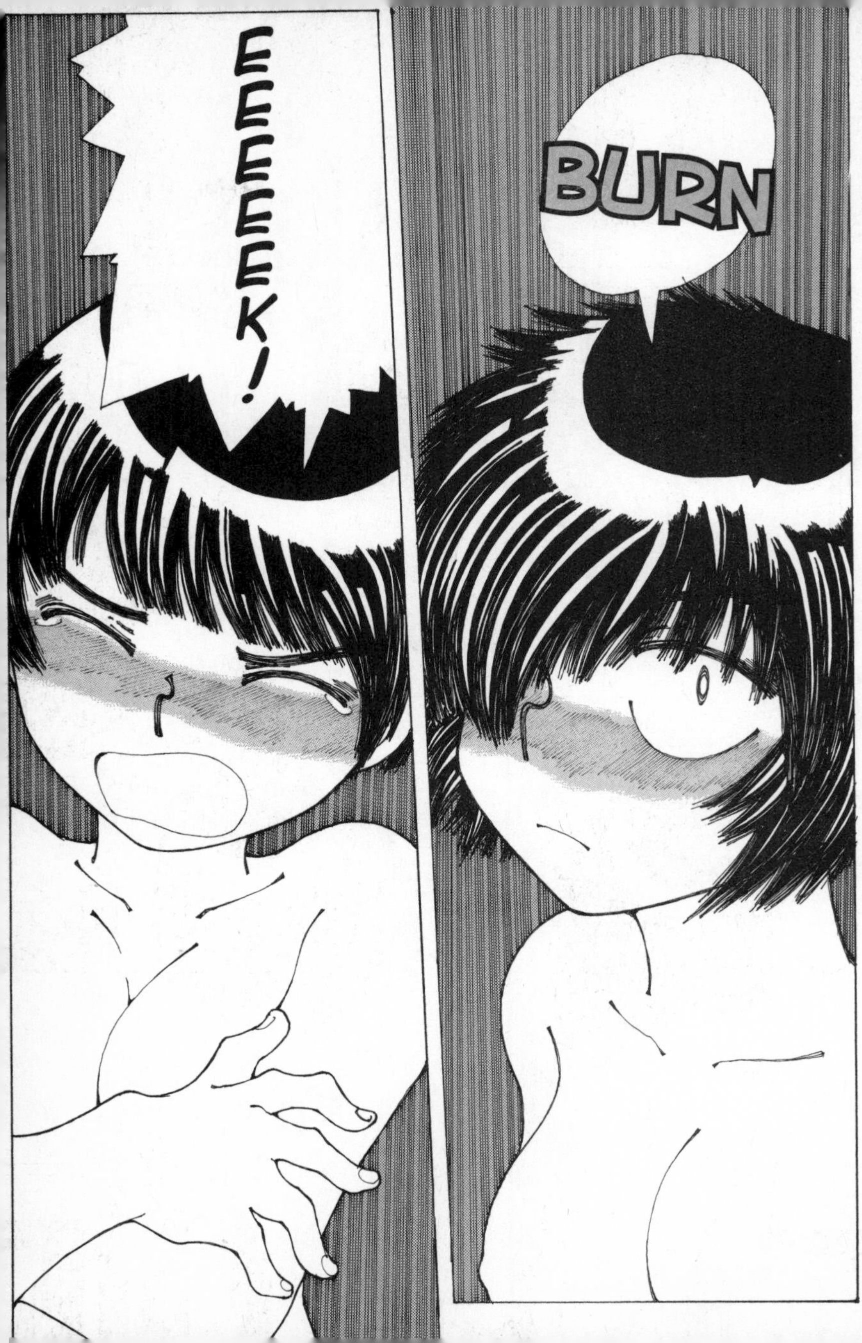
BURN
EEEEEK!

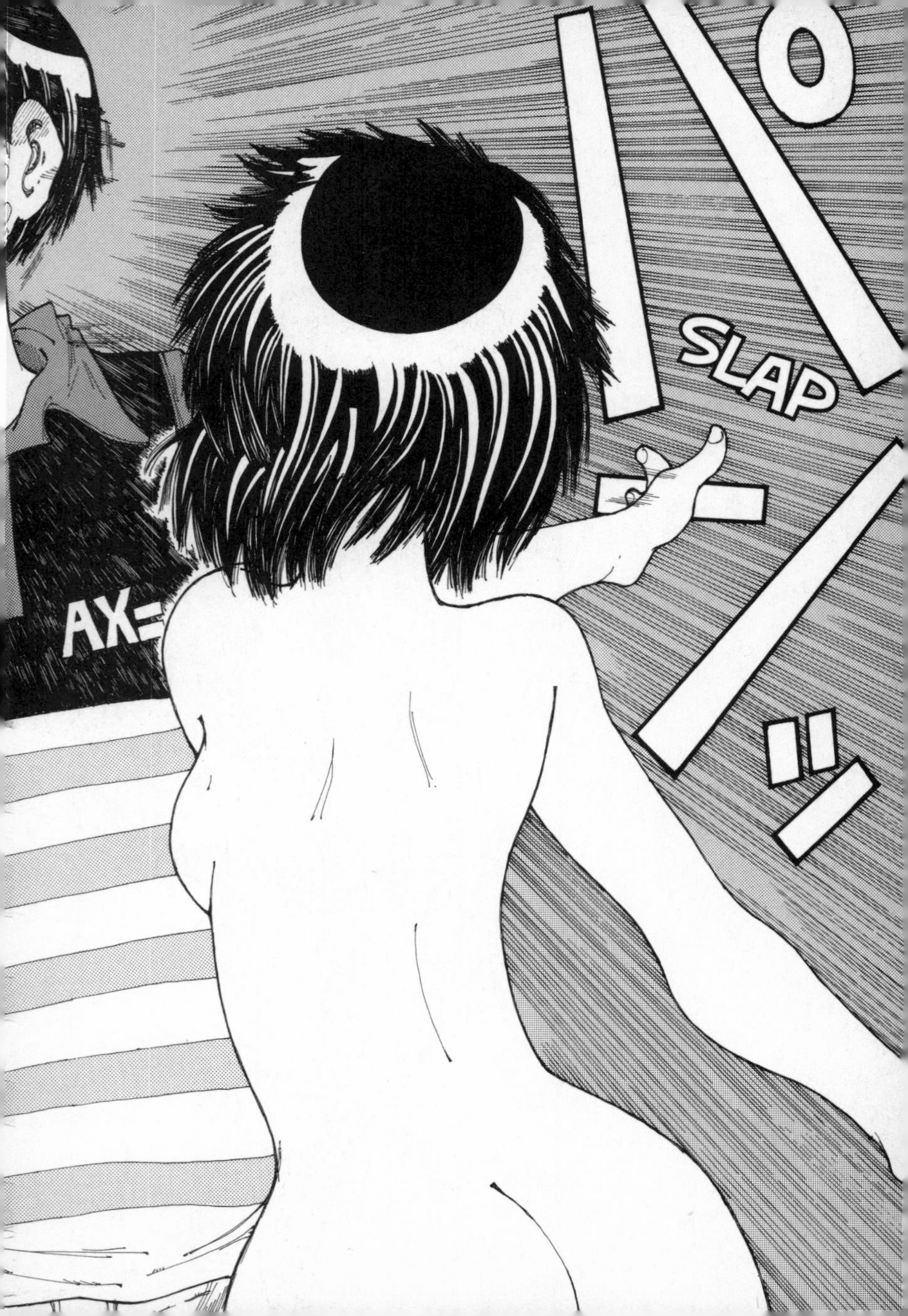
SLAP
AX=

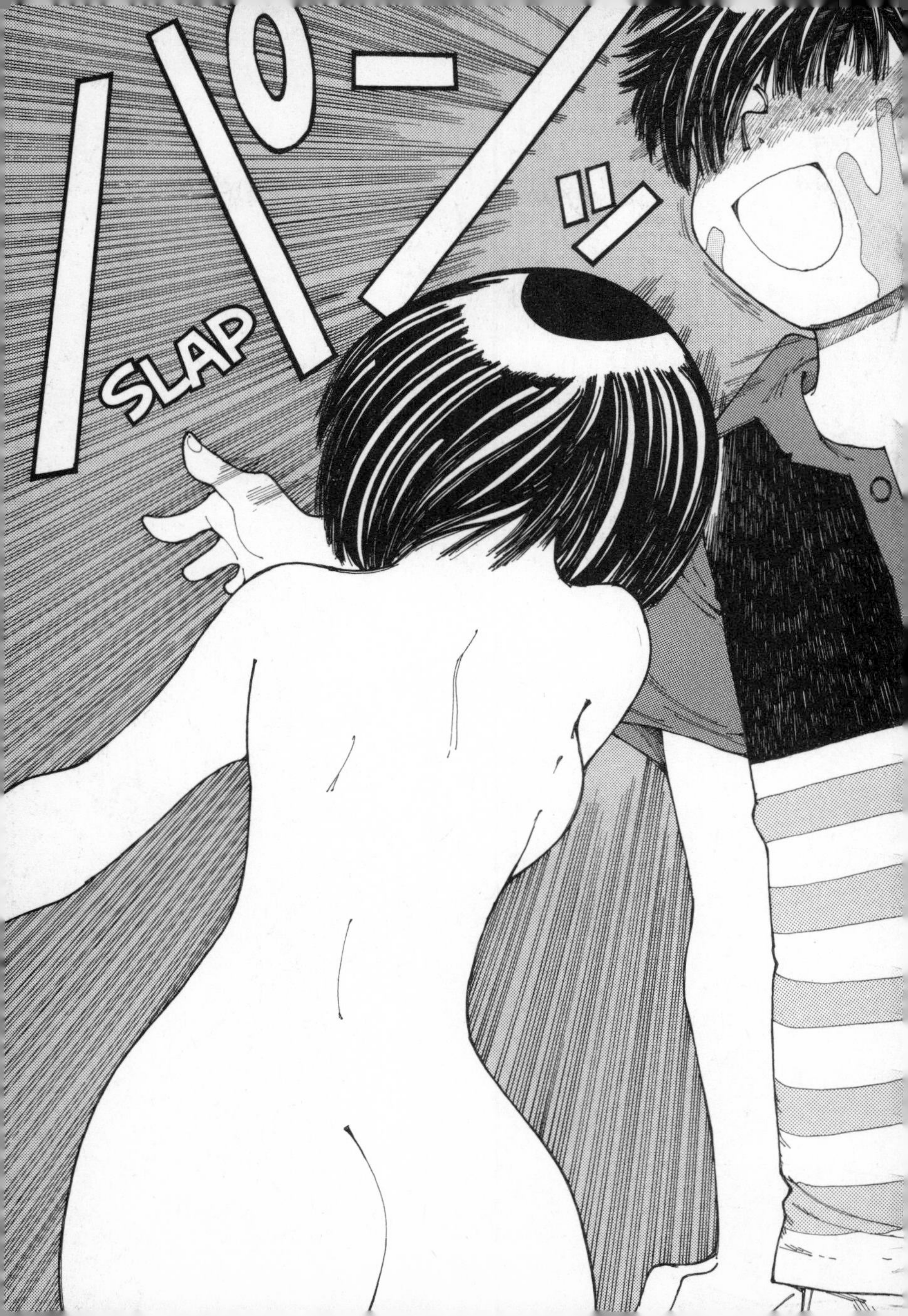
SLAP

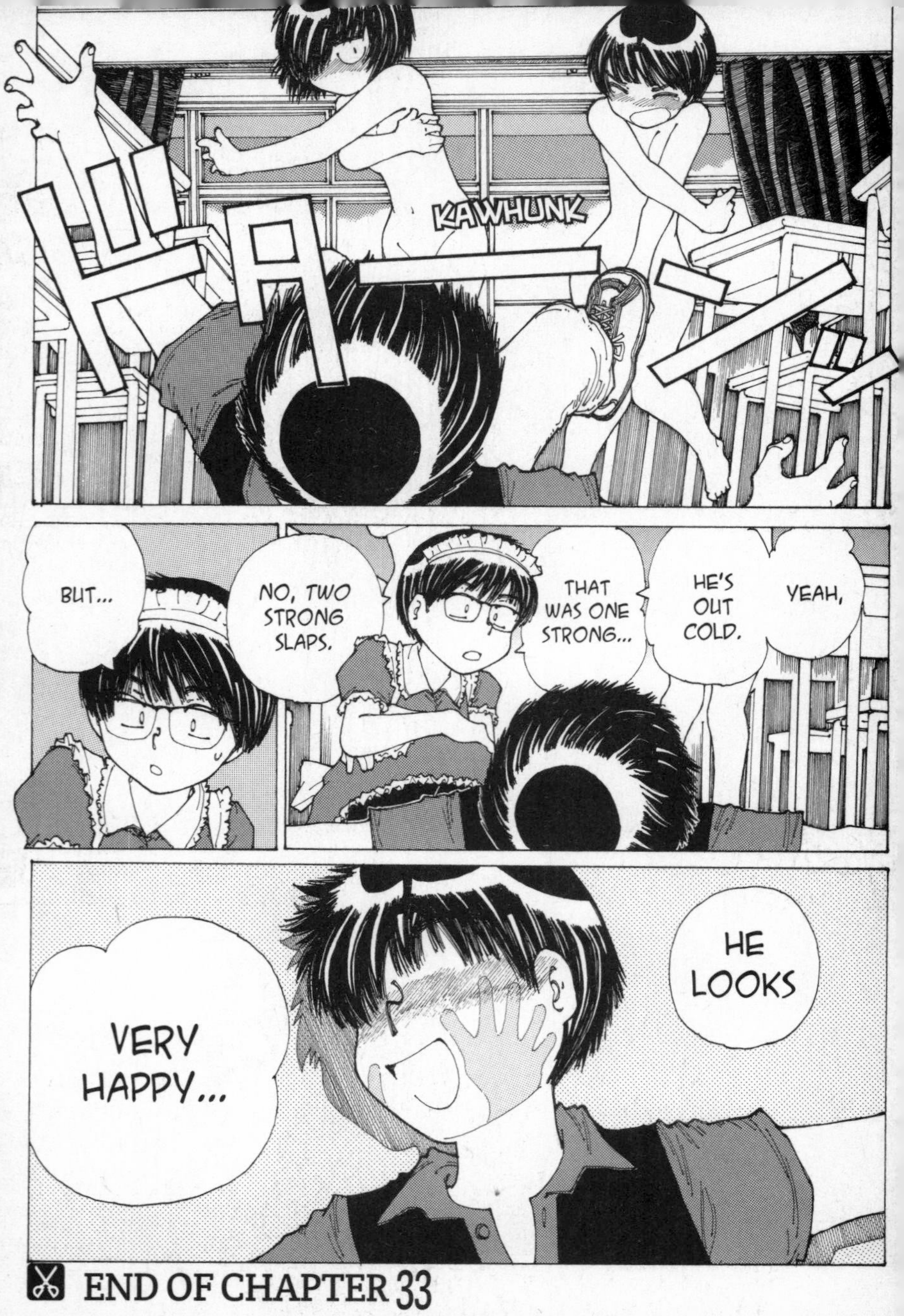
KAWHUNK
YEAH,
HE'S OUT COLD.
THAT WAS ONE STRONG...
NO, TWO STRONG SLAPS.
BUT...
HE LOOKS
VERY HAPPY...

END OF CHAPTER 33

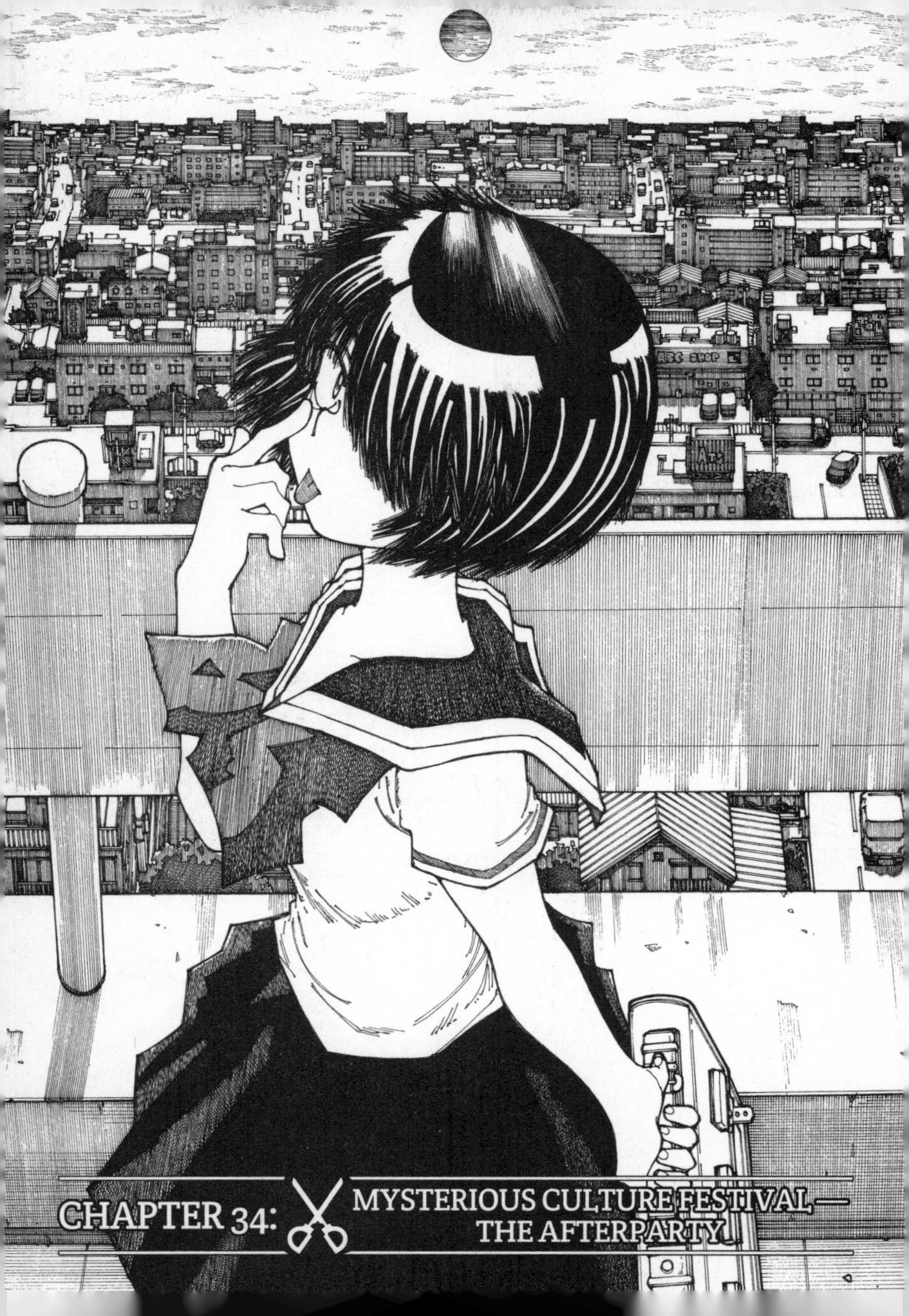
ABC SHOP

CHAPTER 34: MYSTERIOUS CULTURE FESTIVAL— THE AFTERPARTY

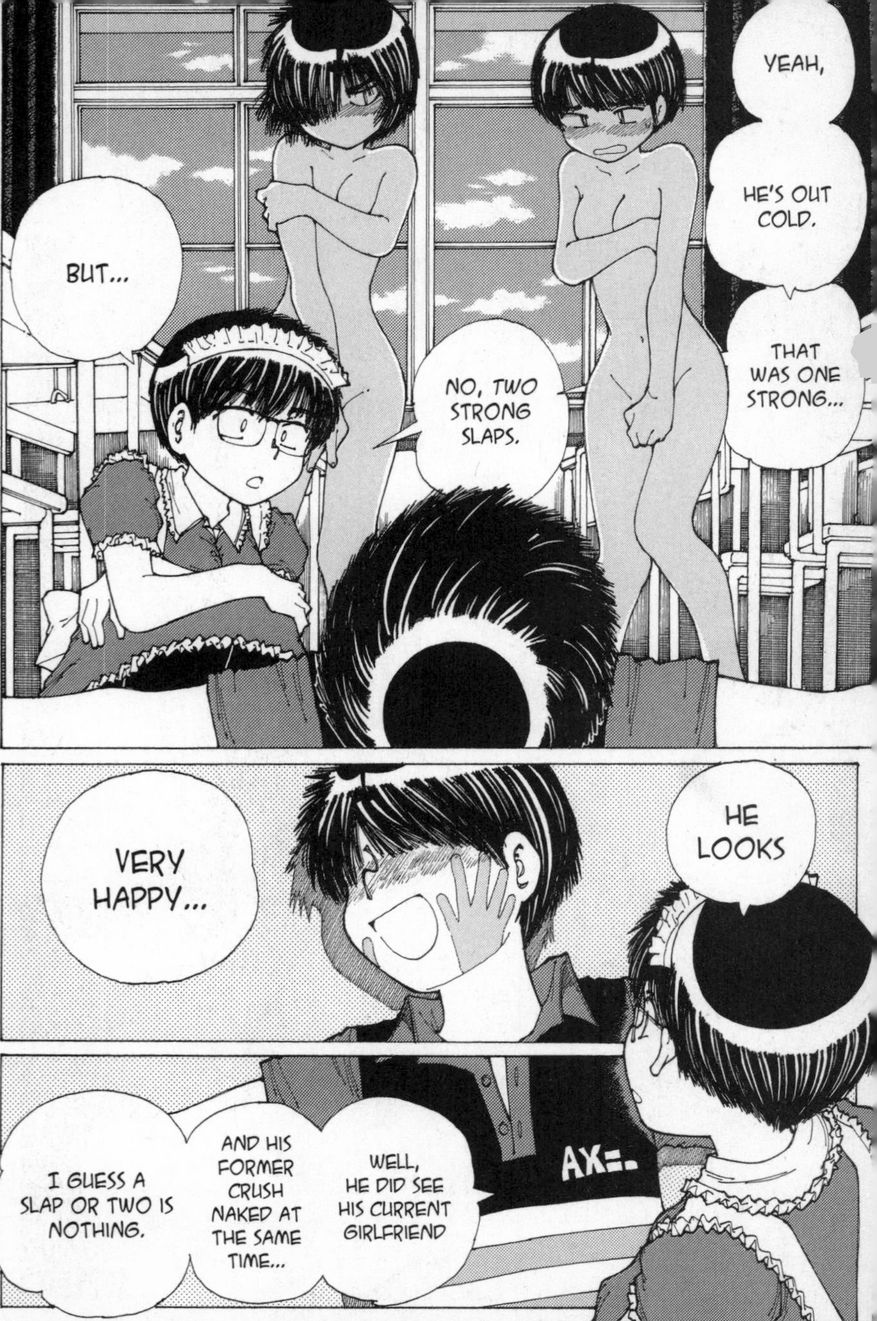
YEAH,
HE'S OUT COLD.
THAT WAS ONE STRONG...
NO, TWO STRONG SLAPS.
BUT...
HE LOOKS
VERY HAPPY...
WELL, HE DID SEE HIS CURRENT GIRLFRIEND
AND HIS FORMER CRUSH NAKED AT THE SAME TIME...
I GUESS A SLAP OR TWO IS NOTHING.

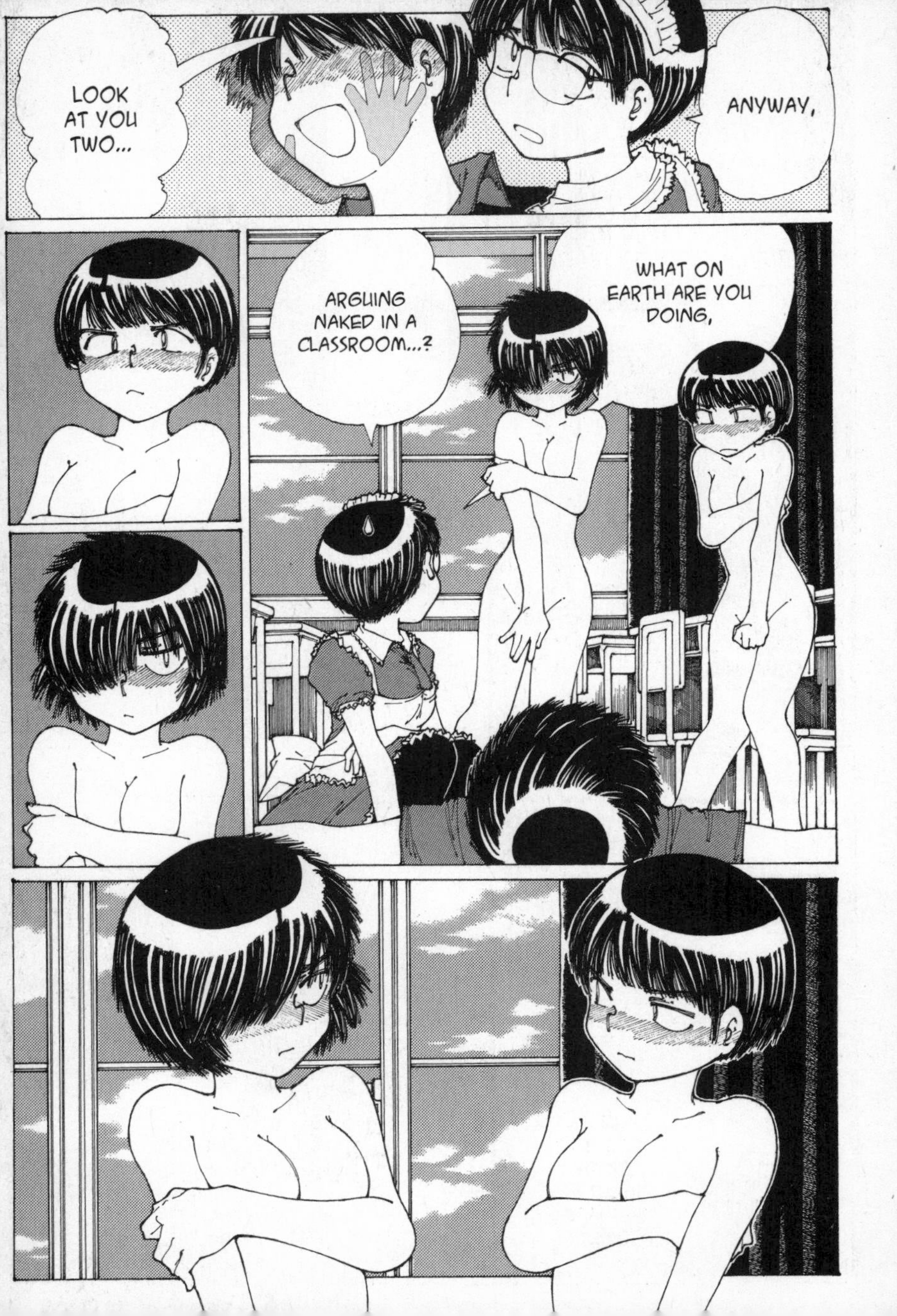
ANYWAY,
LOOK AT YOU TWO...
WHAT ON EARTH ARE YOU DOING,
ARGUING NAKED IN A CLASSROOM...?

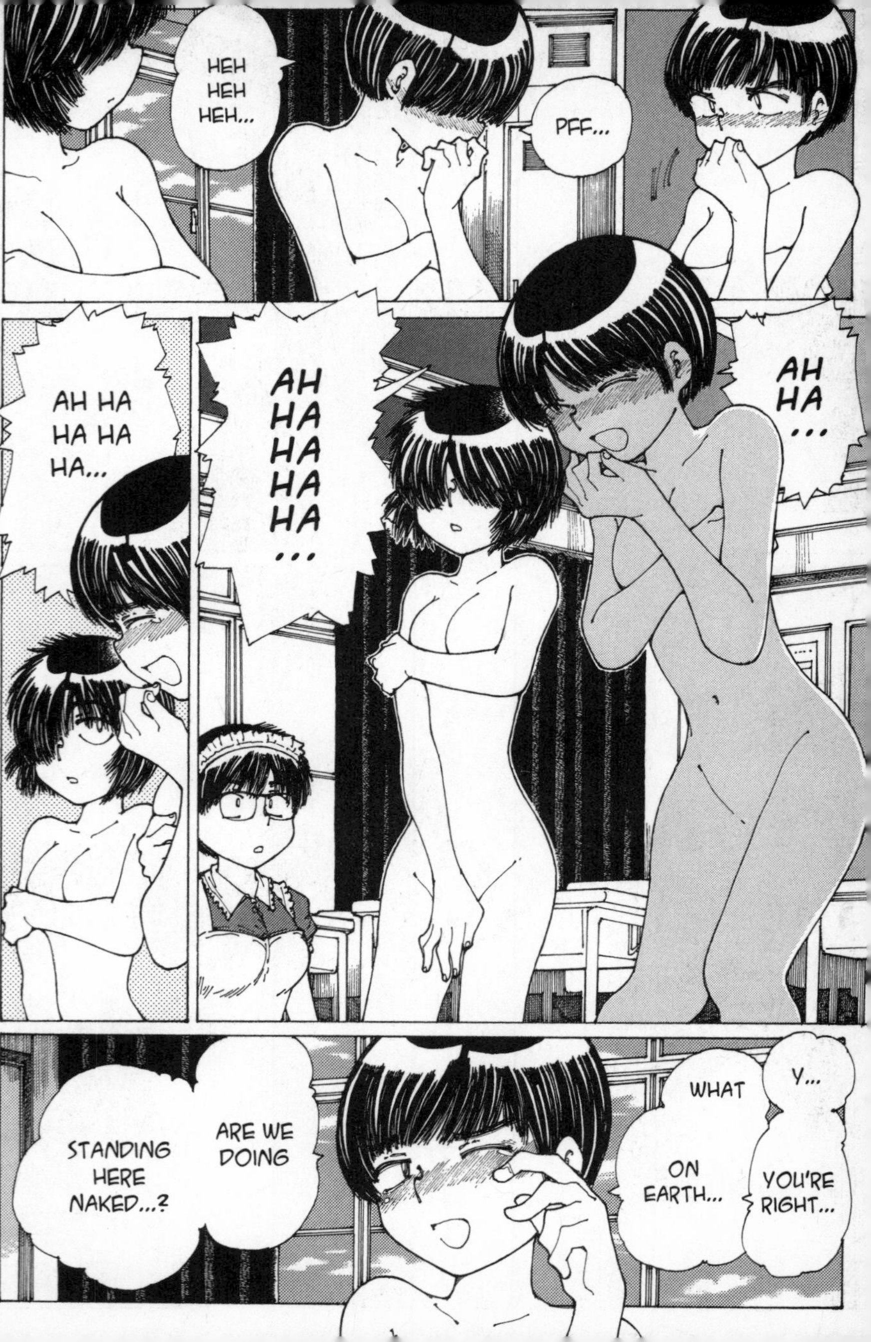
PFF...
HEH HEH HEH...
AH HA...
AH HA HA HA HA...
AH HA HA HA HA...
Y... YOU'RE RIGHT...
WHAT ON EARTH...
ARE WE DOING
STANDING HERE NAKED...?

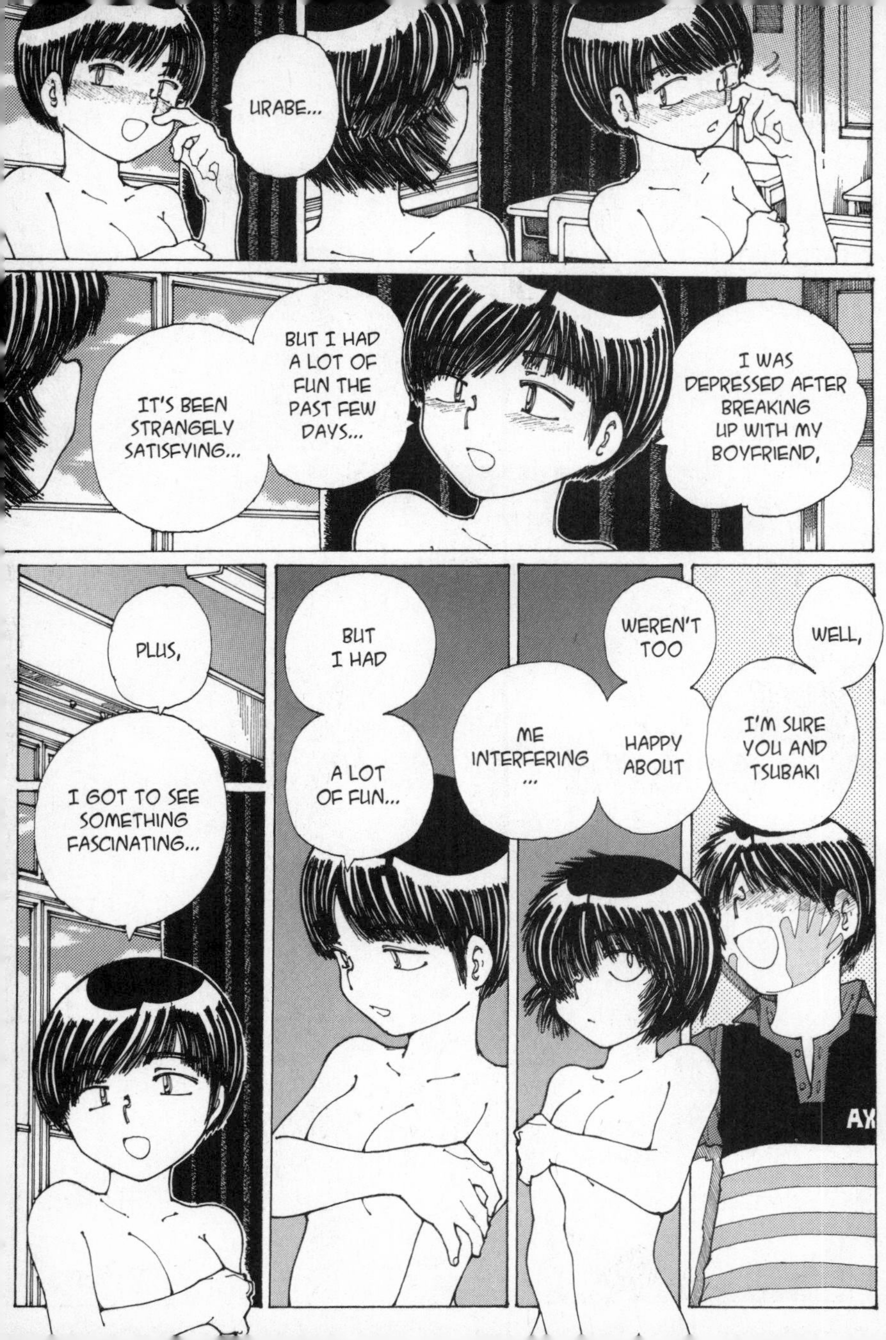
URABE...
I WAS DEPRESSED AFTER BREAKING UP WITH MY BOYFRIEND,
BUT I HAD A LOT OF FUN THE PAST FEW DAYS...
IT'S BEEN STRANGELY SATISFYING...
WELL,
I'M SURE YOU AND TSUBAKI
WEREN'T TOO
HAPPY ABOUT
ME INTERFERING ...
BUT I HAD
A LOT OF FUN...
PLUS,
I GOT TO SEE SOMETHING FASCINATING...

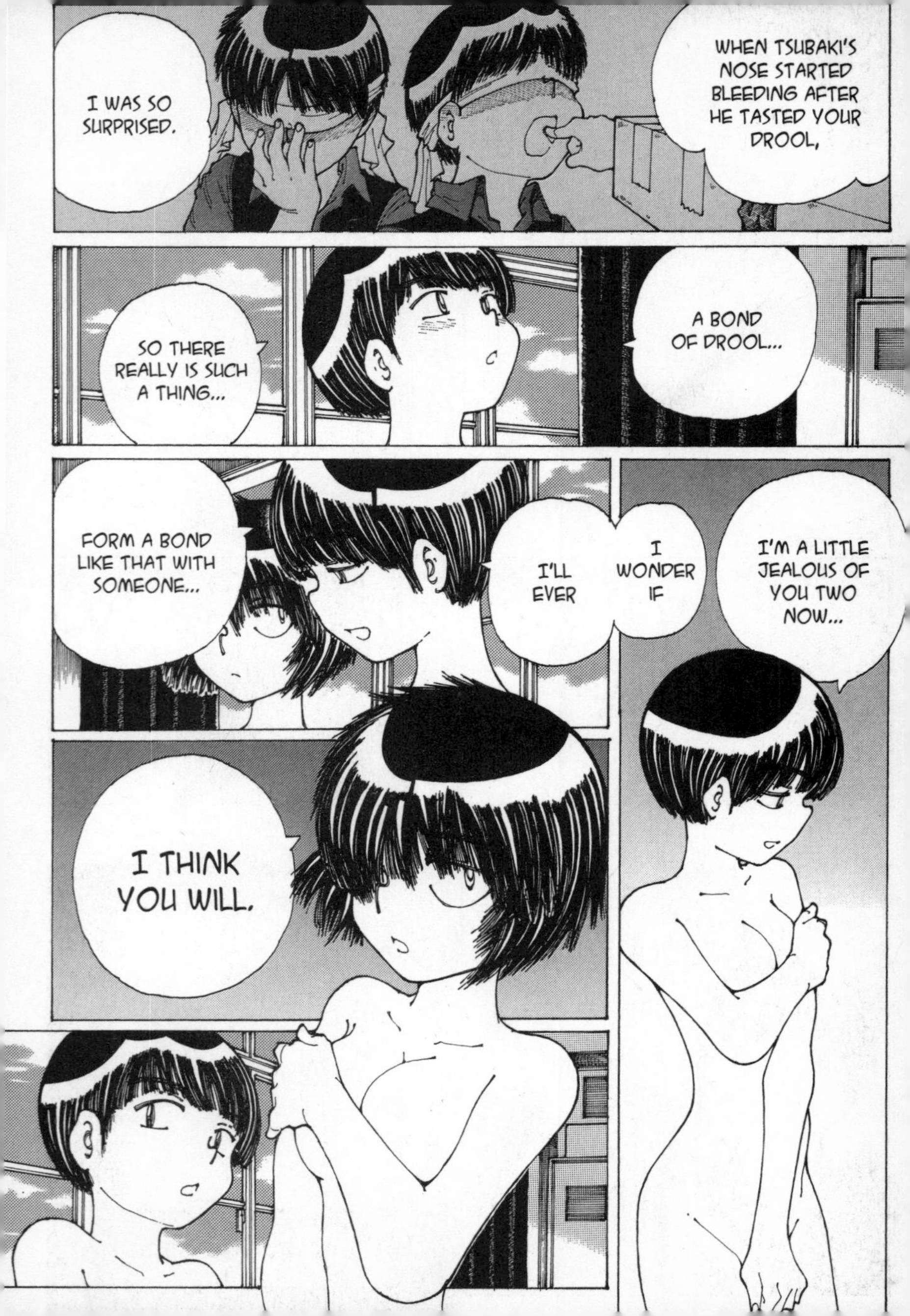
WHEN TSUBAKI'S NOSE STARTED BLEEDING AFTER HE TASTED YOUR DROOL,
I WAS SO SURPRISED.
A BOND OF DROOL...
SO THERE REALLY IS SUCH A THING...
I'M A LITTLE JEALOUS OF YOU TWO NOW...
I WONDER IF
I'LL EVER
FORM A BOND LIKE THAT WITH SOMEONE...
I THINK YOU WILL.

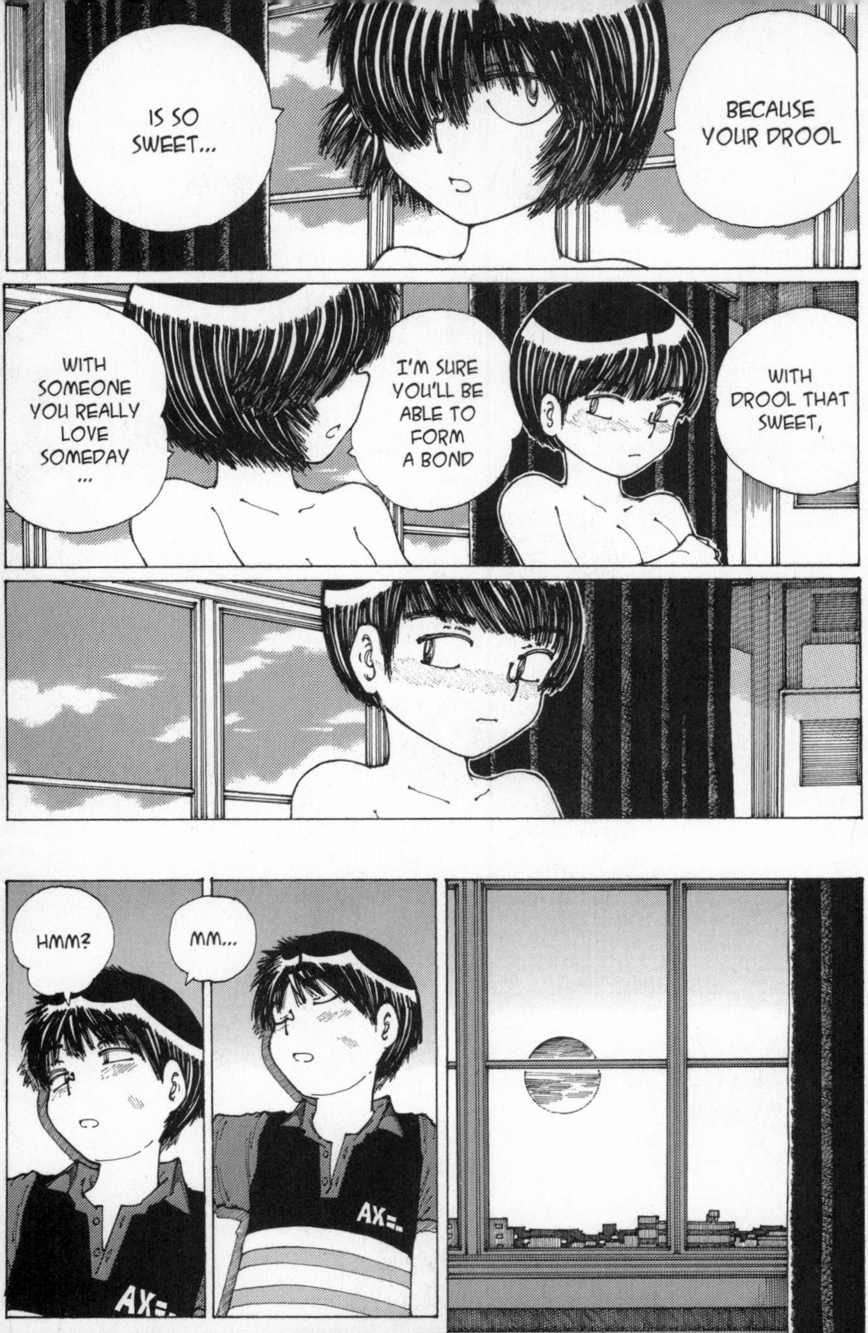
BECAUSE YOUR DROOL
IS SO SWEET...
WITH DROOL THAT SWEET,
I'M SURE YOU'LL BE ABLE TO FORM A BOND
WITH SOMEONE YOU REALLY LOVE SOMEDAY ...
MM...
HMM?

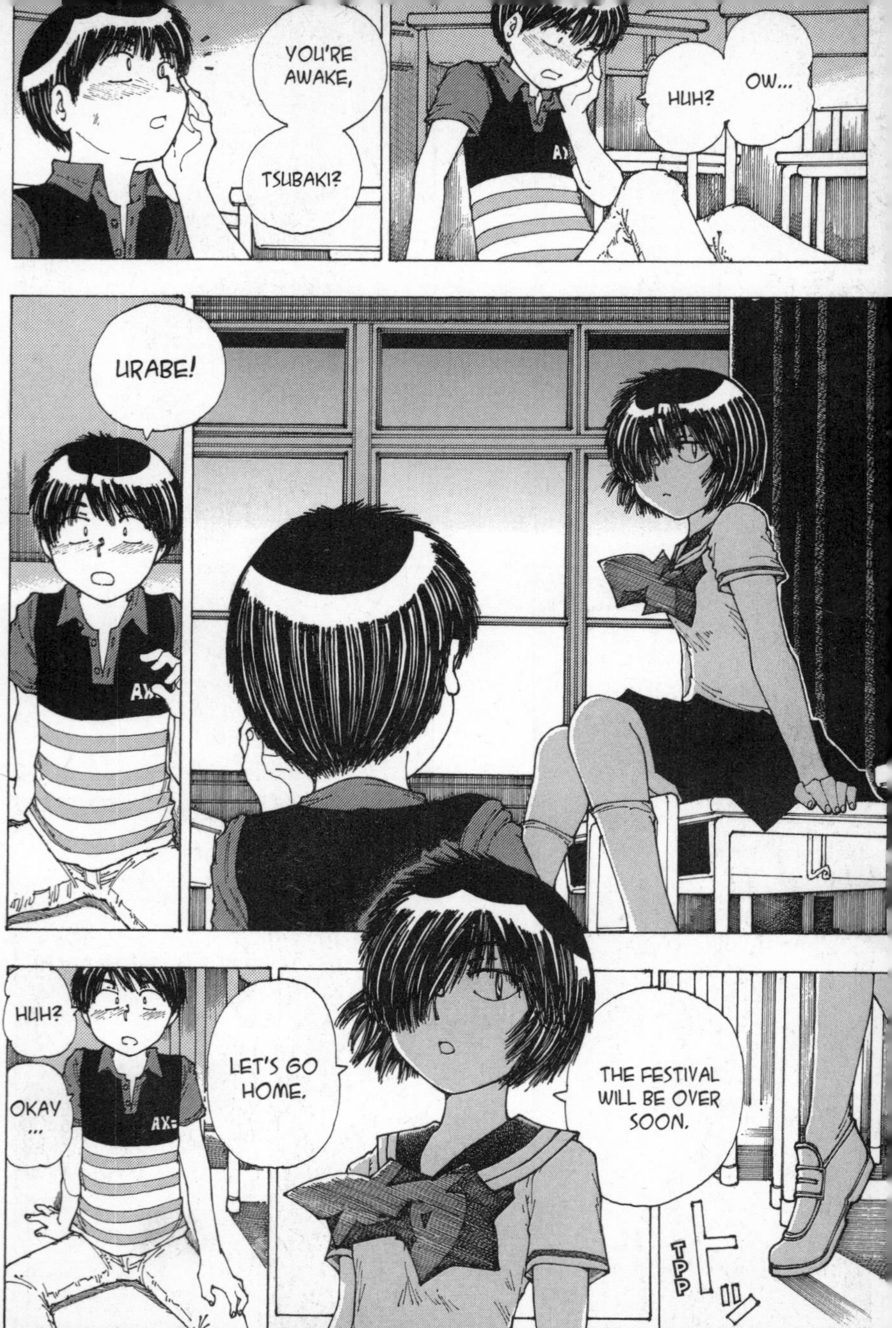
OW...
HUH?
YOU'RE AWAKE, TSUBAKI?
URABE!
TPP
THE FESTIVAL WILL BE OVER SOON.
LET'S GO HOME.
HUH?
OKAY ...

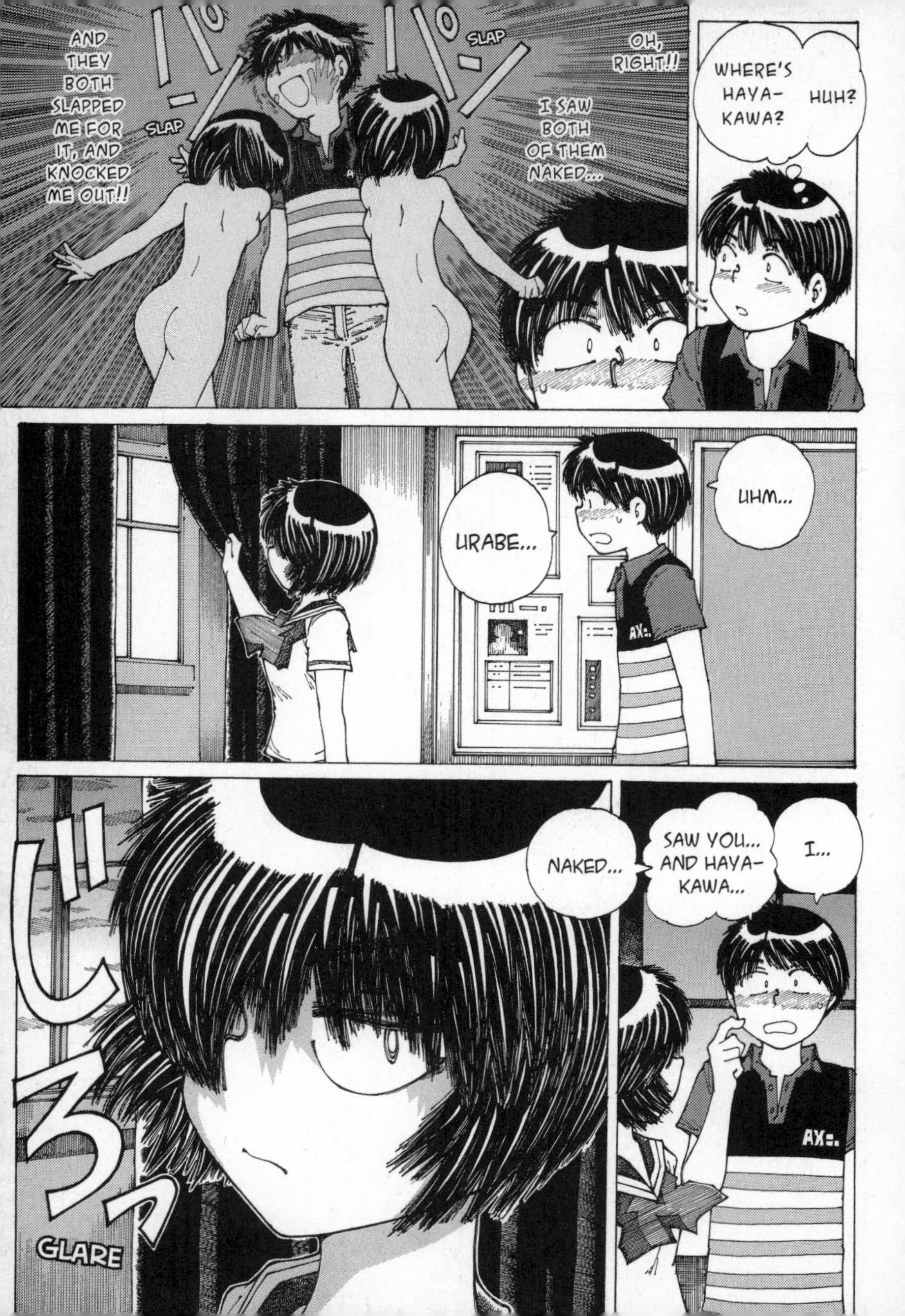

WHERE'S HAYA-KAWA?
HUH?
OH, RIGHT!!
I SAW BOTH OF THEM NAKED...
パー
SLAP
パー
SLAP
AND THEY BOTH SLAPPED ME FOR IT, AND KNOCKED ME OUT!!
UHM...
URABE...
I...
SAW YOU... AND HAYA-KAWA...
NAKED...
じろっ
GLARE

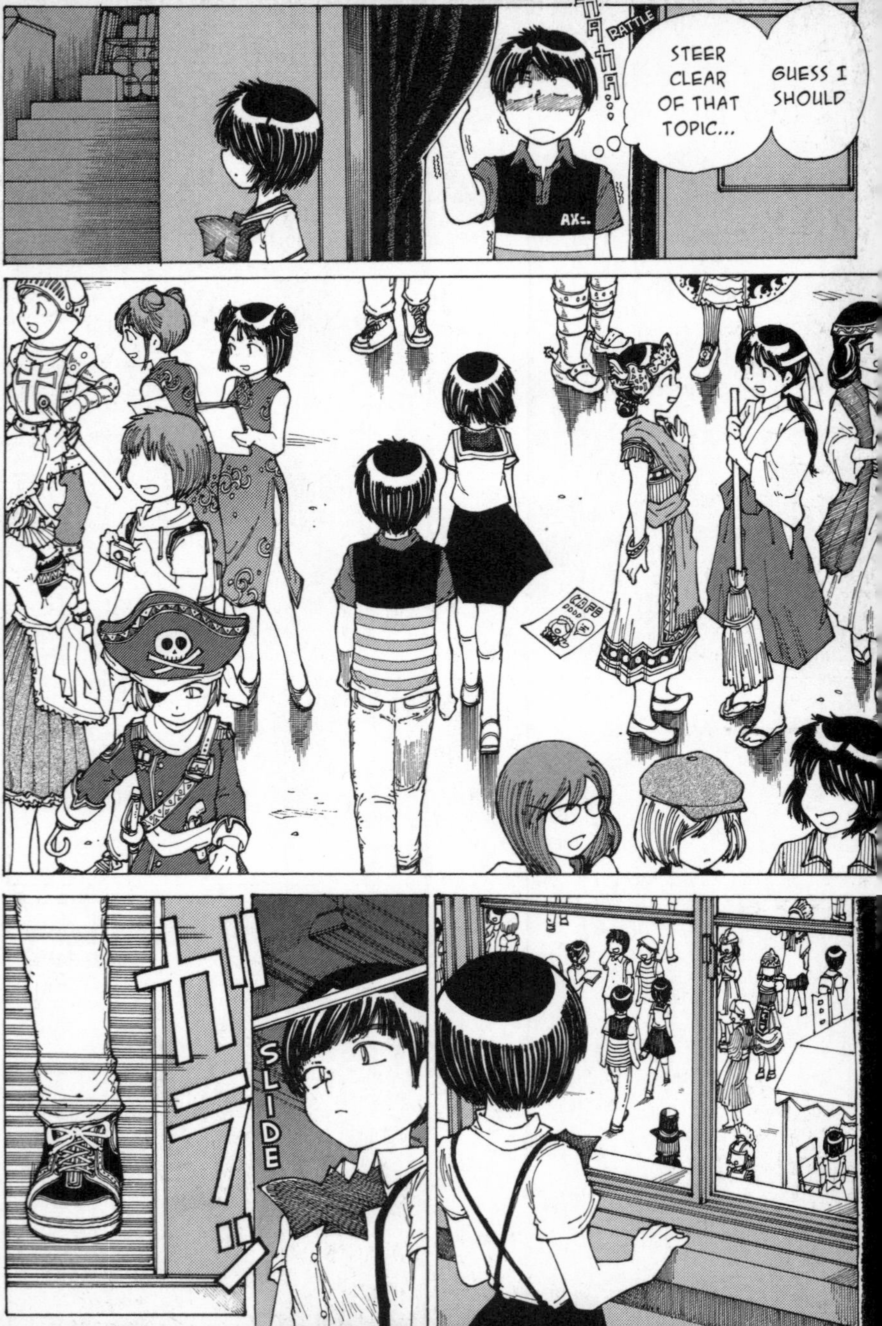
GUESS I SHOULD
STEER CLEAR OF THAT TOPIC...
カタカタ…
RATTLE
ガラッ
SLIDE

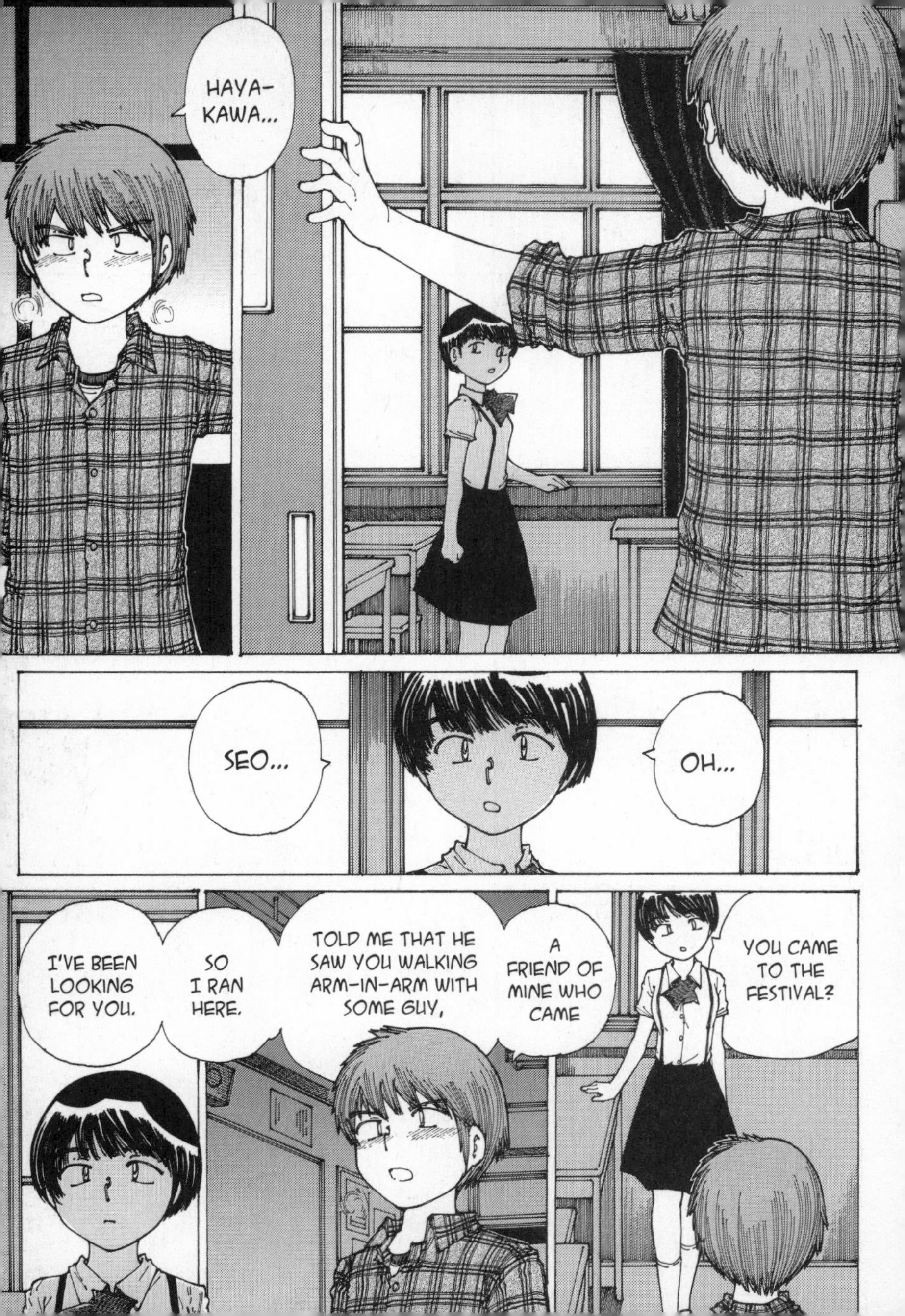
HAYA-KAWA...
OH...
SEO...
YOU CAME TO THE FESTIVAL?
A FRIEND OF MINE WHO CAME
TOLD ME THAT HE SAW YOU WALKING ARM-IN-ARM WITH SOME GUY,
SO I RAN HERE.
I'VE BEEN LOOKING FOR YOU.

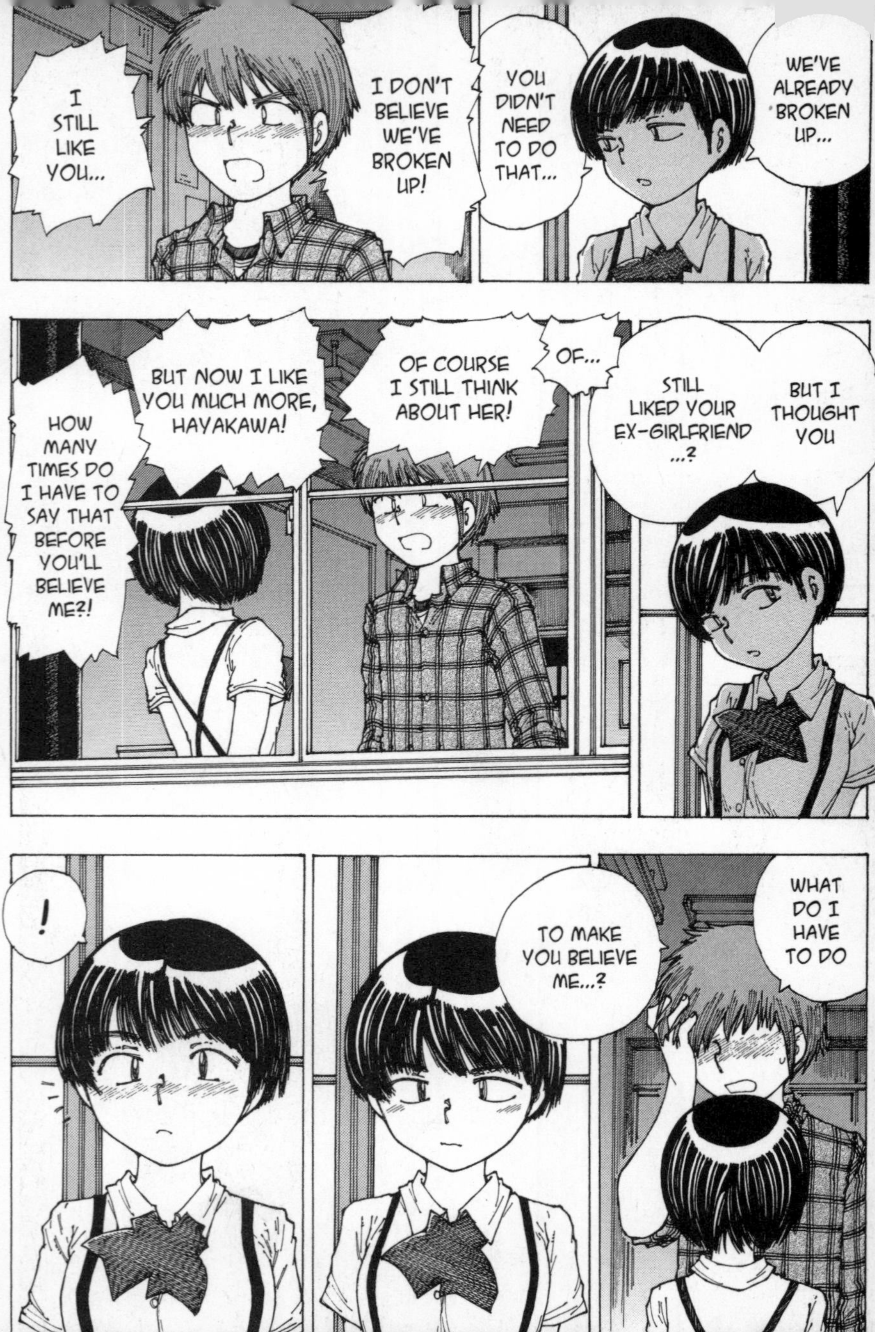
WE'VE ALREADY BROKEN UP...
YOU DIDN'T NEED TO DO THAT...
I DON'T BELIEVE WE'VE BROKEN UP!
I STILL LIKE YOU...
BUT I THOUGHT YOU
STILL LIKED YOUR EX-GIRLFRIEND ...?
OF...
OF COURSE I STILL THINK ABOUT HER!
BUT NOW I LIKE YOU MUCH MORE, HAYAKAWA!
HOW MANY TIMES DO I HAVE TO SAY THAT BEFORE YOU'LL BELIEVE ME?!
WHAT DO I HAVE TO DO
TO MAKE YOU BELIEVE ME...?
!

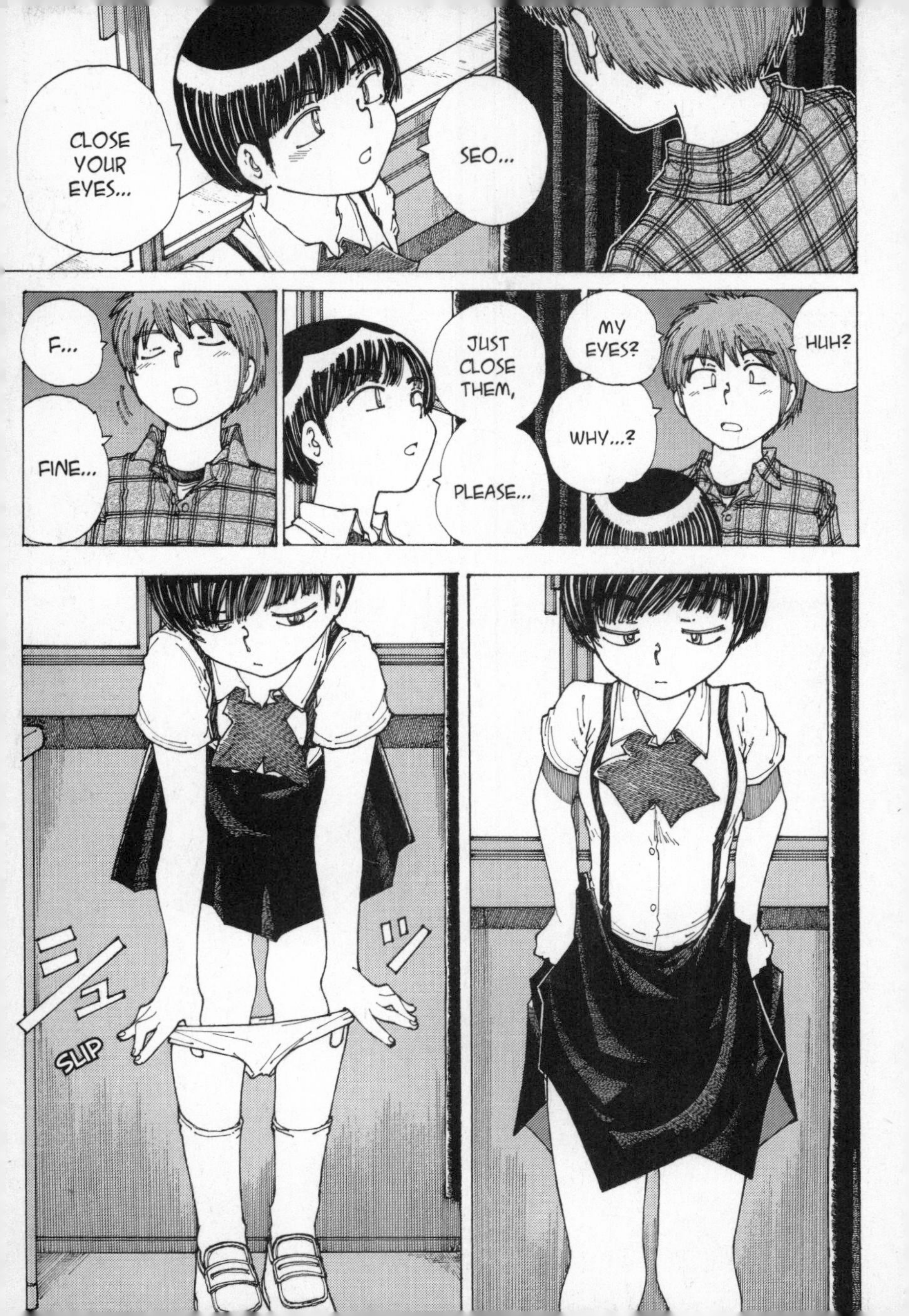
SEO...
CLOSE YOUR EYES...
HUH?
MY EYES?
WHY...?
JUST CLOSE THEM,
PLEASE...
F...
FINE...
SLIP

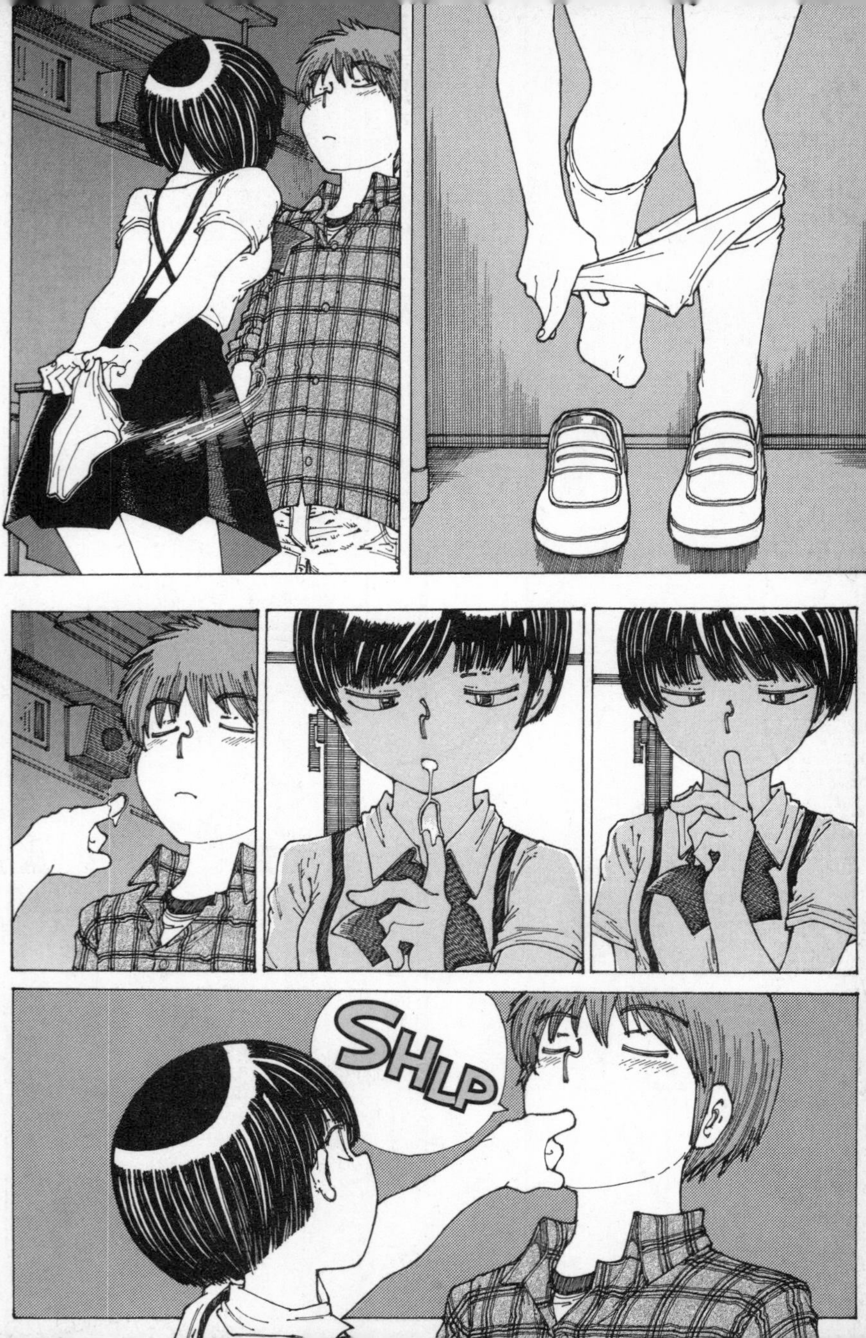
SHLP

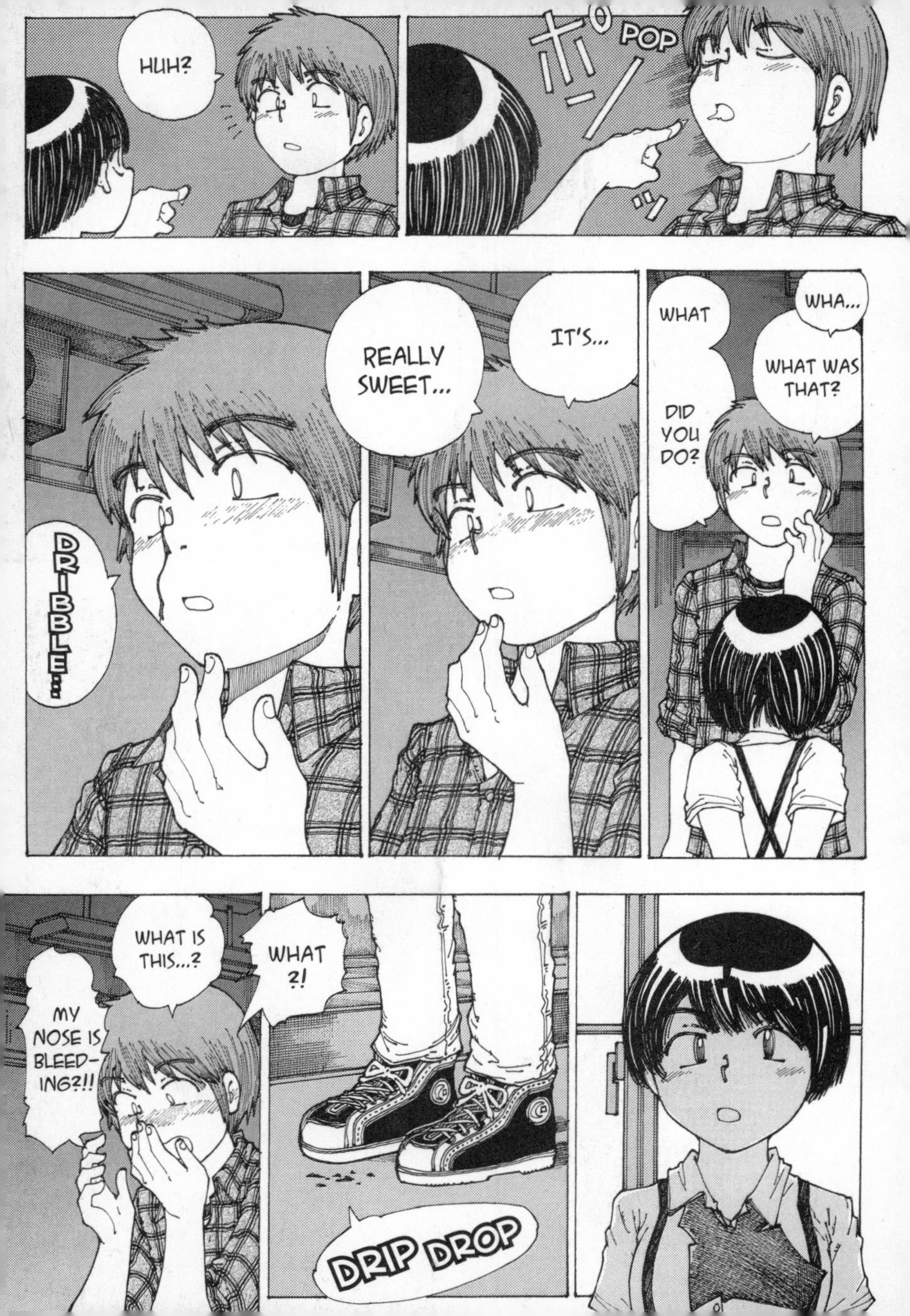
POP
HUH?
WHA...
WHAT WAS THAT?
WHAT
DID YOU DO?
IT'S...
REALLY SWEET...
DRIBBLE...
DRIP DROP
WHAT ?!
WHAT IS THIS...?
MY NOSE IS BLEED-ING?!!

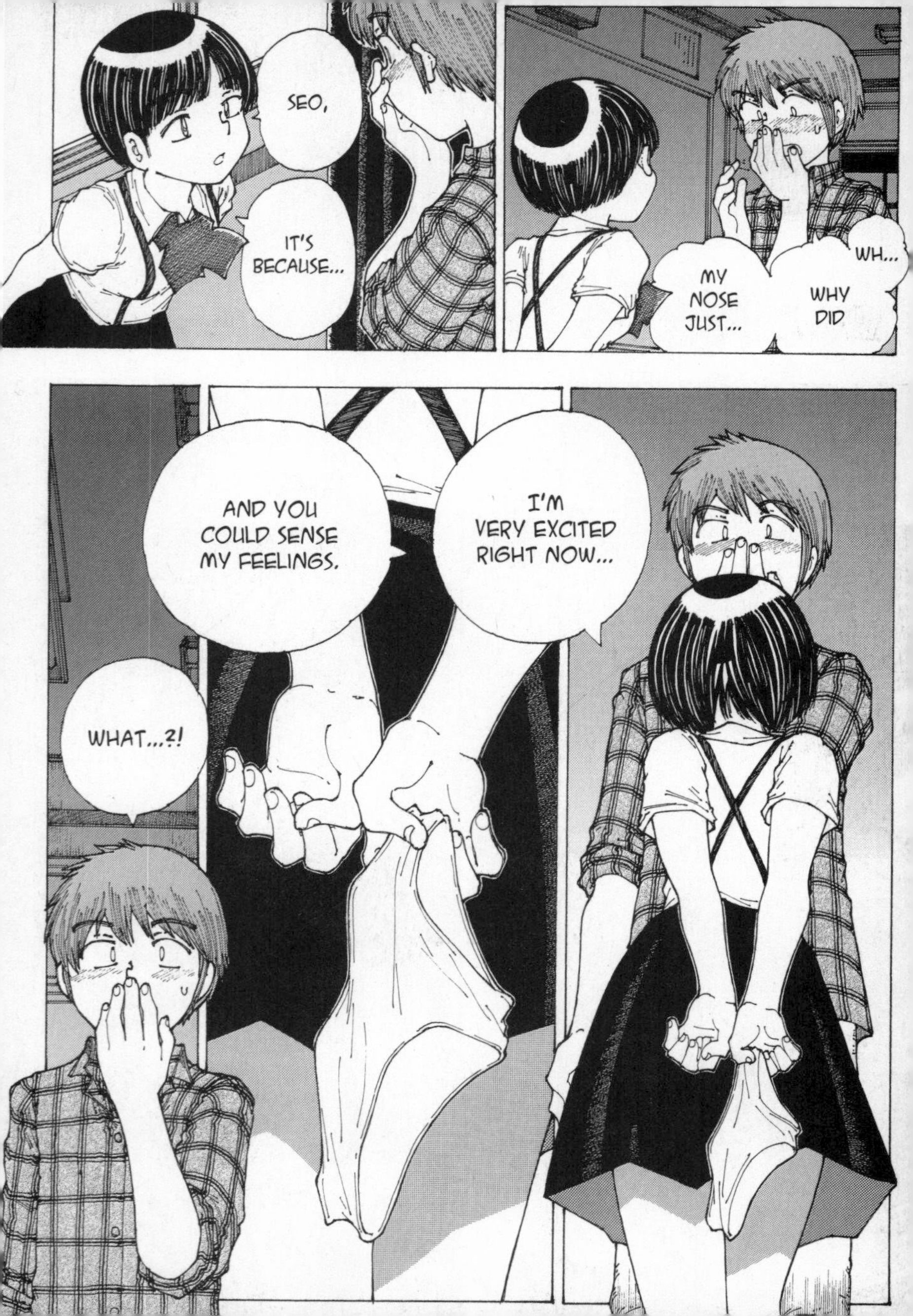
WH... WHY DID
MY NOSE JUST...
SEO,
IT'S BECAUSE...
I'M VERY EXCITED RIGHT NOW...
AND YOU COULD SENSE MY FEELINGS.
WHAT...?!

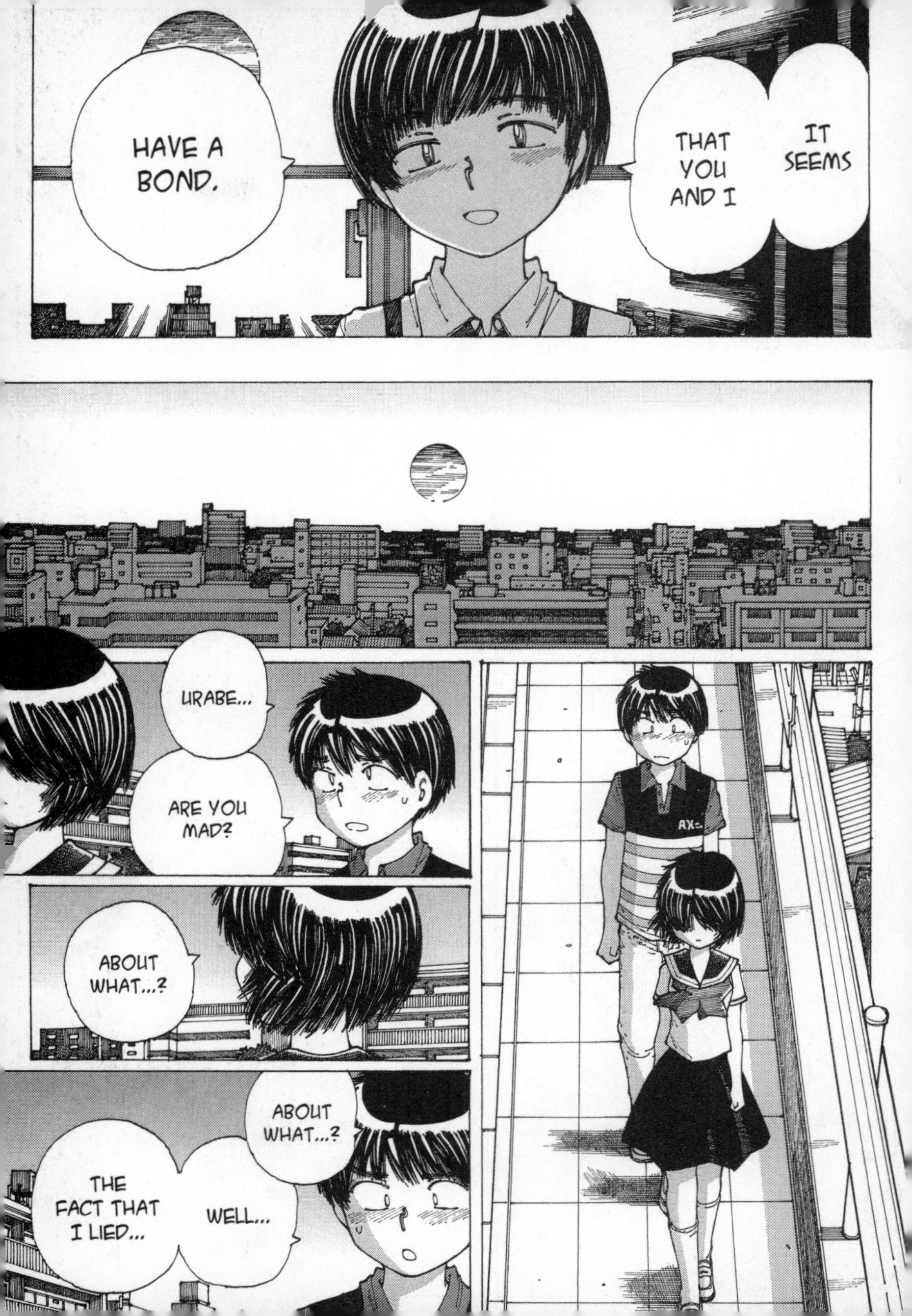
IT SEEMS
THAT YOU AND I
HAVE A BOND.
URABE...
ARE YOU MAD?
ABOUT WHAT...?
ABOUT WHAT...?
WELL...
THE FACT THAT I LIED...

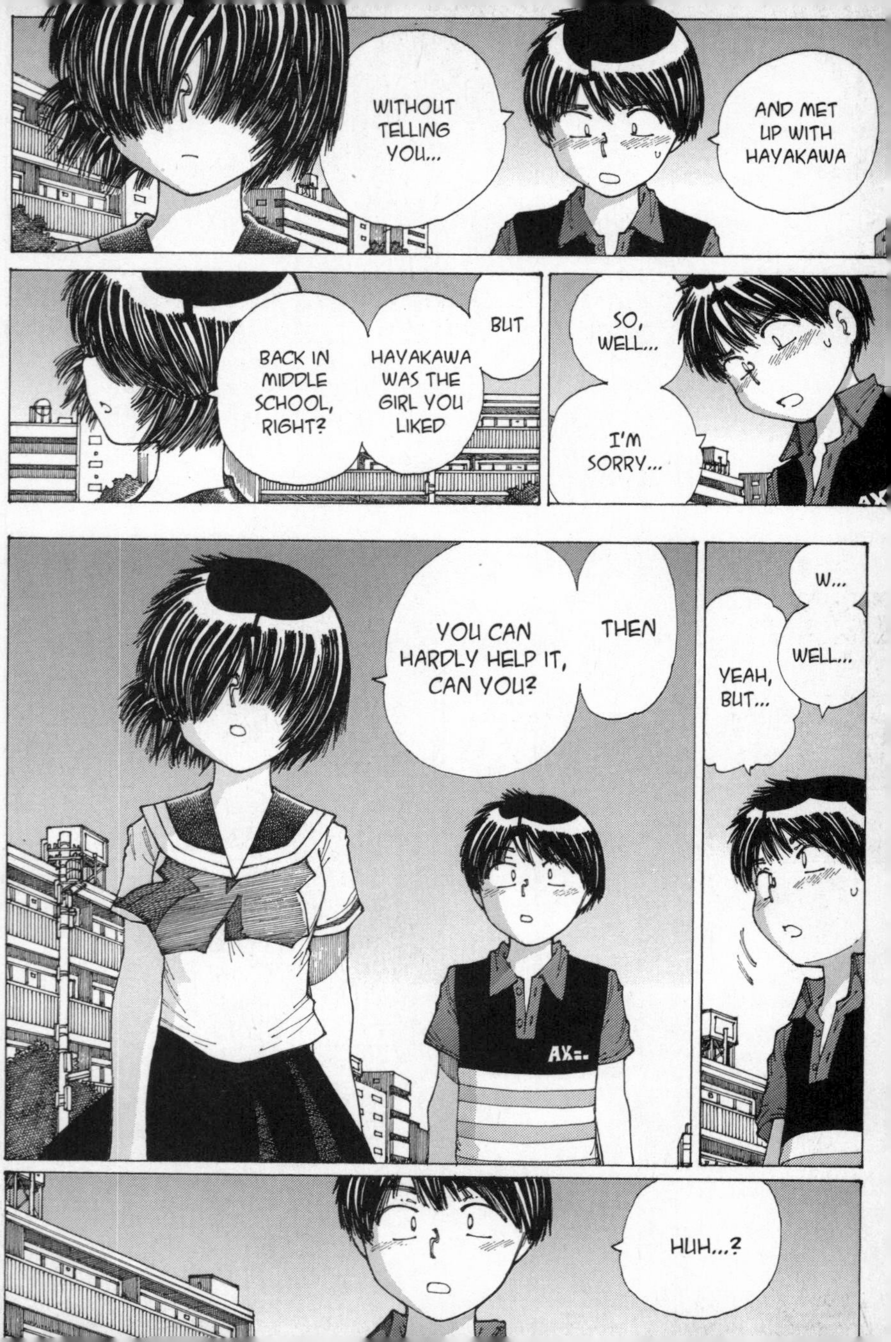
AND MET UP WITH HAYAKAWA
WITHOUT TELLING YOU...
SO, WELL...
I'M SORRY...
BUT
HAYAKAWA WAS THE GIRL YOU LIKED
BACK IN MIDDLE SCHOOL, RIGHT?
W...
WELL...
YEAH, BUT...
THEN
YOU CAN HARDLY HELP IT, CAN YOU?
HUH...?

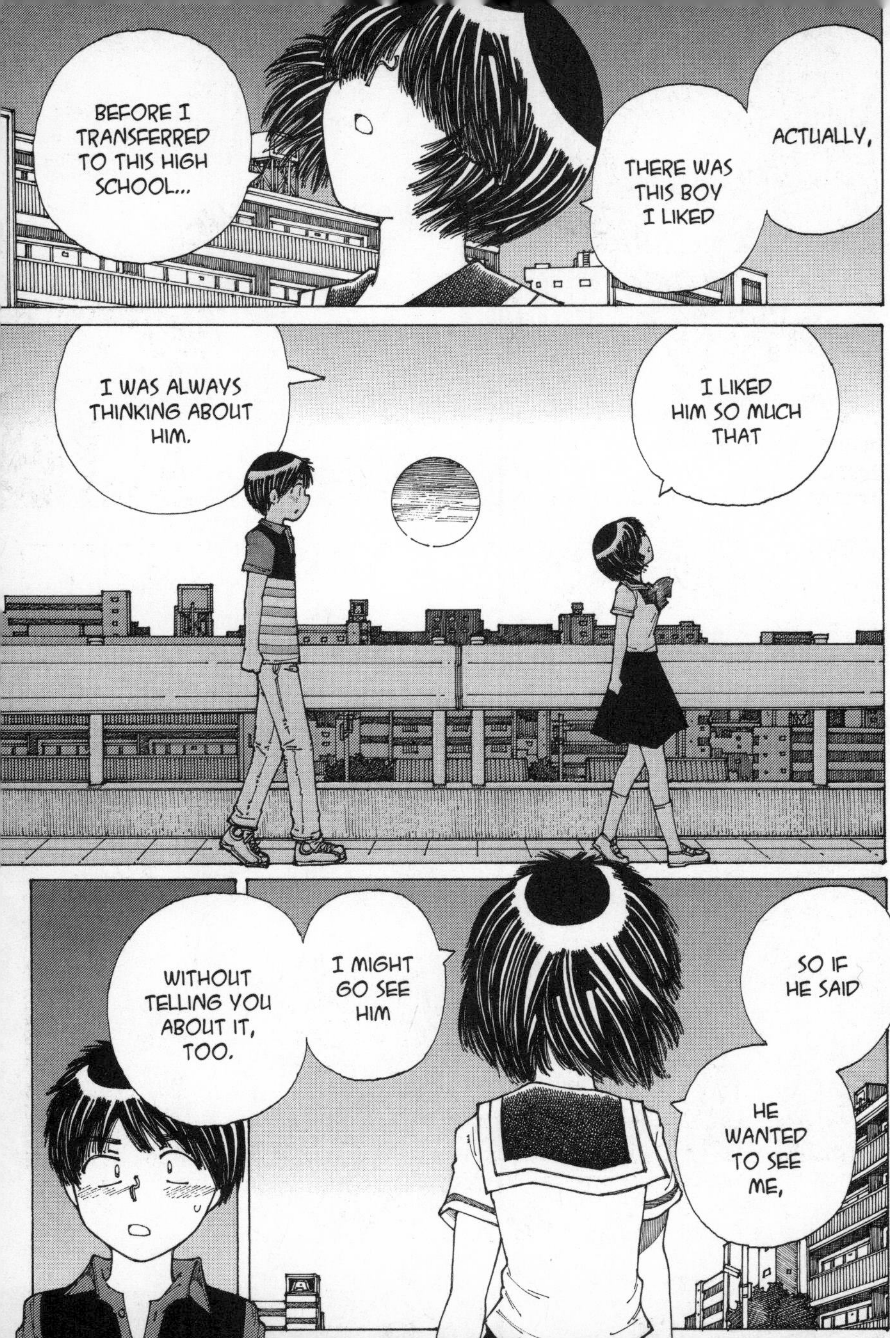
ACTUALLY,
THERE WAS THIS BOY I LIKED
BEFORE I TRANSFERRED TO THIS HIGH SCHOOL...
I LIKED HIM SO MUCH THAT
I WAS ALWAYS THINKING ABOUT HIM.
SO IF HE SAID
HE WANTED TO SEE ME,
I MIGHT GO SEE HIM
WITHOUT TELLING YOU ABOUT IT, TOO.

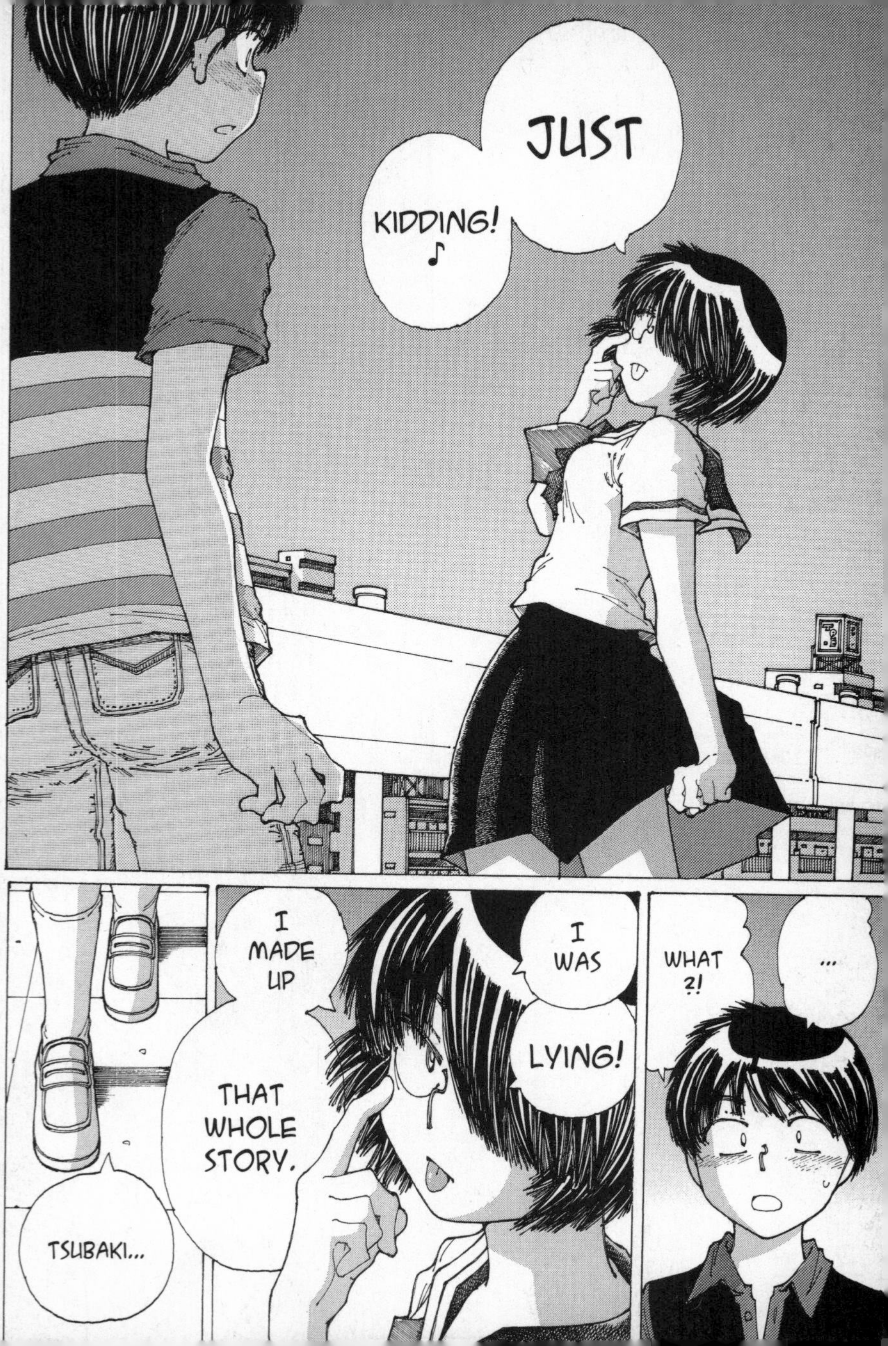
JUST
KIDDING! ♪
...
WHAT ?!
I WAS
LYING!
I MADE UP
THAT WHOLE STORY.
TSUBAKI...

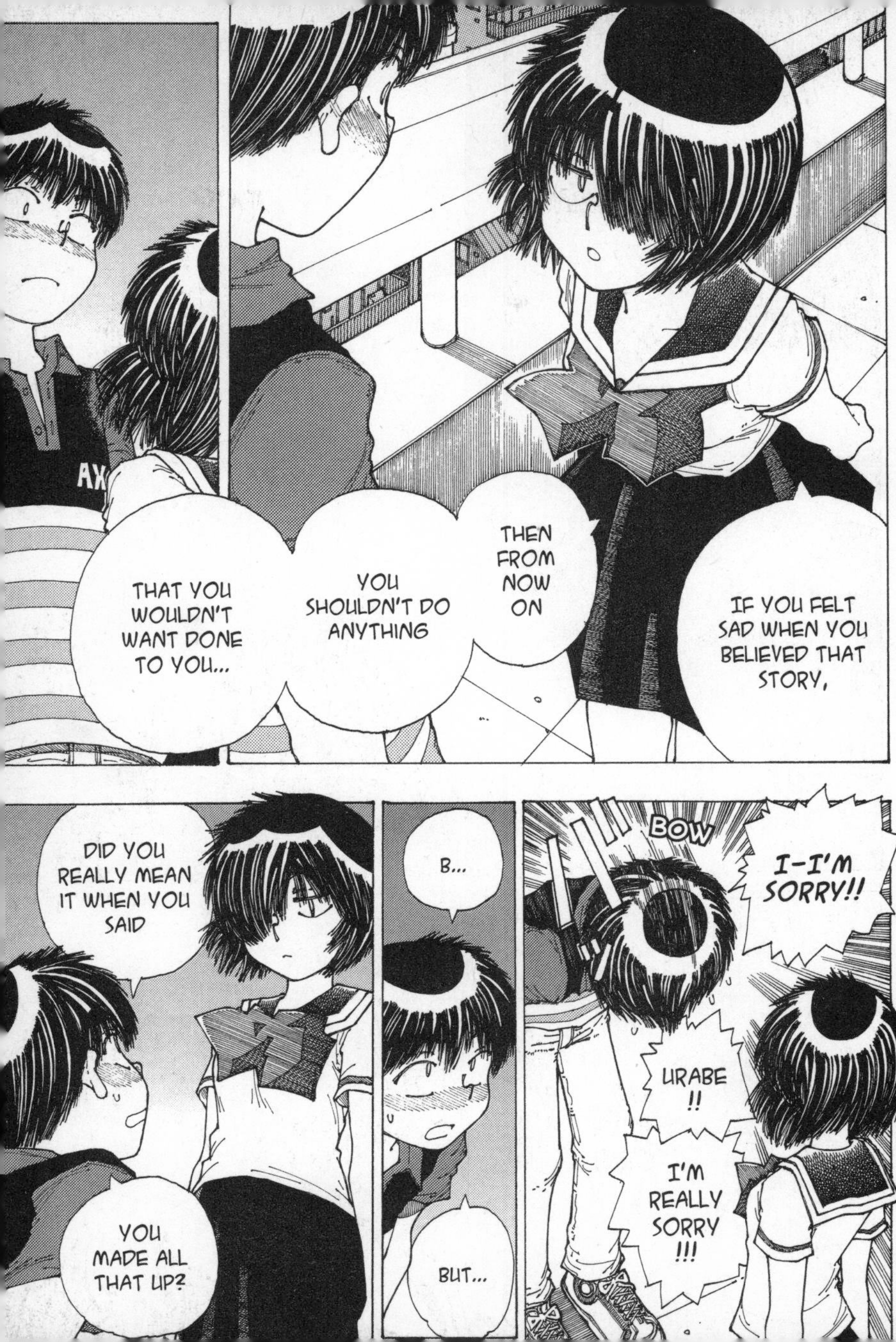
IF YOU FELT SAD WHEN YOU BELIEVED THAT STORY,
THEN FROM NOW ON
YOU SHOULDN'T DO ANYTHING
THAT YOU WOULDN'T WANT DONE TO YOU...
BOW
I-I'M SORRY!!
URABE !!
I'M REALLY SORRY !!!
B...
BUT...
DID YOU REALLY MEAN IT WHEN YOU SAID
YOU MADE ALL THAT UP?

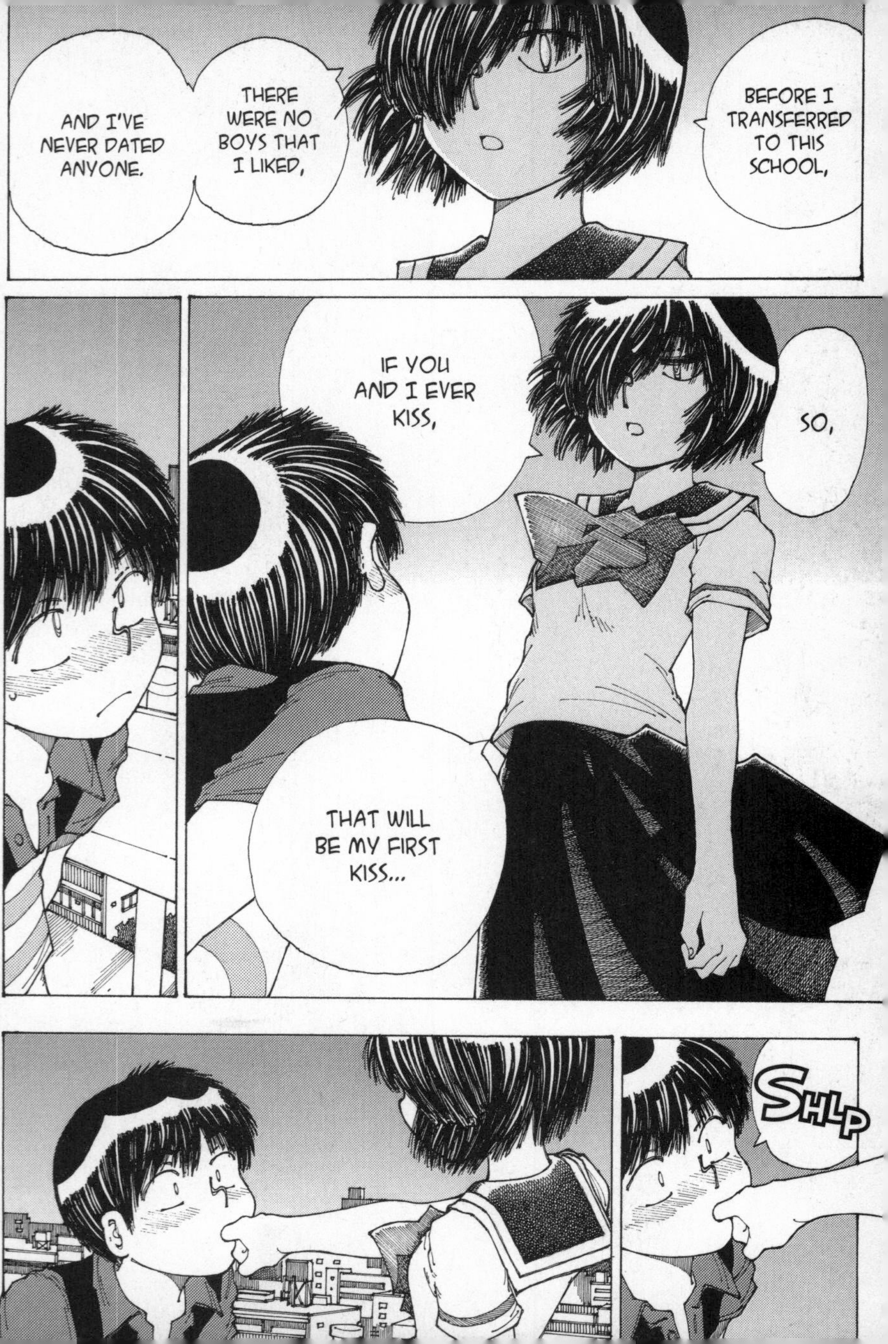
BEFORE I TRANSFERRED TO THIS SCHOOL,
THERE WERE NO BOYS THAT I LIKED,
AND I'VE NEVER DATED ANYONE.
SO,
IF YOU AND I EVER KISS,
THAT WILL BE MY FIRST KISS...
SHLP

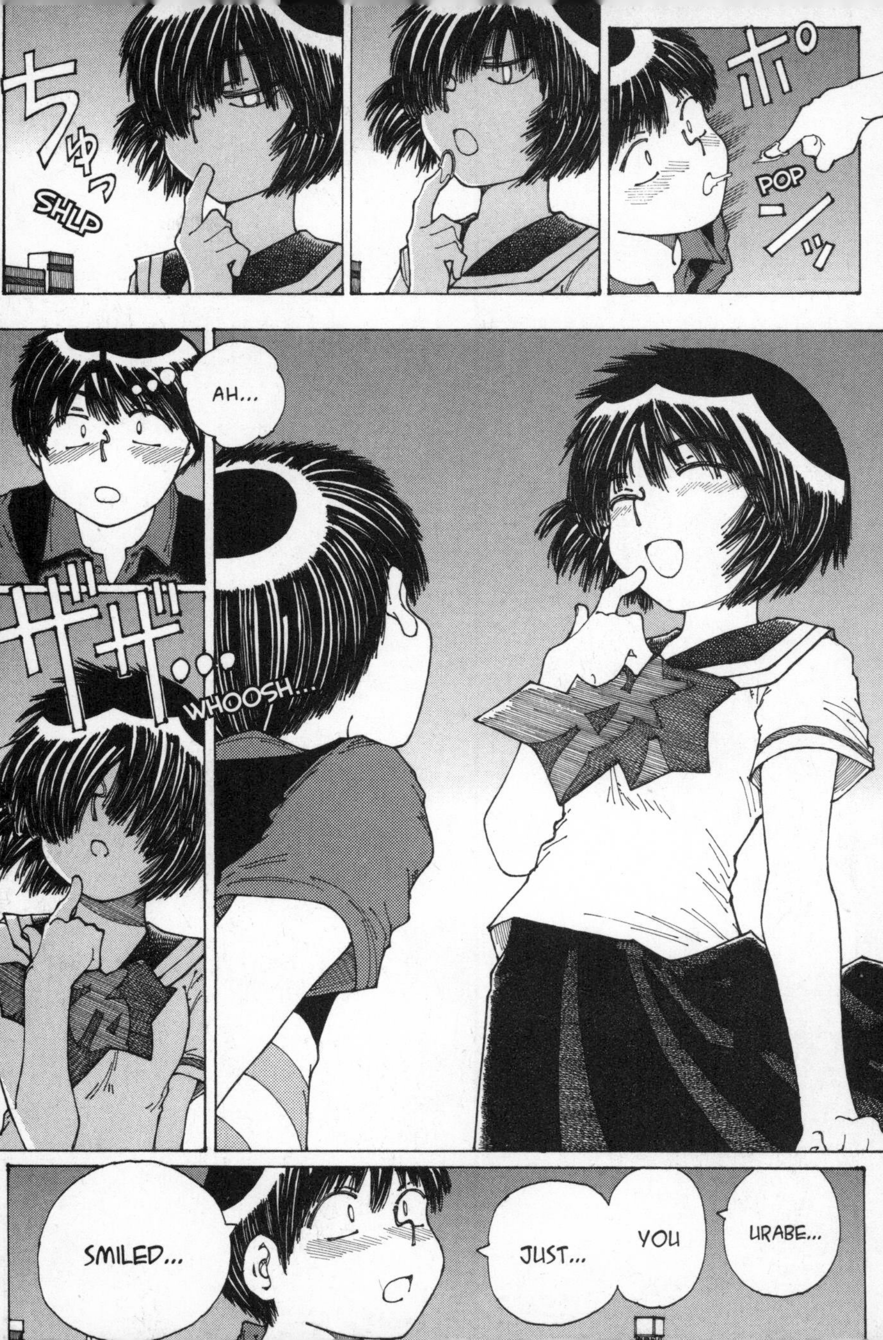
ポ
POP
ーンッ
ちゅっ
SHLP
AH...
ザザ...
WHOOSH...
URABE...
YOU
JUST...
SMILED...

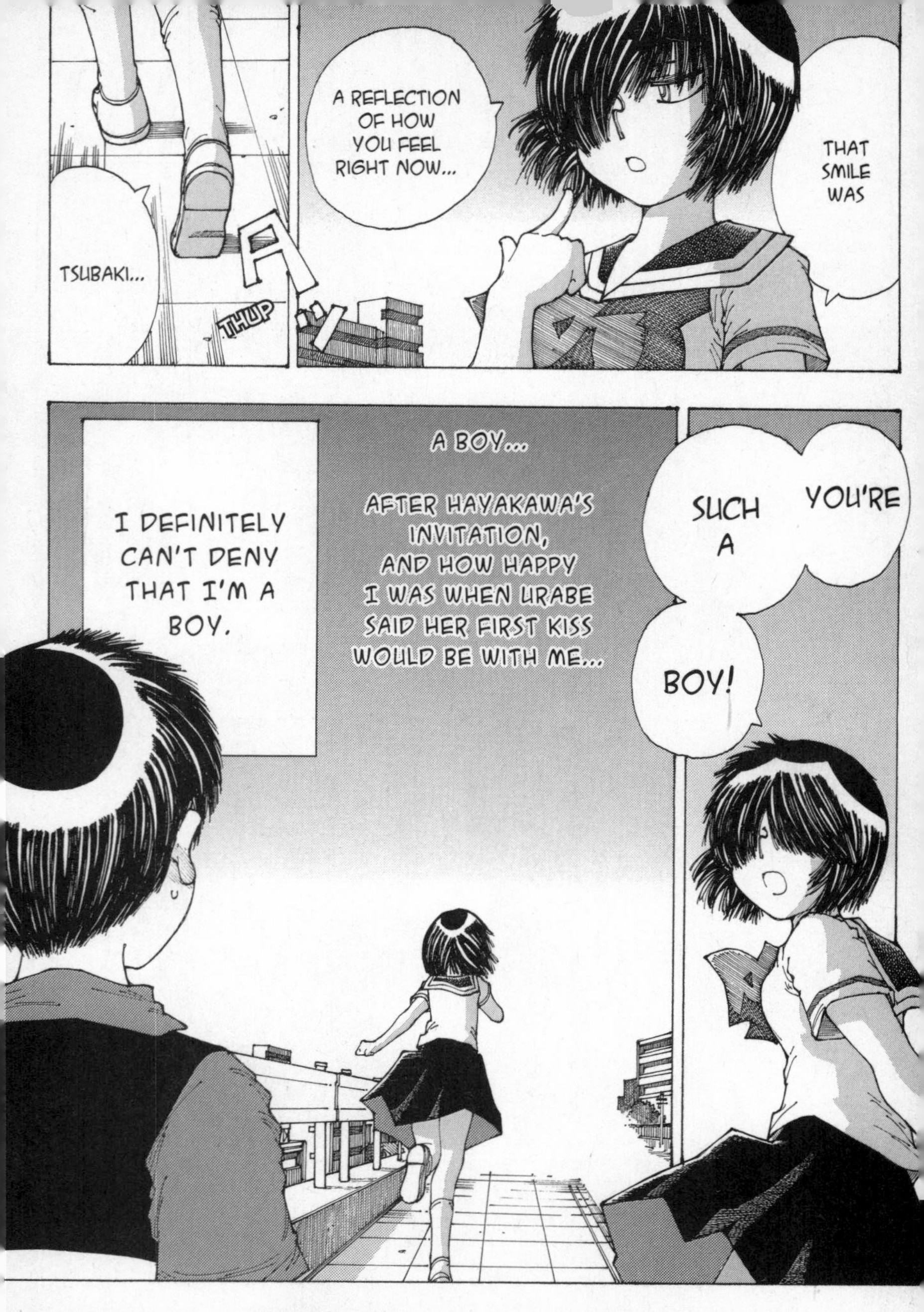
THAT SMILE WAS
A REFLECTION OF HOW YOU FEEL RIGHT NOW...
TSUBAKI...
THUP
YOU'RE SUCH A BOY!
A BOY...
AFTER HAYAKAWA'S INVITATION, AND HOW HAPPY I WAS WHEN URABE SAID HER FIRST KISS WOULD BE WITH ME...
I DEFINITELY CAN'T DENY THAT I'M A BOY.

Mysterious Culture Festival – The Afterparty – Postscript

OKA X UENO

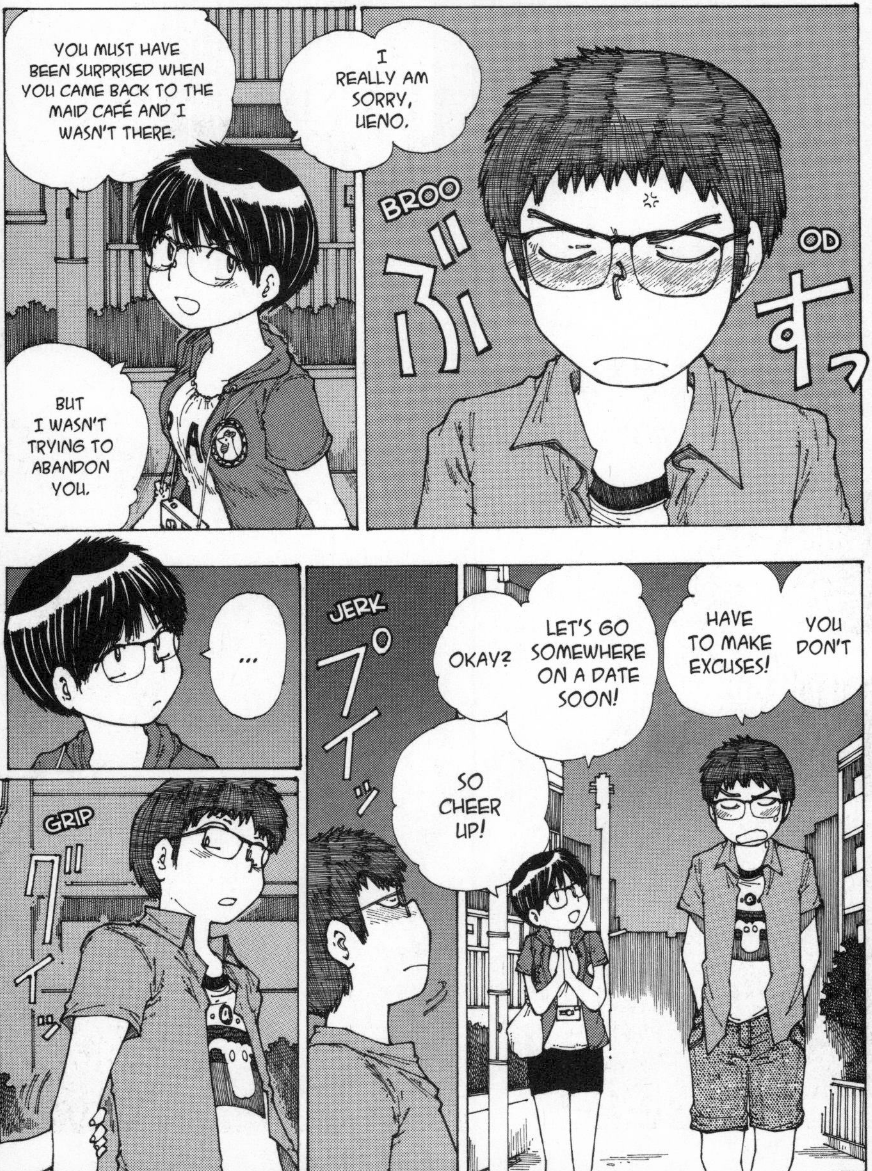
I REALLY AM SORRY, UENO.
BROO
OD
YOU MUST HAVE BEEN SURPRISED WHEN YOU CAME BACK TO THE MAID CAFÉ AND I WASN'T THERE.
BUT I WASN'T TRYING TO ABANDON YOU.
YOU DON'T HAVE TO MAKE EXCUSES!
LET'S GO SOMEWHERE ON A DATE SOON!
OKAY?
SO CHEER UP!
JERK
...
GRIP

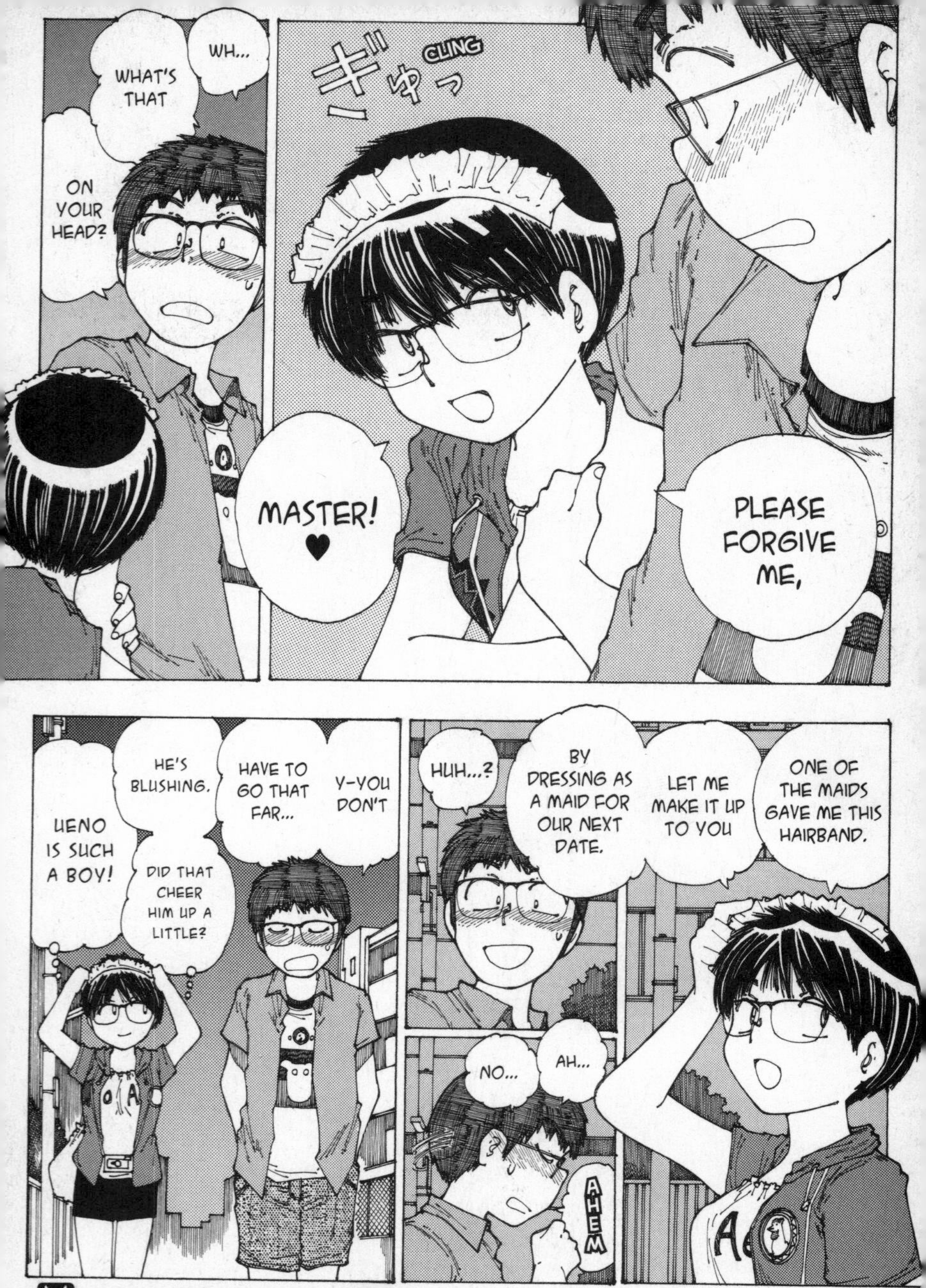
ギゅっ
CLING
PLEASE FORGIVE ME,
MASTER! ♥
WH...
WHAT'S THAT
ON YOUR HEAD?
ONE OF THE MAIDS GAVE ME THIS HAIRBAND.
LET ME MAKE IT UP TO YOU
BY DRESSING AS A MAID FOR OUR NEXT DATE.
HUH...?
AH...
NO...
AHEM
Y-YOU DON'T
HAVE TO GO THAT FAR...
HE'S BLUSHING.
DID THAT CHEER HIM UP A LITTLE?
UENO IS SUCH A BOY!

END OF CHAPTER 34

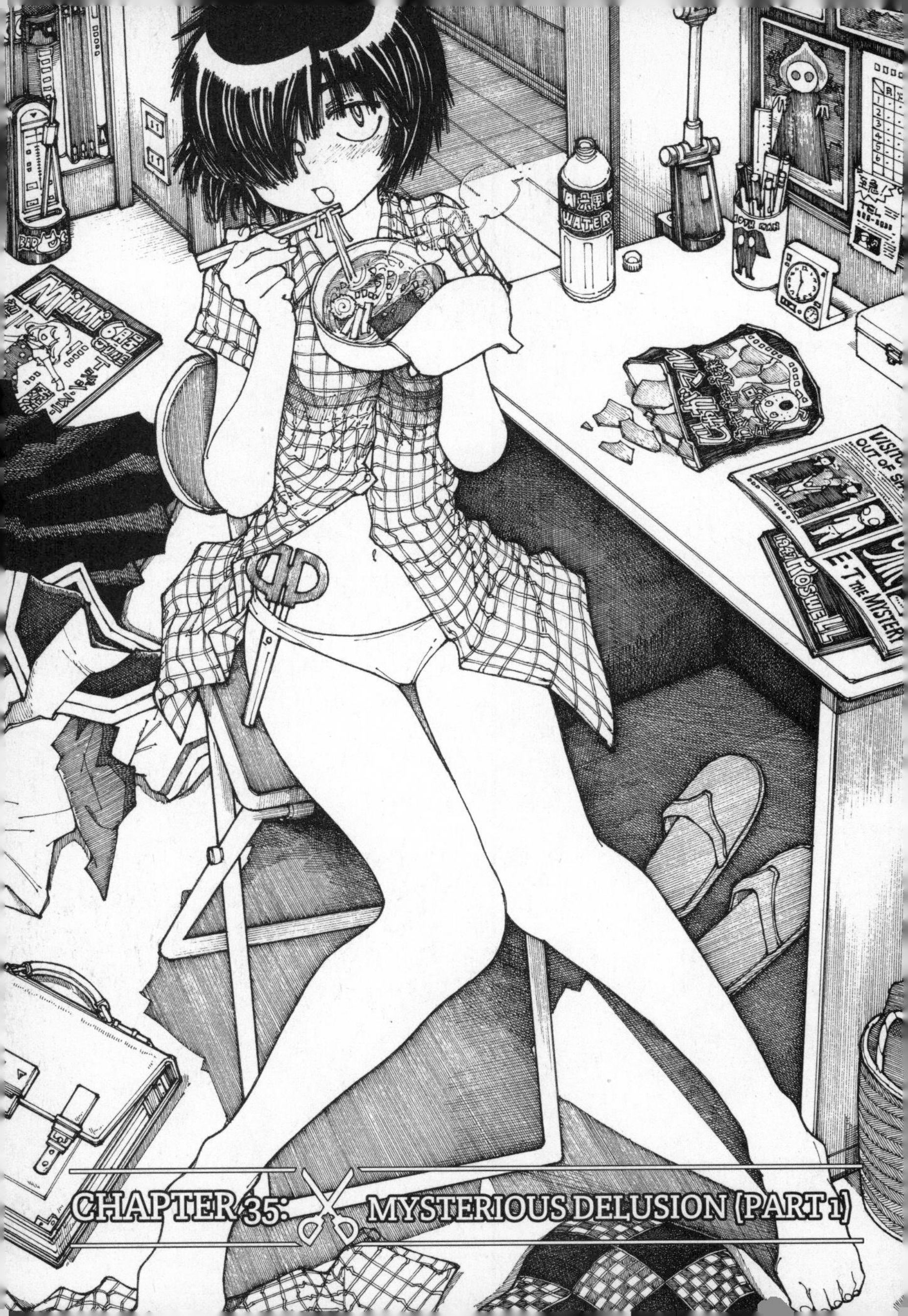
WATER
VISITO
OUT OF S
E.T THE MYSTERY
1947 ROSWELL

CHAPTER 35: MYSTERIOUS DELUSION (PART 1)

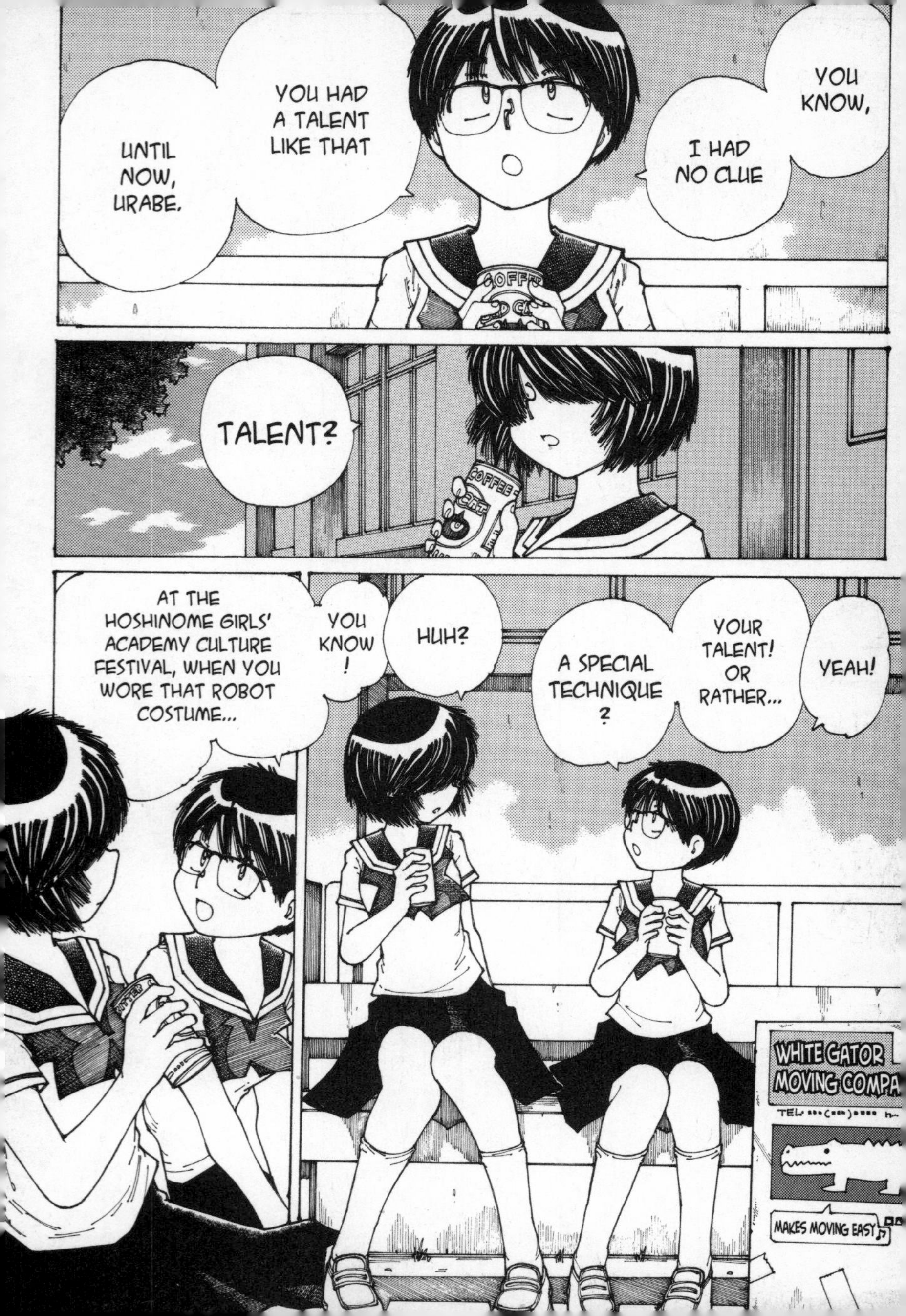
YOU KNOW,
I HAD NO CLUE
YOU HAD A TALENT LIKE THAT
UNTIL NOW, URABE.
TALENT?
COFFEE
YEAH!
YOUR TALENT! OR RATHER...
A SPECIAL TECHNIQUE ?
HUH?
YOU KNOW !
AT THE HOSHINOME GIRLS' ACADEMY CULTURE FESTIVAL, WHEN YOU WORE THAT ROBOT COSTUME...
WHITE GATOR MOVING COMPA
MAKES MOVING EASY

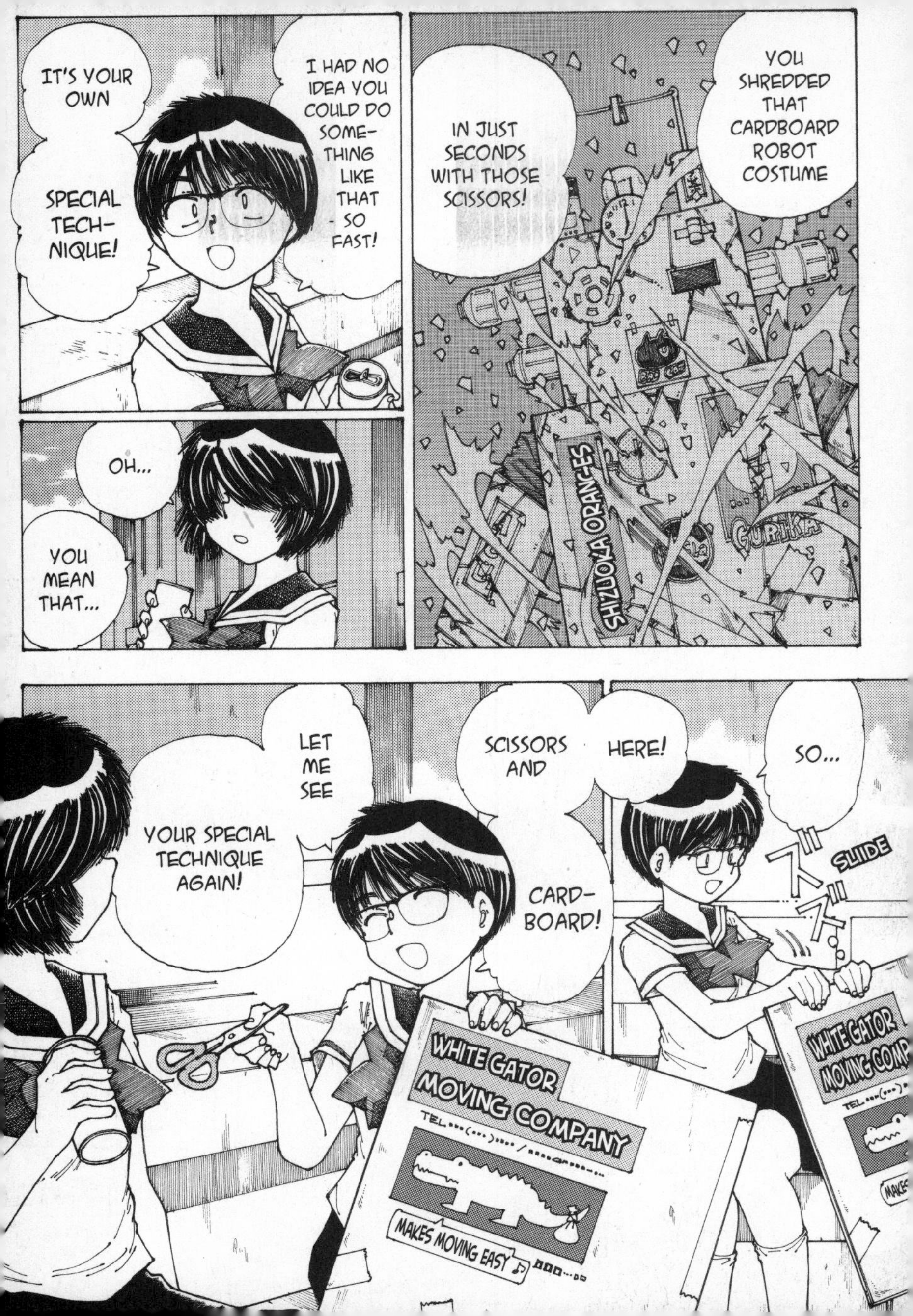
YOU SHREDDED THAT CARDBOARD ROBOT COSTUME
IN JUST SECONDS WITH THOSE SCISSORS!
SHIZUOKA ORANGES
GURIKA
I HAD NO IDEA YOU COULD DO SOMETHING LIKE THAT - SO FAST!
IT'S YOUR OWN
SPECIAL TECHNIQUE!
OH...
YOU MEAN THAT...
SO...
SLIDE
WHITE GATOR MOVING COMP
HERE!
SCISSORS AND
CARDBOARD!
LET ME SEE
YOUR SPECIAL TECHNIQUE AGAIN!
WHITE GATOR MOVING COMPANY
MAKES MOVING EASY

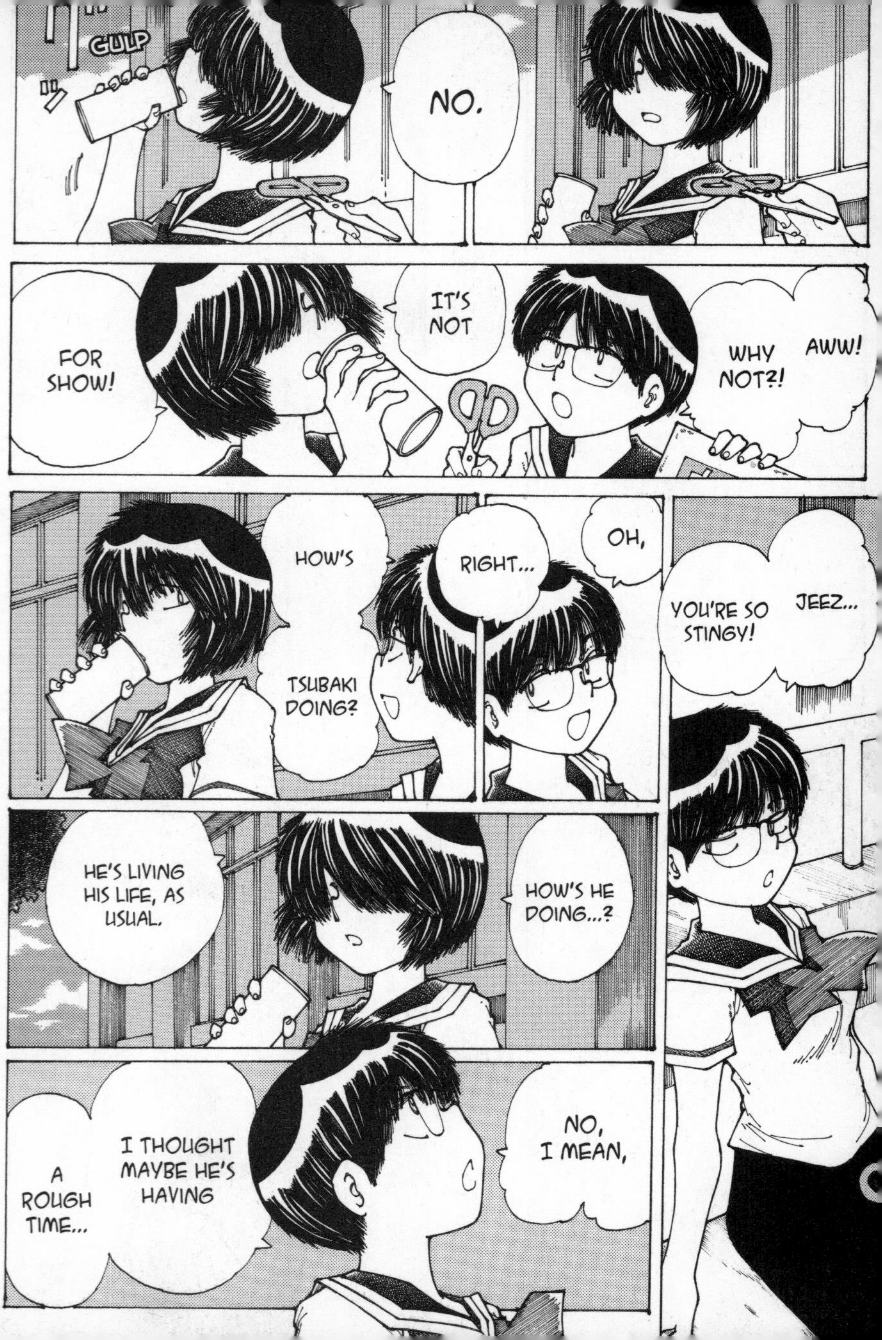
GULP
NO.
AWW!
WHY NOT?!
IT'S NOT
FOR SHOW!
JEEZ...
YOU'RE SO STINGY!
OH,
RIGHT...
HOW'S
TSUBAKI DOING?
HOW'S HE DOING...?
HE'S LIVING HIS LIFE, AS USUAL.
NO, I MEAN,
I THOUGHT MAYBE HE'S HAVING
A ROUGH TIME...

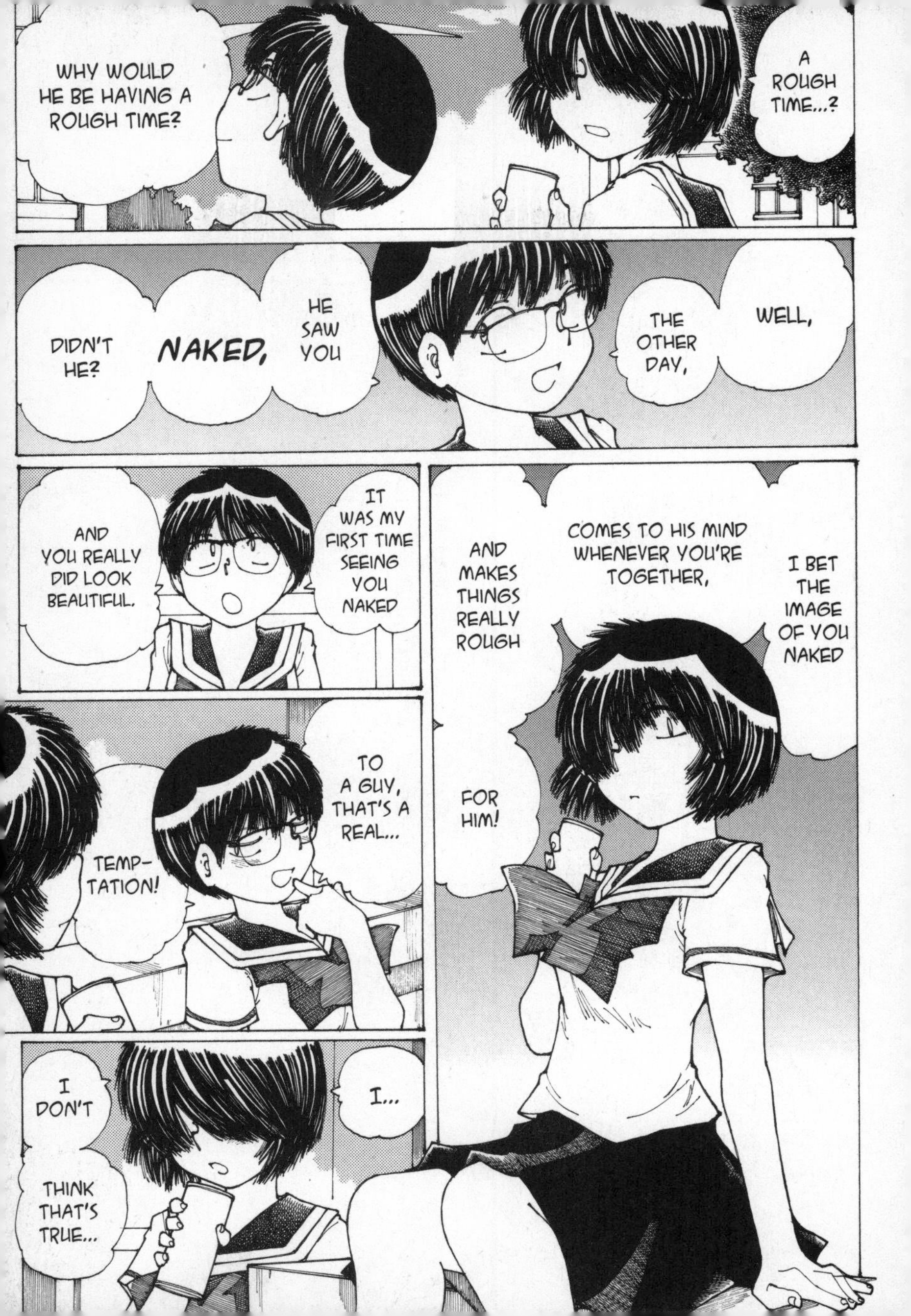
A ROUGH TIME...?
WHY WOULD HE BE HAVING A ROUGH TIME?
WELL,
THE OTHER DAY,
HE SAW YOU
NAKED,
DIDN'T HE?
I BET THE IMAGE OF YOU NAKED
COMES TO HIS MIND WHENEVER YOU'RE TOGETHER,
AND MAKES THINGS REALLY ROUGH
FOR HIM!
IT WAS MY FIRST TIME SEEING YOU NAKED
AND YOU REALLY DID LOOK BEAUTIFUL.
TO A GUY, THAT'S A REAL...
TEMP-TATION!
I...
I DON'T THINK THAT'S TRUE...

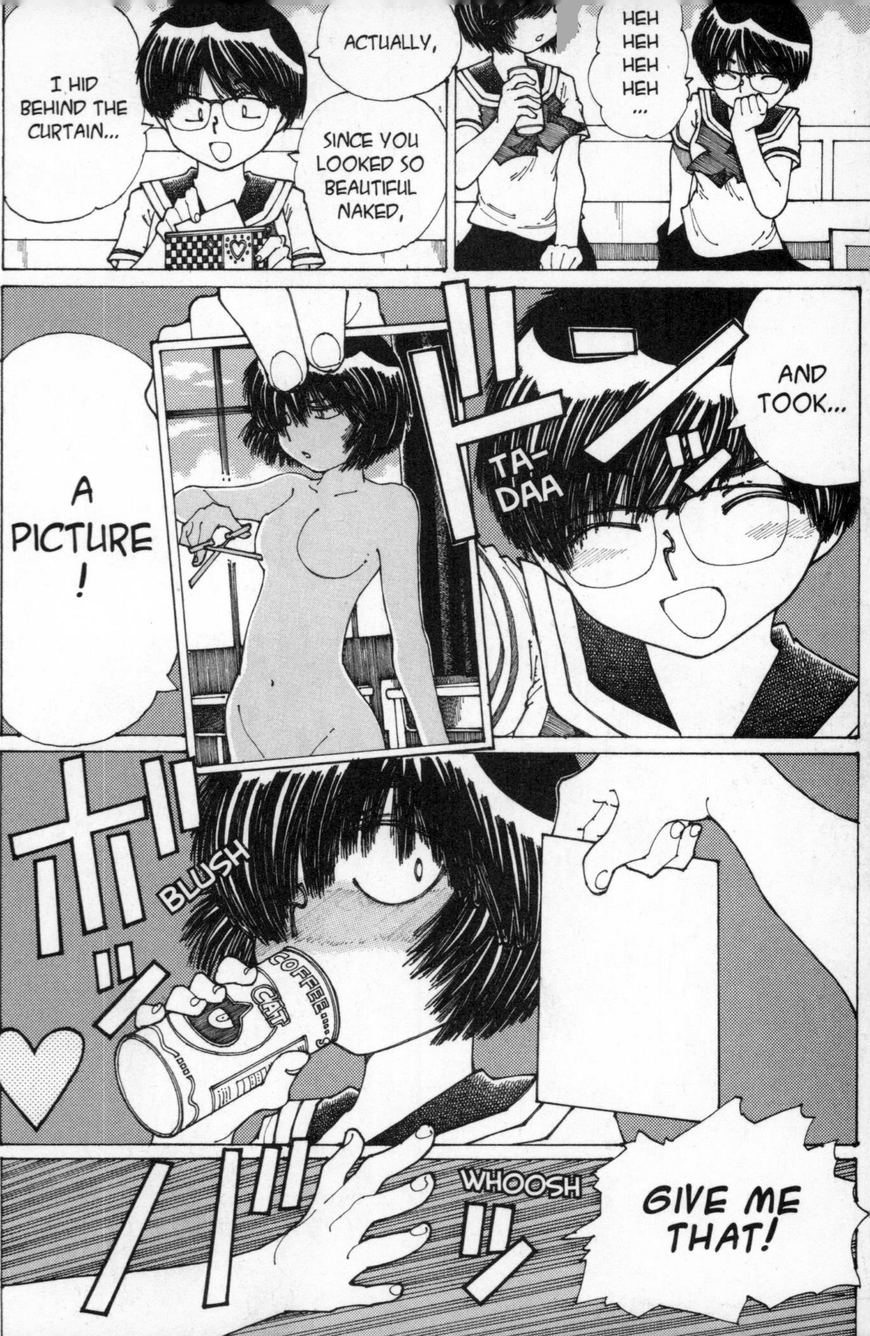
HEH HEH HEH HEH ...
ACTUALLY,
SINCE YOU LOOKED SO BEAUTIFUL NAKED,
I HID BEHIND THE CURTAIN...
AND TOOK...
TA-DAA
A PICTURE!
BLUSH
COFFEE
CAT
GIVE ME THAT!
WHOOSH

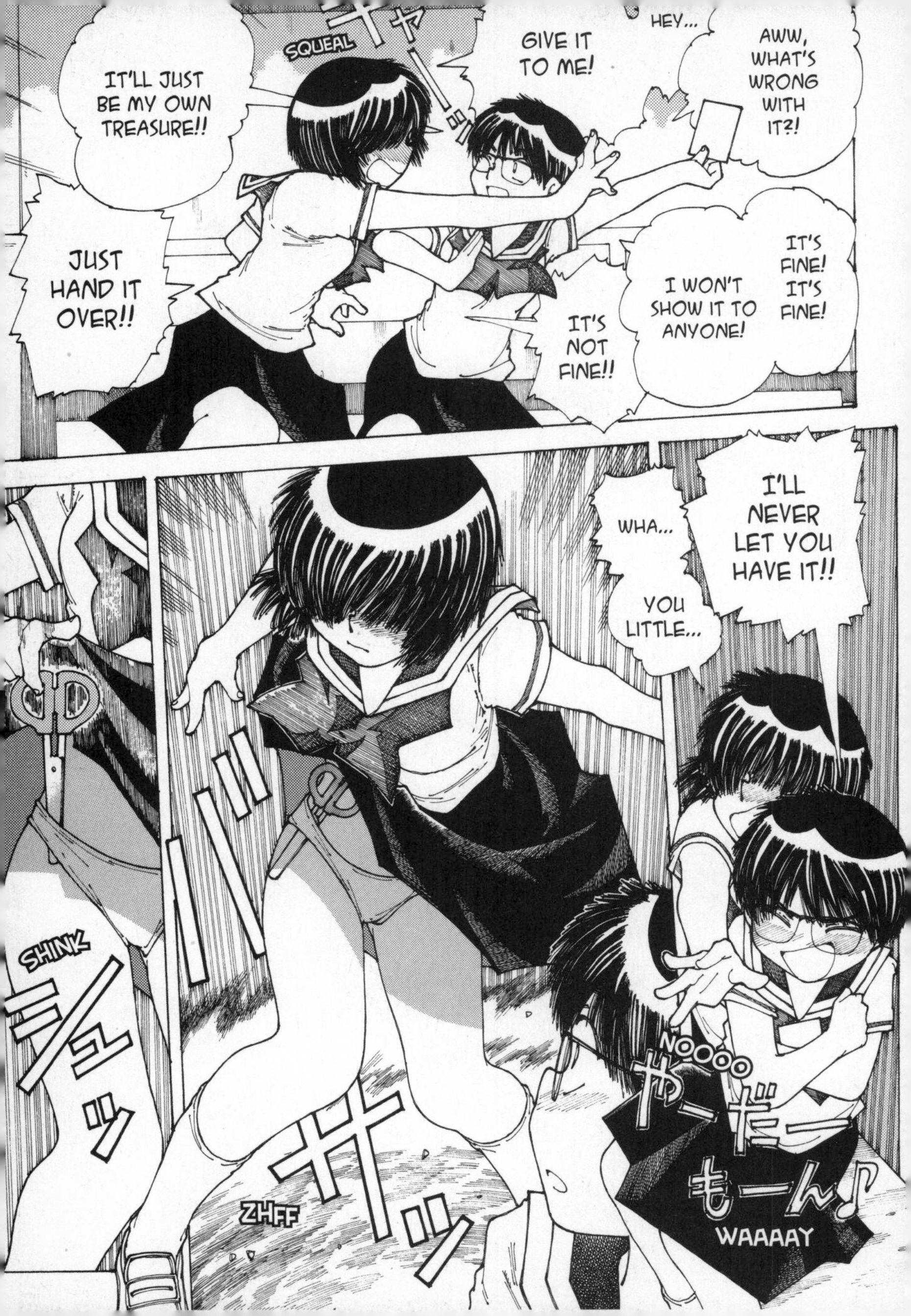
HEY...
AWW, WHAT'S WRONG WITH IT?!
GIVE IT TO ME!
SQUEAL
IT'LL JUST BE MY OWN TREASURE!!
IT'S FINE! IT'S FINE!
I WON'T SHOW IT TO ANYONE!
IT'S NOT FINE!!
JUST HAND IT OVER!!
I'LL NEVER LET YOU HAVE IT!!
WHA...
YOU LITTLE...
NOOOO
やーだーもーん♪
WAAAAY
SHINK
ZHFF

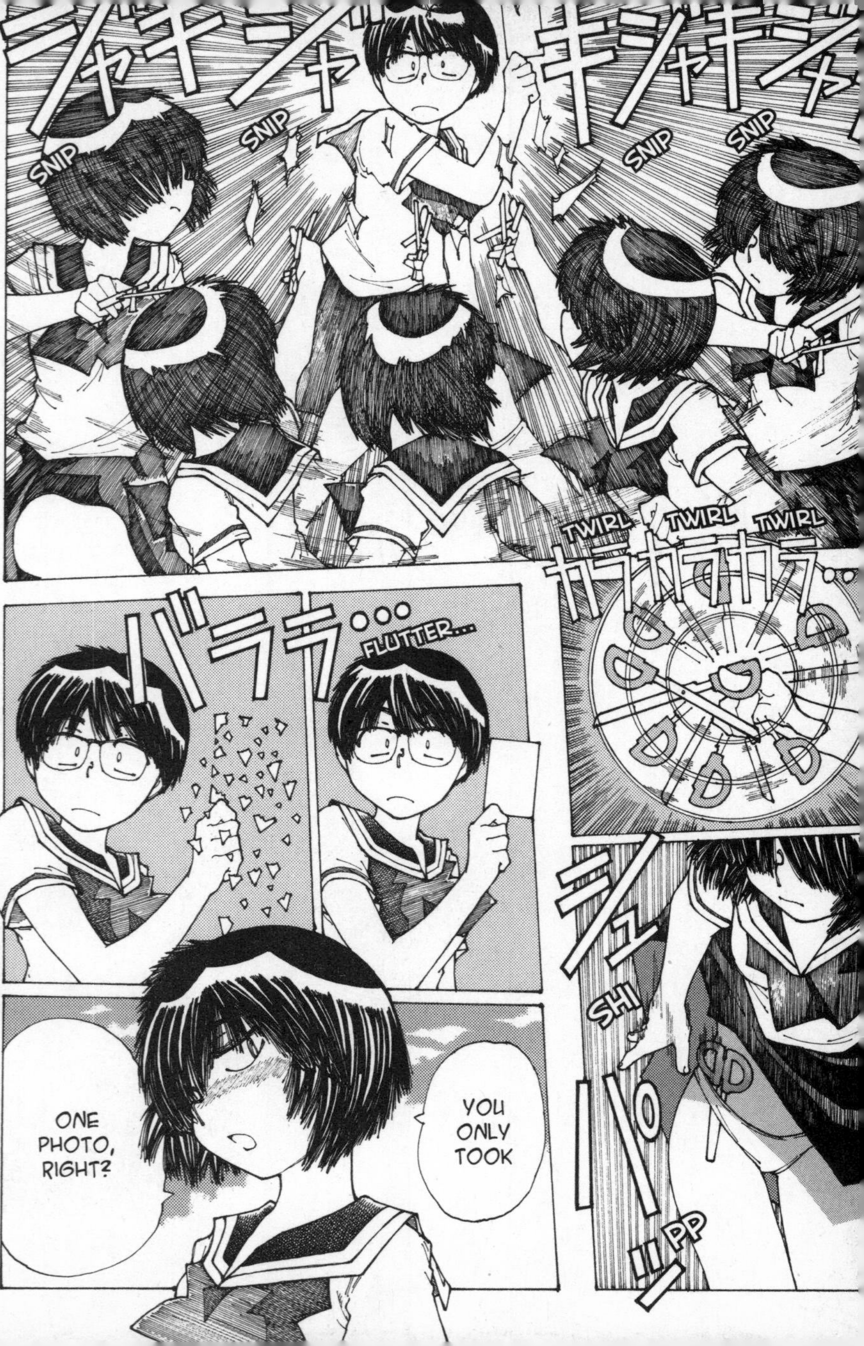

SNIP SNIP
SNIP SNIP
TWIRL TWIRL TWIRL
カラカラカラ…
バララ…
FLUTTER…
シュ
SHI
パッ
PP
YOU ONLY TOOK
ONE PHOTO, RIGHT?

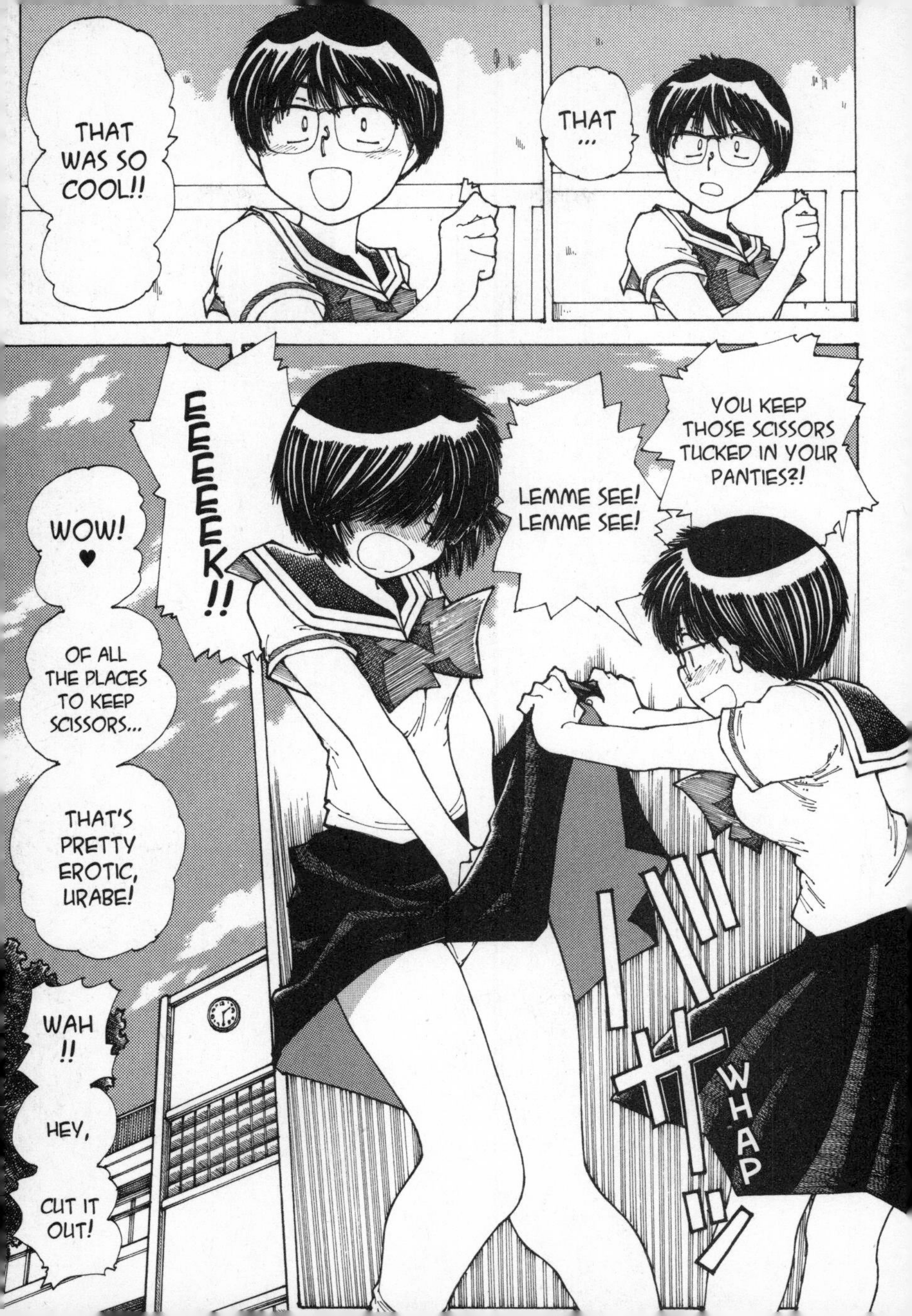
THAT ...
THAT WAS SO COOL!!
YOU KEEP THOSE SCISSORS TUCKED IN YOUR PANTIES?!
LEMME SEE! LEMME SEE!
EEEEEK!!
WOW! ♥
OF ALL THE PLACES TO KEEP SCISSORS...
THAT'S PRETTY EROTIC, URABE!
WHAP
WAH!!
HEY,
CUT IT OUT!

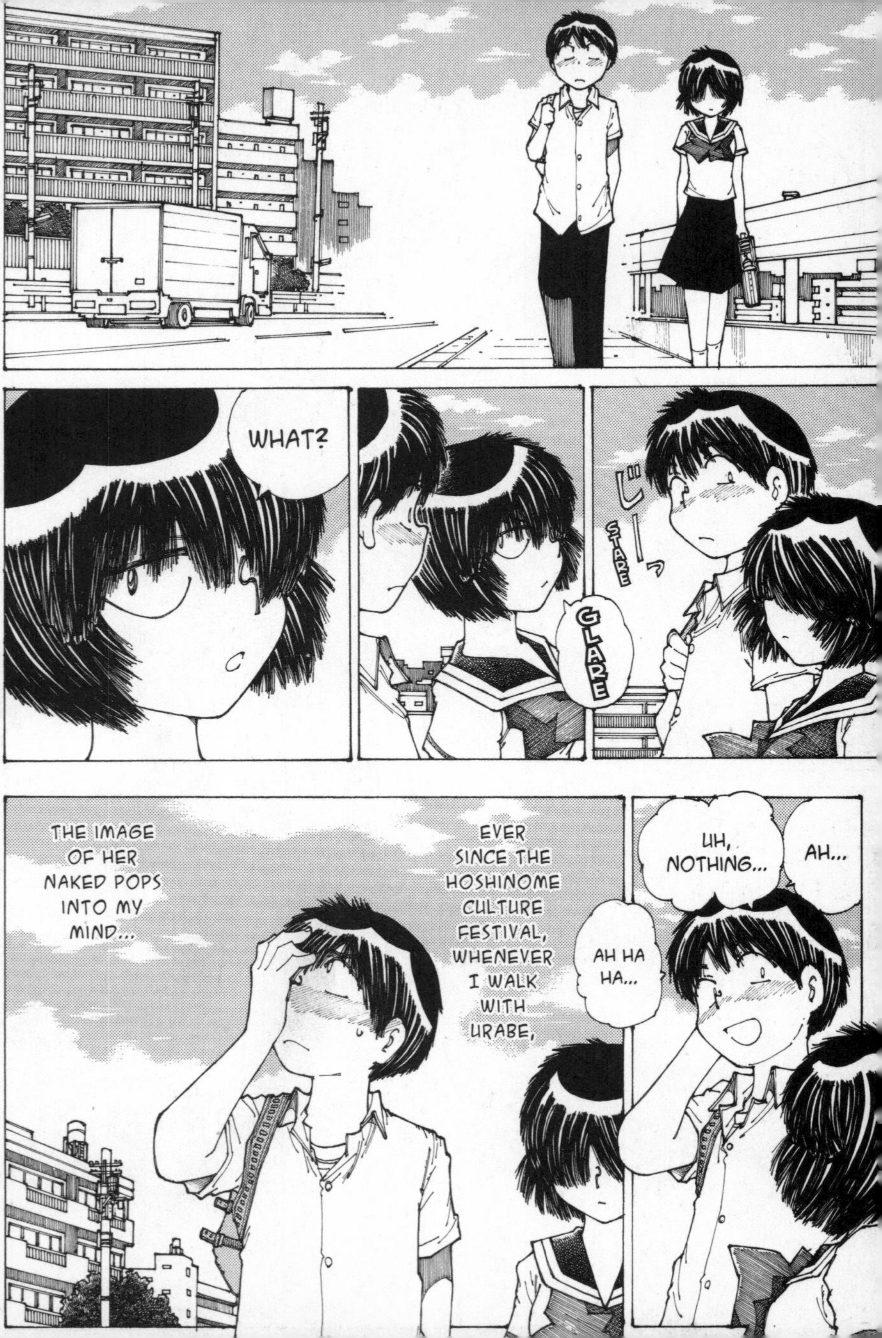
じーっ
STARE
GLARE
WHAT?
AH...
UH, NOTHING...
AH HA HA...
EVER SINCE THE HOSHINOME CULTURE FESTIVAL, WHENEVER I WALK WITH URABE,
THE IMAGE OF HER NAKED POPS INTO MY MIND...

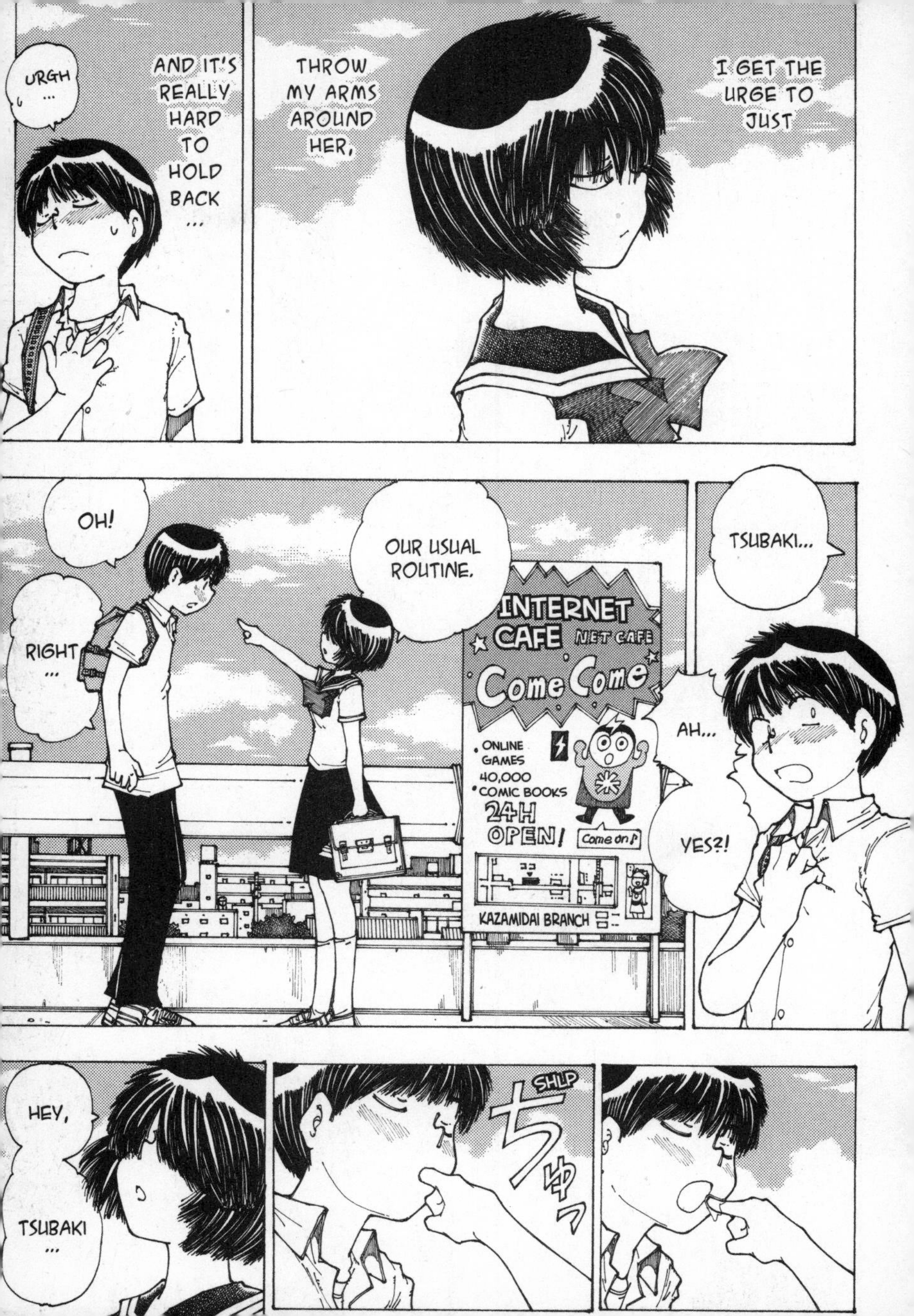
I GET THE URGE TO JUST
THROW MY ARMS AROUND HER,
AND IT'S REALLY HARD TO HOLD BACK ...
URGH ...
TSUBAKI...
AH...
YES?!
OUR USUAL ROUTINE.
INTERNET CAFE
NET CAFE
Come Come
ONLINE GAMES
40,000 COMIC BOOKS
24H OPEN!
Come on♪
KAZAMIDAI BRANCH
OH!
RIGHT ...
SHLP
ちゅっ
HEY,
TSUBAKI ...

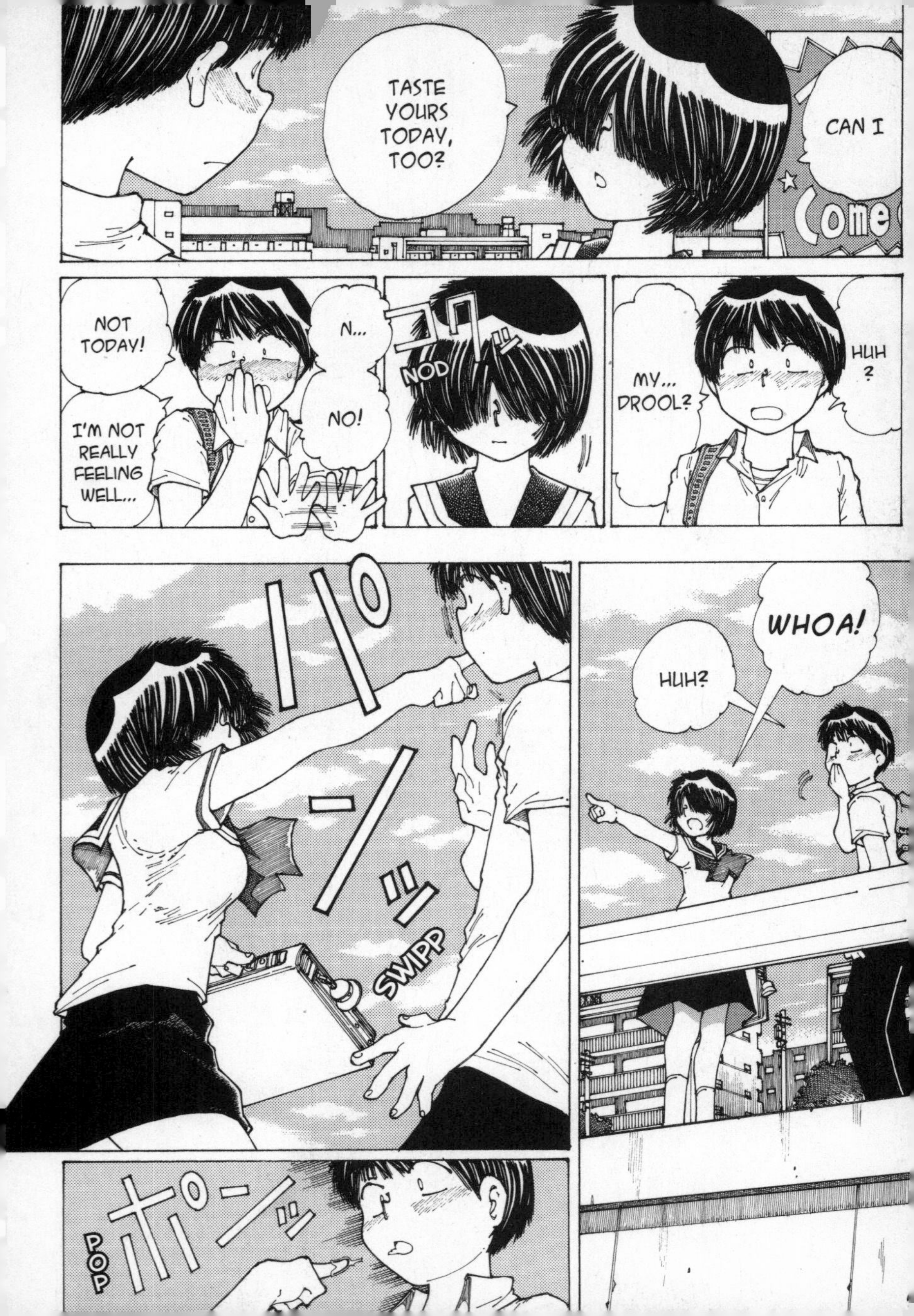
CAN I
TASTE YOURS TODAY, TOO?
HUH?
MY... DROOL?
コクッ
NOD
N...
NOT TODAY!
NO!
I'M NOT REALLY FEELING WELL...
WHOA!
HUH?
パーッ
SWIPP
ポーンッ
POP

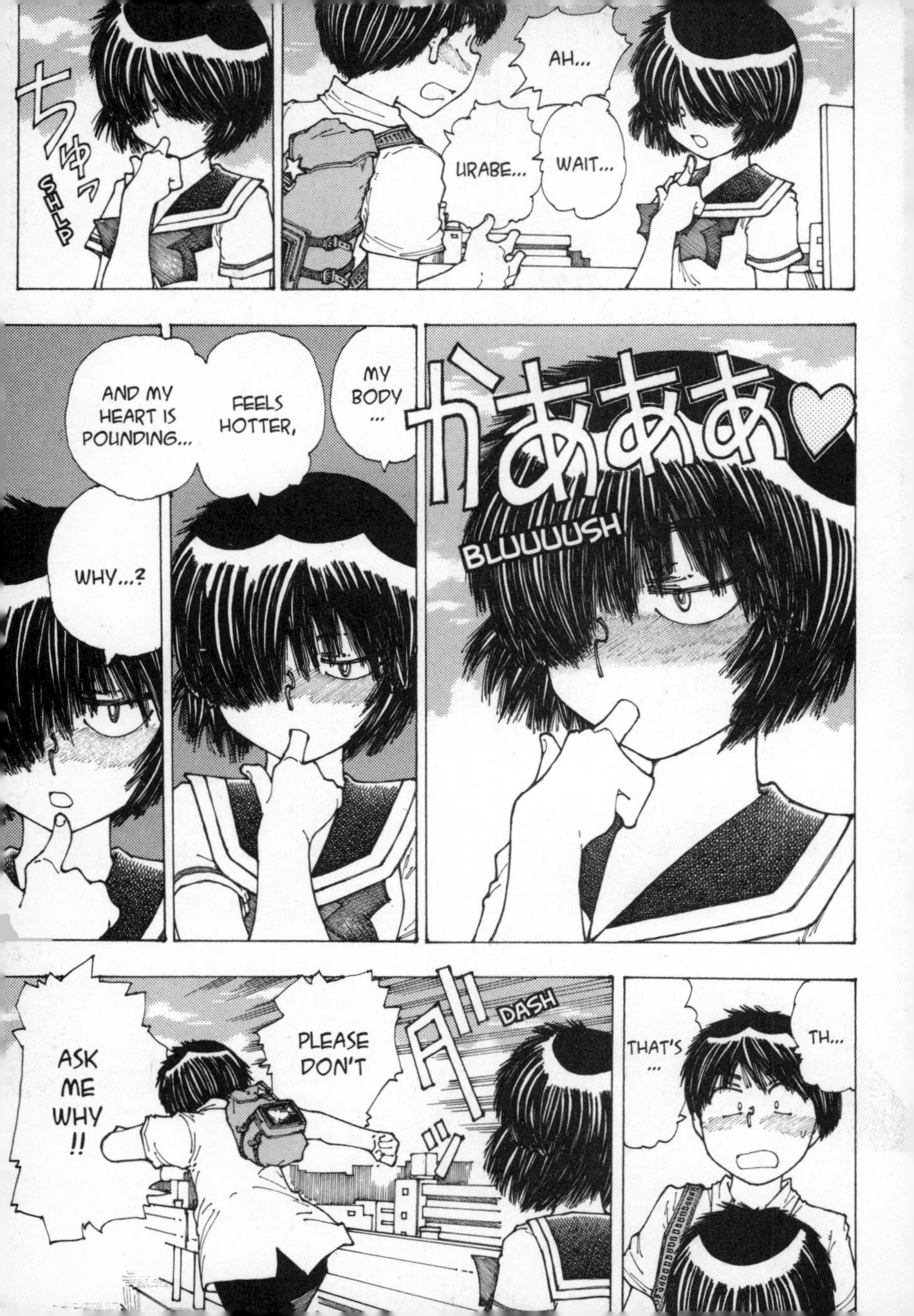
AH...
WAIT...
URABE...
ちゅっ
SHLP
かあああ♥
BLUUUUSH
MY BODY ...
FEELS HOTTER,
AND MY HEART IS POUNDING...
WHY...?
TH...
THAT'S ...
ダッ
DASH
PLEASE DON'T
ASK ME WHY !!

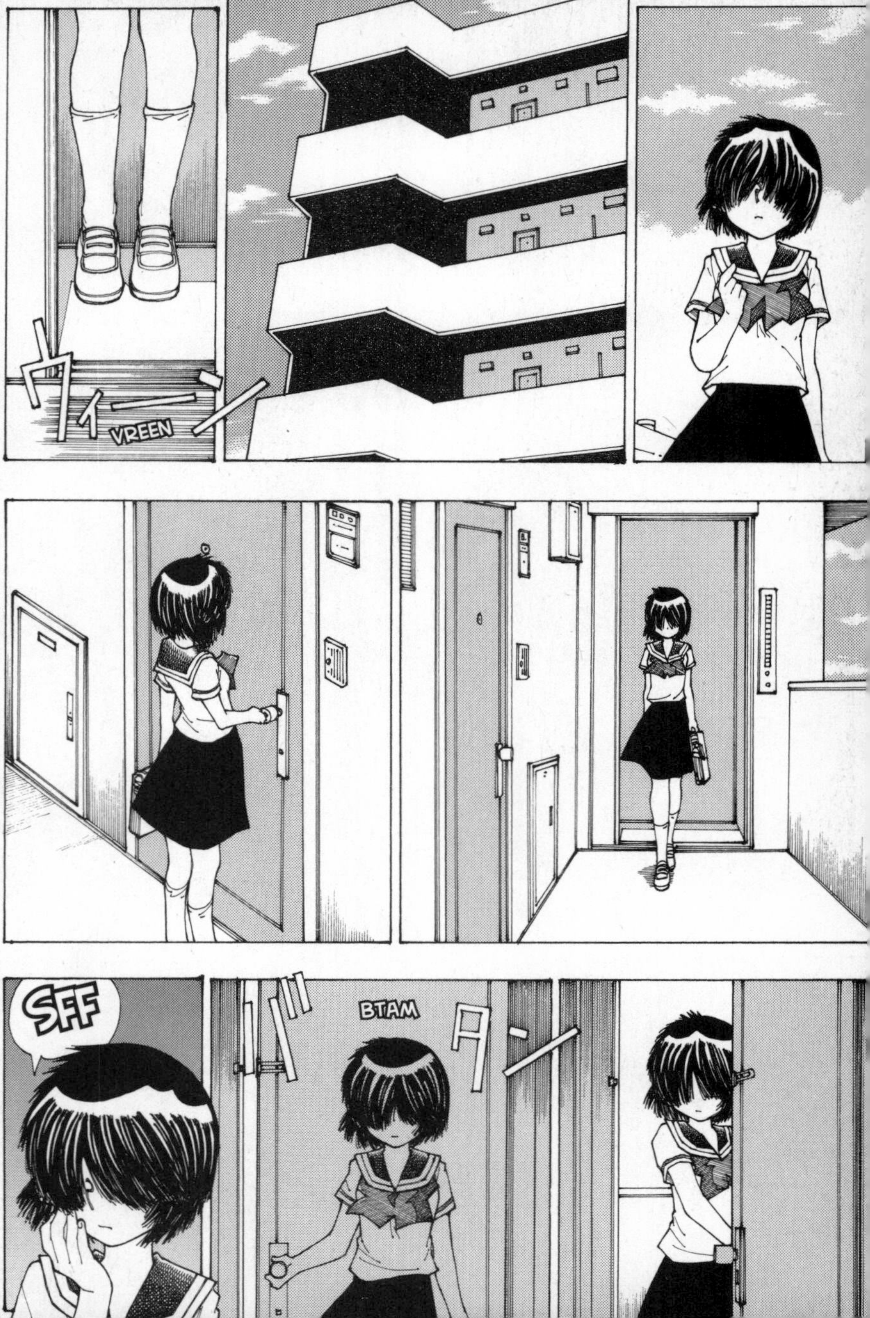
VREEN
BTAM
SFF

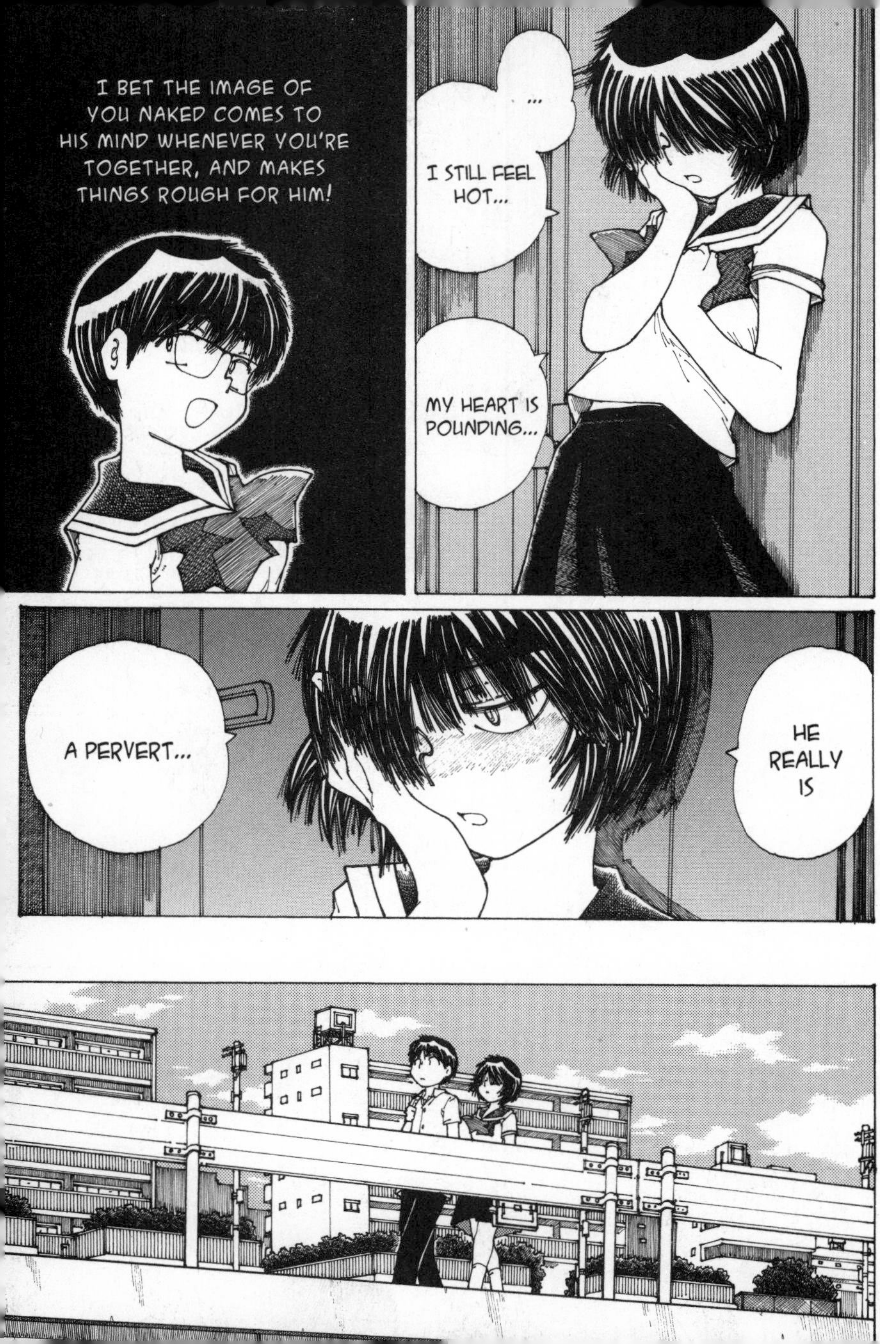
...
I STILL FEEL HOT...
MY HEART IS POUNDING...
I BET THE IMAGE OF YOU NAKED COMES TO HIS MIND WHENEVER YOU'RE TOGETHER, AND MAKES THINGS ROUGH FOR HIM!
HE REALLY IS
A PERVERT...

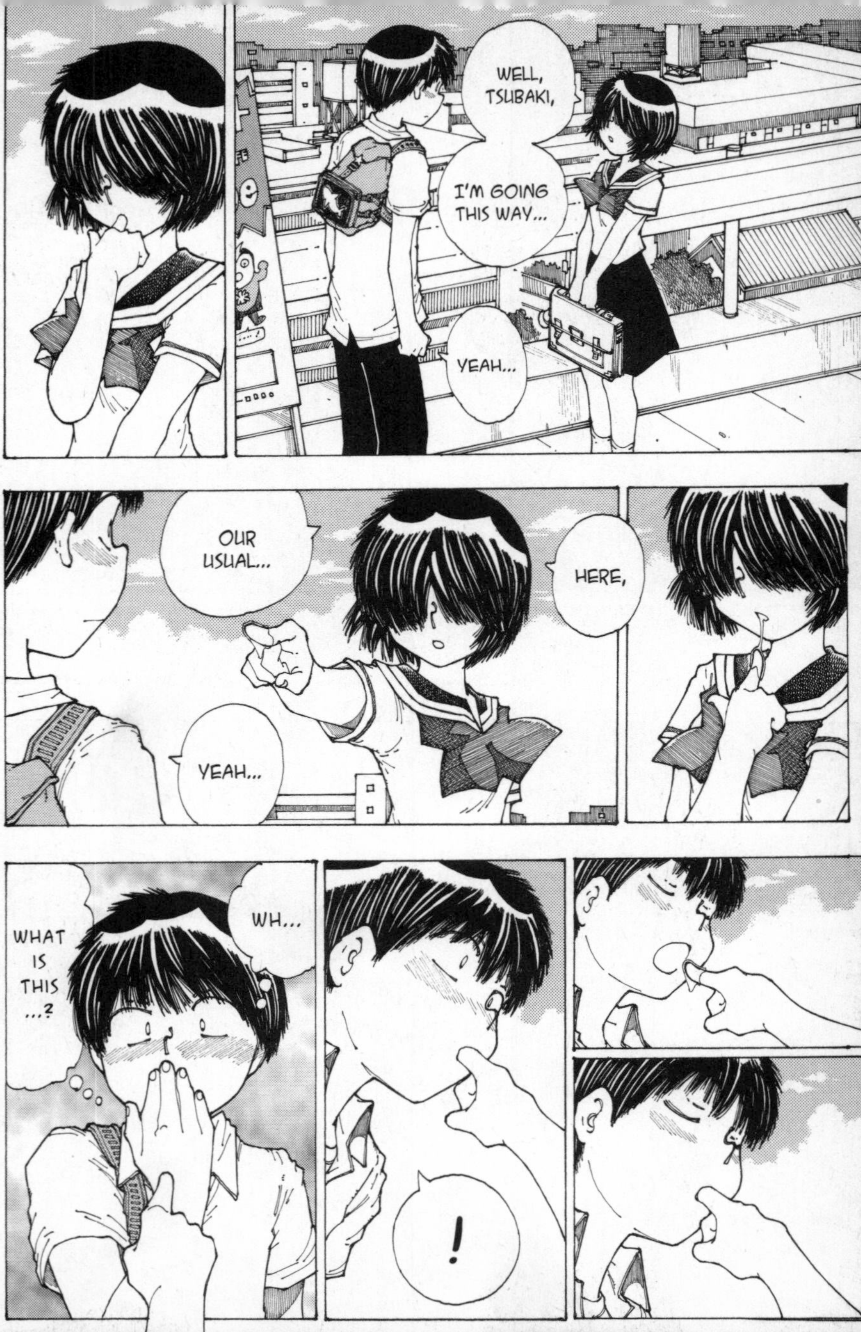
WELL, TSUBAKI,
I'M GOING THIS WAY...
YEAH...
HERE,
OUR USUAL...
YEAH...
!
WH...
WHAT IS THIS ...?

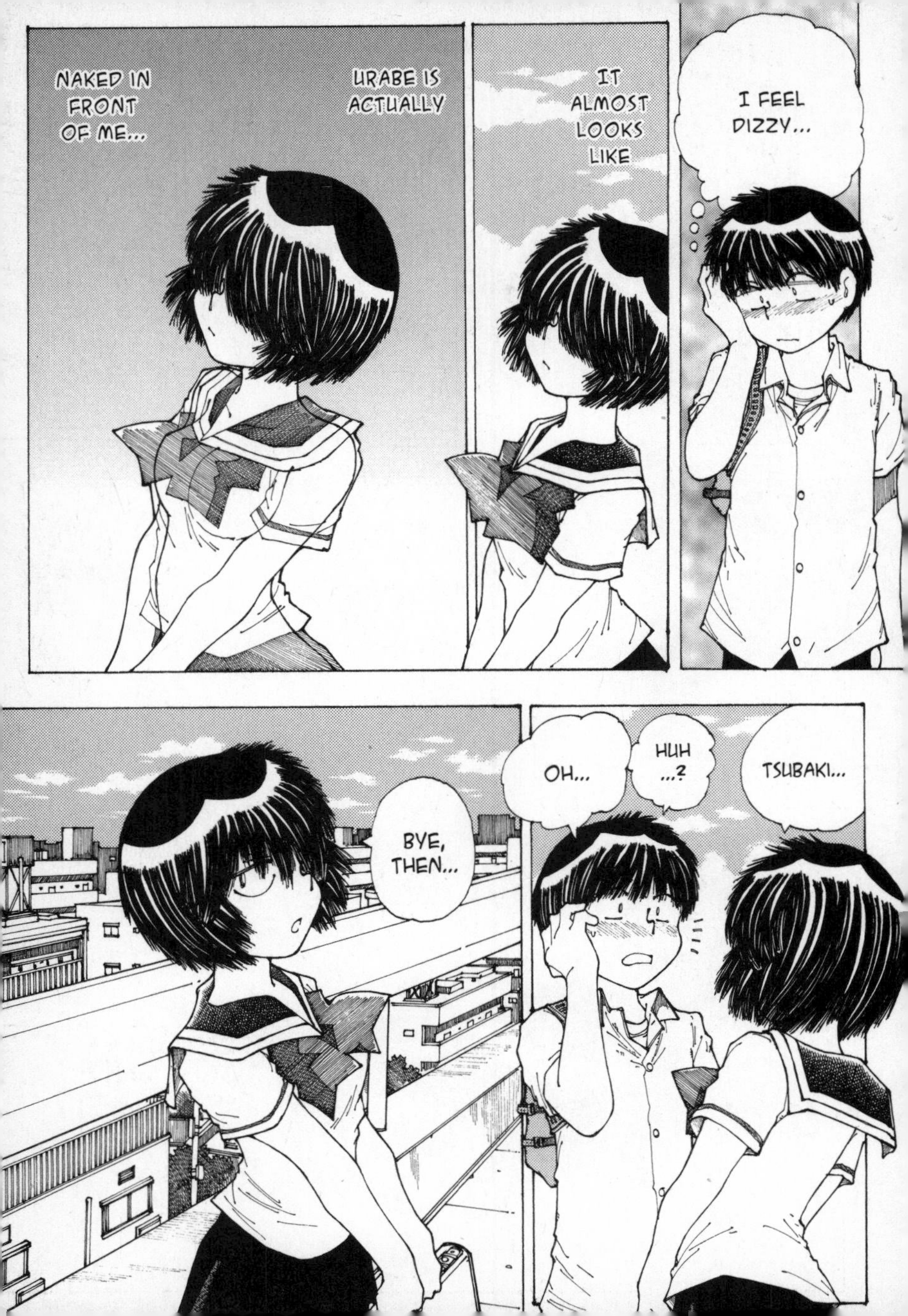
I FEEL DIZZY...
IT ALMOST LOOKS LIKE
URABE IS ACTUALLY
NAKED IN FRONT OF ME...
TSUBAKI...
HUH ...?
OH...
BYE, THEN...

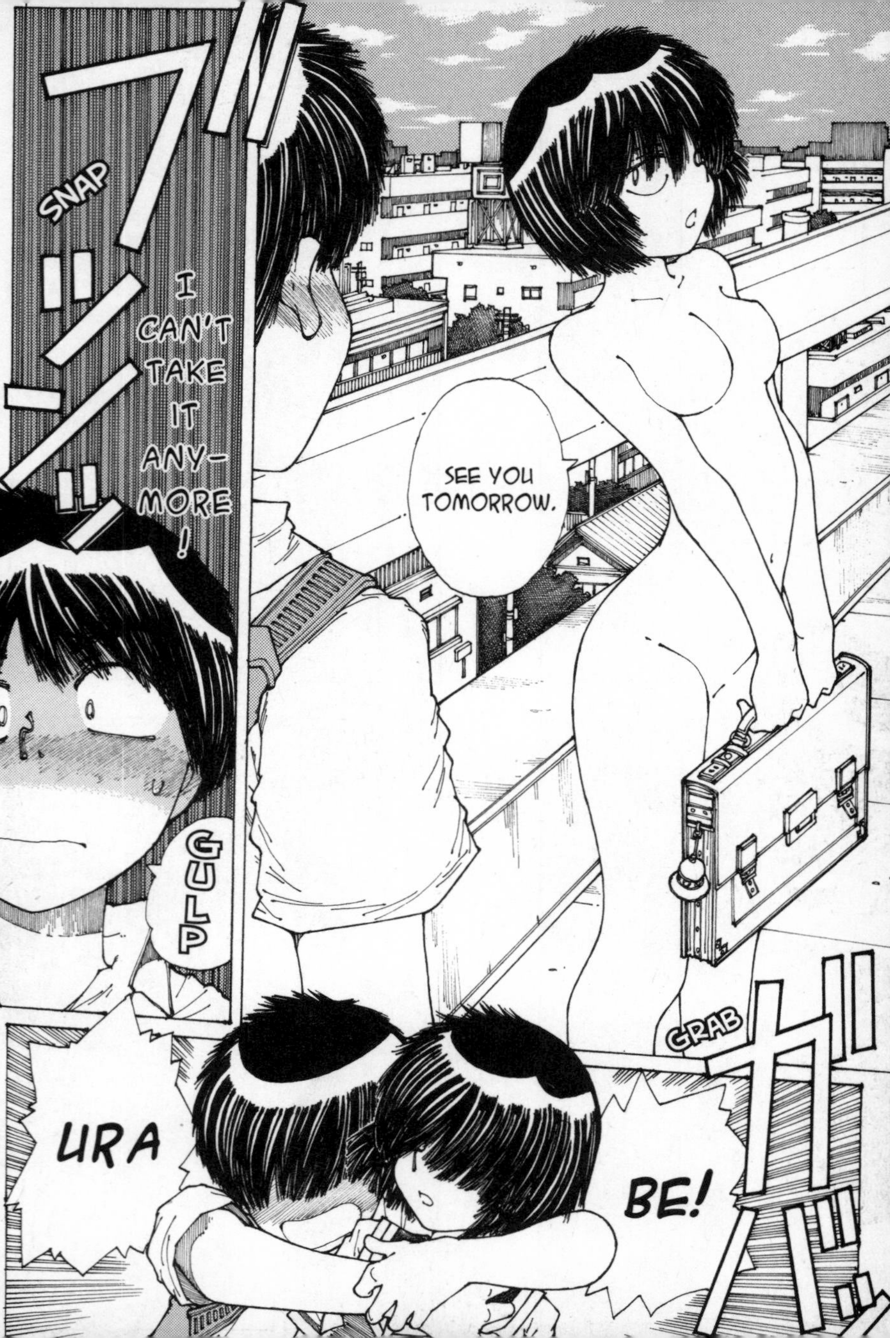
SEE YOU TOMORROW.
SNAP
I CAN'T TAKE IT ANY-MORE!
GULP
GRAB
URA
BE!

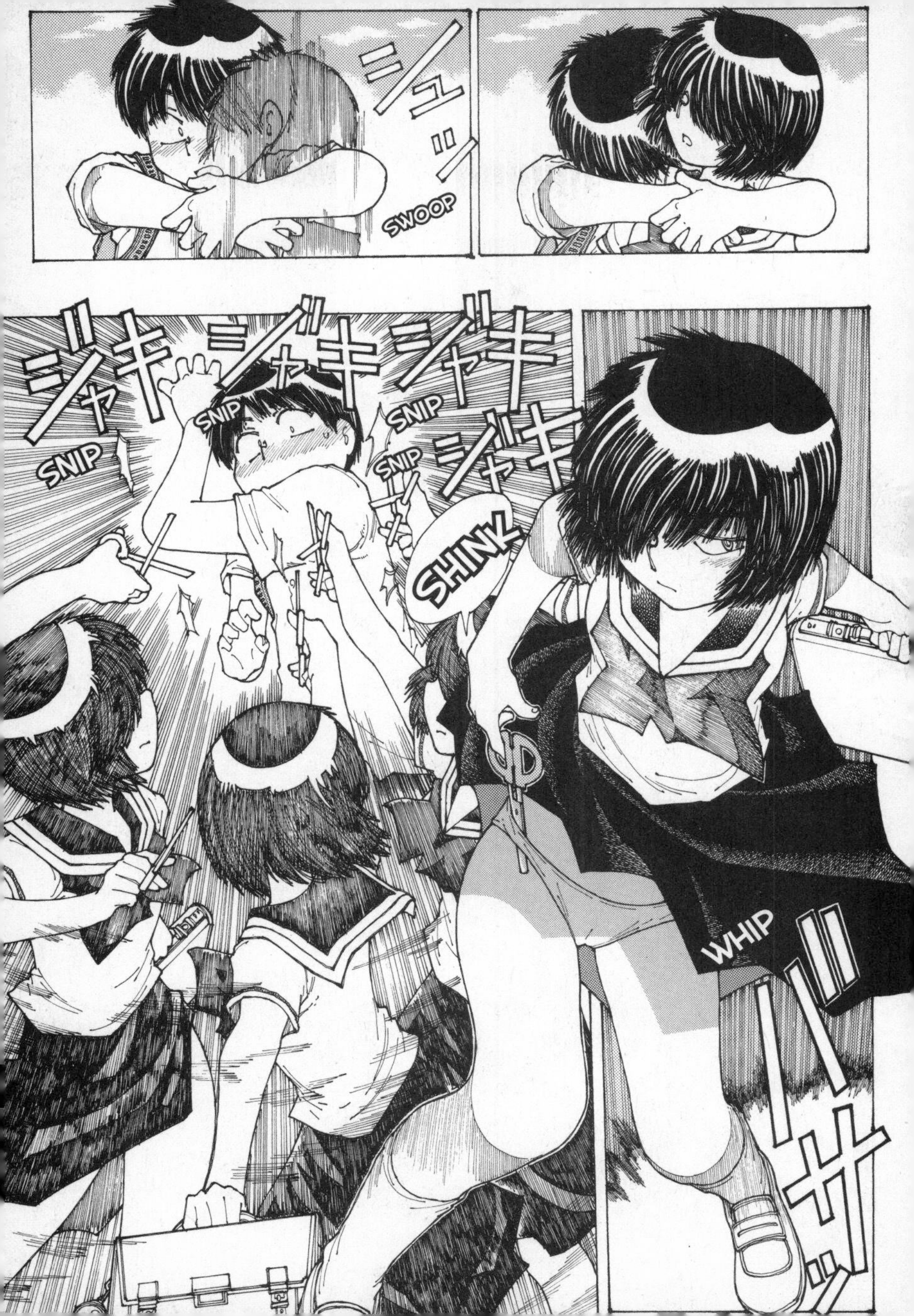
シュッ
SWOOP
バサッ
WHIP
ジャキ
SNIP
SHINK
ジャキ
SNIP
ジャキ
SNIP
ジャキ
SNIP

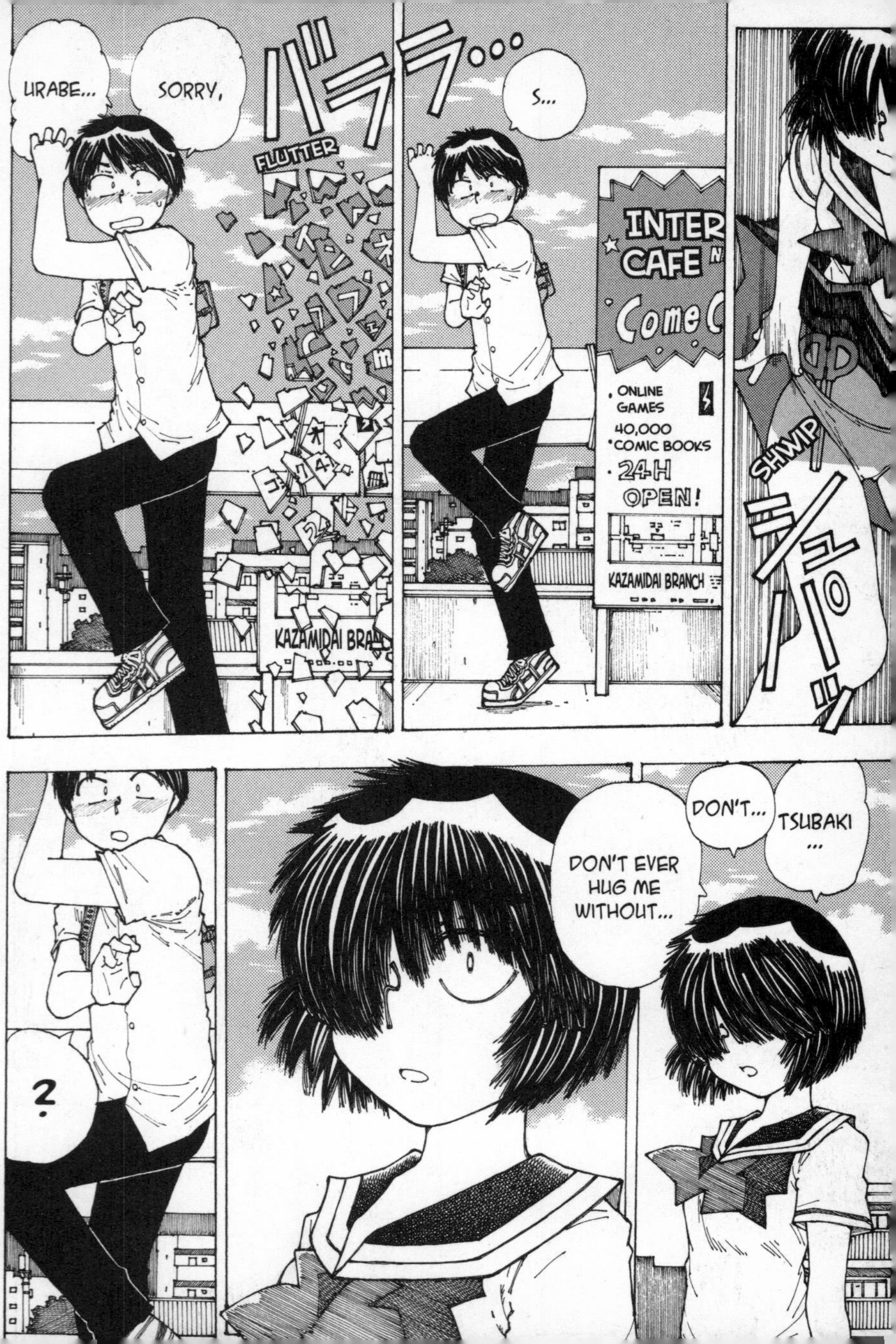
SHWIP
S...
INTER
CAFE
Come C
ONLINE GAMES
40,000 COMIC BOOKS
24H OPEN!
KAZAMIDAI BRANCH
URABE...
SORRY,
バララ…
FLUTTER
KAZAMIDAI BRAN
TSUBAKI ...
DON'T...
DON'T EVER HUG ME WITHOUT...
?

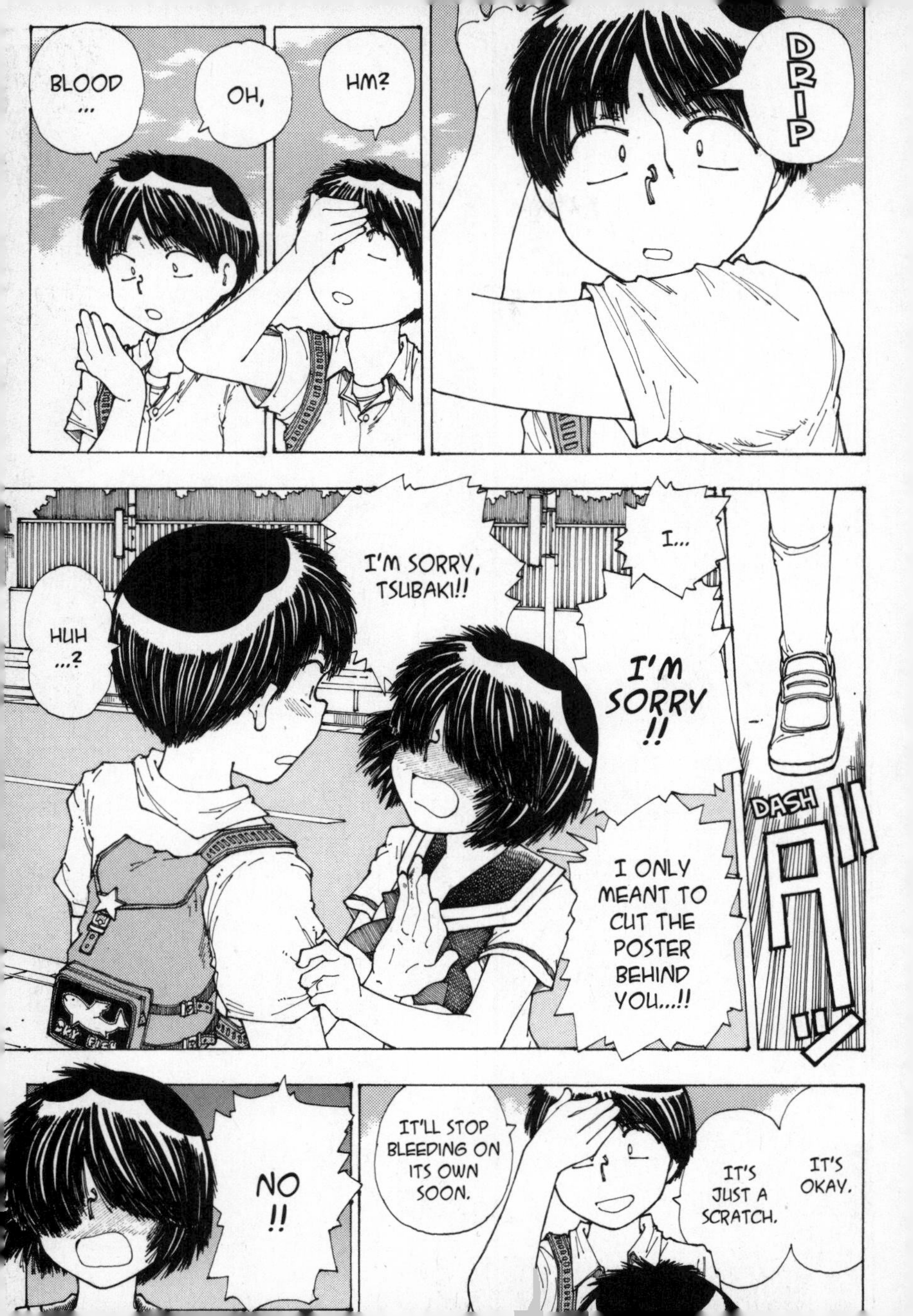
DRIP
HM?
OH,
BLOOD ...
DASH
I...
I'M SORRY !!
I ONLY MEANT TO CUT THE POSTER BEHIND YOU...!!
I'M SORRY, TSUBAKI!!
HUH ...?
IT'S OKAY.
IT'S JUST A SCRATCH.
IT'LL STOP BLEEDING ON ITS OWN SOON.
NO !!

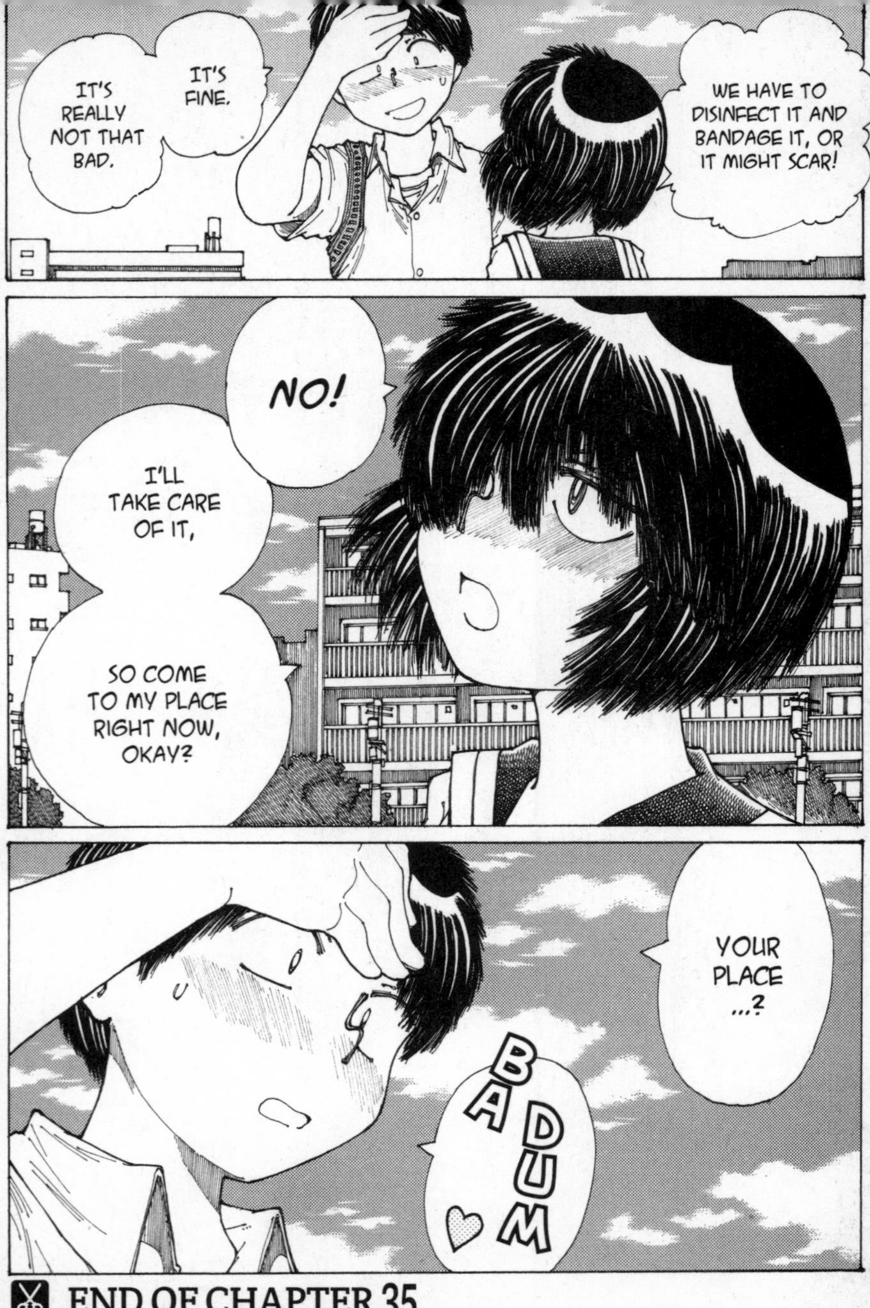
WE HAVE TO DISINFECT IT AND BANDAGE IT, OR IT MIGHT SCAR!
IT'S FINE.
IT'S REALLY NOT THAT BAD.
NO!
I'LL TAKE CARE OF IT,
SO COME TO MY PLACE RIGHT NOW, OKAY?
YOUR PLACE ...?
BADUM

END OF CHAPTER 35

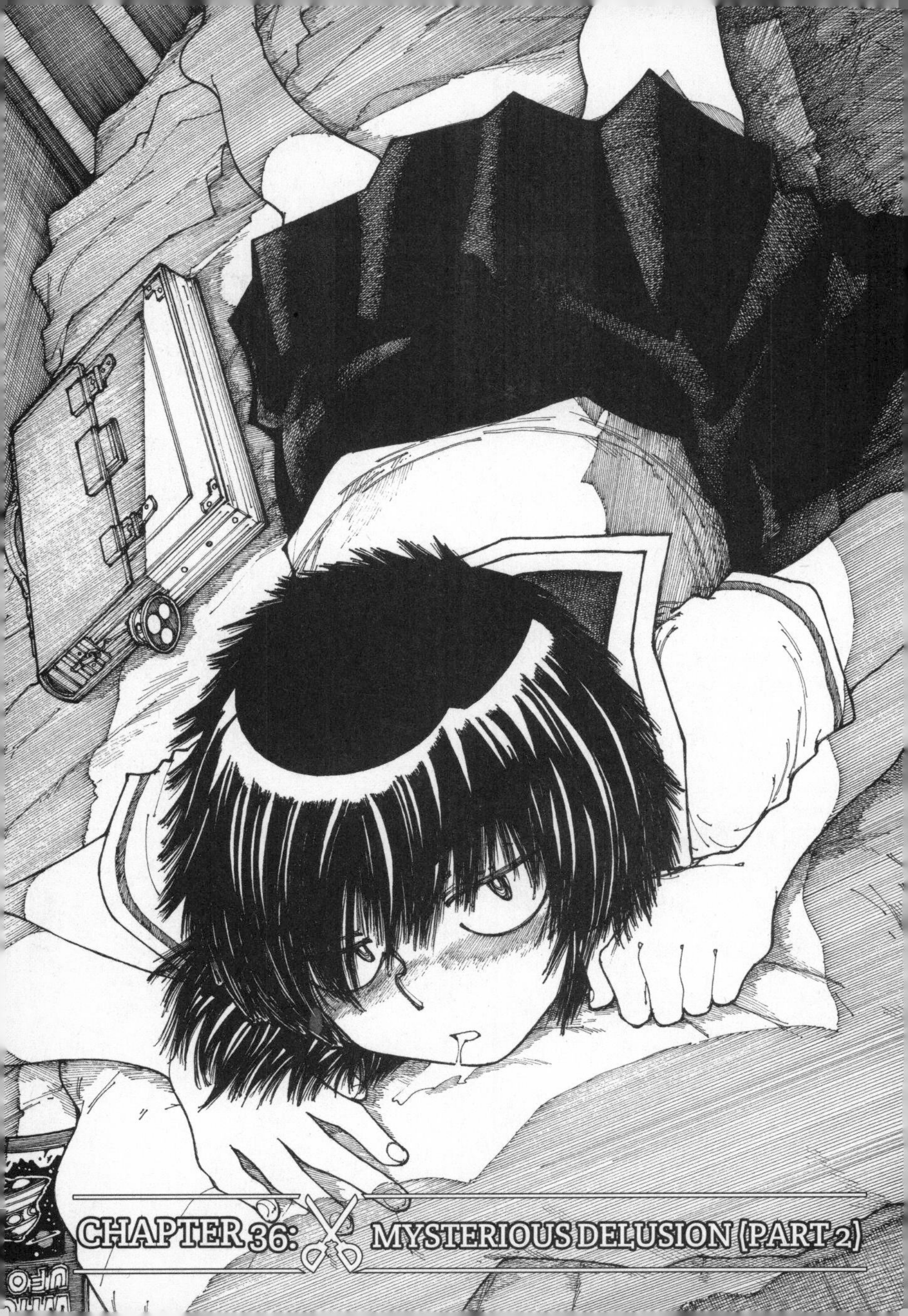
CHAPTER 36: MYSTERIOUS DELUSION (PART 2)

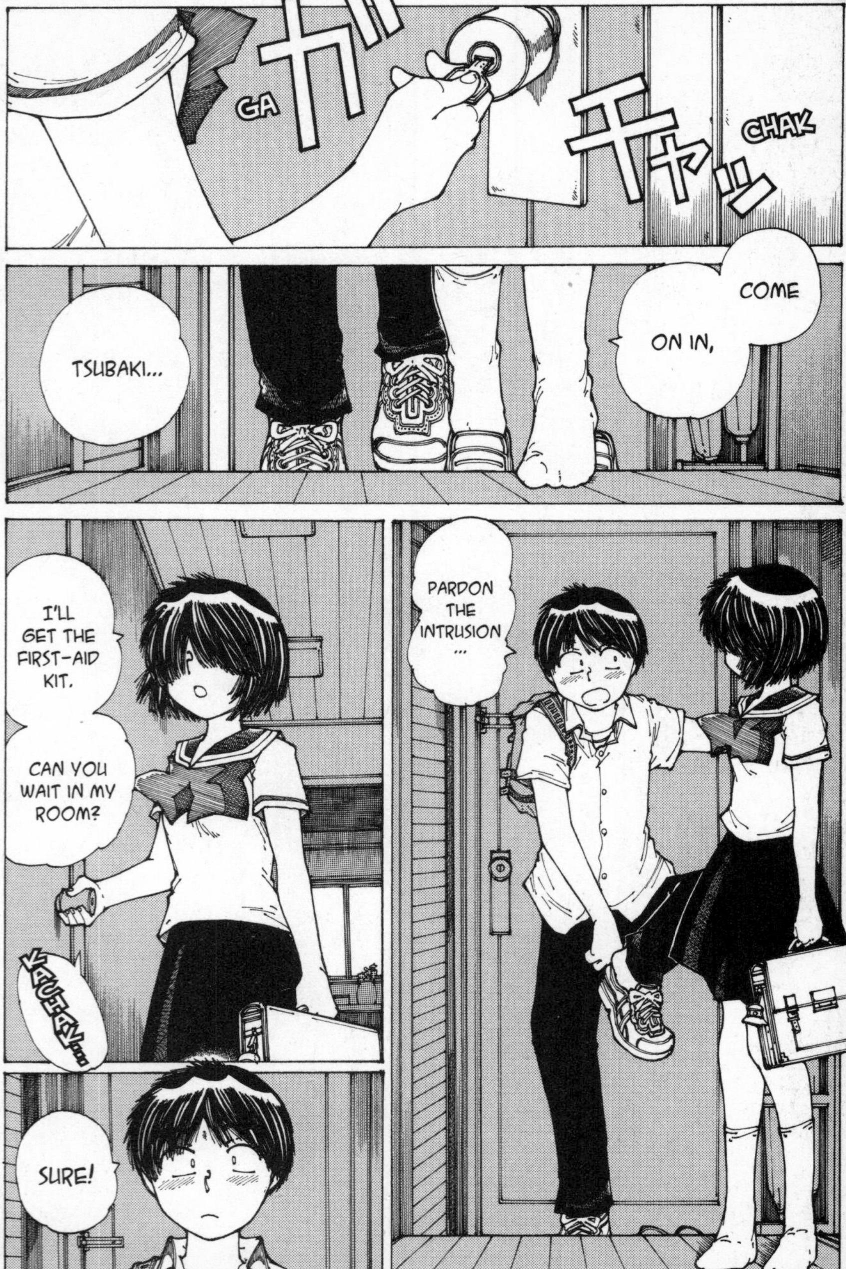
ガ゛
GA
チャッ
CHAK
COME ON IN,
TSUBAKI...
PARDON THE INTRUSION ...
I'LL GET THE FIRST-AID KIT.
CAN YOU WAIT IN MY ROOM?
KACHAK...
SURE!

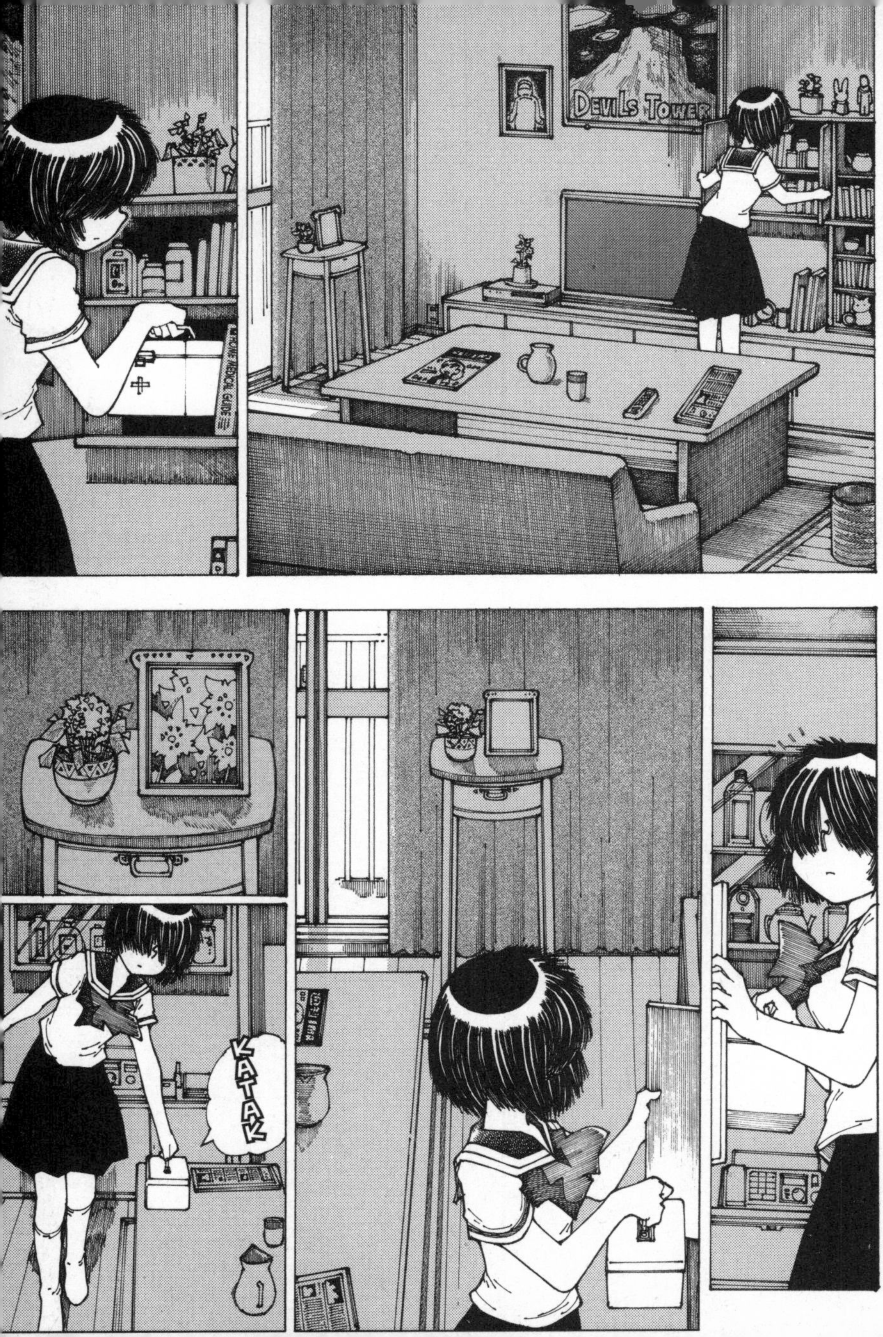
DEVILS TOWER
HOME MEDICAL GUIDE
KATAK

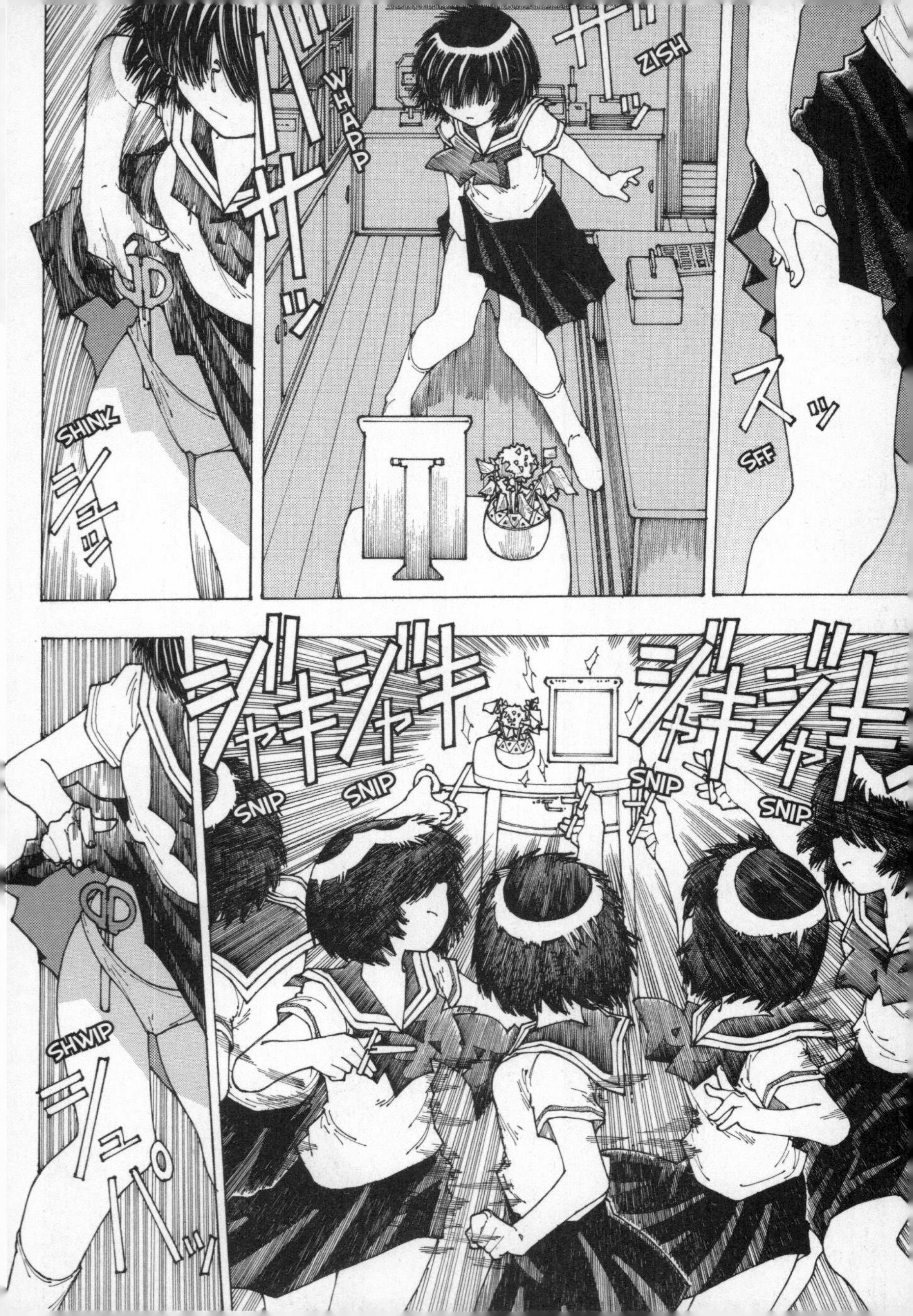
スッ
SFF
ZISH
WHAPP
SHINK
シュッ
ジャキジャキ
ジャキジャキ
SNIP
SNIP
SNIP
SNIP
SHWIP
シュパッ

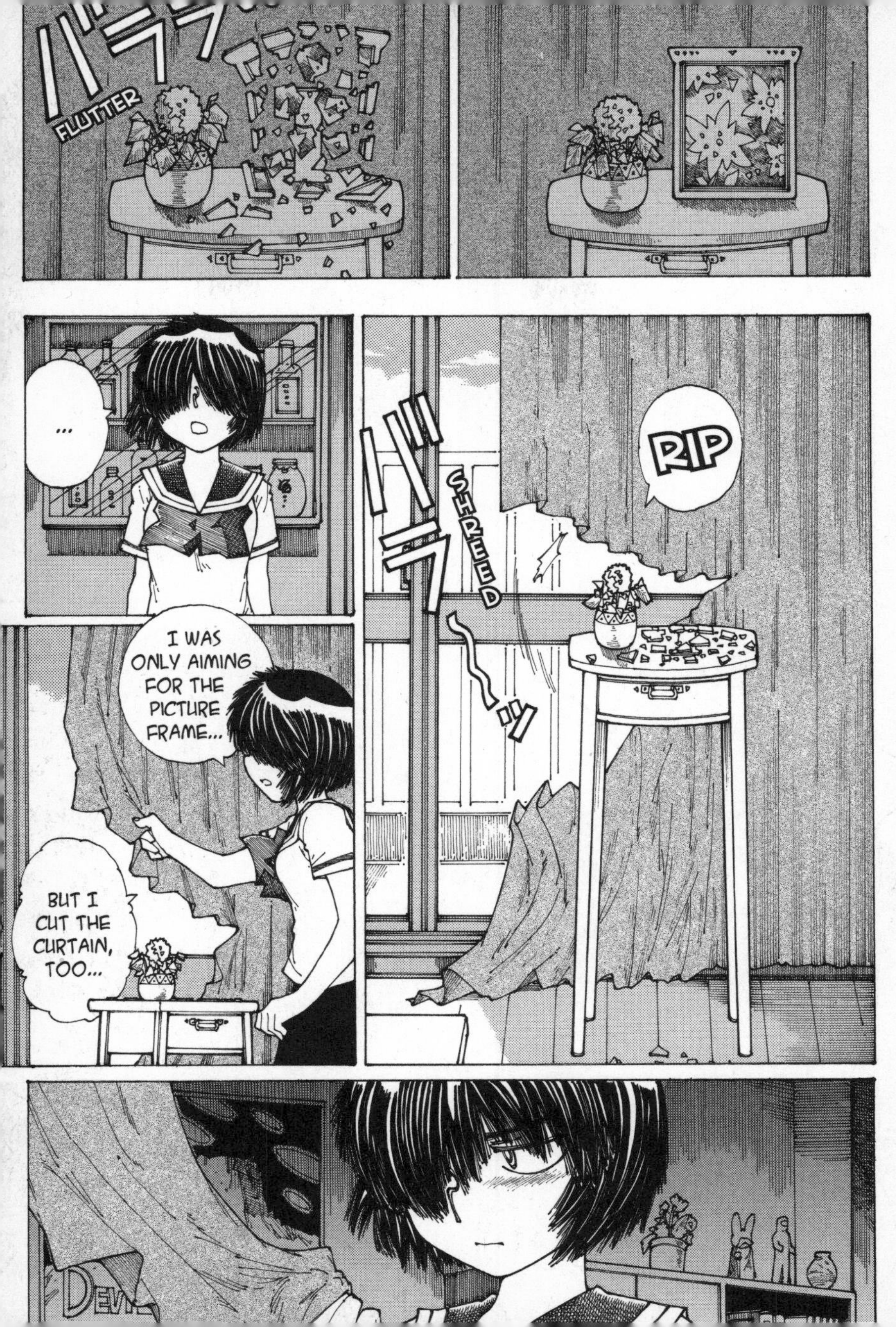
FLUTTER
RIP
SHREED
...
I WAS ONLY AIMING FOR THE PICTURE FRAME...
BUT I CUT THE CURTAIN, TOO...

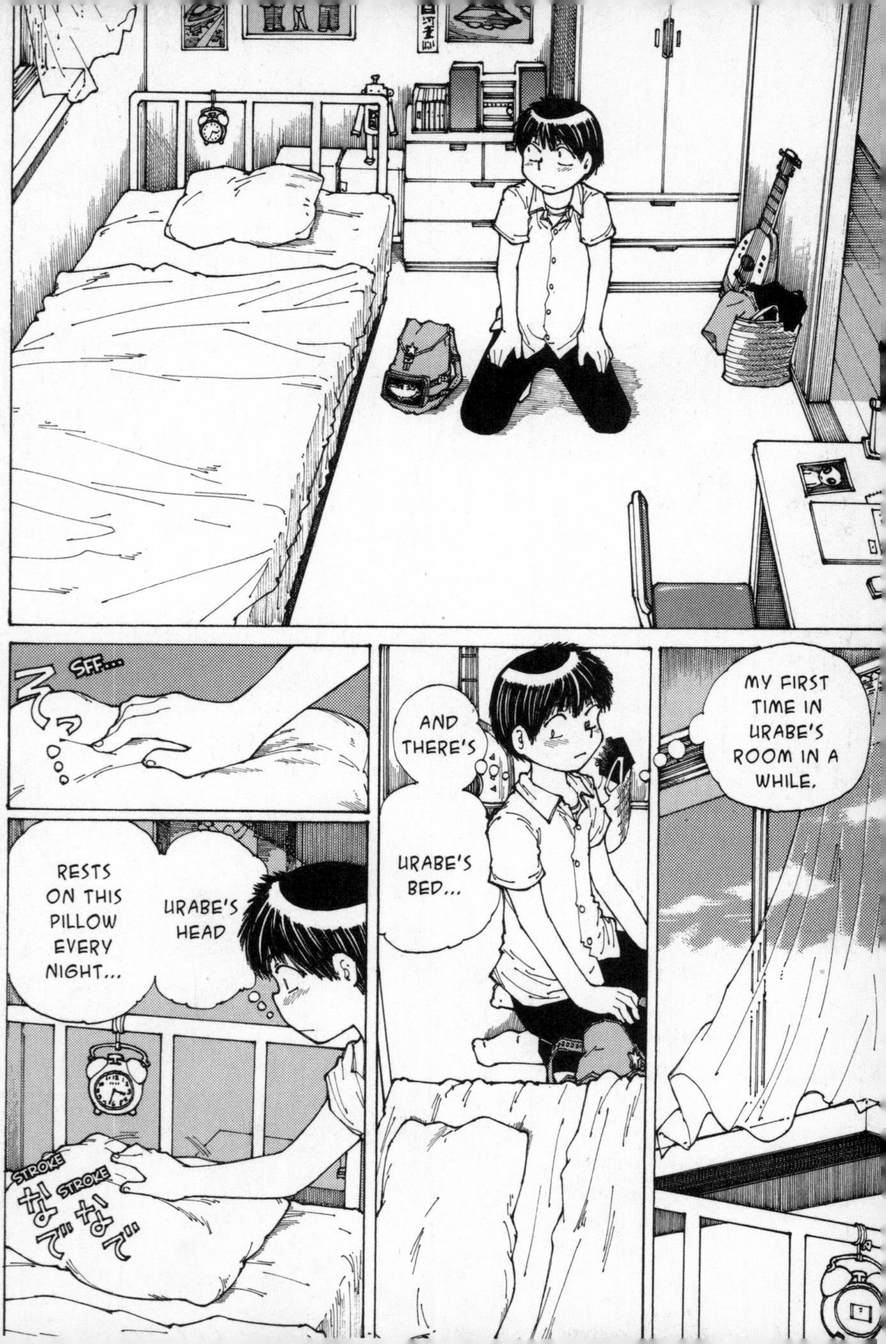
MY FIRST TIME IN URABE'S ROOM IN A WHILE.
AND THERE'S
URABE'S BED...
SFF...
URABE'S HEAD
RESTS ON THIS PILLOW EVERY NIGHT...
STROKE
STROKE
なでなで

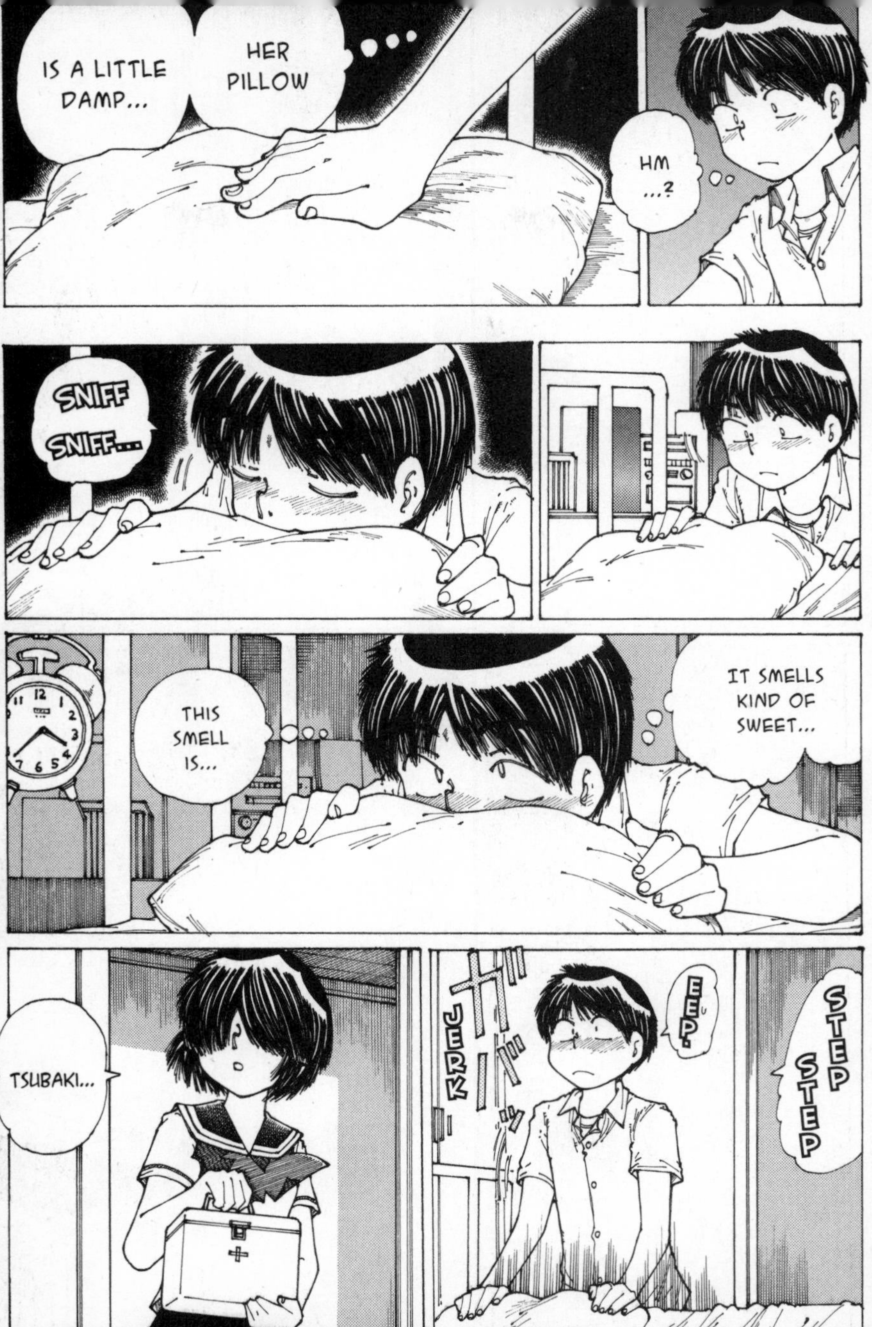
HM ...?
HER PILLOW
IS A LITTLE DAMP...
SNIFF SNIFF...
IT SMELLS KIND OF SWEET...
THIS SMELL IS...
STEP STEP
EEP!
JERK
TSUBAKI...

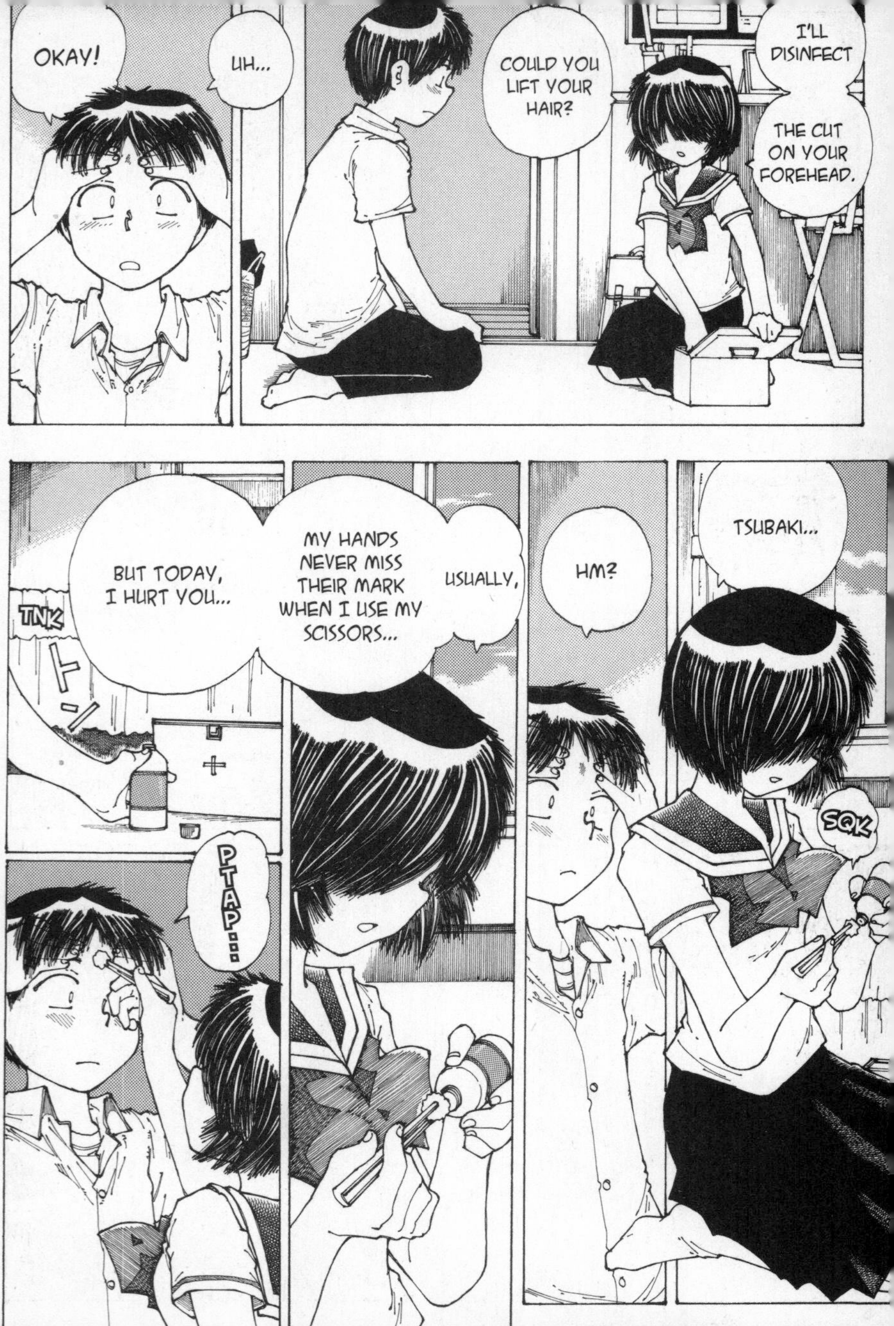
I'LL DISINFECT
THE CUT ON YOUR FOREHEAD.
COULD YOU LIFT YOUR HAIR?
UH...
OKAY!
TSUBAKI...
HM?
SQK
USUALLY,
MY HANDS NEVER MISS THEIR MARK WHEN I USE MY SCISSORS...
BUT TODAY, I HURT YOU...
TNK
PTAP...

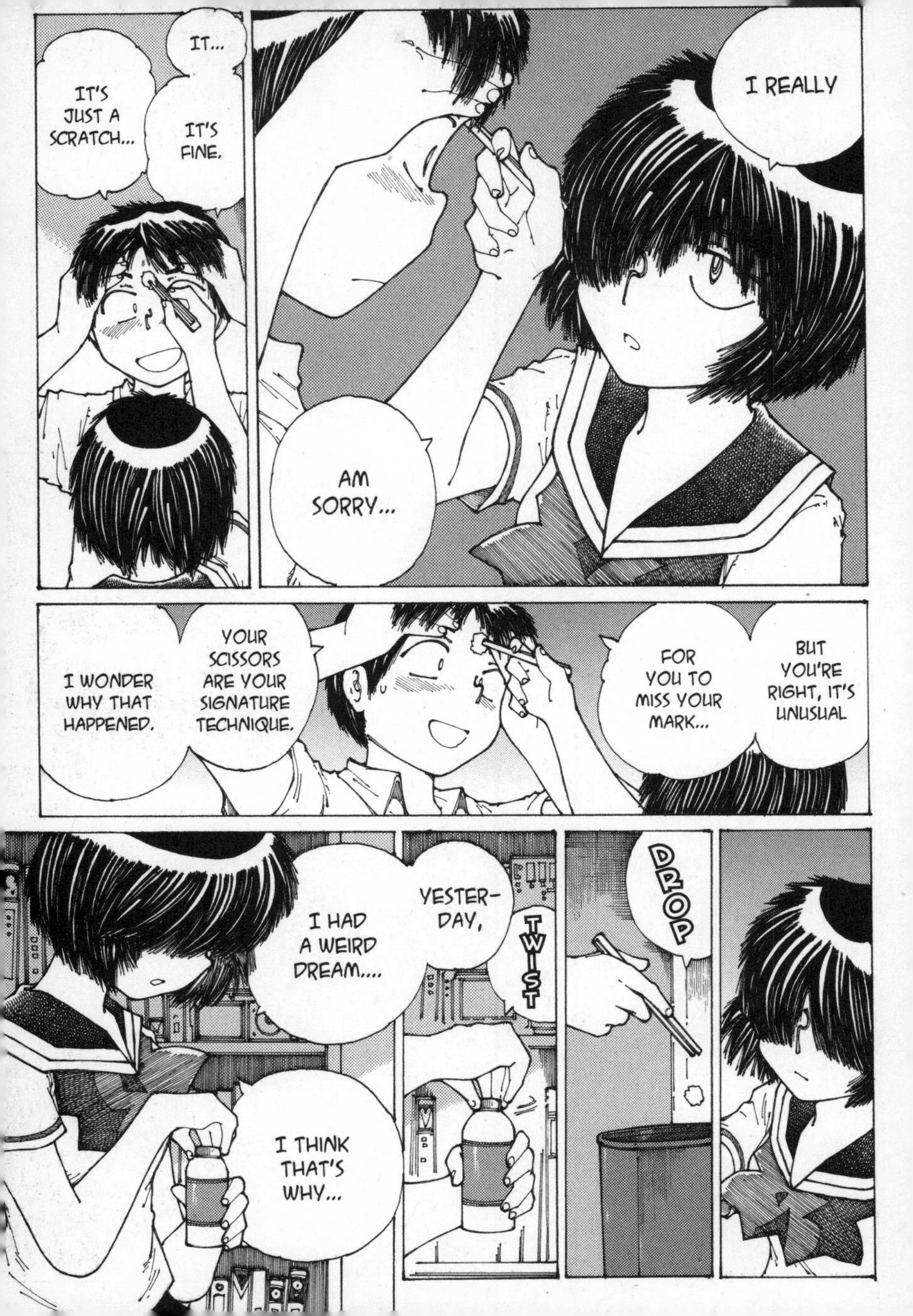
I REALLY
AM SORRY...
IT...
IT'S FINE.
IT'S JUST A SCRATCH...
BUT YOU'RE RIGHT, IT'S UNUSUAL
FOR YOU TO MISS YOUR MARK...
YOUR SCISSORS ARE YOUR SIGNATURE TECHNIQUE.
I WONDER WHY THAT HAPPENED.
DROP
YESTER-DAY,
TWIST
I HAD A WEIRD DREAM....
I THINK THAT'S WHY...

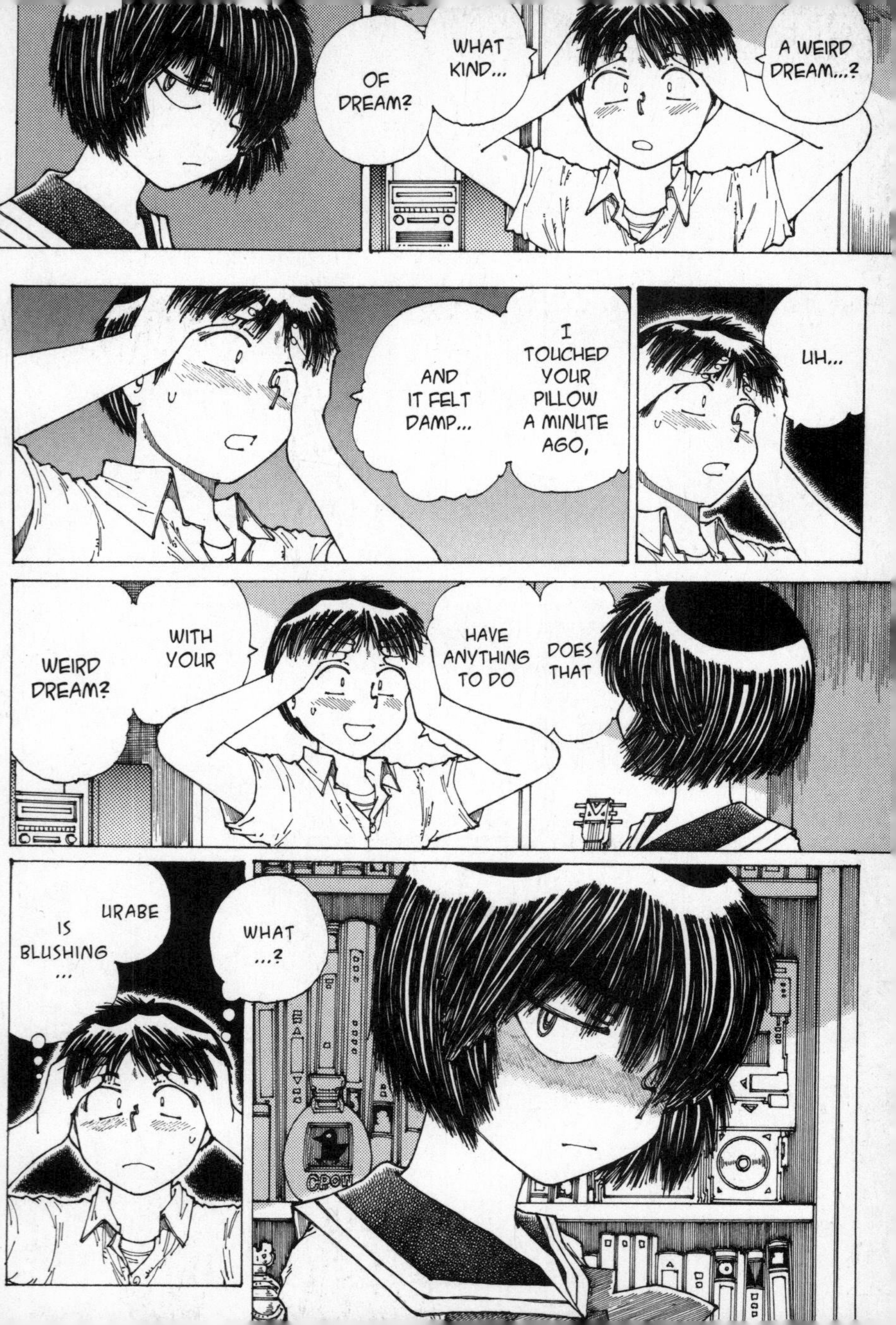
A WEIRD DREAM...?
WHAT KIND... OF DREAM?
UH...
I TOUCHED YOUR PILLOW A MINUTE AGO,
AND IT FELT DAMP...
DOES THAT HAVE ANYTHING TO DO
WITH YOUR WEIRD DREAM?
WHAT ...?
URABE IS BLUSHING ...
CROW

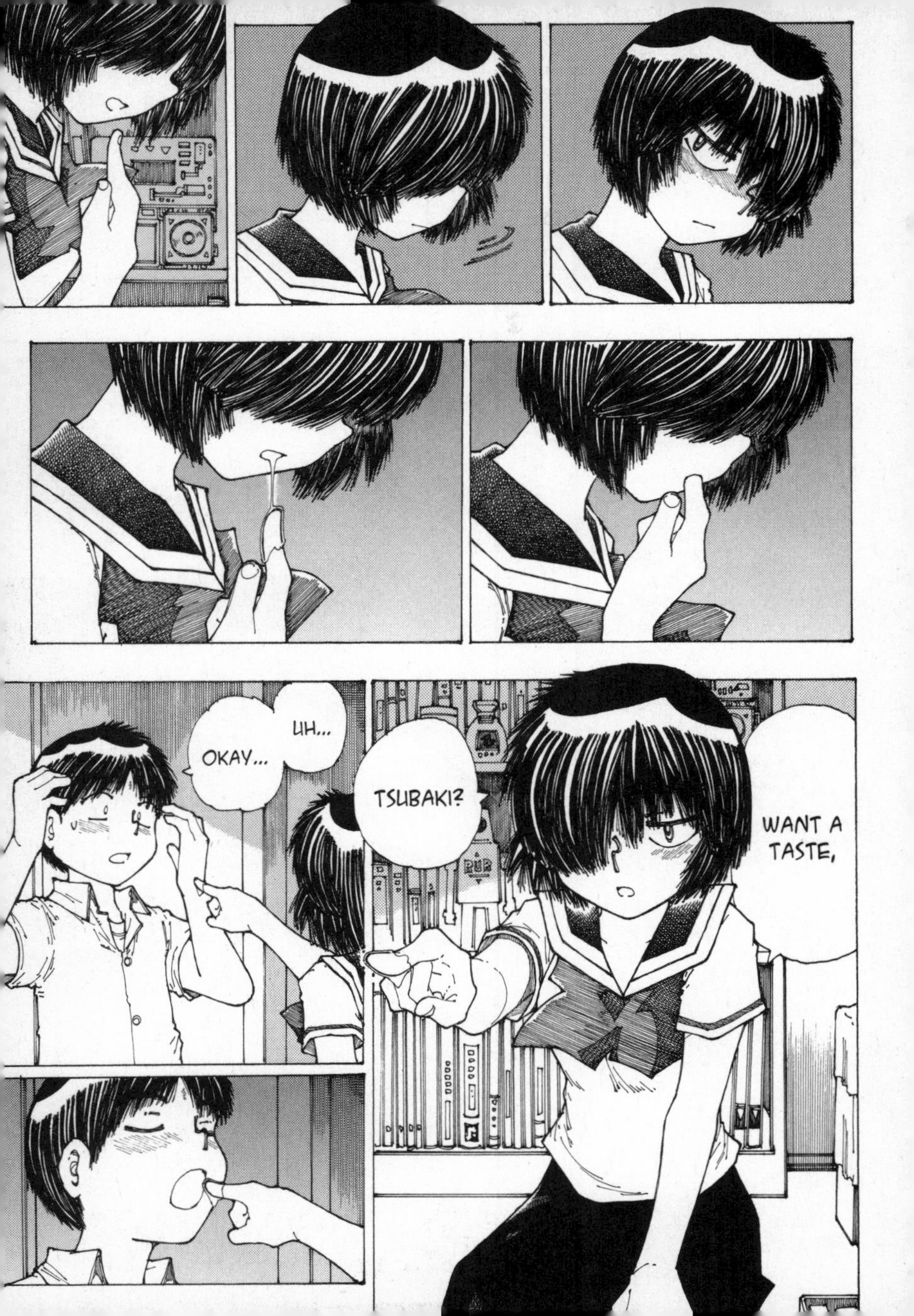
WANT A TASTE,
TSUBAKI?
UH... OKAY...

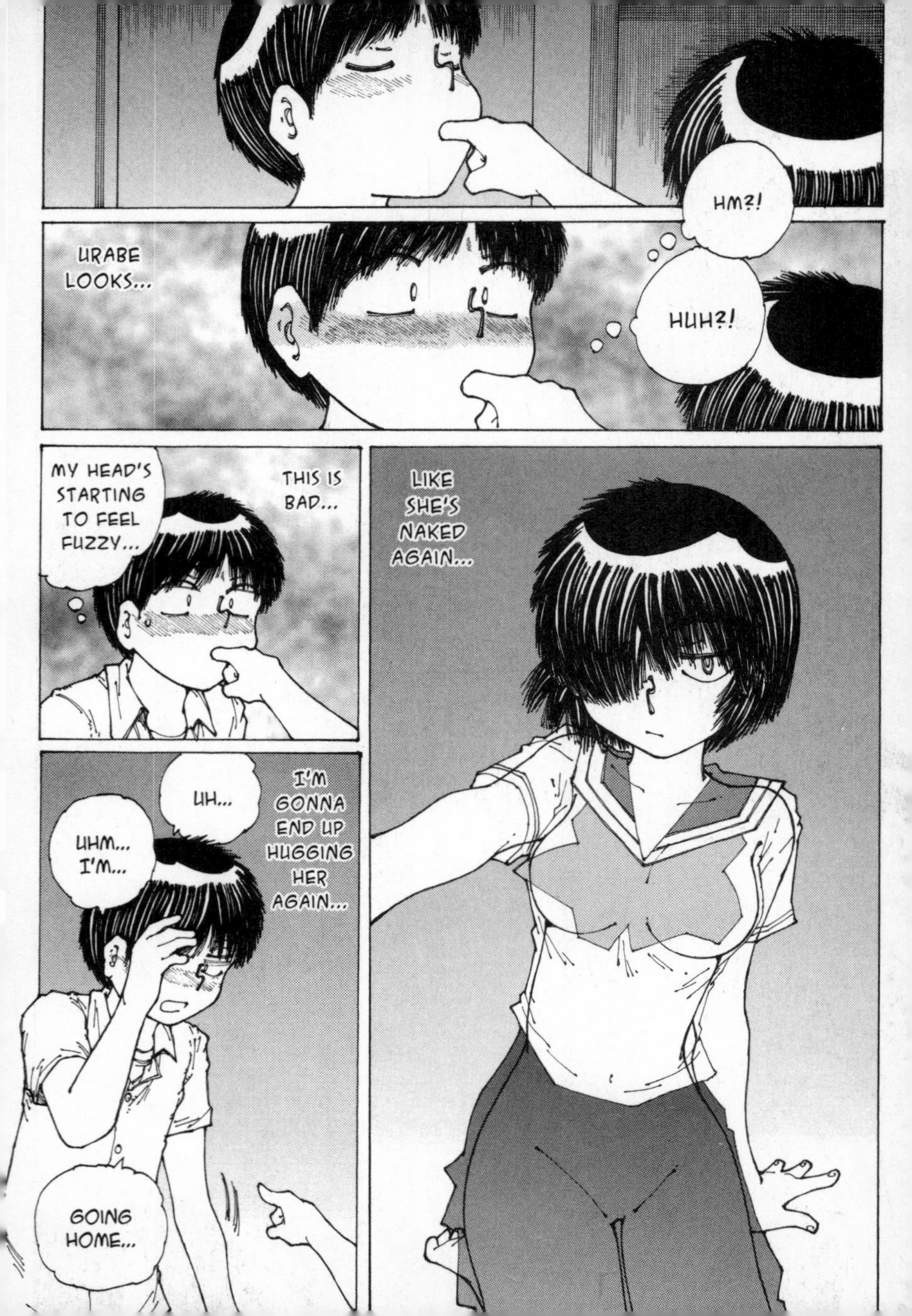
HM?!
HUH?!
URABE LOOKS...
LIKE SHE'S NAKED AGAIN...
THIS IS BAD...
MY HEAD'S STARTING TO FEEL FUZZY...
I'M GONNA END UP HUGGING HER AGAIN...
UH...
UHM... I'M...
GOING HOME...

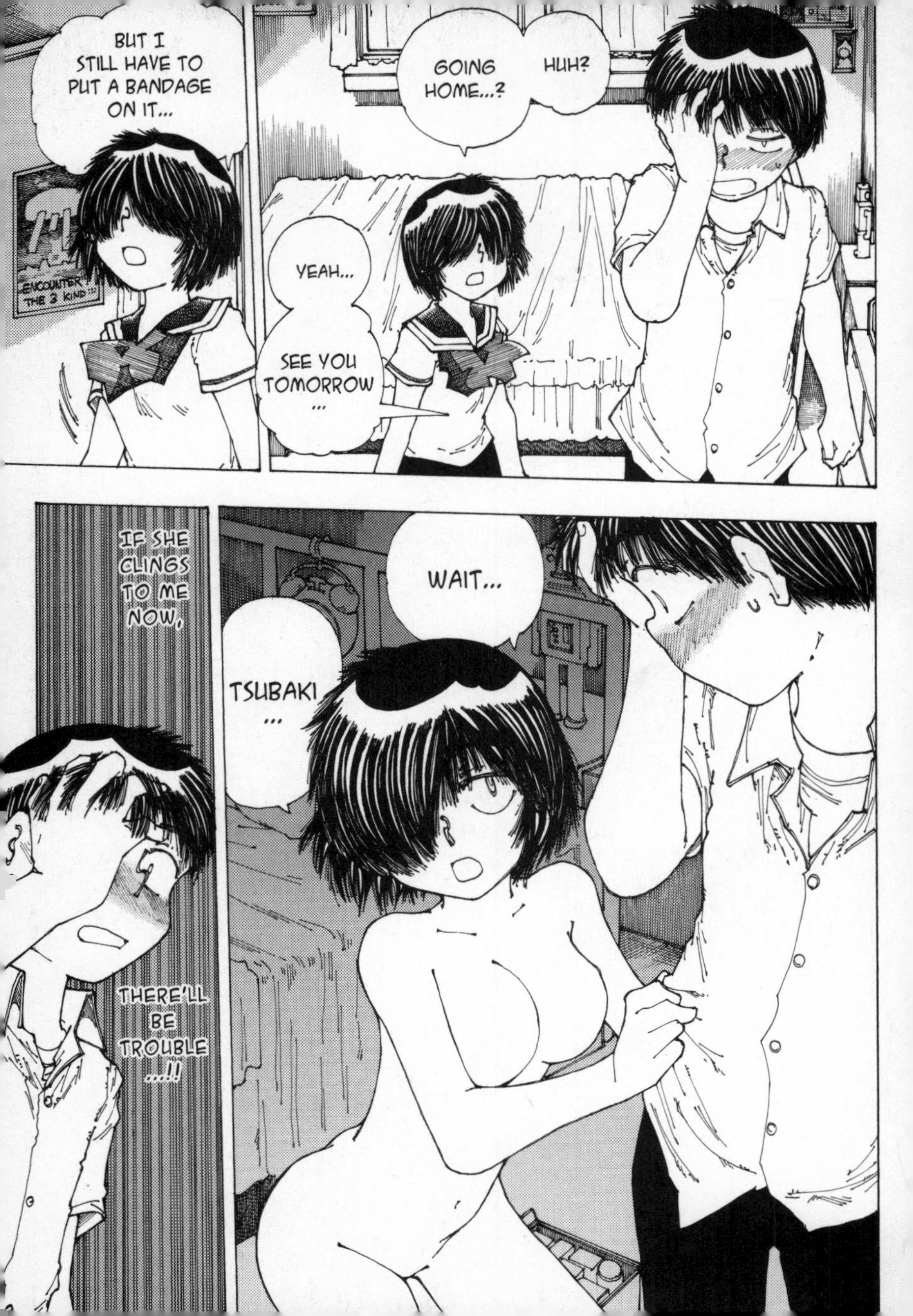
HUH?
GOING HOME...?
YEAH...
SEE YOU TOMORROW ...
BUT I STILL HAVE TO PUT A BANDAGE ON IT...
ENCOUNTER THE 3 KIND
WAIT...
TSUBAKI ...
IF SHE CLINGS TO ME NOW,
THERE'LL BE TROUBLE ...!!

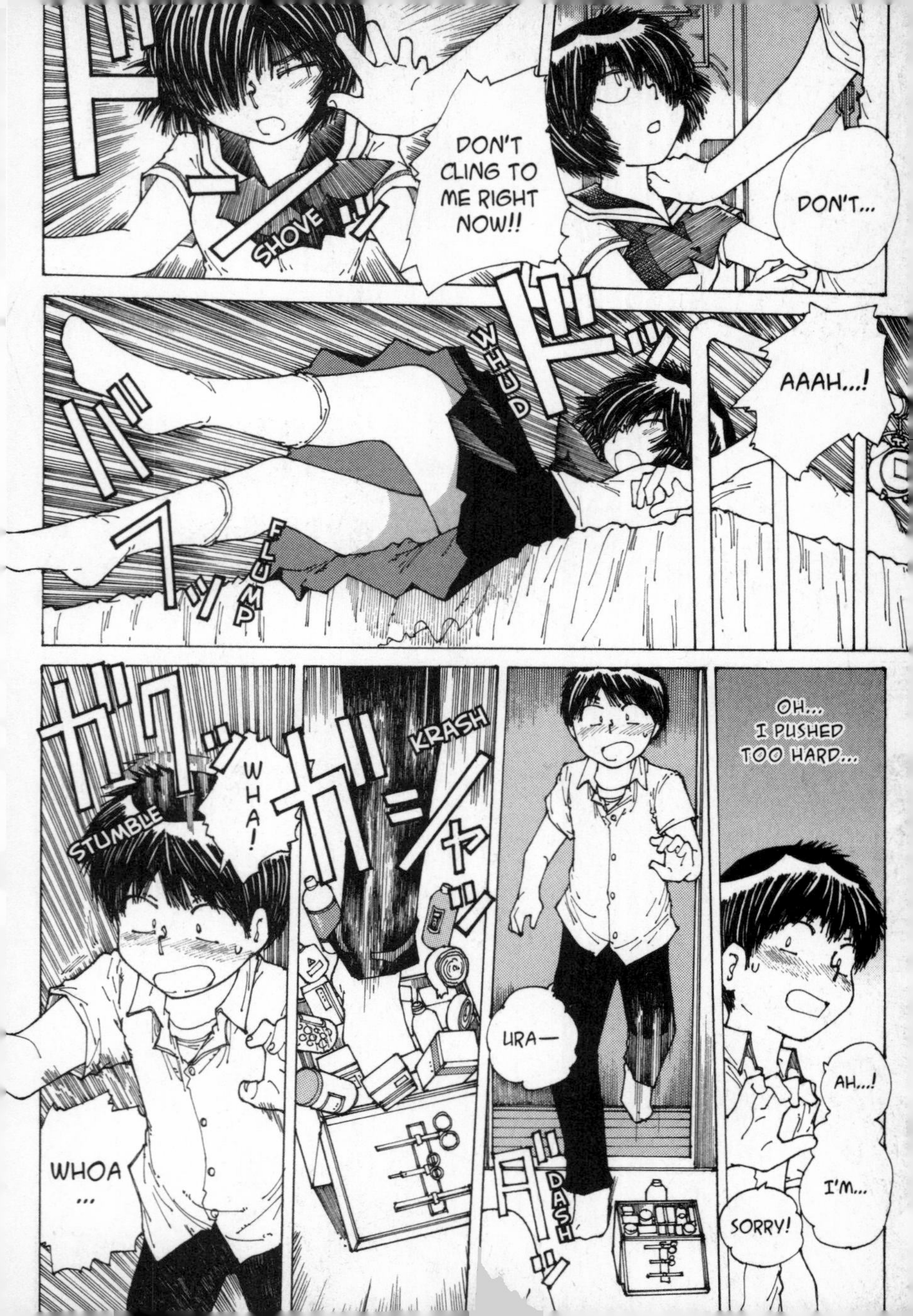
DON'T...
DON'T CLING TO ME RIGHT NOW!!
SHOVE
AAAH...!
WHUD
FLUMP
OH... I PUSHED TOO HARD...
AH...!
I'M...
SORRY!
URA—
DASH
KRASH
STUMBLE
WHA!
WHOA...

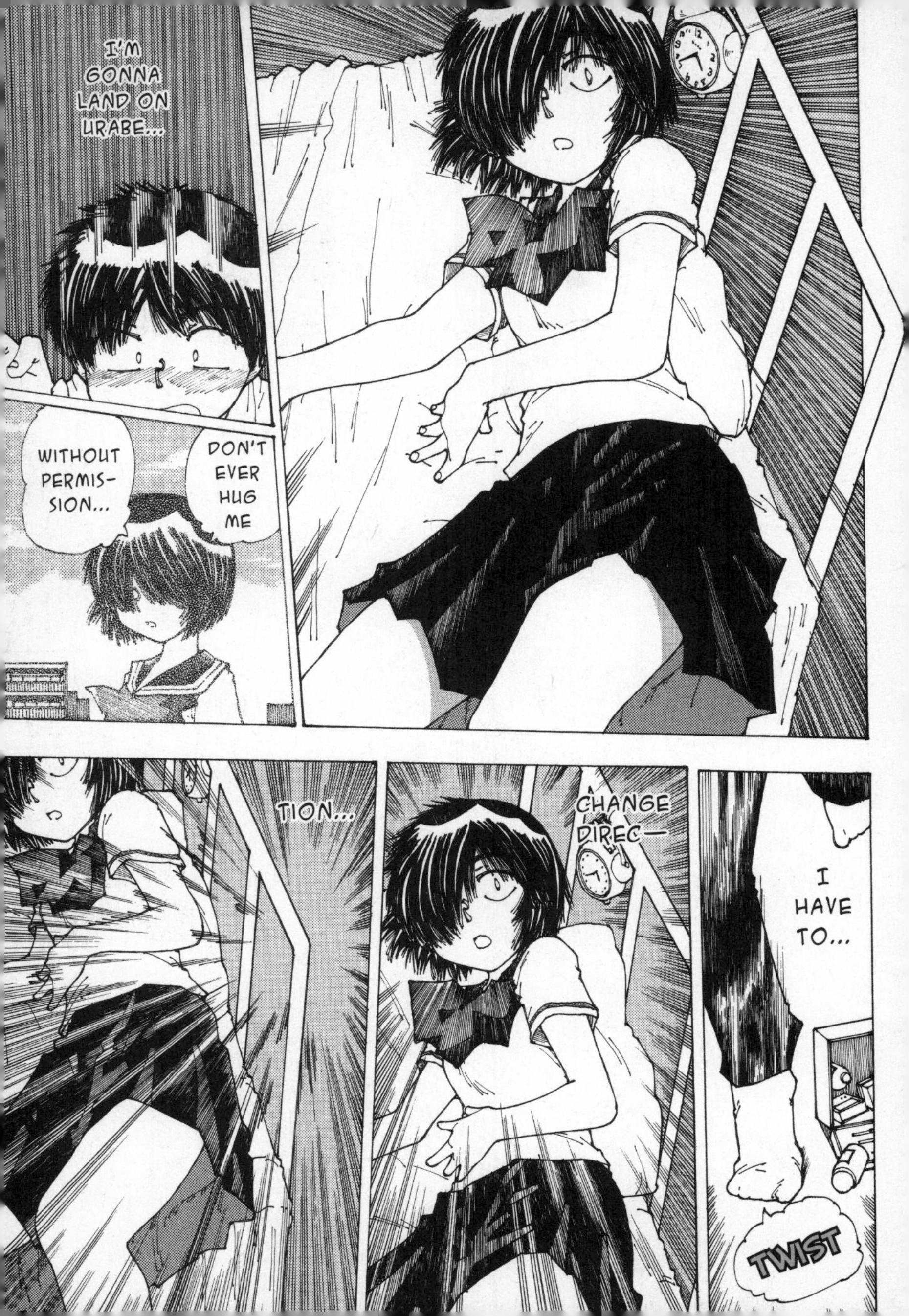
I'M GONNA LAND ON URABE...
DON'T EVER HUG ME
WITHOUT PERMIS-SION...
I HAVE TO...
TWIST
CHANGE DIREC—
TION...

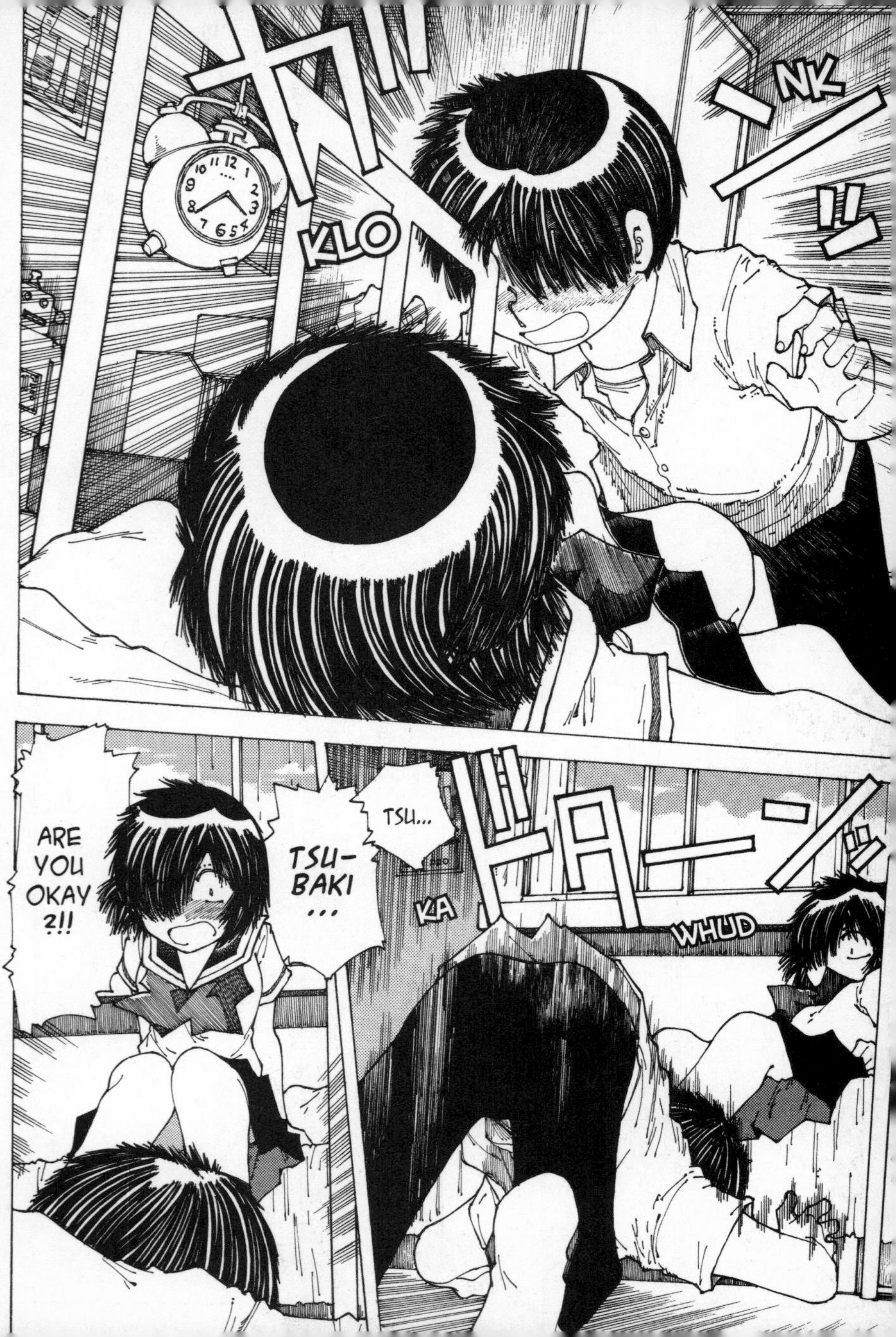

NK
KLO
WHUD
KA
TSU...
TSU-BAKI...
ARE YOU OKAY?!!

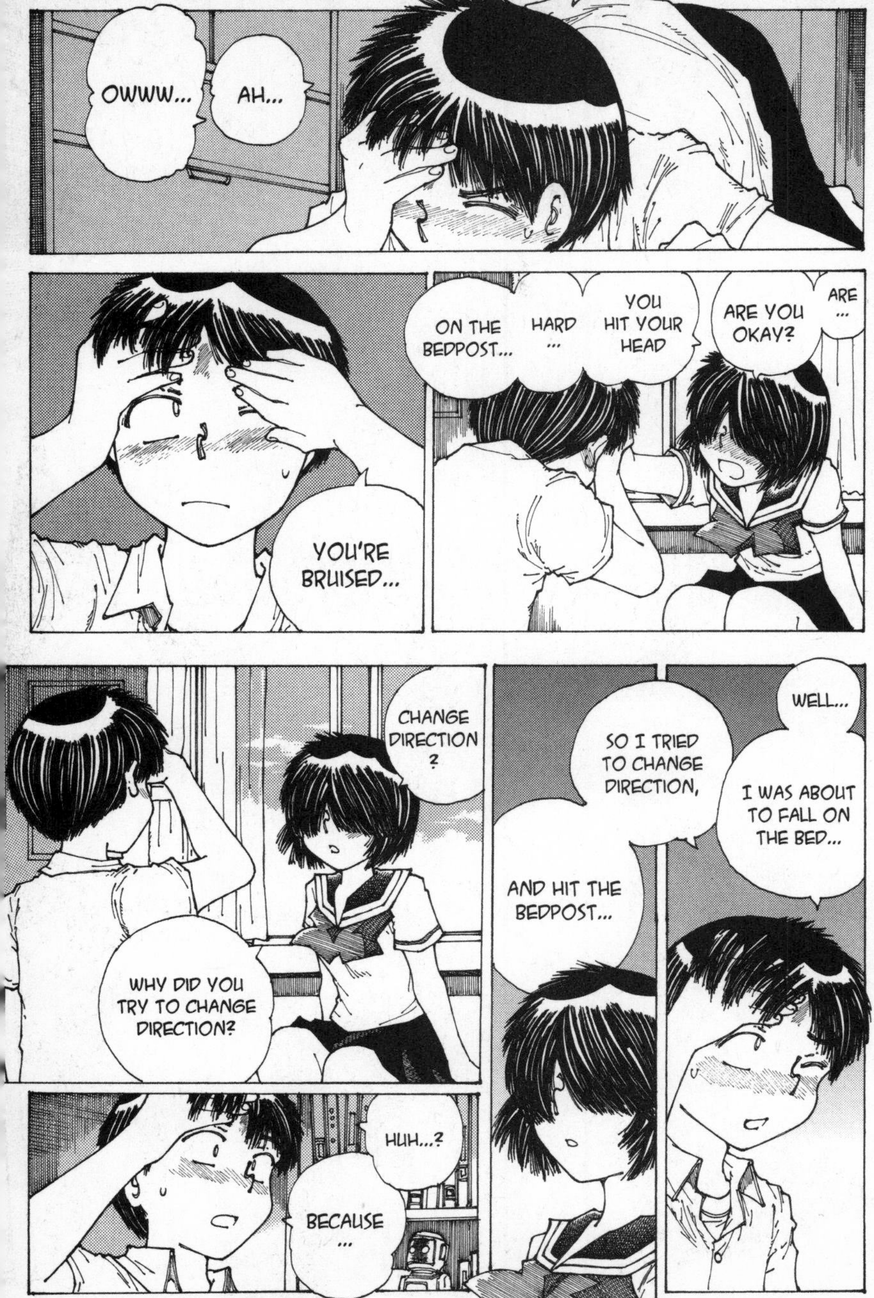
AH...
OWWW...
ARE ...
ARE YOU OKAY?
YOU HIT YOUR HEAD
HARD ...
ON THE BEDPOST...
YOU'RE BRUISED...
WELL...
I WAS ABOUT TO FALL ON THE BED...
SO I TRIED TO CHANGE DIRECTION,
AND HIT THE BEDPOST...
CHANGE DIRECTION ?
WHY DID YOU TRY TO CHANGE DIRECTION?
HUH...?
BECAUSE ...

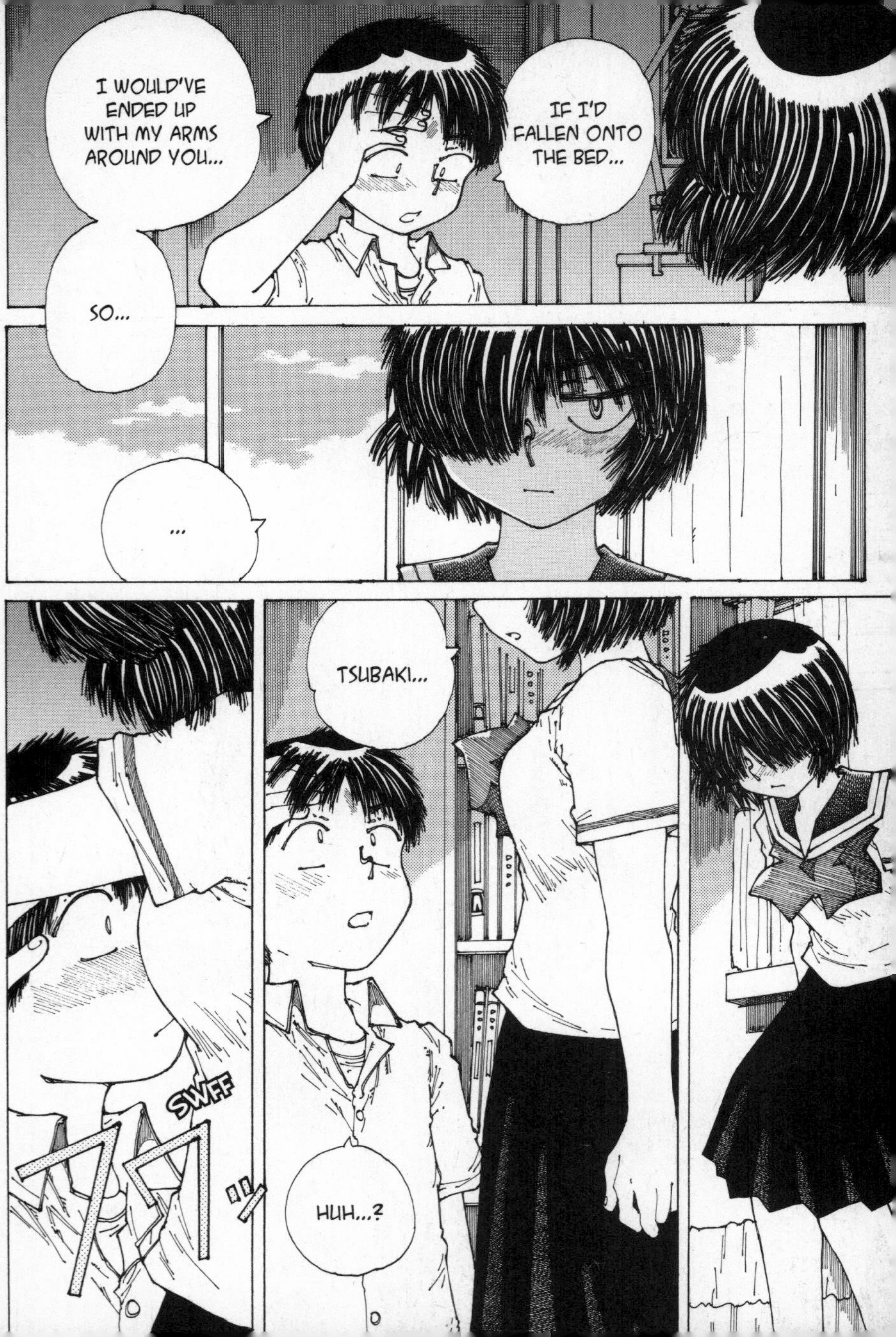
IF I'D FALLEN ONTO THE BED...
I WOULD'VE ENDED UP WITH MY ARMS AROUND YOU...
SO...
...
TSUBAKI...
HUH...?
SWFF

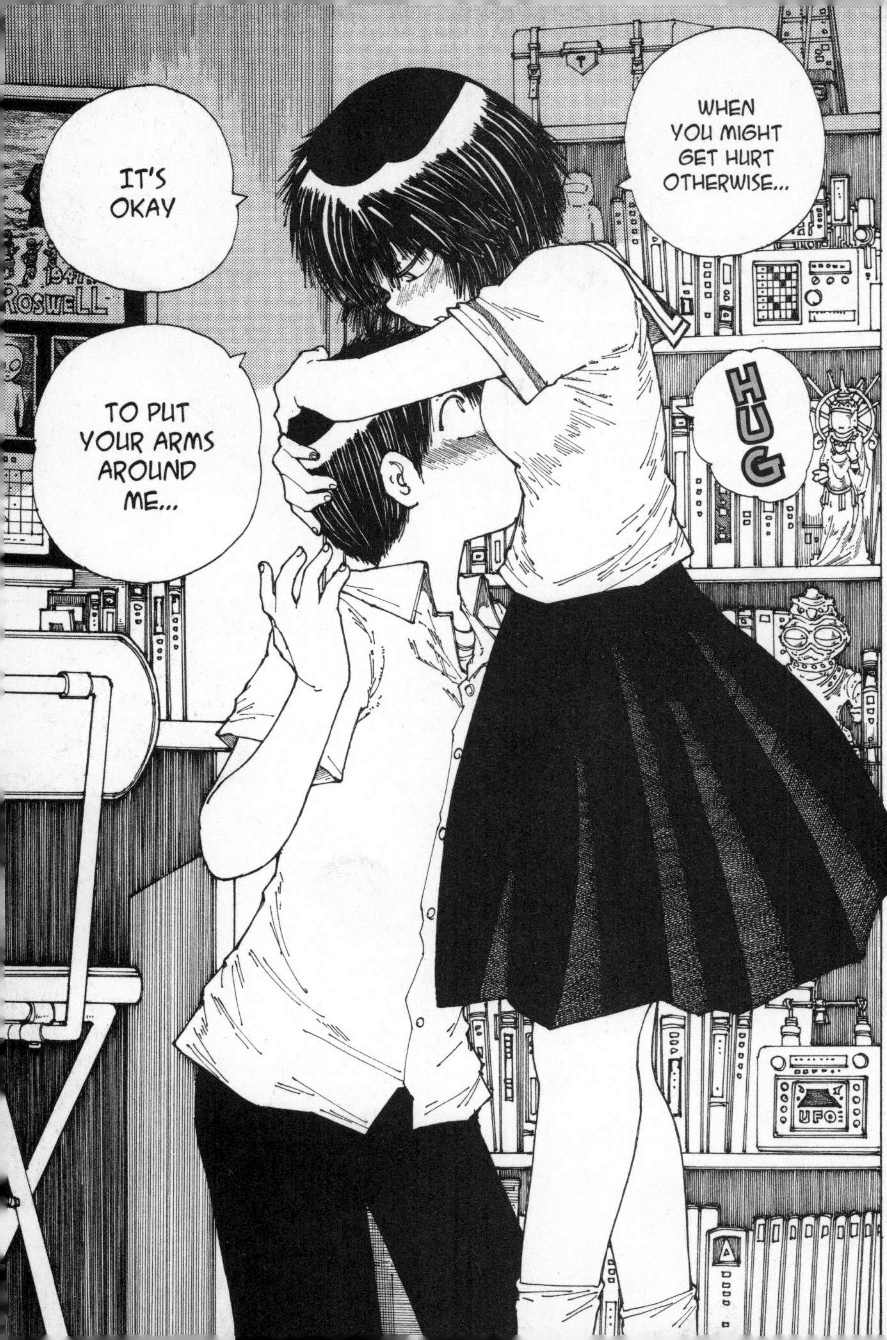
WHEN YOU MIGHT GET HURT OTHERWISE...
HUG
IT'S OKAY
ROSWELL
TO PUT YOUR ARMS AROUND ME...
UFO

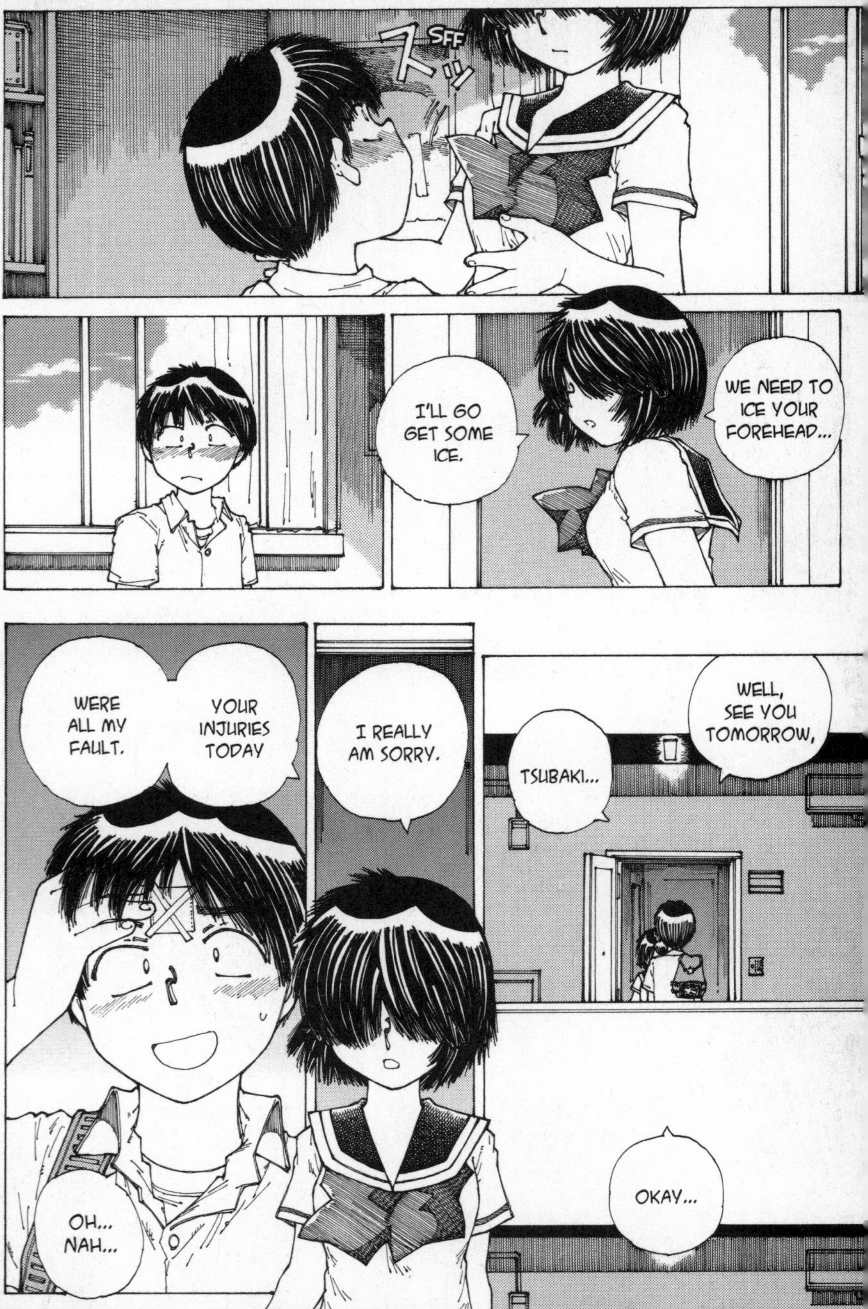
SFF
WE NEED TO ICE YOUR FOREHEAD...
I'LL GO GET SOME ICE.
WELL, SEE YOU TOMORROW,
TSUBAKI...
OKAY...
I REALLY AM SORRY.
YOUR INJURIES TODAY
WERE ALL MY FAULT.
OH... NAH...

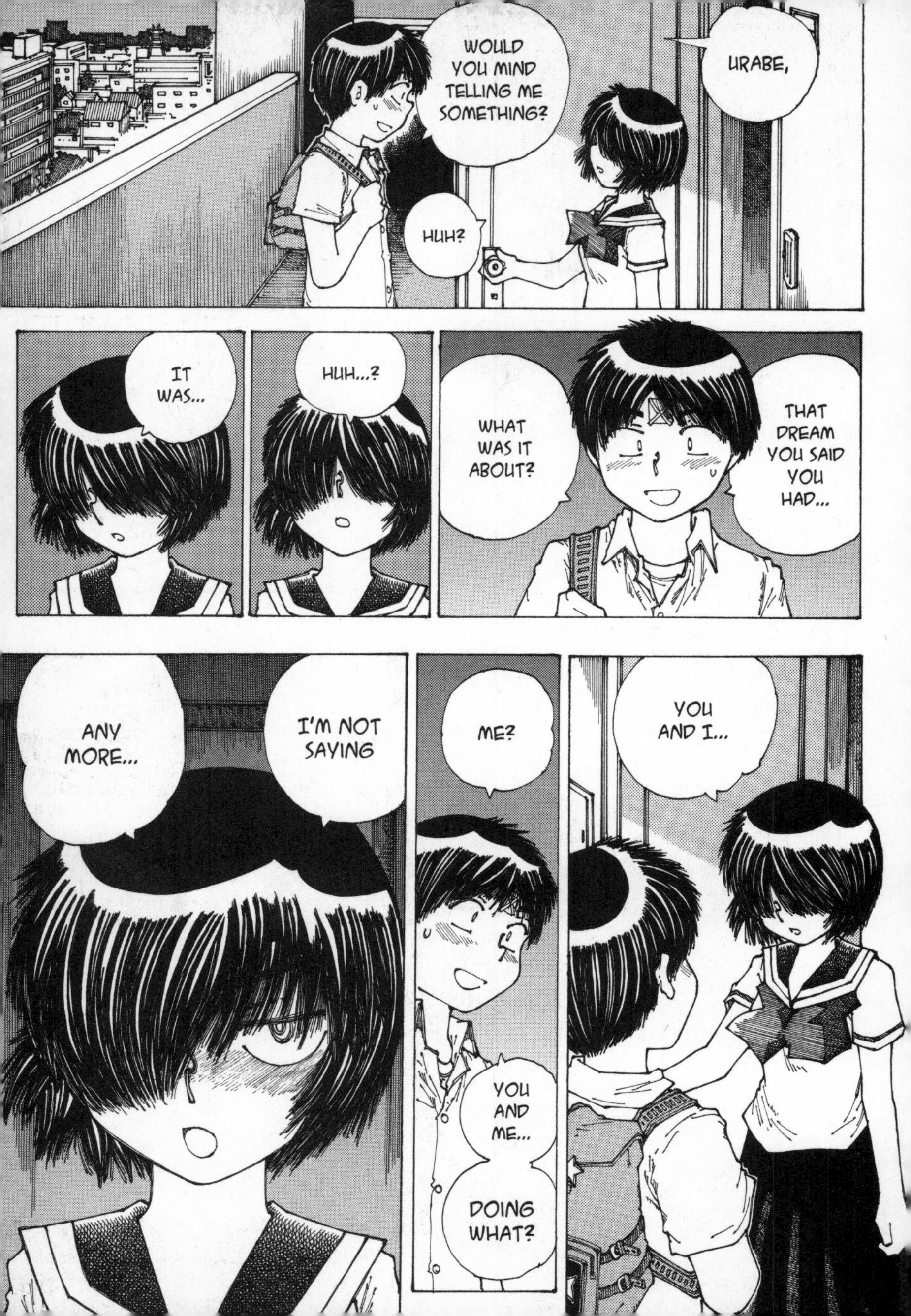
URABE,
WOULD YOU MIND TELLING ME SOMETHING?
HUH?
THAT DREAM YOU SAID YOU HAD...
WHAT WAS IT ABOUT?
HUH...?
IT WAS...
YOU AND I...
ME?
YOU AND ME...
DOING WHAT?
I'M NOT SAYING
ANY MORE...

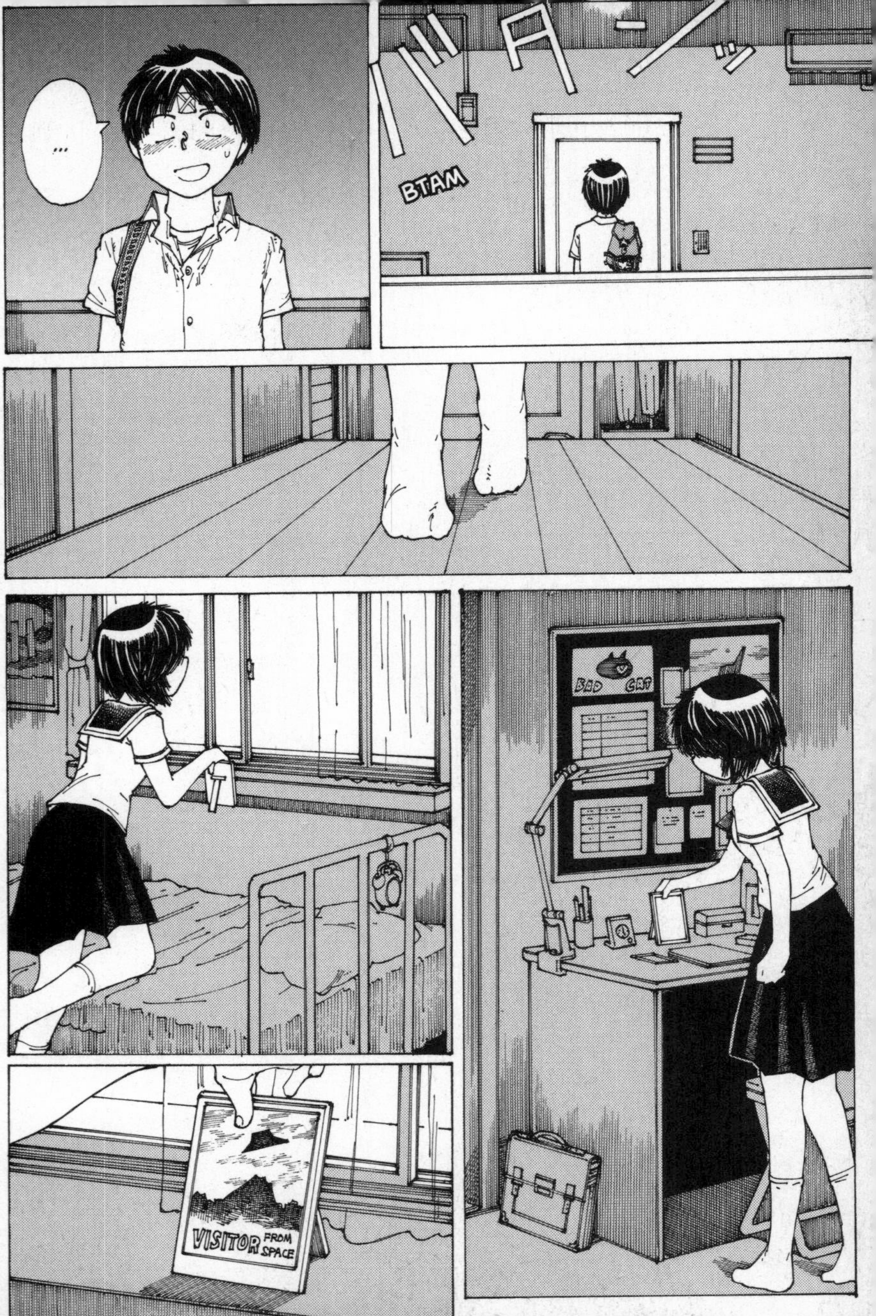
BTAM
...
BAD CAT
VISITOR FROM SPACE

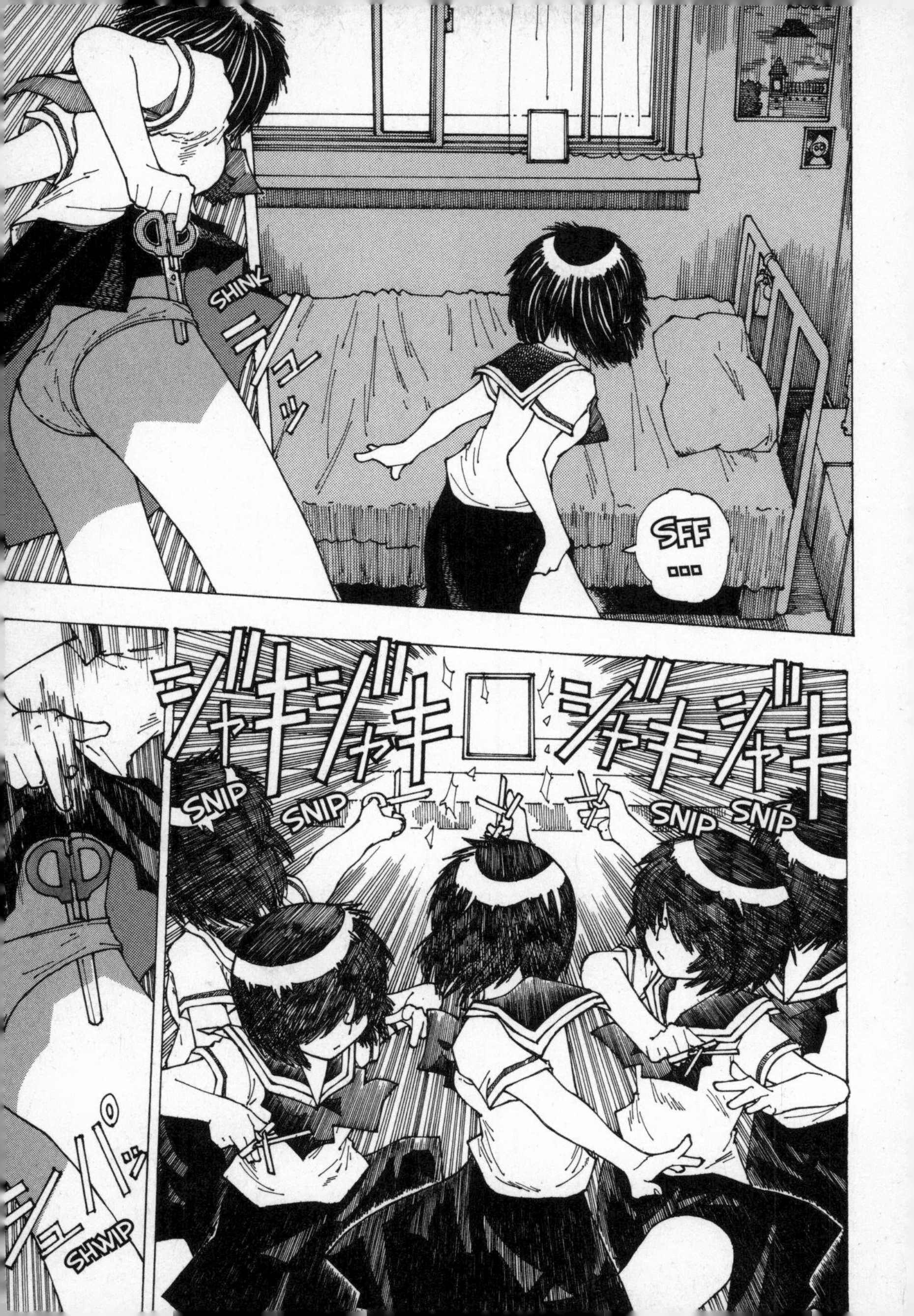
SFF ...
SHINK
シュッ
ジャキジャキ
ジャキジャキ
SNIP SNIP
SNIP SNIP
シュパッ
SHWIP

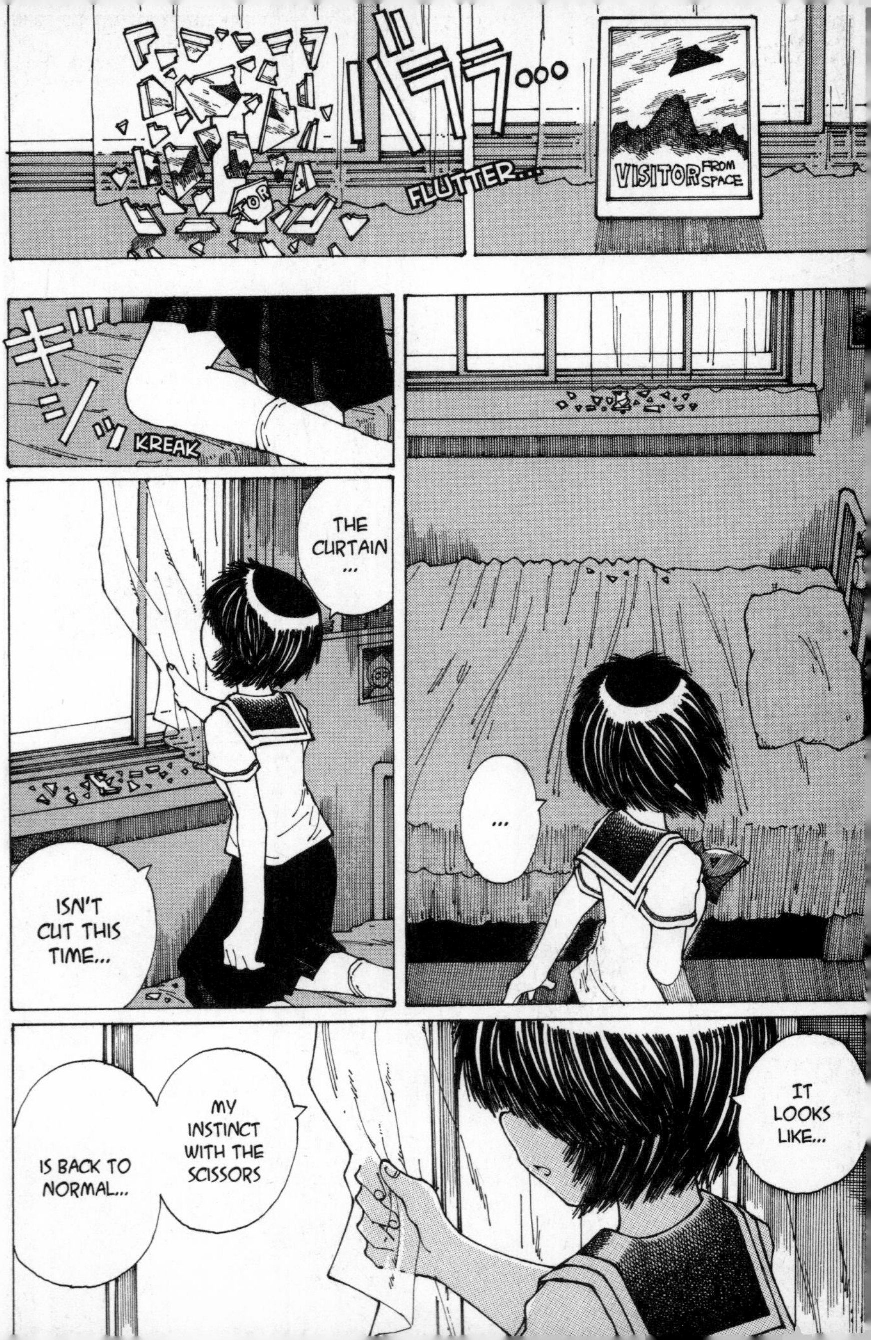
VISITOR FROM SPACE
バララ…
FLUTTER...
...
ギシッ
KREAK
THE CURTAIN ...
ISN'T CUT THIS TIME...
IT LOOKS LIKE...
MY INSTINCT WITH THE SCISSORS
IS BACK TO NORMAL...

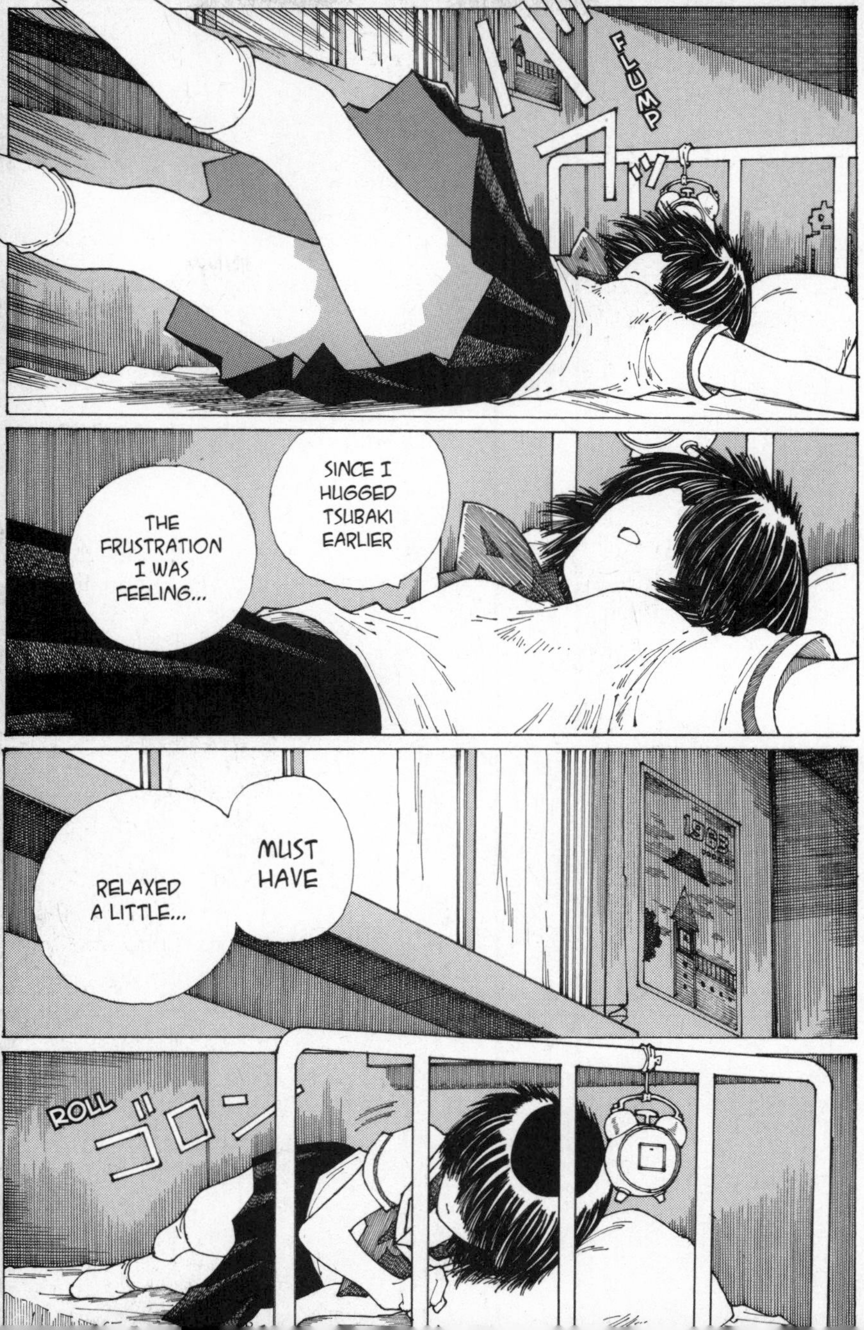
FLUMP
SINCE I HUGGED TSUBAKI EARLIER
THE FRUSTRATION I WAS FEELING...
MUST HAVE
RELAXED A LITTLE...
ROLL
ゴロー

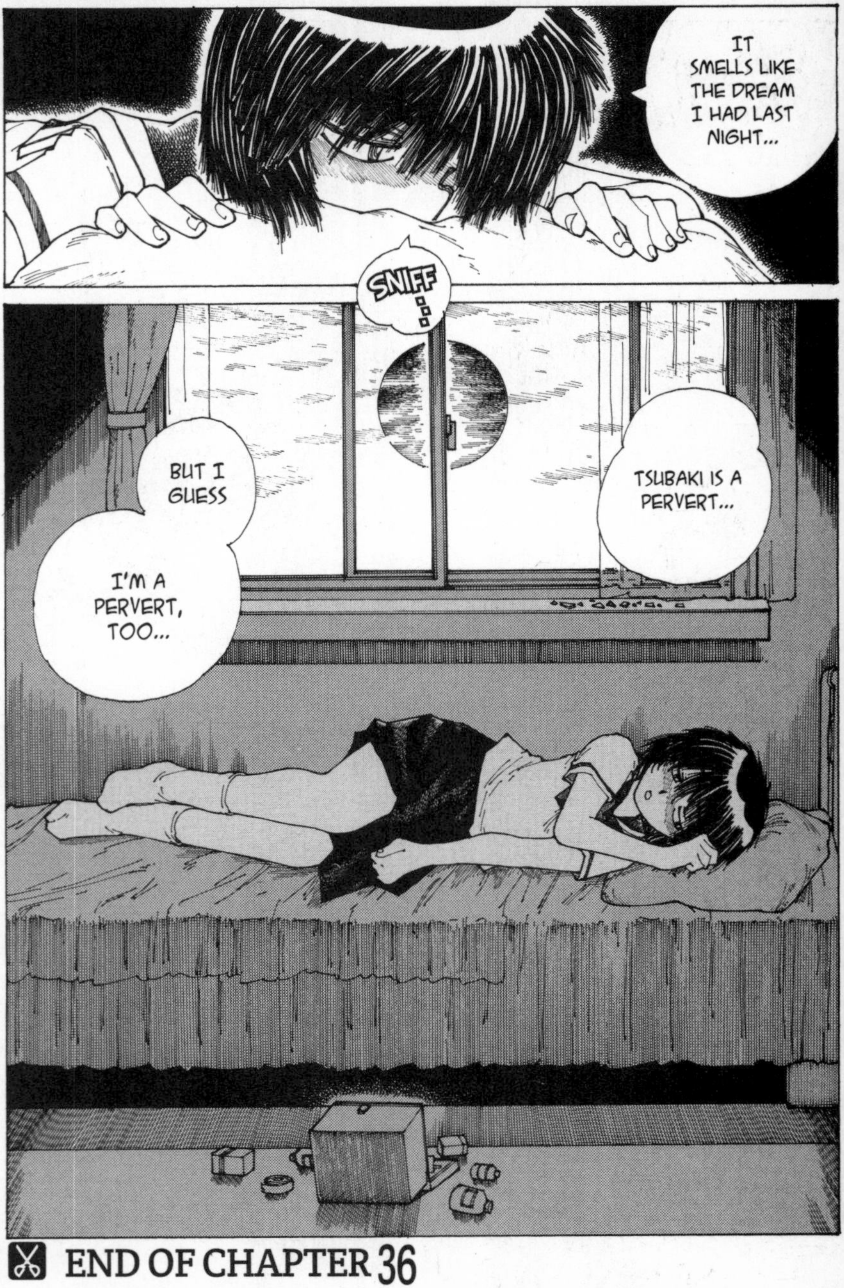
IT SMELLS LIKE THE DREAM I HAD LAST NIGHT...
SNIFF...
TSUBAKI IS A PERVERT...
BUT I GUESS
I'M A PERVERT, TOO...

END OF CHAPTER 36

"X" VOLUME 3 IS NOW ON SALE!!

IT'S ALL THANKS TO THE READERS♡

SO, LOOKING OVER VOLUME 3, THE PART THAT STANDS OUT TO ME IS OKA'S **SEXUAL HARASSMENT (?) SCENE.**

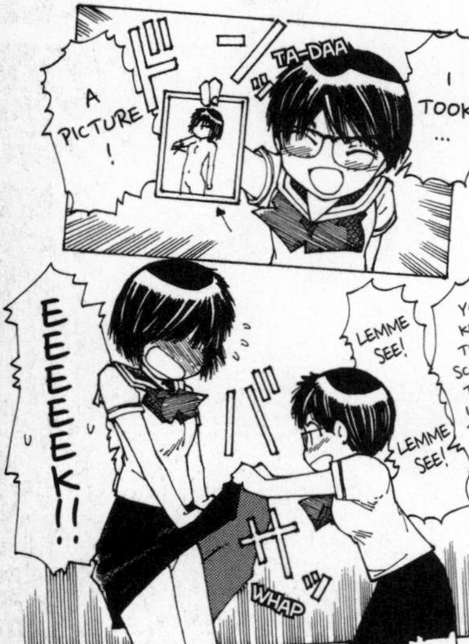
TA-DAA
I TOOK ...
A PICTURE !
YOU KEEP THOSE SCISSORS TUCKED IN YOUR PANTIES ?!
LEMME SEE!
LEMME SEE!
EEEEEEK!!
WHAP

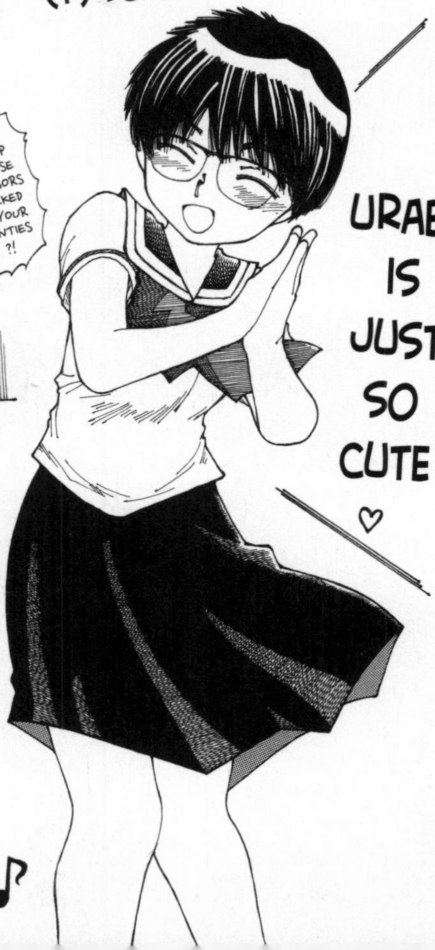

URABE IS JUST SO CUTE♡

LATELY, FROM THE LOOKS SHE GIVES URABE, IT SEEMS LIKE OKA IS TURNING INTO A **"DIRTY OLD MAN"** CHARACTER... SO ON THAT NOTE, HERE'S A BONUS COMIC **EXCLUSIVE TO THIS VOLUME** ILLUSTRATING A DAY IN THE LIFE OF OKA AND URABE, **CHAPTER 36.5!**

STARTING ON THE NEXT PAGE ♪

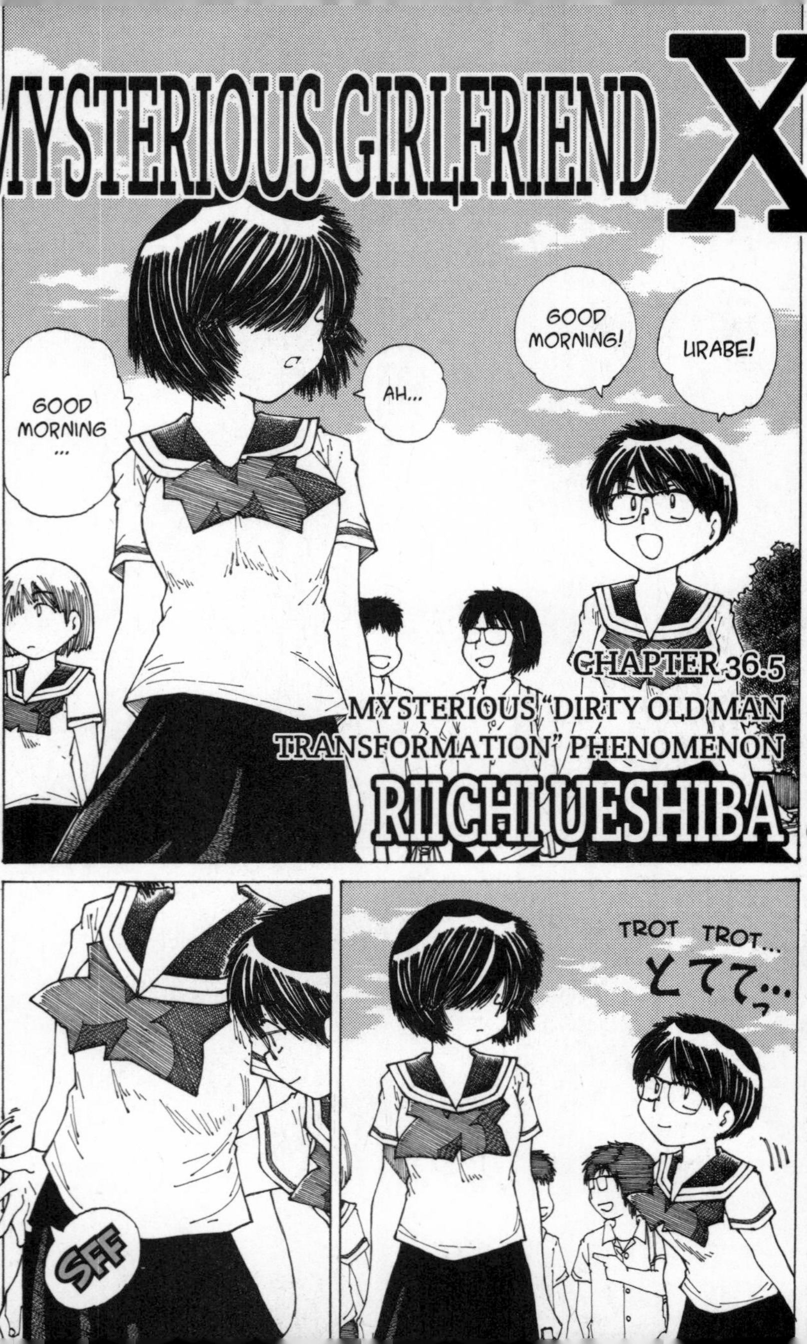

MYSTERIOUS GIRLFRIEND X
URABE!
GOOD MORNING!
AH...
GOOD MORNING ...
CHAPTER 36.5
MYSTERIOUS "DIRTY OLD MAN TRANSFORMATION" PHENOMENON
RIICHI UESHIBA
TROT TROT...
とてて…
SFF

They're good friends now. But nothing should ever be taken too far!!

The Latest from the Author

Riichi Ueshiba

WHEN I CREATE A STORY, FIRST A SINGLE SCENE COMES TO MY MIND, AND I DEVELOP THE REST FROM THERE. IN THE CASE OF "MYSTERIOUS GIRLFRIEND X," THE FIRST SCENE THAT CAME TO MY MIND WAS: "IN A CLASSROOM AT SUNSET, A BOY LICKS THE DROOL LEFT ON THE DESK OF A GIRL WHO FELL ASLEEP IN HER SEAT." (CONTINUED...)

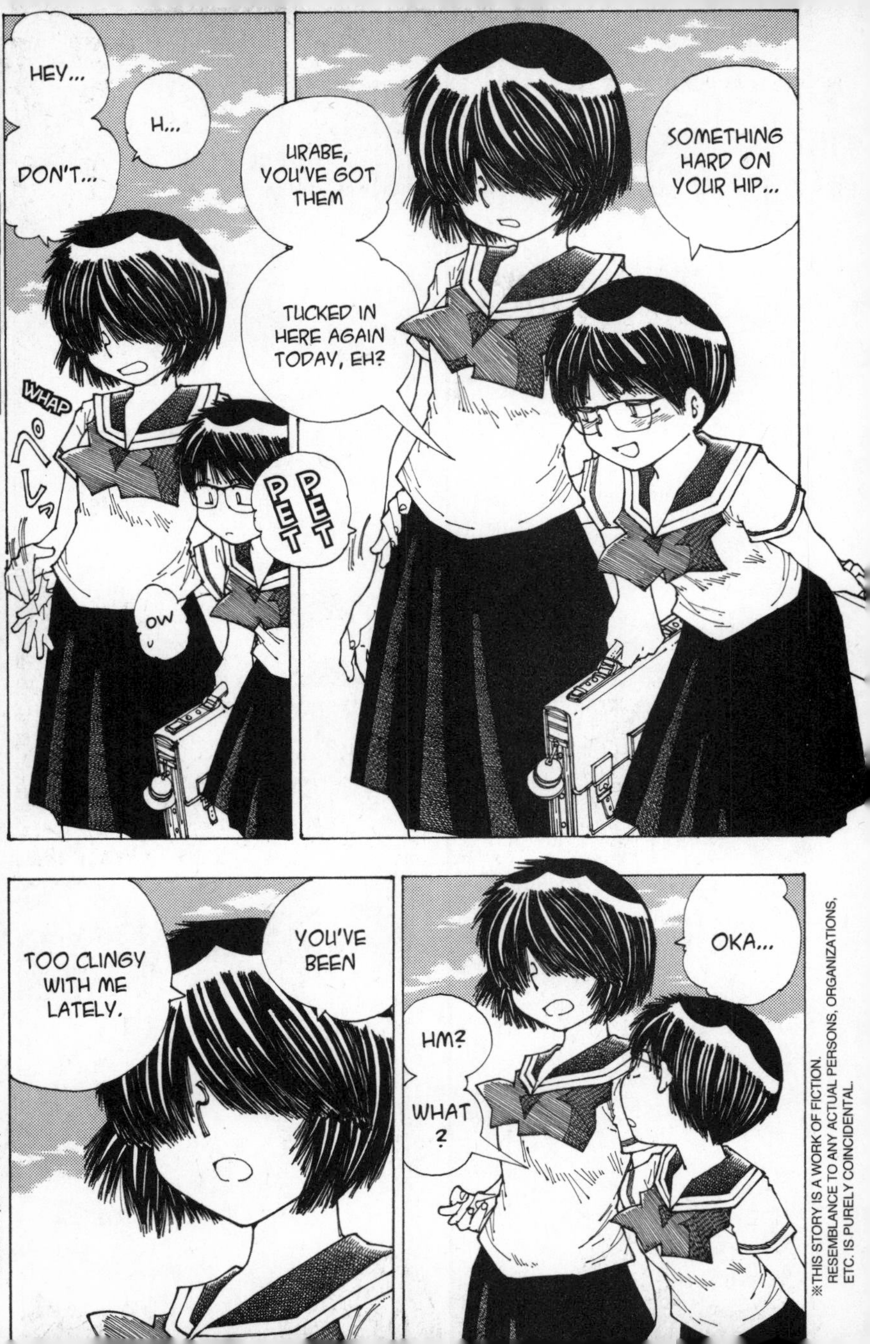
SOMETHING HARD ON YOUR HIP...
URABE, YOU'VE GOT THEM
TUCKED IN HERE AGAIN TODAY, EH?
HEY...
H...
DON'T...
WHAP
PET PET
OW
OKA...
HM?
WHAT?
YOU'VE BEEN
TOO CLINGY WITH ME LATELY.

※THIS STORY IS A WORK OF FICTION. RESEMBLANCE TO ANY ACTUAL PERSONS, ORGANIZATIONS, ETC. IS PURELY COINCIDENTAL.

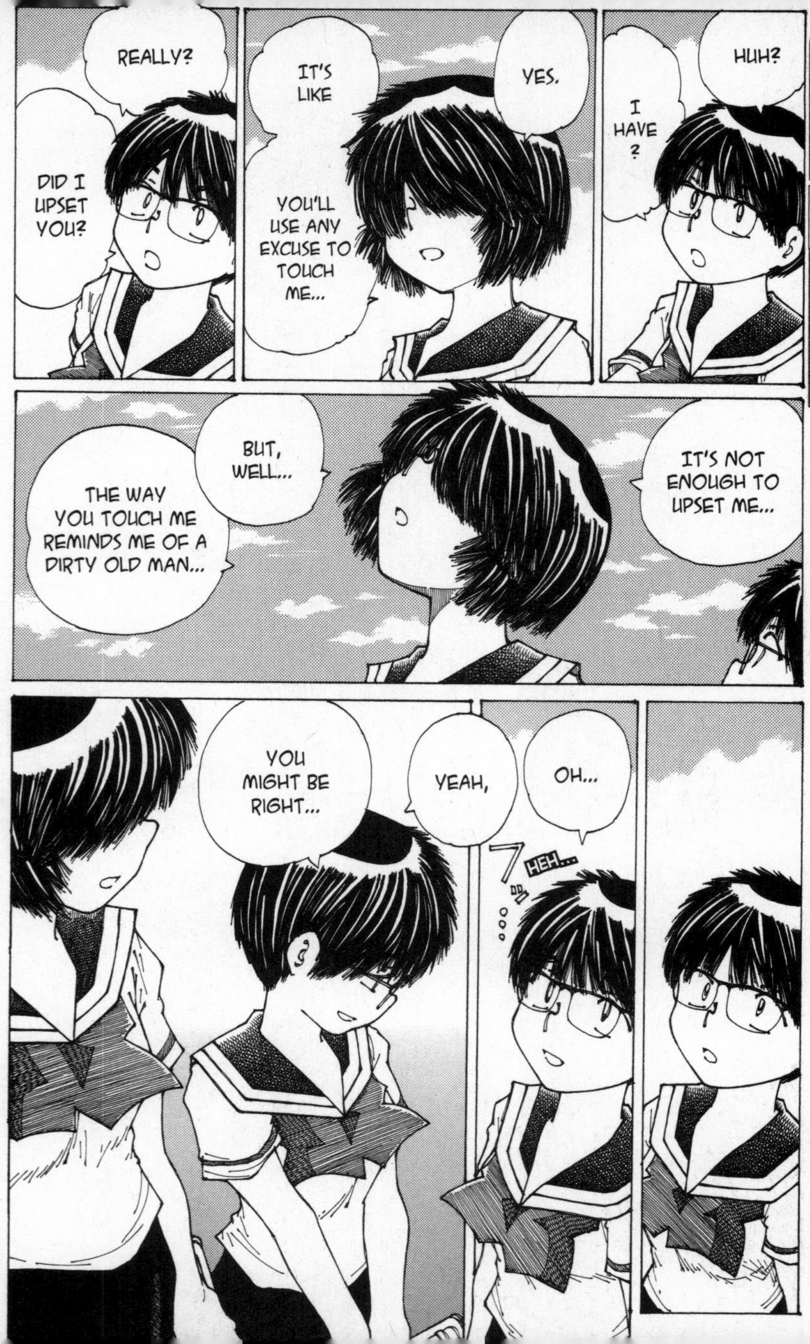

HUH?
I HAVE?
YES.
IT'S LIKE
YOU'LL USE ANY EXCUSE TO TOUCH ME...
REALLY?
DID I UPSET YOU?
IT'S NOT ENOUGH TO UPSET ME...
BUT, WELL...
THE WAY YOU TOUCH ME REMINDS ME OF A DIRTY OLD MAN...
OH...
HEH...
YEAH,
YOU MIGHT BE RIGHT...

The Latest from the Author

Riichi Ueshiba

IT WAS THE SCENE IN VOLUME 1 WHERE TSUBAKI GOT HIS FIRST REAL LOOK AT URABE'S FACE. ANYWAY, RECENTLY I'VE BEEN THINKING ABOUT "EXPERIENCES." AS I WROTE IN MY ESSAY FOR VOLUME 1, I DIDN'T HAVE A GIRLFRIEND IN HIGH SCHOOL. IF I'D HAD A GIRLFRIEND THEN, THE REALITY OF MY EXPERIENCE PROBABLY WOULD HAVE INFLUENCED ME... (CONTINUED...)

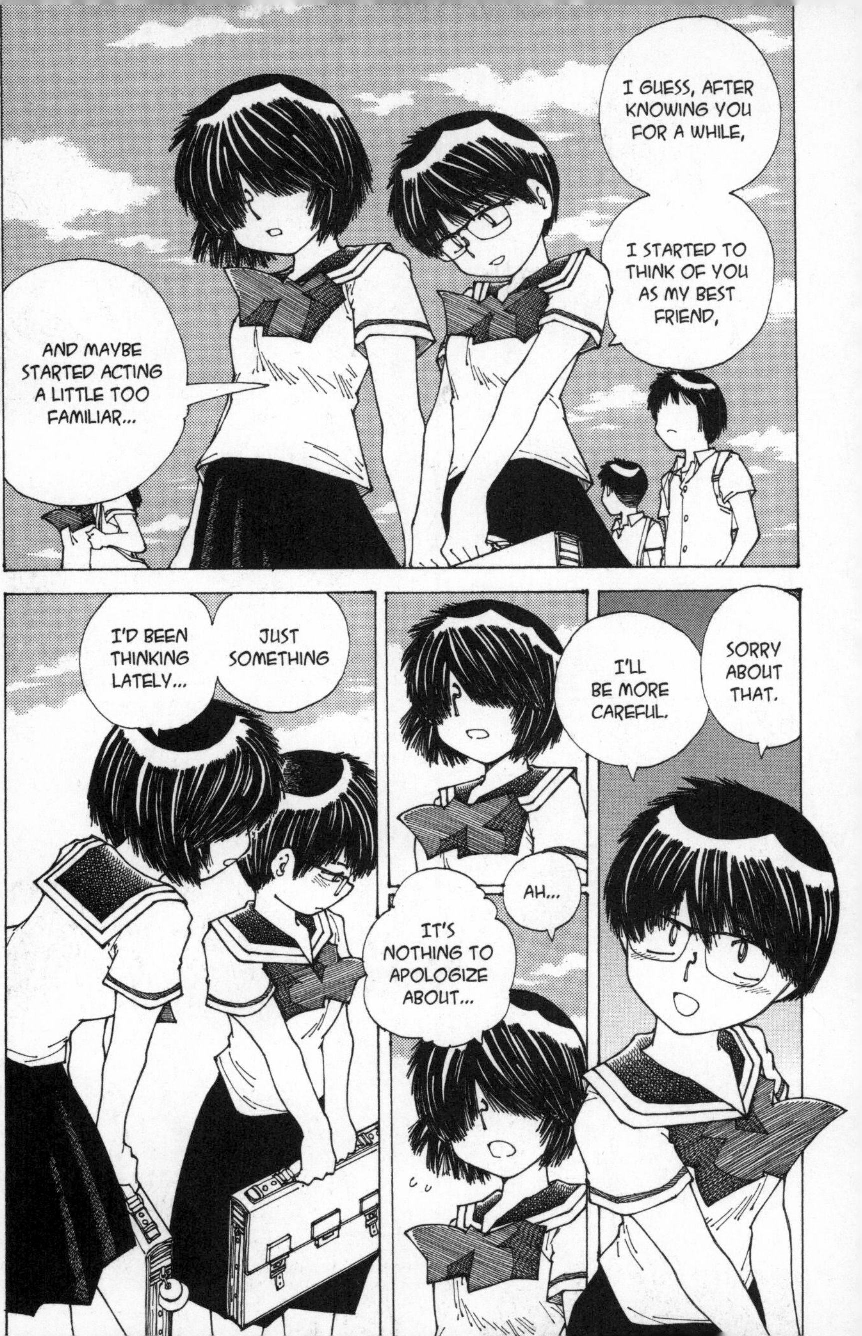
I GUESS, AFTER KNOWING YOU FOR A WHILE,
I STARTED TO THINK OF YOU AS MY BEST FRIEND,
AND MAYBE STARTED ACTING A LITTLE TOO FAMILIAR...
SORRY ABOUT THAT.
I'LL BE MORE CAREFUL.
AH...
IT'S NOTHING TO APOLOGIZE ABOUT...
JUST SOMETHING
I'D BEEN THINKING LATELY...

The Latest from the Author

Riichi Ueshiba

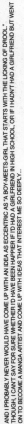

AND I PROBABLY NEVER WOULD HAVE COME UP WITH AN IDEA AS ECCENTRIC AS "A BOY-MEETS-GIRL THAT STARTS WITH THE LICKING OF DROOL." THOUGH, I CAN'T SAY FOR SURE WHETHER I'D HAVE BEEN HAPPIER IF I'D HAD A GIRLFRIEND IN HIGH SCHOOL, OR IF I HADN'T HAD A GIRLFRIEND BUT WENT ON TO BECOME A MANGA ARTIST AND COME UP WITH IDEAS THAT INTEREST ME SO DEEPLY...

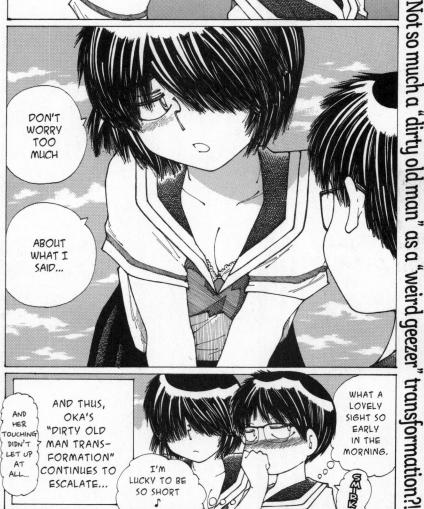

DON'T WORRY TOO MUCH
ABOUT WHAT I SAID...
WHAT A LOVELY SIGHT SO EARLY IN THE MORNING.
SMIRK
I'M LUCKY TO BE SO SHORT ♪
AND THUS, OKA'S "DIRTY OLD MAN TRANS-FORMATION" CONTINUES TO ESCALATE...
AND HER TOUCHING DIDN'T LET UP AT ALL...

Not so much a "dirty old man" as a "weird geezer" transformation?!

MYSTERIOUS GIRLFRIEND X

END OF CHAPTER 36.5

NEXT TIME, A NEW DEVELOPMENT PRESENTED IN COLOR! IS TSUBAKI'S RELATIONSHIP WITH URABE CHANGING?!

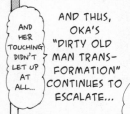

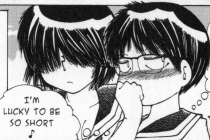

DON'T YOU THINK A GIRL WHO DROOLS WHEN SHE FALLS ASLEEP IS CUTE?

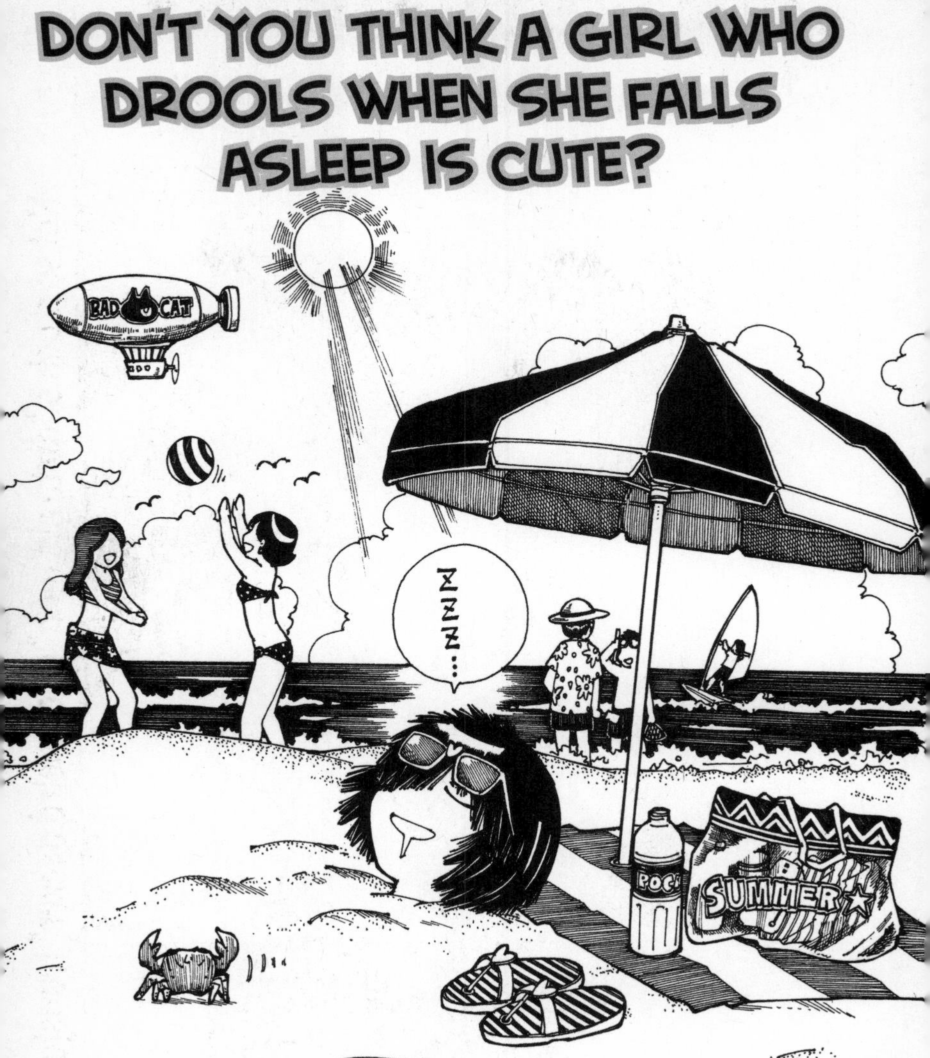
BAD CAT
ZZZ...
SUMMER

WELL, THIS IS A COMIC ABOUT THAT SORT OF GIRL.

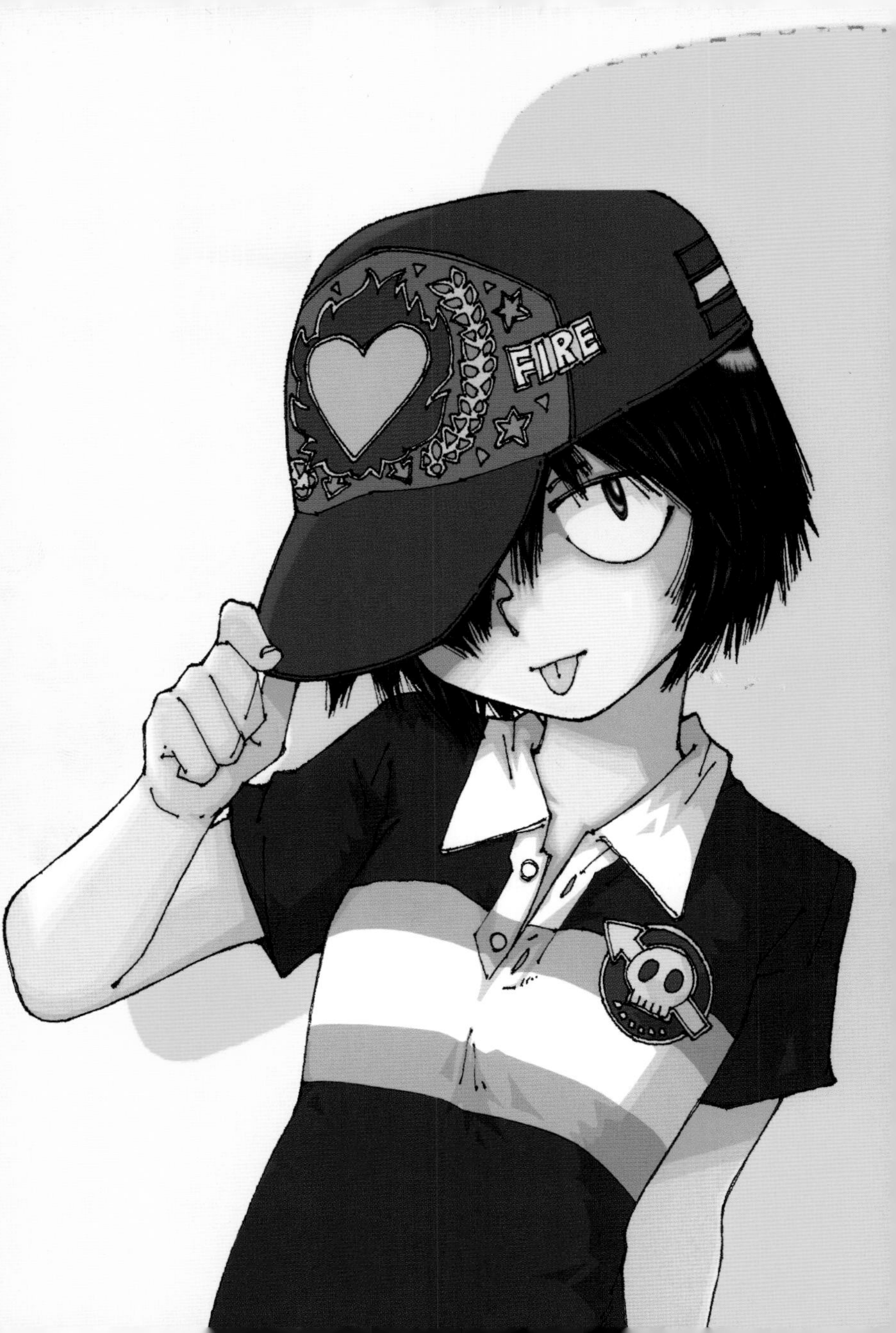
FIRE

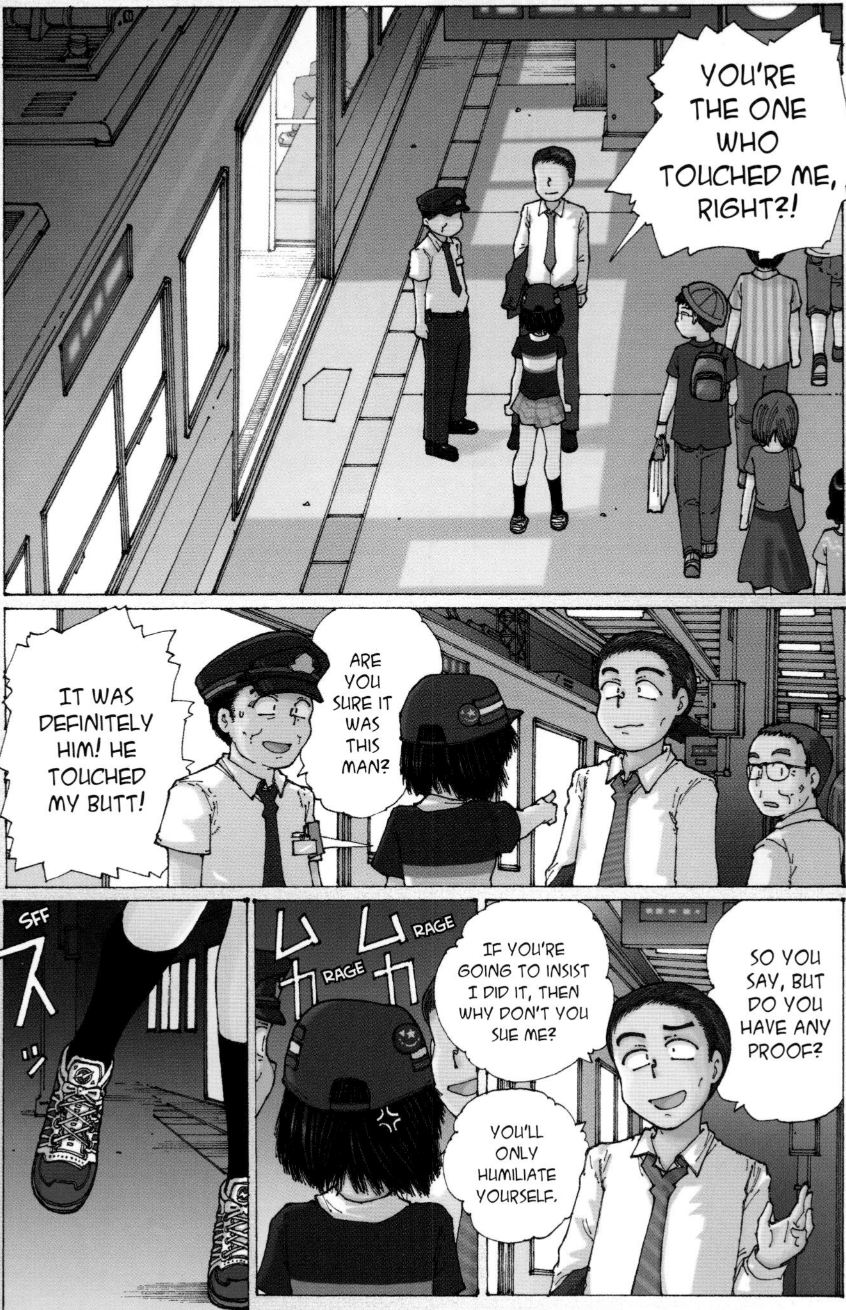
YOU'RE THE ONE WHO TOUCHED ME, RIGHT?!
ARE YOU SURE IT WAS THIS MAN?
IT WAS DEFINITELY HIM! HE TOUCHED MY BUTT!
SO YOU SAY, BUT DO YOU HAVE ANY PROOF?
IF YOU'RE GOING TO INSIST I DID IT, THEN WHY DON'T YOU SUE ME?
YOU'LL ONLY HUMILIATE YOURSELF.
ムカ RAGE
ムカ RAGE
スッ SFF

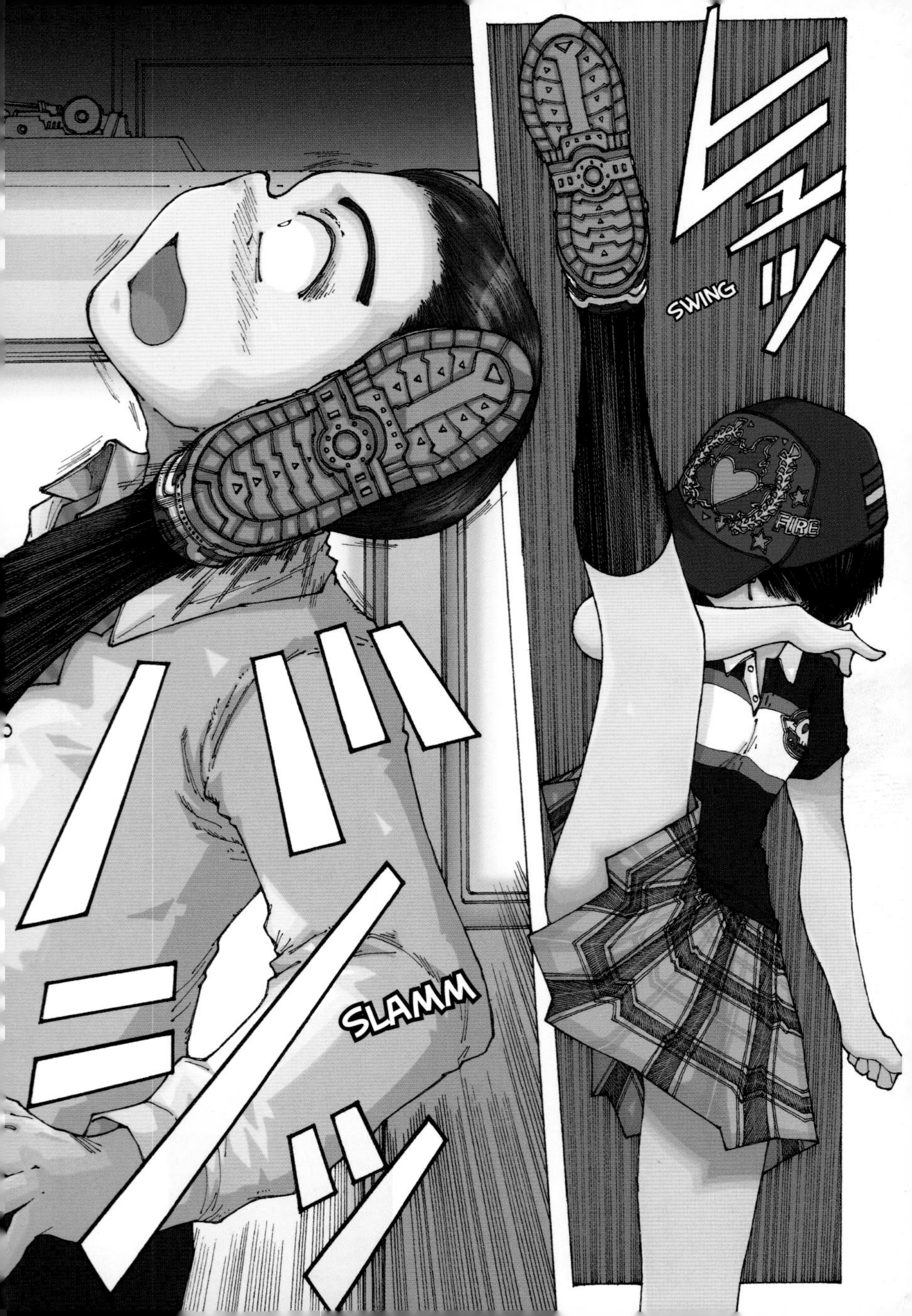
ヒュッ
SWING
FIRE
SLAMM

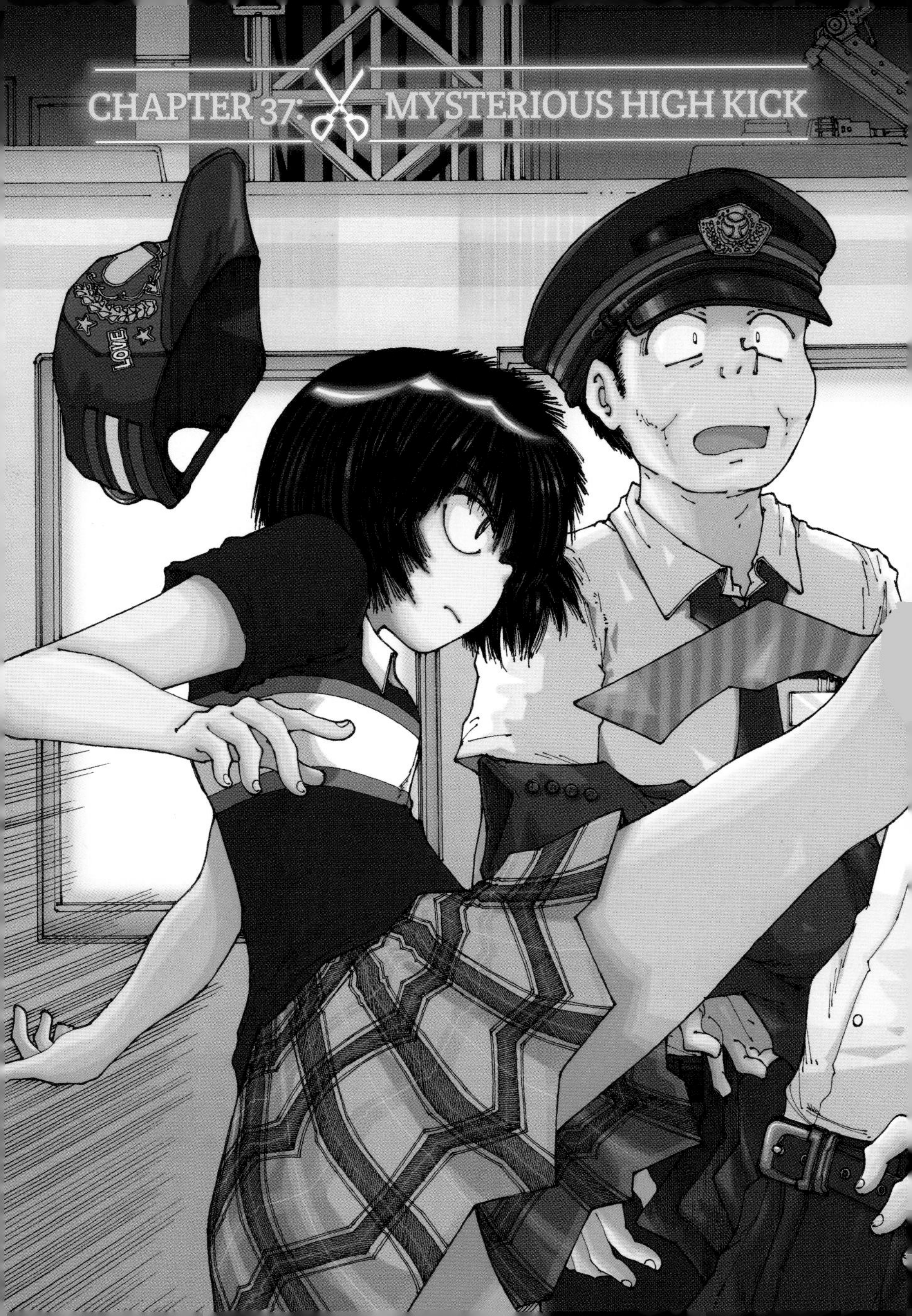
CHAPTER 37: MYSTERIOUS HIGH KICK
LOVE

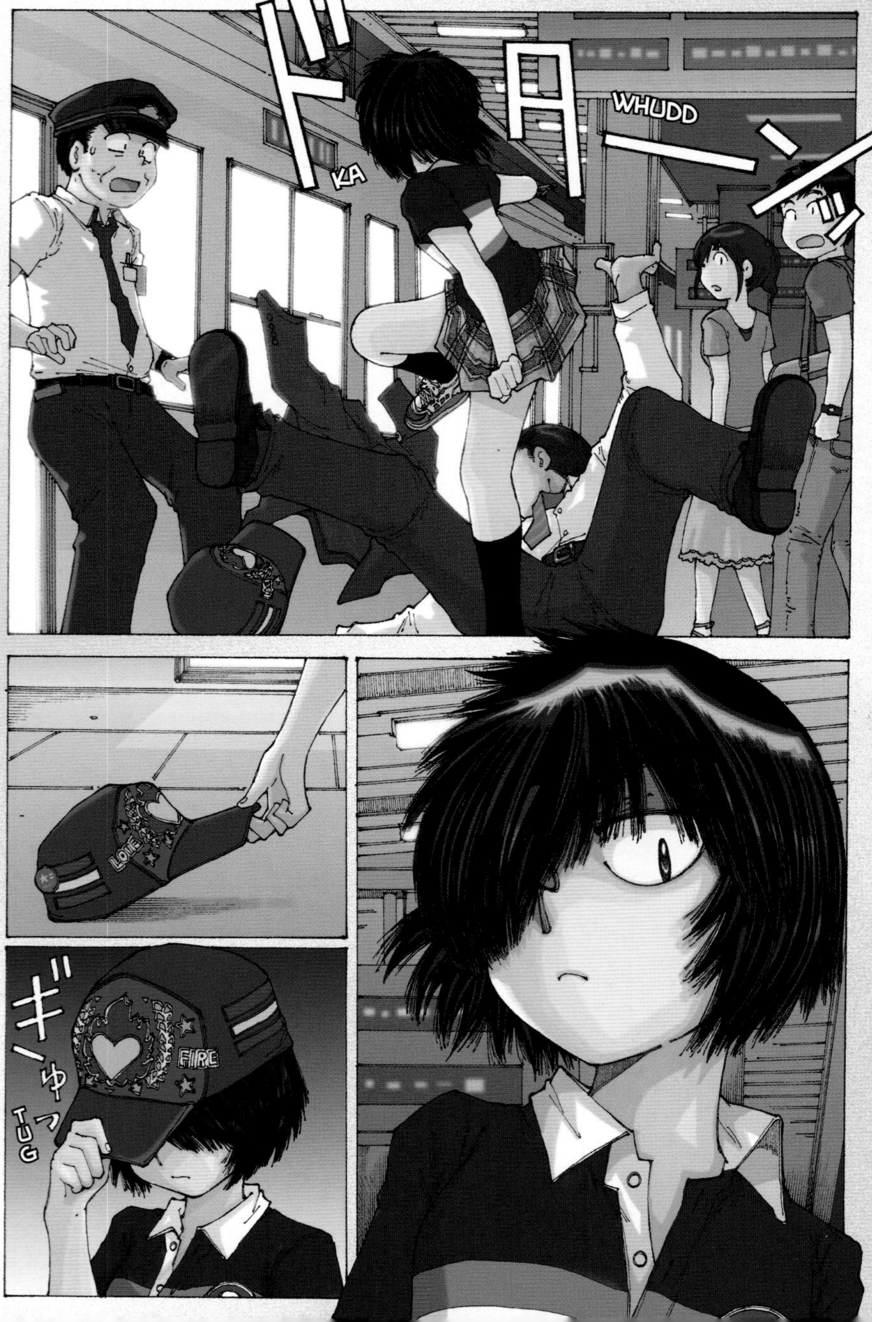
KA
WHUDD
LOVE
ギゅっ
TUG
FIRE

VERTICAL COMICS

MYSTERIOUS GIRLFRIEND X

RIICHI UESHIBA

CHARACTERS

Mikoto Urabe (17)

A transfer student who joined Tsubaki's class. She can convey her own feelings through her drool, as well as pick up on Tsubaki's feelings through his. She's anti-social and everything she says and does is mysterious, but her ideas about love are very pure. Her hobby is using scissors, which she can use to cut up anything.

Akira Tsubaki (17)

The protagonist of the story. His bizarre relationship with Urabe began after he licked her drool one day. He is as interested in girls as any boy his age, but Urabe takes the lead in their relationship and Tsubaki can't seem to initiate any progress between them.

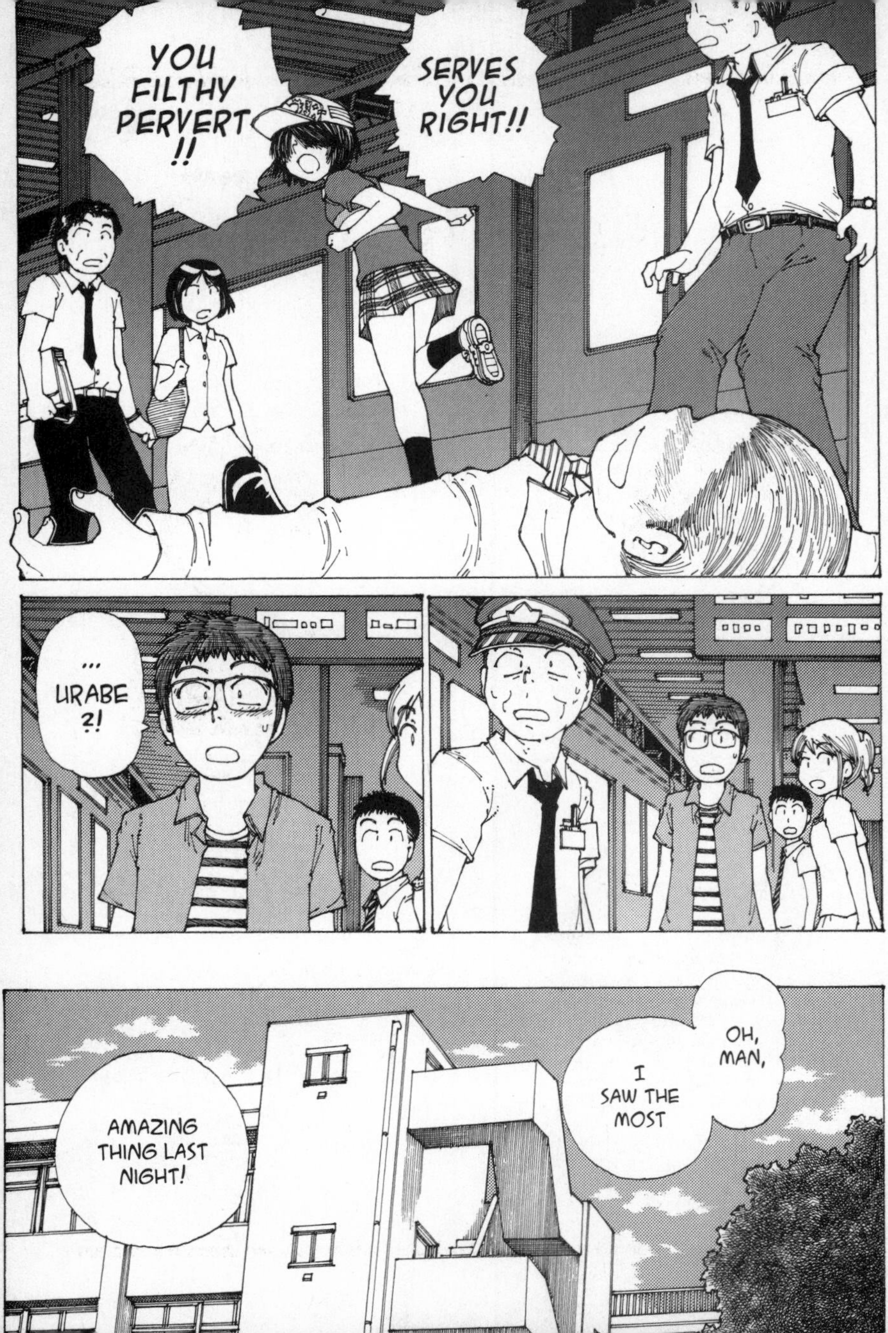
SERVES YOU RIGHT!!
YOU FILTHY PERVERT !!
... URABE ?!
OH, MAN,
I SAW THE MOST
AMAZING THING LAST NIGHT!

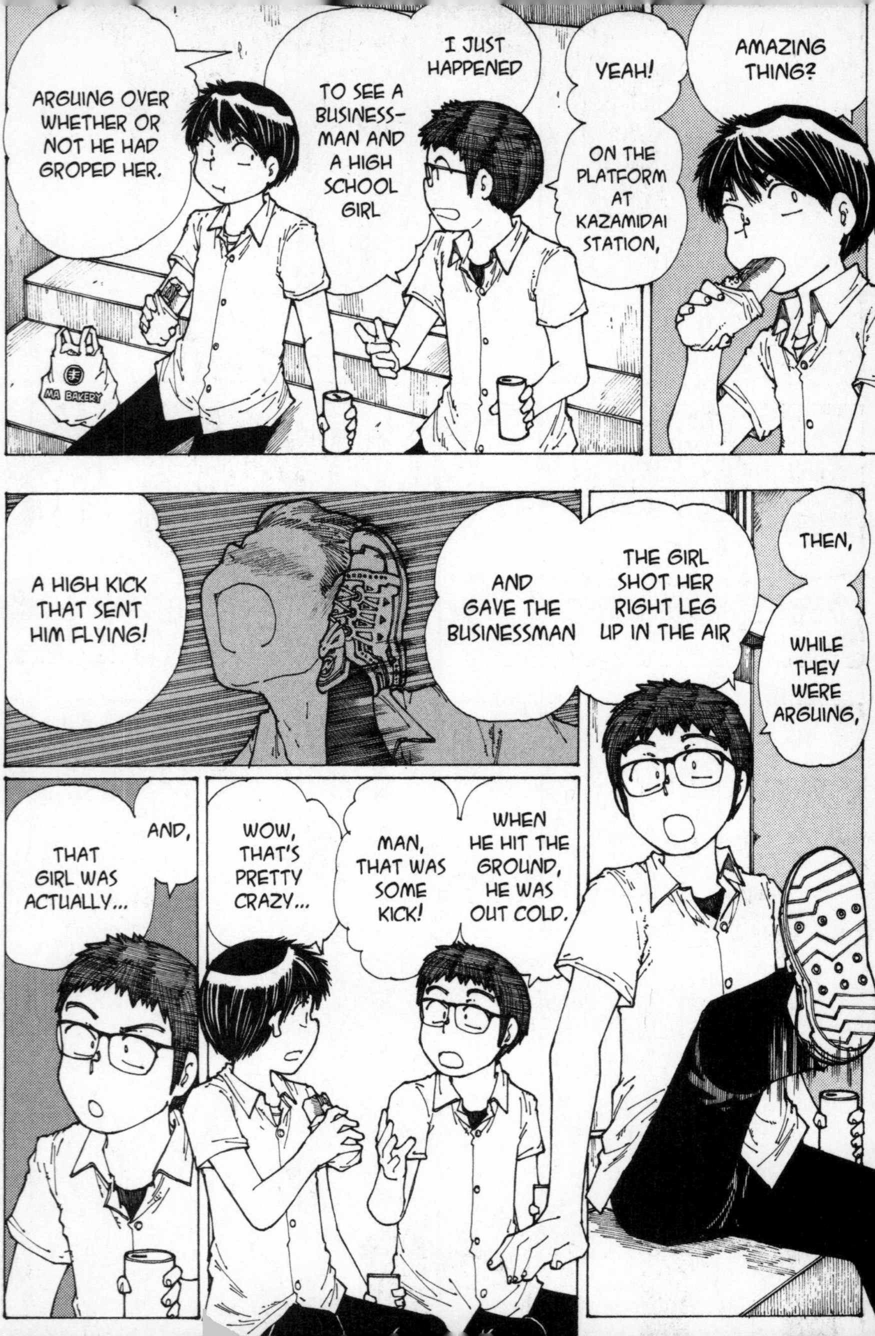
AMAZING THING?
YEAH!
ON THE PLATFORM AT KAZAMIDAI STATION,
I JUST HAPPENED
TO SEE A BUSINESS-MAN AND A HIGH SCHOOL GIRL
ARGUING OVER WHETHER OR NOT HE HAD GROPED HER.
THEN,
WHILE THEY WERE ARGUING,
THE GIRL SHOT HER RIGHT LEG UP IN THE AIR
AND GAVE THE BUSINESSMAN
A HIGH KICK THAT SENT HIM FLYING!
WHEN HE HIT THE GROUND, HE WAS OUT COLD.
MAN, THAT WAS SOME KICK!
WOW, THAT'S PRETTY CRAZY...
AND,
THAT GIRL WAS ACTUALLY...
MA BAKERY

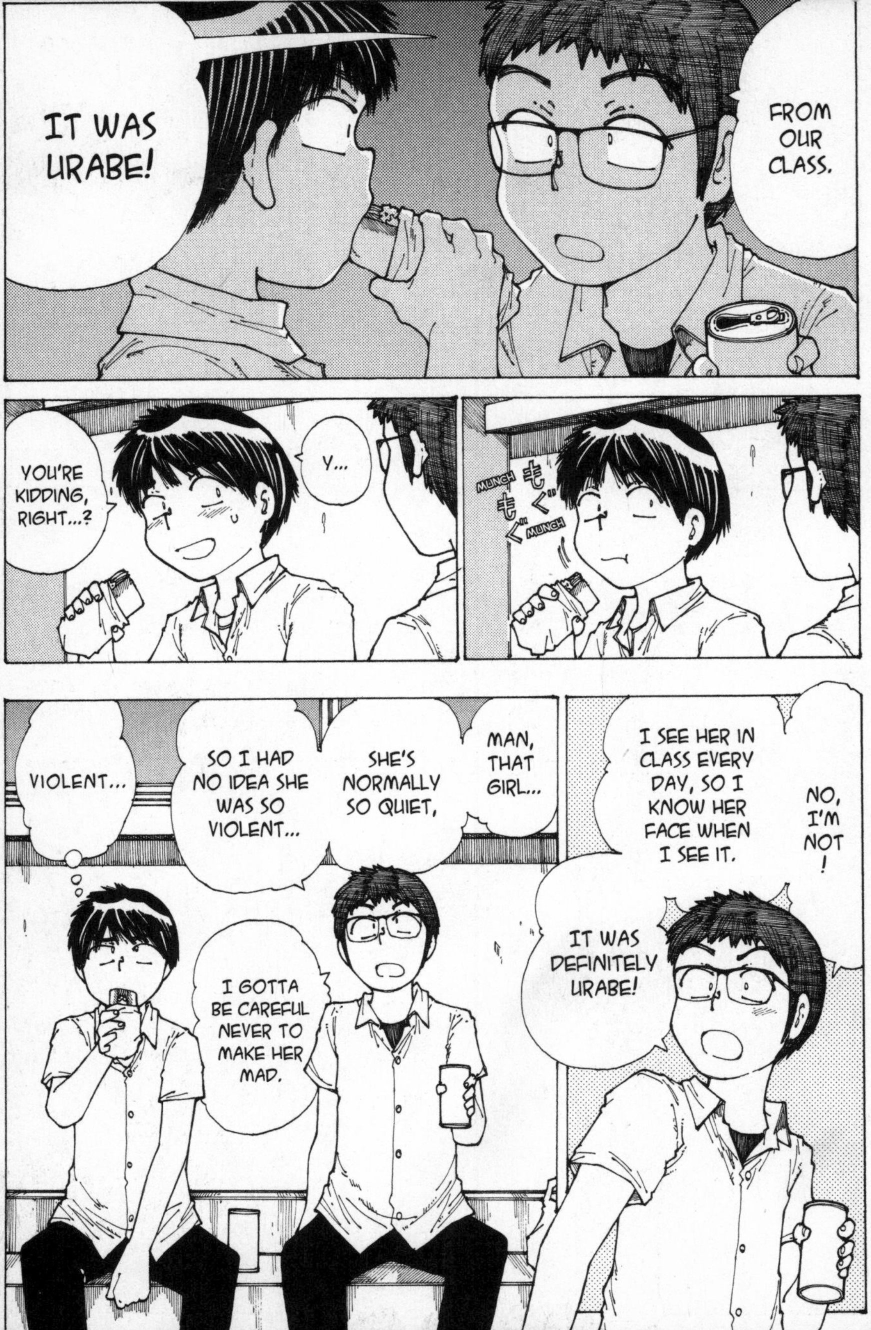
FROM OUR CLASS.
IT WAS URABE!
もぐ
MUNCH
もぐ
MUNCH
Y...
YOU'RE KIDDING, RIGHT...?
NO, I'M NOT!
I SEE HER IN CLASS EVERY DAY, SO I KNOW HER FACE WHEN I SEE IT.
IT WAS DEFINITELY URABE!
MAN, THAT GIRL...
SHE'S NORMALLY SO QUIET,
SO I HAD NO IDEA SHE WAS SO VIOLENT...
I GOTTA BE CAREFUL NEVER TO MAKE HER MAD.
VIOLENT...

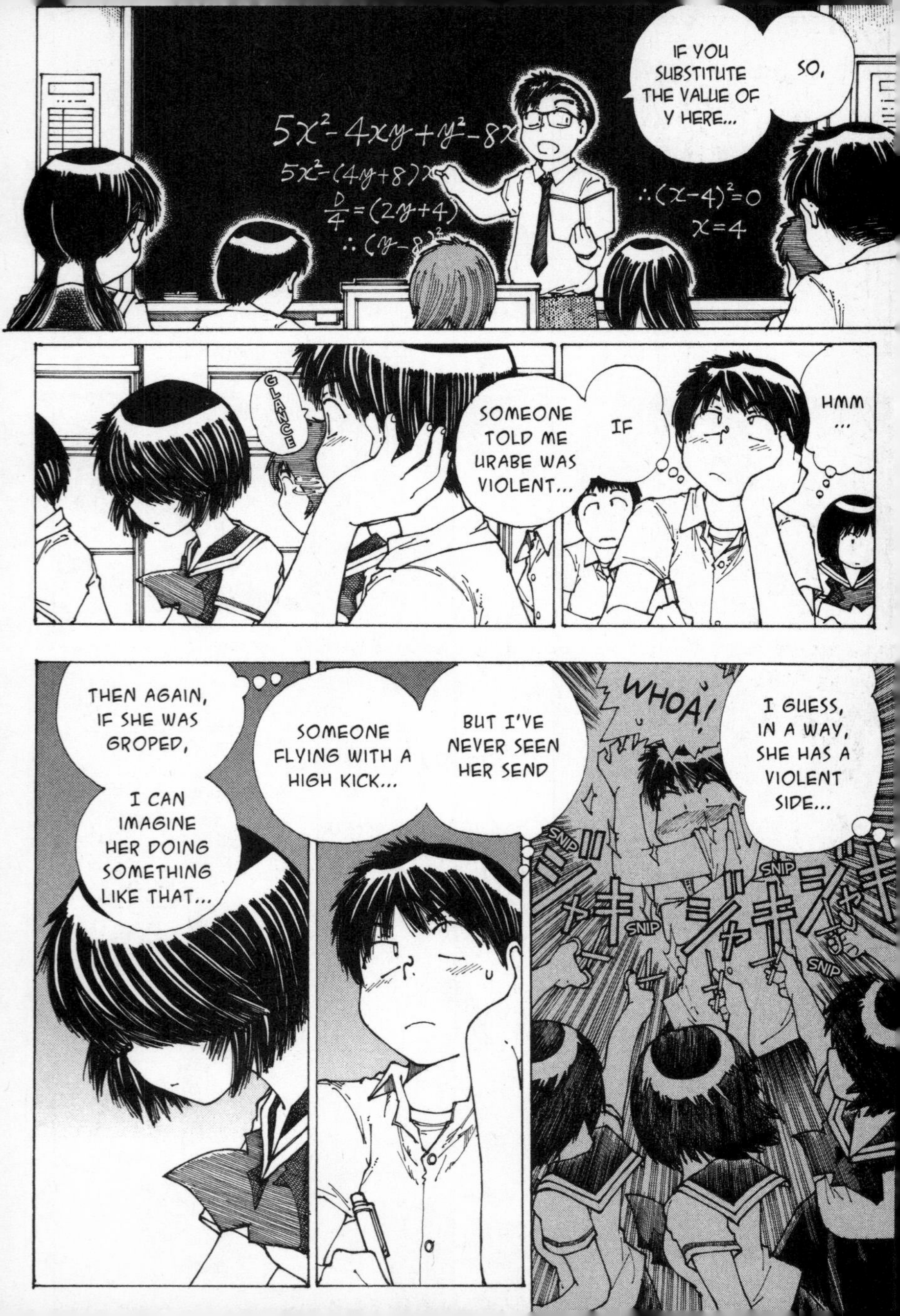
SO,
IF YOU SUBSTITUTE THE VALUE OF Y HERE...
HMM ...
IF
SOMEONE TOLD ME URABE WAS VIOLENT...
GLANCE
I GUESS, IN A WAY, SHE HAS A VIOLENT SIDE...
WHOA!
SNIP
SNIP
SNIP
SNIP
BUT I'VE NEVER SEEN HER SEND
SOMEONE FLYING WITH A HIGH KICK...
THEN AGAIN, IF SHE WAS GROPED,
I CAN IMAGINE HER DOING SOMETHING LIKE THAT...

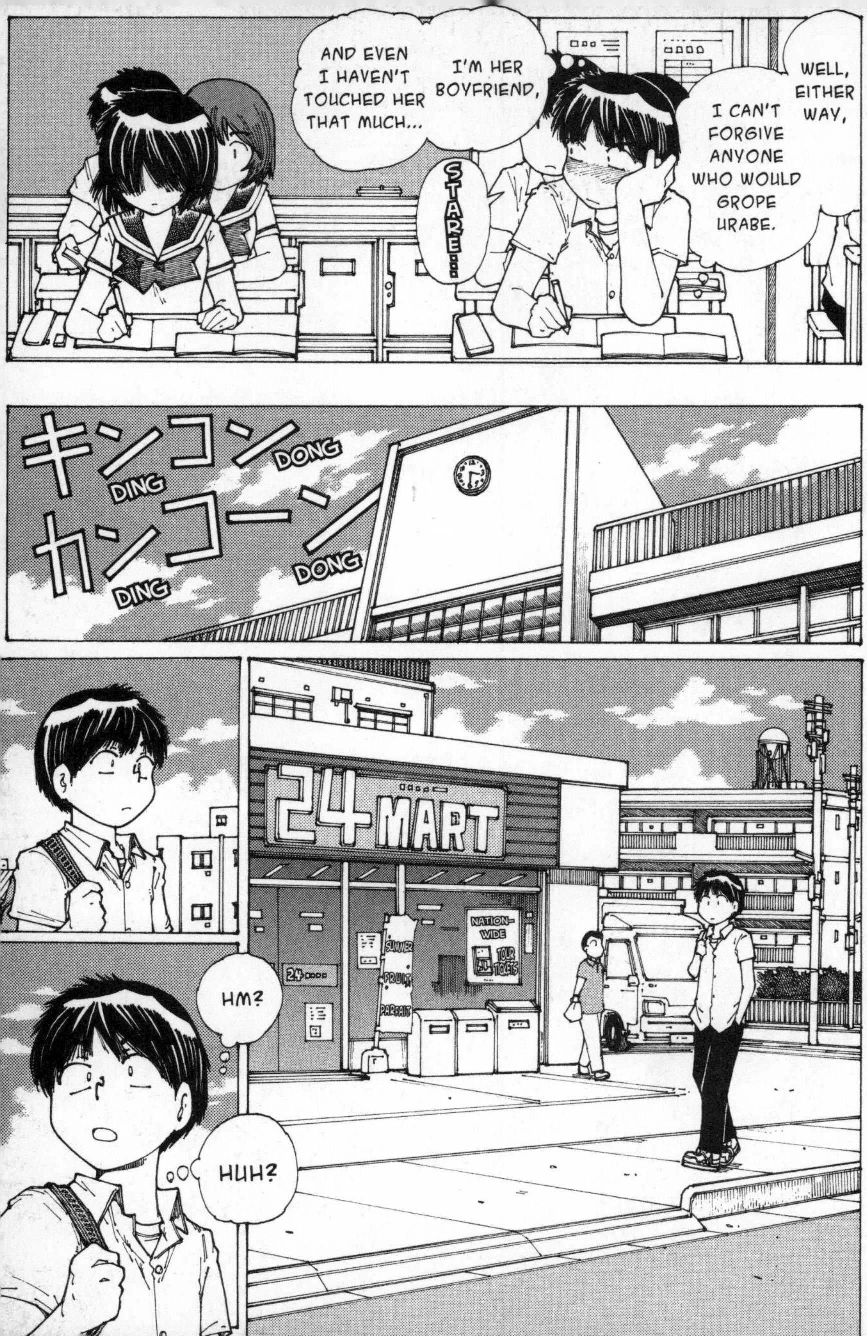
WELL, EITHER WAY,
I CAN'T FORGIVE ANYONE WHO WOULD GROPE URABE.
I'M HER BOYFRIEND,
AND EVEN I HAVEN'T TOUCHED HER THAT MUCH...
STARE...
キンコン
DING
DONG
カンコーン
DING
DONG
24 MART
NATION-WIDE
TOUR TICKETS
SUMMER FRUIT PARFAIT
HM?
HUH?

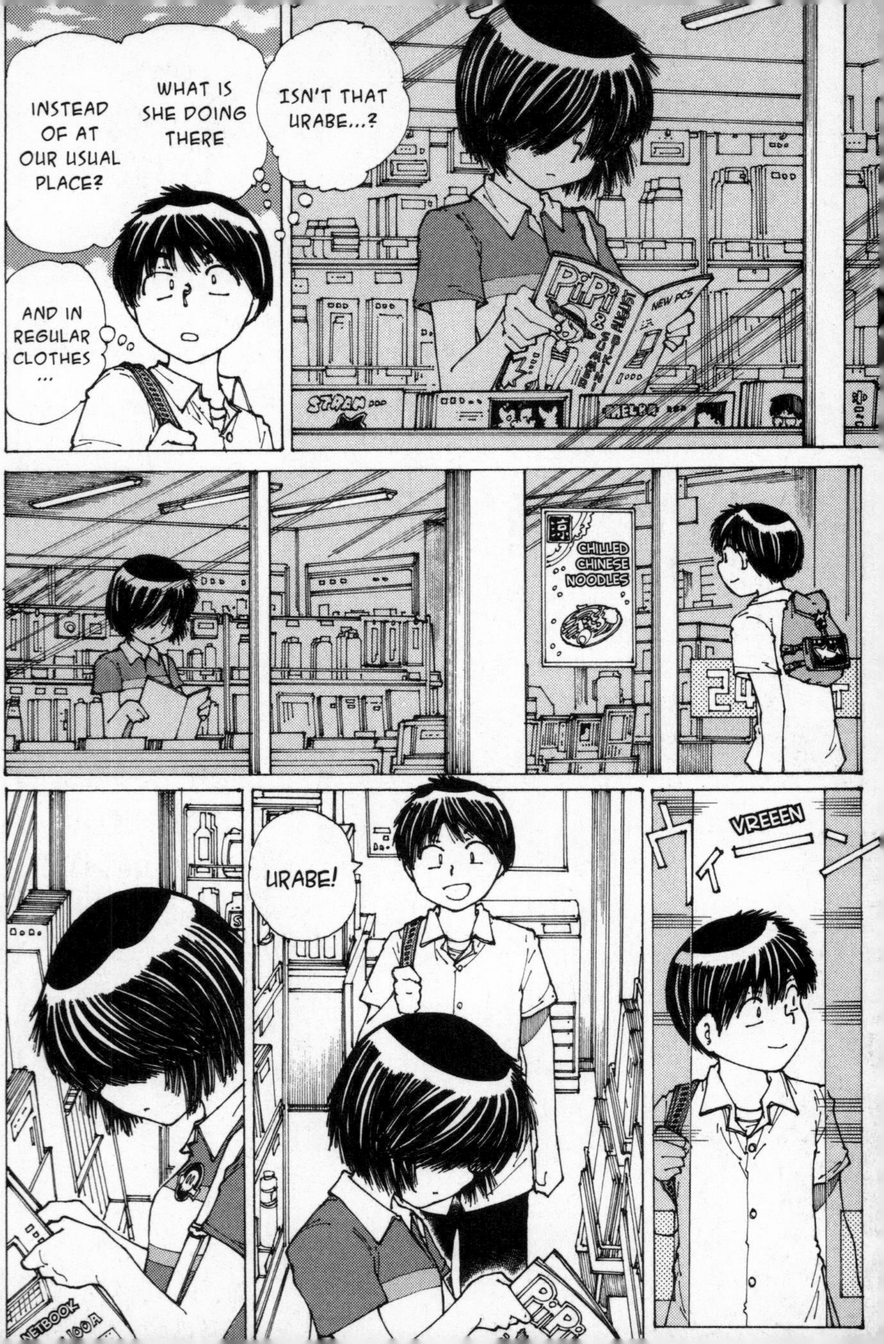
ISN'T THAT URABE...?
WHAT IS SHE DOING THERE
INSTEAD OF AT OUR USUAL PLACE?
AND IN REGULAR CLOTHES ...
PiPi
NEW PCS
CHILLED CHINESE NOODLES
VREEEN
URABE!
NETBOOK

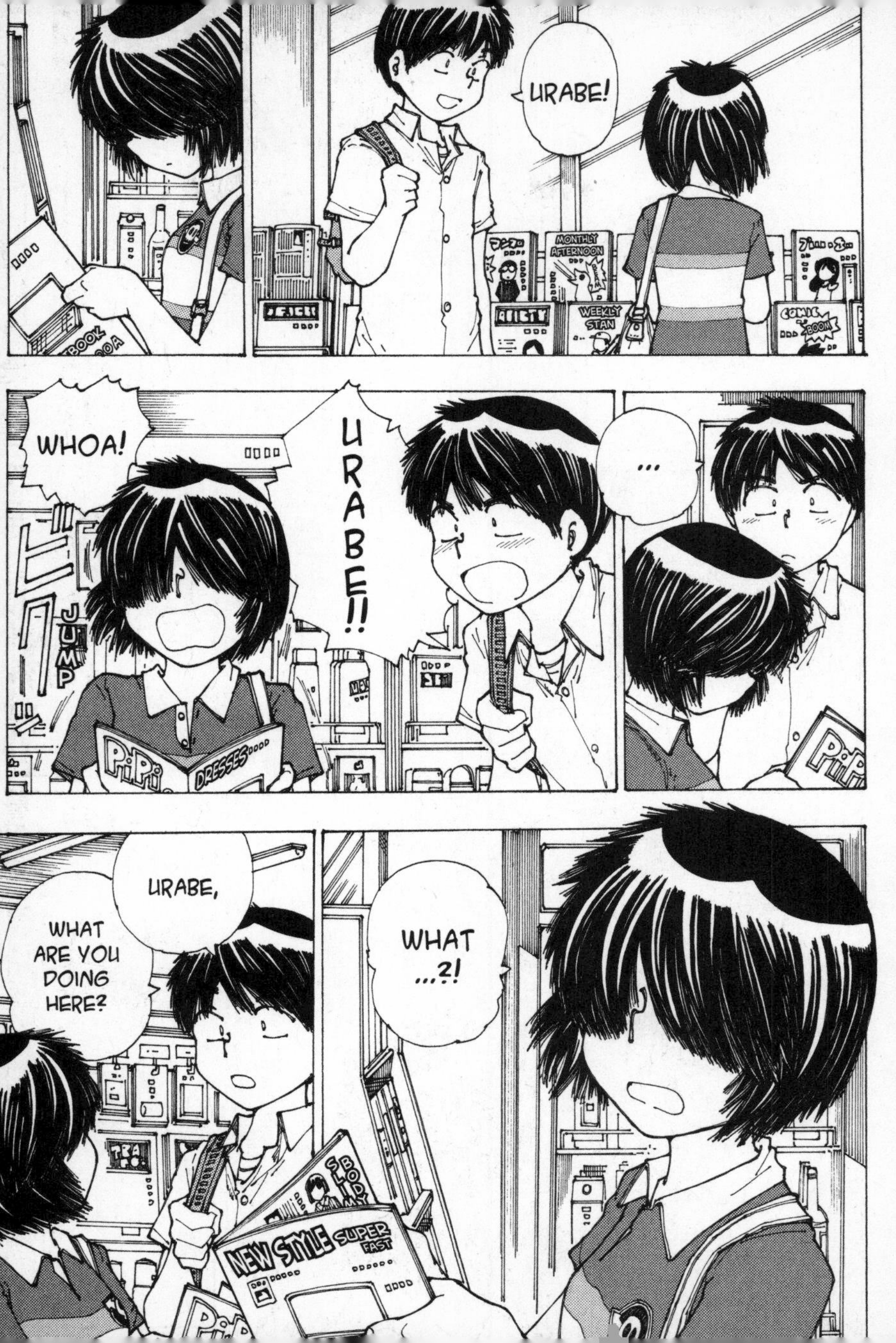
URABE!
MONTHLY AFTERNOON
WEEKLY STAN
COMIC BOOM
...
PiPi
URABE!!
WHOA!
JUMP
PiPi
DRESSES
WHAT ...?!
URABE,
WHAT ARE YOU DOING HERE?
NEW STYLE
SUPER FAST

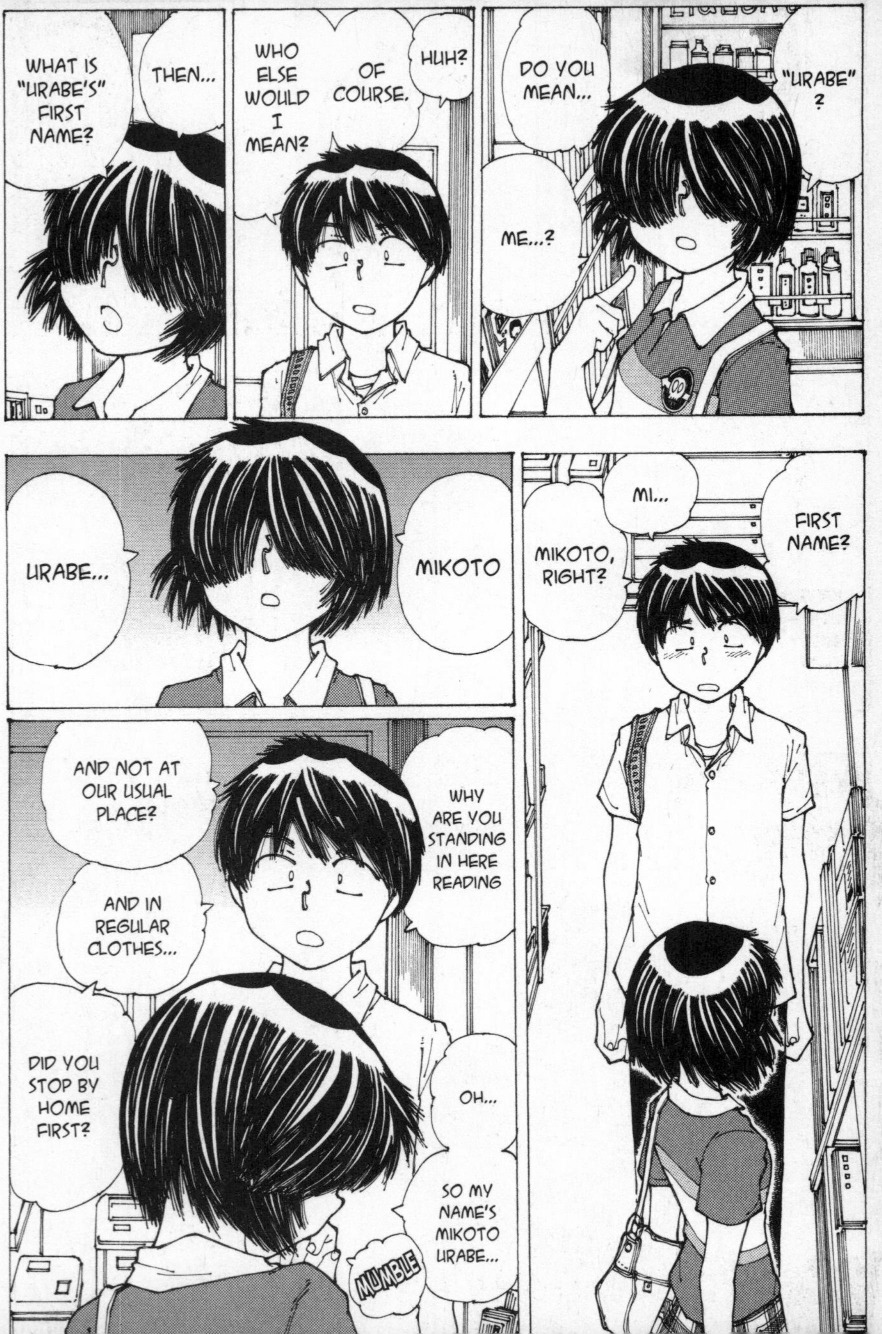
"URABE" ?
DO YOU MEAN...
ME...?
HUH?
OF COURSE.
WHO ELSE WOULD I MEAN?
THEN...
WHAT IS "URABE'S" FIRST NAME?
FIRST NAME?
MI...
MIKOTO, RIGHT?
MIKOTO
URABE...
WHY ARE YOU STANDING IN HERE READING
AND NOT AT OUR USUAL PLACE?
AND IN REGULAR CLOTHES...
OH...
DID YOU STOP BY HOME FIRST?
SO MY NAME'S MIKOTO URABE...
MUMBLE

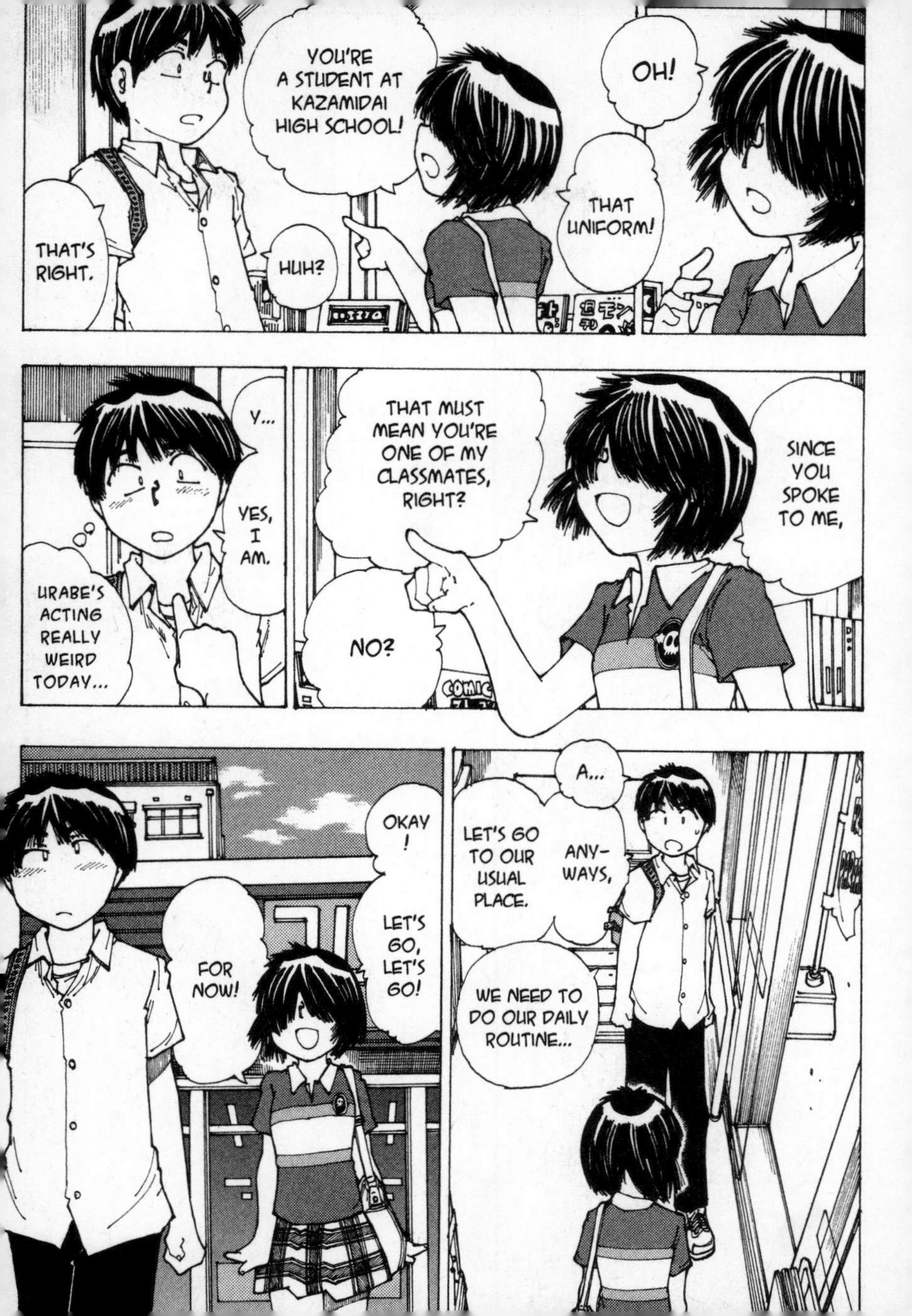
OH!
THAT UNIFORM!
YOU'RE A STUDENT AT KAZAMIDAI HIGH SCHOOL!
HUH?
THAT'S RIGHT.
SINCE YOU SPOKE TO ME,
THAT MUST MEAN YOU'RE ONE OF MY CLASSMATES, RIGHT?
NO?
Y...
YES, I AM.
URABE'S ACTING REALLY WEIRD TODAY...
A...
ANY-WAYS,
LET'S GO TO OUR USUAL PLACE.
WE NEED TO DO OUR DAILY ROUTINE...
OKAY!
LET'S GO, LET'S GO!
FOR NOW!

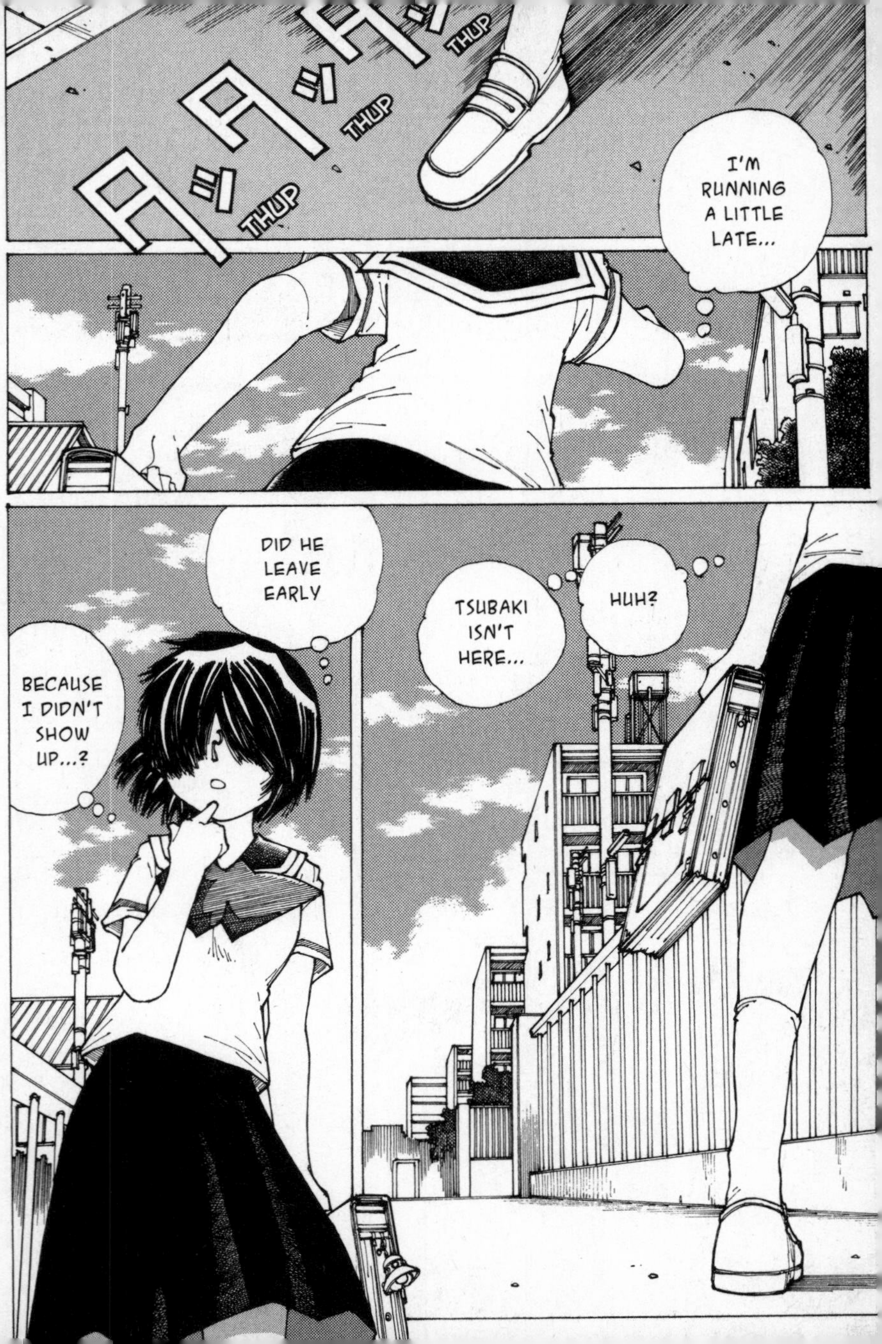
THUP
THUP
THUP
I'M RUNNING A LITTLE LATE...
HUH?
TSUBAKI ISN'T HERE...
DID HE LEAVE EARLY
BECAUSE I DIDN'T SHOW UP...?

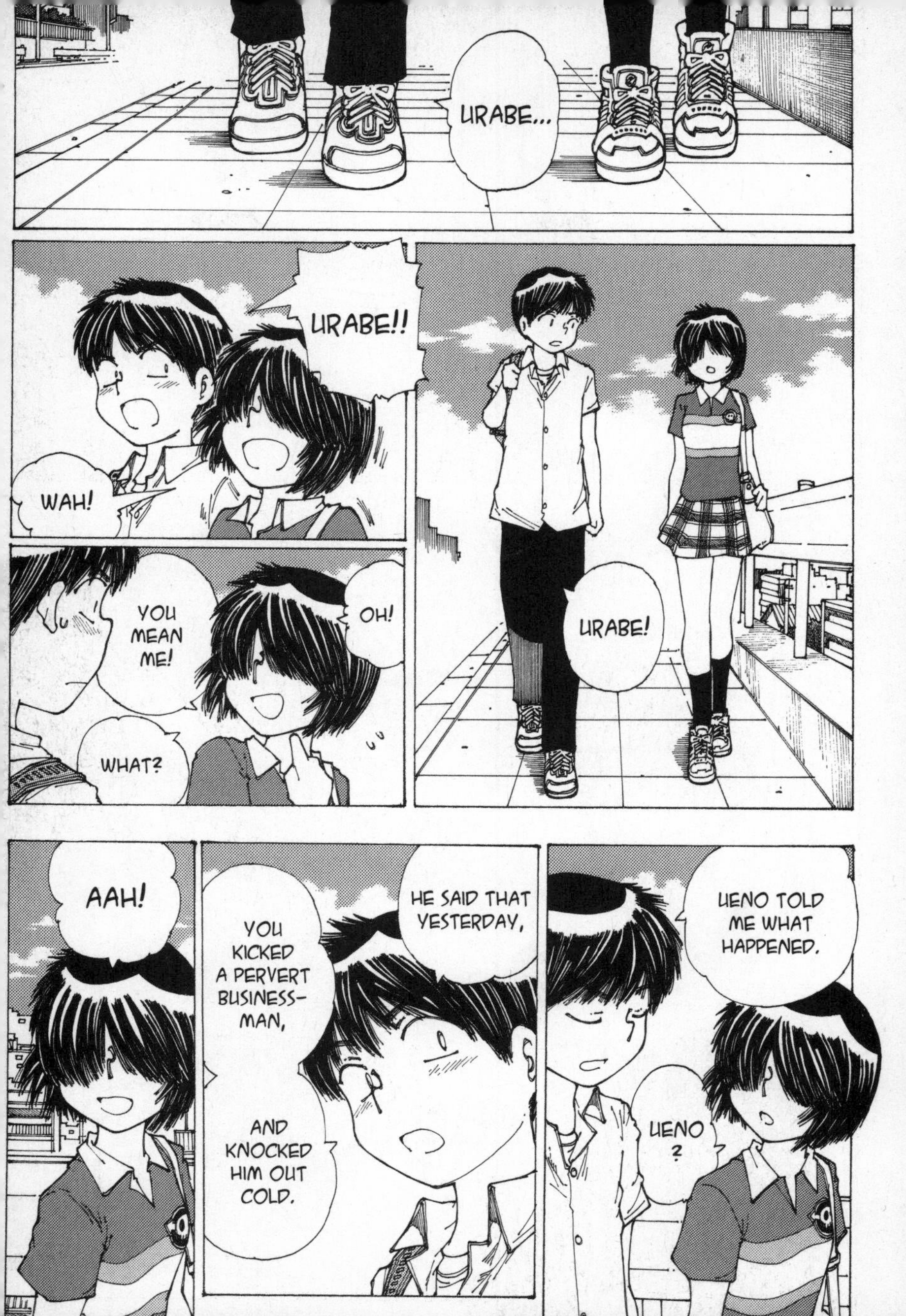
URABE...
URABE!
URABE!!
WAH!
OH!
YOU MEAN ME!
WHAT?
UENO TOLD ME WHAT HAPPENED.
UENO ?
HE SAID THAT YESTERDAY,
YOU KICKED A PERVERT BUSINESS-MAN,
AND KNOCKED HIM OUT COLD.
AAH!

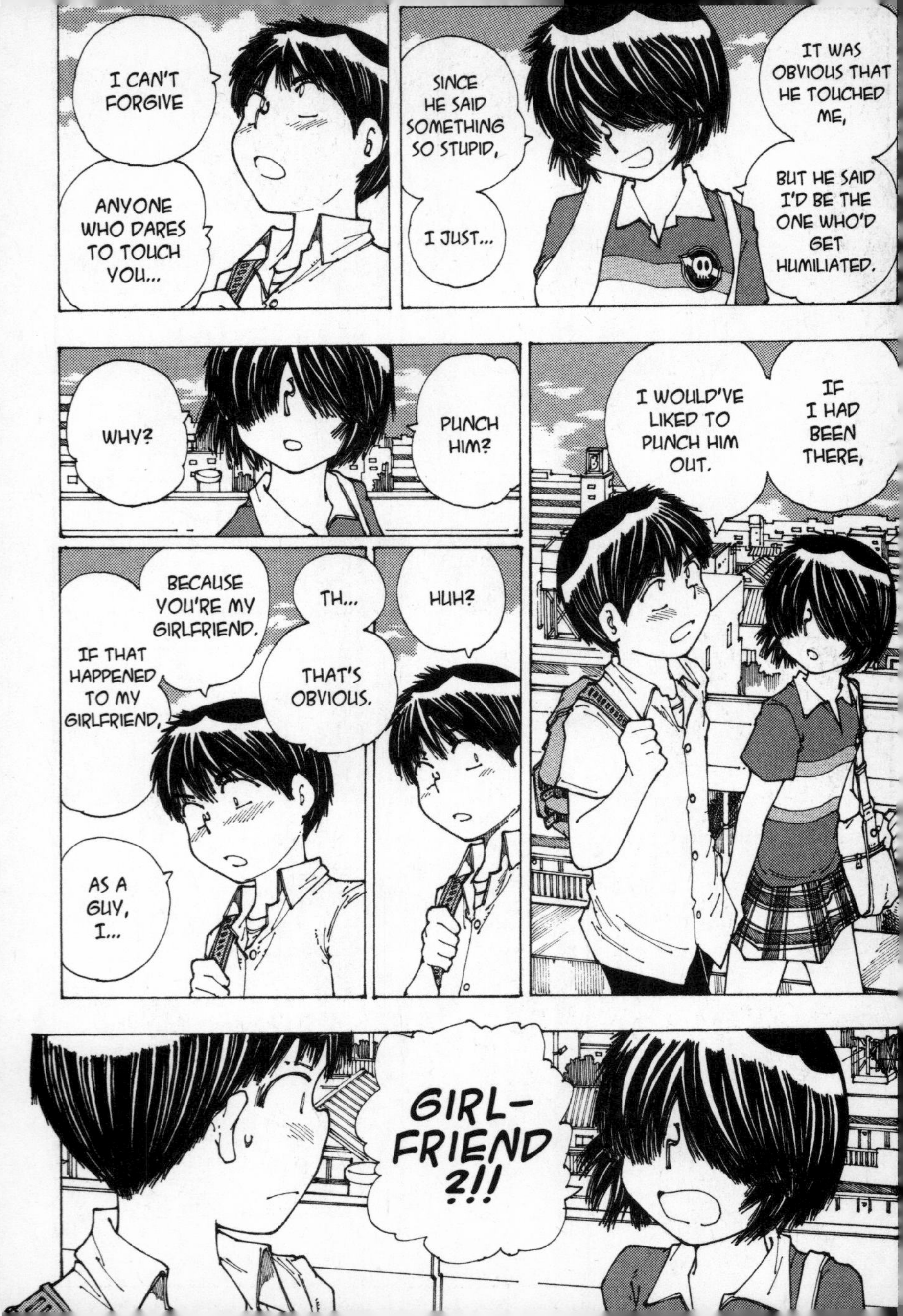

IT WAS OBVIOUS THAT HE TOUCHED ME,
BUT HE SAID I'D BE THE ONE WHO'D GET HUMILIATED.
SINCE HE SAID SOMETHING SO STUPID,
I JUST...
I CAN'T FORGIVE
ANYONE WHO DARES TO TOUCH YOU...
IF I HAD BEEN THERE,
I WOULD'VE LIKED TO PUNCH HIM OUT.
PUNCH HIM?
WHY?
HUH?
TH...
THAT'S OBVIOUS.
BECAUSE YOU'RE MY GIRLFRIEND.
IF THAT HAPPENED TO MY GIRLFRIEND,
AS A GUY, I...
GIRL-FRIEND ?!!

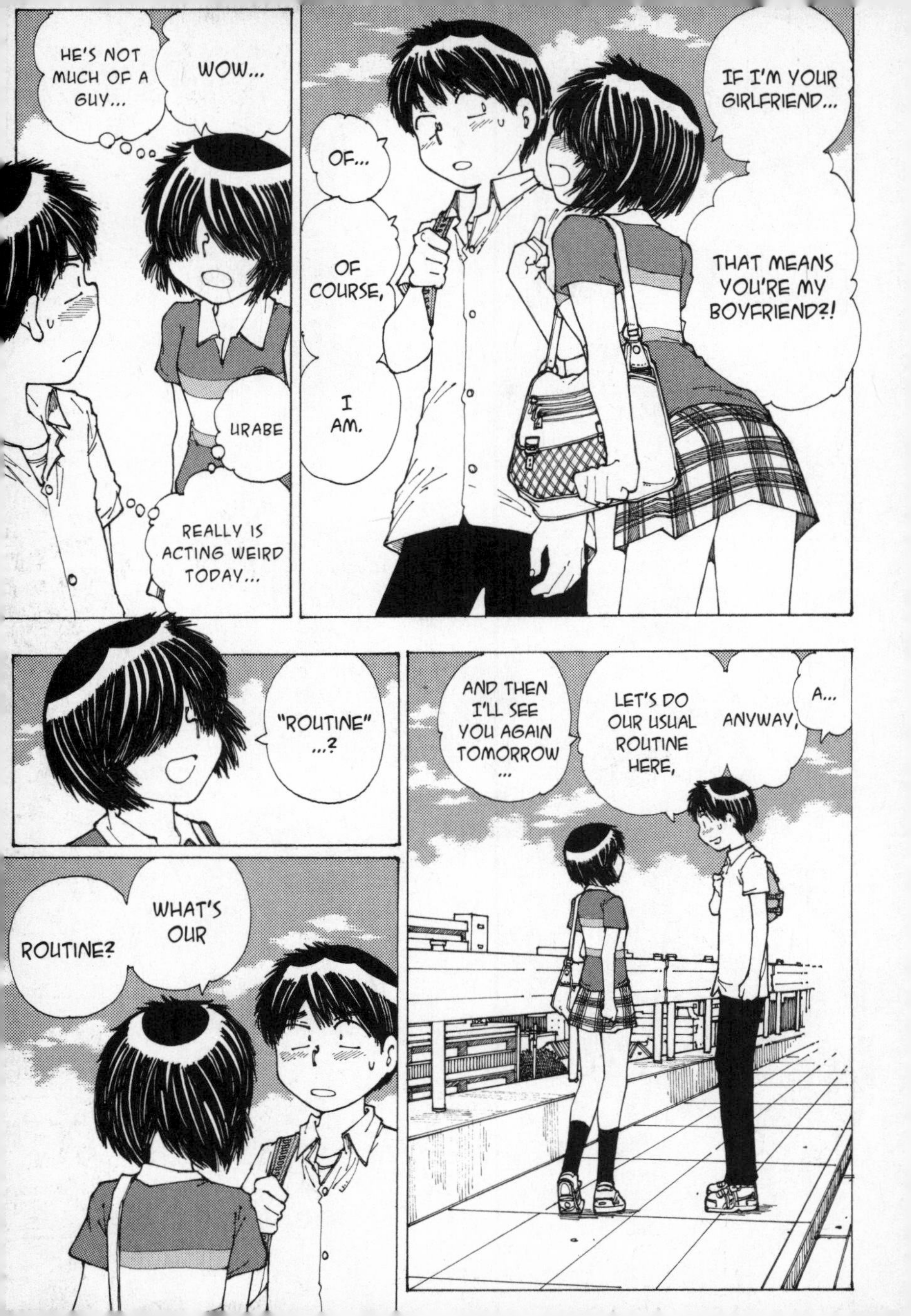
IF I'M YOUR GIRLFRIEND...
THAT MEANS YOU'RE MY BOYFRIEND?!
OF...
OF COURSE,
I AM.
WOW...
HE'S NOT MUCH OF A GUY...
URABE
REALLY IS ACTING WEIRD TODAY...
A...
ANYWAY,
LET'S DO OUR USUAL ROUTINE HERE,
AND THEN I'LL SEE YOU AGAIN TOMORROW ...
"ROUTINE" ...?
WHAT'S OUR
ROUTINE?

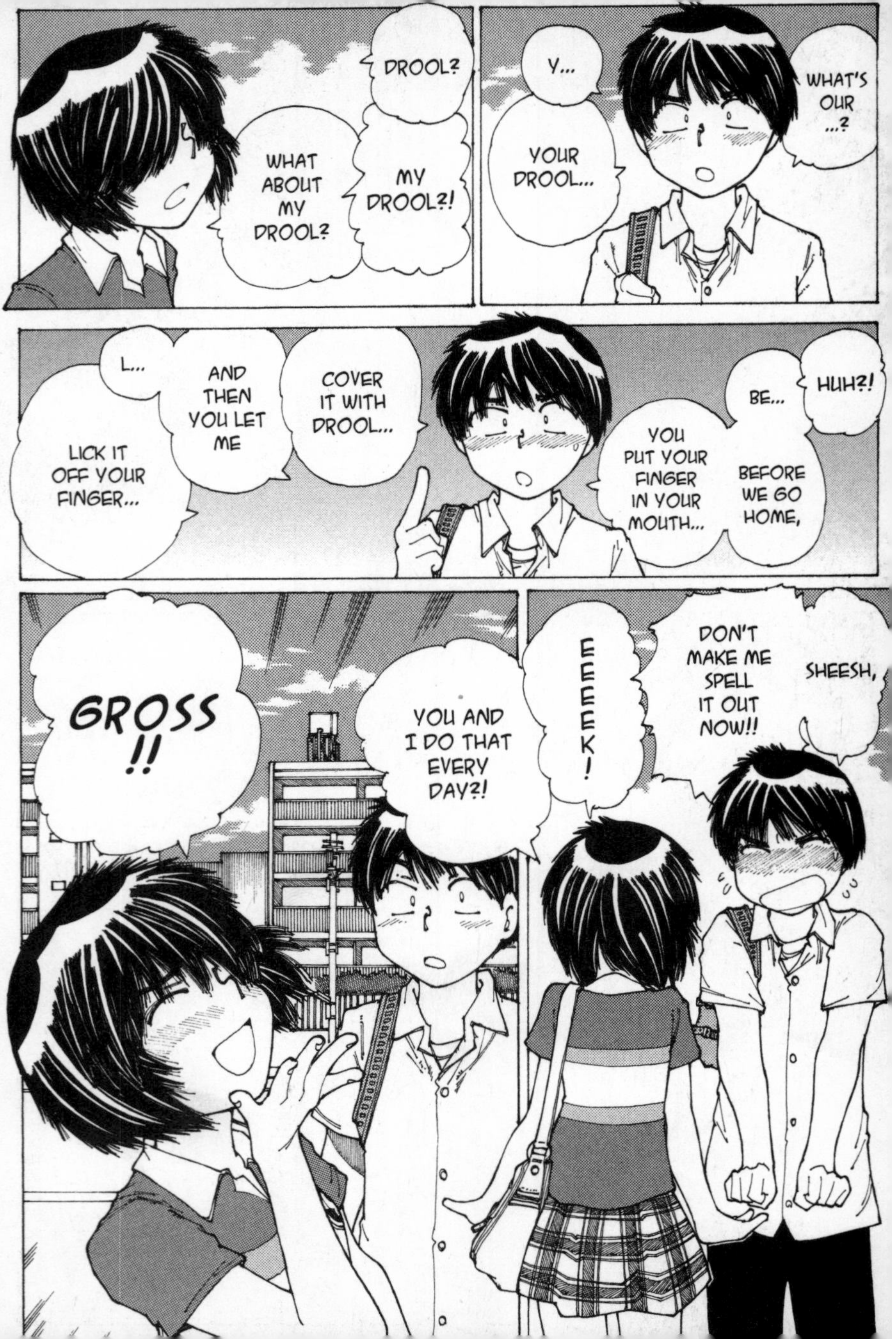
WHAT'S OUR ...?
Y...
YOUR DROOL...
DROOL?
MY DROOL?!
WHAT ABOUT MY DROOL?
HUH?!
BE...
BEFORE WE GO HOME,
YOU PUT YOUR FINGER IN YOUR MOUTH...
COVER IT WITH DROOL...
AND THEN YOU LET ME
L...
LICK IT OFF YOUR FINGER...
SHEESH,
DON'T MAKE ME SPELL IT OUT NOW!!
EEEEK!
YOU AND I DO THAT EVERY DAY?!
GROSS!!

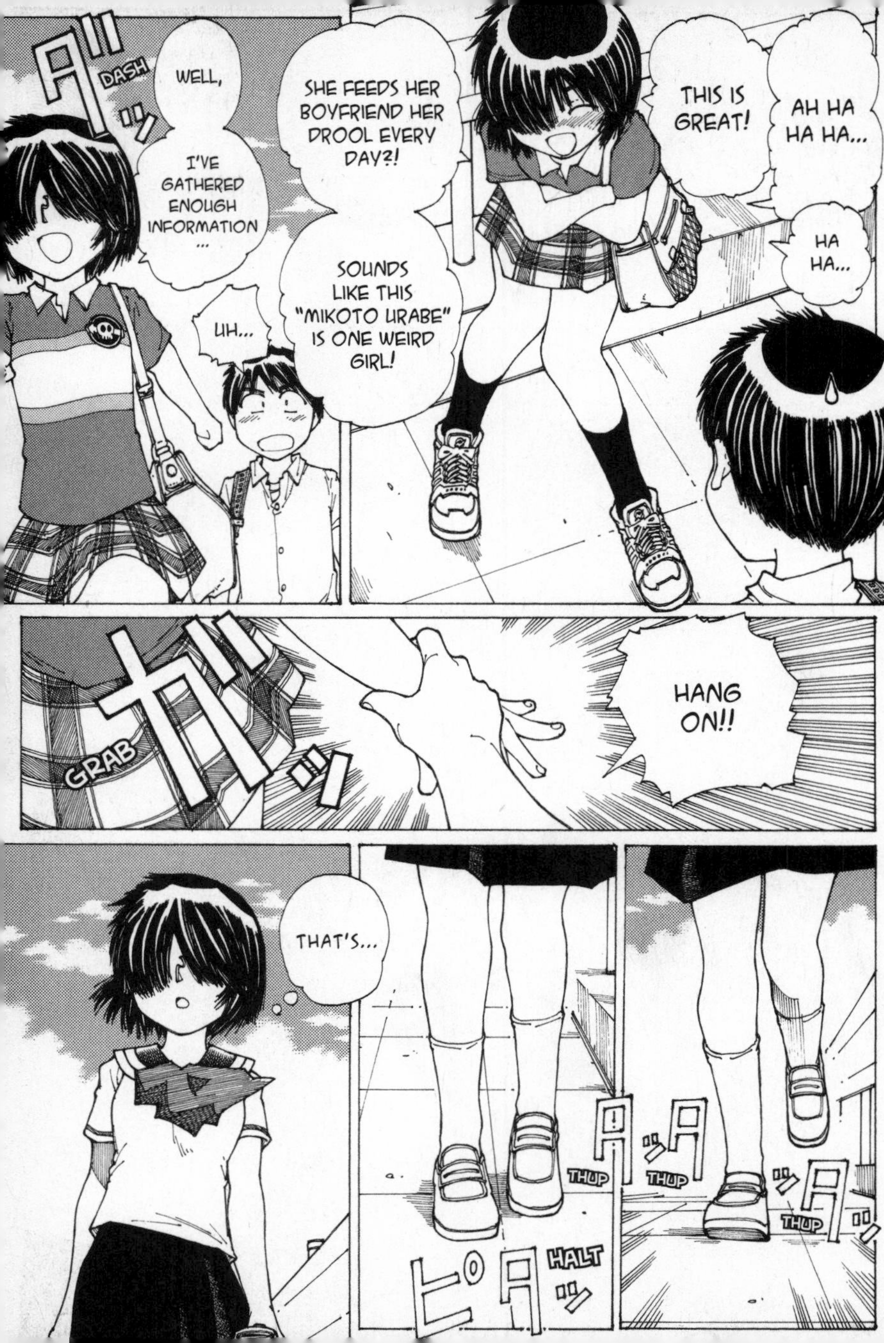
AH HA HA HA...
HA HA...
THIS IS GREAT!
SHE FEEDS HER BOYFRIEND HER DROOL EVERY DAY?!
SOUNDS LIKE THIS "MIKOTO URABE" IS ONE WEIRD GIRL!
DASH
WELL,
I'VE GATHERED ENOUGH INFORMATION ...
UH...
HANG ON!!
GRAB
THUP
THUP
THUP
HALT
THAT'S...

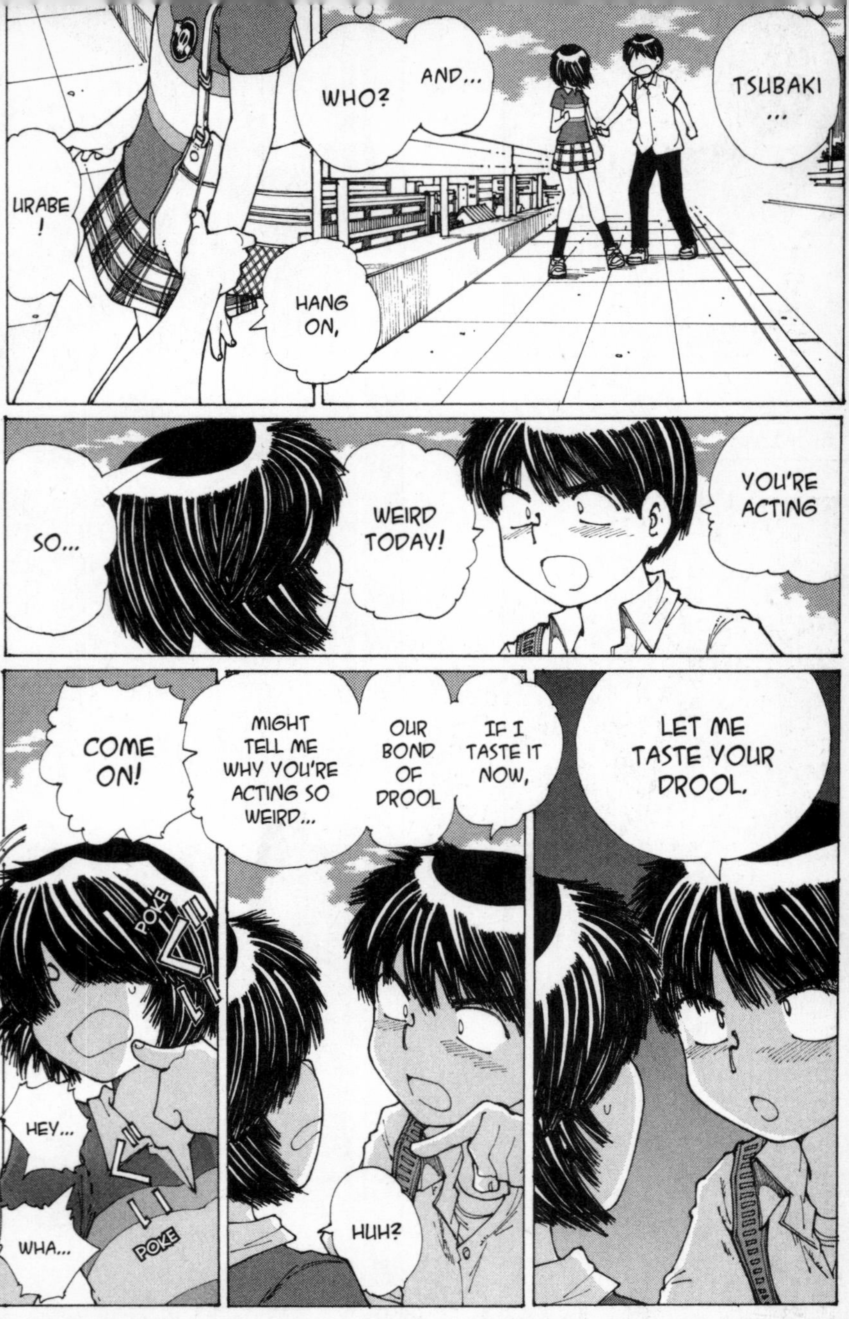
TSUBAKI ...
AND... WHO?
HANG ON,
URABE!
YOU'RE ACTING
WEIRD TODAY!
SO...
LET ME TASTE YOUR DROOL.
IF I TASTE IT NOW,
OUR BOND OF DROOL
MIGHT TELL ME WHY YOU'RE ACTING SO WEIRD...
HUH?
COME ON!
POKE
HEY...
WHA...
POKE

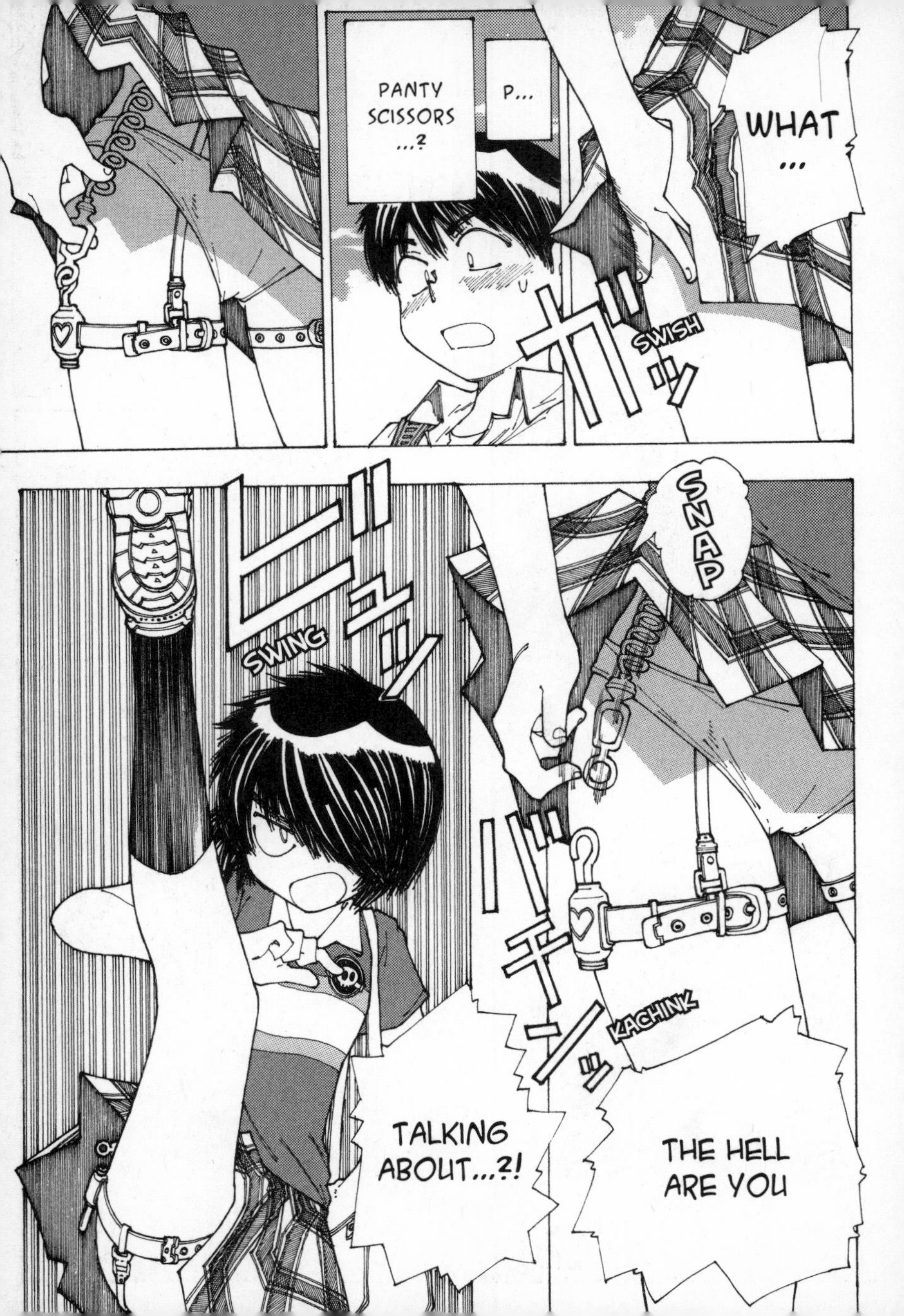
WHAT ...
SWISH
P...
PANTY SCISSORS ...?
SNAP
KACHINK
THE HELL ARE YOU
SWING
TALKING ABOUT...?!

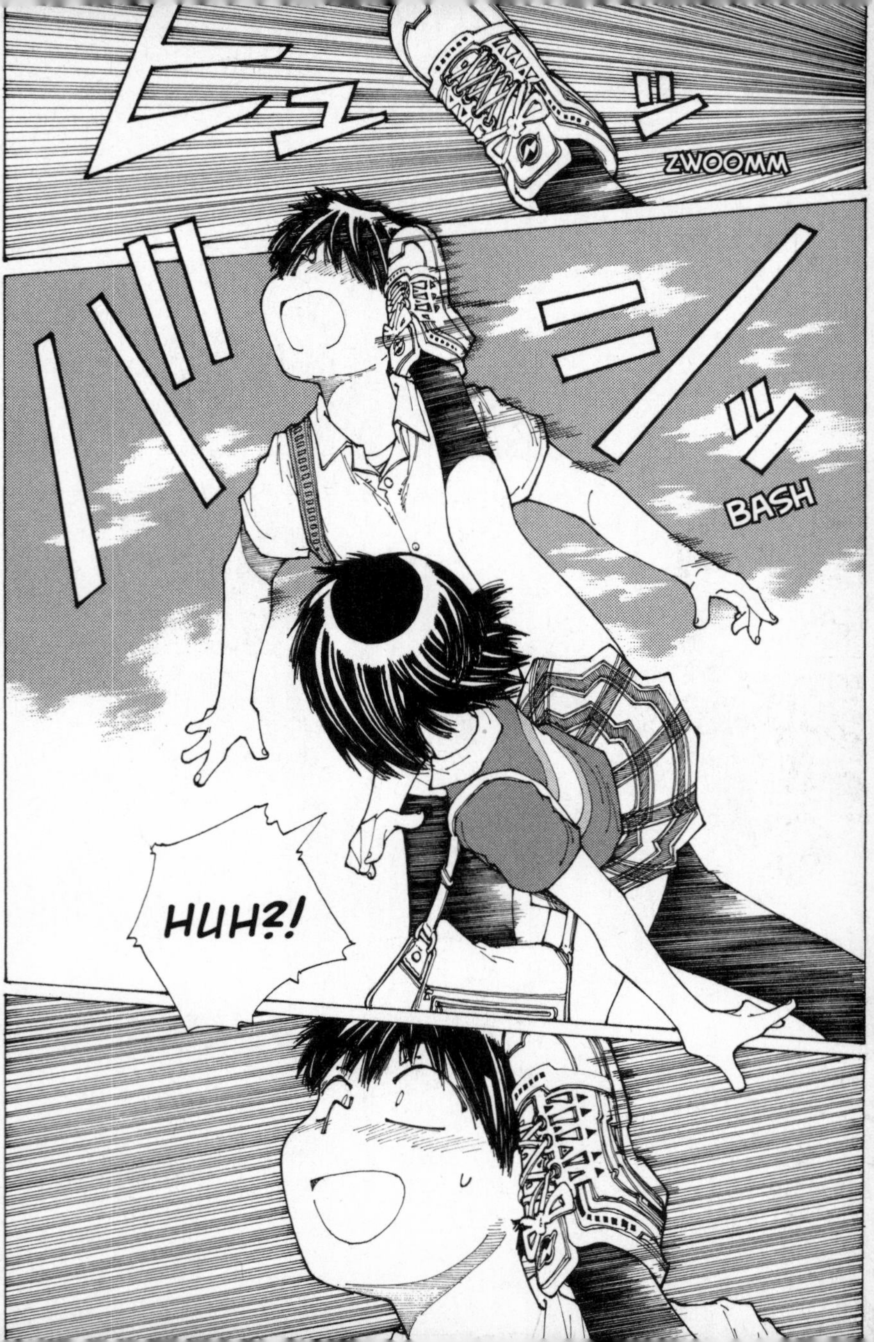

ヒュッ
ZWOOMM
BASH
HUH?!

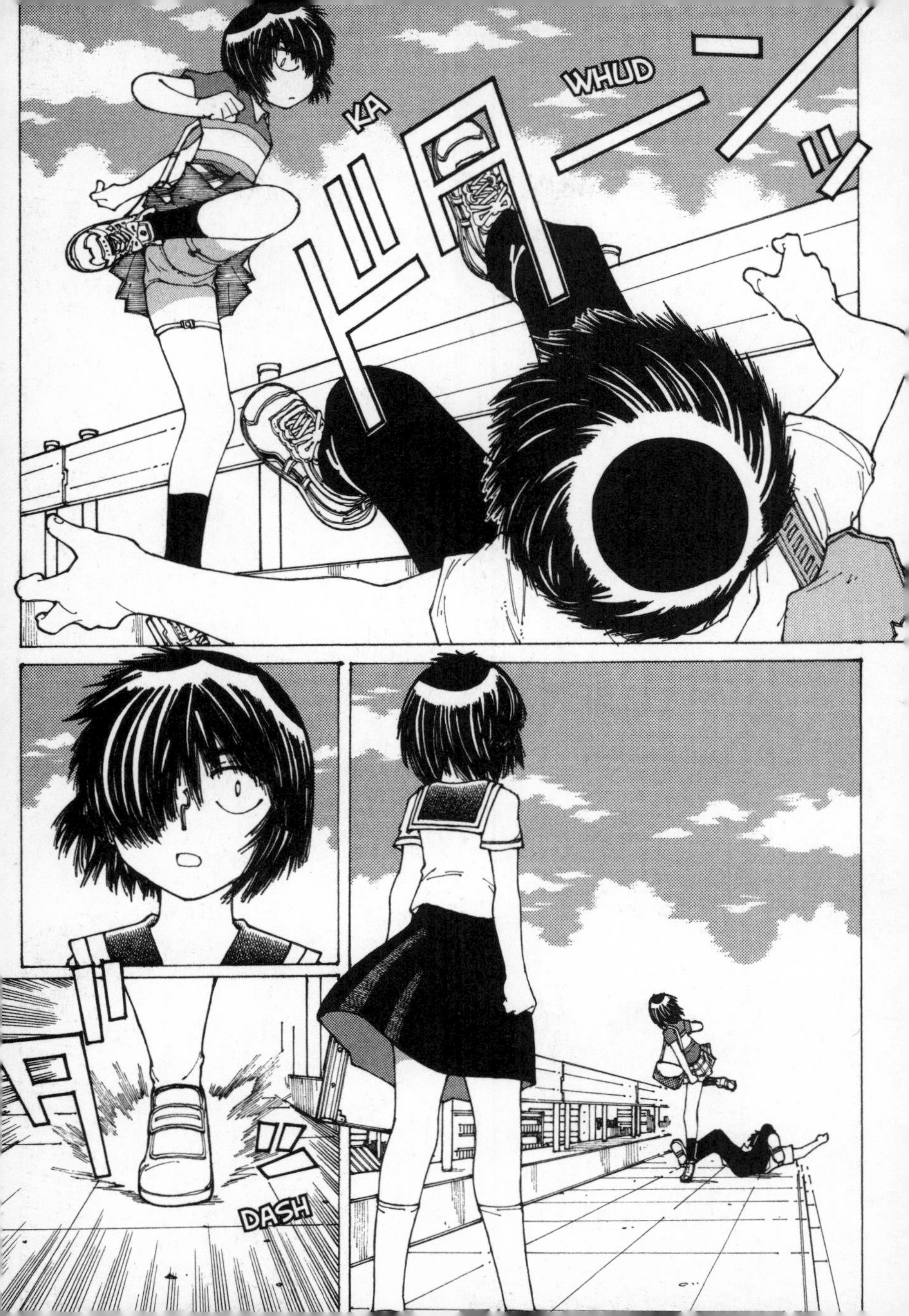
WHUD
KA
DASH

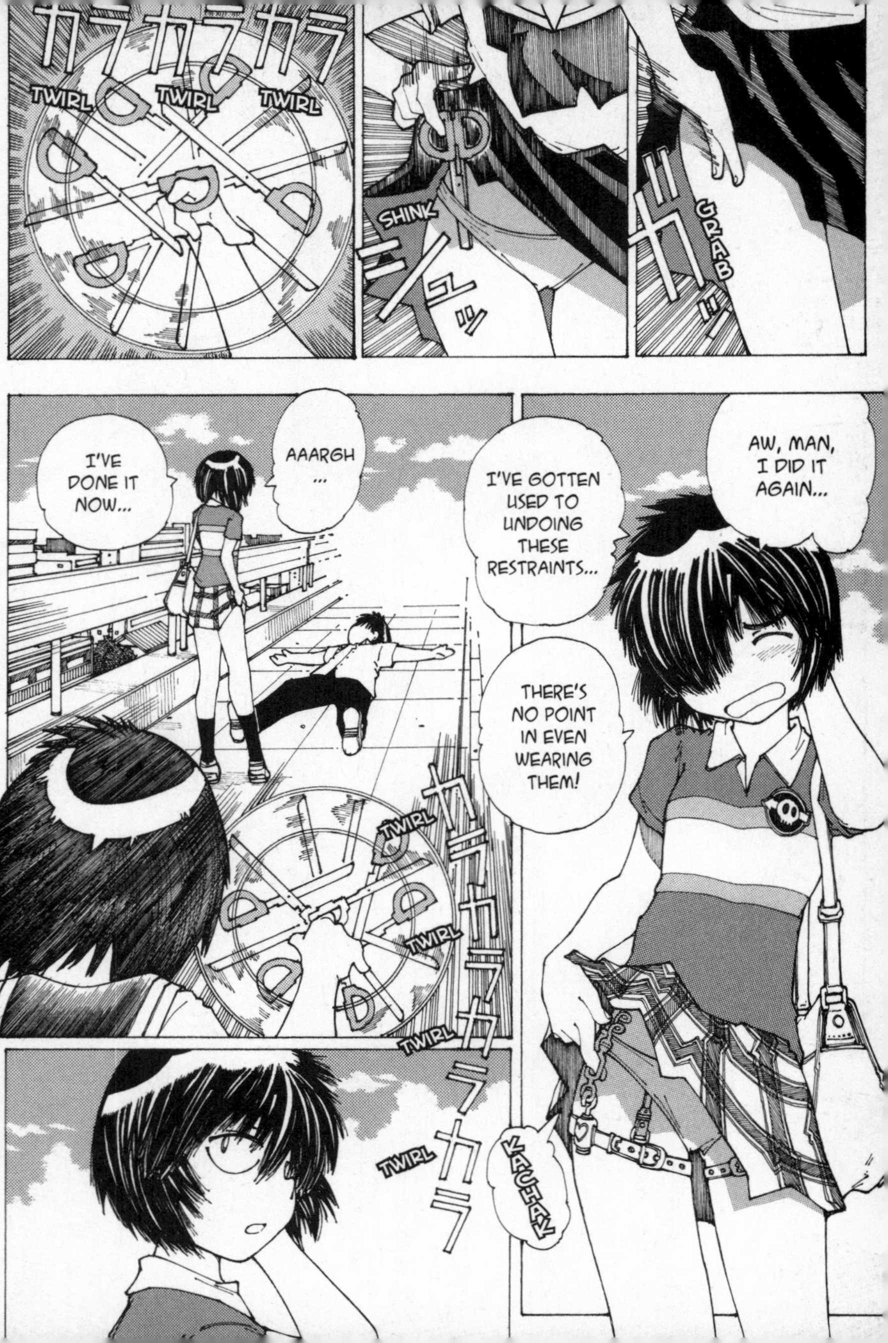
GRAB
SHINK
カラカラカラ
TWIRL
TWIRL
TWIRL
AW, MAN, I DID IT AGAIN...
I'VE GOTTEN USED TO UNDOING THESE RESTRAINTS...
THERE'S NO POINT IN EVEN WEARING THEM!
KACHAK
AAARGH ...
I'VE DONE IT NOW...
TWIRL
TWIRL
TWIRL
TWIRL

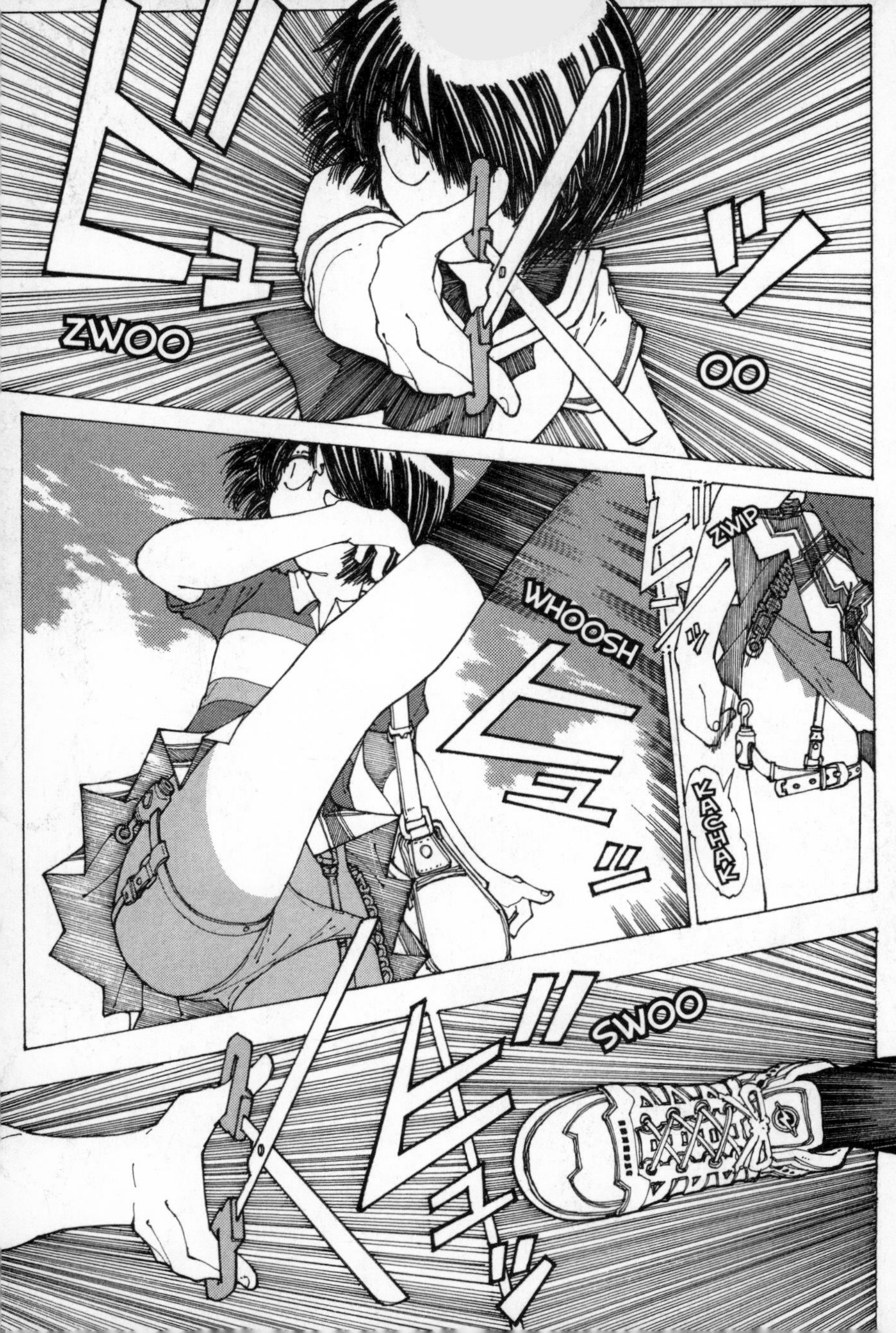
ZWOO
OO
ZWIP
KACHAK
WHOOSH
SWOO

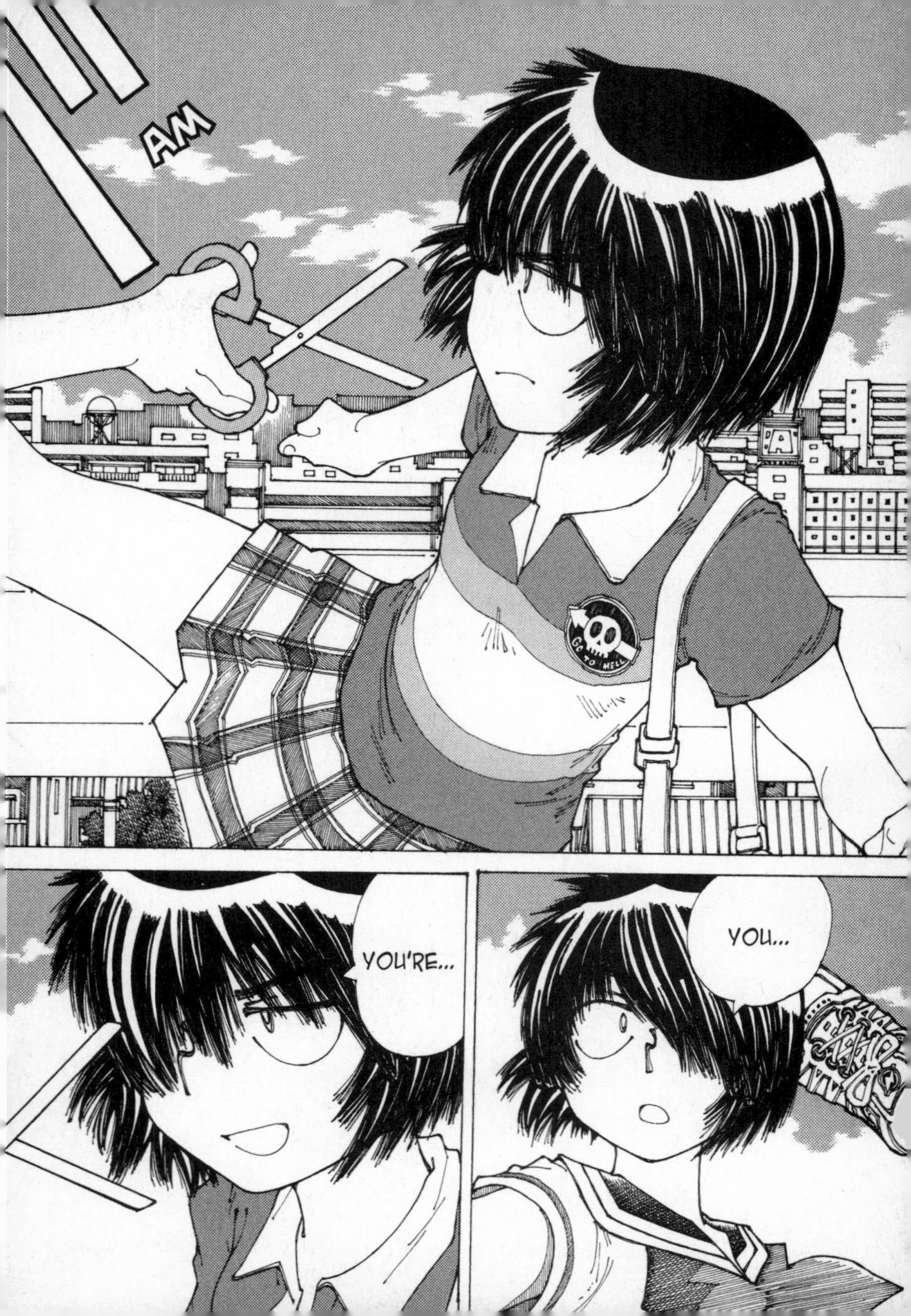
AM
GO TO HELL
A
YOU...
YOU'RE...

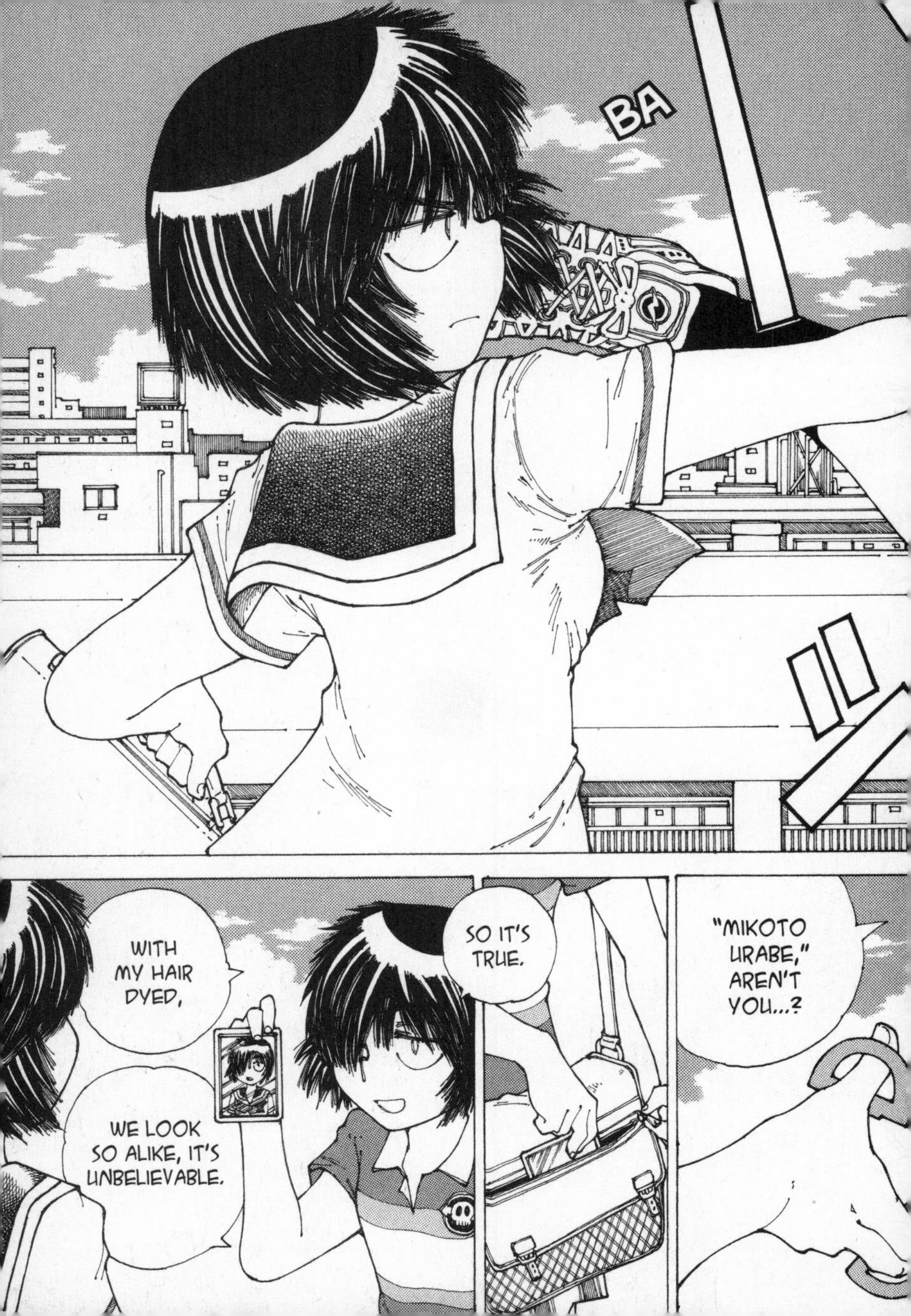
BA
"MIKOTO URABE," AREN'T YOU...?
SO IT'S TRUE.
WITH MY HAIR DYED,
WE LOOK SO ALIKE, IT'S UNBELIEVABLE.

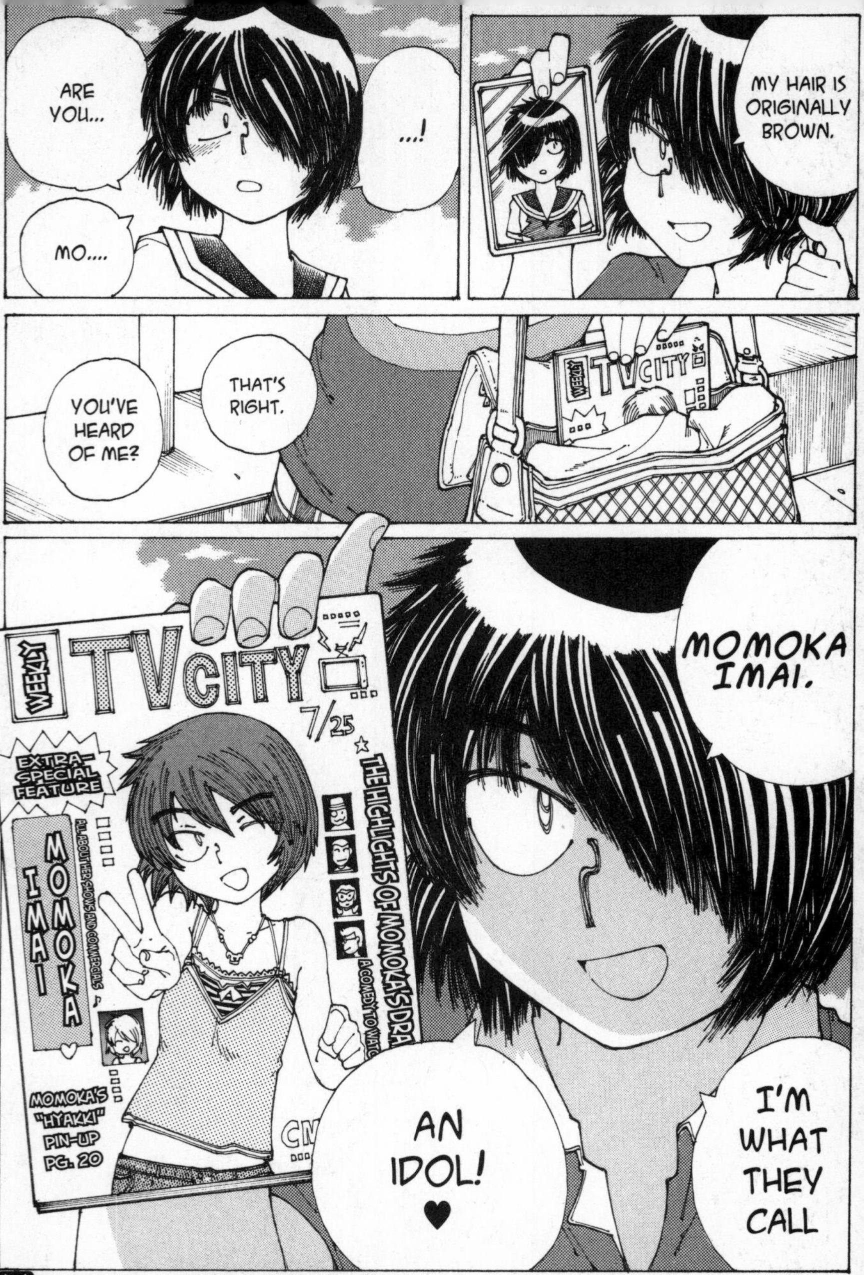
MY HAIR IS ORIGINALLY BROWN.
...!
ARE YOU...
MO....
THAT'S RIGHT.
YOU'VE HEARD OF ME?
WEEKLY TV CITY
MOMOKA IMAI.
WEEKLY TV CITY
7/25
EXTRA-SPECIAL FEATURE
MOMOKA IMAI
ALL ABOUT HER SHOWS AND COMMERCIALS
MOMOKA'S "HYAKKI" PIN-UP PG. 20
I'M WHAT THEY CALL
AN IDOL! ♥

END OF CHAPTER 37

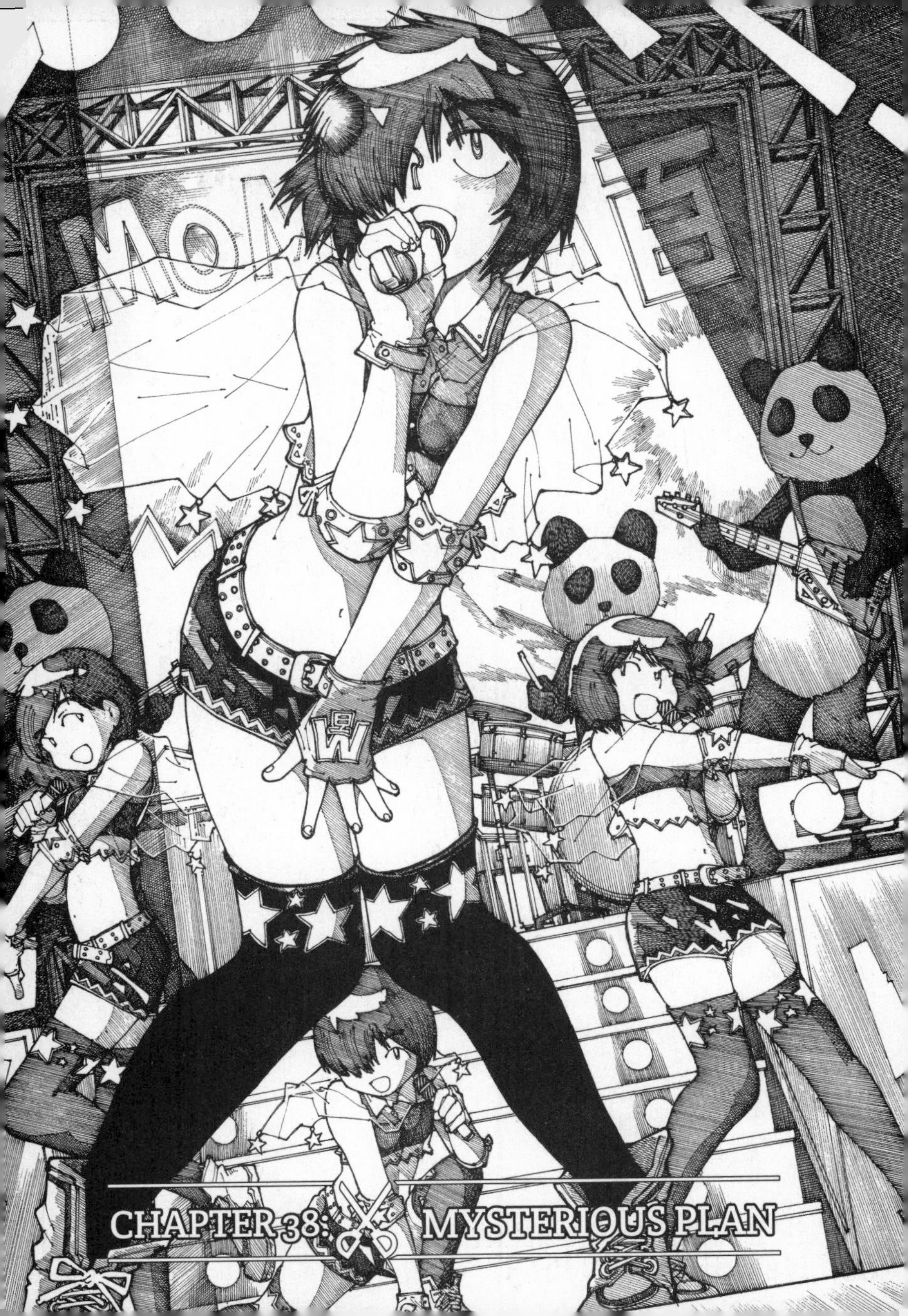

CHAPTER 38: MYSTERIOUS PLAN

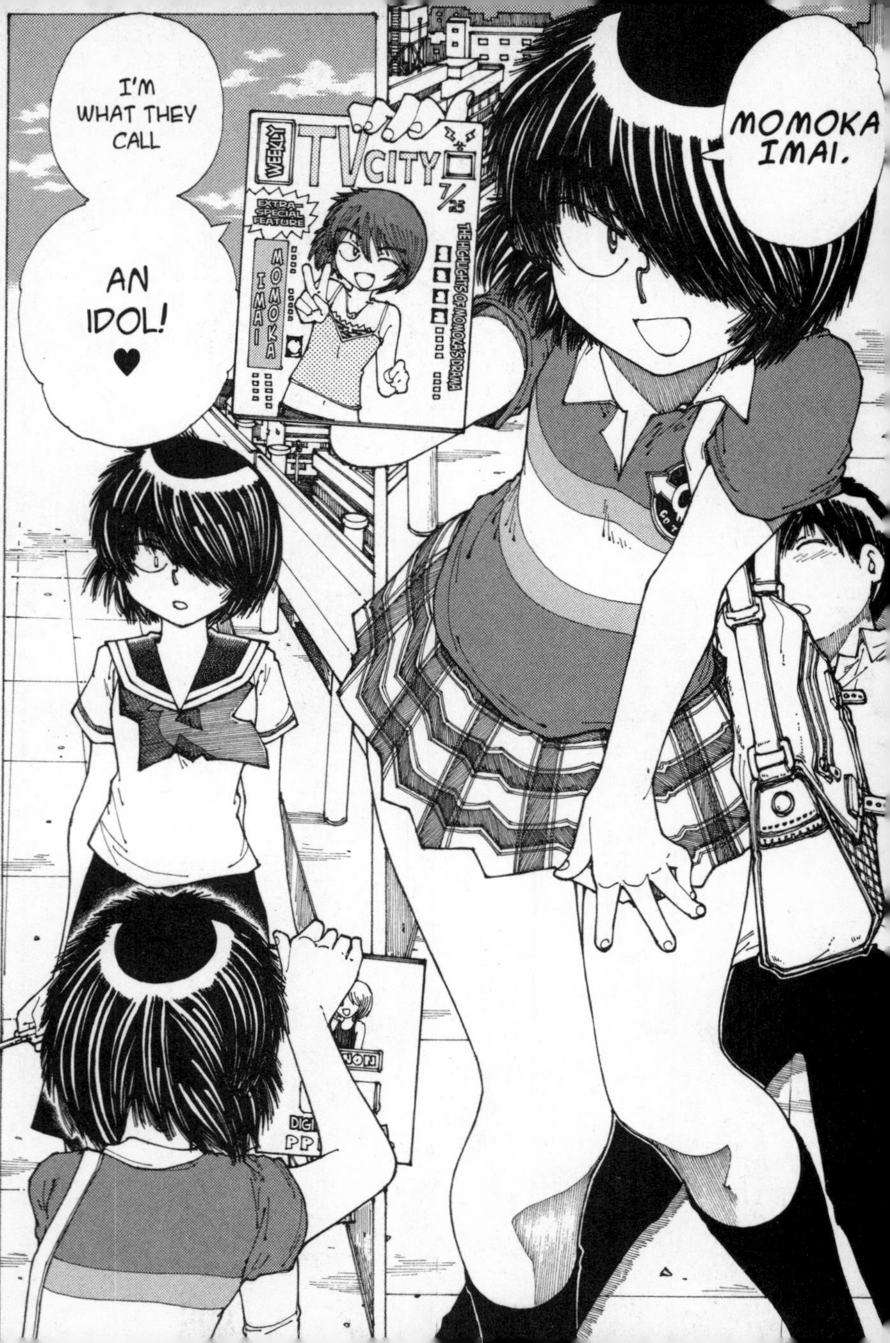
MOMOKA IMAI.
I'M WHAT THEY CALL
AN IDOL! ♥
WEEKLY
TV CITY
7/25
EXTRA-SPECIAL FEATURE
MOMOKA IMAI
THE HIGHLIGHTS OF MOMOKA'S DRAMA

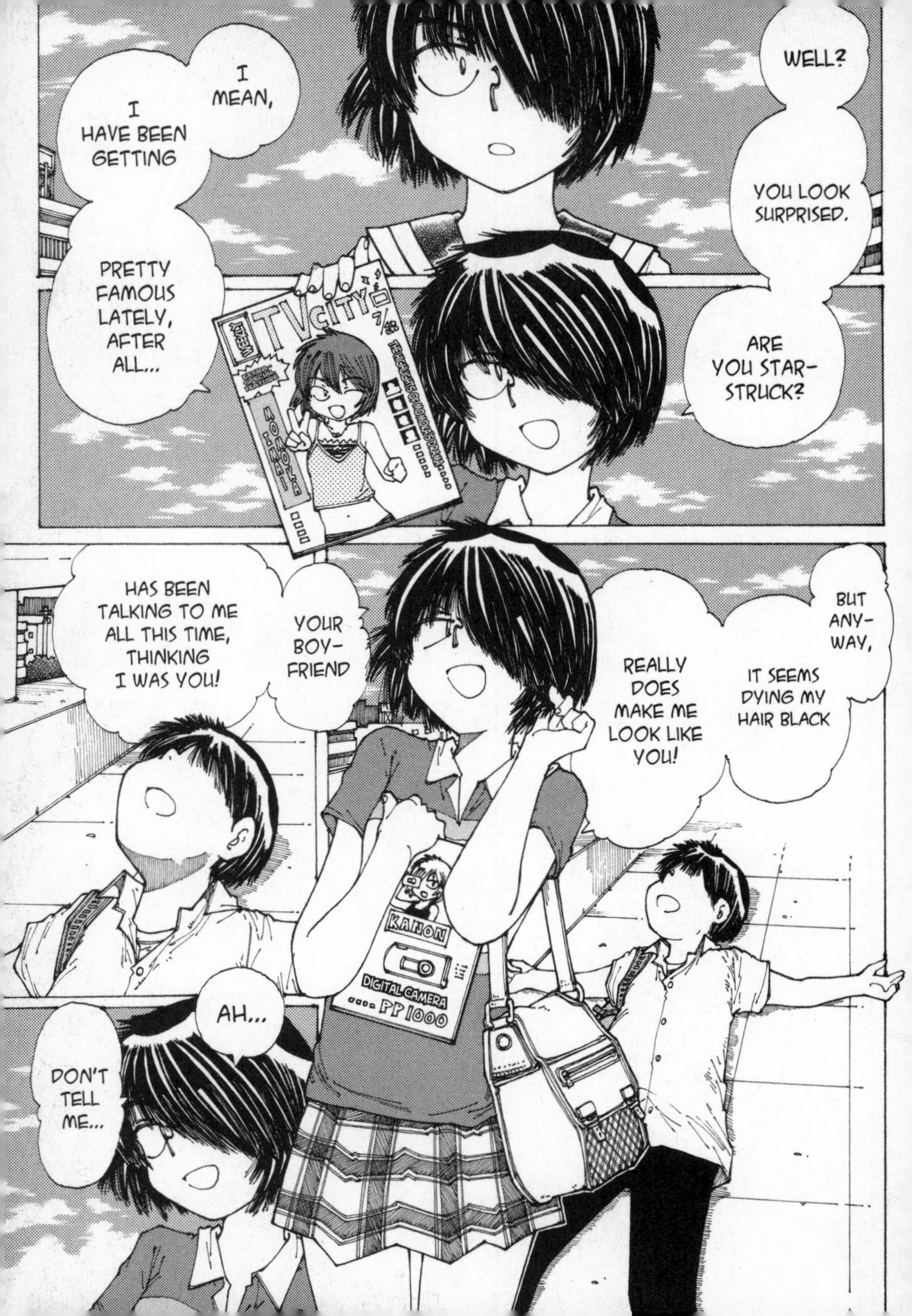
WELL?
YOU LOOK SURPRISED.
ARE YOU STAR-STRUCK?
I MEAN,
I HAVE BEEN GETTING
PRETTY FAMOUS LATELY, AFTER ALL...
WEEKLY TV CITY
BUT ANYWAY,
IT SEEMS DYING MY HAIR BLACK
REALLY DOES MAKE ME LOOK LIKE YOU!
YOUR BOY-FRIEND
HAS BEEN TALKING TO ME ALL THIS TIME, THINKING I WAS YOU!
KANON
DIGITAL CAMERA
PP1000
AH...
DON'T TELL ME...

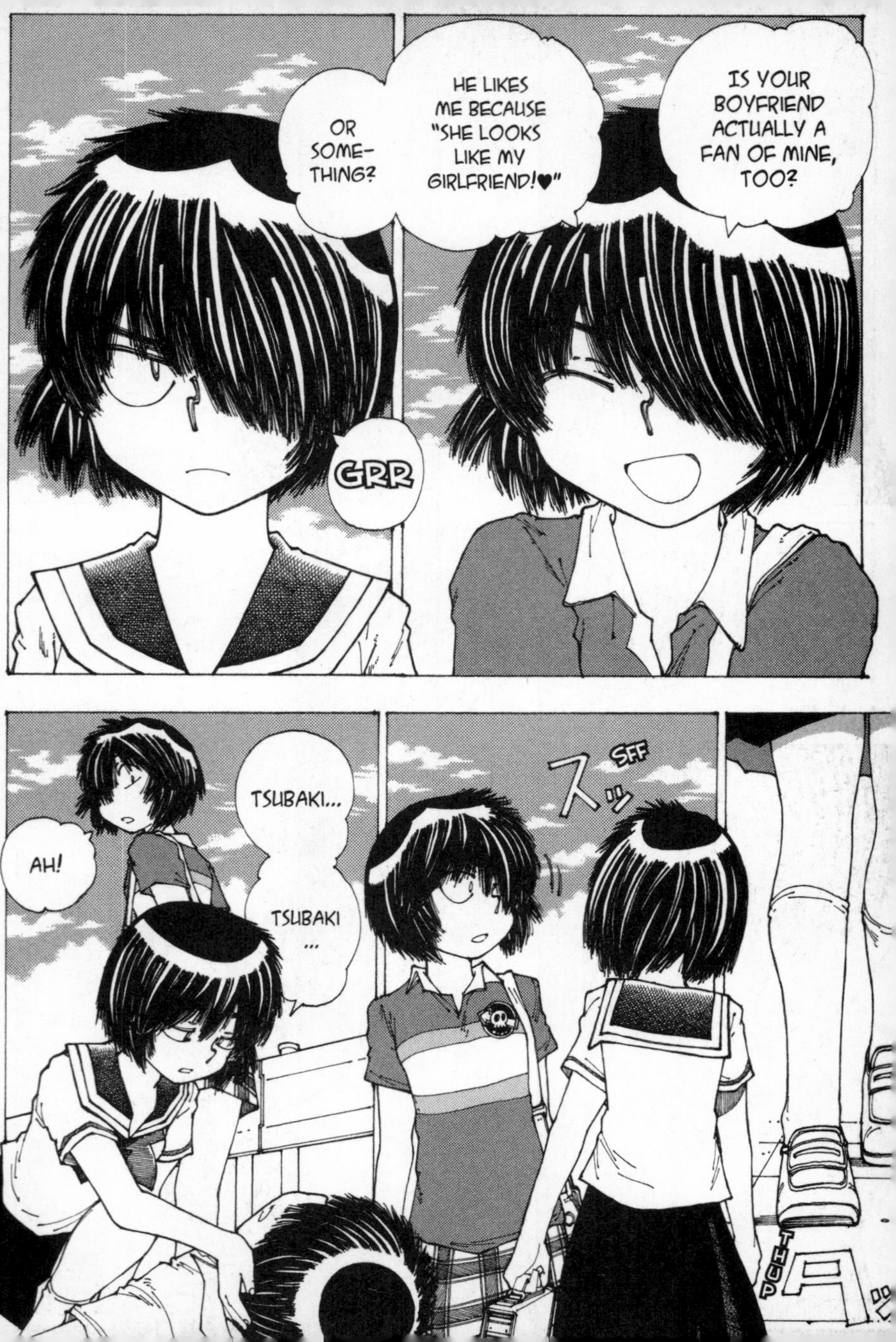
IS YOUR BOYFRIEND ACTUALLY A FAN OF MINE, TOO?
HE LIKES ME BECAUSE "SHE LOOKS LIKE MY GIRLFRIEND!♥"
OR SOME-THING?
GRR
THUP
SFF
TSUBAKI...
TSUBAKI ...
AH!

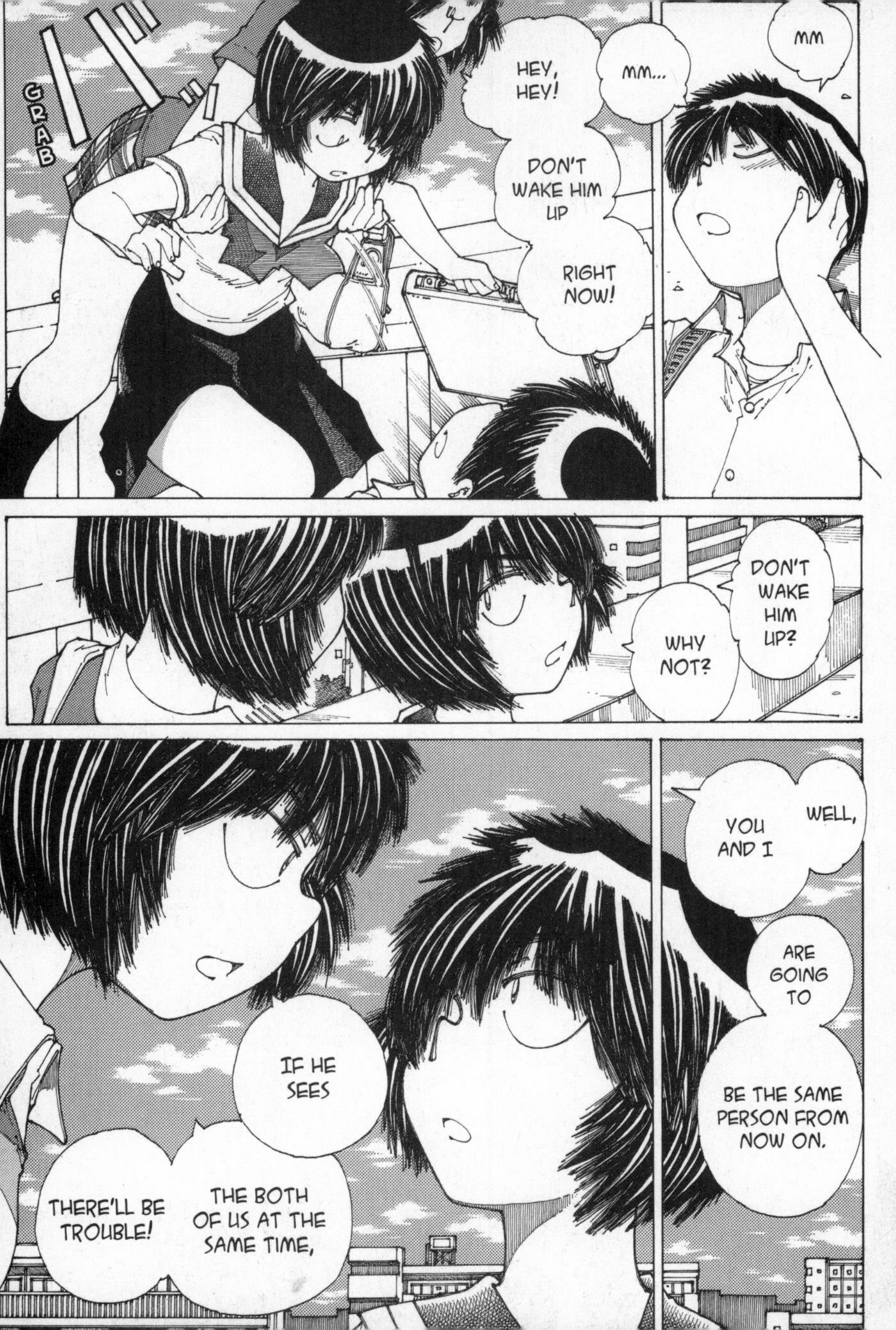
MM
MM...
HEY, HEY!
DON'T WAKE HIM UP
RIGHT NOW!
GRAB
DON'T WAKE HIM UP?
WHY NOT?
WELL,
YOU AND I
ARE GOING TO
BE THE SAME PERSON FROM NOW ON.
IF HE SEES
THE BOTH OF US AT THE SAME TIME,
THERE'LL BE TROUBLE!

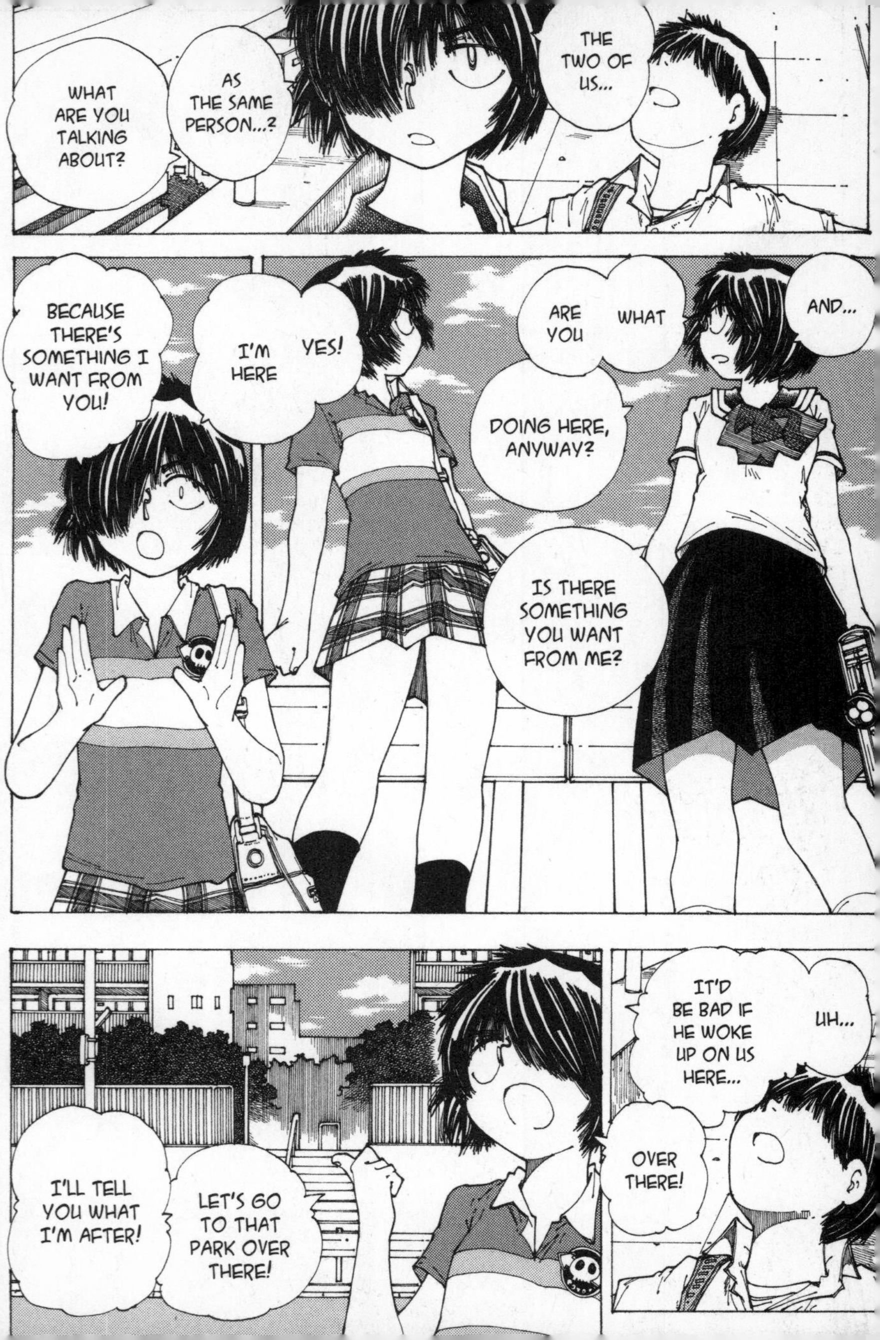
THE TWO OF US...
AS THE SAME PERSON...?
WHAT ARE YOU TALKING ABOUT?
AND...
WHAT
ARE YOU
DOING HERE, ANYWAY?
IS THERE SOMETHING YOU WANT FROM ME?
YES!
I'M HERE
BECAUSE THERE'S SOMETHING I WANT FROM YOU!
UH...
IT'D BE BAD IF HE WOKE UP ON US HERE...
OVER THERE!
LET'S GO TO THAT PARK OVER THERE!
I'LL TELL YOU WHAT I'M AFTER!

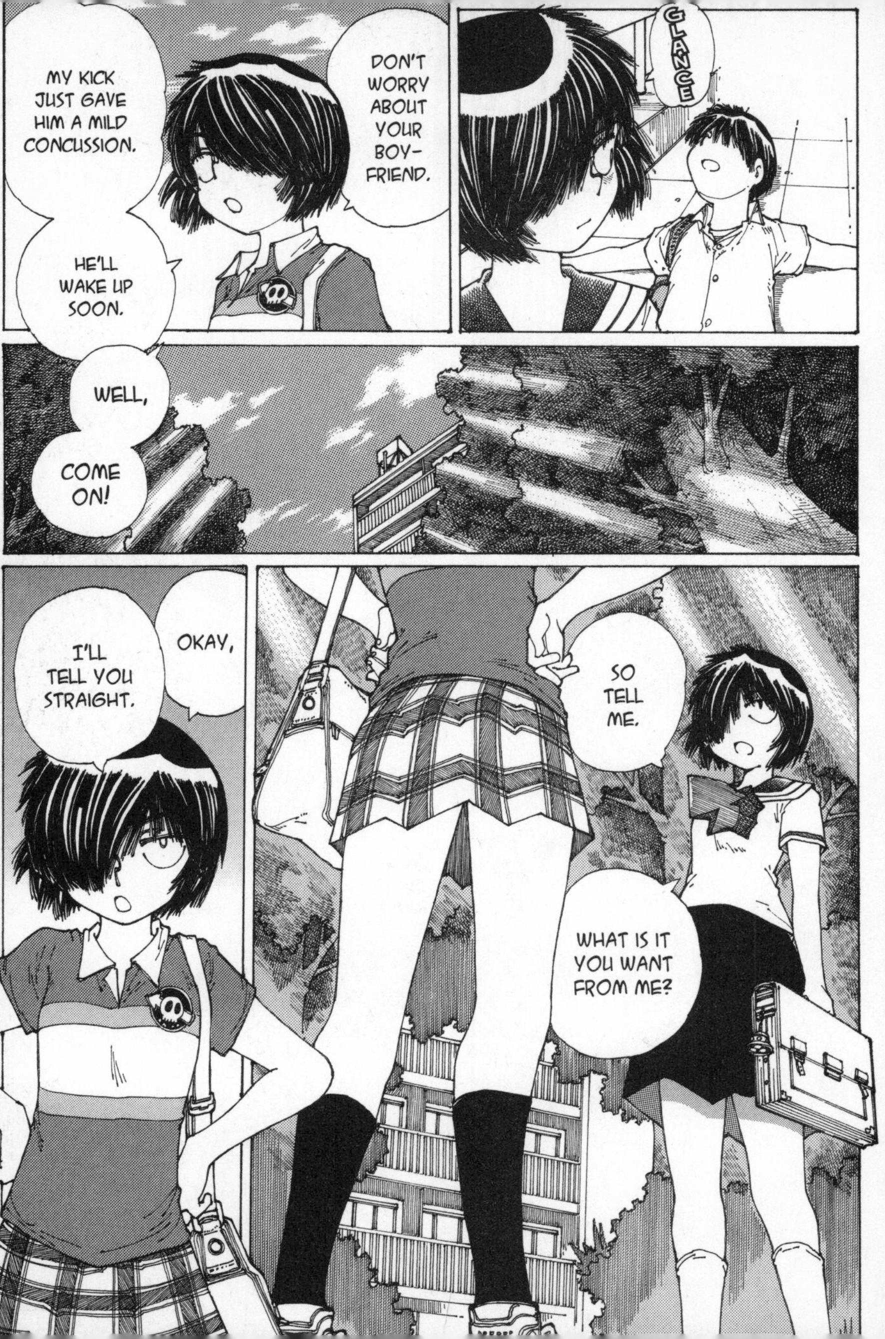
GLANCE
DON'T WORRY ABOUT YOUR BOY-FRIEND.
MY KICK JUST GAVE HIM A MILD CONCUSSION.
HE'LL WAKE UP SOON.
WELL,
COME ON!
SO TELL ME.
WHAT IS IT YOU WANT FROM ME?
OKAY,
I'LL TELL YOU STRAIGHT.

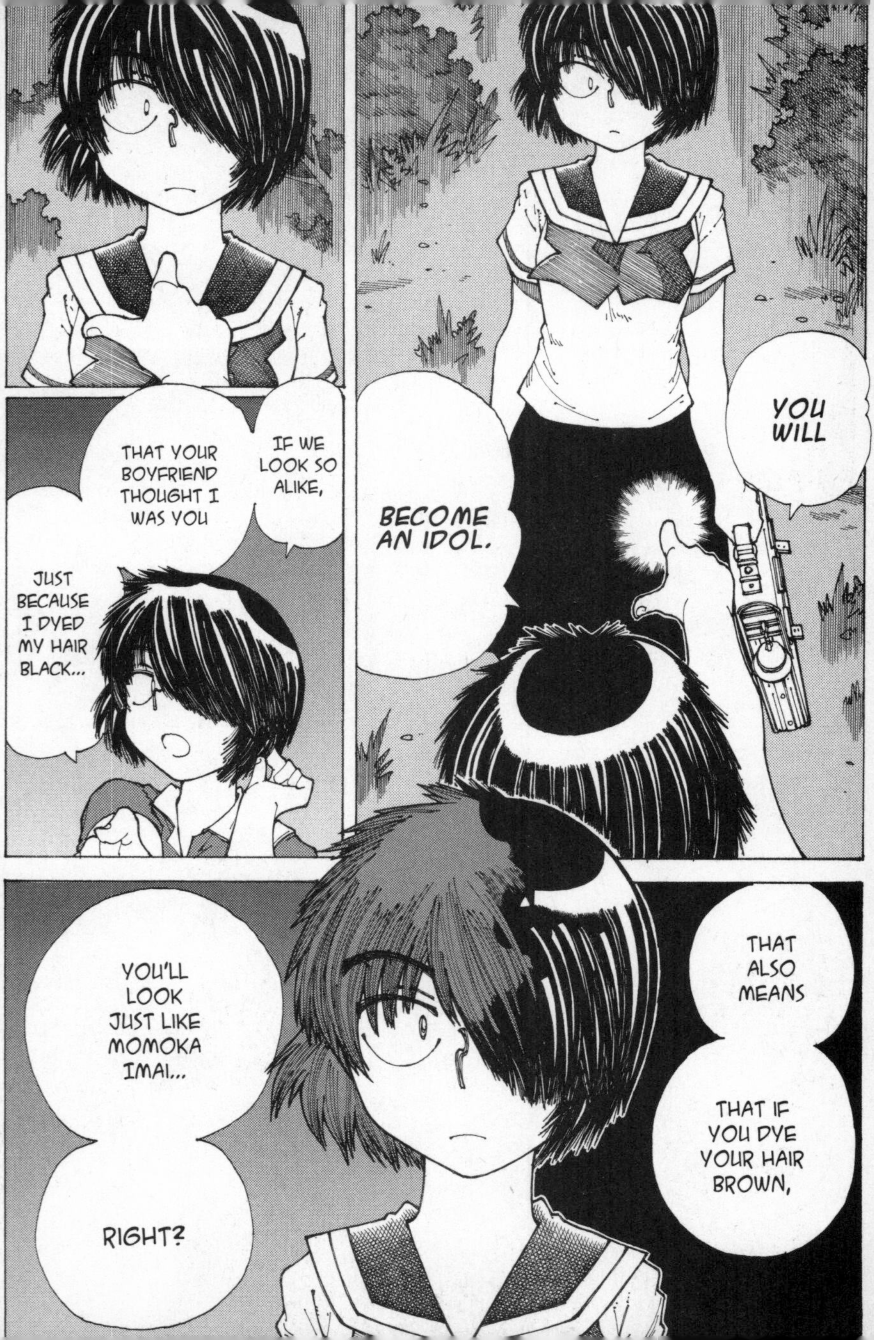
YOU WILL
BECOME AN IDOL.
IF WE LOOK SO ALIKE,
THAT YOUR BOYFRIEND THOUGHT I WAS YOU
JUST BECAUSE I DYED MY HAIR BLACK...
THAT ALSO MEANS
THAT IF YOU DYE YOUR HAIR BROWN,
YOU'LL LOOK JUST LIKE MOMOKA IMAI...
RIGHT?

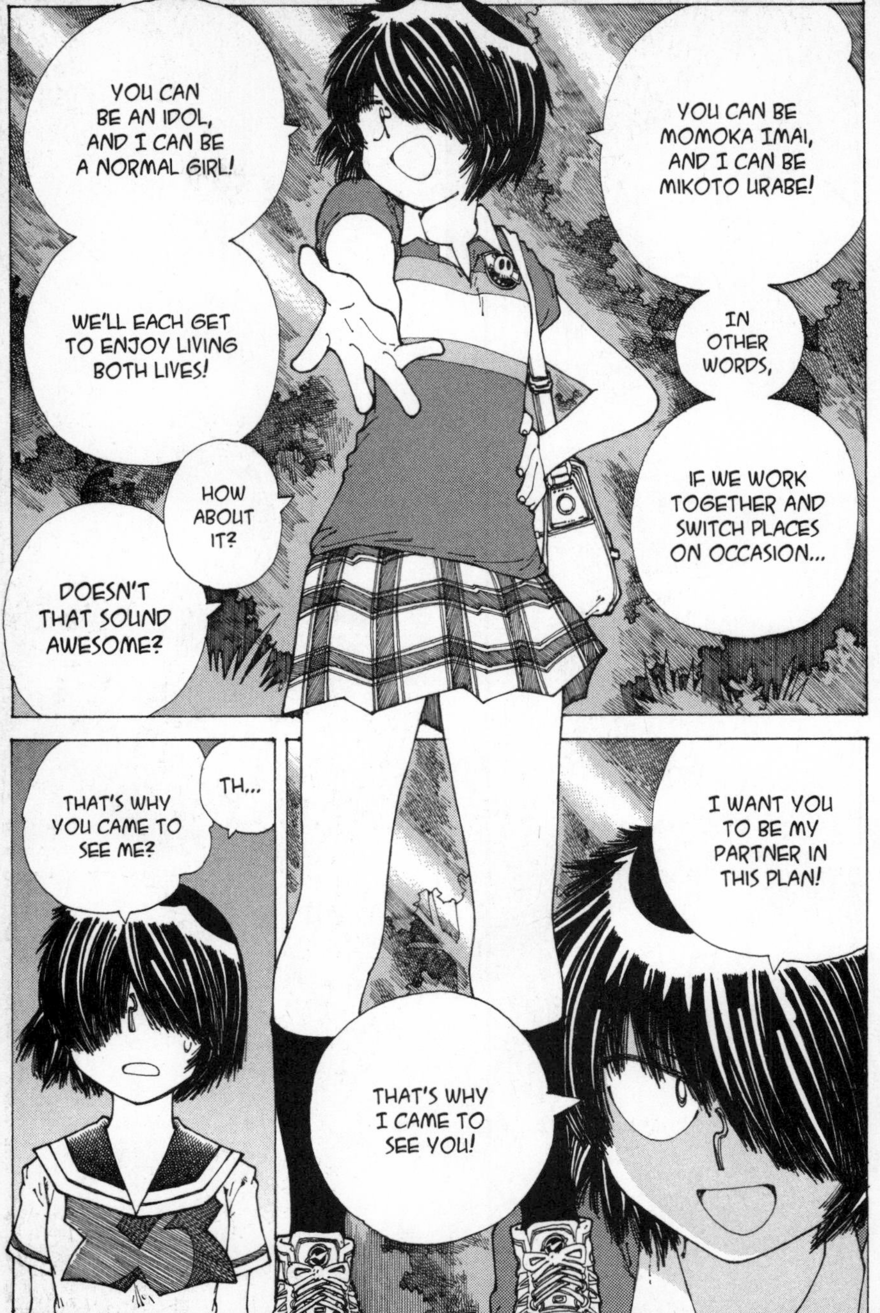
YOU CAN BE MOMOKA IMAI, AND I CAN BE MIKOTO URABE!
IN OTHER WORDS,
IF WE WORK TOGETHER AND SWITCH PLACES ON OCCASION...
YOU CAN BE AN IDOL, AND I CAN BE A NORMAL GIRL!
WE'LL EACH GET TO ENJOY LIVING BOTH LIVES!
HOW ABOUT IT?
DOESN'T THAT SOUND AWESOME?
I WANT YOU TO BE MY PARTNER IN THIS PLAN!
TH...
THAT'S WHY YOU CAME TO SEE ME?
THAT'S WHY I CAME TO SEE YOU!

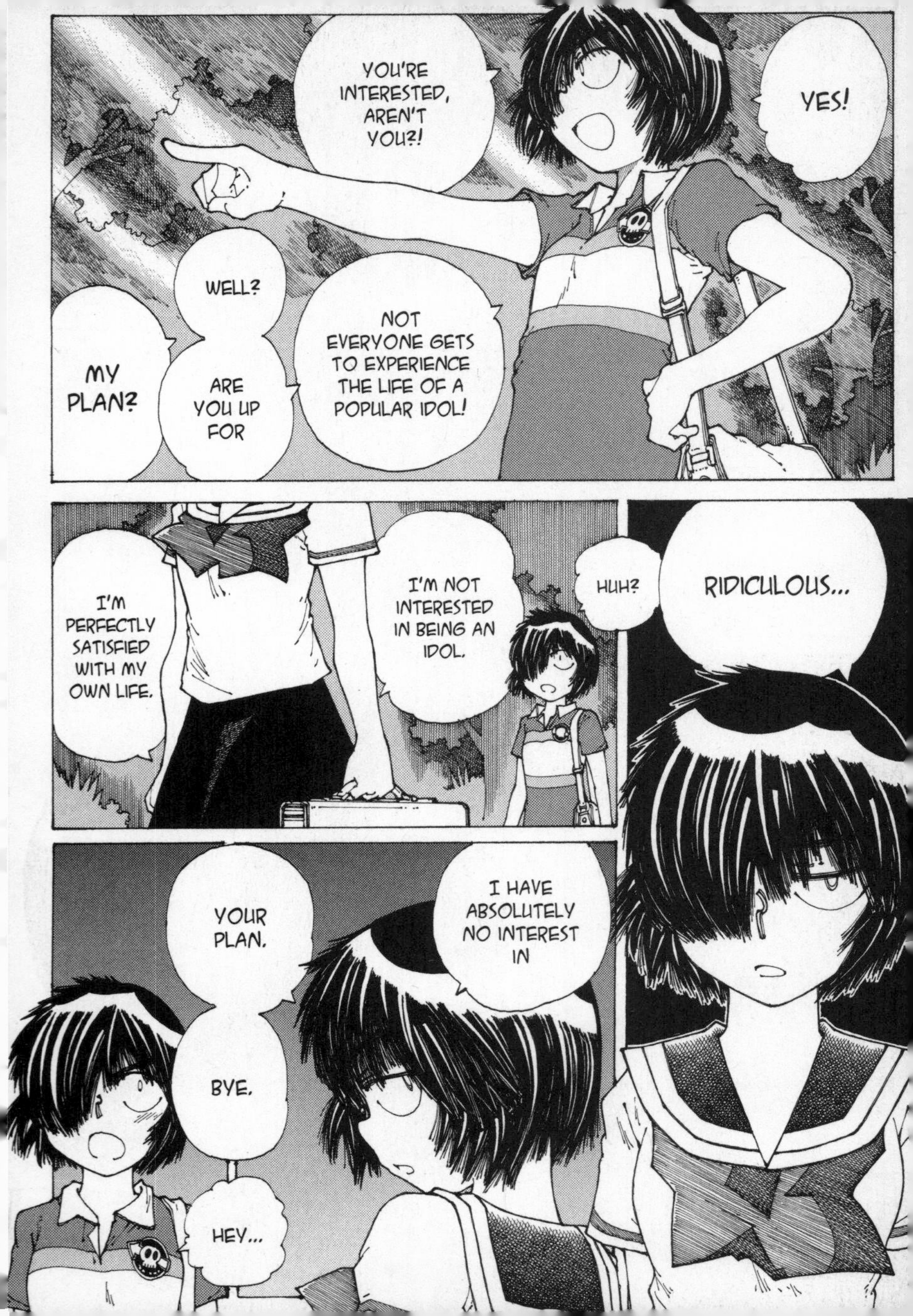
YES!
YOU'RE INTERESTED, AREN'T YOU?!
NOT EVERYONE GETS TO EXPERIENCE THE LIFE OF A POPULAR IDOL!
WELL?
ARE YOU UP FOR
MY PLAN?
RIDICULOUS...
HUH?
I'M NOT INTERESTED IN BEING AN IDOL.
I'M PERFECTLY SATISFIED WITH MY OWN LIFE.
I HAVE ABSOLUTELY NO INTEREST IN
YOUR PLAN.
BYE.
HEY...

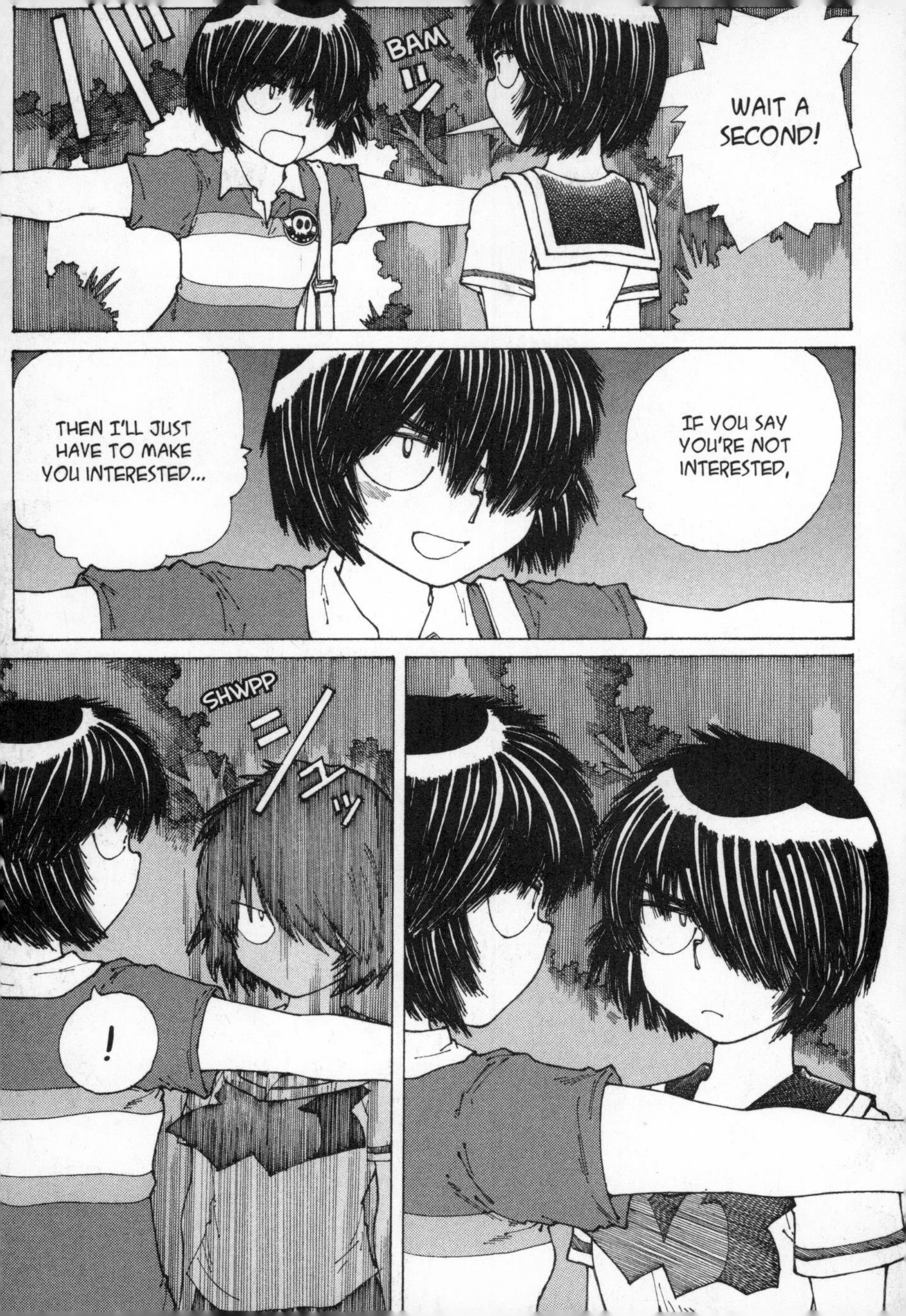
WAIT A SECOND!
BAM
IF YOU SAY YOU'RE NOT INTERESTED,
THEN I'LL JUST HAVE TO MAKE YOU INTERESTED...
SHWPP
!

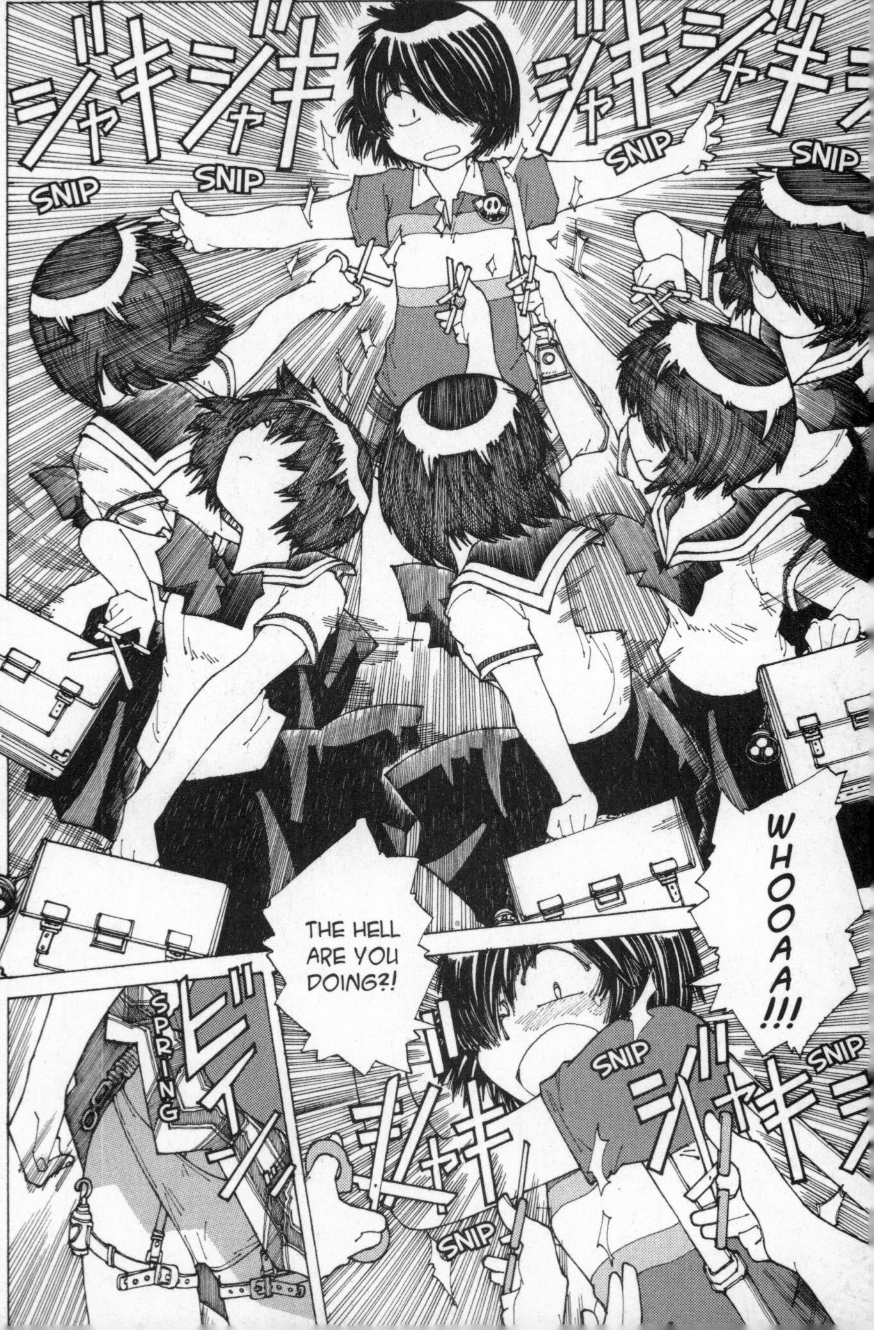
SNIP
SNIP
SNIP
SNIP
WHOOAAA!!!
THE HELL ARE YOU DOING?!
SNIP
SNIP
SNIP
SPRING

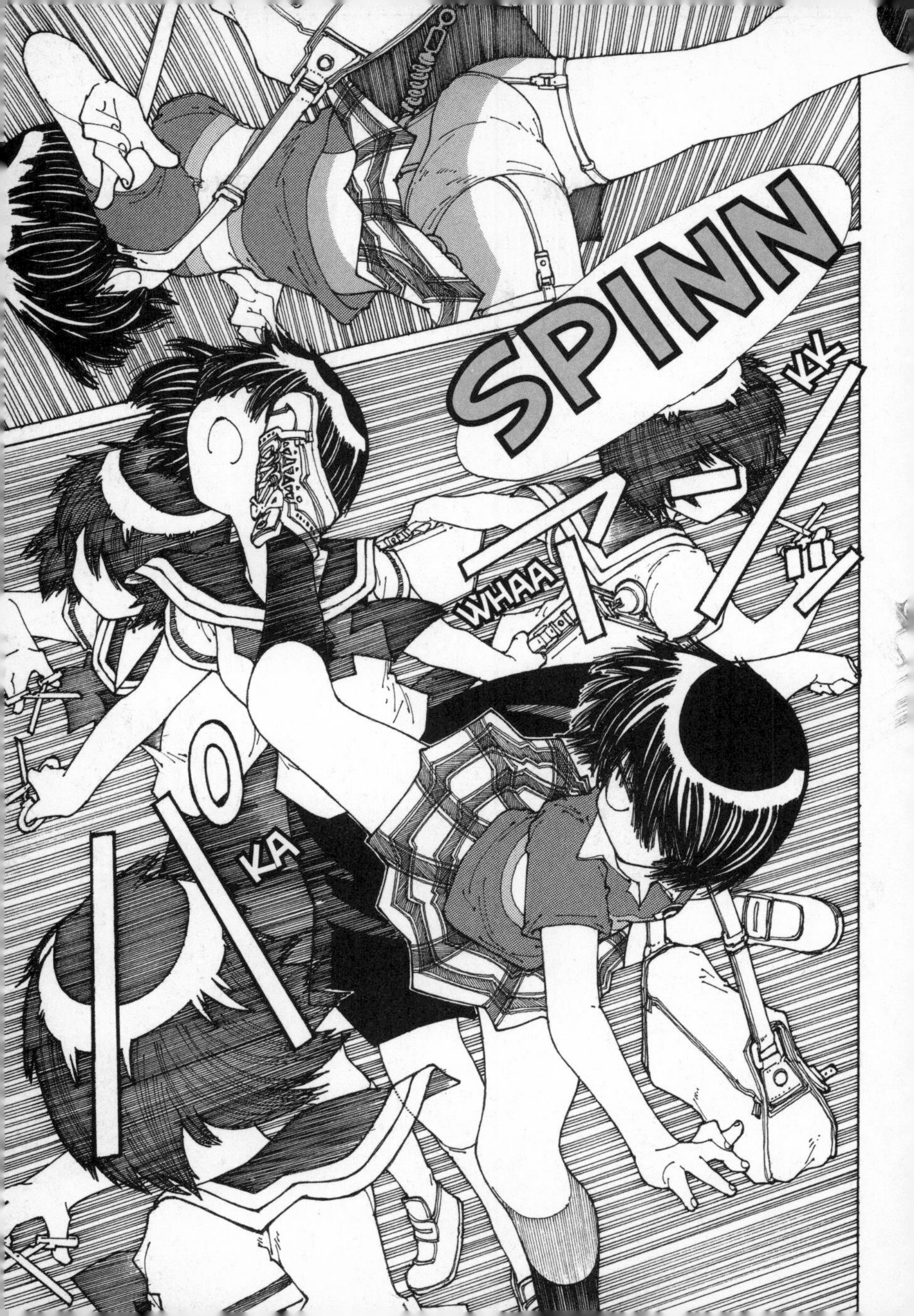
SPINN
KAK
WHAA
KA

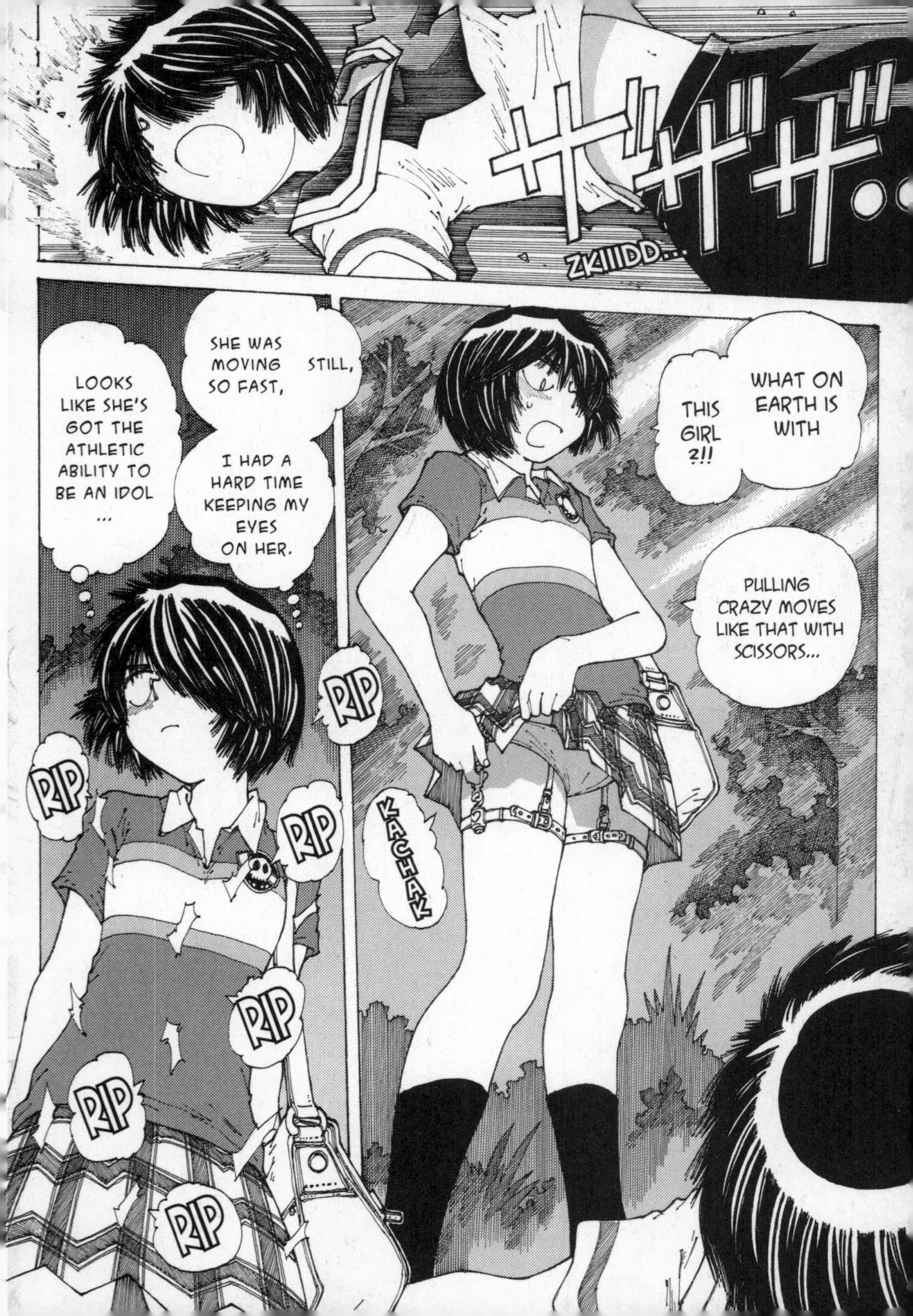
ザザザ…
ZKIIIDD…
WHAT ON EARTH IS WITH THIS GIRL ?!!
PULLING CRAZY MOVES LIKE THAT WITH SCISSORS...
KACHAK
STILL, SHE WAS MOVING SO FAST,
I HAD A HARD TIME KEEPING MY EYES ON HER.
LOOKS LIKE SHE'S GOT THE ATHLETIC ABILITY TO BE AN IDOL ...
RIP
RIP
RIP
RIP
RIP
RIP

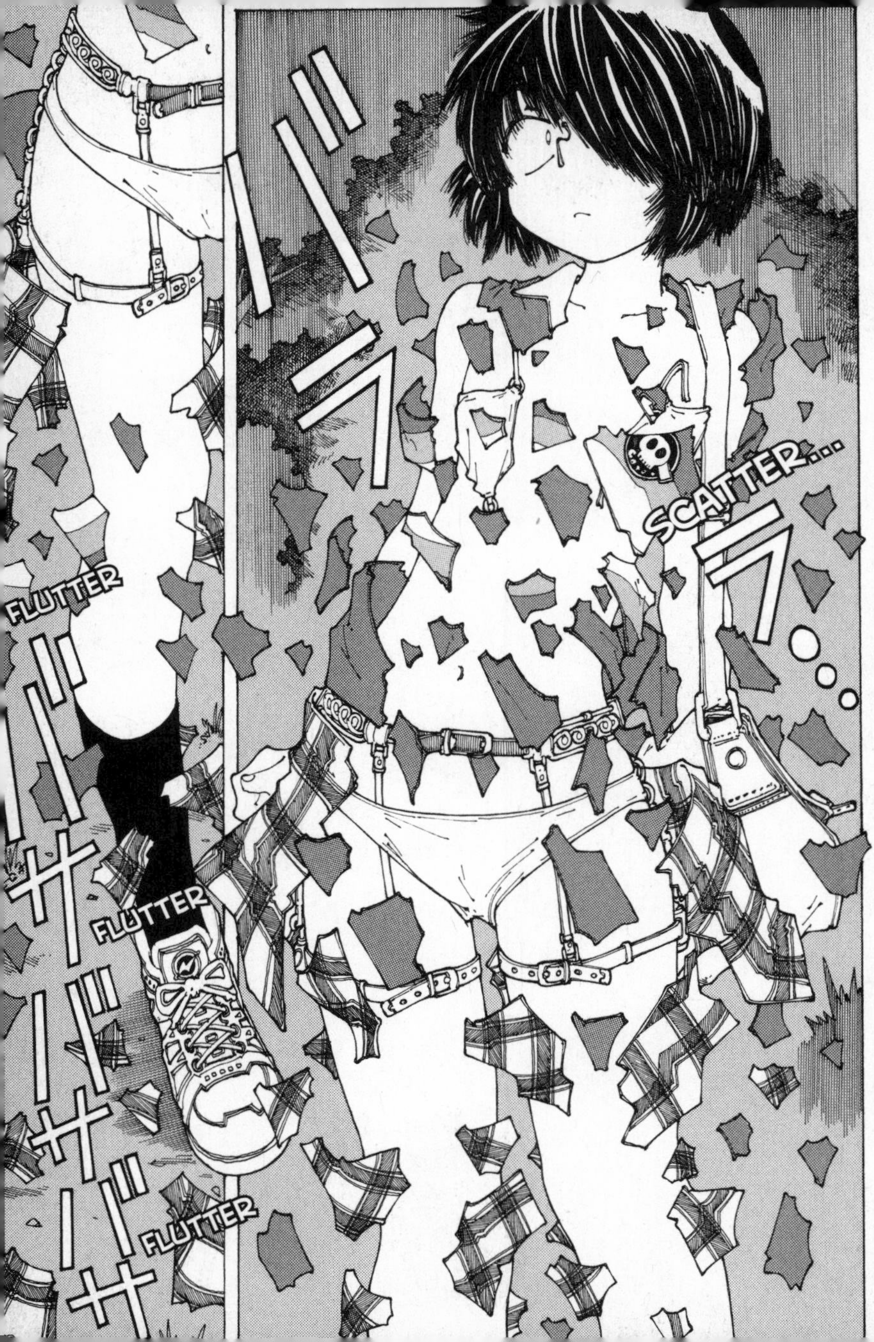
SCATTER...
FLUTTER
FLUTTER
FLUTTER

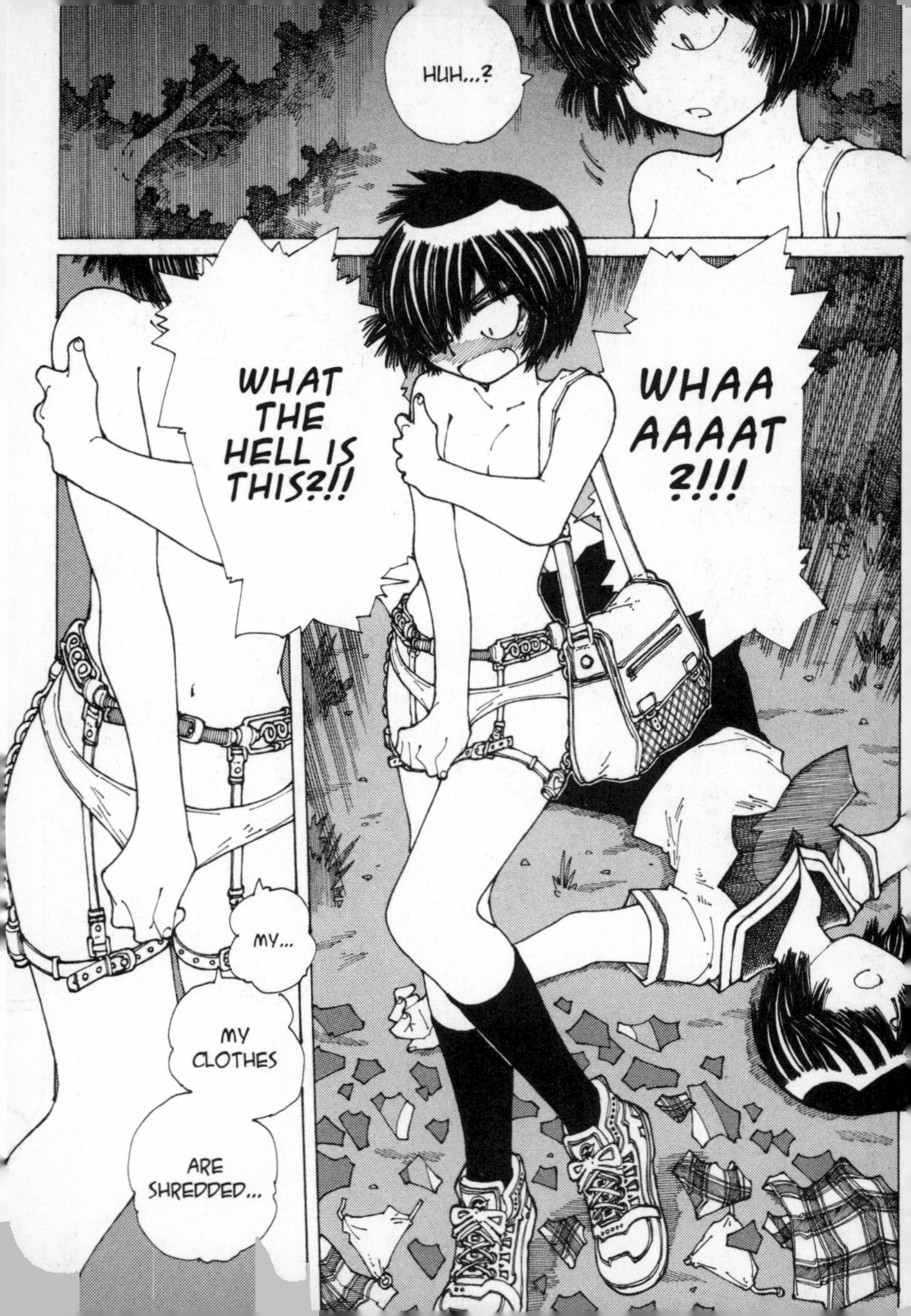
HUH...?
WHAA AAAAT ?!!!
WHAT THE HELL IS THIS?!!
MY...
MY CLOTHES
ARE SHREDDED...

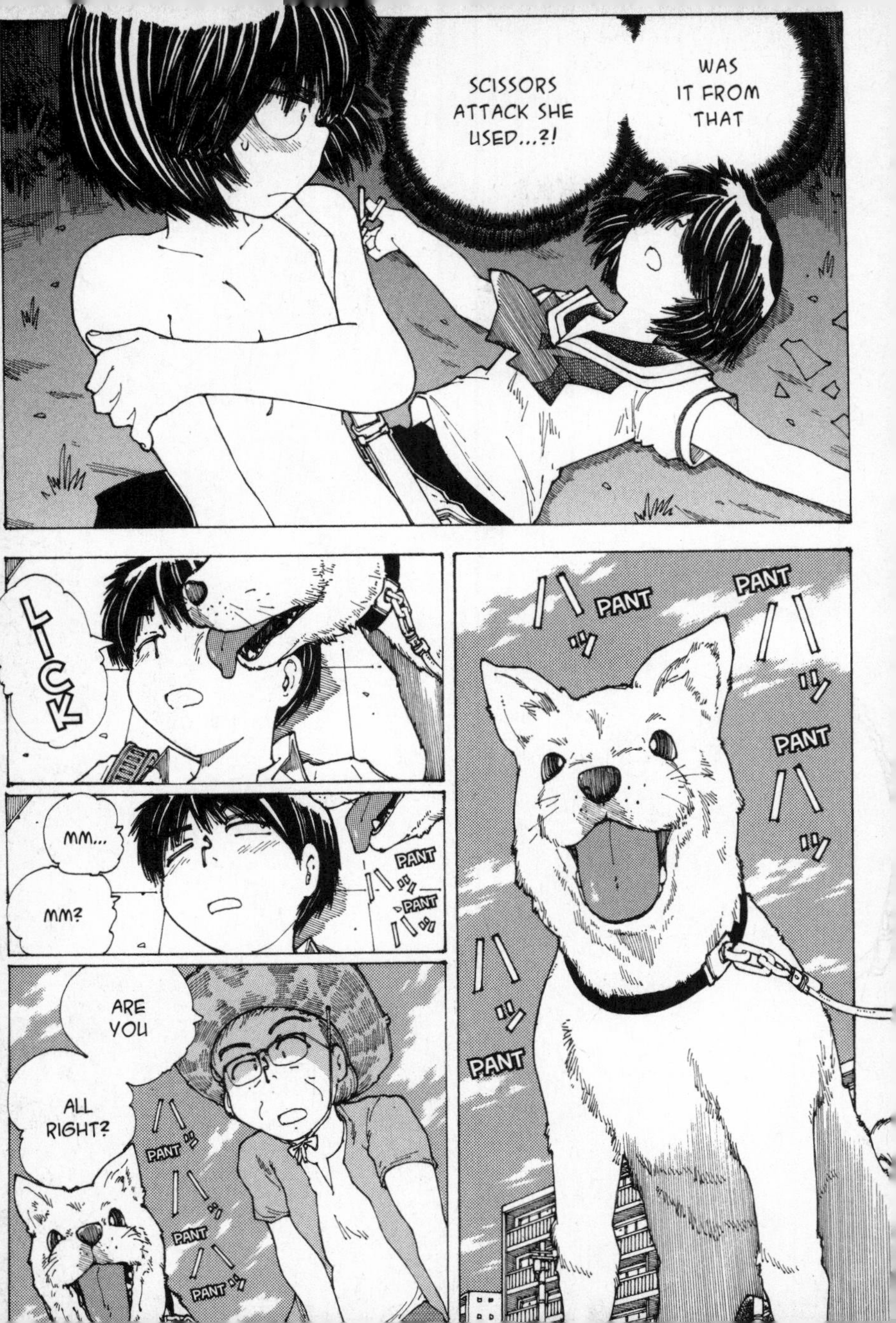
WAS IT FROM THAT
SCISSORS ATTACK SHE USED...?!
PANT
PANT
ハッ
ハッ
PANT
ハッ
ハッ
PANT
LICK
MM...
MM?
PANT
PANT
ARE YOU
ALL RIGHT?
PANT
PANT
PANT

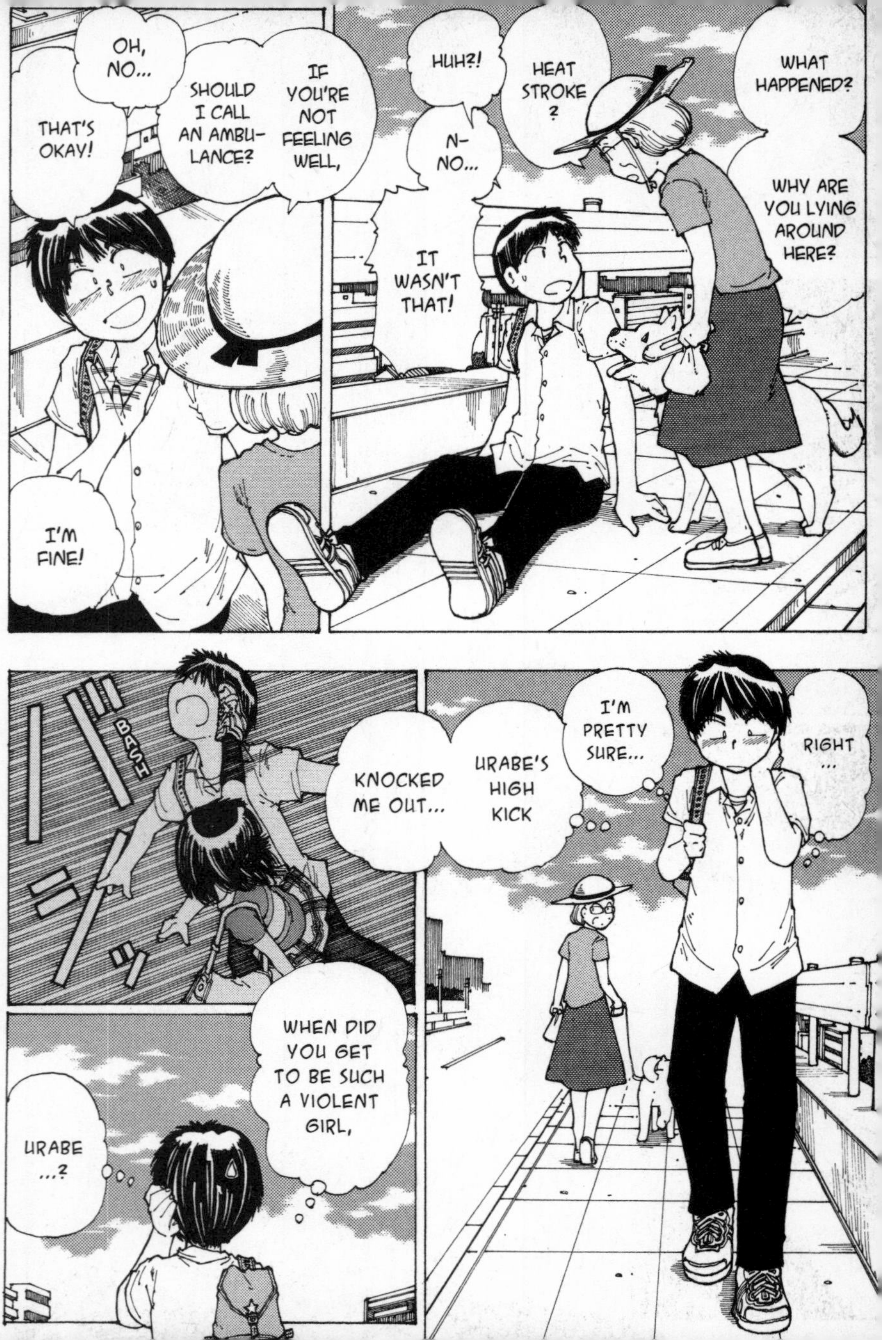
WHAT HAPPENED?
WHY ARE YOU LYING AROUND HERE?
HEAT STROKE?
HUH?!
N-NO...
IT WASN'T THAT!
IF YOU'RE NOT FEELING WELL,
SHOULD I CALL AN AMBULANCE?
OH, NO...
THAT'S OKAY!
I'M FINE!
RIGHT ...
I'M PRETTY SURE...
URABE'S HIGH KICK
KNOCKED ME OUT...
BASH
WHEN DID YOU GET TO BE SUCH A VIOLENT GIRL,
URABE ...?

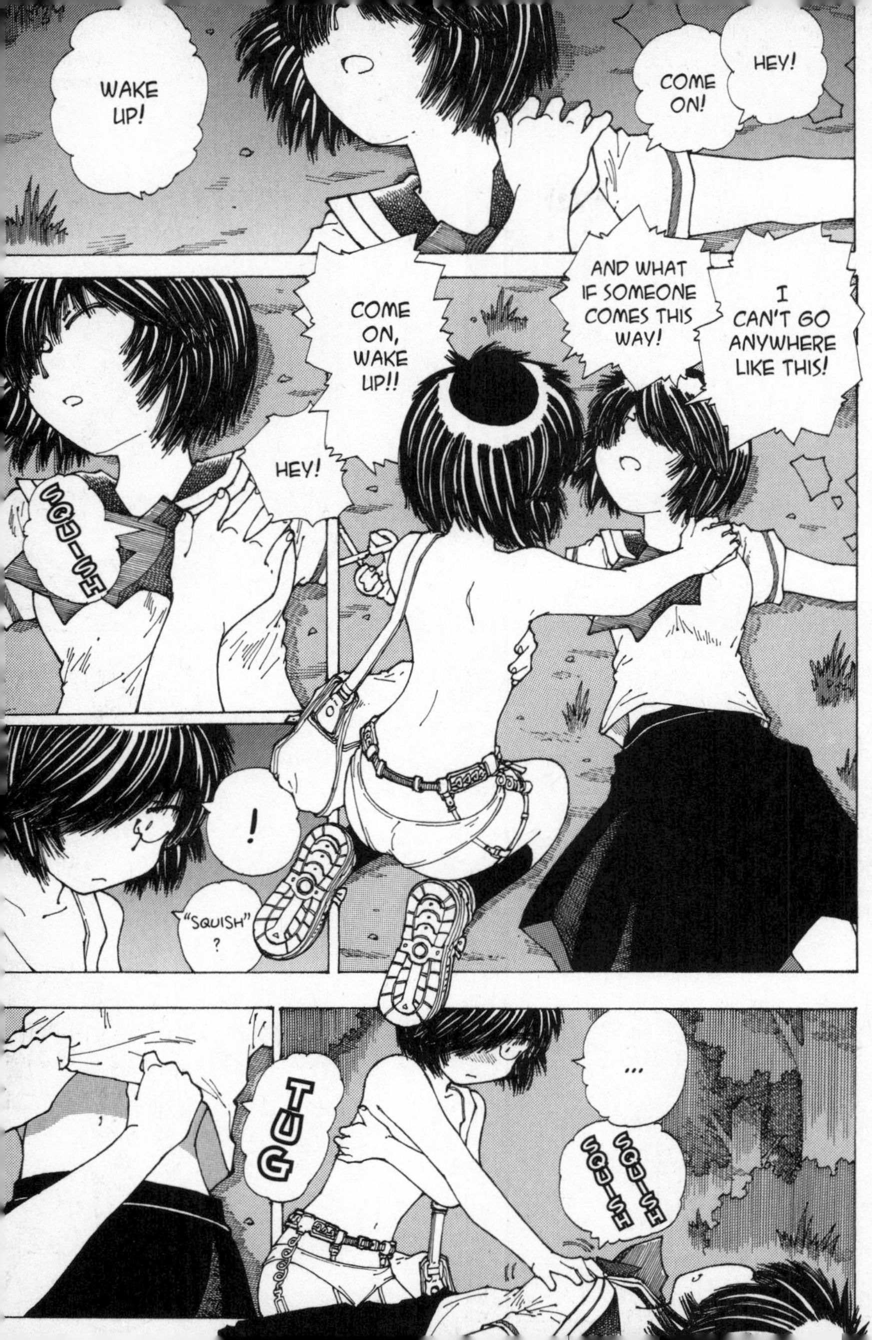
HEY!
COME ON!
WAKE UP!
I CAN'T GO ANYWHERE LIKE THIS!
AND WHAT IF SOMEONE COMES THIS WAY!
COME ON, WAKE UP!!
HEY!
SQUISH
!
"SQUISH" ?
...
SQUISH SQUISH
TUG

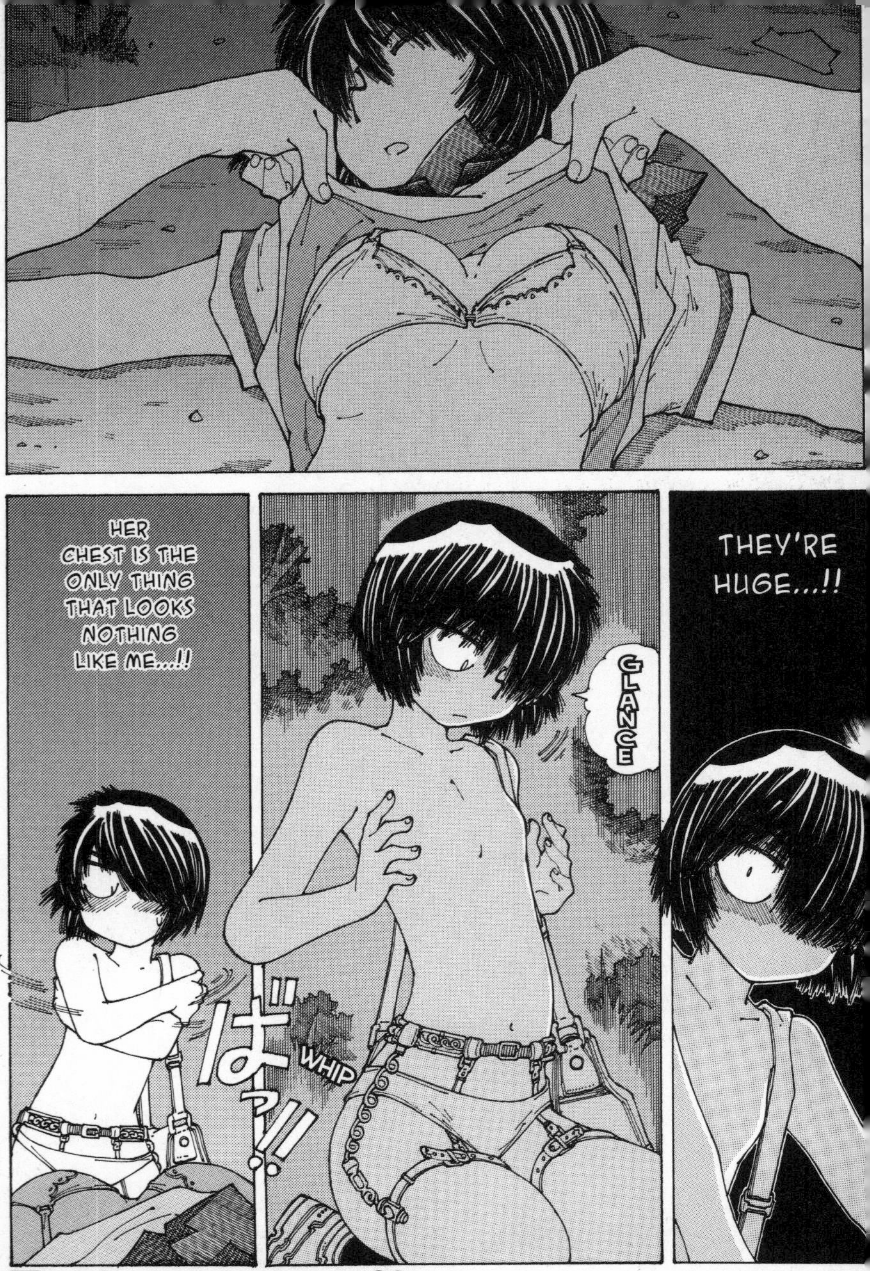
THEY'RE HUGE...!!
GLANCE
HER CHEST IS THE ONLY THING THAT LOOKS NOTHING LIKE ME...!!
ばっ!!
WHIP

END OF CHAPTER 38

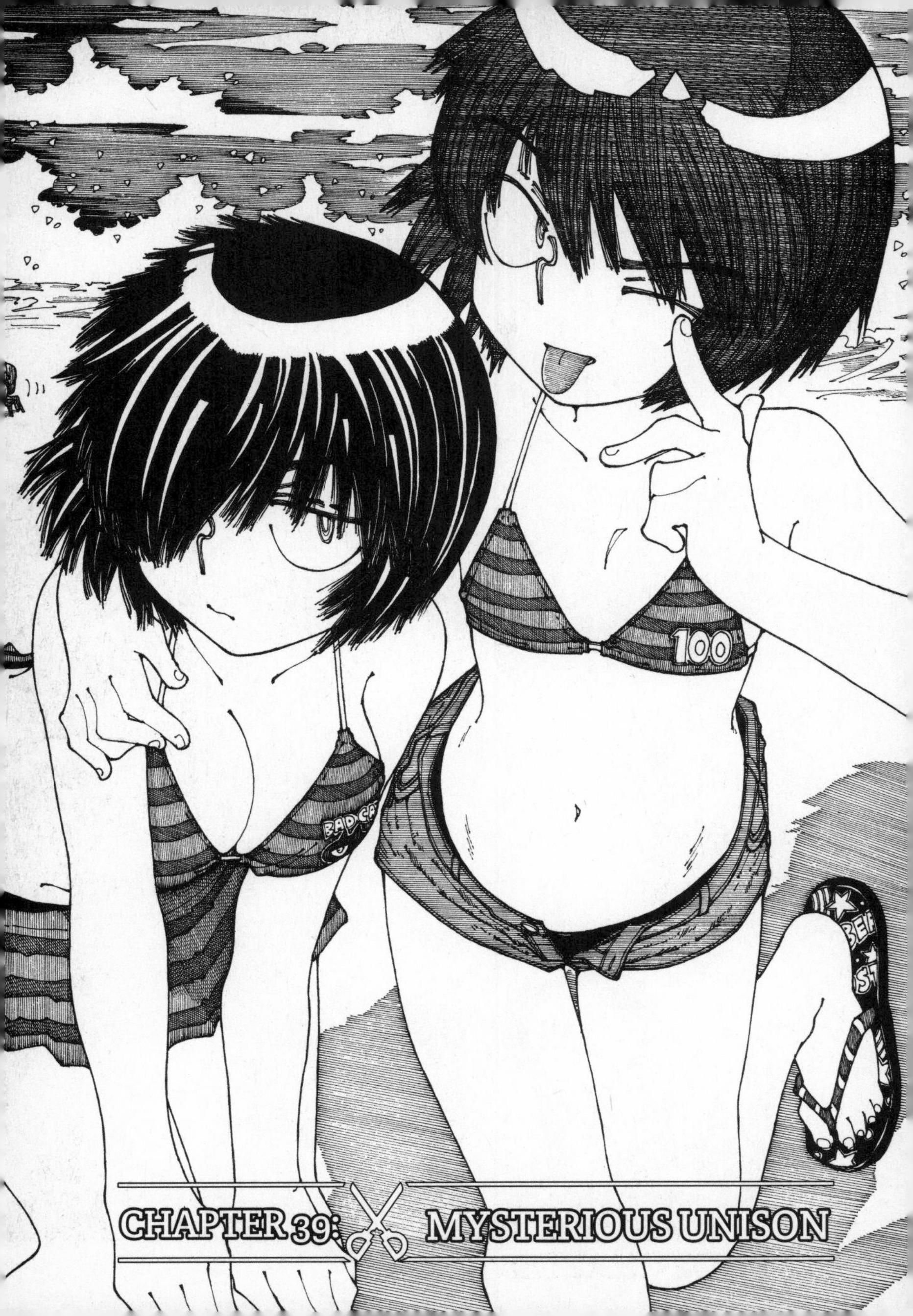
100
BAD CAT
CHAPTER 39: MYSTERIOUS UNISON

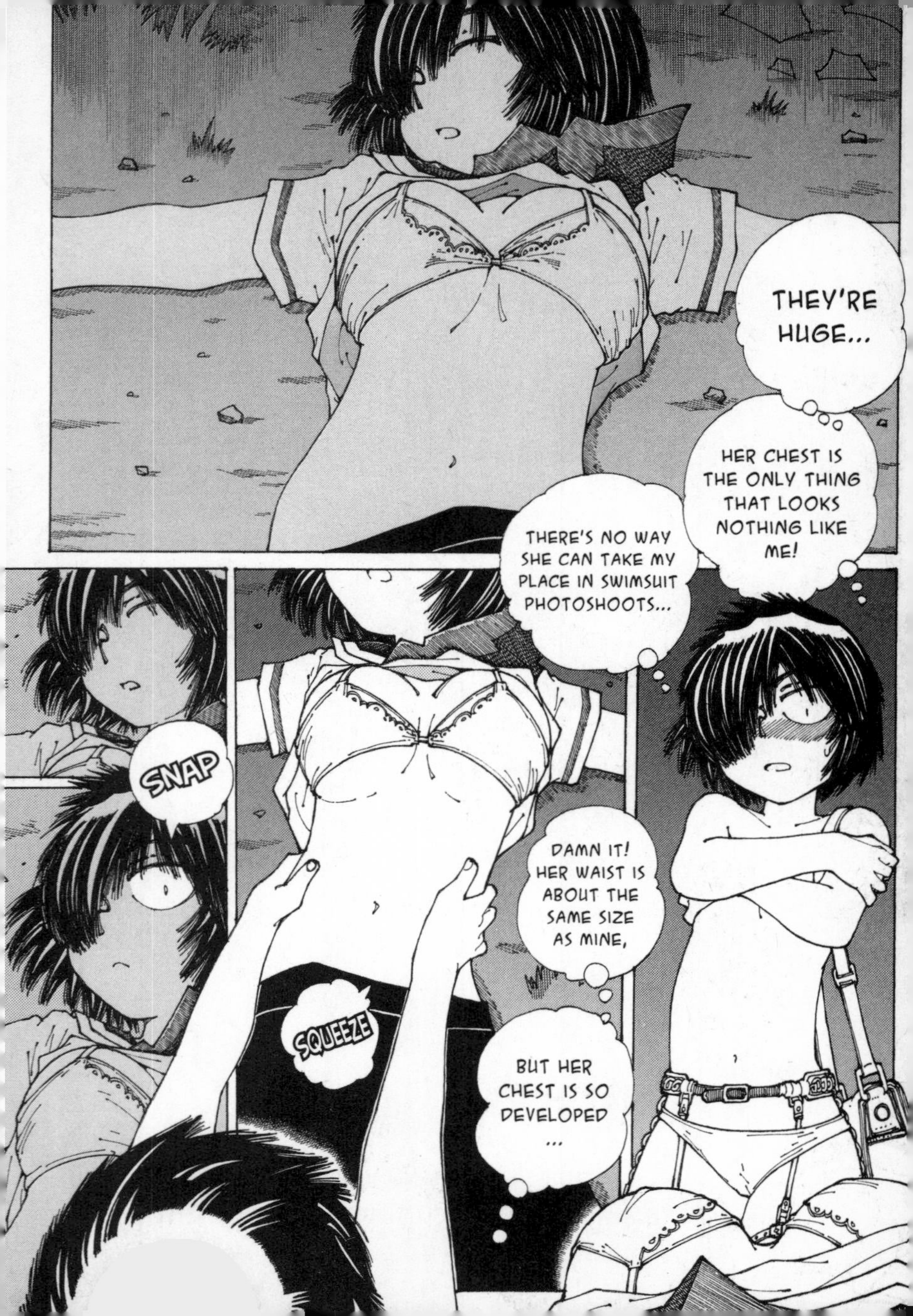
THEY'RE HUGE...
HER CHEST IS THE ONLY THING THAT LOOKS NOTHING LIKE ME!
THERE'S NO WAY SHE CAN TAKE MY PLACE IN SWIMSUIT PHOTOSHOOTS...
DAMN IT! HER WAIST IS ABOUT THE SAME SIZE AS MINE,
BUT HER CHEST IS SO DEVELOPED ...
SQUEEZE
SNAP

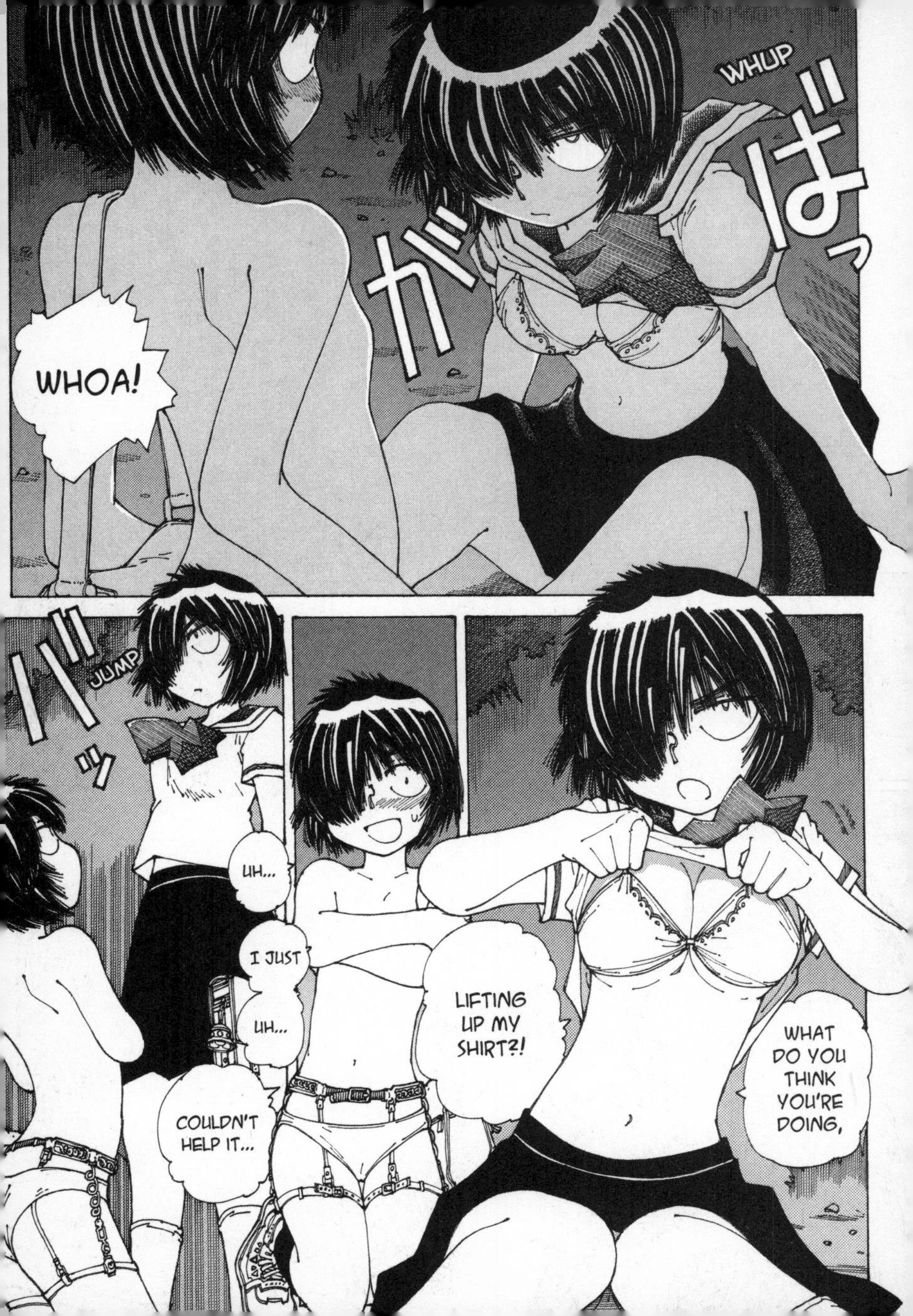
WHUP
ばっ
が
WHOA!
WHAT DO YOU THINK YOU'RE DOING,
LIFTING UP MY SHIRT?!
UH...
I JUST
UH...
COULDN'T HELP IT...
バッ
JUMP

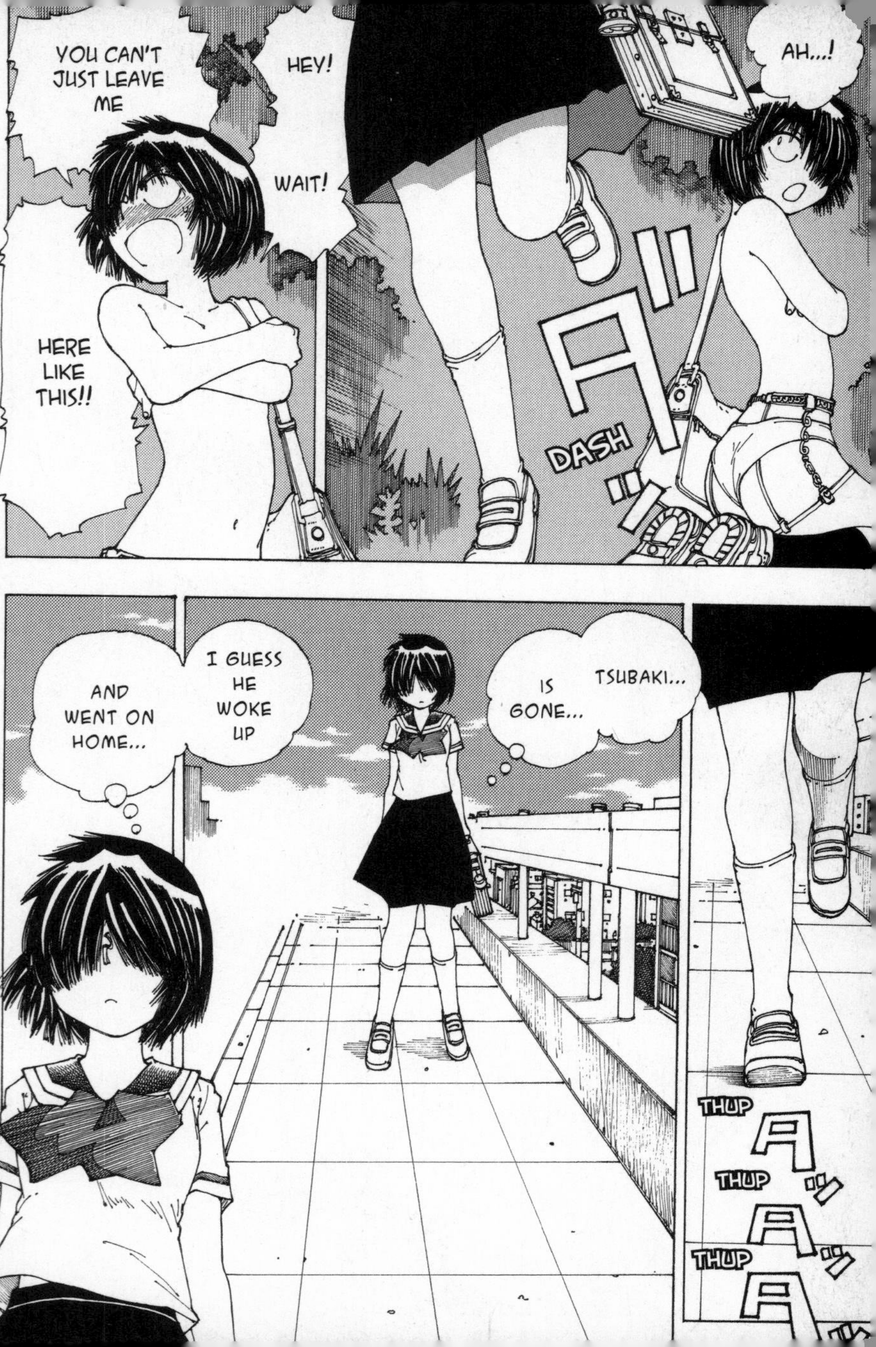
AH...!
DASH
HEY!
YOU CAN'T JUST LEAVE ME
WAIT!
HERE LIKE THIS!!
THUP
THUP
THUP
TSUBAKI... IS GONE...
I GUESS HE WOKE UP
AND WENT ON HOME...

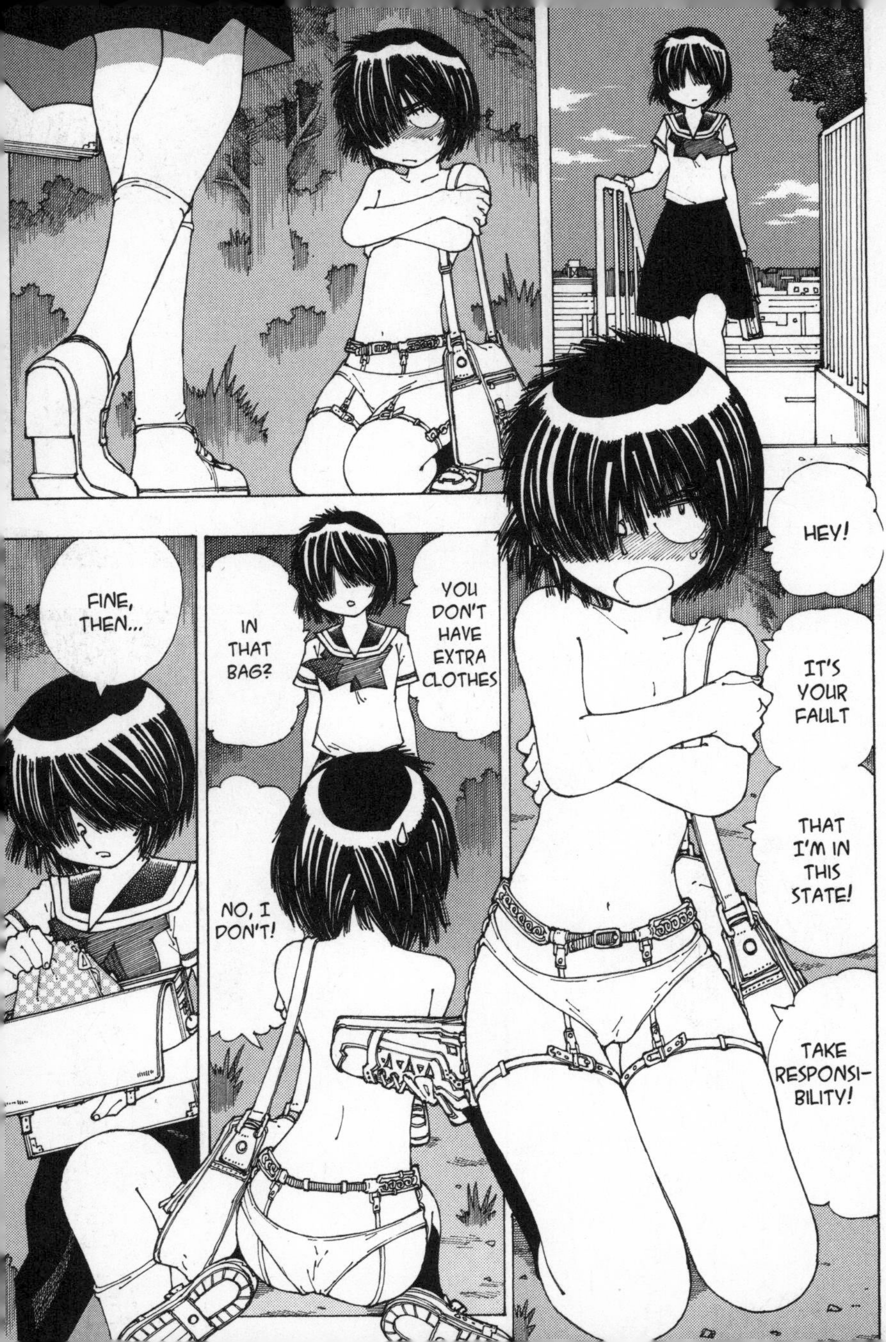
HEY!
IT'S YOUR FAULT
THAT I'M IN THIS STATE!
TAKE RESPONSI-BILITY!
YOU DON'T HAVE EXTRA CLOTHES
IN THAT BAG?
NO, I DON'T!
FINE, THEN...

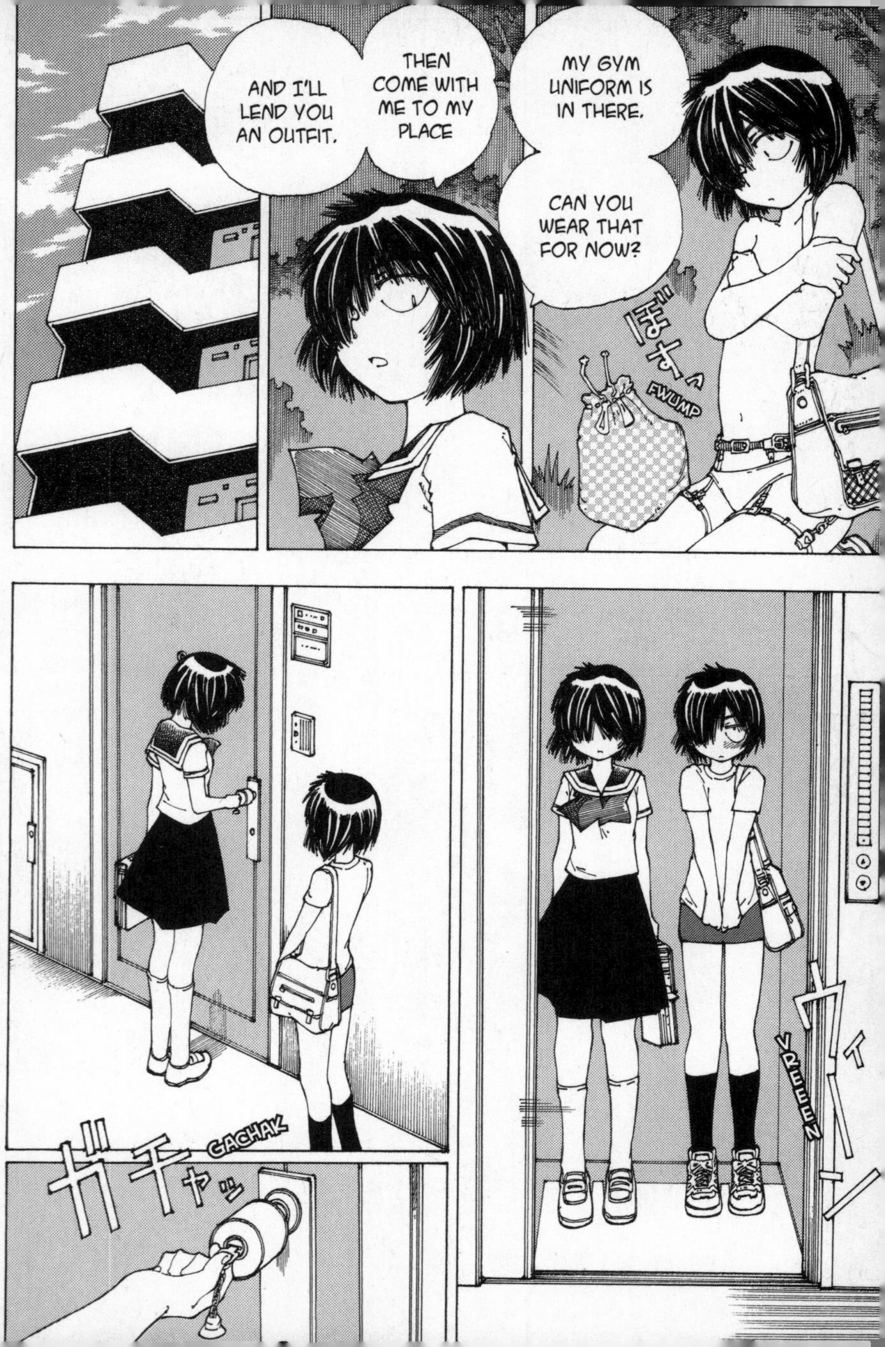
MY GYM UNIFORM IS IN THERE.
CAN YOU WEAR THAT FOR NOW?
ぼさ
FWUMP
THEN COME WITH ME TO MY PLACE
AND I'LL LEND YOU AN OUTFIT.
ウィーン
VREEEN
ガチャッ
GACHAK

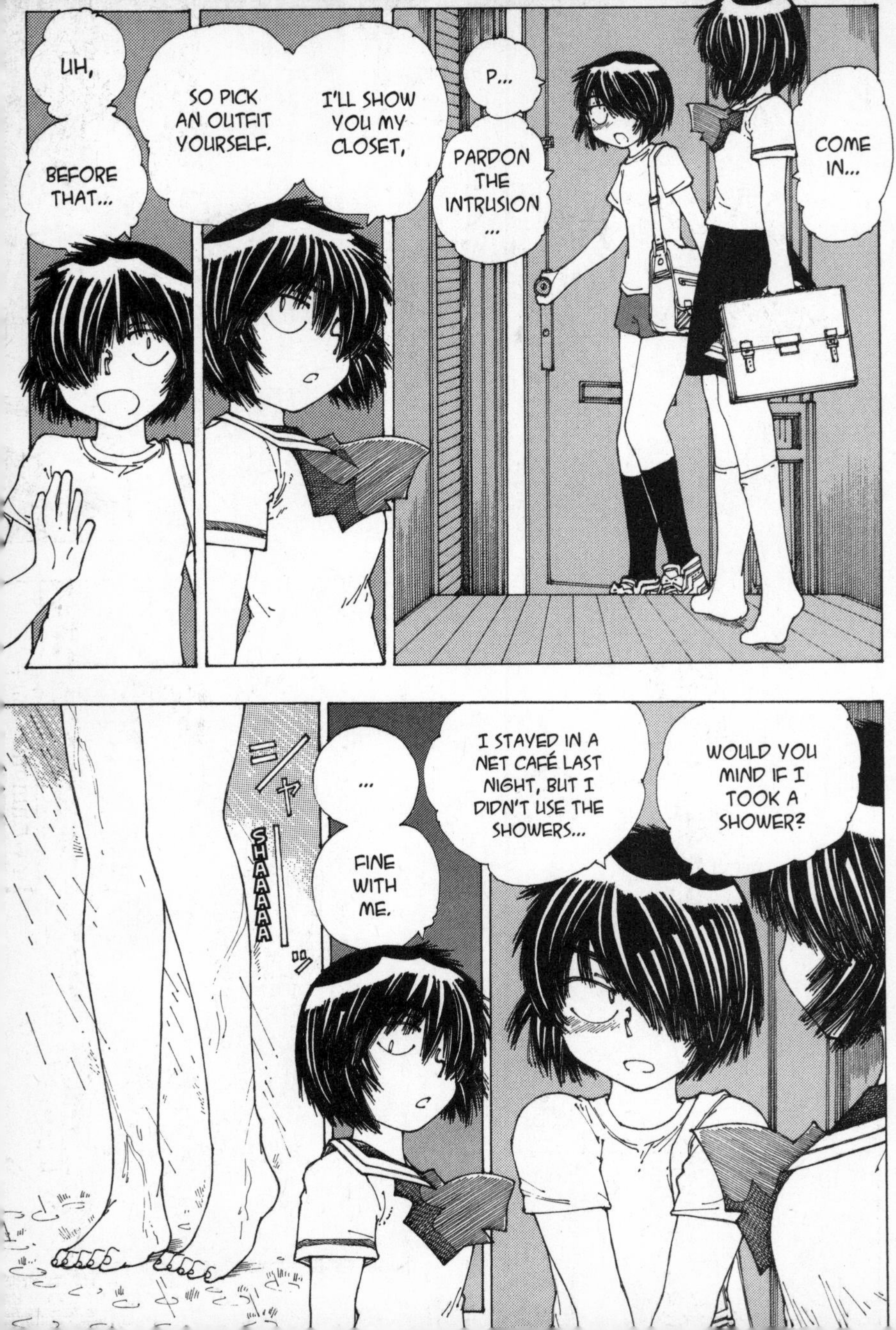
COME IN...
P...
PARDON THE INTRUSION ...
I'LL SHOW YOU MY CLOSET,
SO PICK AN OUTFIT YOURSELF.
UH,
BEFORE THAT...
WOULD YOU MIND IF I TOOK A SHOWER?
I STAYED IN A NET CAFÉ LAST NIGHT, BUT I DIDN'T USE THE SHOWERS...
...
FINE WITH ME.
SHAAAAA

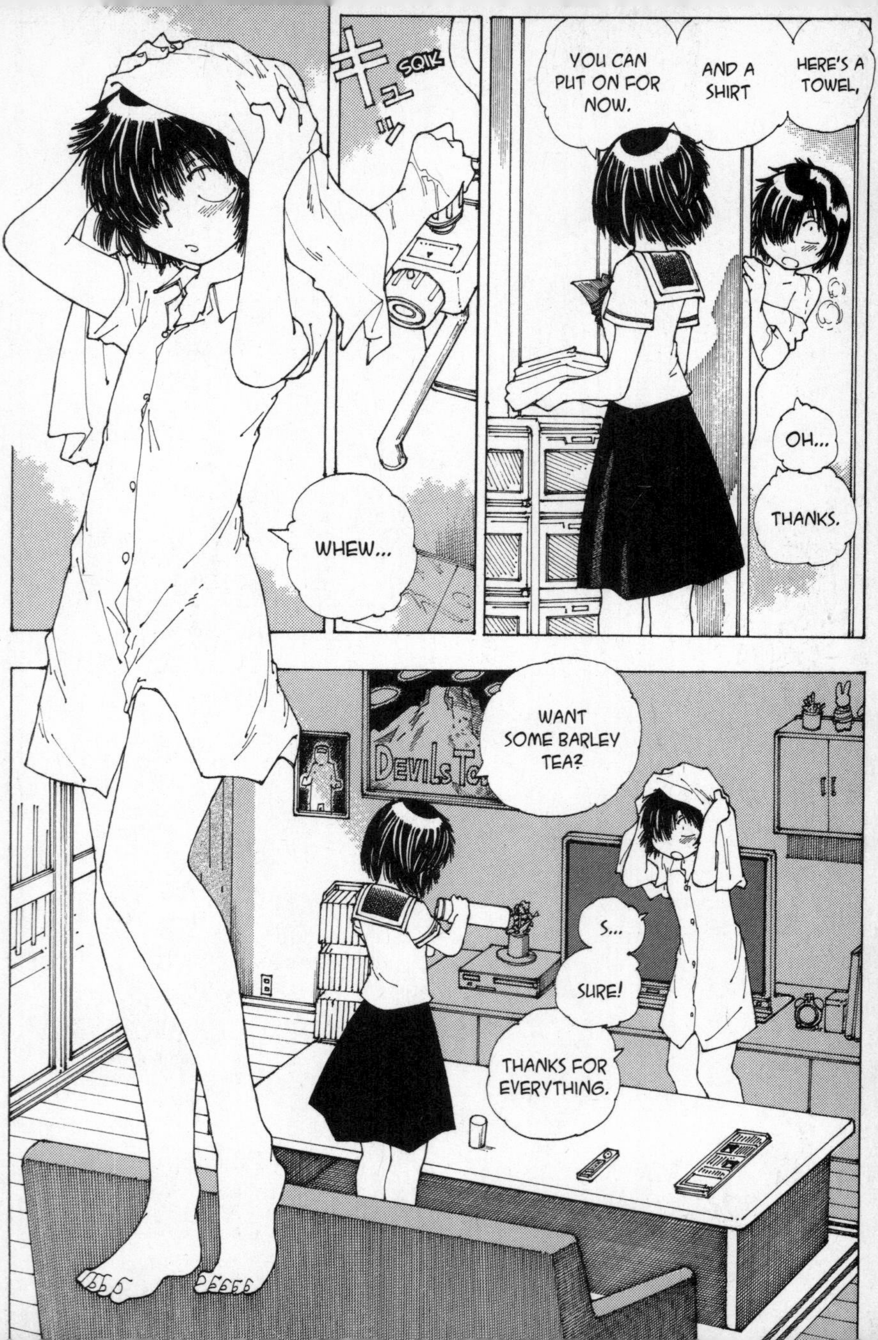
HERE'S A TOWEL,
AND A SHIRT
YOU CAN PUT ON FOR NOW.
OH...
THANKS.
キュッ
SQIK
WHEW...
WANT SOME BARLEY TEA?
S...
SURE!
THANKS FOR EVERYTHING.

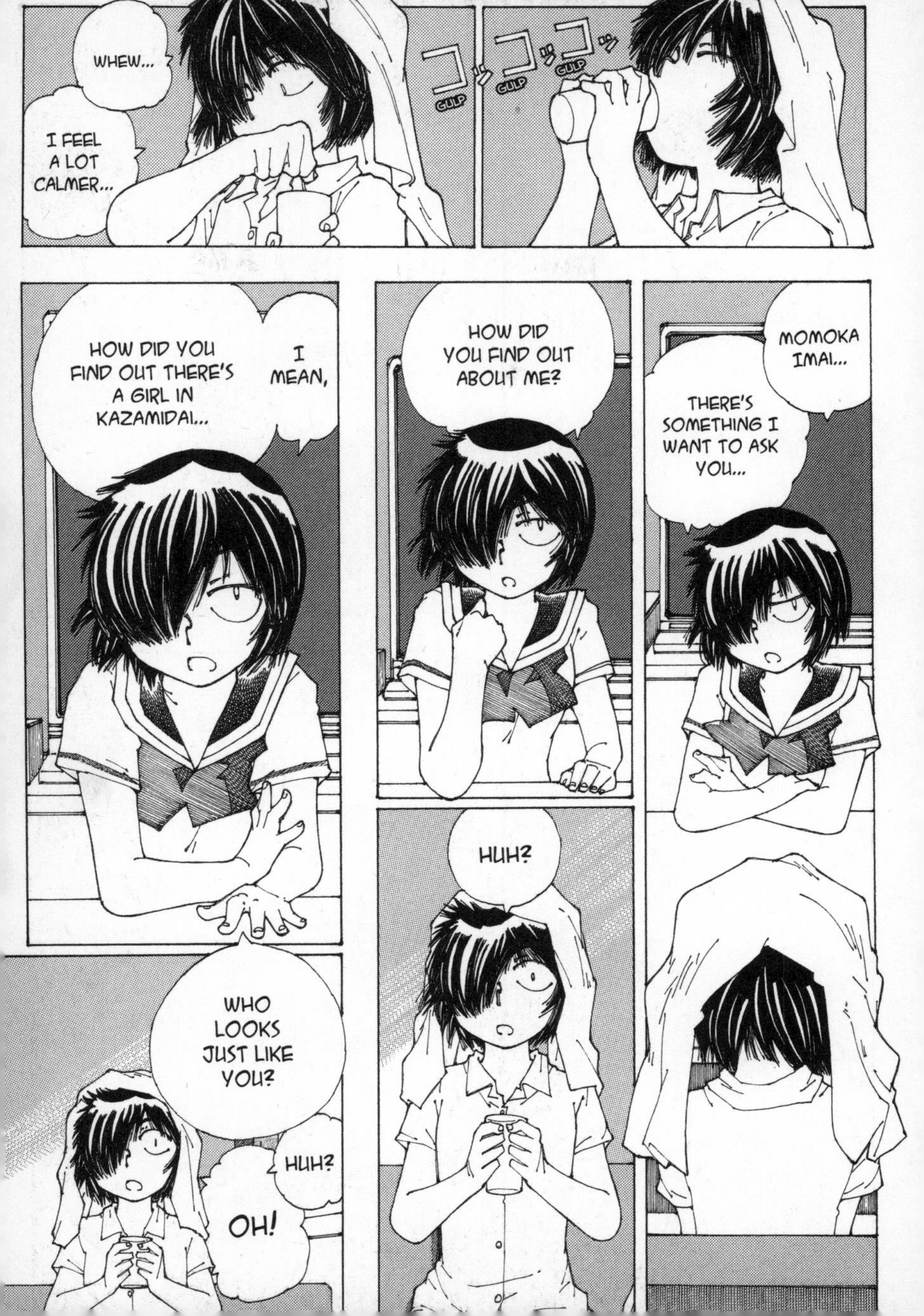

コッ
GULP
コッ
GULP
コッ
GULP
WHEW...
I FEEL A LOT CALMER...
MOMOKA IMAI...
THERE'S SOMETHING I WANT TO ASK YOU...
HOW DID YOU FIND OUT ABOUT ME?
I MEAN,
HOW DID YOU FIND OUT THERE'S A GIRL IN KAZAMIDAI...
HUH?
WHO LOOKS JUST LIKE YOU?
HUH?
OH!

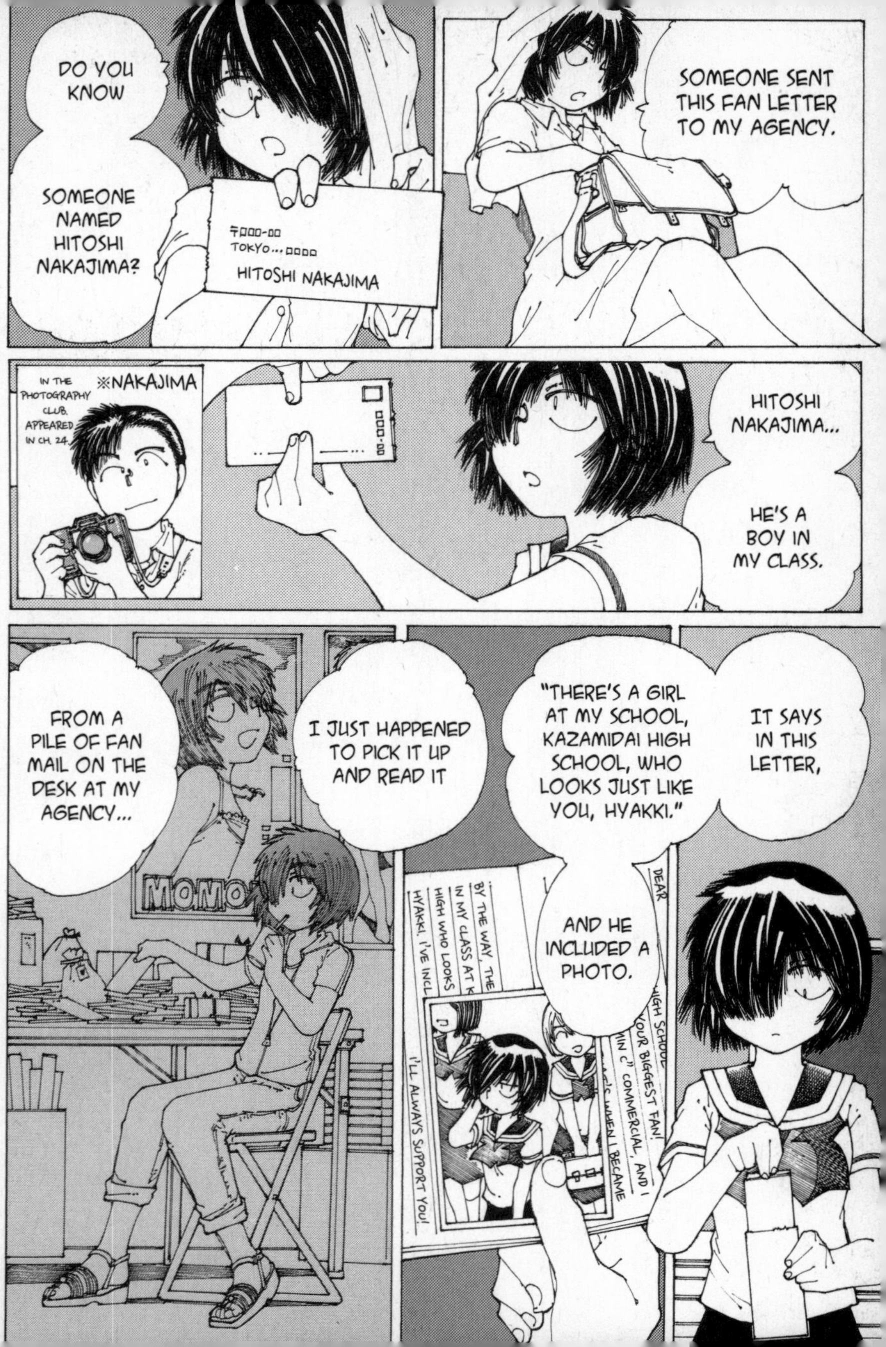
SOMEONE SENT THIS FAN LETTER TO MY AGENCY.
DO YOU KNOW
SOMEONE NAMED HITOSHI NAKAJIMA?
TOKYO...
HITOSHI NAKAJIMA
HITOSHI NAKAJIMA...
HE'S A BOY IN MY CLASS.
※NAKAJIMA IN THE PHOTOGRAPHY CLUB. APPEARED IN CH. 24.
IT SAYS IN THIS LETTER,
"THERE'S A GIRL AT MY SCHOOL, KAZAMIDAI HIGH SCHOOL, WHO LOOKS JUST LIKE YOU, HYAKKI."
AND HE INCLUDED A PHOTO.
DEAR
YOUR BIGGEST FAN!
I'LL ALWAYS SUPPORT YOU!
BY THE WAY, THE
IN MY CLASS AT K
HIGH WHO LOOKS
HYAKKI. I'VE INCL
I JUST HAPPENED TO PICK IT UP AND READ IT
FROM A PILE OF FAN MAIL ON THE DESK AT MY AGENCY...

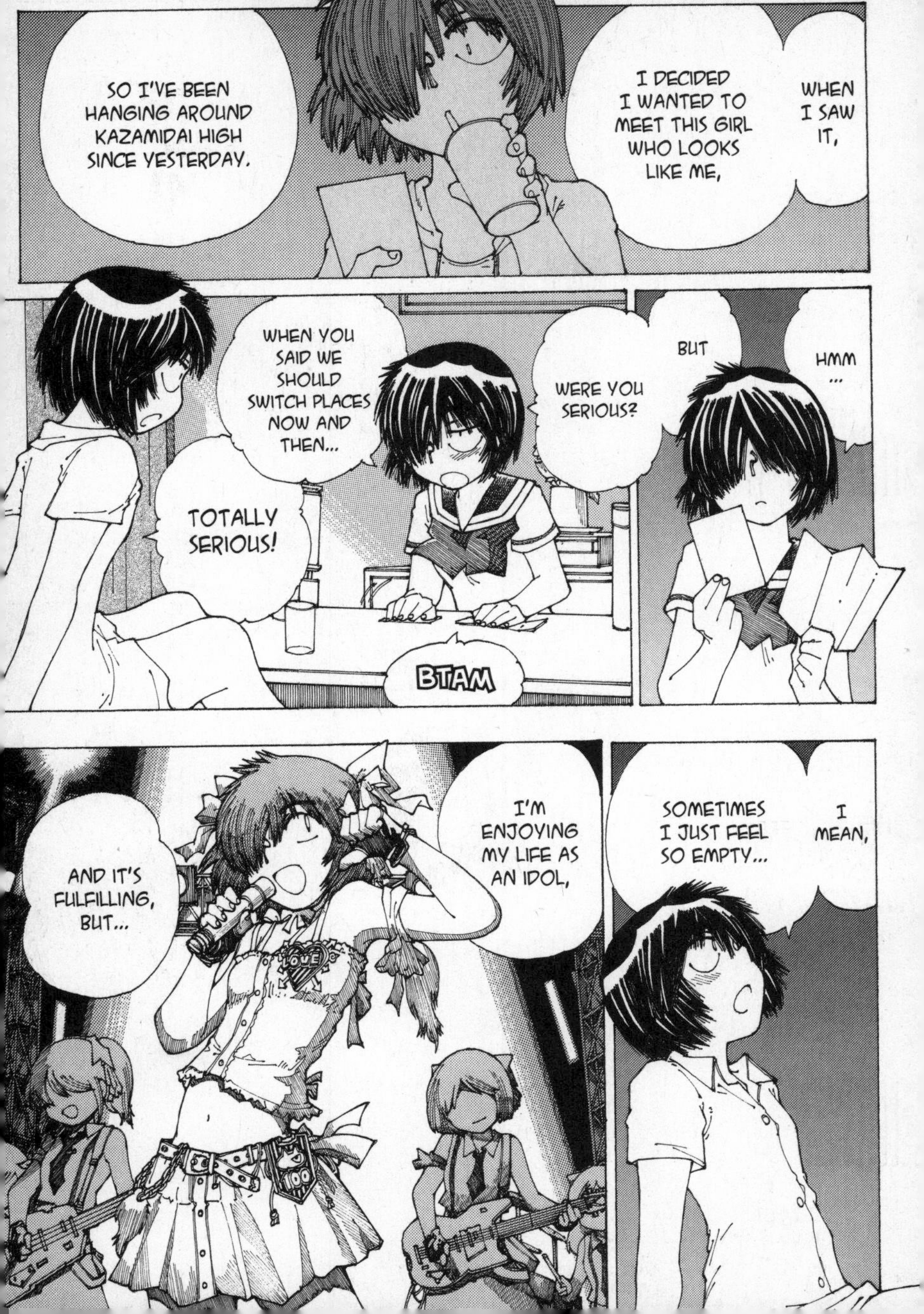
WHEN I SAW IT,
I DECIDED I WANTED TO MEET THIS GIRL WHO LOOKS LIKE ME,
SO I'VE BEEN HANGING AROUND KAZAMIDAI HIGH SINCE YESTERDAY.
HMM ...
BUT
WERE YOU SERIOUS?
WHEN YOU SAID WE SHOULD SWITCH PLACES NOW AND THEN...
TOTALLY SERIOUS!
BTAM
I MEAN,
SOMETIMES I JUST FEEL SO EMPTY...
I'M ENJOYING MY LIFE AS AN IDOL,
AND IT'S FULFILLING, BUT...

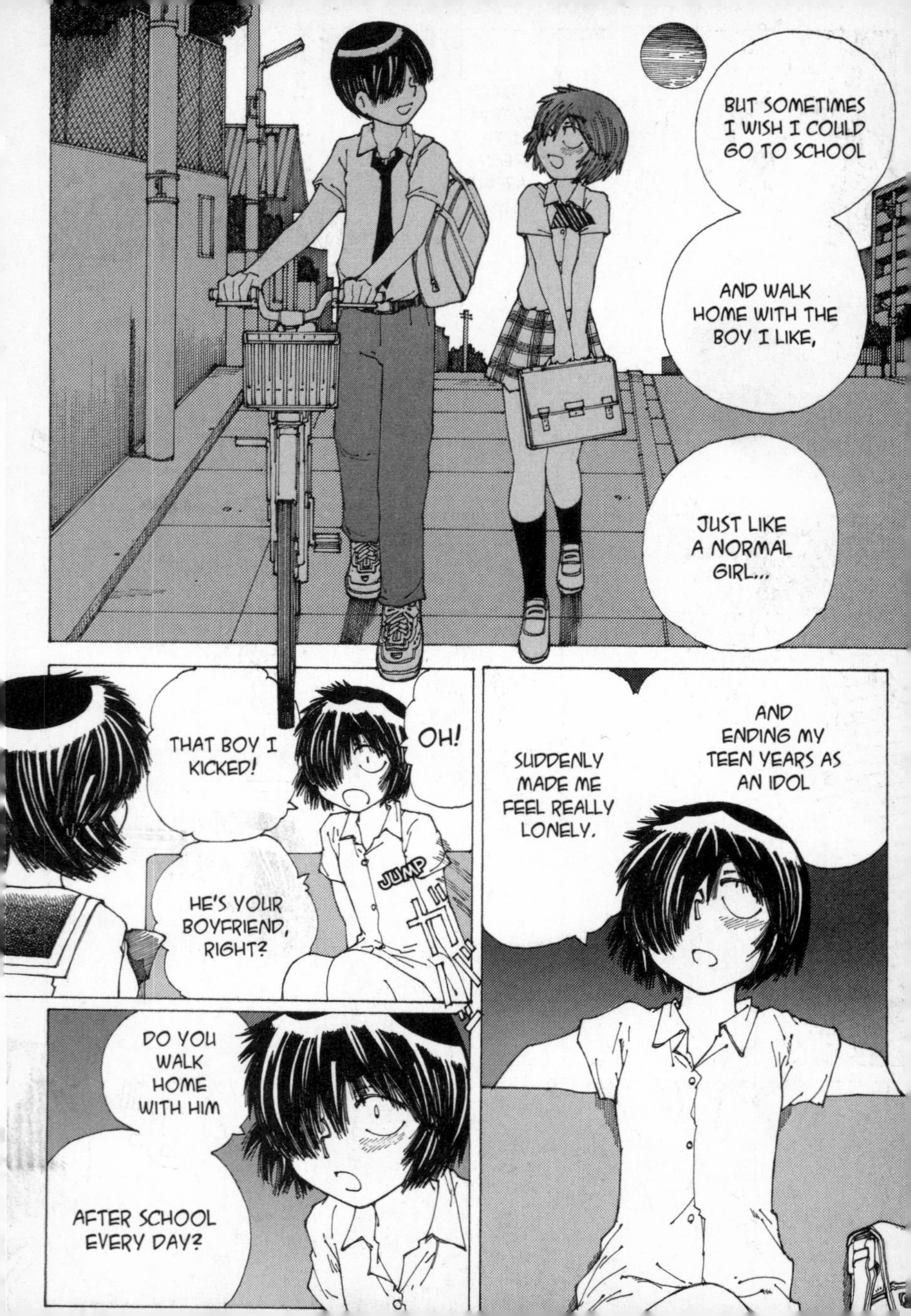
BUT SOMETIMES I WISH I COULD GO TO SCHOOL
AND WALK HOME WITH THE BOY I LIKE,
JUST LIKE A NORMAL GIRL...
AND ENDING MY TEEN YEARS AS AN IDOL
SUDDENLY MADE ME FEEL REALLY LONELY.
OH!
THAT BOY I KICKED!
HE'S YOUR BOYFRIEND, RIGHT?
DO YOU WALK HOME WITH HIM
AFTER SCHOOL EVERY DAY?

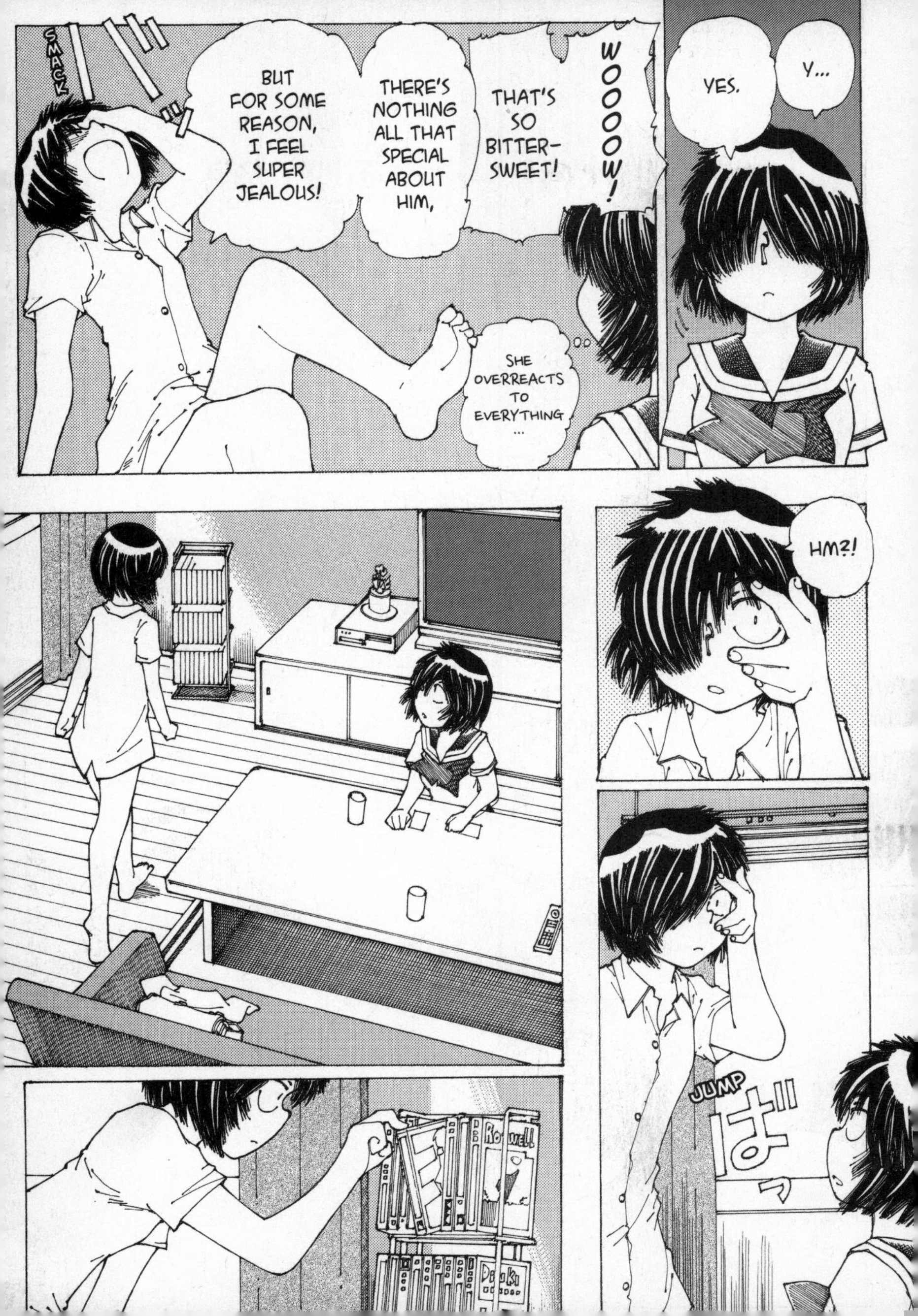

Y...
YES.
WOOOOOW!
THAT'S SO BITTER-SWEET!
THERE'S NOTHING ALL THAT SPECIAL ABOUT HIM,
BUT FOR SOME REASON, I FEEL SUPER JEALOUS!
SMACK
SHE OVERREACTS TO EVERYTHING ...
HM?!
JUMP
ばっ
Roswell

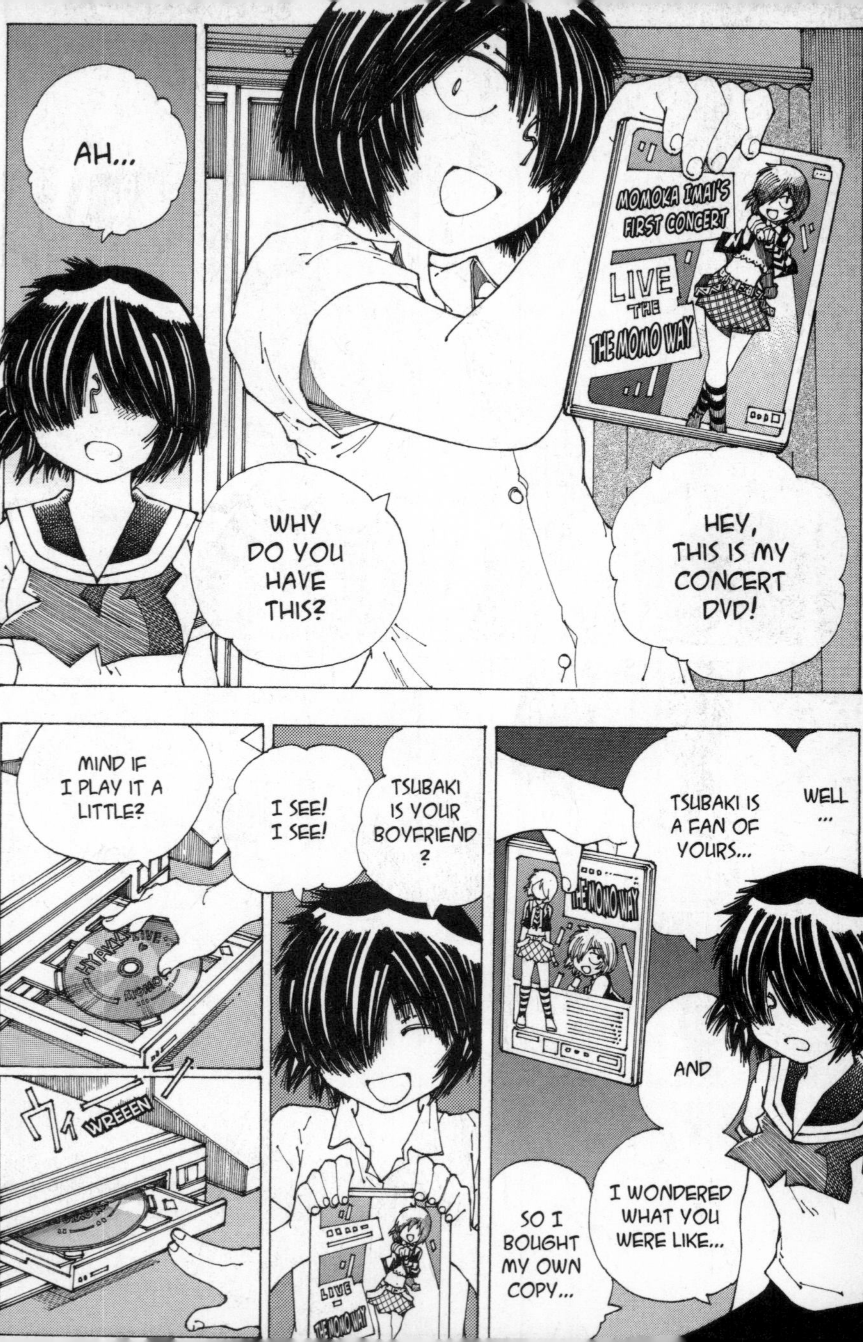
HEY, THIS IS MY CONCERT DVD!
MOMOKA IMAI'S FIRST CONCERT
LIVE THE THE MOMO WAY
WHY DO YOU HAVE THIS?
AH...
WELL ...
TSUBAKI IS A FAN OF YOURS...
AND
I WONDERED WHAT YOU WERE LIKE...
SO I BOUGHT MY OWN COPY...
THE MOMO WAY
TSUBAKI IS YOUR BOYFRIEND?
I SEE! I SEE!
LIVE
THE MOMO WAY
MIND IF I PLAY IT A LITTLE?
WREEEN

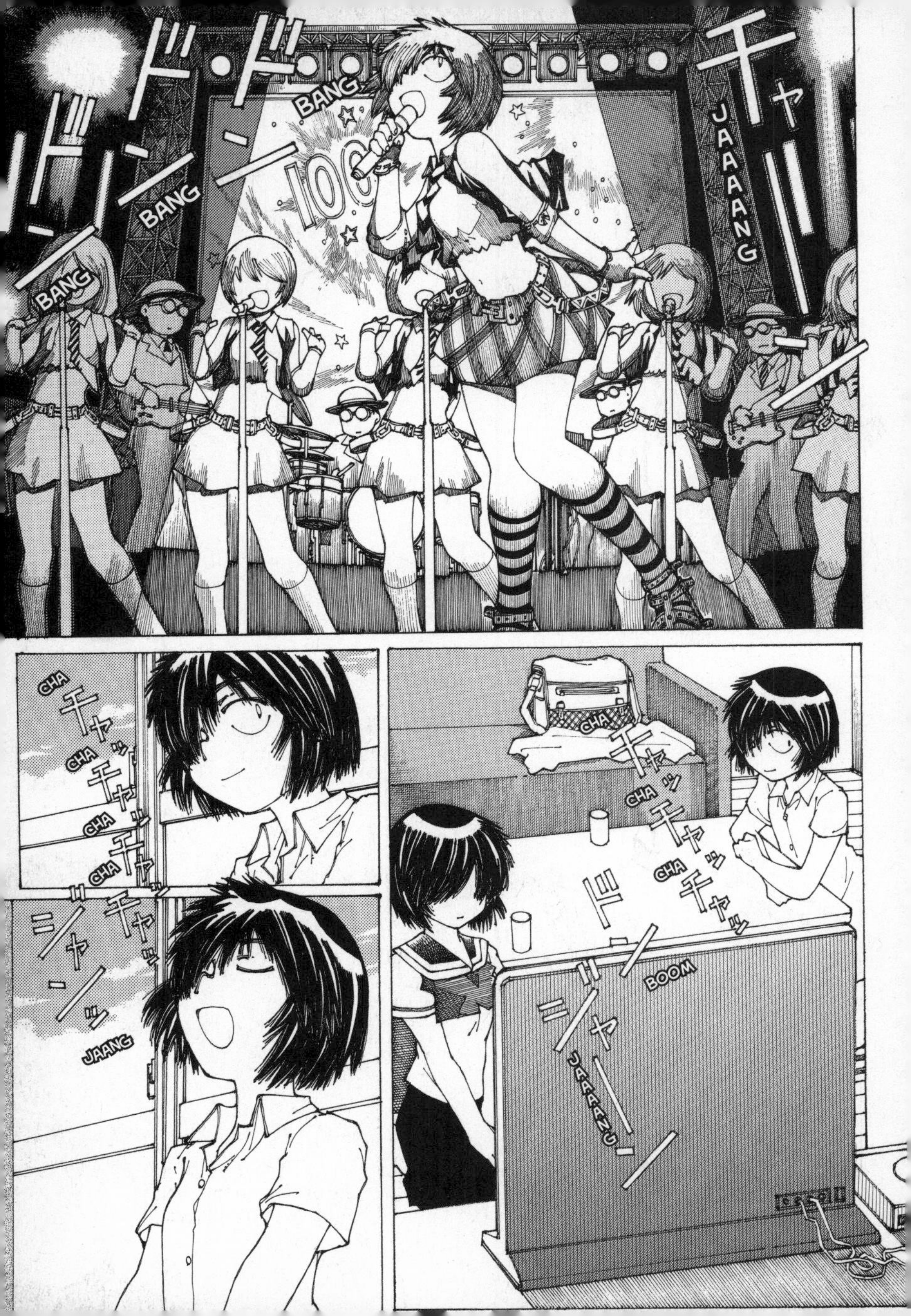

チャーン
JAAAAANG
BANG
BANG
BANG
ドドドーン
100
CHA
チャッ
CHA
チャッ
CHA
チャッ
ドーン
BOOM
ジャーン
JAAAAANG
CHA
チャッ
CHA
チャッ
CHA
チャッ
CHA
チャッ
ジャーンッ
JAANG

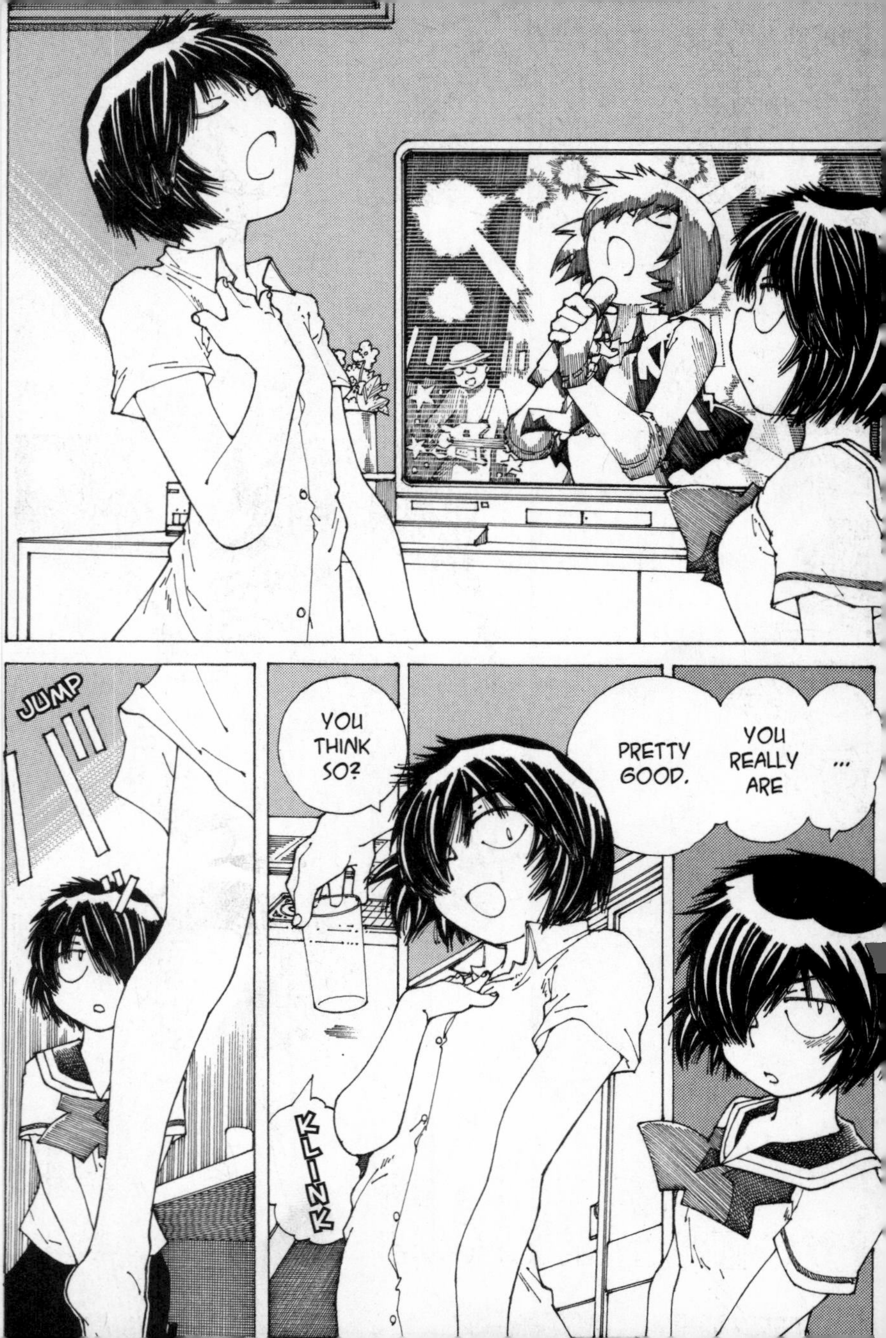
PRETTY GOOD. YOU REALLY ARE ...
YOU THINK SO?
KLINK
JUMP

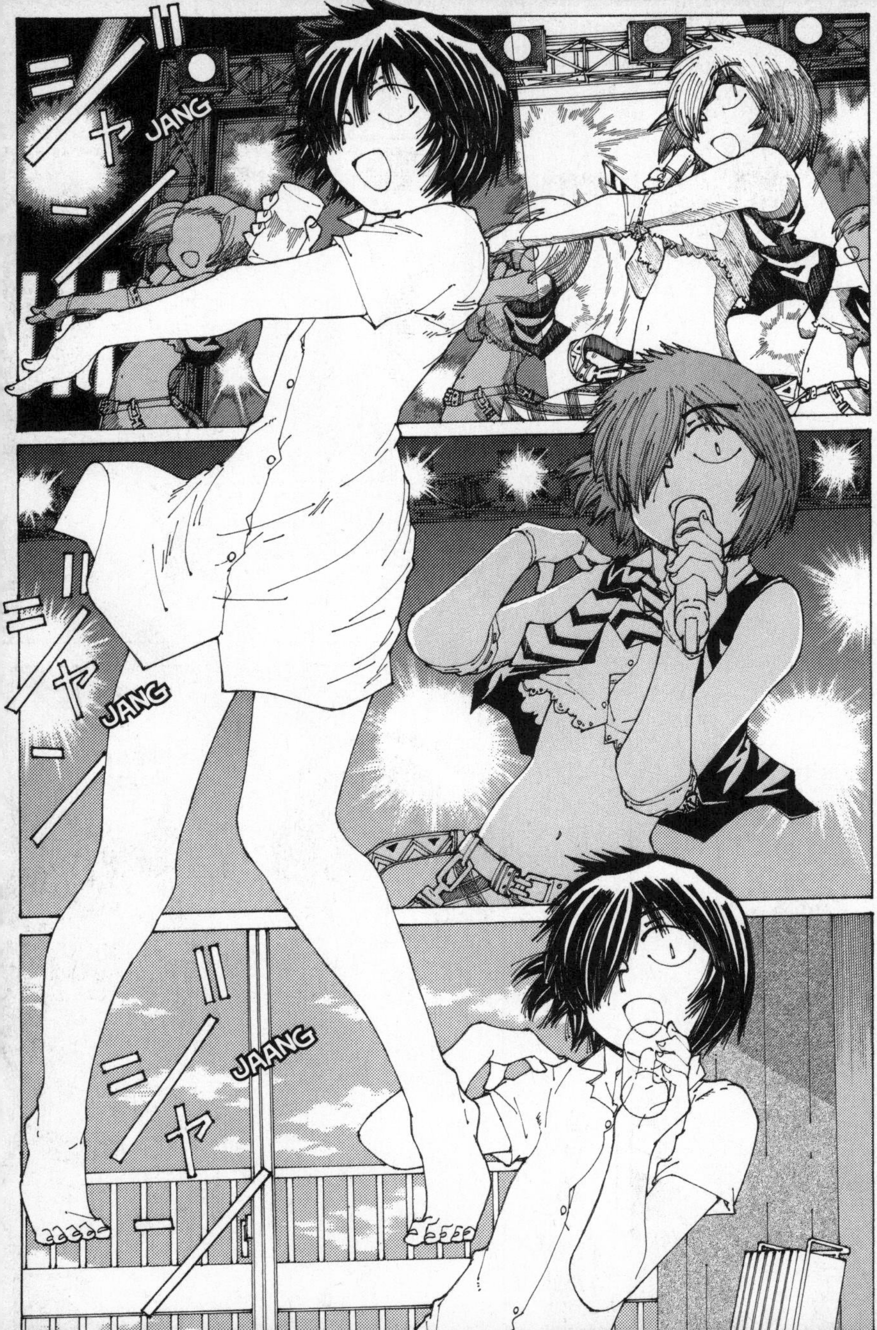
JANG
JANG
JAANG

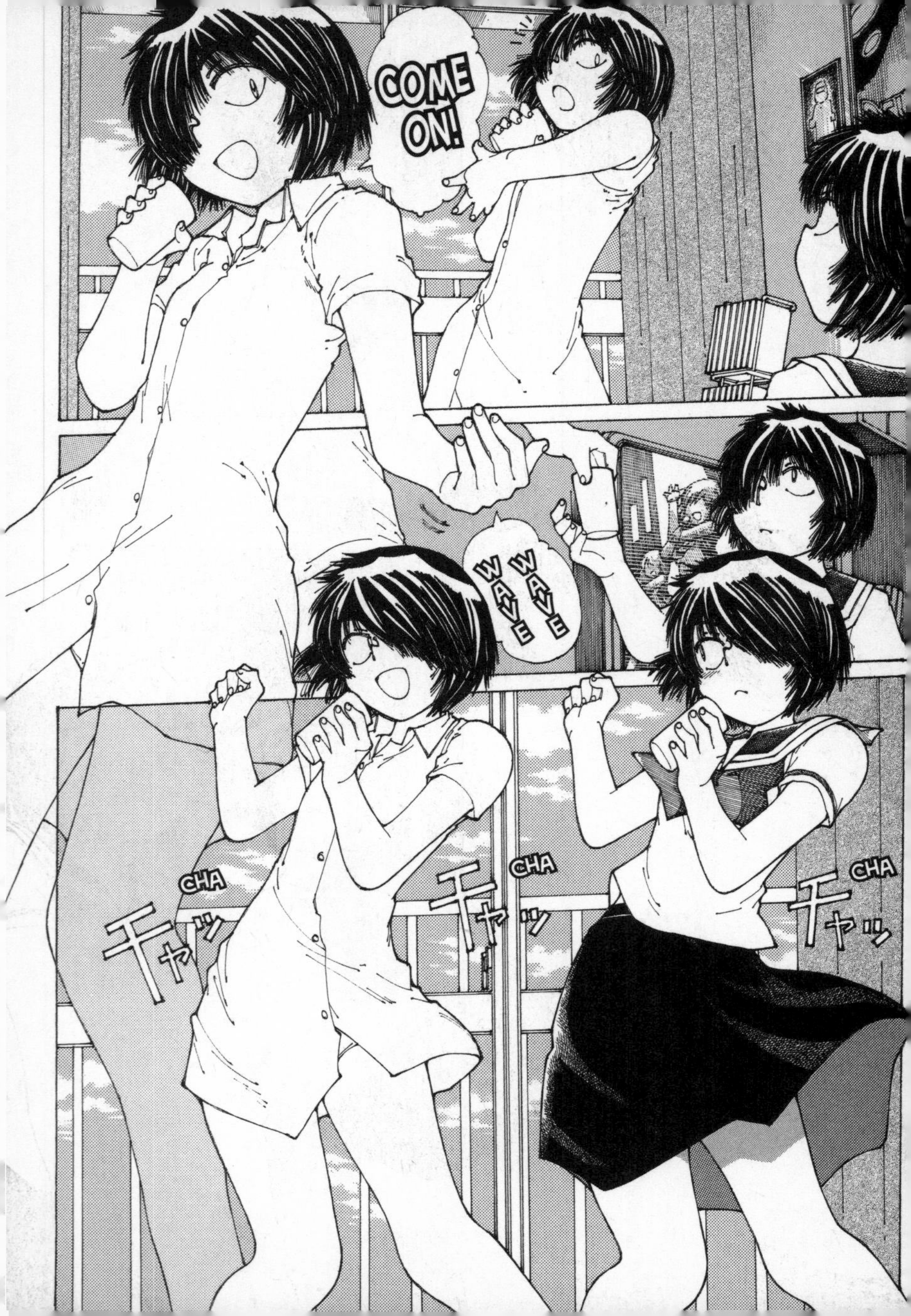
COME ON!
WAVE WAVE
CHA
チャッ
CHA
チャッ
CHA
チャッ

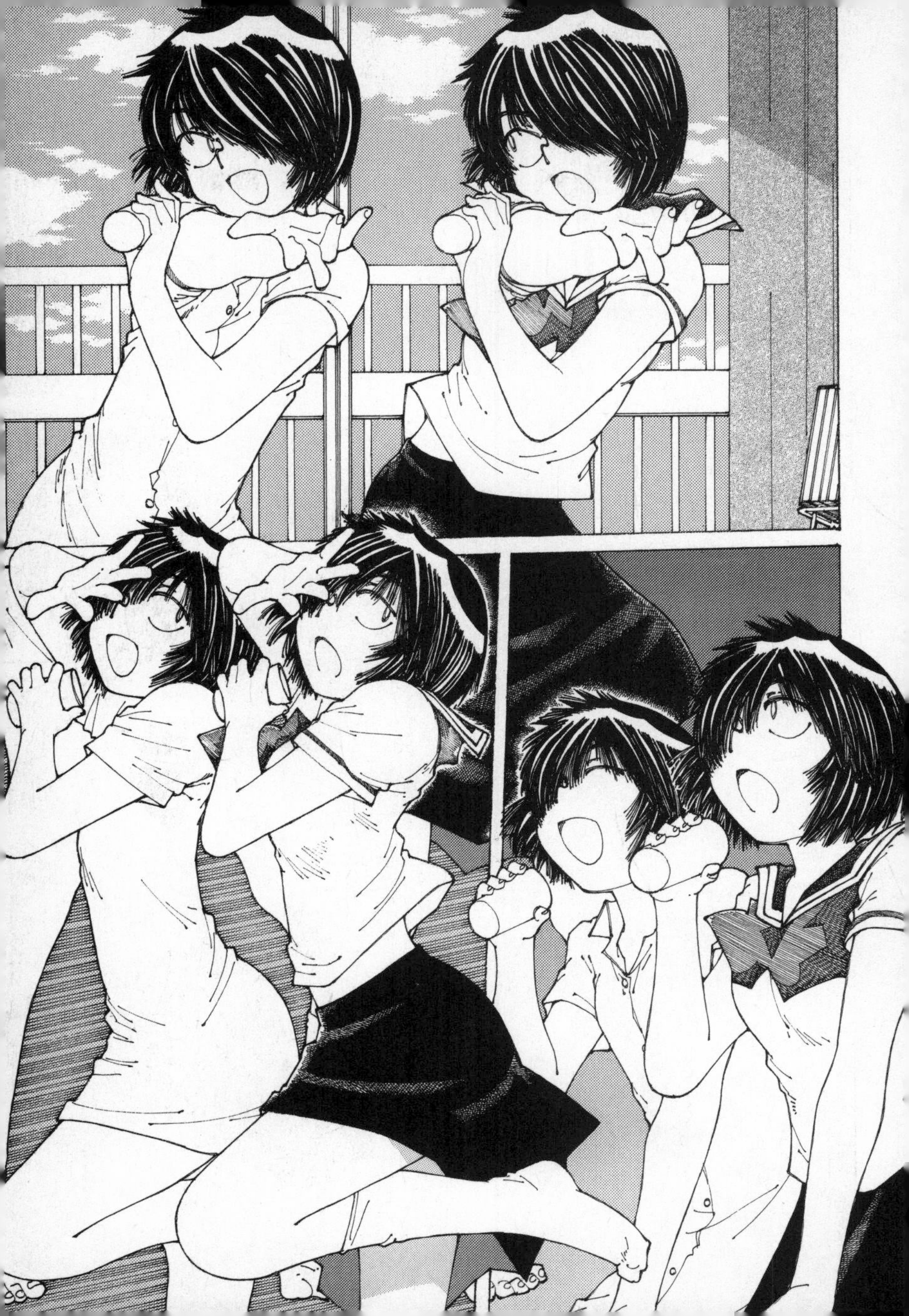

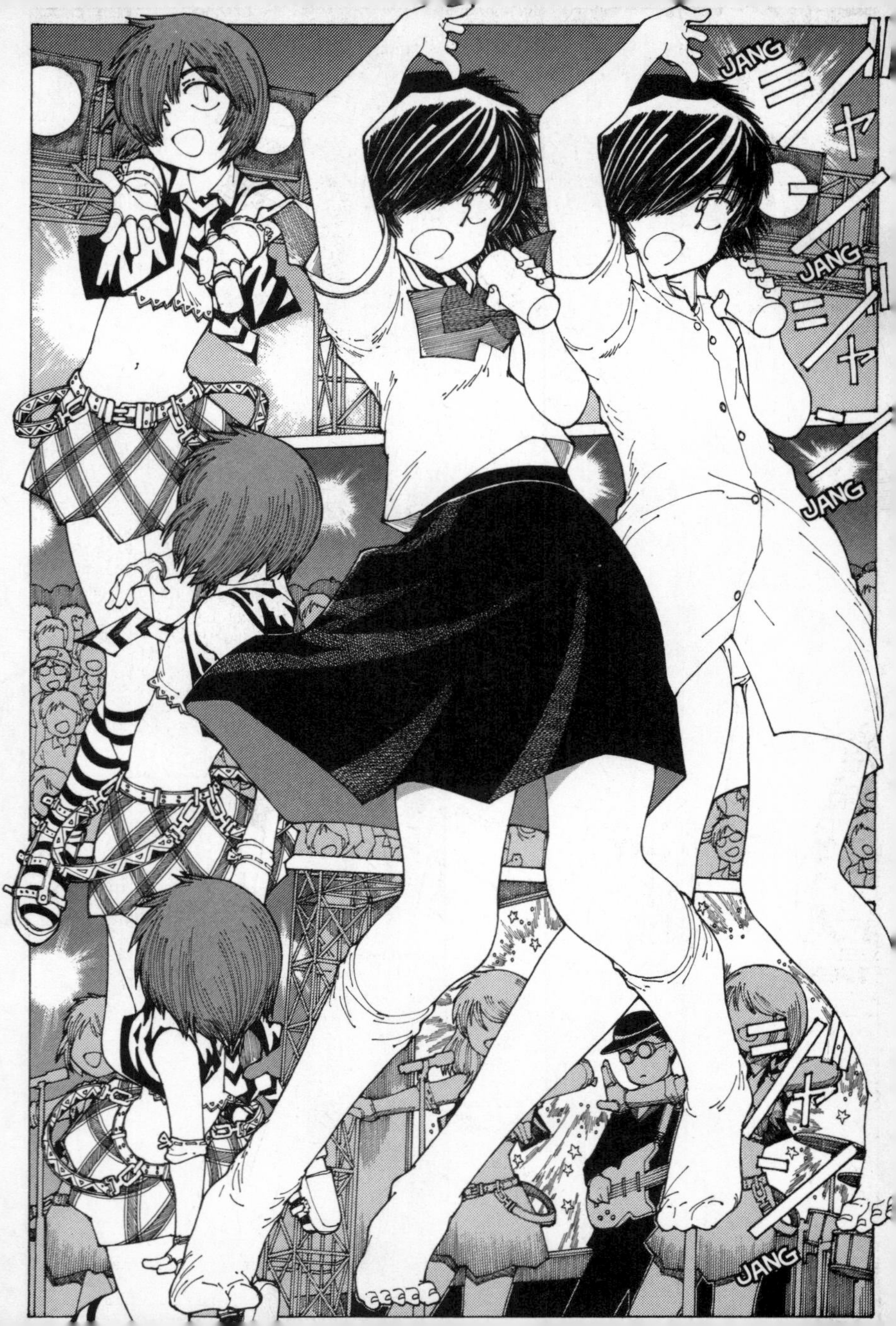
JANG
JANG
JANG
JANG

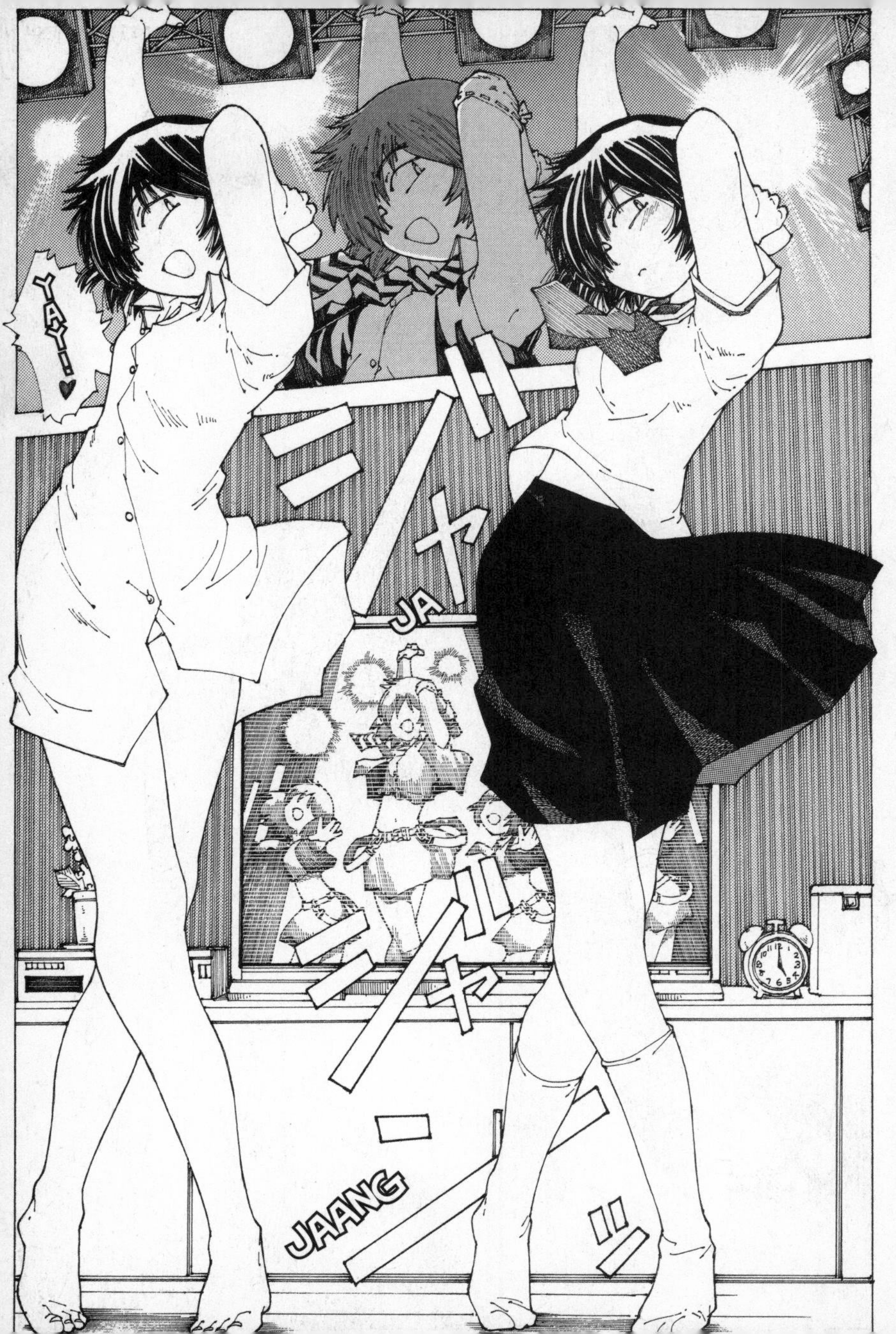
ジャ
JA
YAY!♥
ジャーン
JAANG

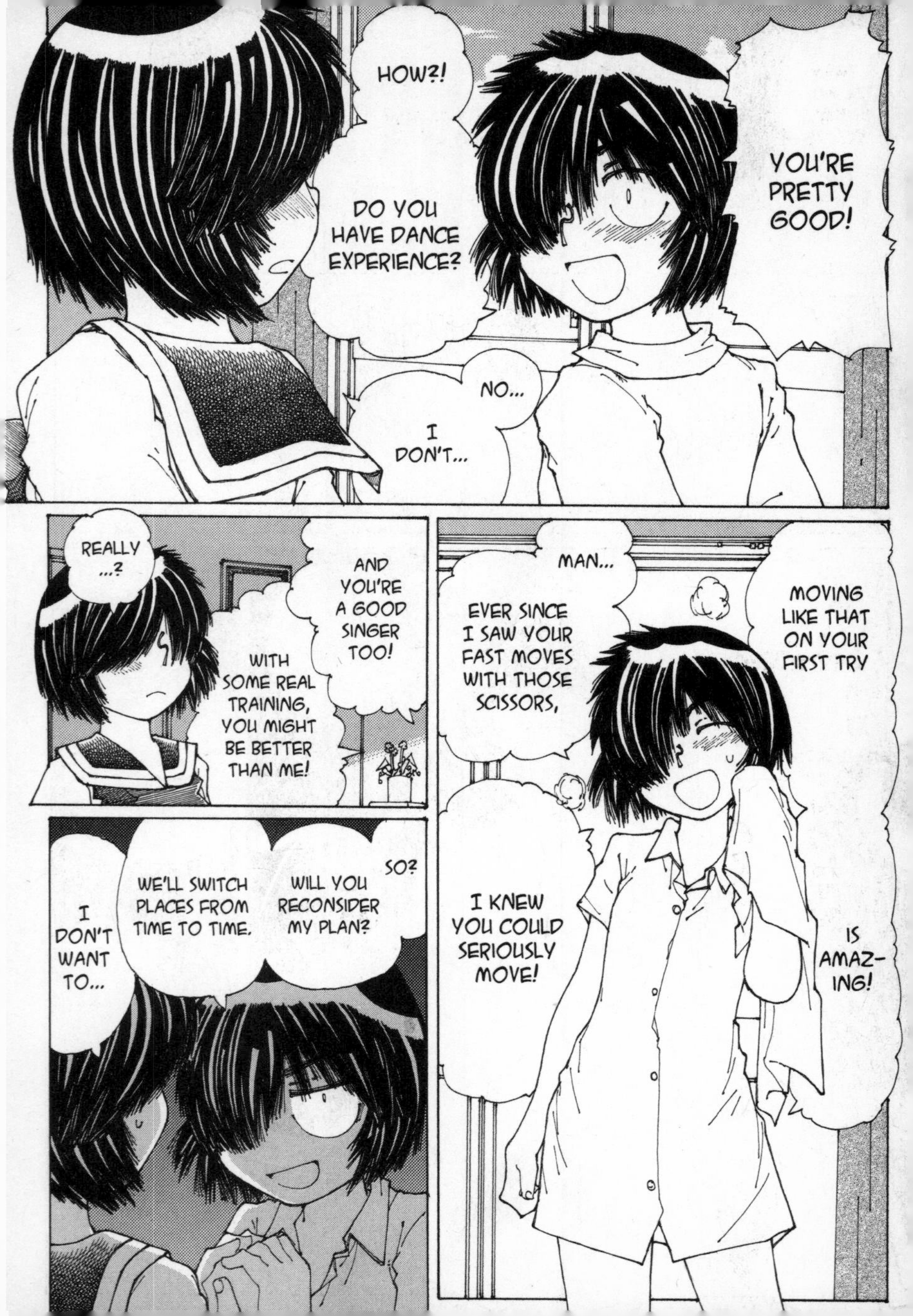
YOU'RE PRETTY GOOD!
HOW?!
DO YOU HAVE DANCE EXPERIENCE?
NO...
I DON'T...
MOVING LIKE THAT ON YOUR FIRST TRY
IS AMAZ-ING!
MAN...
EVER SINCE I SAW YOUR FAST MOVES WITH THOSE SCISSORS,
I KNEW YOU COULD SERIOUSLY MOVE!
AND YOU'RE A GOOD SINGER TOO!
WITH SOME REAL TRAINING, YOU MIGHT BE BETTER THAN ME!
REALLY ...?
SO?
WILL YOU RECONSIDER MY PLAN?
WE'LL SWITCH PLACES FROM TIME TO TIME.
I DON'T WANT TO...

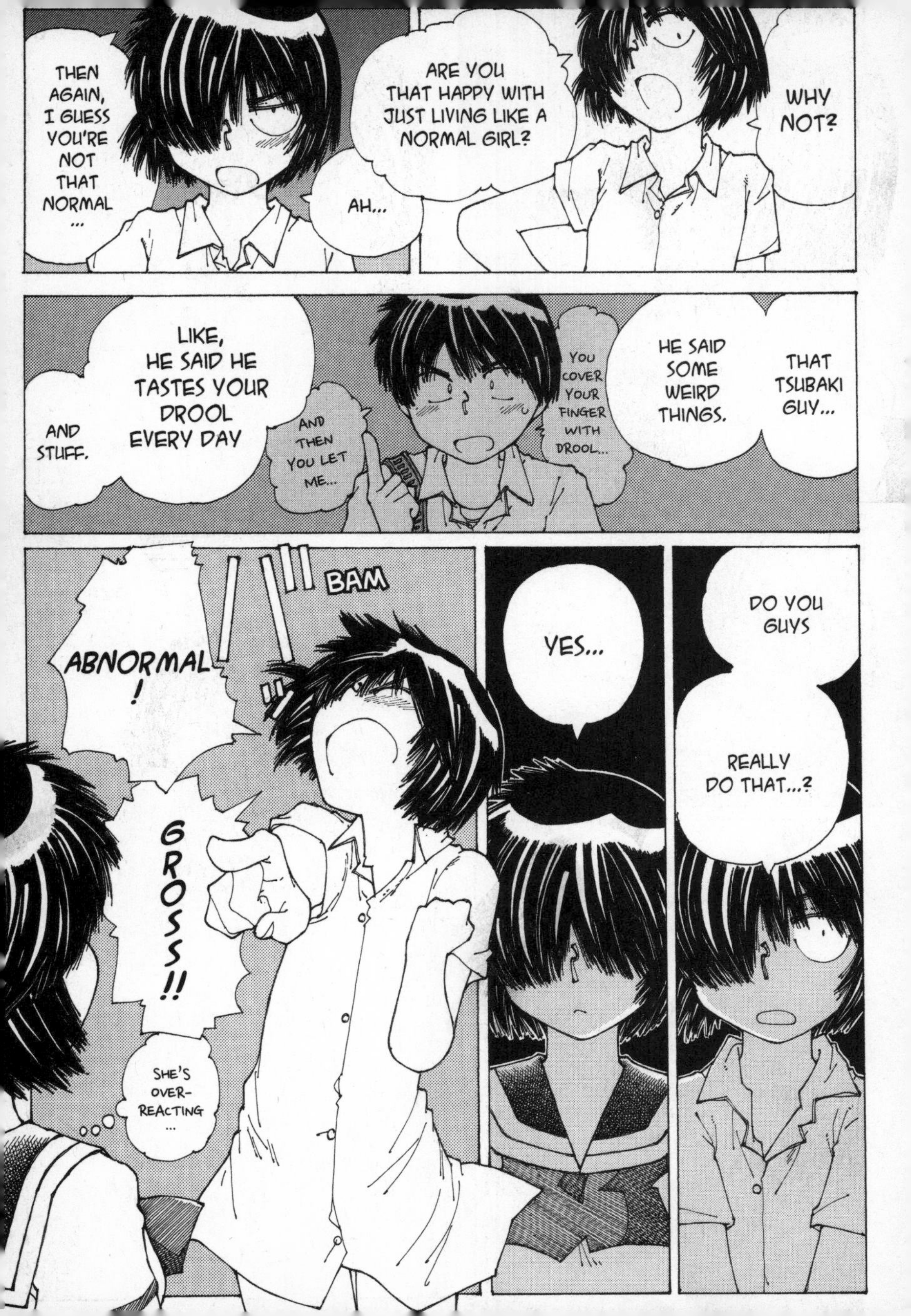
ARE YOU THAT HAPPY WITH JUST LIVING LIKE A NORMAL GIRL?
WHY NOT?
AH...
THEN AGAIN, I GUESS YOU'RE NOT THAT NORMAL...
THAT TSUBAKI GUY...
HE SAID SOME WEIRD THINGS.
YOU COVER YOUR FINGER WITH DROOL...
AND THEN YOU LET ME...
LIKE, HE SAID HE TASTES YOUR DROOL EVERY DAY
AND STUFF.
DO YOU GUYS
REALLY DO THAT...?
YES...
BAM
ABNORMAL!
GROSS!!
SHE'S OVER-REACTING...

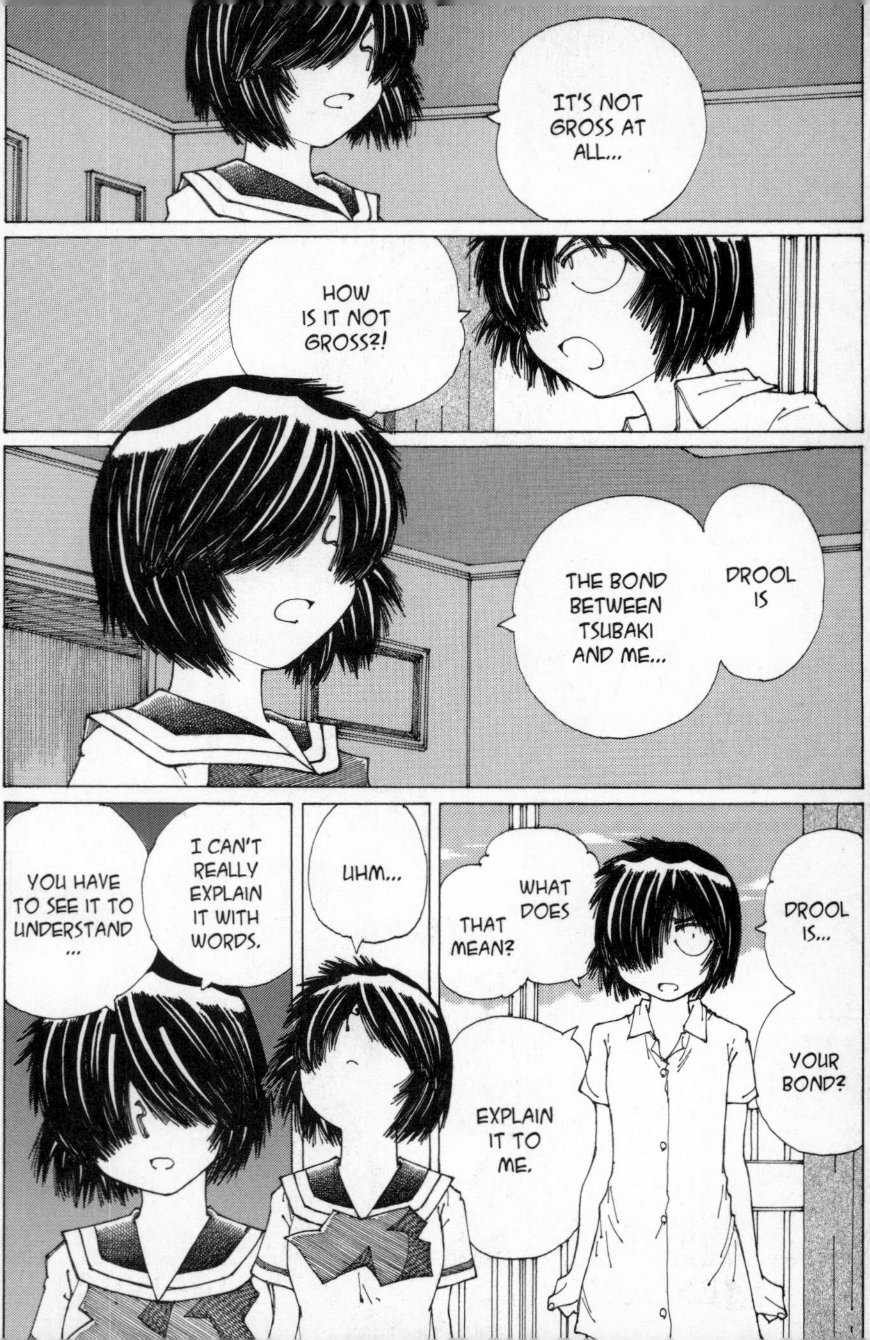
IT'S NOT GROSS AT ALL...
HOW IS IT NOT GROSS?!
DROOL IS
THE BOND BETWEEN TSUBAKI AND ME...
DROOL IS...
YOUR BOND?
WHAT DOES THAT MEAN?
EXPLAIN IT TO ME.
UHM...
I CAN'T REALLY EXPLAIN IT WITH WORDS.
YOU HAVE TO SEE IT TO UNDERSTAND...

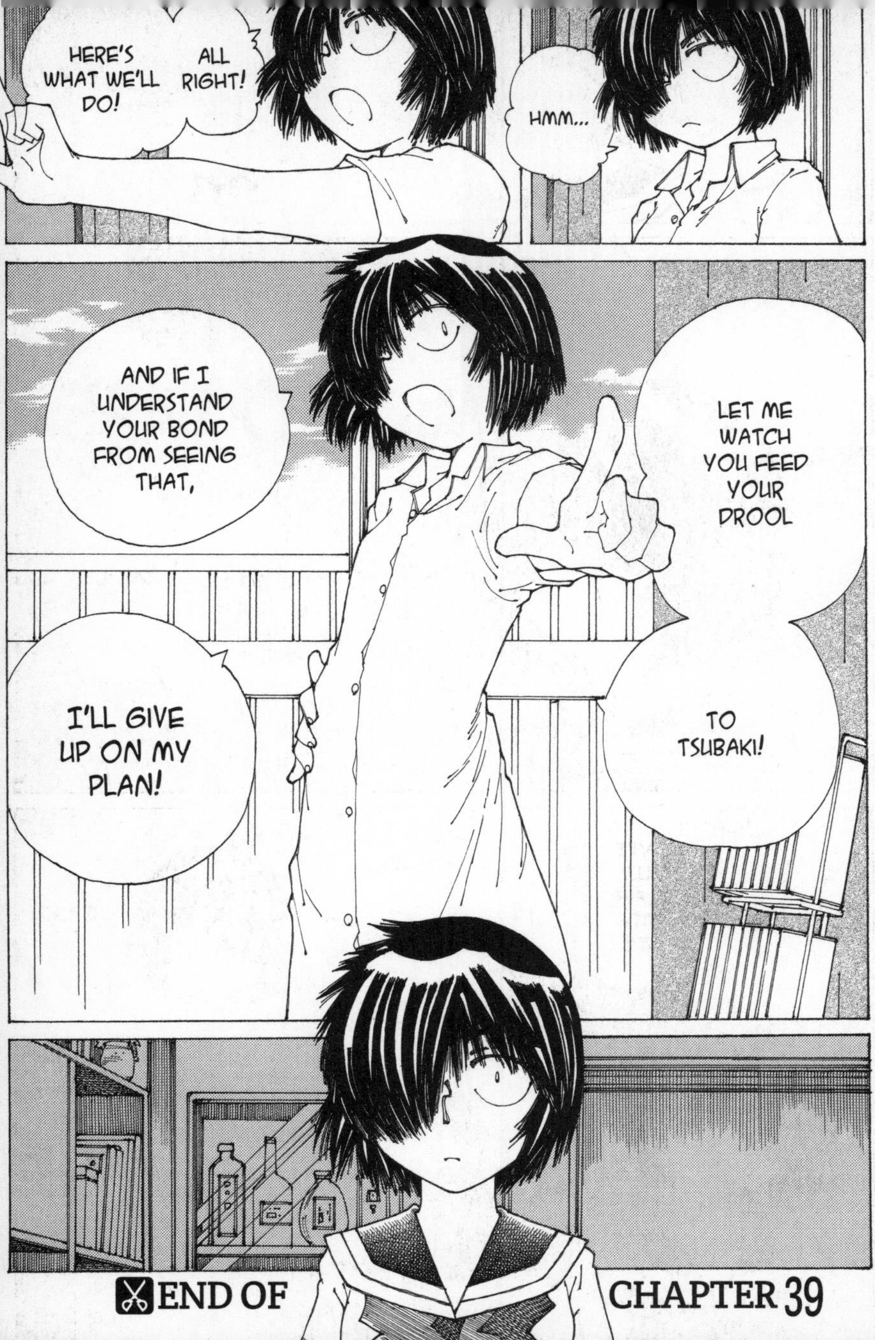
HMM...
ALL RIGHT!
HERE'S WHAT WE'LL DO!
LET ME WATCH YOU FEED YOUR DROOL
TO TSUBAKI!
AND IF I UNDERSTAND YOUR BOND FROM SEEING THAT,
I'LL GIVE UP ON MY PLAN!
END OF CHAPTER 39

Since the story in this volume is about an idol,
I decided to make the theme of these bonus pages
about idols, or in other words, people I admire.

MY IDOL: ①

MIKAKO TABE

(1989~)

She's an actress.

I suffered from a slipped disk last year, and during my frequent visits to the orthopedic surgeon, I often saw the NHK serial drama "Tsubasa" on the waiting room TV. She's the one who played the title character, Tsubasa. I wound up becoming her fan over the course of all those hospital visits.

Her face usually looks a bit sullen, but I think it's really cute when she smiles. Apparently, I've always liked girls who look a little sullen. People often tell me that Urabe's face in "X" has been looking scarier recently, so it may be that my own tastes are becoming increasingly apparent as the story's serialization continues.

BUT NOW HAVING A LOT OF WHITE SHOWING IS THE DEFAULT.

HER PUPILS WERE LARGER WHEN SERIALIZATION FIRST STARTED,

IT DOESN'T NECESSARILY MEAN SHE'S ANGRY!

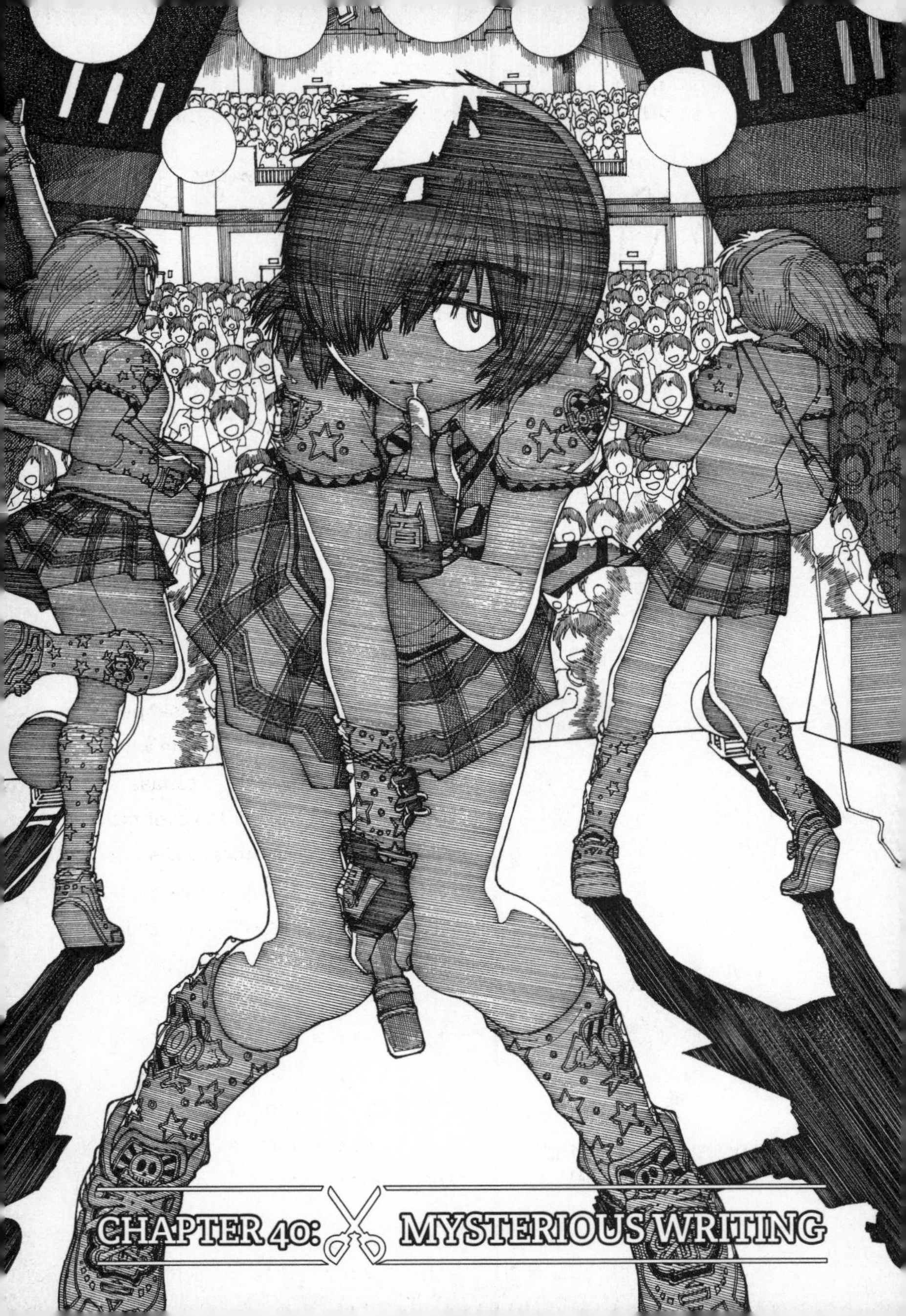
CHAPTER 40: MYSTERIOUS WRITING

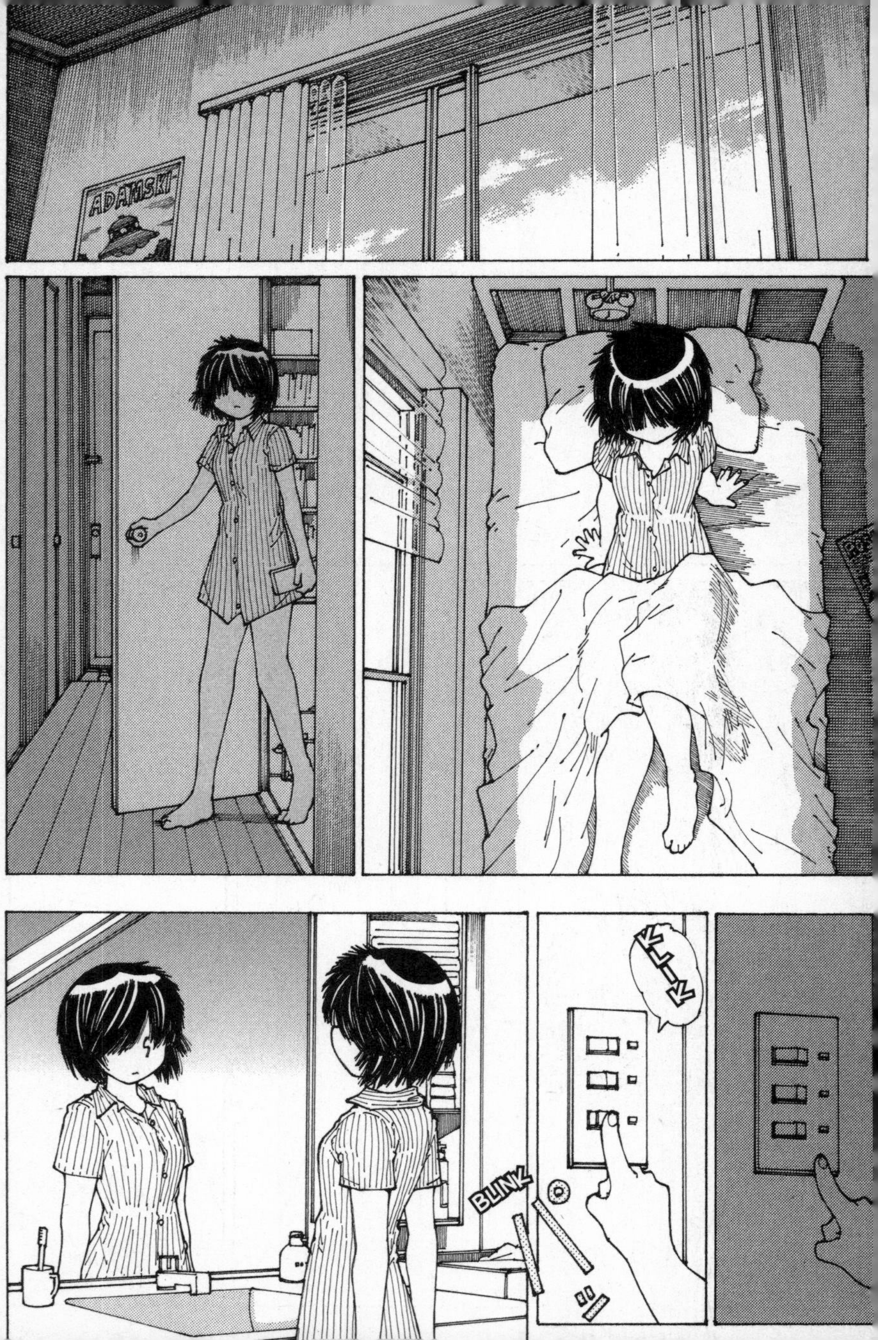
ADAMSKI
KLIK
BLINK

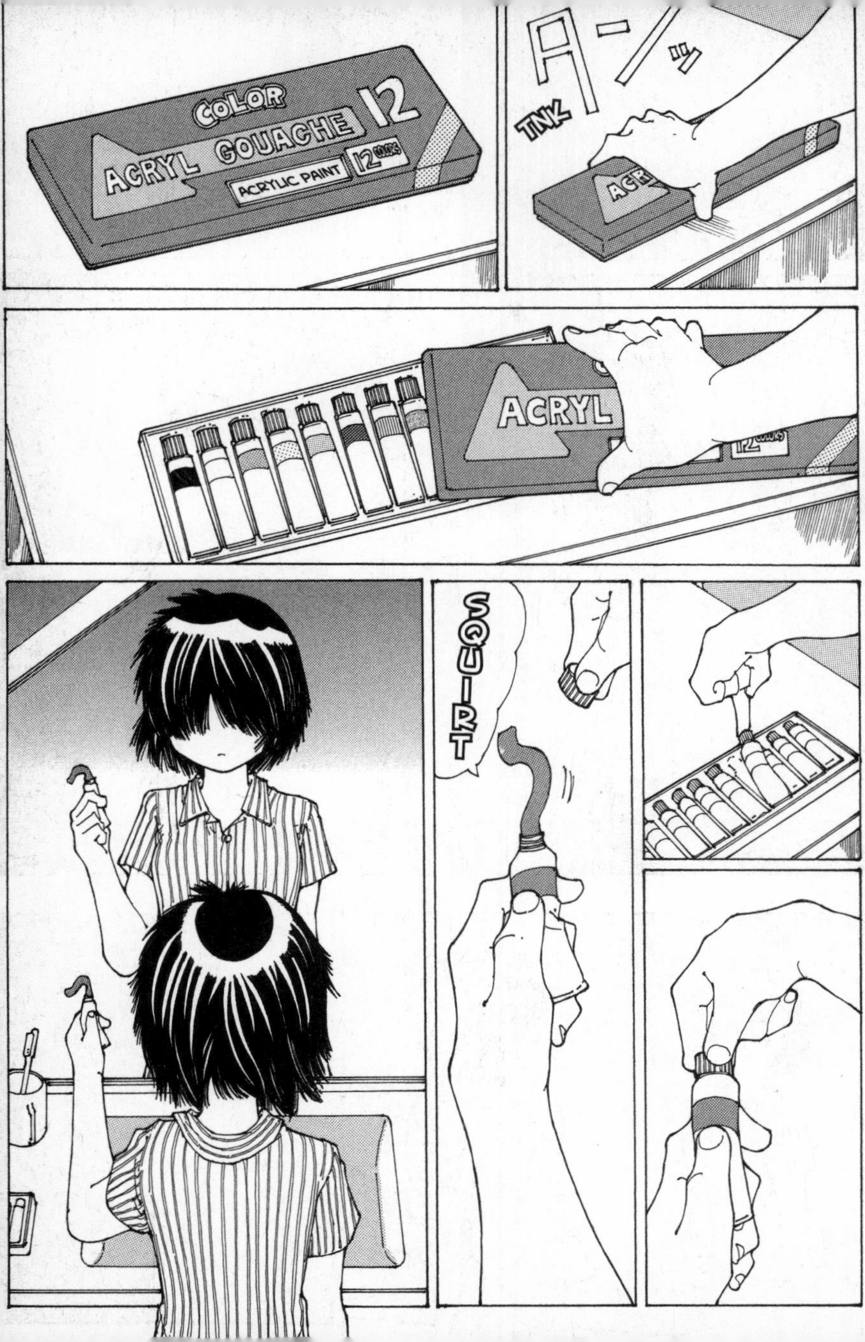
TNK
COLOR
ACRYL GOUACHE 12
12 COLORS
ACRYLIC PAINT
ACRYL
SQUIRT

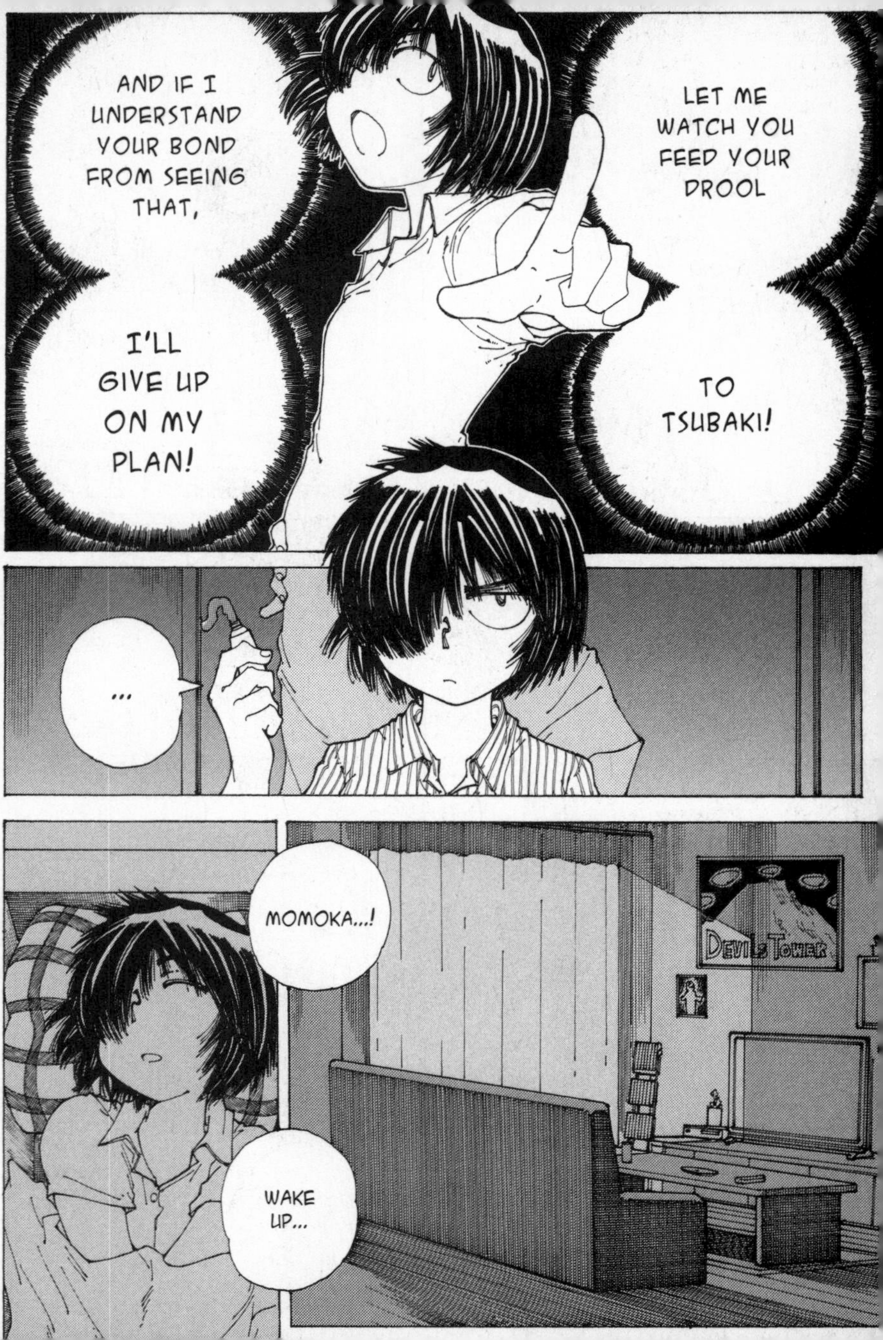
LET ME WATCH YOU FEED YOUR DROOL
TO TSUBAKI!
AND IF I UNDERSTAND YOUR BOND FROM SEEING THAT,
I'LL GIVE UP ON MY PLAN!
...
DEVILS TOWER
MOMOKA...!
WAKE UP...

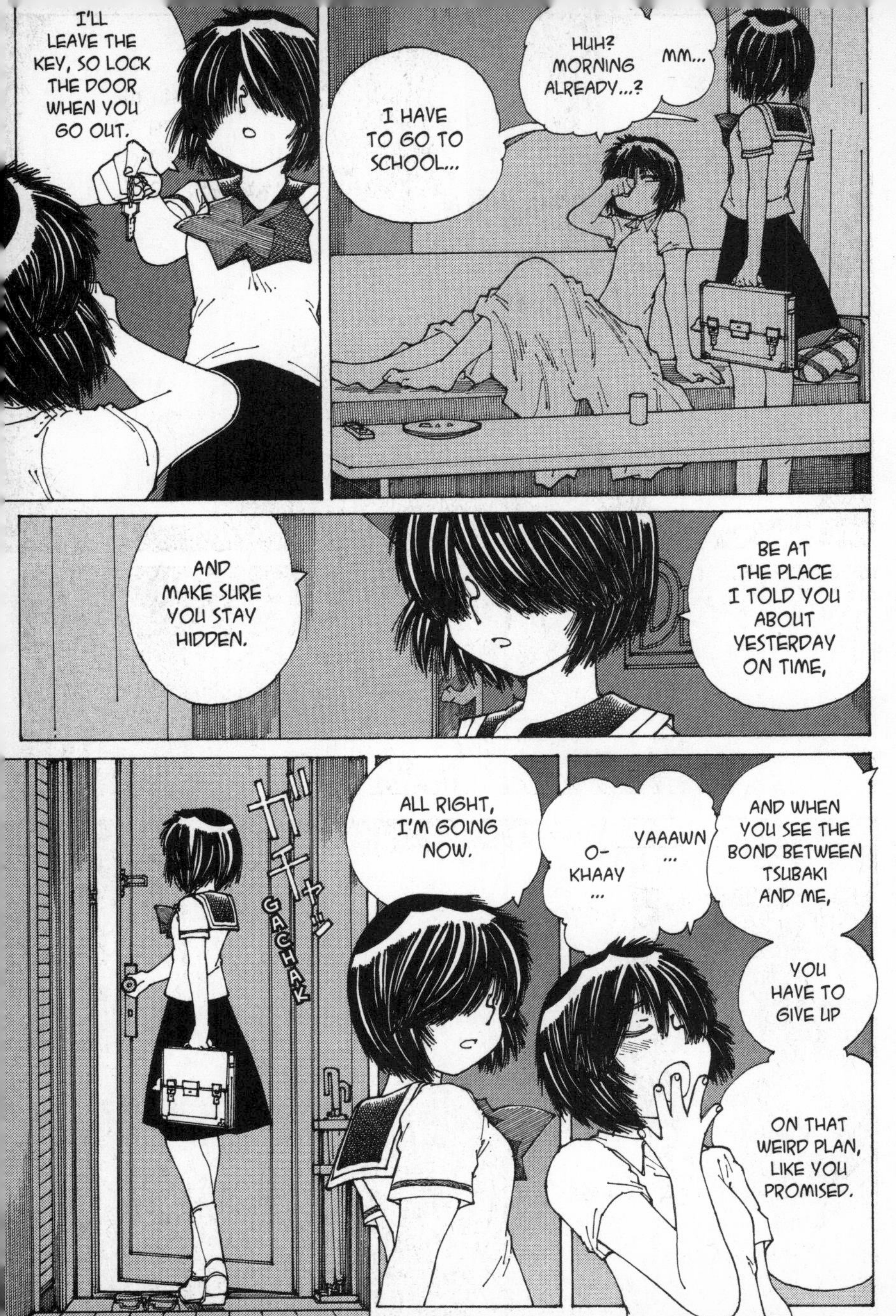
MM...
HUH? MORNING ALREADY...?
I HAVE TO GO TO SCHOOL...
I'LL LEAVE THE KEY, SO LOCK THE DOOR WHEN YOU GO OUT.
BE AT THE PLACE I TOLD YOU ABOUT YESTERDAY ON TIME,
AND MAKE SURE YOU STAY HIDDEN.
AND WHEN YOU SEE THE BOND BETWEEN TSUBAKI AND ME,
YOU HAVE TO GIVE UP
ON THAT WEIRD PLAN, LIKE YOU PROMISED.
YAAAWN ...
O-KHAAY ...
ALL RIGHT, I'M GOING NOW.
GACHAK

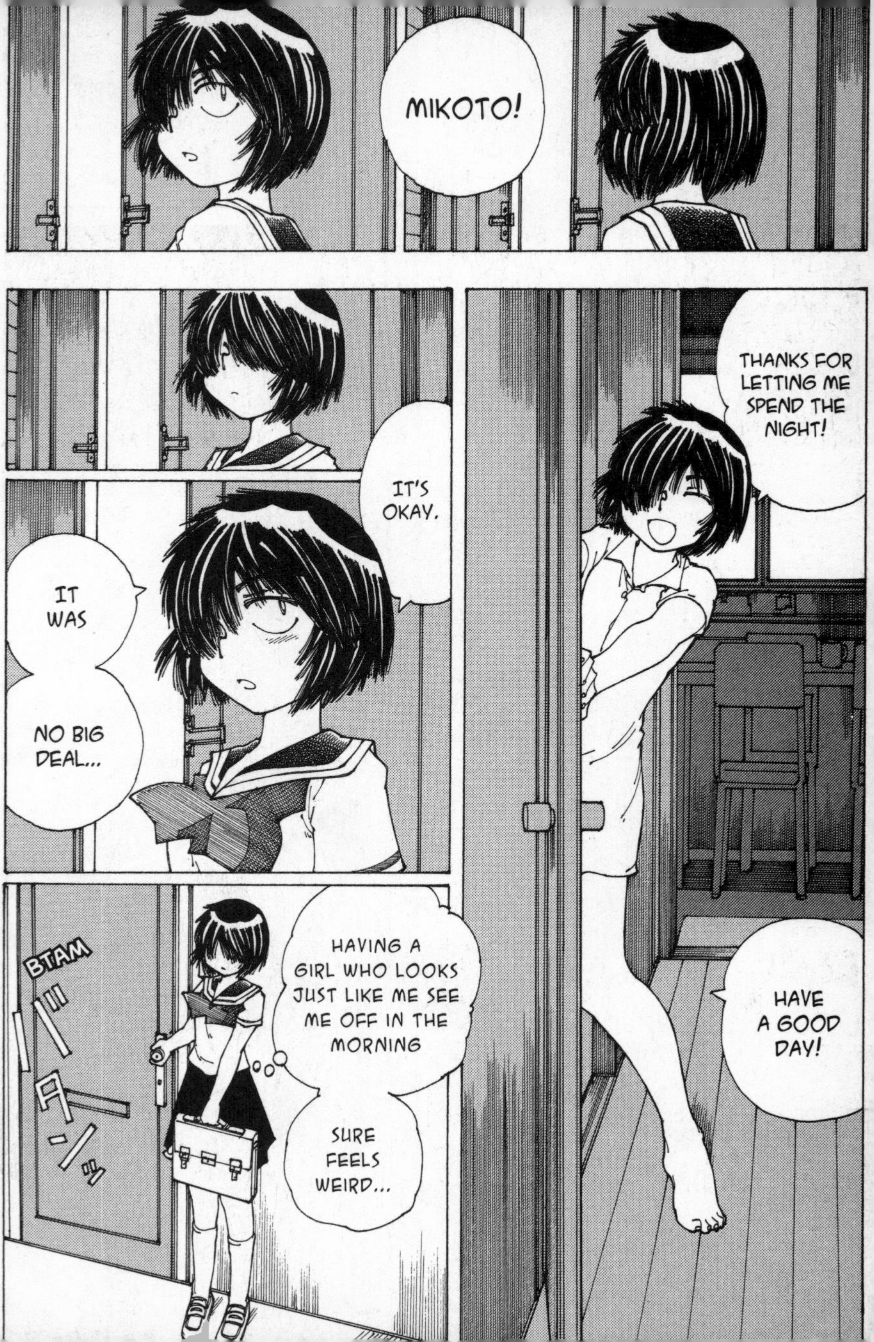
MIKOTO!
THANKS FOR LETTING ME SPEND THE NIGHT!
HAVE A GOOD DAY!
IT'S OKAY.
IT WAS
NO BIG DEAL...
BTAM
HAVING A GIRL WHO LOOKS JUST LIKE ME SEE ME OFF IN THE MORNING
SURE FEELS WEIRD...

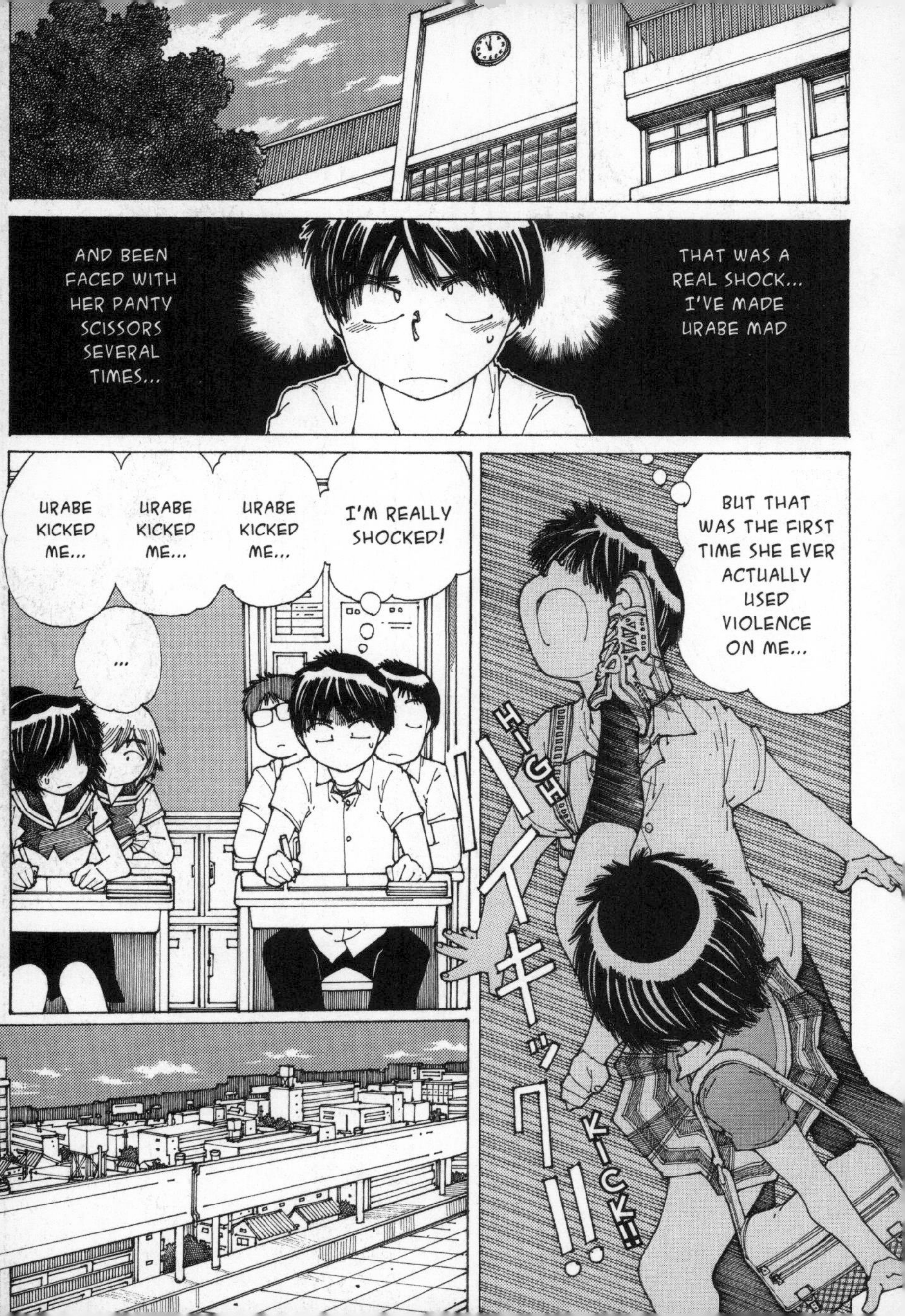
THAT WAS A REAL SHOCK... I'VE MADE URABE MAD
AND BEEN FACED WITH HER PANTY SCISSORS SEVERAL TIMES...
BUT THAT WAS THE FIRST TIME SHE EVER ACTUALLY USED VIOLENCE ON ME...
HI-UGH
KICK!!
I'M REALLY SHOCKED!
URABE KICKED ME...
URABE KICKED ME...
URABE KICKED ME...
...

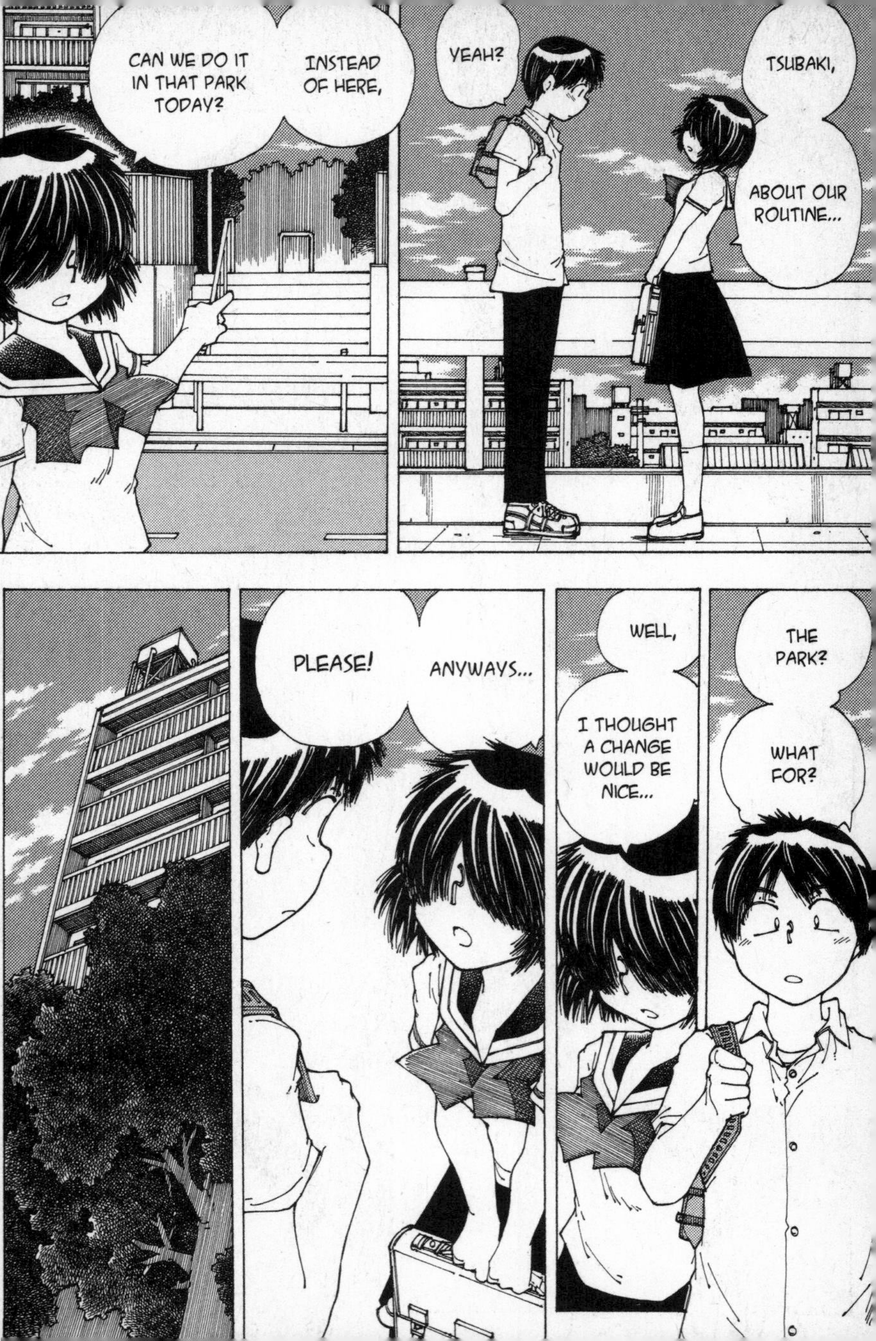
TSUBAKI,
ABOUT OUR ROUTINE...
YEAH?
INSTEAD OF HERE,
CAN WE DO IT IN THAT PARK TODAY?
THE PARK?
WHAT FOR?
WELL,
I THOUGHT A CHANGE WOULD BE NICE...
ANYWAYS...
PLEASE!

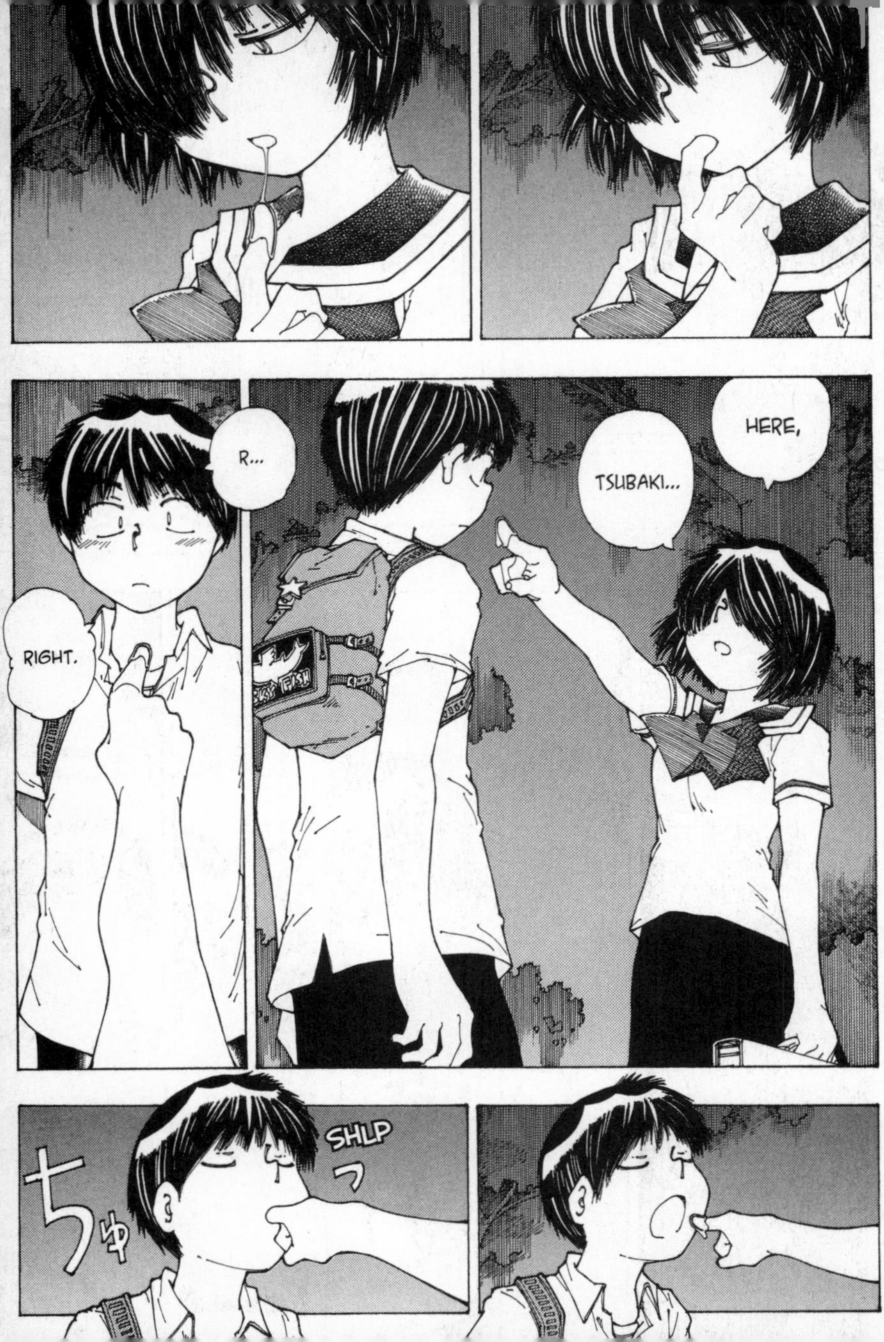
HERE,
TSUBAKI...
R...
RIGHT.
SHLP
ちゅ

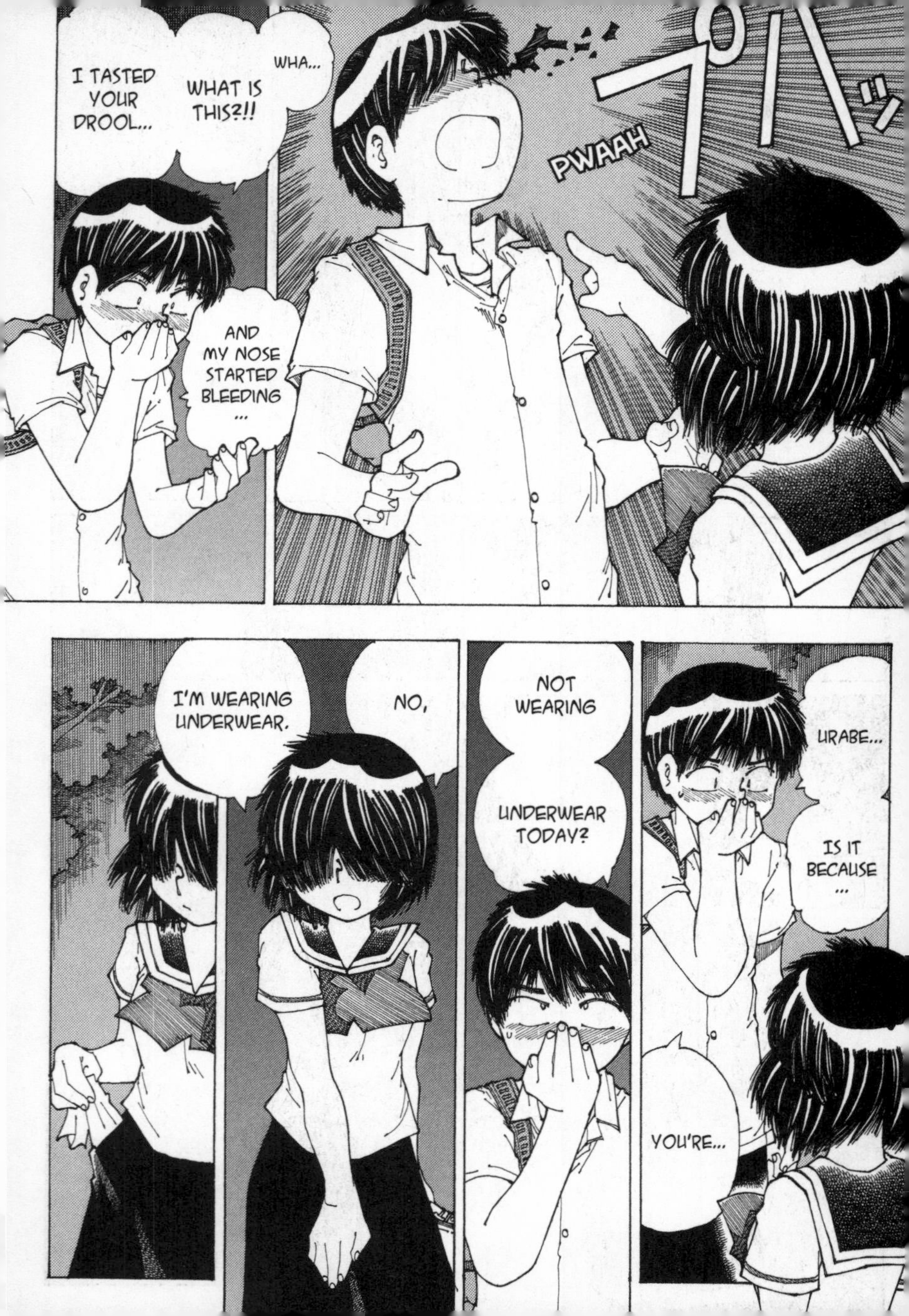
プハッ
PWAAH
WHA...
WHAT IS THIS?!!
I TASTED YOUR DROOL...
AND MY NOSE STARTED BLEEDING...
URABE...
IS IT BECAUSE...
YOU'RE...
NOT WEARING
UNDERWEAR TODAY?
NO,
I'M WEARING UNDERWEAR.

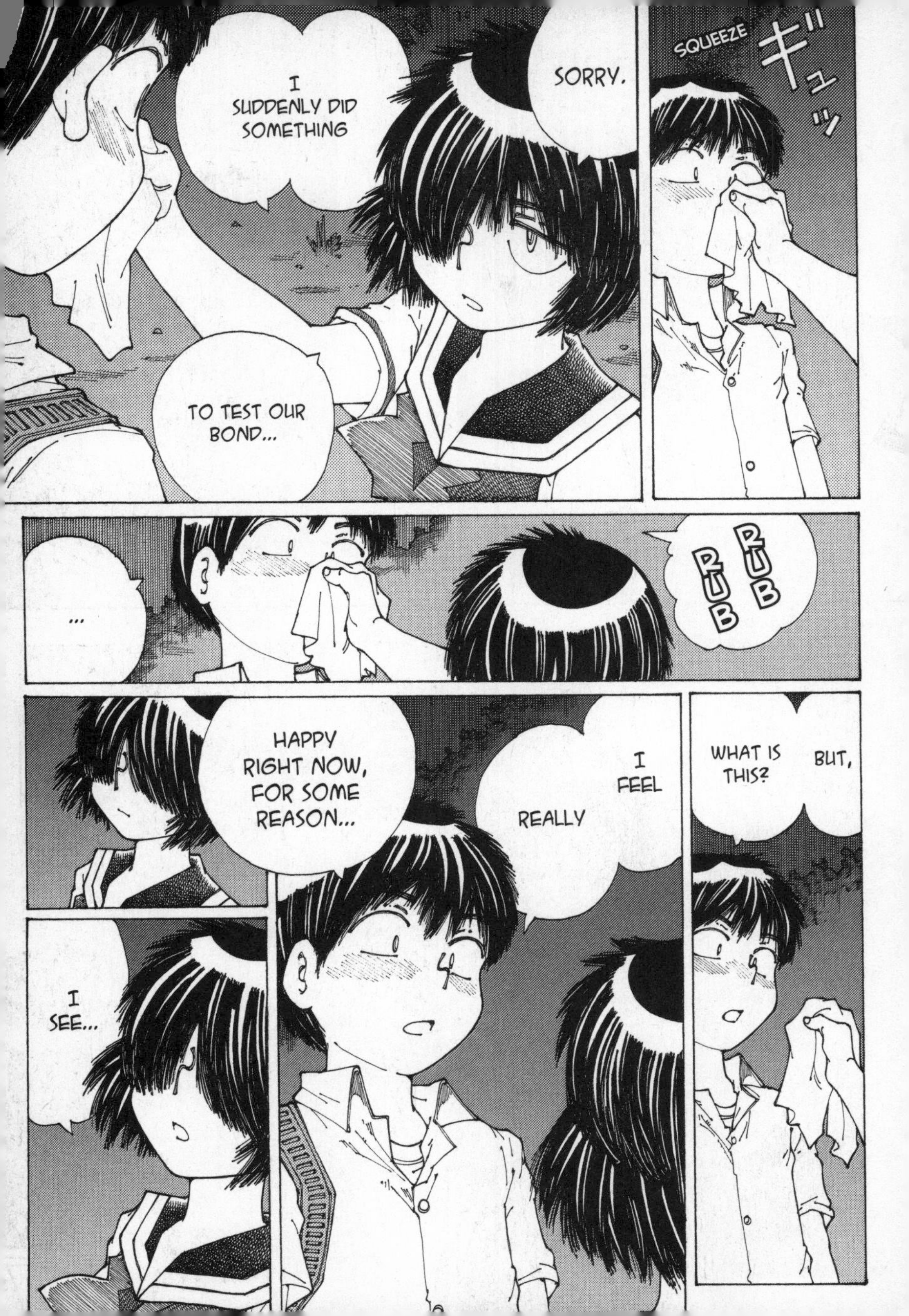
SQUEEZE
ギュッ
SORRY.
I SUDDENLY DID SOMETHING
TO TEST OUR BOND...
RUB RUB
...
BUT,
WHAT IS THIS?
I FEEL
REALLY
HAPPY RIGHT NOW, FOR SOME REASON...
I SEE...

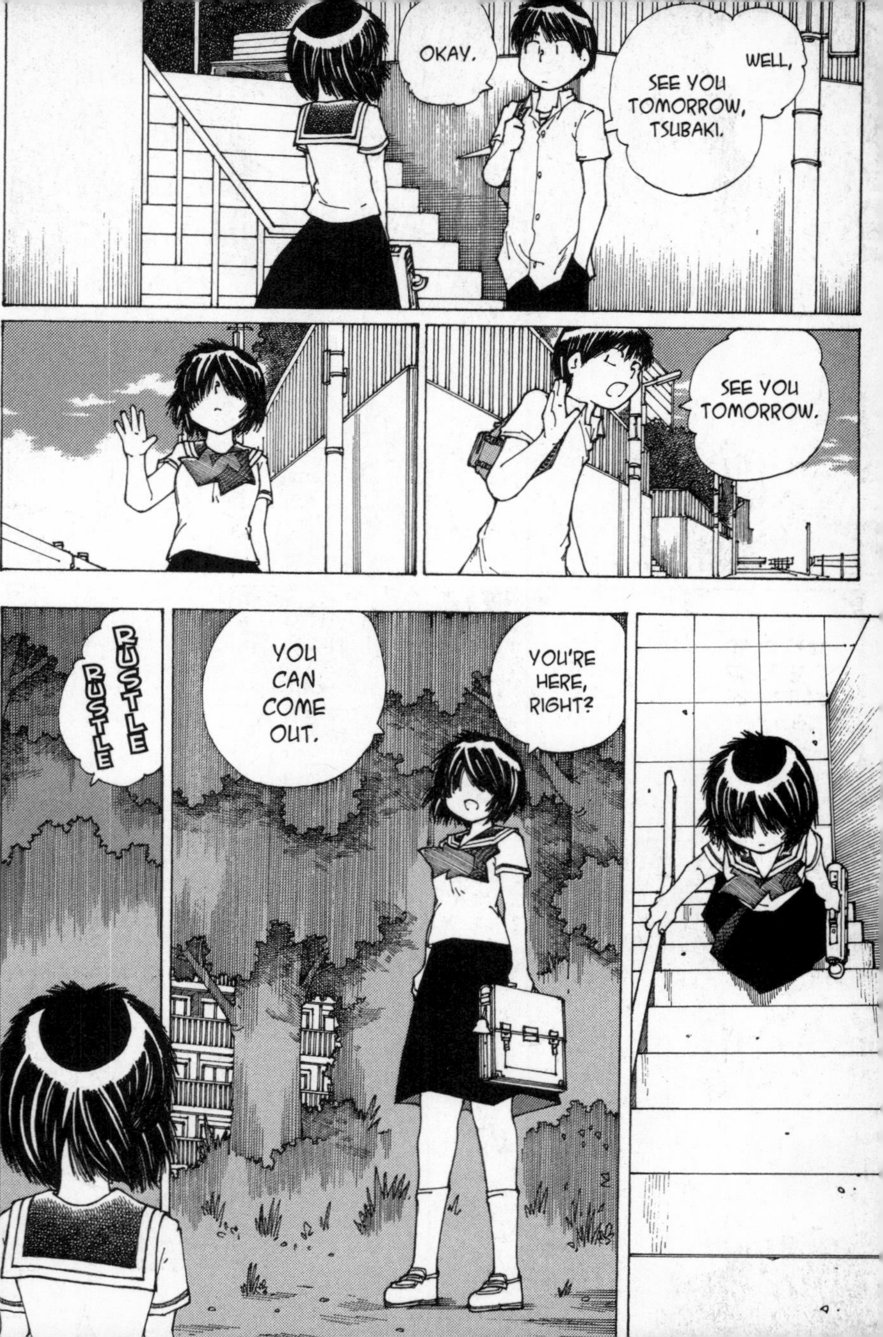
WELL, SEE YOU TOMORROW, TSUBAKI.
OKAY.
SEE YOU TOMORROW.
YOU'RE HERE, RIGHT?
YOU CAN COME OUT.
RUSTLE RUSTLE

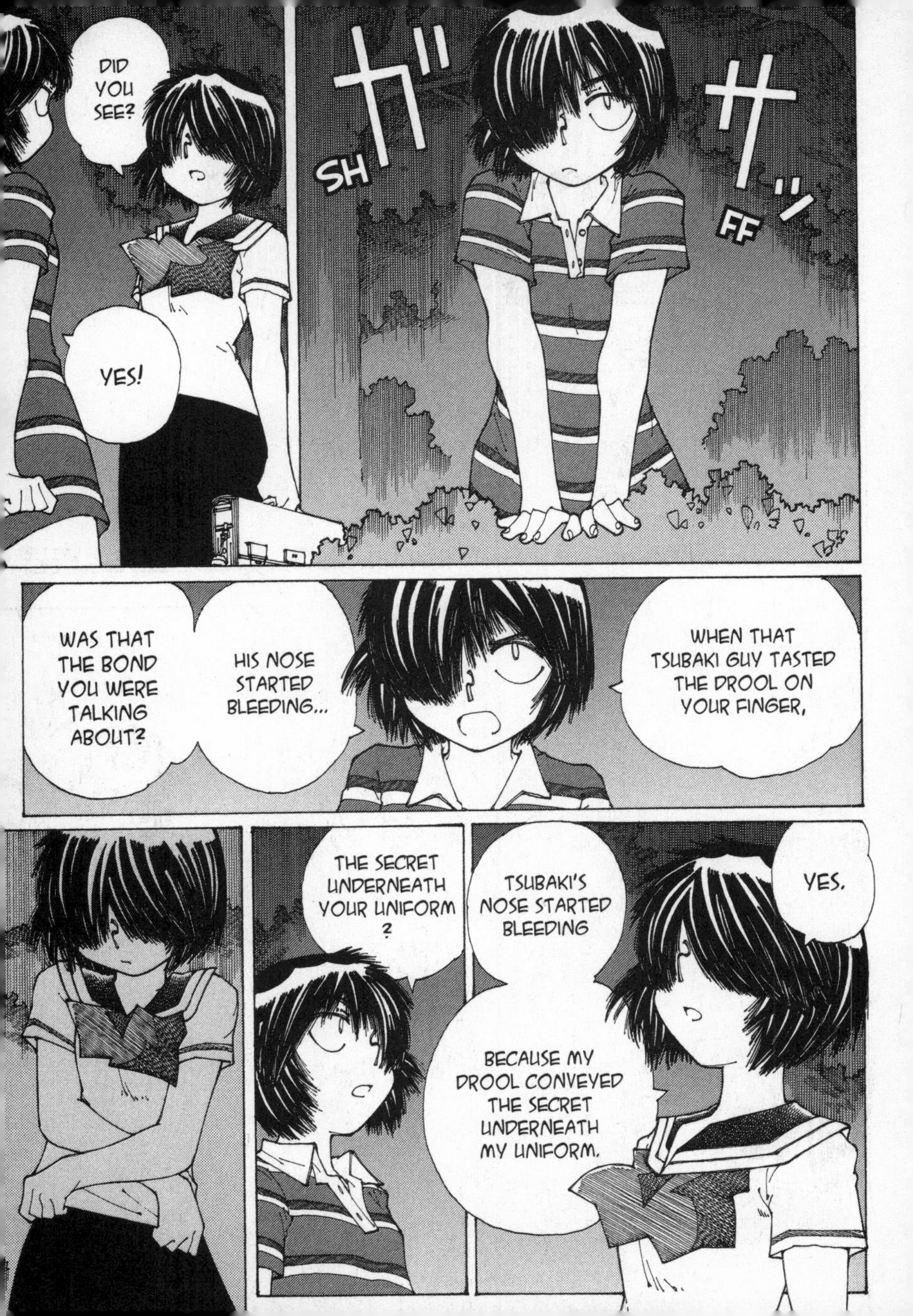
ガサッ
SH
FF
DID YOU SEE?
YES!
WHEN THAT TSUBAKI GUY TASTED THE DROOL ON YOUR FINGER,
HIS NOSE STARTED BLEEDING...
WAS THAT THE BOND YOU WERE TALKING ABOUT?
YES.
TSUBAKI'S NOSE STARTED BLEEDING
BECAUSE MY DROOL CONVEYED THE SECRET UNDERNEATH MY UNIFORM.
THE SECRET UNDERNEATH YOUR UNIFORM ?

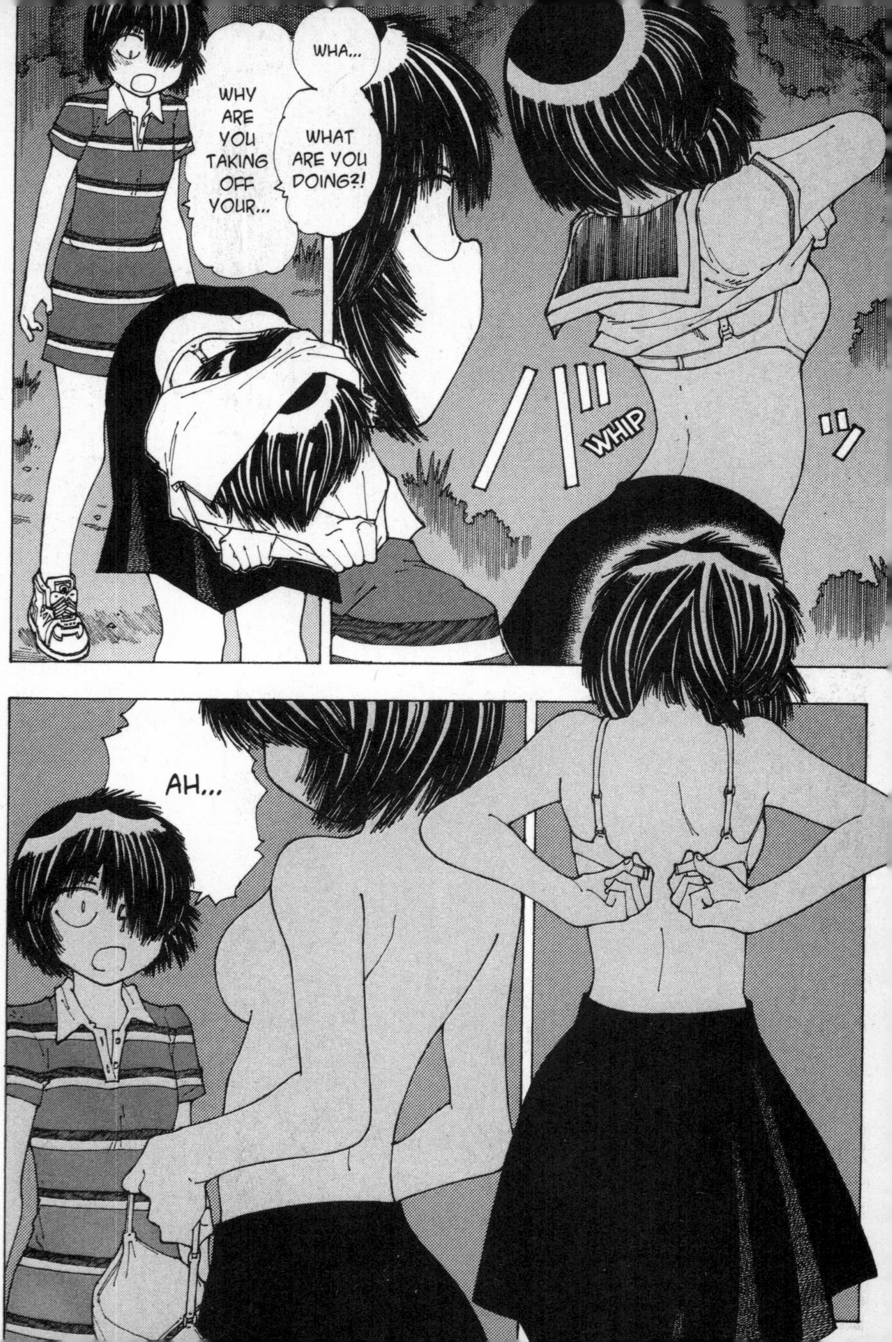
WHIP
WHA...
WHAT ARE YOU DOING?!
WHY ARE YOU TAKING OFF YOUR...
AH...

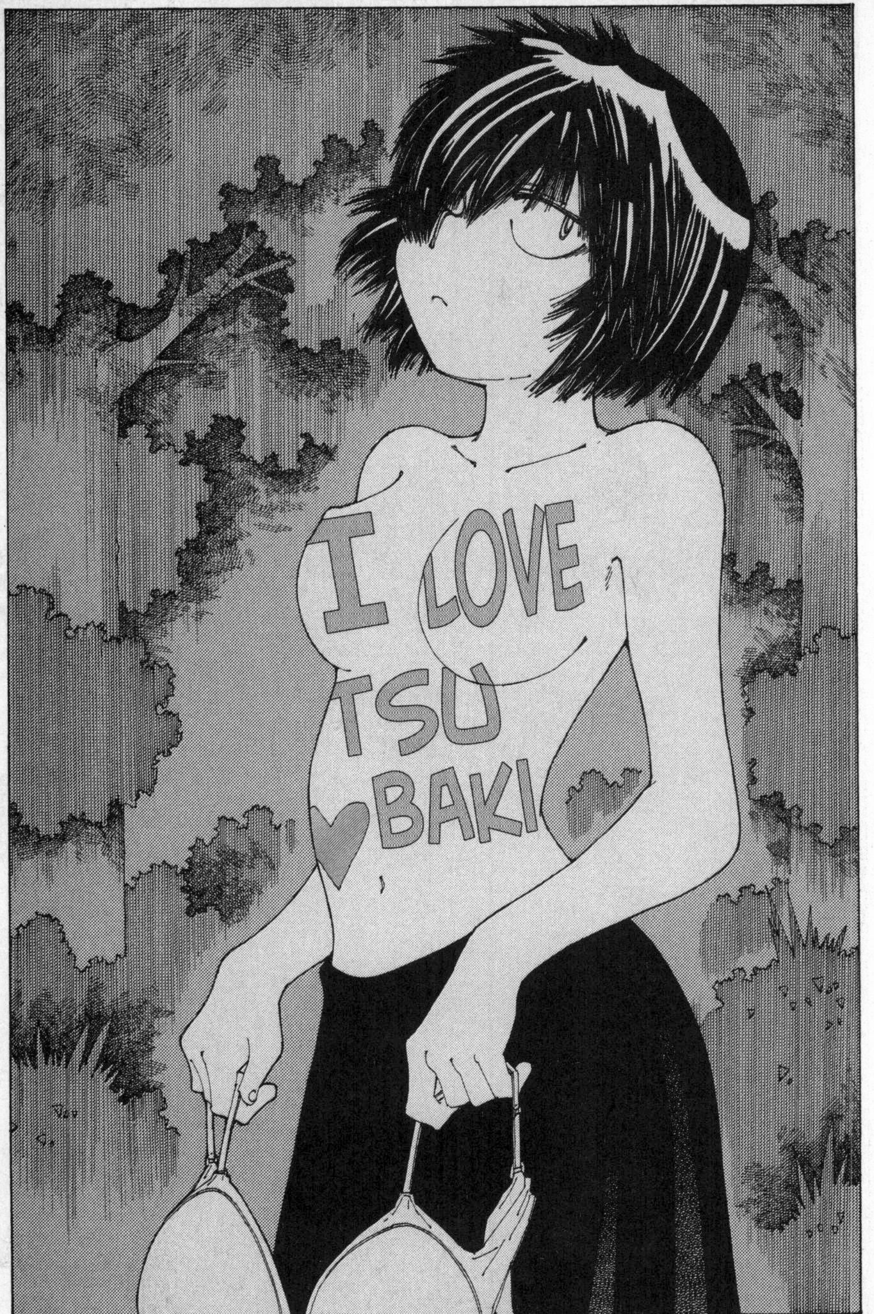
I LOVE
TSU
BAKI

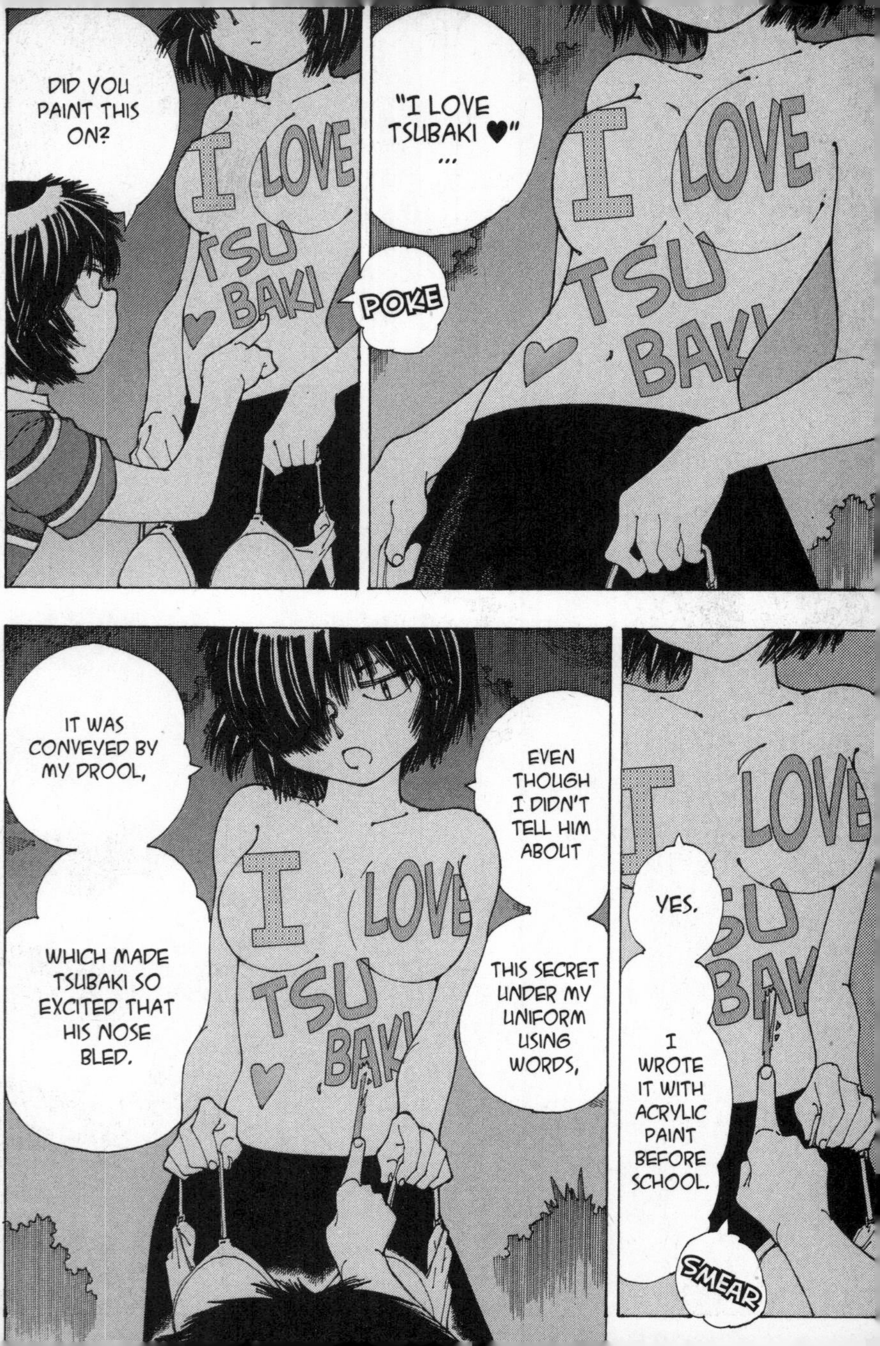
"I LOVE TSUBAKI ♥" ...
DID YOU PAINT THIS ON?
POKE
YES.
I WROTE IT WITH ACRYLIC PAINT BEFORE SCHOOL.
SMEAR
EVEN THOUGH I DIDN'T TELL HIM ABOUT
THIS SECRET UNDER MY UNIFORM USING WORDS,
IT WAS CONVEYED BY MY DROOL,
WHICH MADE TSUBAKI SO EXCITED THAT HIS NOSE BLED.

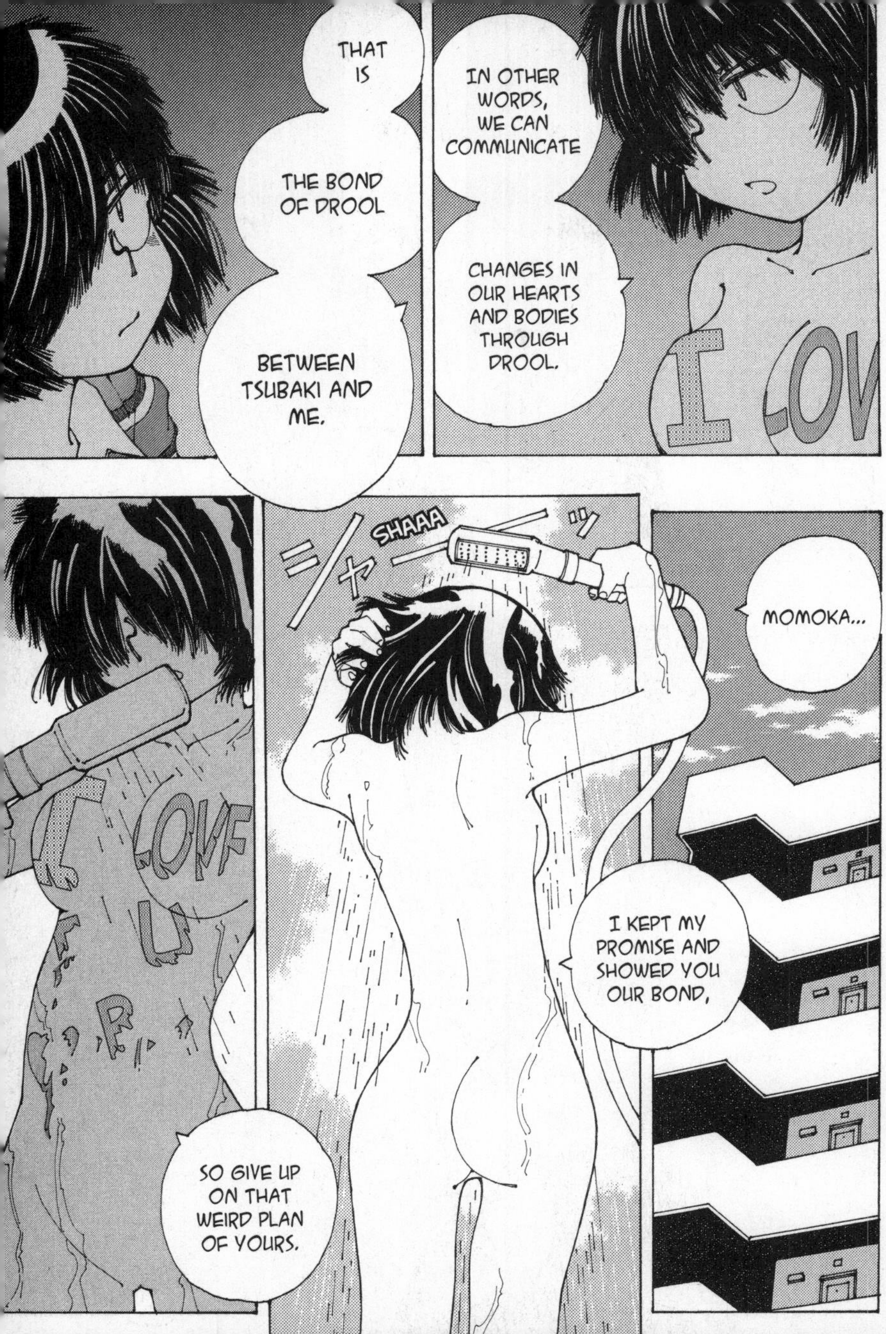
IN OTHER WORDS, WE CAN COMMUNICATE
CHANGES IN OUR HEARTS AND BODIES THROUGH DROOL.
THAT IS
THE BOND OF DROOL
BETWEEN TSUBAKI AND ME.
MOMOKA...
SHAAA
I KEPT MY PROMISE AND SHOWED YOU OUR BOND,
SO GIVE UP ON THAT WEIRD PLAN OF YOURS.

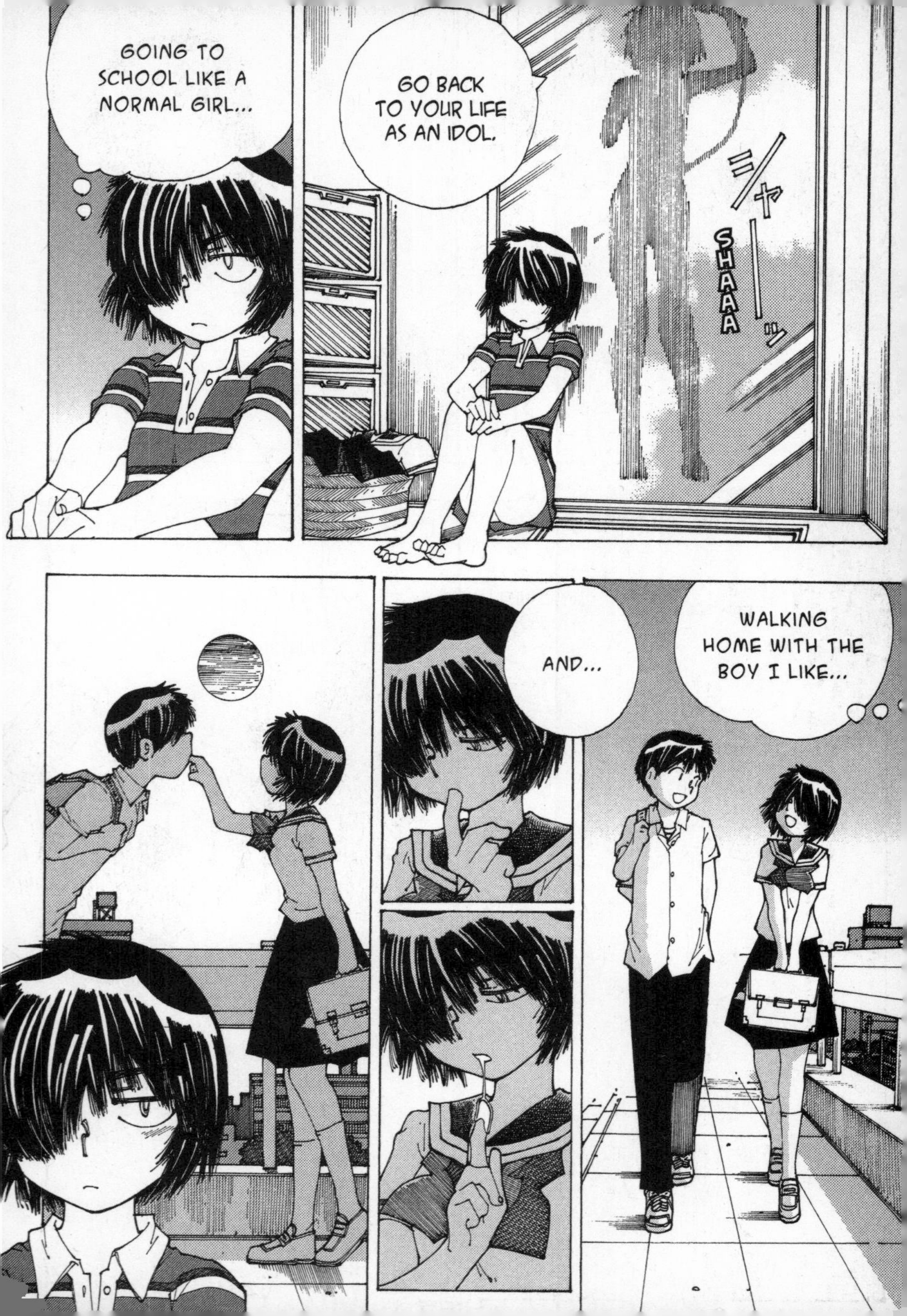
GO BACK TO YOUR LIFE AS AN IDOL.
シャーッ
SHAAA
GOING TO SCHOOL LIKE A NORMAL GIRL...
WALKING HOME WITH THE BOY I LIKE...
AND...

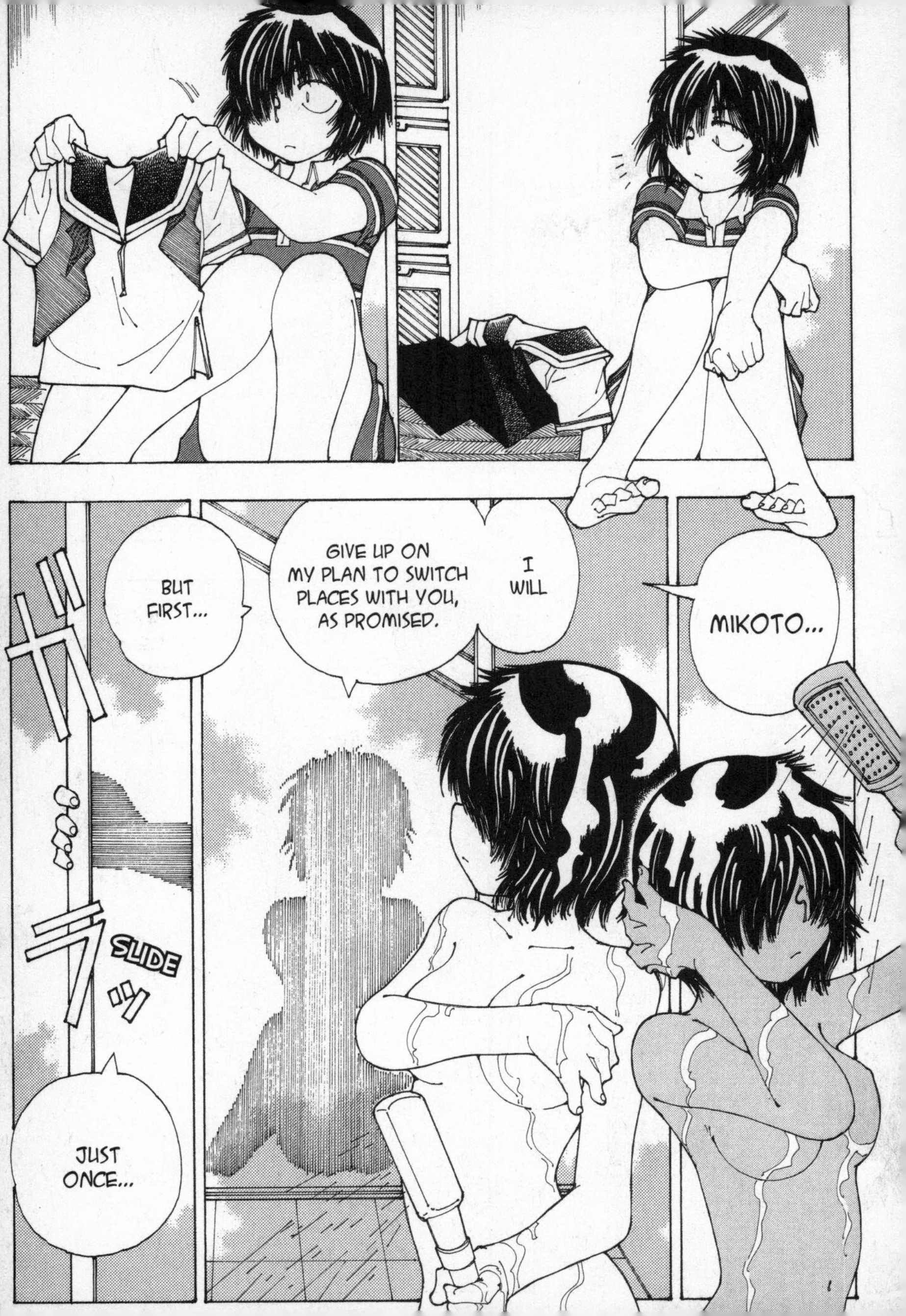
MIKOTO...
I WILL
GIVE UP ON MY PLAN TO SWITCH PLACES WITH YOU, AS PROMISED.
BUT FIRST...
SLIDE
JUST ONCE...

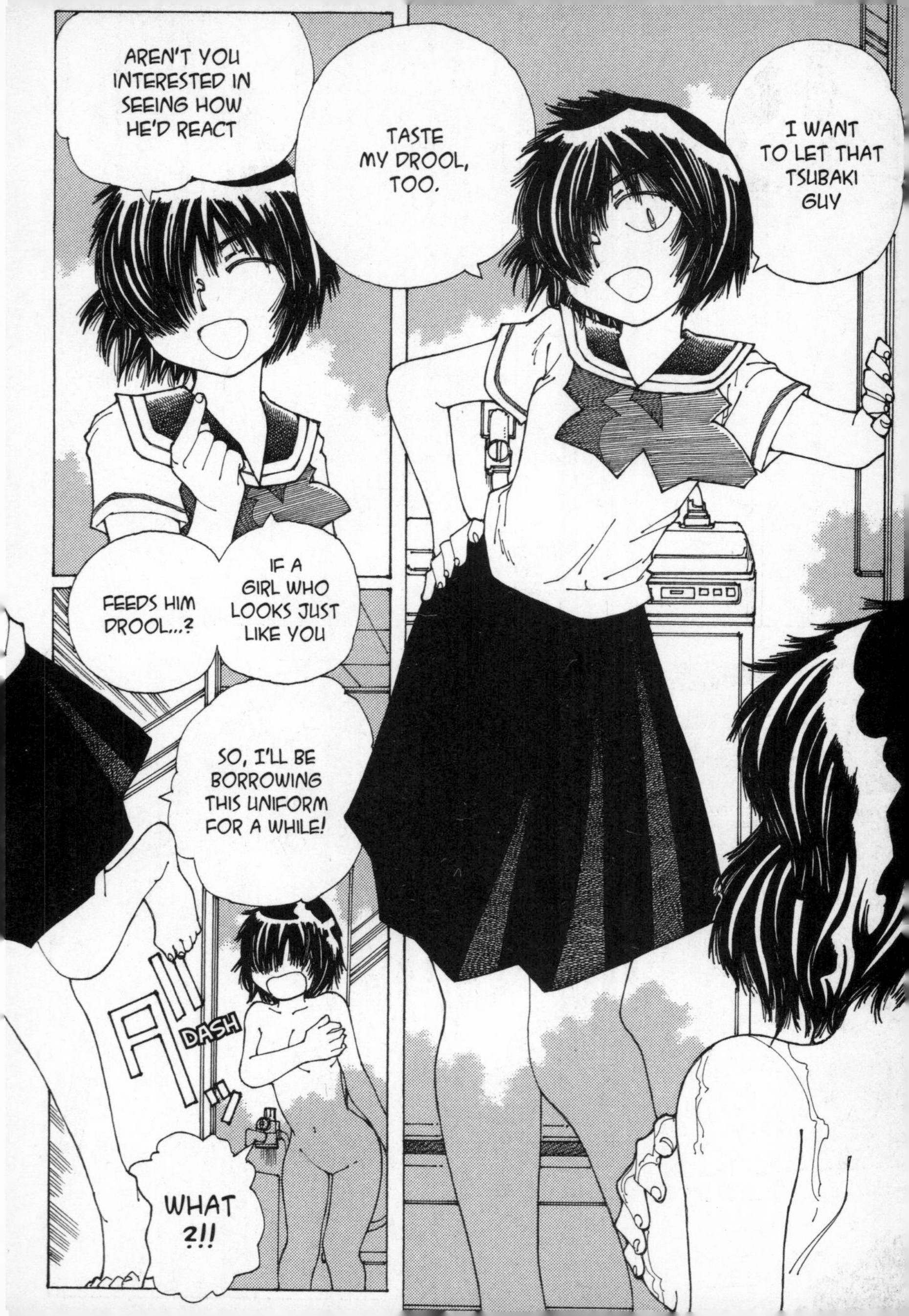
I WANT TO LET THAT TSUBAKI GUY
TASTE MY DROOL, TOO.
AREN'T YOU INTERESTED IN SEEING HOW HE'D REACT
IF A GIRL WHO LOOKS JUST LIKE YOU
FEEDS HIM DROOL...?
SO, I'LL BE BORROWING THIS UNIFORM FOR A WHILE!
DASH
WHAT ?!!

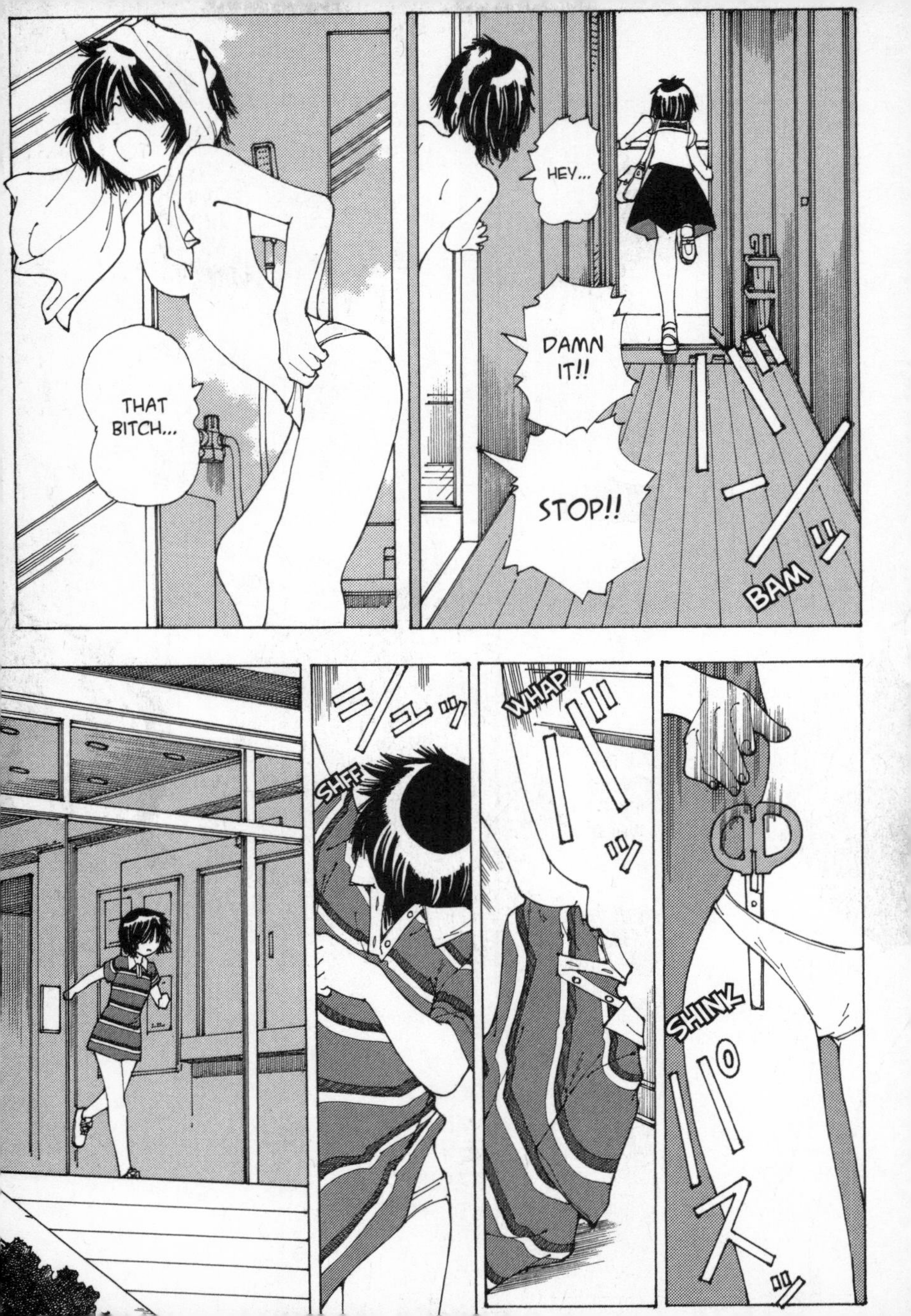
HEY...
DAMN IT!!
STOP!!
BAM
THAT BITCH...
SHINK
WHAP
SHFF

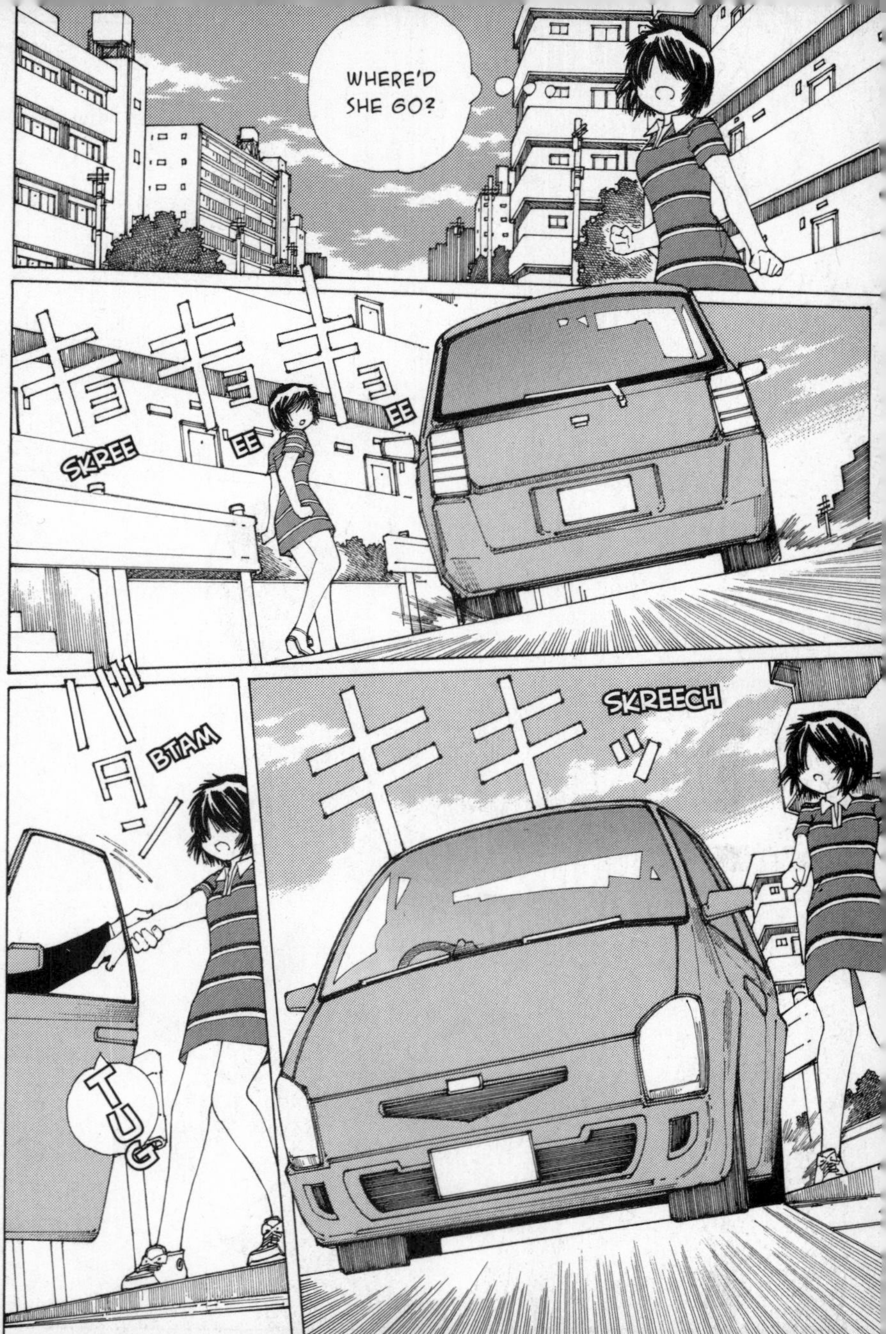
WHERE'D SHE GO?
SKREE
EE
EE
SKREECH
BTAM
TUG

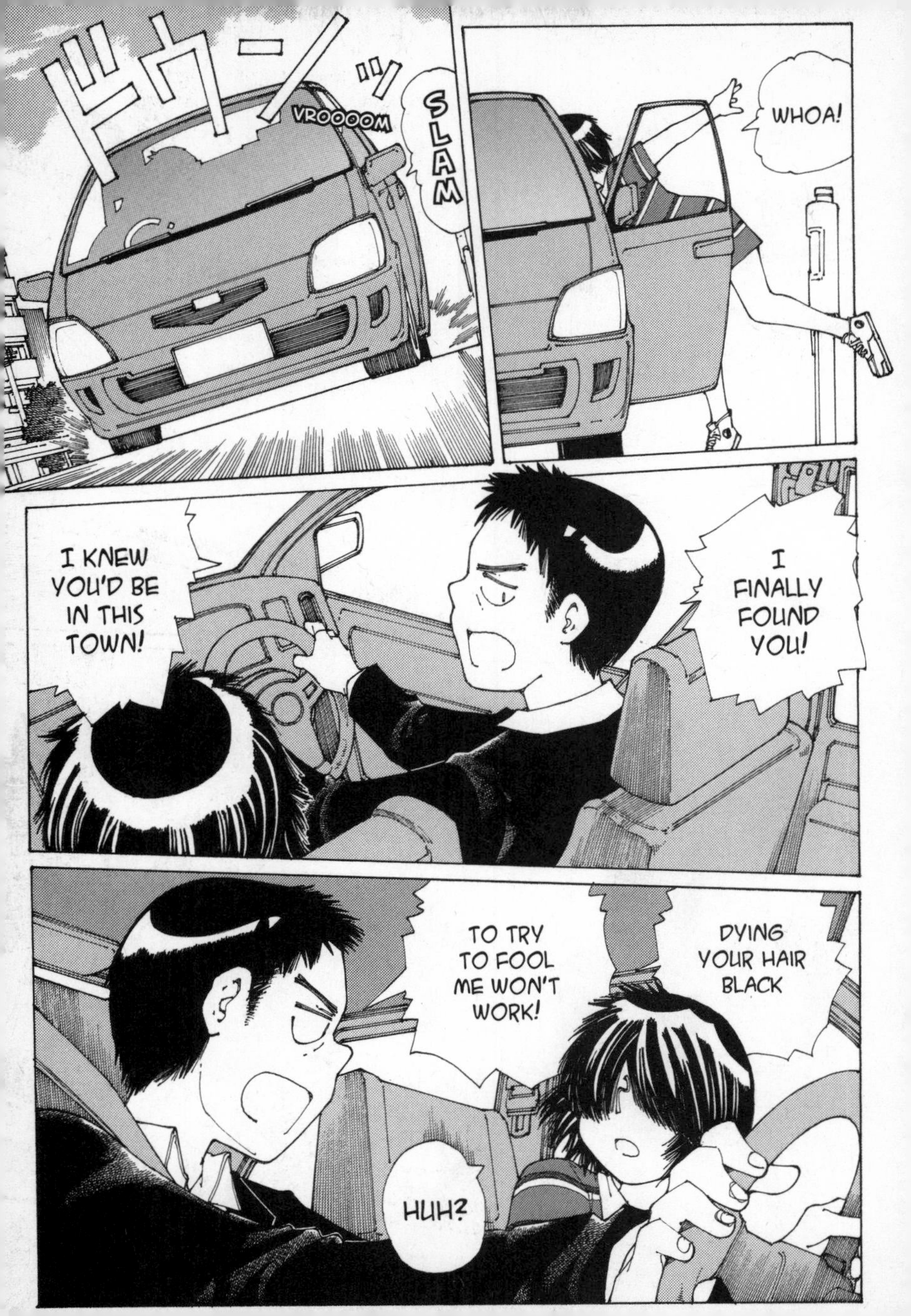
WHOA!
SLAM
VROOOOM
I FINALLY FOUND YOU!
I KNEW YOU'D BE IN THIS TOWN!
DYING YOUR HAIR BLACK
TO TRY TO FOOL ME WON'T WORK!
HUH?

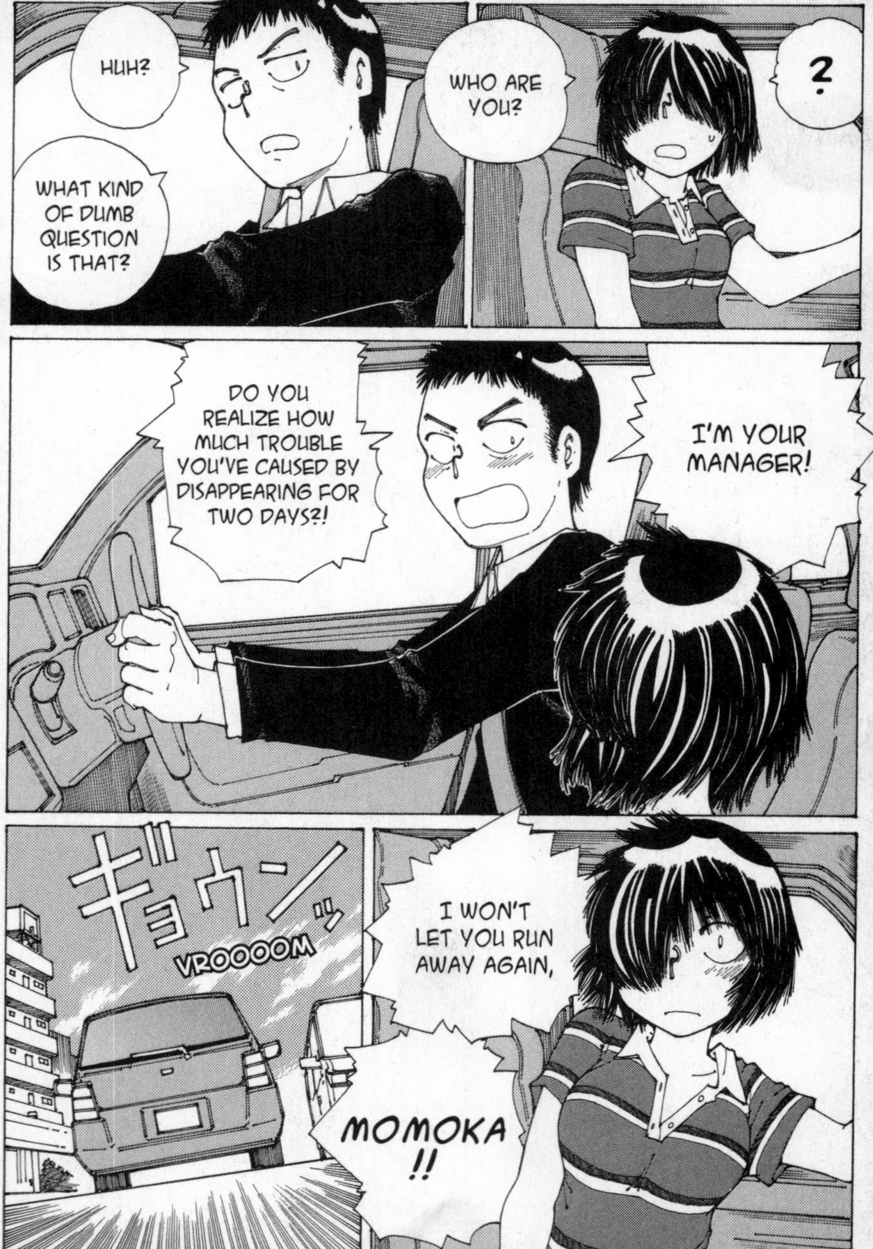
?
WHO ARE YOU?
HUH?
WHAT KIND OF DUMB QUESTION IS THAT?
I'M YOUR MANAGER!
DO YOU REALIZE HOW MUCH TROUBLE YOU'VE CAUSED BY DISAPPEARING FOR TWO DAYS?!
I WON'T LET YOU RUN AWAY AGAIN,
MOMOKA !!
ギョウーンッ
VROOOOM

END OF CHAPTER 40

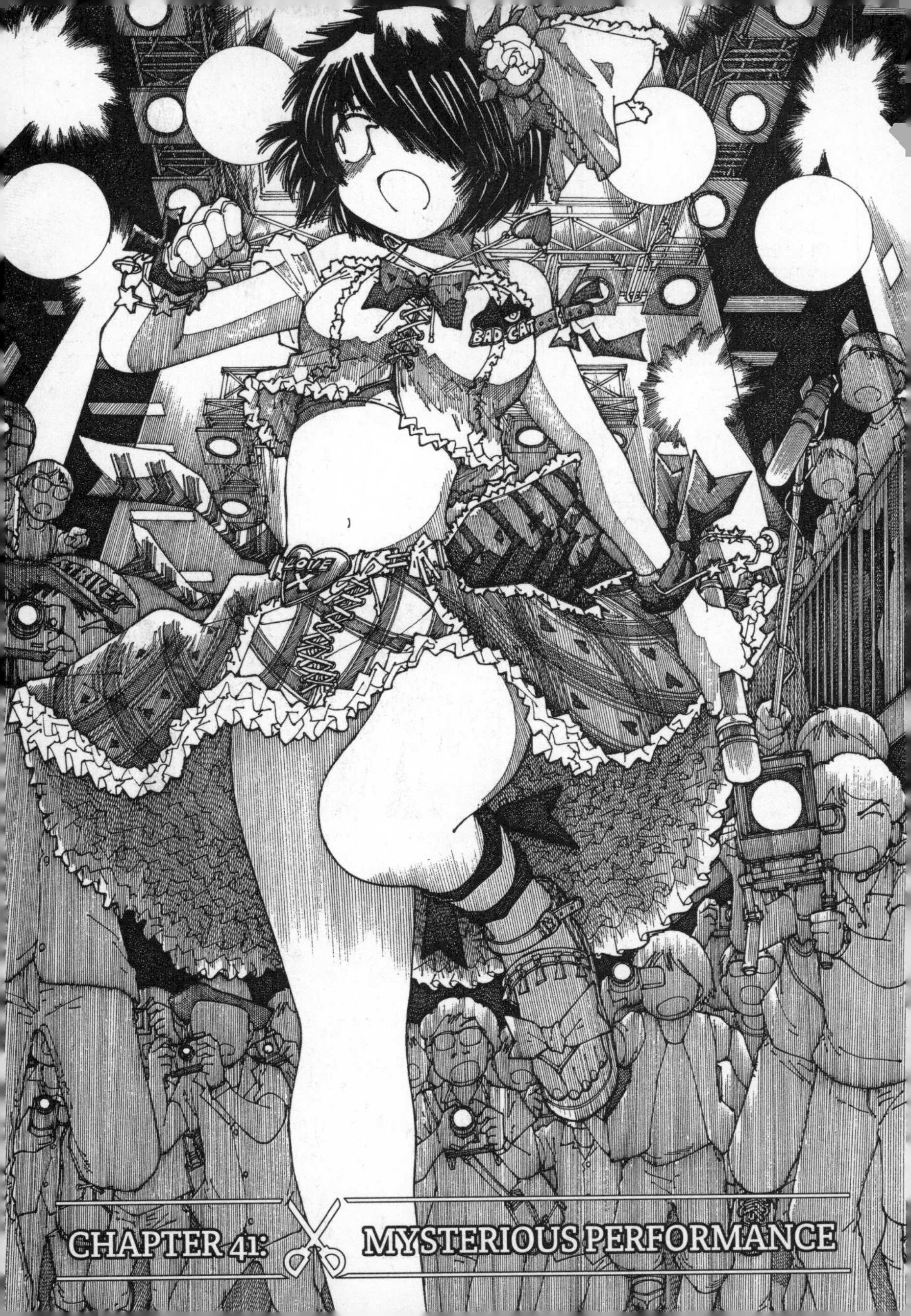
BAD-CAT
LOVE
STRIKE

CHAPTER 41: MYSTERIOUS PERFORMANCE

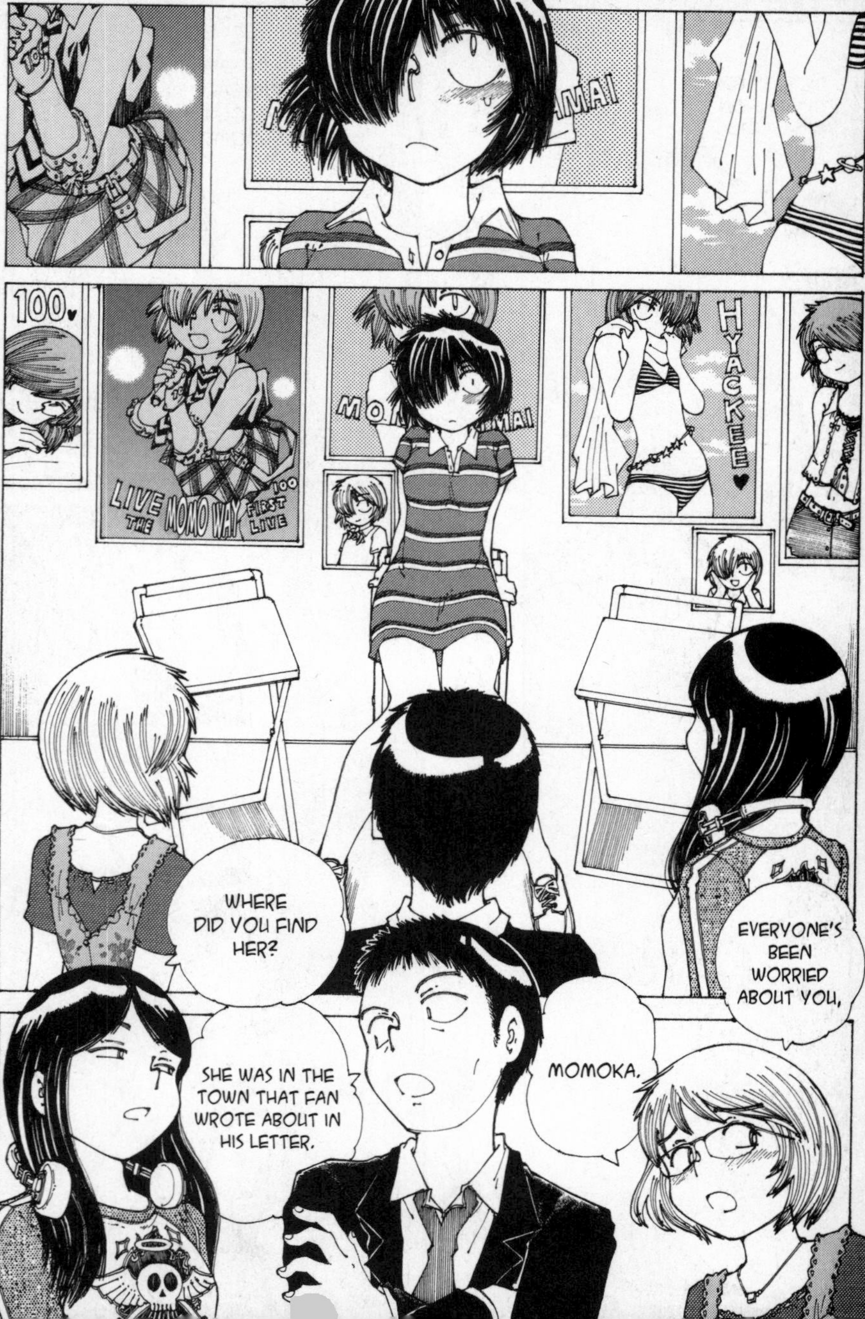
HYACKEE
LIVE THE MOMO WAY
100 FIRST LIVE
100
EVERYONE'S BEEN WORRIED ABOUT YOU,
WHERE DID YOU FIND HER?
MOMOKA.
SHE WAS IN THE TOWN THAT FAN WROTE ABOUT IN HIS LETTER.

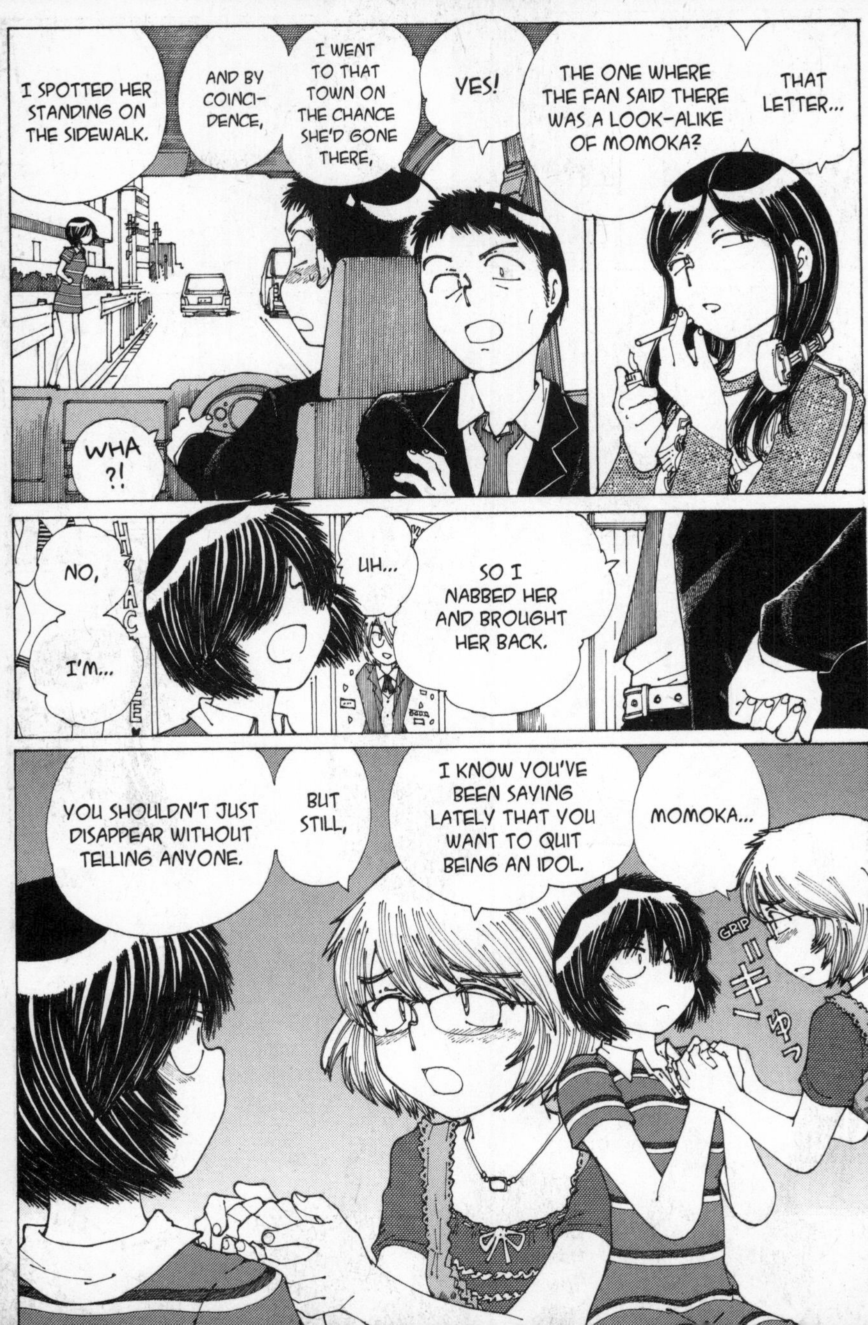
THAT LETTER...
THE ONE WHERE THE FAN SAID THERE WAS A LOOK-ALIKE OF MOMOKA?
YES!
I WENT TO THAT TOWN ON THE CHANCE SHE'D GONE THERE,
AND BY COINCI-DENCE,
I SPOTTED HER STANDING ON THE SIDEWALK.
WHA ?!
SO I NABBED HER AND BROUGHT HER BACK.
UH...
NO,
I'M...
MOMOKA...
I KNOW YOU'VE BEEN SAYING LATELY THAT YOU WANT TO QUIT BEING AN IDOL.
BUT STILL,
YOU SHOULDN'T JUST DISAPPEAR WITHOUT TELLING ANYONE.
GRIP

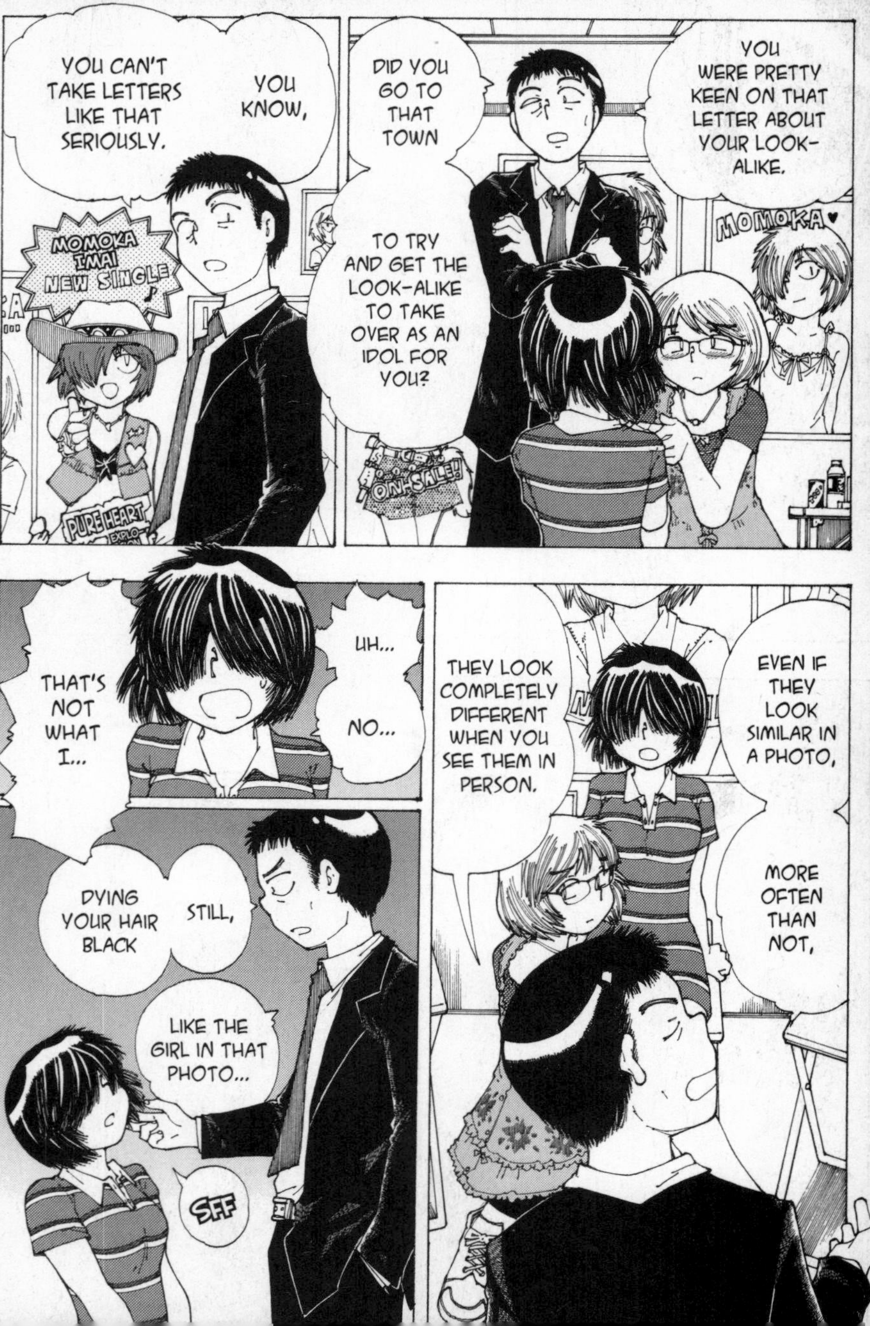
YOU WERE PRETTY KEEN ON THAT LETTER ABOUT YOUR LOOK-ALIKE.
MOMOKA
DID YOU GO TO THAT TOWN
TO TRY AND GET THE LOOK-ALIKE TO TAKE OVER AS AN IDOL FOR YOU?
ON SALE!
YOU KNOW,
YOU CAN'T TAKE LETTERS LIKE THAT SERIOUSLY.
MOMOKA IMAI NEW SINGLE
PURE HEART
EVEN IF THEY LOOK SIMILAR IN A PHOTO,
MORE OFTEN THAN NOT,
THEY LOOK COMPLETELY DIFFERENT WHEN YOU SEE THEM IN PERSON.
UH...
NO...
THAT'S NOT WHAT I...
STILL,
DYING YOUR HAIR BLACK
LIKE THE GIRL IN THAT PHOTO...
SFF

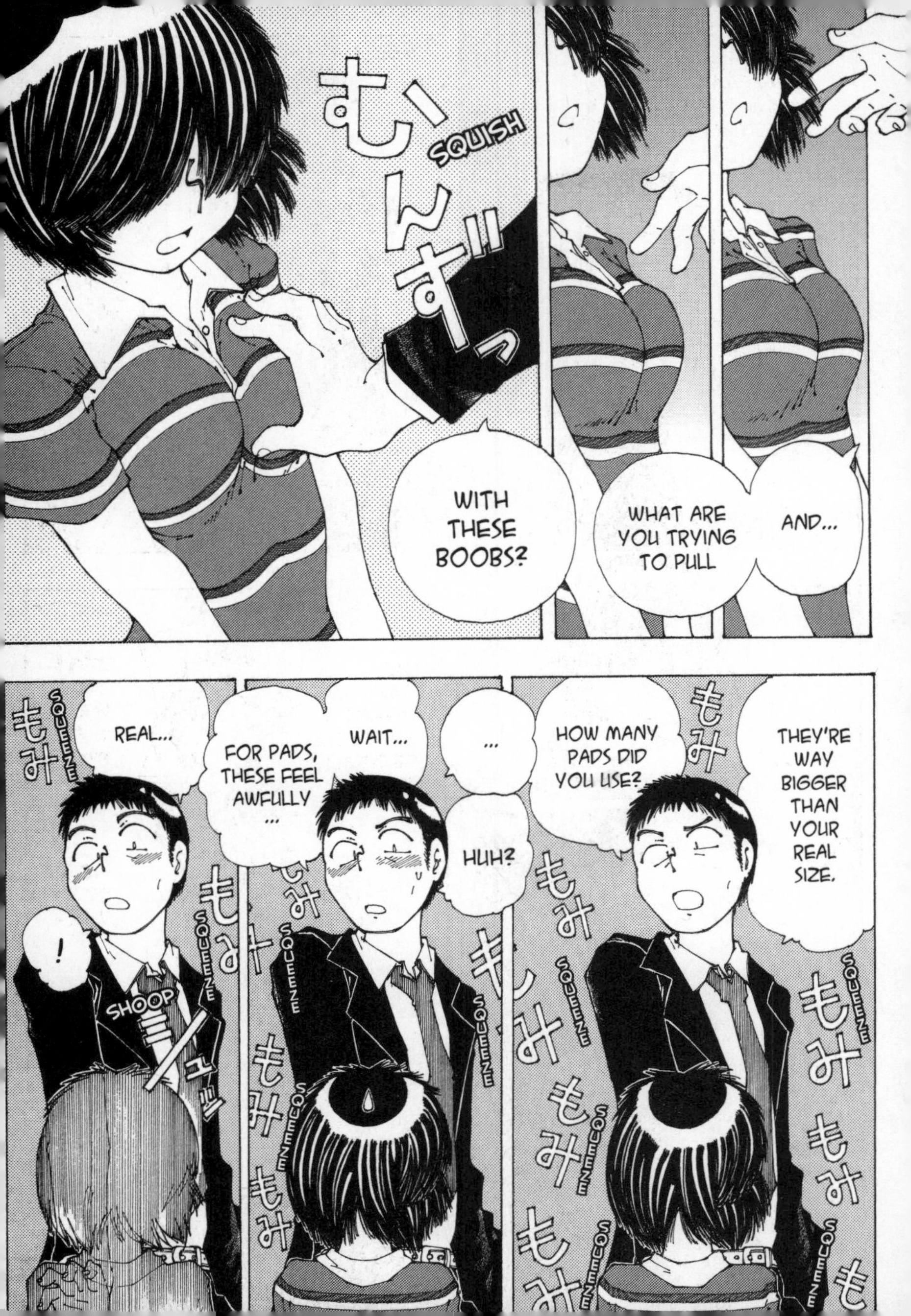
AND...
WHAT ARE YOU TRYING TO PULL
むんずっ
SQUISH
WITH THESE BOOBS?
THEY'RE WAY BIGGER THAN YOUR REAL SIZE.
HOW MANY PADS DID YOU USE?
もみ
SQUEEZE
...
HUH?
WAIT...
FOR PADS, THESE FEEL AWFULLY ...
もみ
SQUEEZE
REAL...
!
SHOOP
もみ
SQUEEZE

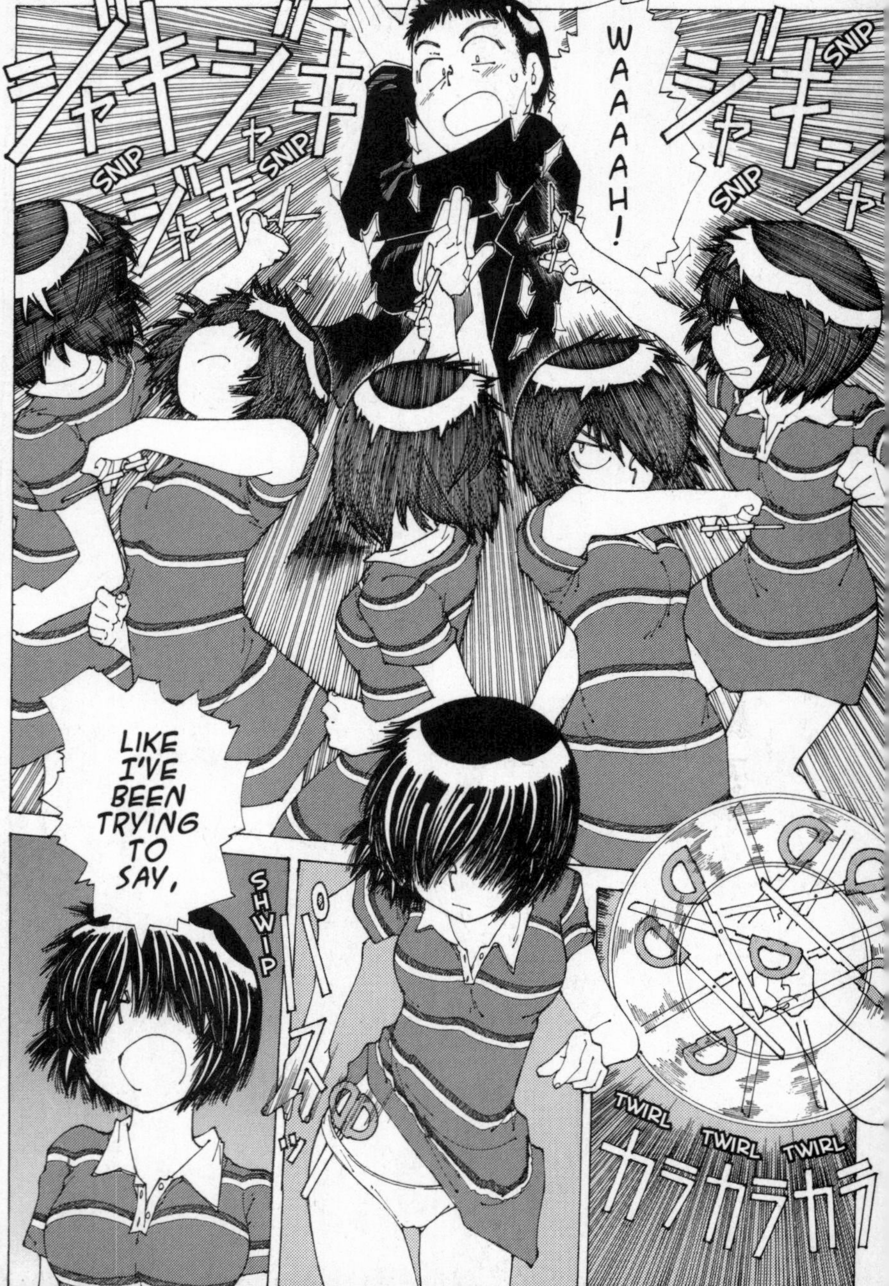
ジャキジャキ
SNIP SNIP
WAAAAAH!
ジャキジャキ
SNIP SNIP
ジャキジャキ
TWIRL TWIRL TWIRL
カラカラカラ
LIKE I'VE BEEN TRYING TO SAY,
SHWIP

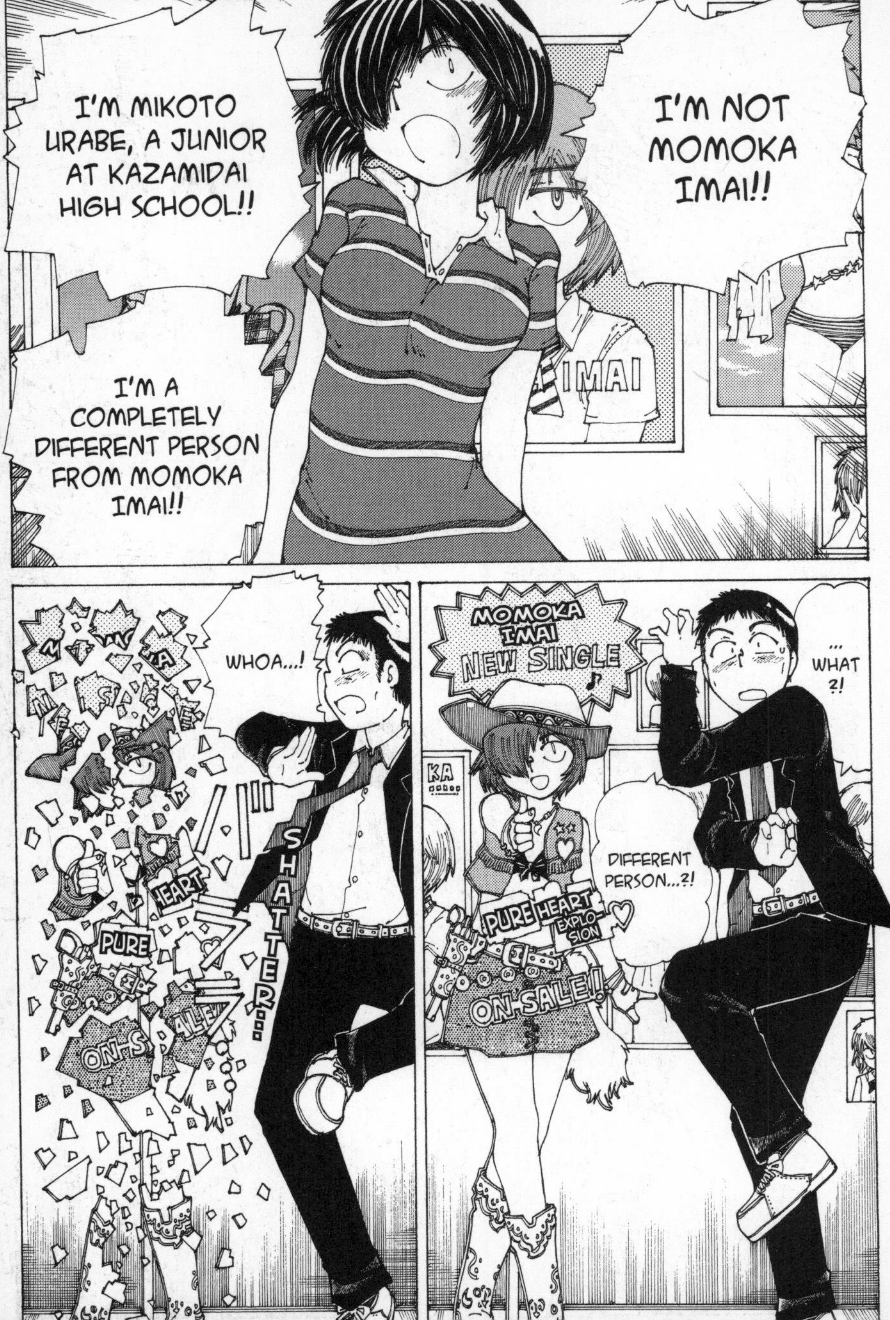
I'M NOT MOMOKA IMAI!!
I'M MIKOTO URABE, A JUNIOR AT KAZAMIDAI JUNIOR HIGH SCHOOL!!
IMAI
I'M A COMPLETELY DIFFERENT PERSON FROM MOMOKA IMAI!!
MOMOKA IMAI NEW SINGLE
... WHAT?!
DIFFERENT PERSON...?!
PURE HEART EXPLO-SION
ON SALE!!
WHOA...!
SHATTER...
HEART
PURE

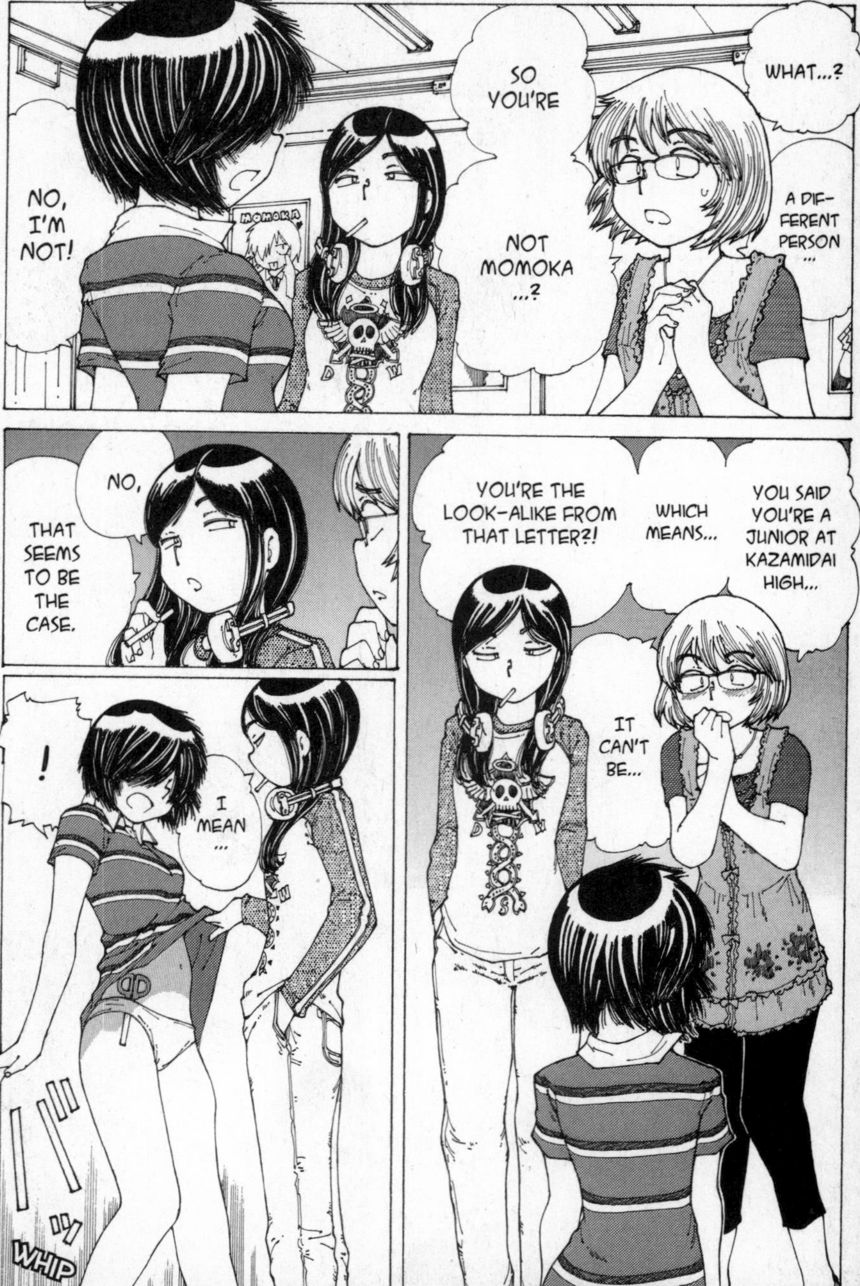
WHAT...?
A DIF-FERENT PERSON ...
SO YOU'RE
NOT MOMOKA ...?
NO, I'M NOT!
MOMOKA
YOU SAID YOU'RE A JUNIOR AT KAZAMIDAI HIGH...
WHICH MEANS...
YOU'RE THE LOOK-ALIKE FROM THAT LETTER?!
IT CAN'T BE...
NO,
THAT SEEMS TO BE THE CASE.
!
I MEAN ...
WHIP

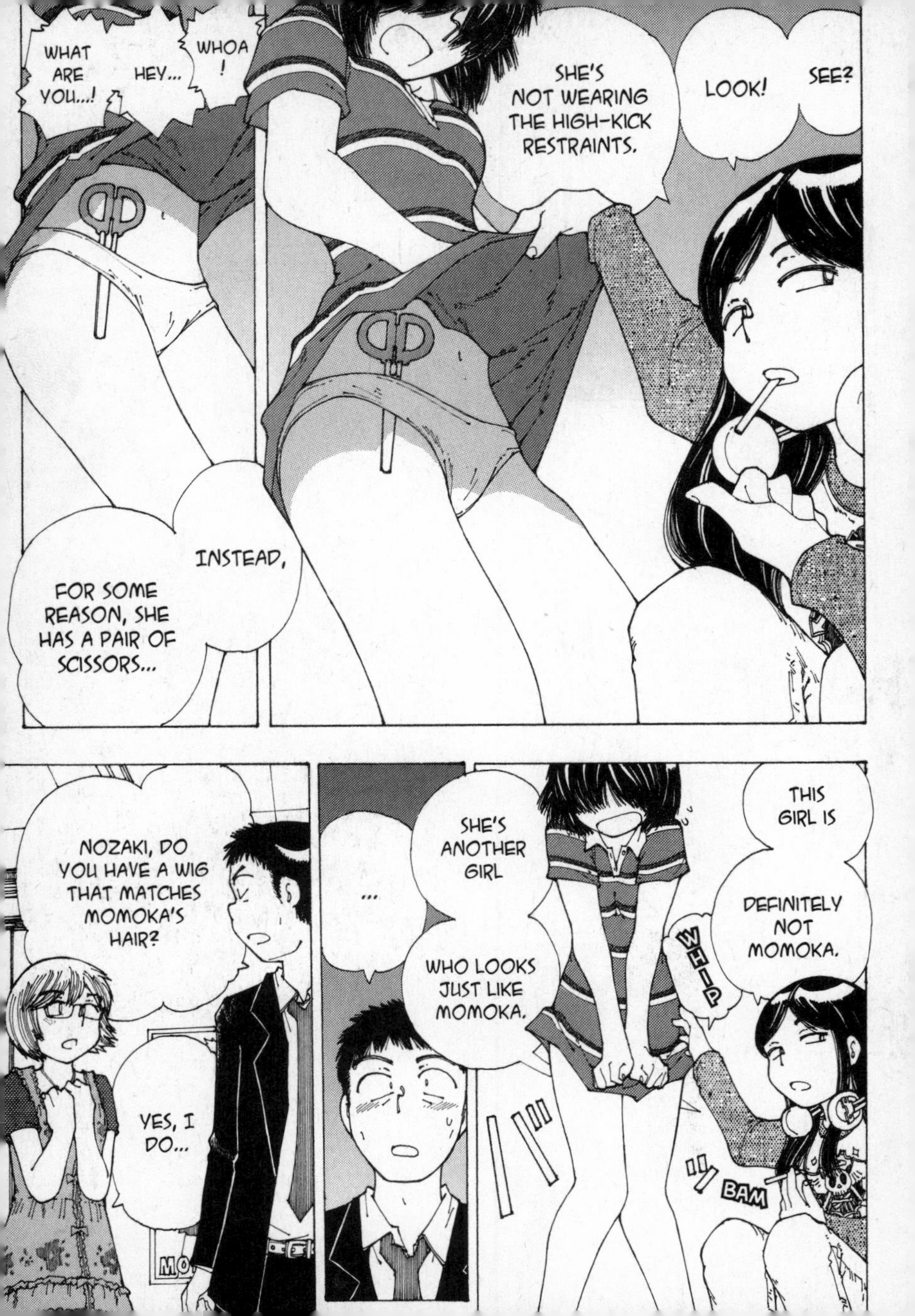
SEE?
LOOK!
SHE'S NOT WEARING THE HIGH-KICK RESTRAINTS.
WHOA!
HEY...
WHAT ARE YOU...!
INSTEAD,
FOR SOME REASON, SHE HAS A PAIR OF SCISSORS...
THIS GIRL IS
DEFINITELY NOT MOMOKA.
WHIP
BAM
SHE'S ANOTHER GIRL
WHO LOOKS JUST LIKE MOMOKA.
...
NOZAKI, DO YOU HAVE A WIG THAT MATCHES MOMOKA'S HAIR?
YES, I DO...

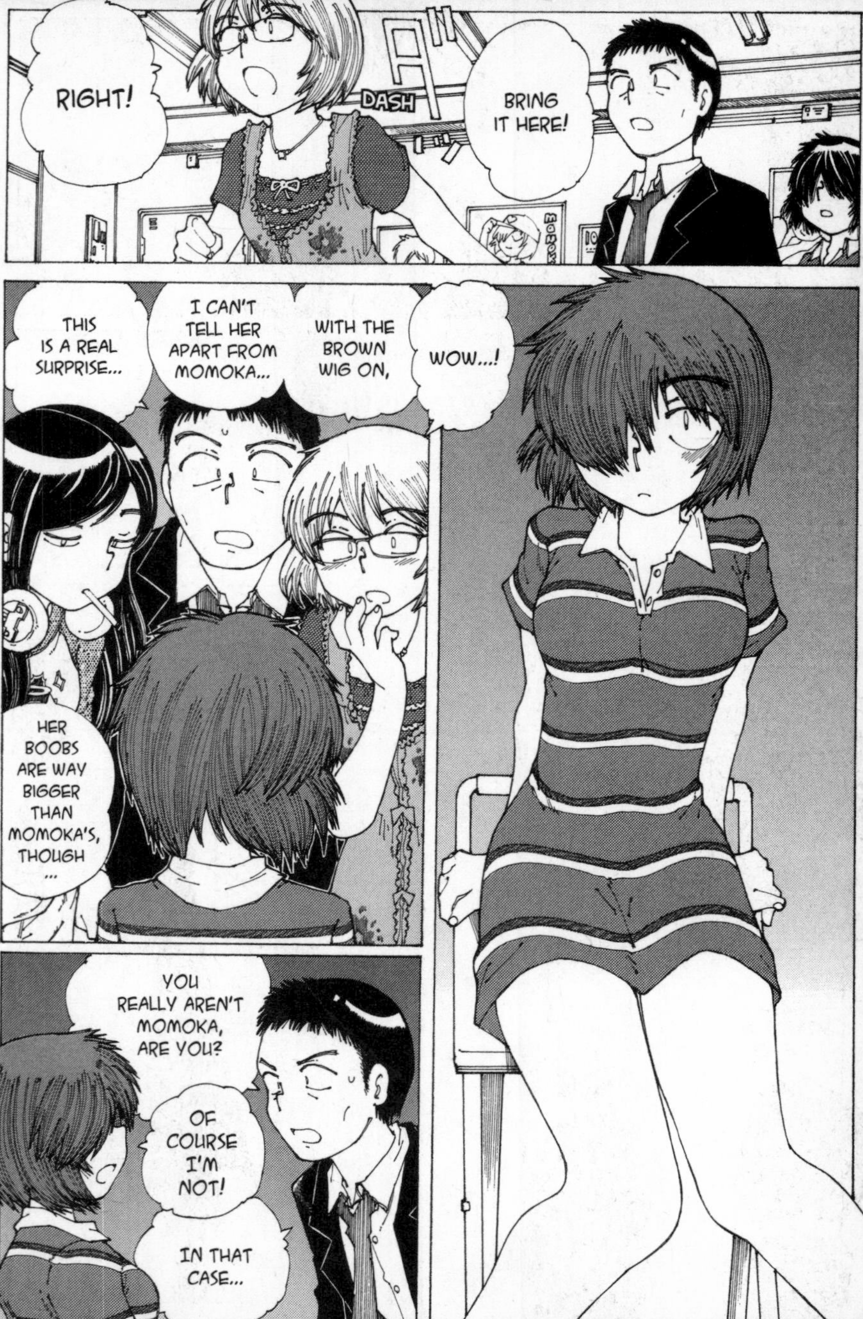
BRING IT HERE!
DASH
RIGHT!
WOW...!
WITH THE BROWN WIG ON,
I CAN'T TELL HER APART FROM MOMOKA...
THIS IS A REAL SURPRISE...
HER BOOBS ARE WAY BIGGER THAN MOMOKA'S, THOUGH ...
YOU REALLY AREN'T MOMOKA, ARE YOU?
OF COURSE I'M NOT!
IN THAT CASE...

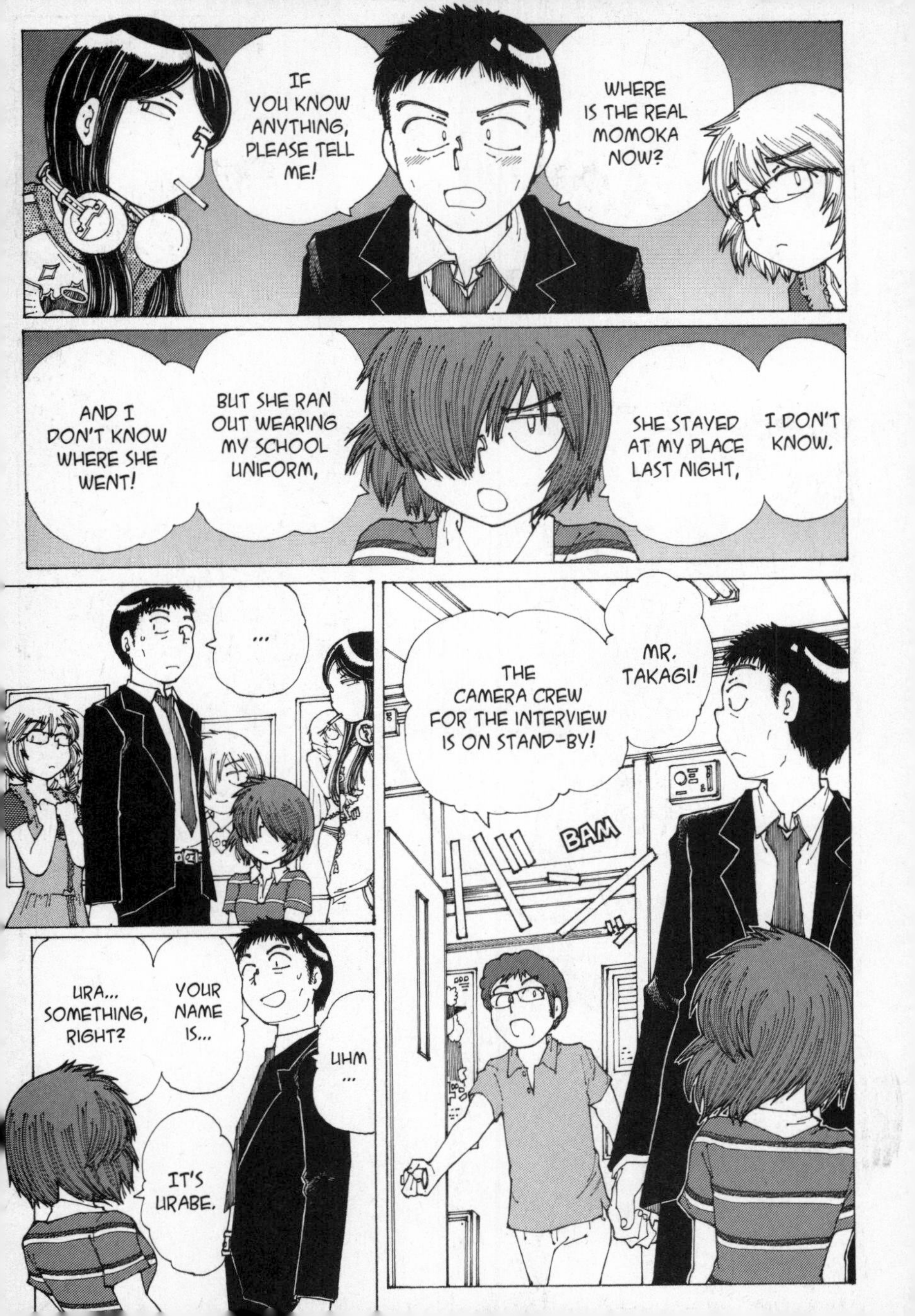
WHERE IS THE REAL MOMOKA NOW?
IF YOU KNOW ANYTHING, PLEASE TELL ME!
I DON'T KNOW.
SHE STAYED AT MY PLACE LAST NIGHT,
BUT SHE RAN OUT WEARING MY SCHOOL UNIFORM,
AND I DON'T KNOW WHERE SHE WENT!
MR. TAKAGI!
THE CAMERA CREW FOR THE INTERVIEW IS ON STAND-BY!
BAM
...
YOUR NAME IS...
URA... SOMETHING, RIGHT?
UHM ...
IT'S URABE.

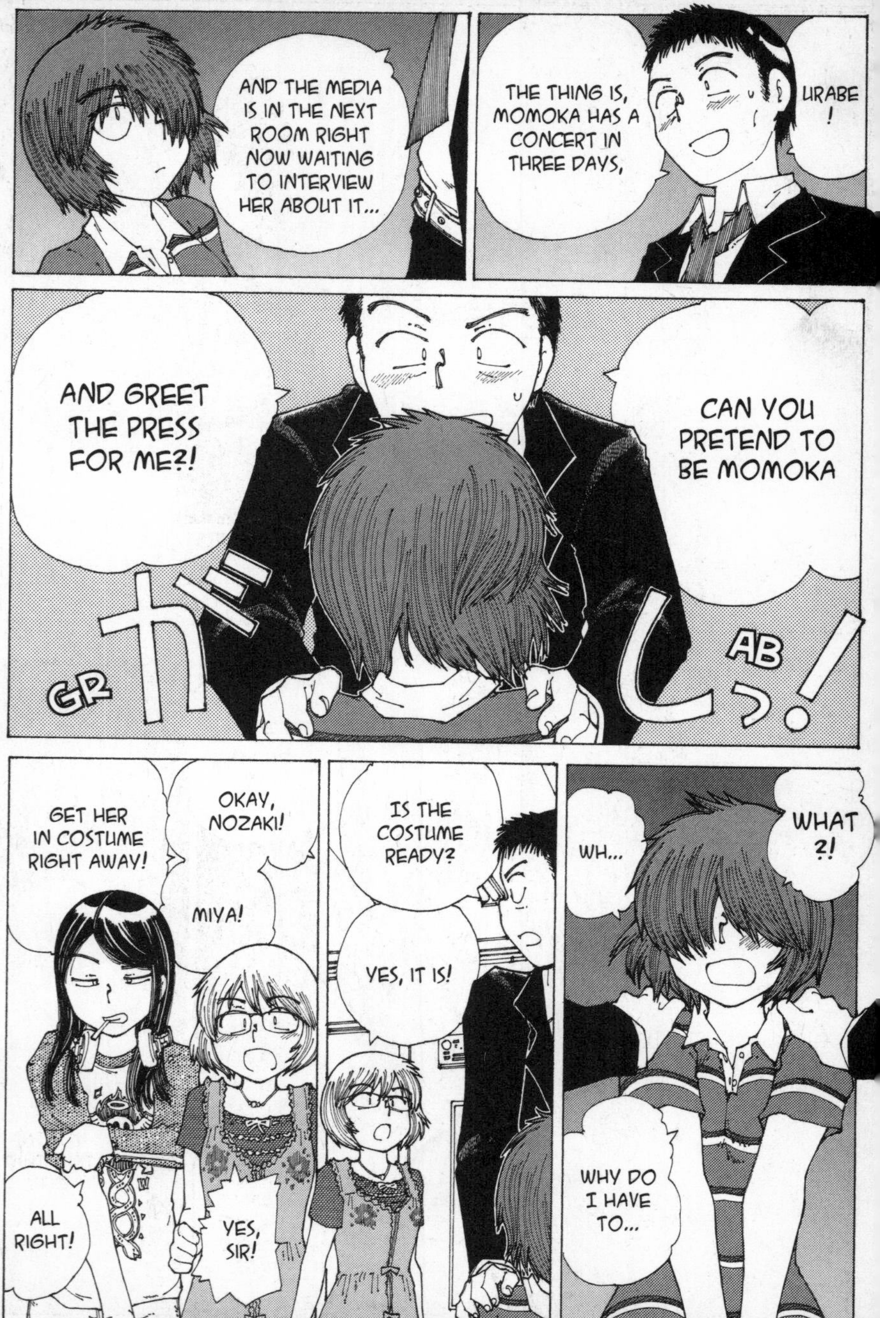
URABE!
THE THING IS, MOMOKA HAS A CONCERT IN THREE DAYS,
AND THE MEDIA IS IN THE NEXT ROOM RIGHT NOW WAITING TO INTERVIEW HER ABOUT IT...
CAN YOU PRETEND TO BE MOMOKA
AND GREET THE PRESS FOR ME?!
ガしっ!
GR
AB
WH...
WHAT?!
WHY DO I HAVE TO...
IS THE COSTUME READY?
YES, IT IS!
OKAY, NOZAKI!
GET HER IN COSTUME RIGHT AWAY!
MIYA!
YES, SIR!
ALL RIGHT!

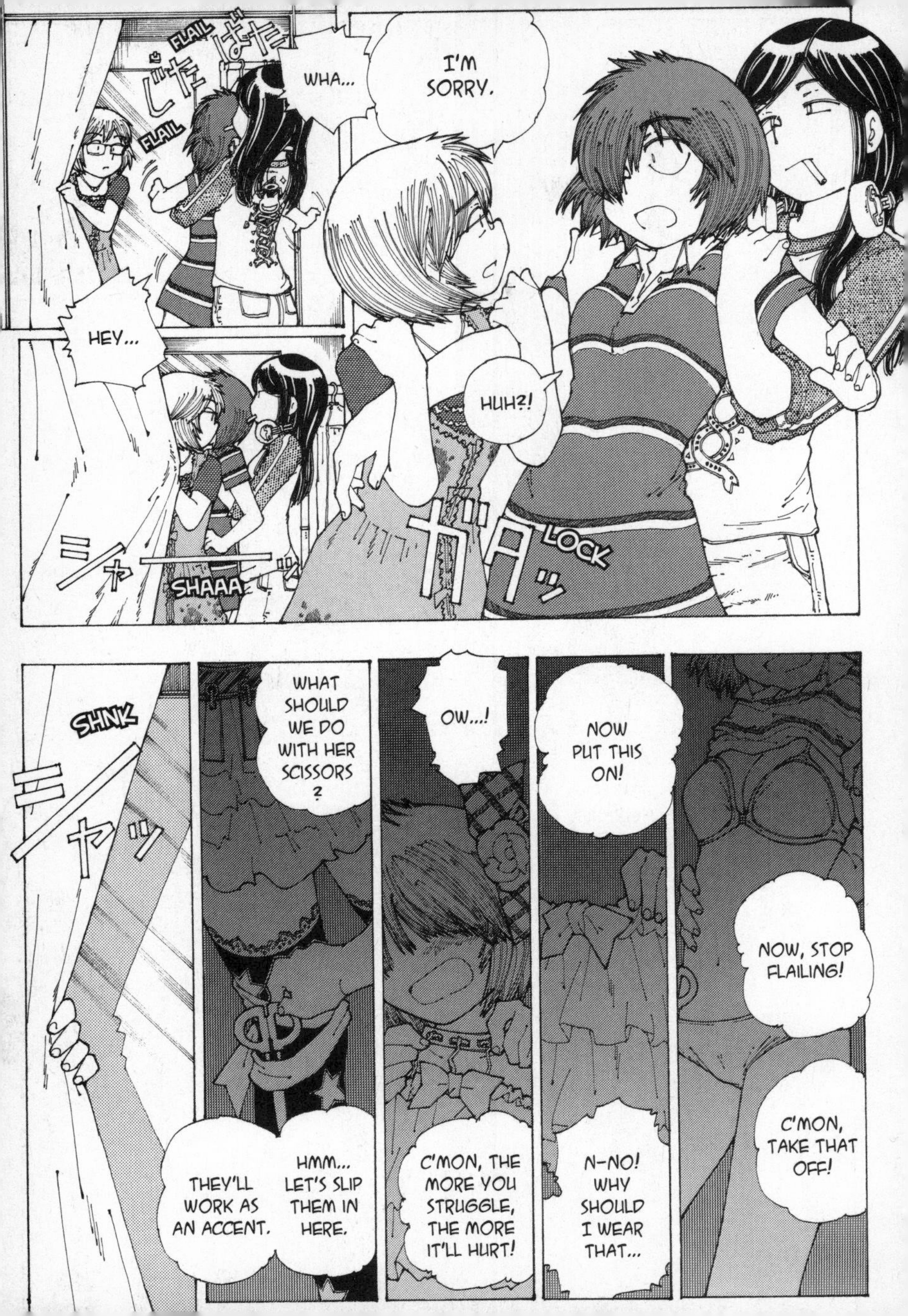
I'M SORRY.
HUH?!
ガッ
LOCK
WHA...
じた ばた
FLAIL
FLAIL
HEY...
シャ
SHAAA
NOW, STOP FLAILING!
C'MON, TAKE THAT OFF!
NOW PUT THIS ON!
N-NO! WHY SHOULD I WEAR THAT...
OW...!
C'MON, THE MORE YOU STRUGGLE, THE MORE IT'LL HURT!
WHAT SHOULD WE DO WITH HER SCISSORS?
HMM... LET'S SLIP THEM IN HERE.
THEY'LL WORK AS AN ACCENT.
シャッ
SHNK

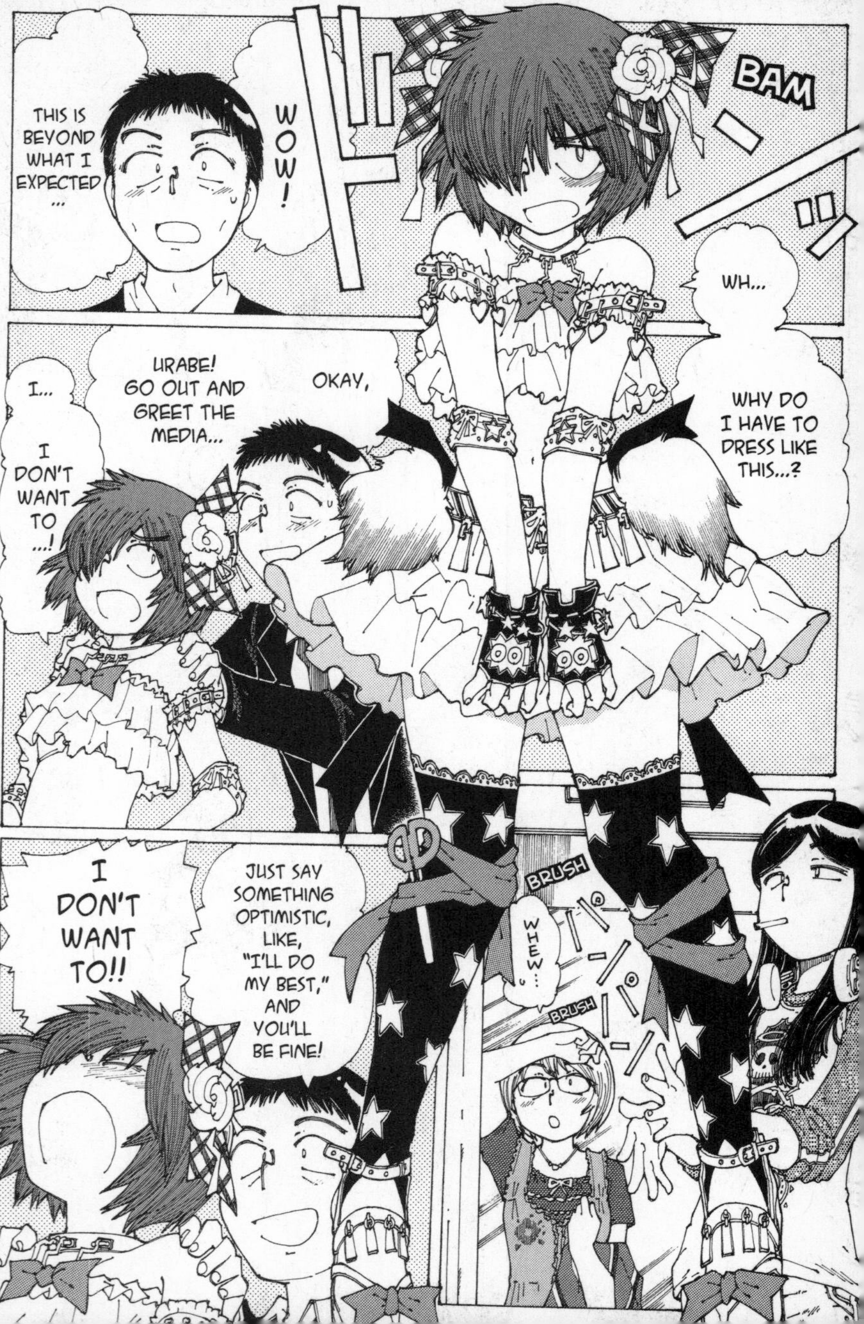
BAM
WH...
WHY DO I HAVE TO DRESS LIKE THIS...?
WOW!
THIS IS BEYOND WHAT I EXPECTED...
OKAY,
URABE! GO OUT AND GREET THE MEDIA...
I...
I DON'T WANT TO...!
BRUSH
BRUSH
WHEW...
JUST SAY SOMETHING OPTIMISTIC, LIKE, "I'LL DO MY BEST," AND YOU'LL BE FINE!
I DON'T WANT TO!!

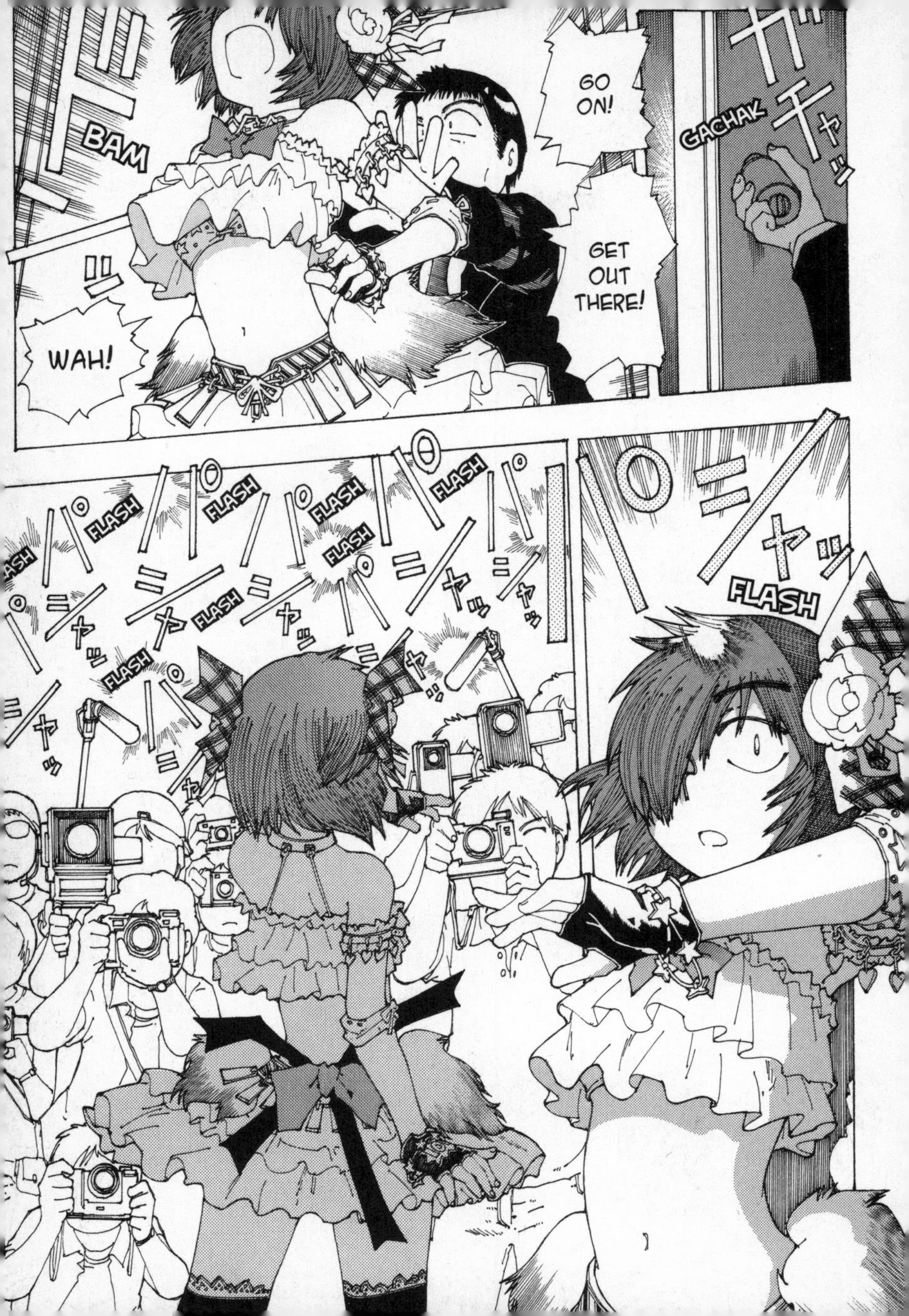

GACHAK
GO ON!
GET OUT THERE!
BAM
WAH!
FLASH
FLASH
FLASH
FLASH
FLASH
FLASH
FLASH
FLASH

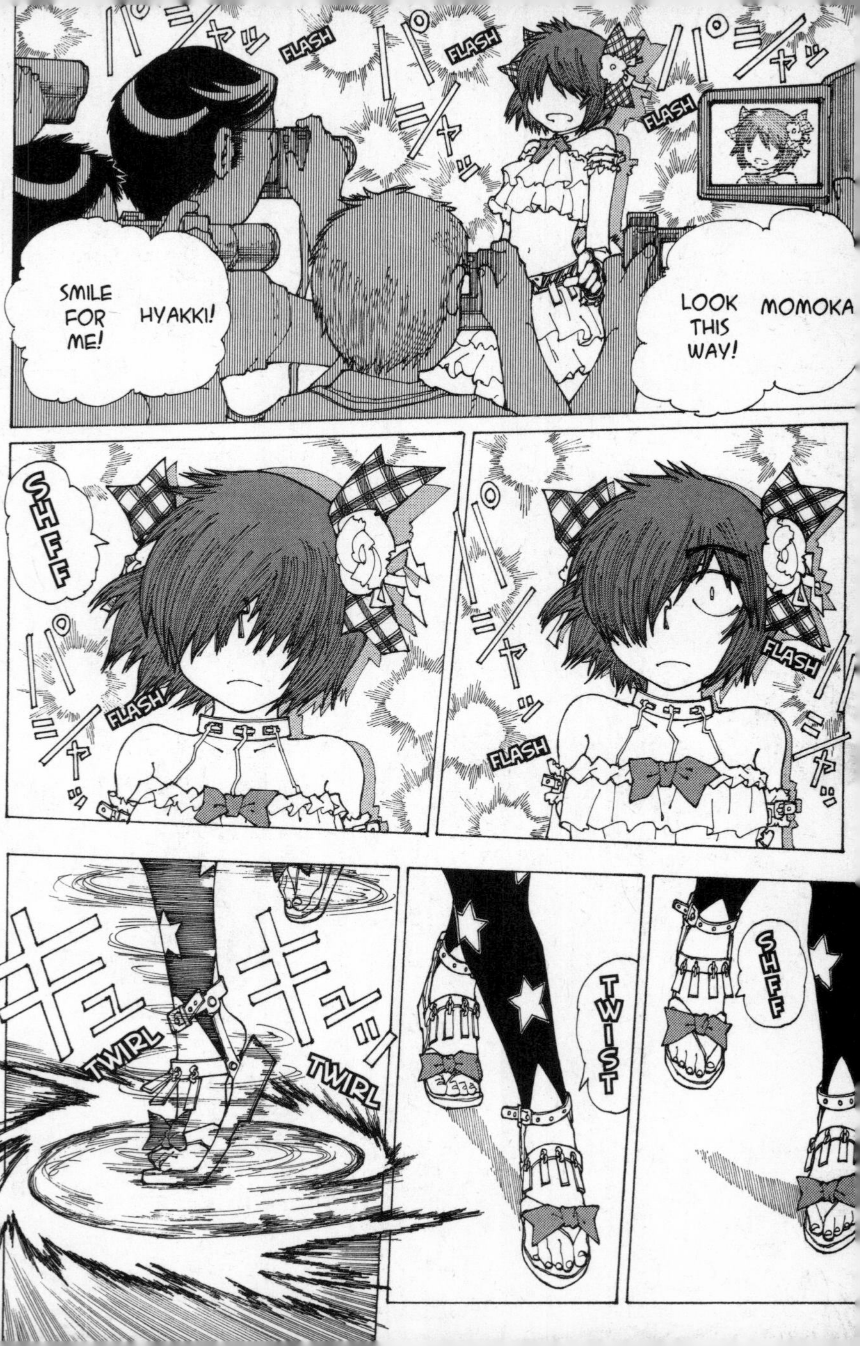

パシャッ
FLASH
パシャッ
FLASH
パシャッ
FLASH
パシャッ
FLASH
LOOK THIS WAY! MOMOKA
SMILE FOR ME! HYAKKI!
パシャッ
FLASH
FLASH
パシャッ
SHFF
パシャッ
FLASH
SHFF
TWIST
キュッ
キュッ
TWIRL
TWIRL

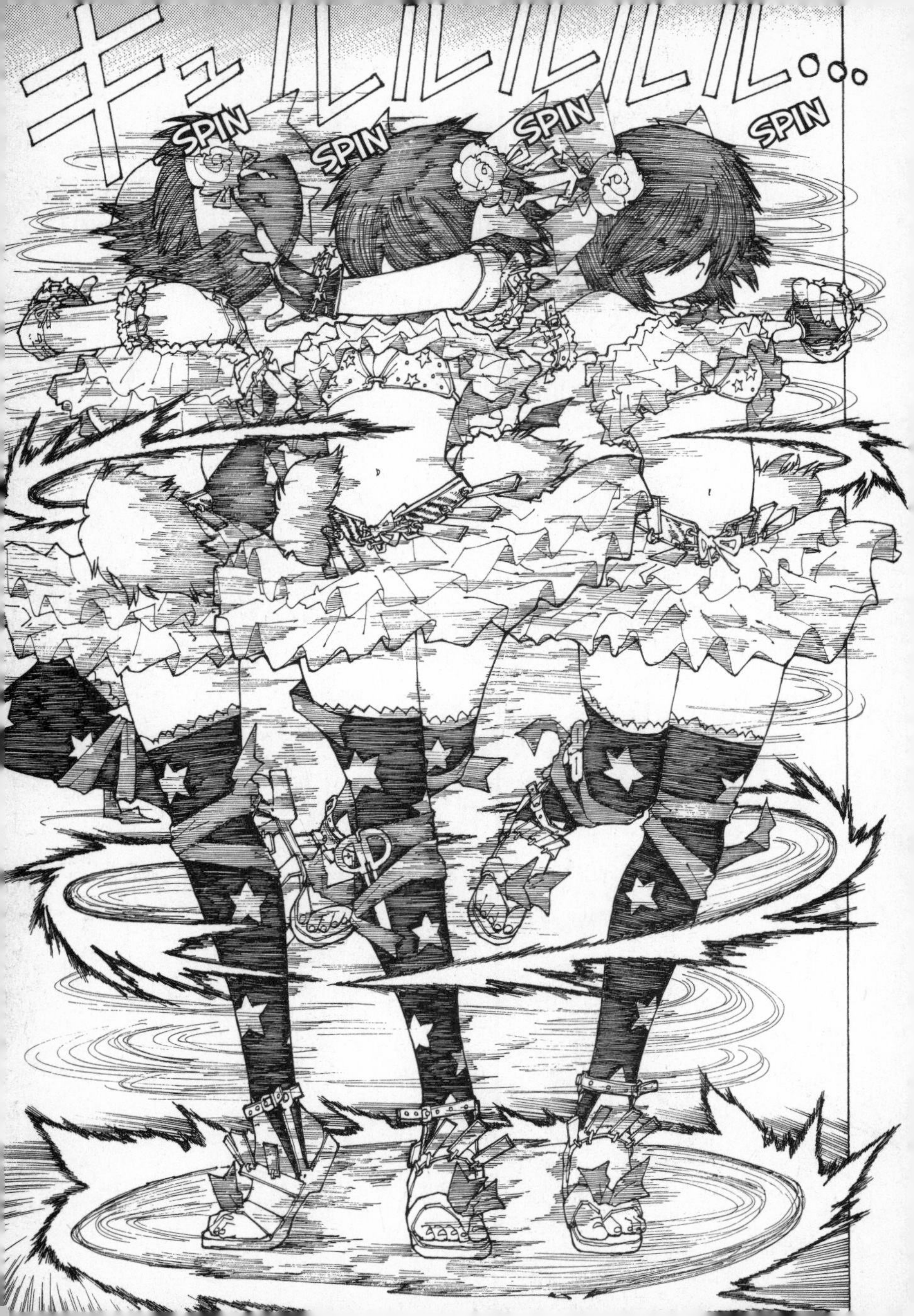
キュィィィィィィ...
SPIN
SPIN
SPIN
SPIN

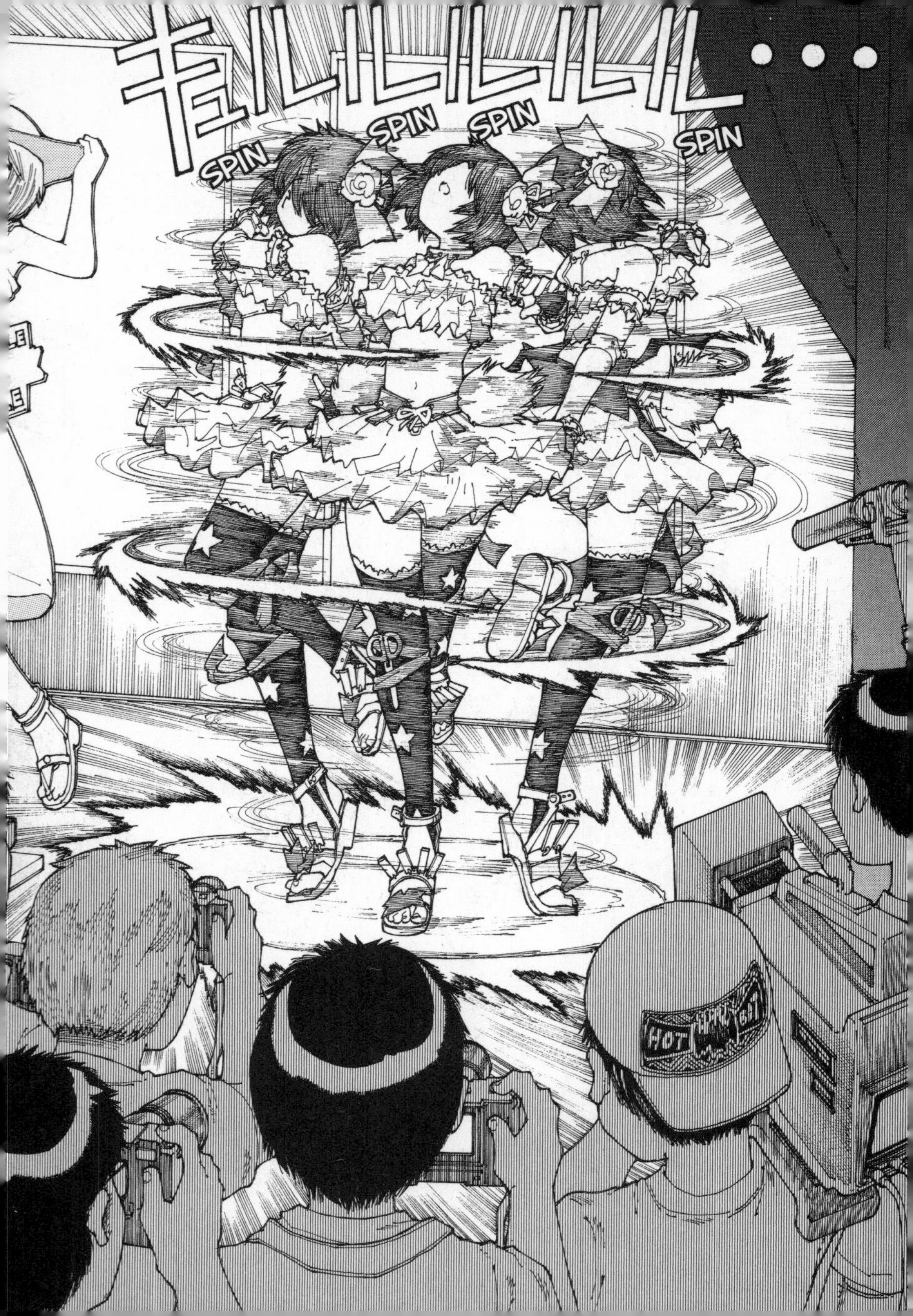
キュルルルル…
SPIN
SPIN
SPIN
SPIN
HOT

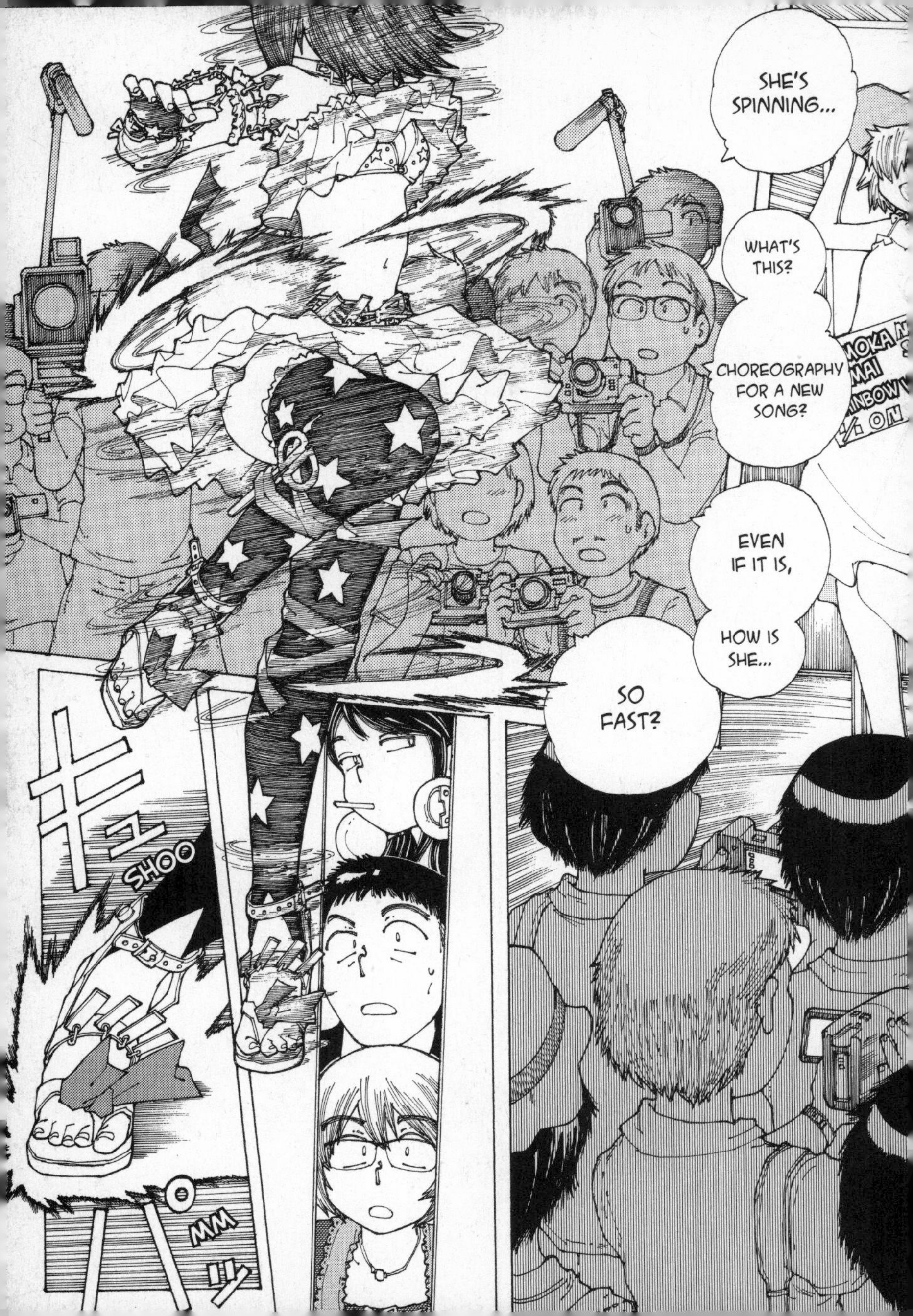
SHE'S SPINNING...
WHAT'S THIS?
CHOREOGRAPHY FOR A NEW SONG?
EVEN IF IT IS,
HOW IS SHE...
SO FAST?
SHOO
MM

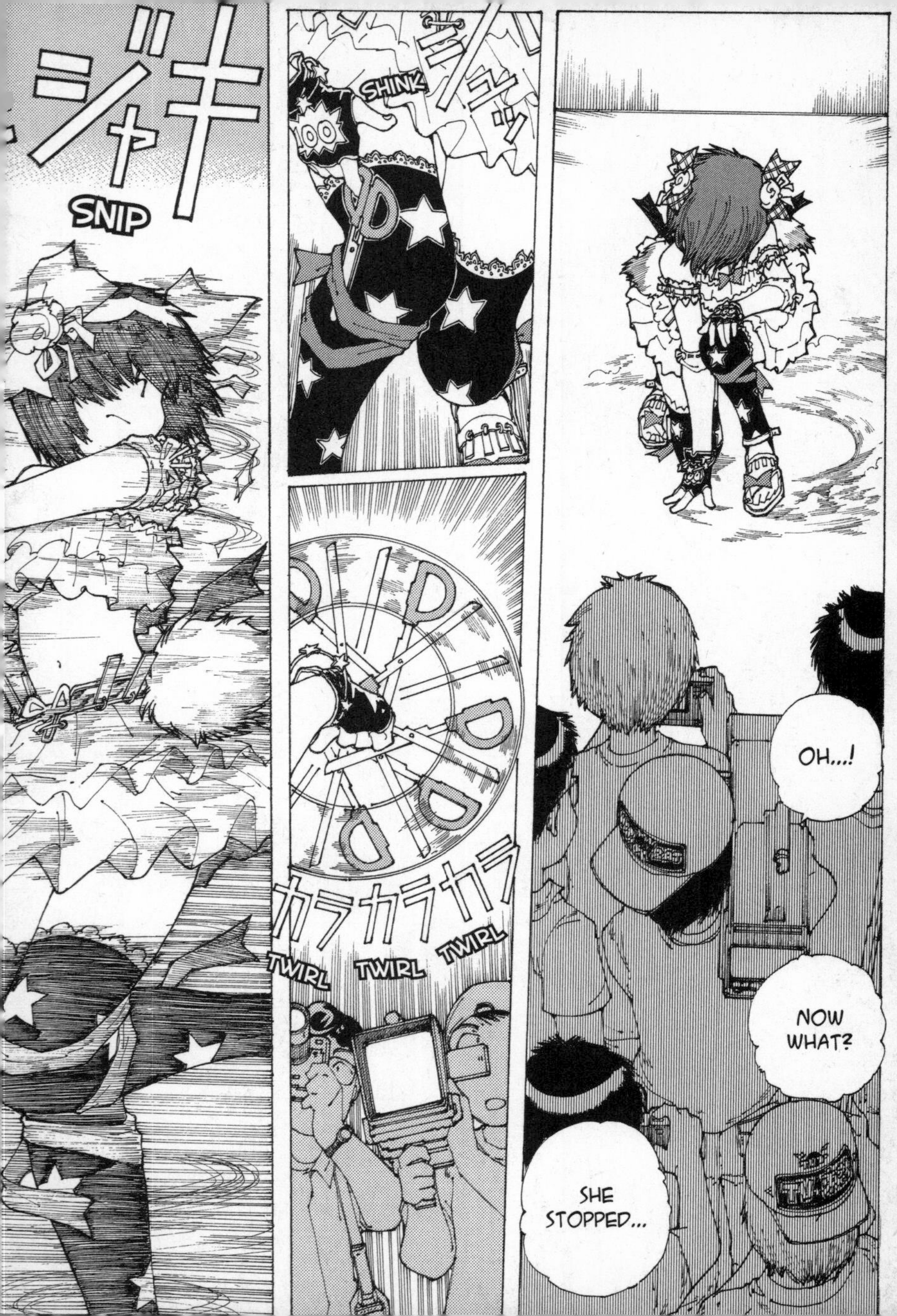
OH...!
NOW WHAT?
SHE STOPPED...
SHINK
100
カラカラカラ
TWIRL TWIRL TWIRL
ジャキ
SNIP

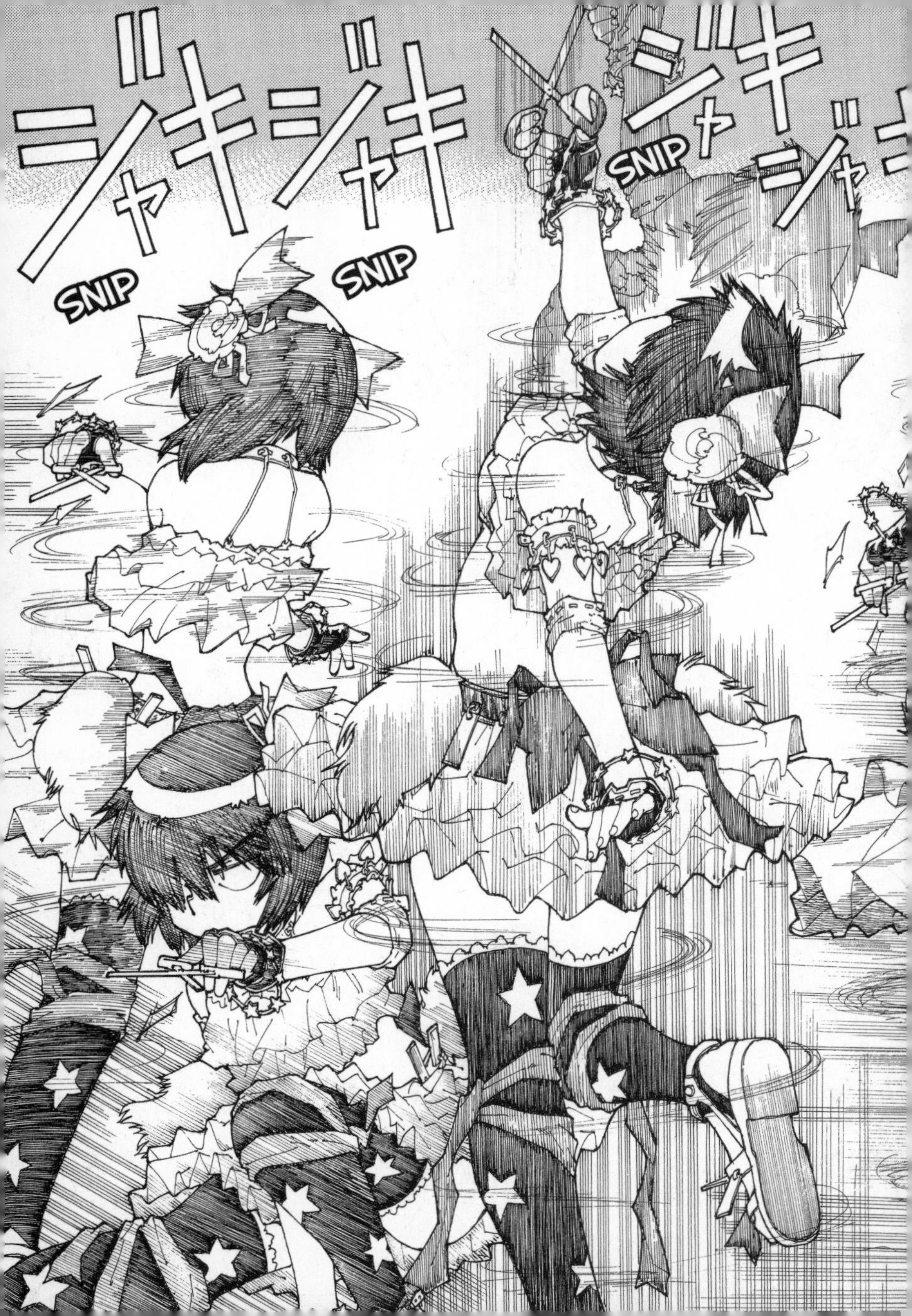

ジャキ
SNIP
ジャキジャキ
SNIP
SNIP

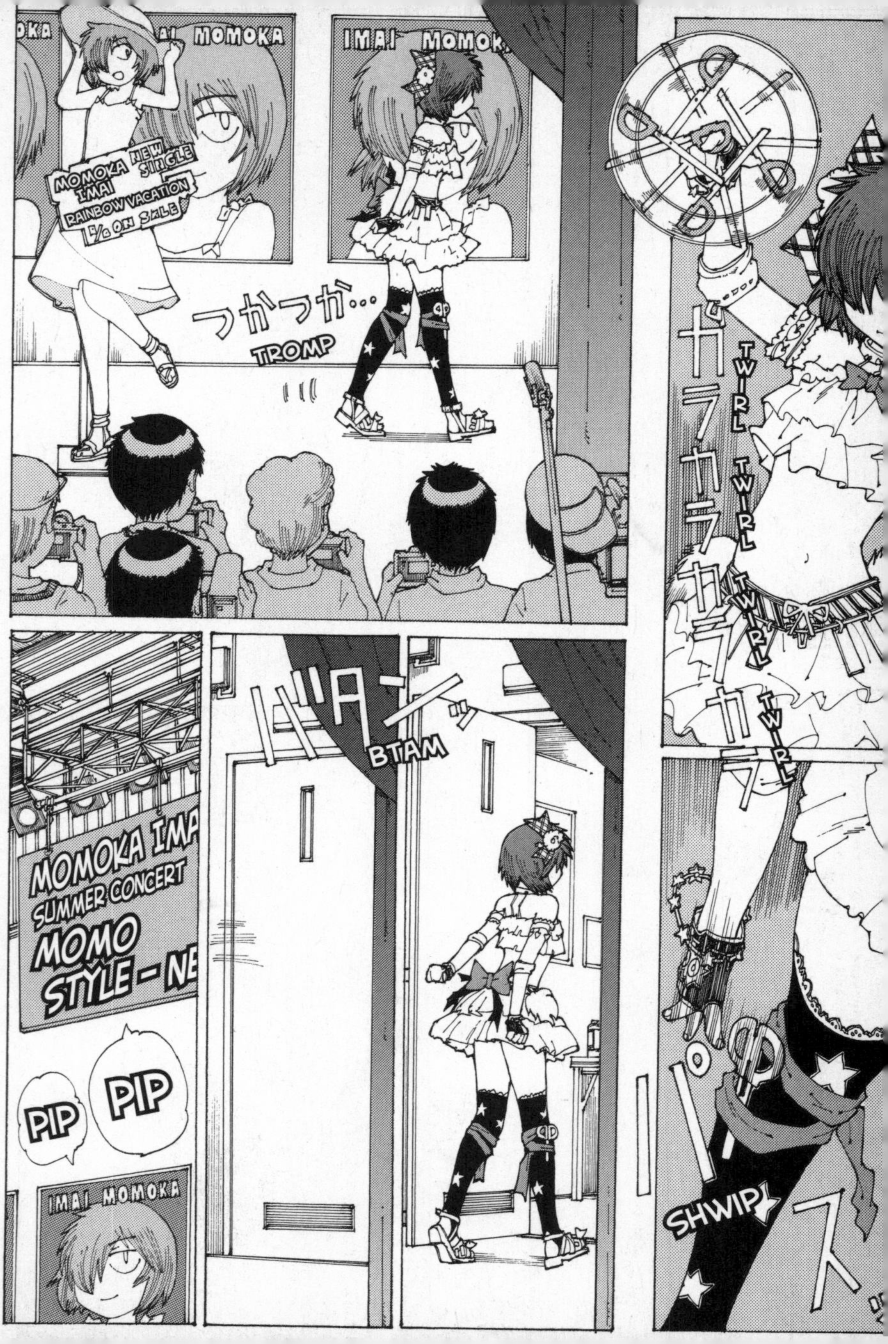
カラカラカラカラ
TWIRL TWIRL TWIRL TWIRL
IMAI MOMOKA
IMAI MOMOKA
MOMOKA IMAI NEW SINGLE
RAINBOW VACATION
ON SALE
つかつか…
TROMP
パ
ス
SHWIP
バタン
BTAM
MOMOKA IMAI
SUMMER CONCERT
MOMO
STYLE - NE
PIP
PIP
IMAI MOMOKA

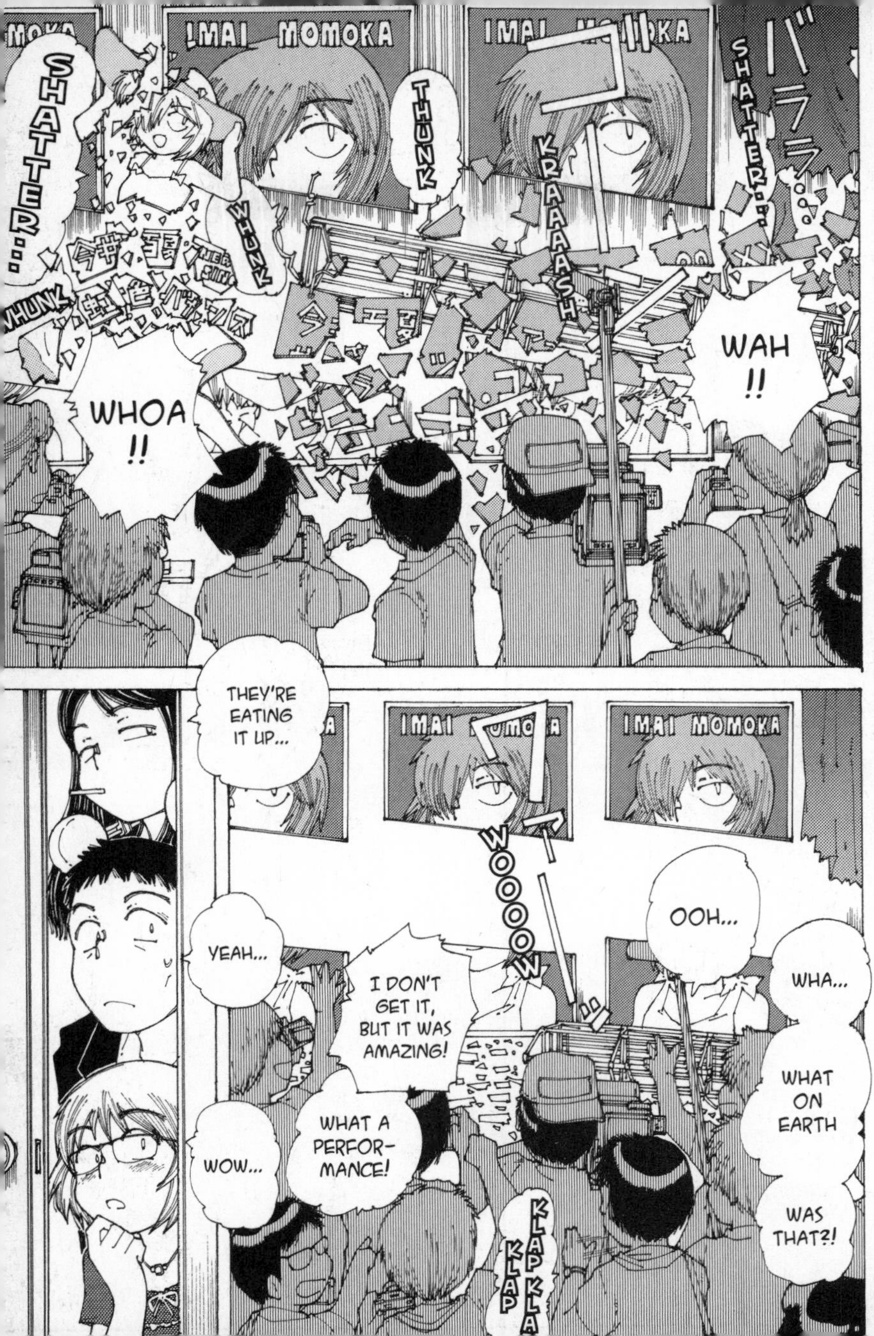
IMAI MOMOKA
IMAI MOMOKA
バラ…
SHATTER…
KRAAAASH
THUNK
WAH !!
WHOA !!
SHATTER…
WHUNK
WHUNK
IMAI MOMOKA
IMAI MOMOKA
OOH…
WHA…
WHAT ON EARTH WAS THAT?!
WOOOOOW
I DON'T GET IT, BUT IT WAS AMAZING!
KLAP KLAP KLA
WHAT A PERFORMANCE!
WOW…
THEY'RE EATING IT UP…
YEAH…

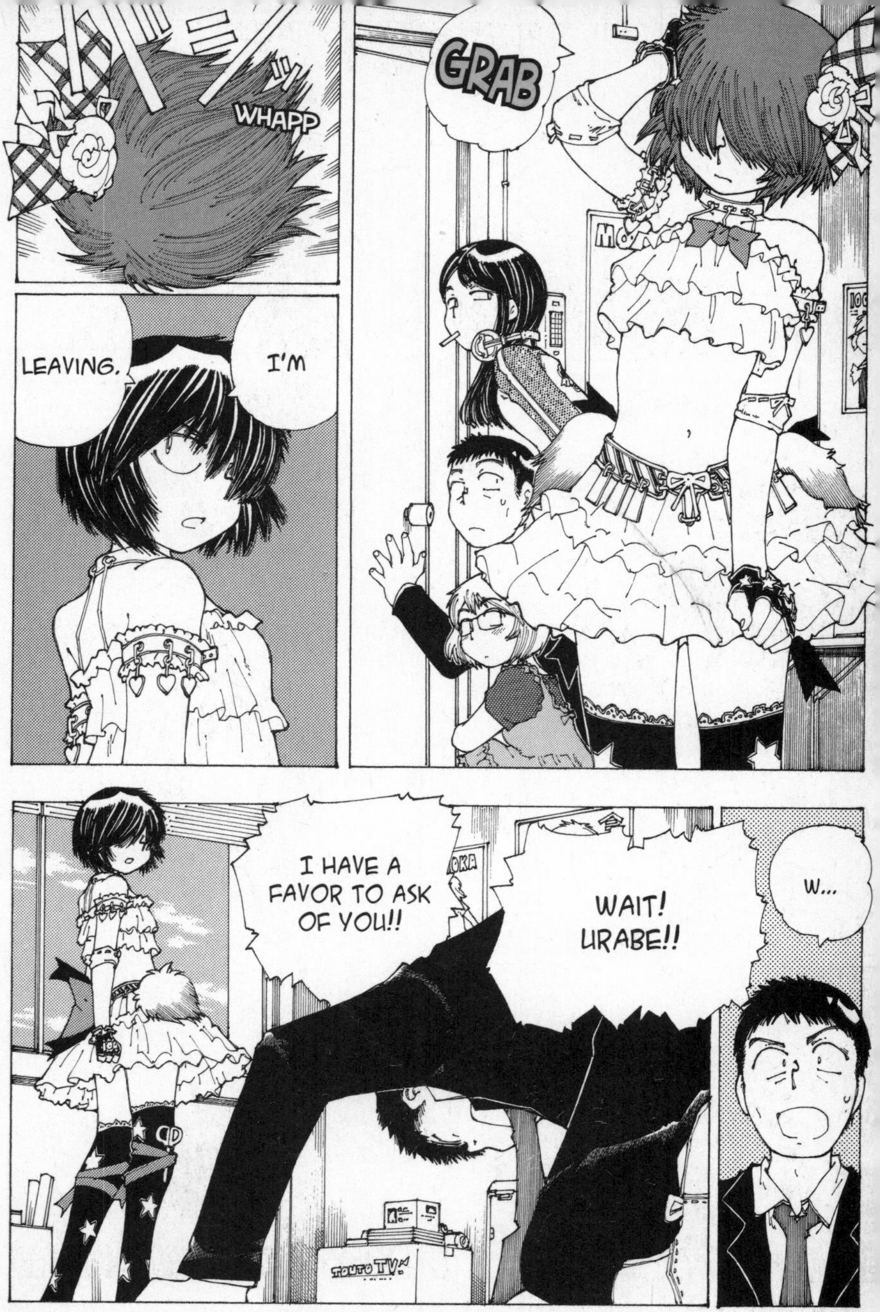
GRAB
WHAPP
I'M
LEAVING.
W...
WAIT! URABE!!
I HAVE A FAVOR TO ASK OF YOU!!
TOUTO TV

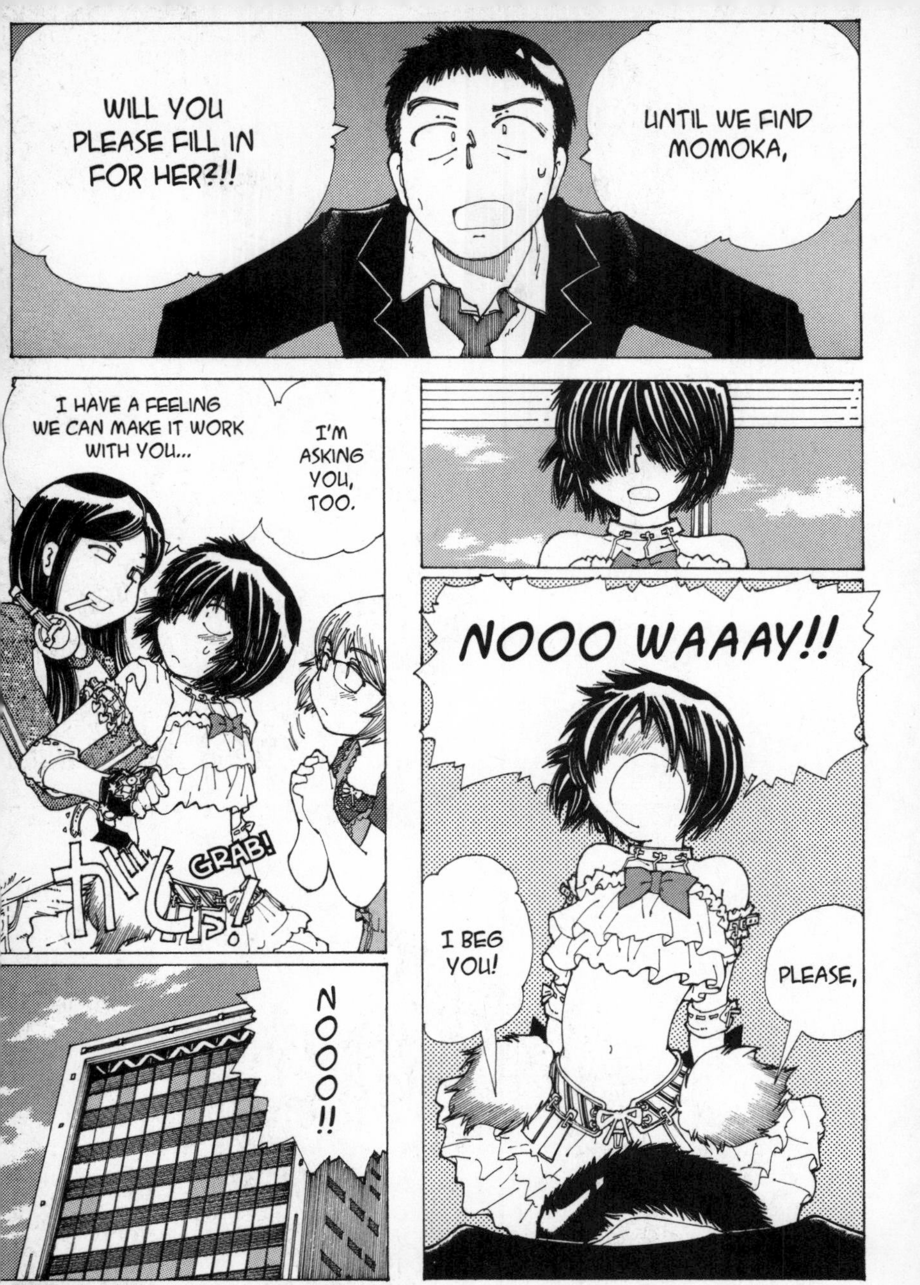
UNTIL WE FIND MOMOKA,
WILL YOU PLEASE FILL IN FOR HER?!!
NOOO WAAAY!!
PLEASE,
I BEG YOU!
I'M ASKING YOU, TOO.
I HAVE A FEELING WE CAN MAKE IT WORK WITH YOU...
わしっ!
GRAB!
NOOOO!!

END OF CHAPTER 41

MY IDOL: 2

I SHALL BRING AMUSEMENT TO A WORLD

IN WHICH THERE IS NONE...

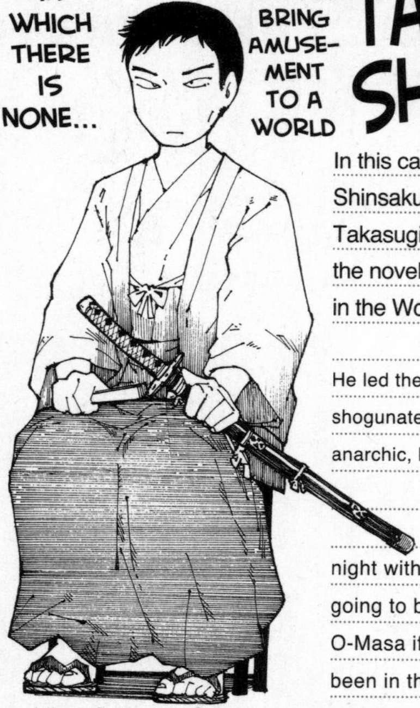

TAKASUGI SHINSAKU (1839~1867)

In this case, my idol is not Takasugi Shinsaku the historical figure, but Takasugi Shinsaku as the character in the novel "Yo ni Sumu Hibi" [Days Spent in the World] by Ryotaro Shiba.

He led the movement to overthrow the shogunate in the Choshu Domain. He was anarchic, but he had a very cute side.

My favorite scene is his first night with his bride, O-Masa. Before going to bed, Shinsaku suddenly asks O-Masa if she remembers what had been in the stew served at their wedding. O-Masa responds by naming rice cakes, daikon, and kelp. Hearing this, Shinsaku's mood grows sour and he falls silent. O-Masa is bewildered, not knowing why Shinsaku won't speak. It turns out that Shinsaku was so nervous during the wedding that he couldn't remember anything that had been in the stew, and hearing his bride easily name the ingredients put him in a bad mood. Am I the only one who feels that dramatic scenes between men and women in Shiba's works have a lot of romantic comedy elements?

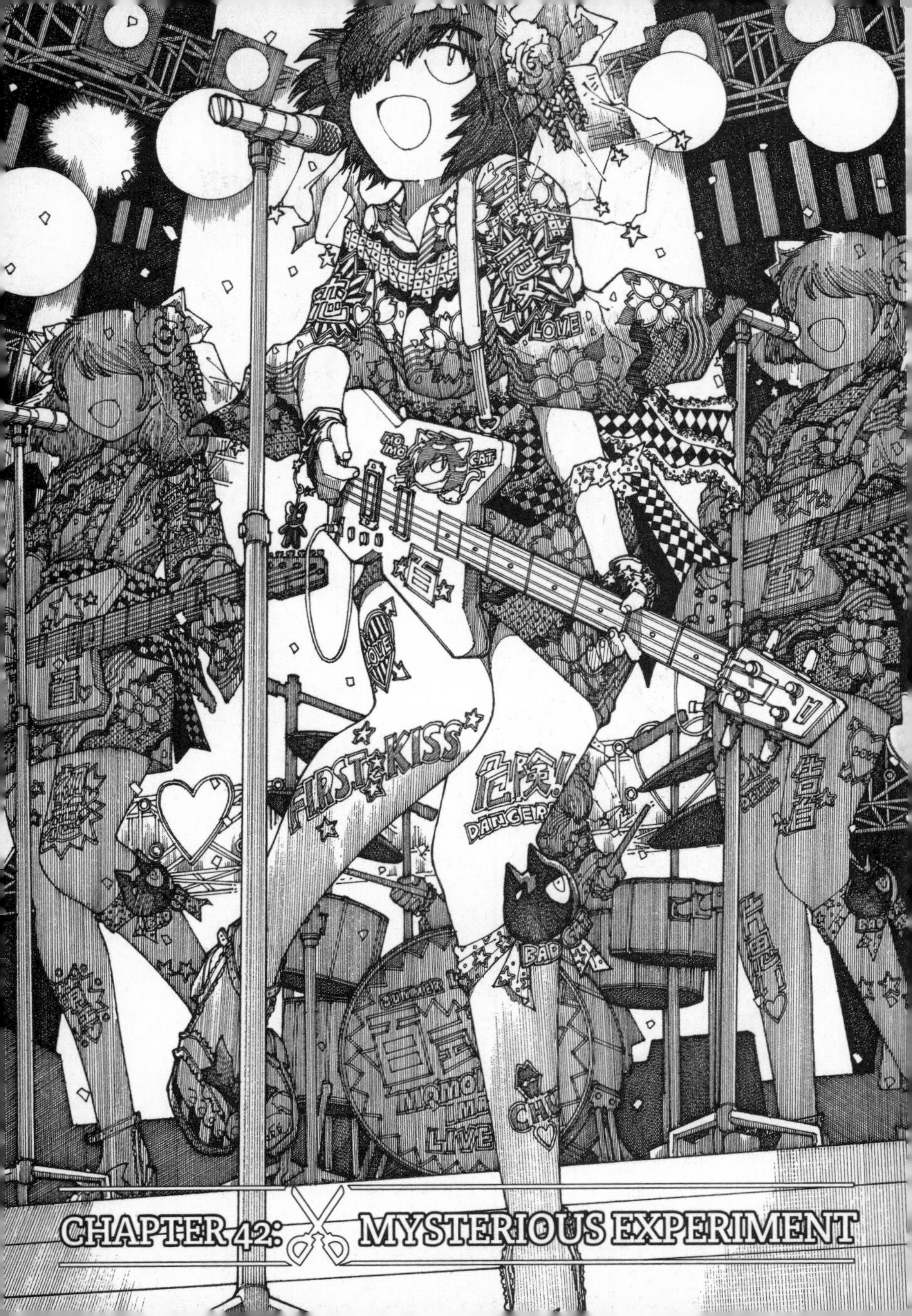
LOVE
CAT
FIRST KISS
危険!
DANGER
BAD

CHAPTER 42: MYSTERIOUS EXPERIMENT

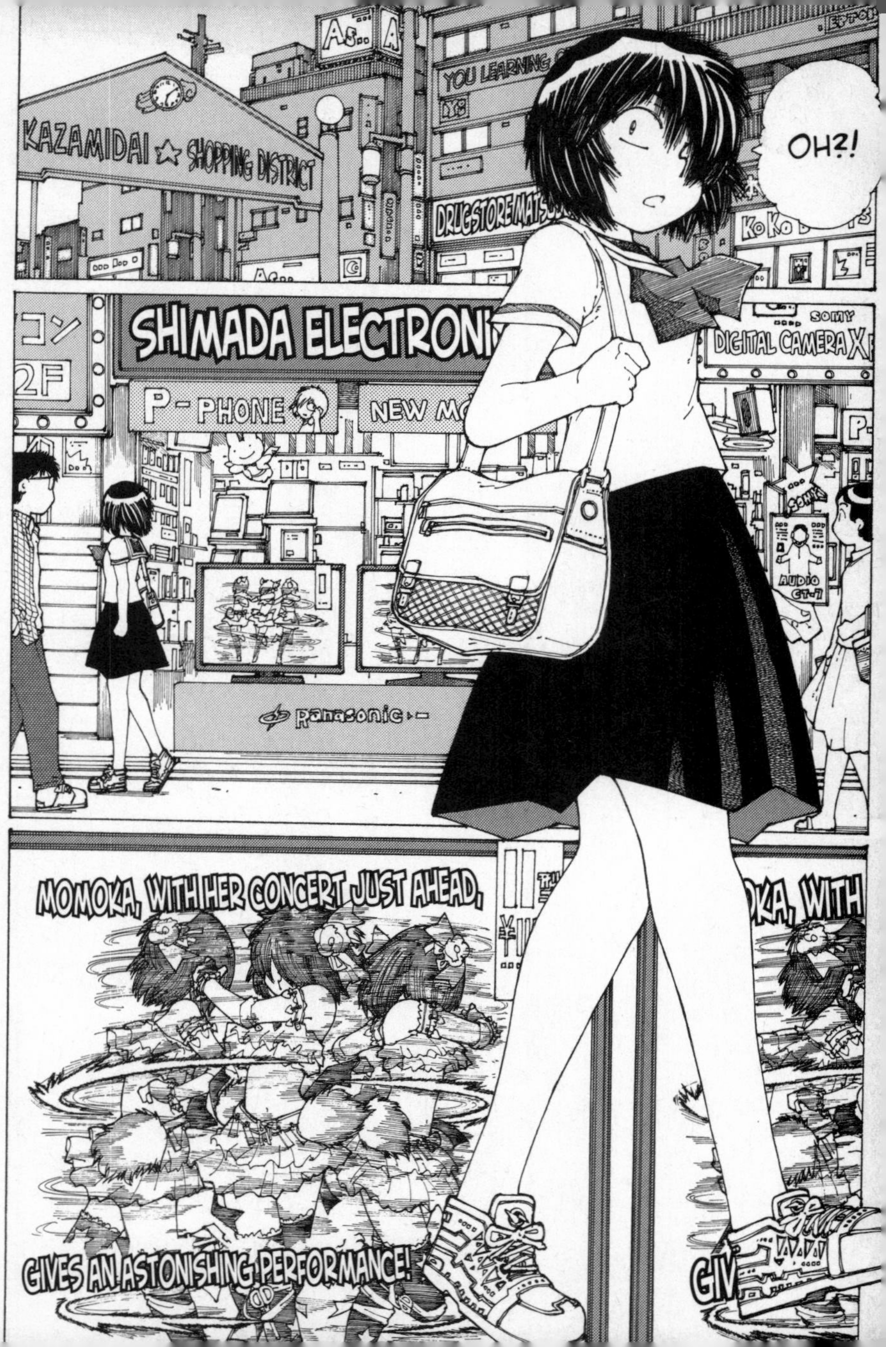
OH?!
YOU LEARNING
KAZAMIDAI ☆ SHOPPING DISTRICT
DRUGSTORE MATSU
SOMY
DIGITAL CAMERA X
SHIMADA ELECTRONI
2F
P-PHONE
NEW MO
AUDIO CT-7
Panasonic
KA, WITH
GIV
MOMOKA, WITH HER CONCERT JUST AHEAD,
GIVES AN ASTONISHING PERFORMANCE!

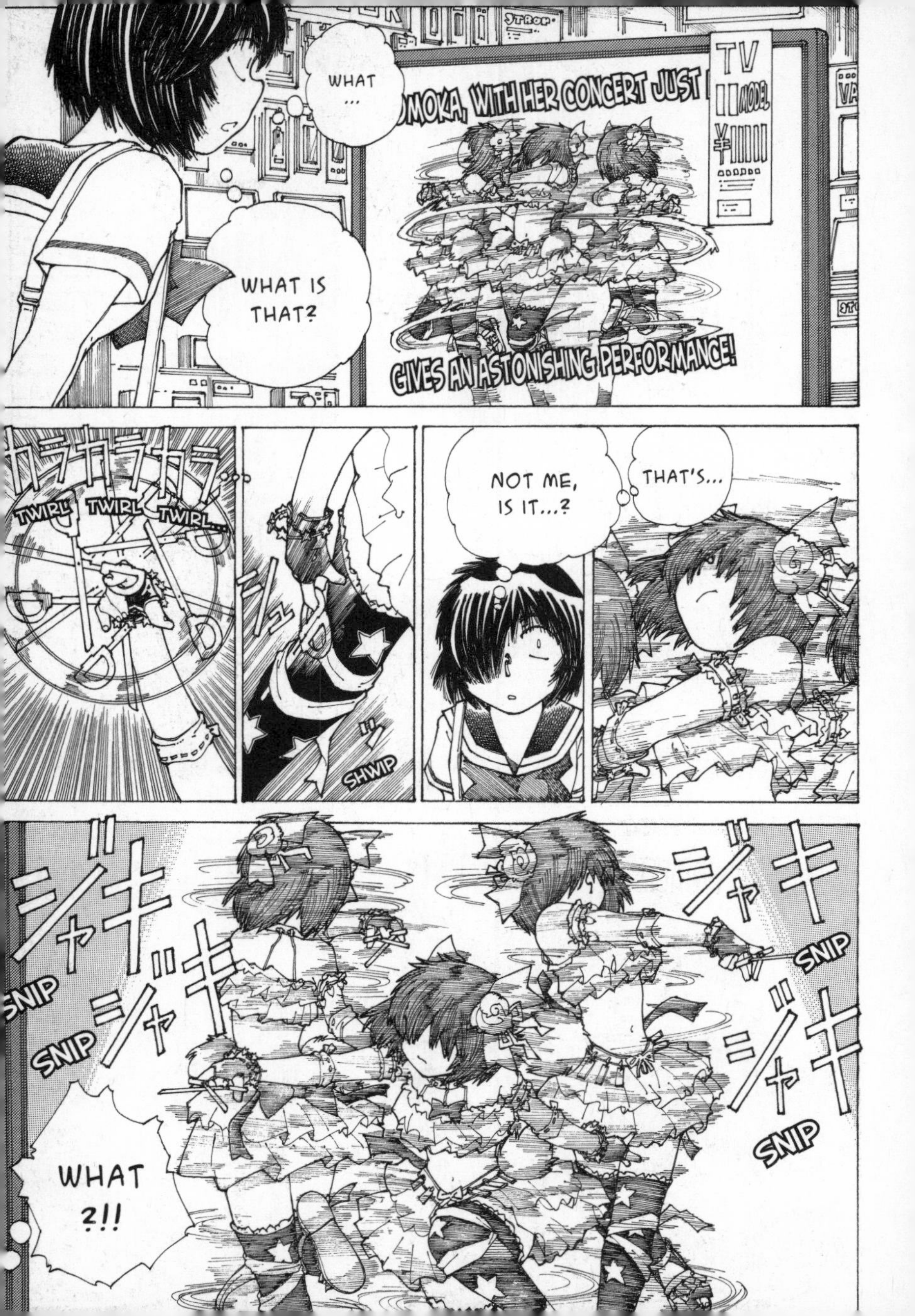
TV
MODEL
OMOKA, WITH HER CONCERT JUST
GIVES AN ASTONISHING PERFORMANCE!
WHAT ...
WHAT IS THAT?
THAT'S...
NOT ME, IS IT...?
シュ
SHWIP
カラカラカラ...
TWIRL TWIRL TWIRL...
ジャキ
SNIP
ジャキ
SNIP
ジャキ
SNIP
ジャキ
SNIP
WHAT ?!!

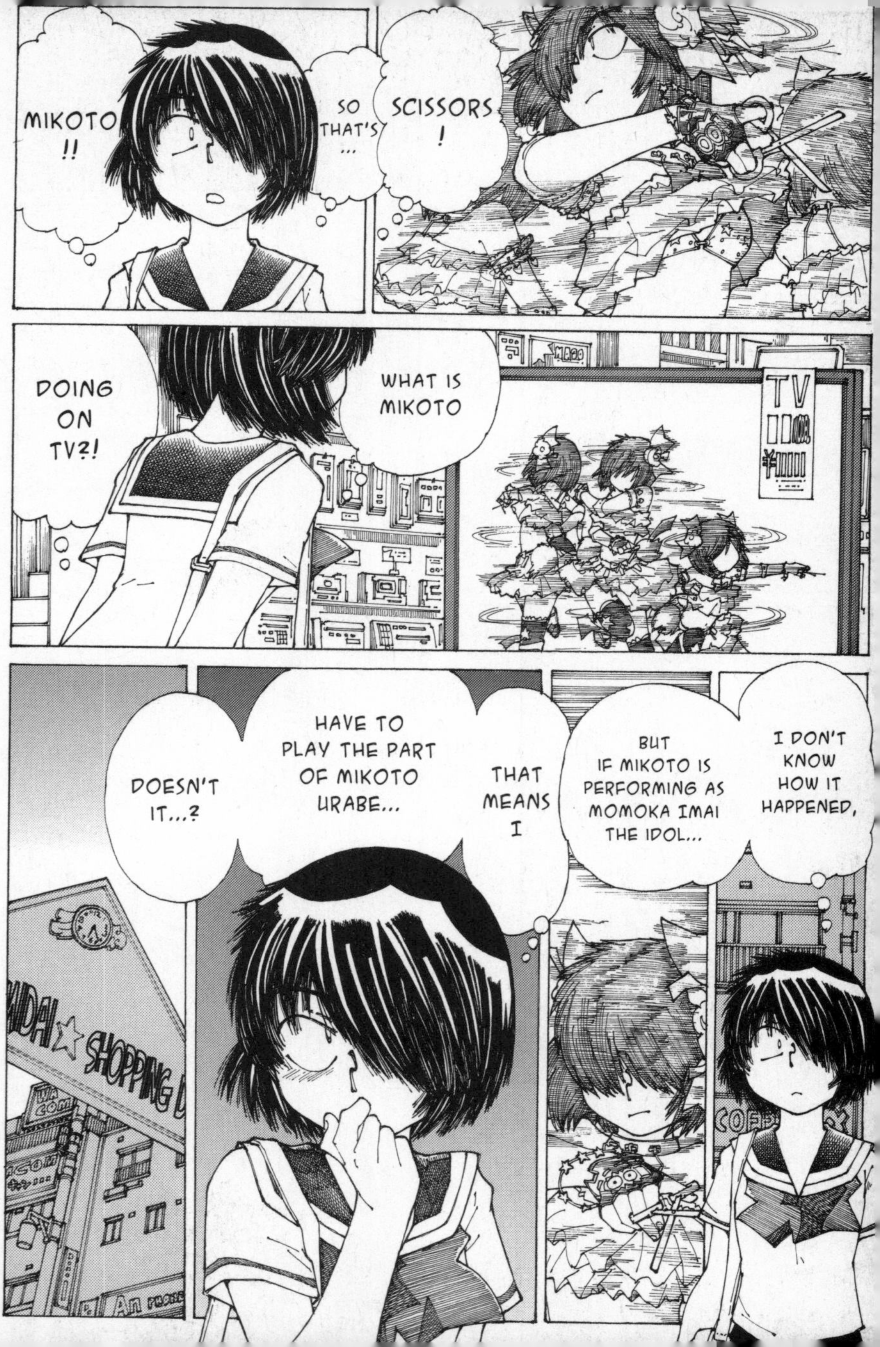
SCISSORS!
SO THAT'S...
MIKOTO!!
WHAT IS MIKOTO
DOING ON TV?!
TV
I DON'T KNOW HOW IT HAPPENED,
BUT IF MIKOTO IS PERFORMING AS MOMOKA IMAI THE IDOL...
THAT MEANS I
HAVE TO PLAY THE PART OF MIKOTO URABE...
DOESN'T IT...?

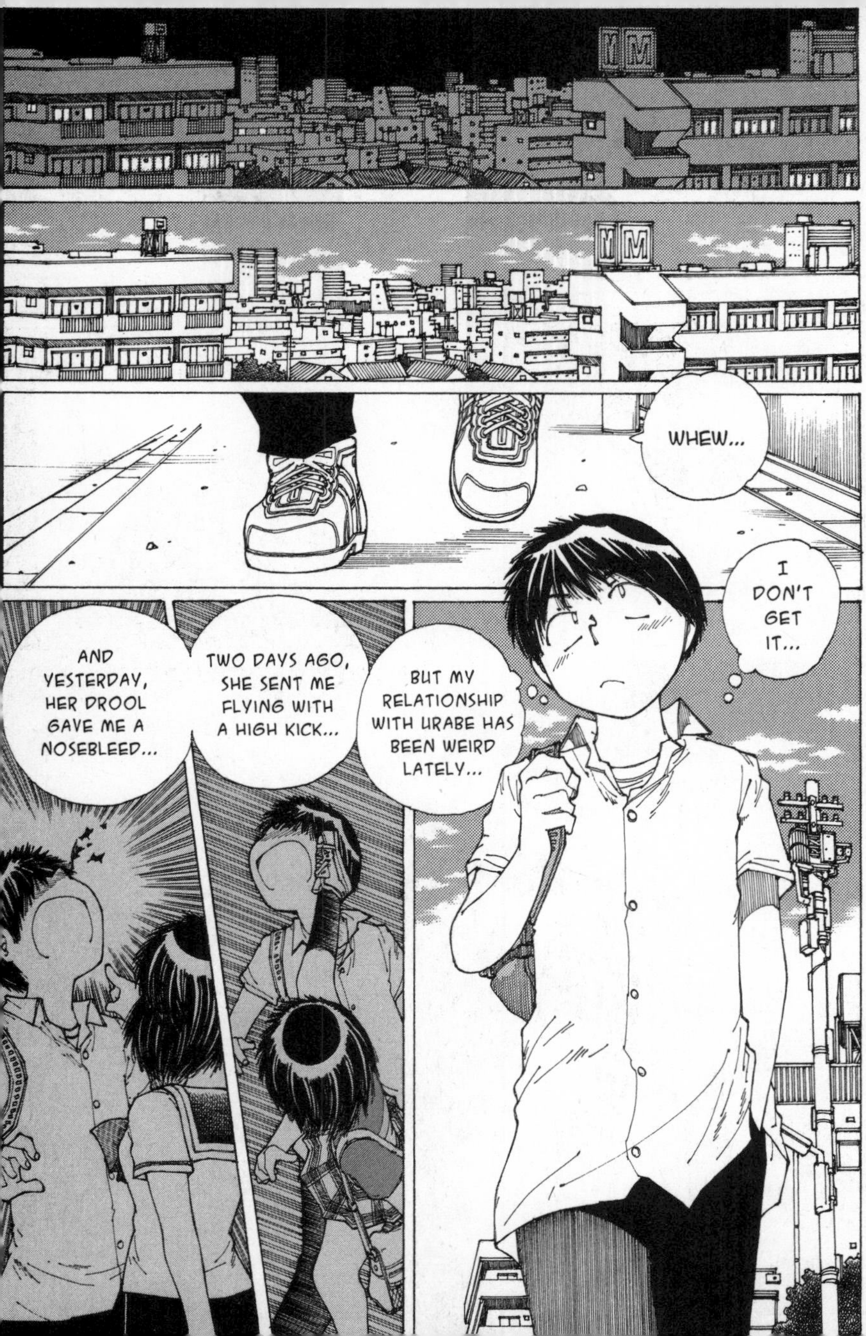
WHEW...
I DON'T GET IT...
BUT MY RELATIONSHIP WITH URABE HAS BEEN WEIRD LATELY...
TWO DAYS AGO, SHE SENT ME FLYING WITH A HIGH KICK...
AND YESTERDAY, HER DROOL GAVE ME A NOSEBLEED...

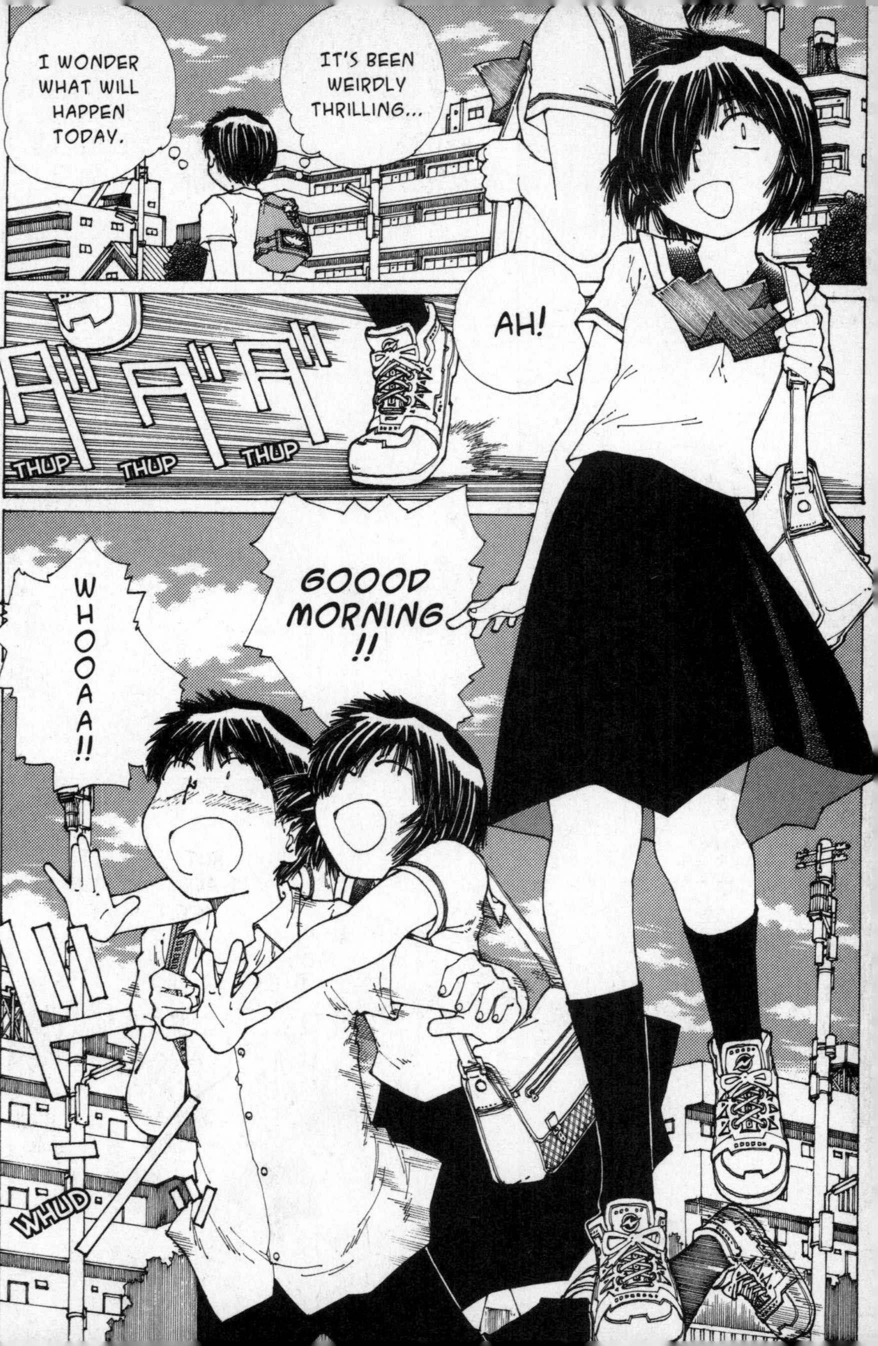
IT'S BEEN WEIRDLY THRILLING...
I WONDER WHAT WILL HAPPEN TODAY.
AH!
THUP
THUP
THUP
GOOOD MORNING!!
WHOOAAA!!
WHUD

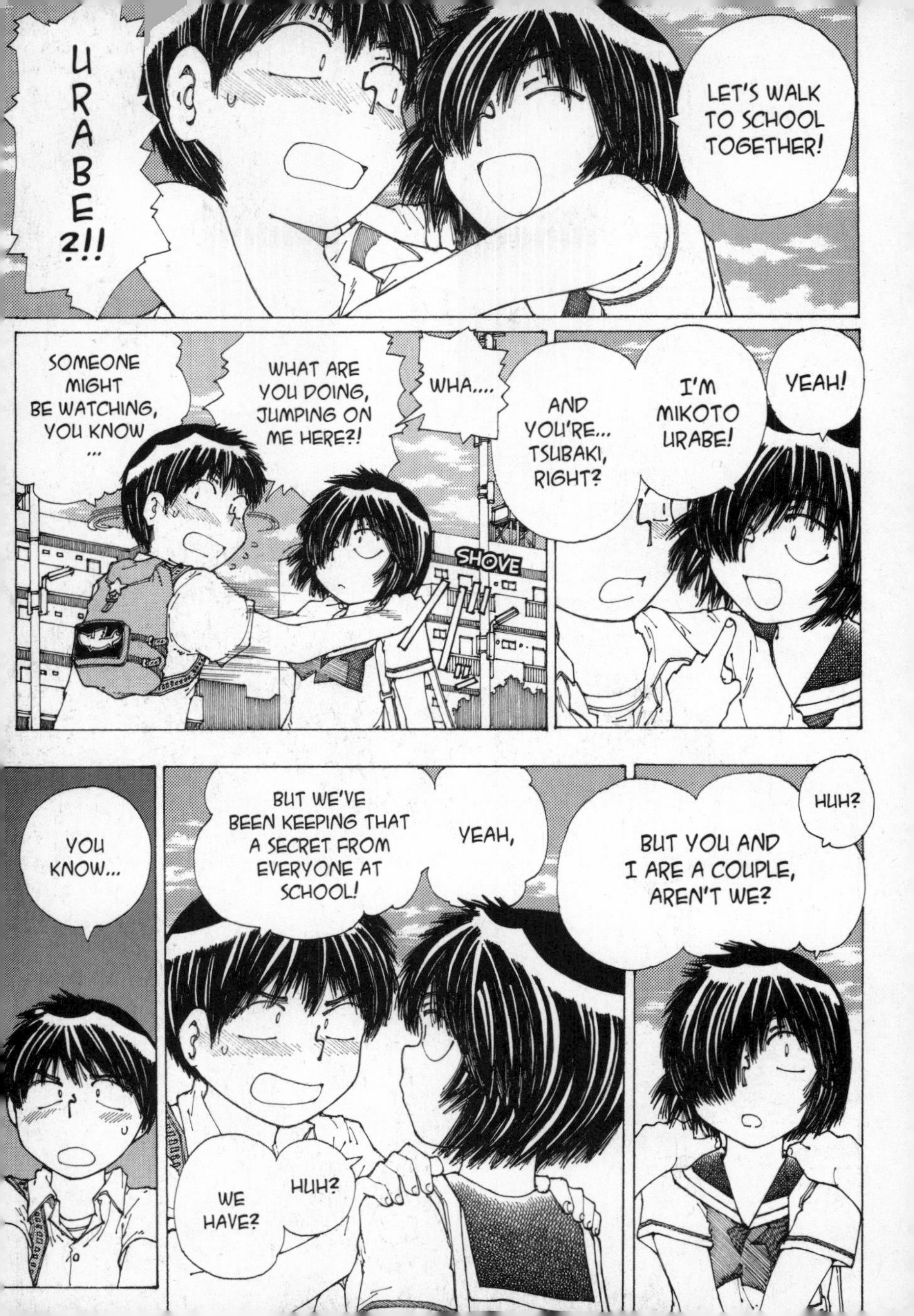
LET'S WALK TO SCHOOL TOGETHER!
URABE?!!
YEAH!
I'M MIKOTO URABE!
AND YOU'RE... TSUBAKI, RIGHT?
WHA....
WHAT ARE YOU DOING, JUMPING ON ME HERE?!
SOMEONE MIGHT BE WATCHING, YOU KNOW ...
SHOVE
HUH?
BUT YOU AND I ARE A COUPLE, AREN'T WE?
YEAH,
BUT WE'VE BEEN KEEPING THAT A SECRET FROM EVERYONE AT SCHOOL!
HUH?
WE HAVE?
YOU KNOW...

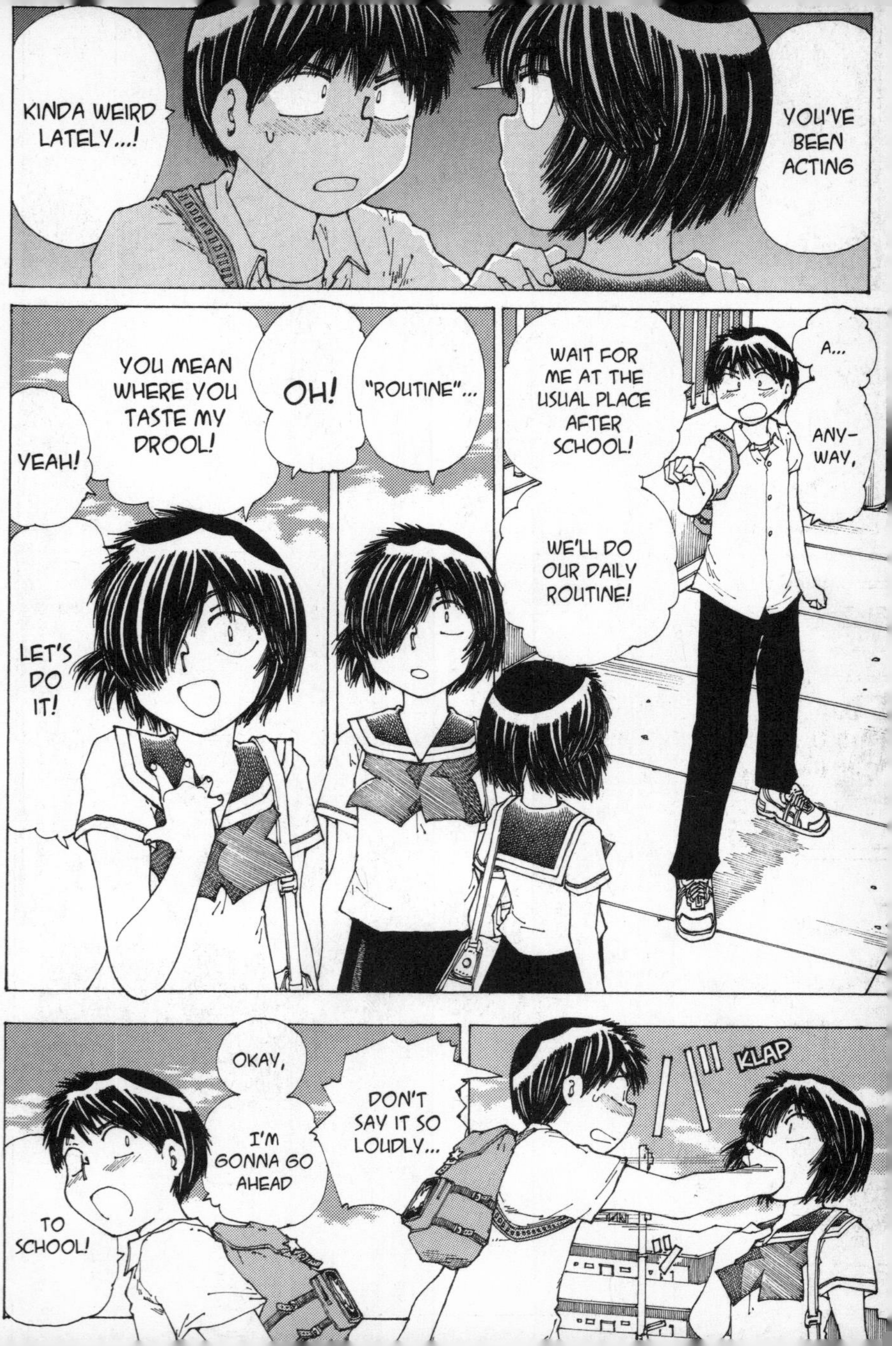
YOU'VE BEEN ACTING
KINDA WEIRD LATELY...!
A... ANY-WAY,
WAIT FOR ME AT THE USUAL PLACE AFTER SCHOOL!
WE'LL DO OUR DAILY ROUTINE!
"ROUTINE"...
OH!
YOU MEAN WHERE YOU TASTE MY DROOL!
YEAH!
LET'S DO IT!
KLAP
DON'T SAY IT SO LOUDLY...
OKAY,
I'M GONNA GO AHEAD
TO SCHOOL!

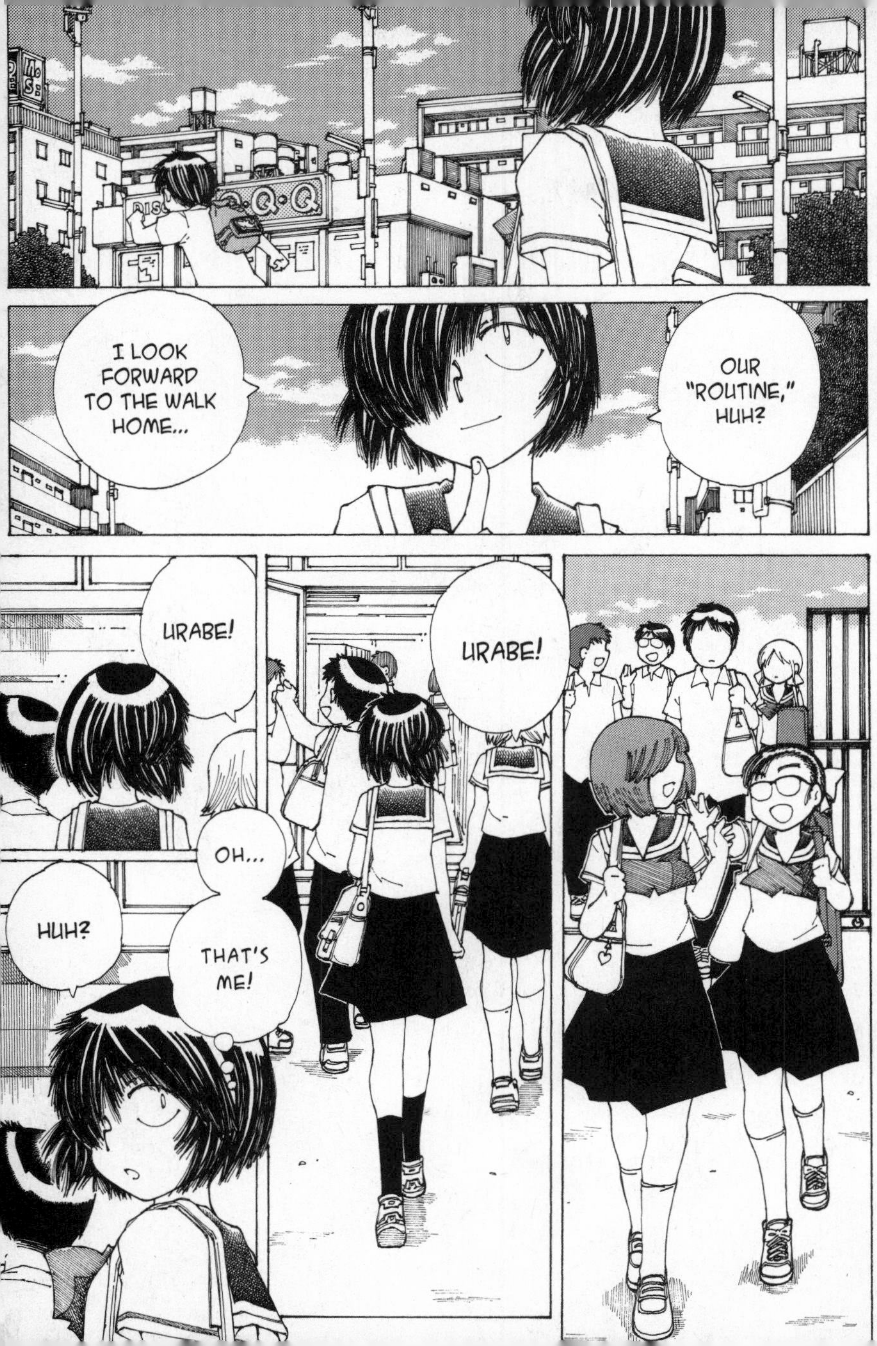
OUR "ROUTINE," HUH?
I LOOK FORWARD TO THE WALK HOME...
URABE!
URABE!
OH...
THAT'S ME!
HUH?

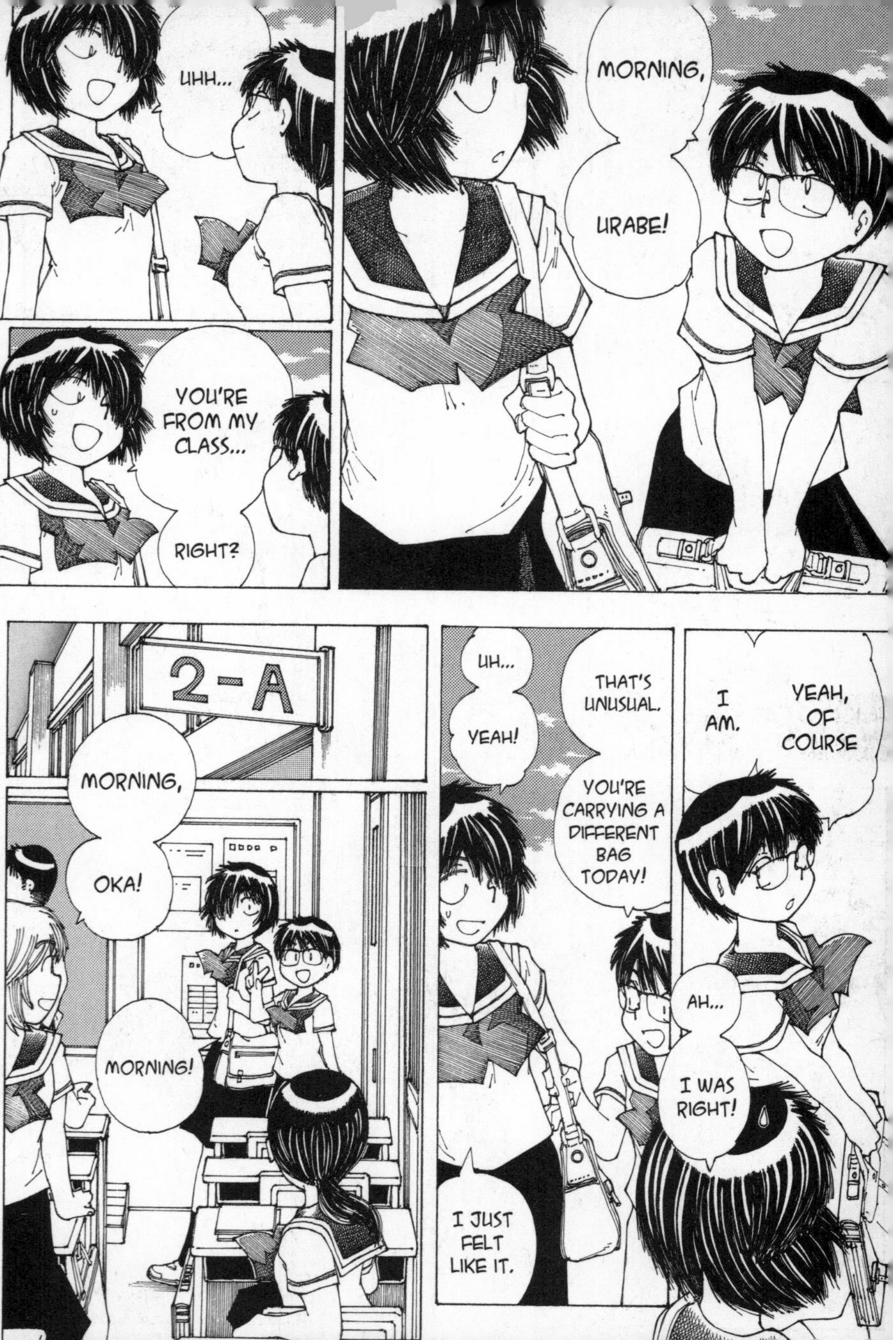
MORNING, URABE!
UHH...
YOU'RE FROM MY CLASS... RIGHT?
YEAH, OF COURSE I AM.
AH... I WAS RIGHT!
THAT'S UNUSUAL.
UH... YEAH!
YOU'RE CARRYING A DIFFERENT BAG TODAY!
I JUST FELT LIKE IT.
2-A
MORNING, OKA!
MORNING!

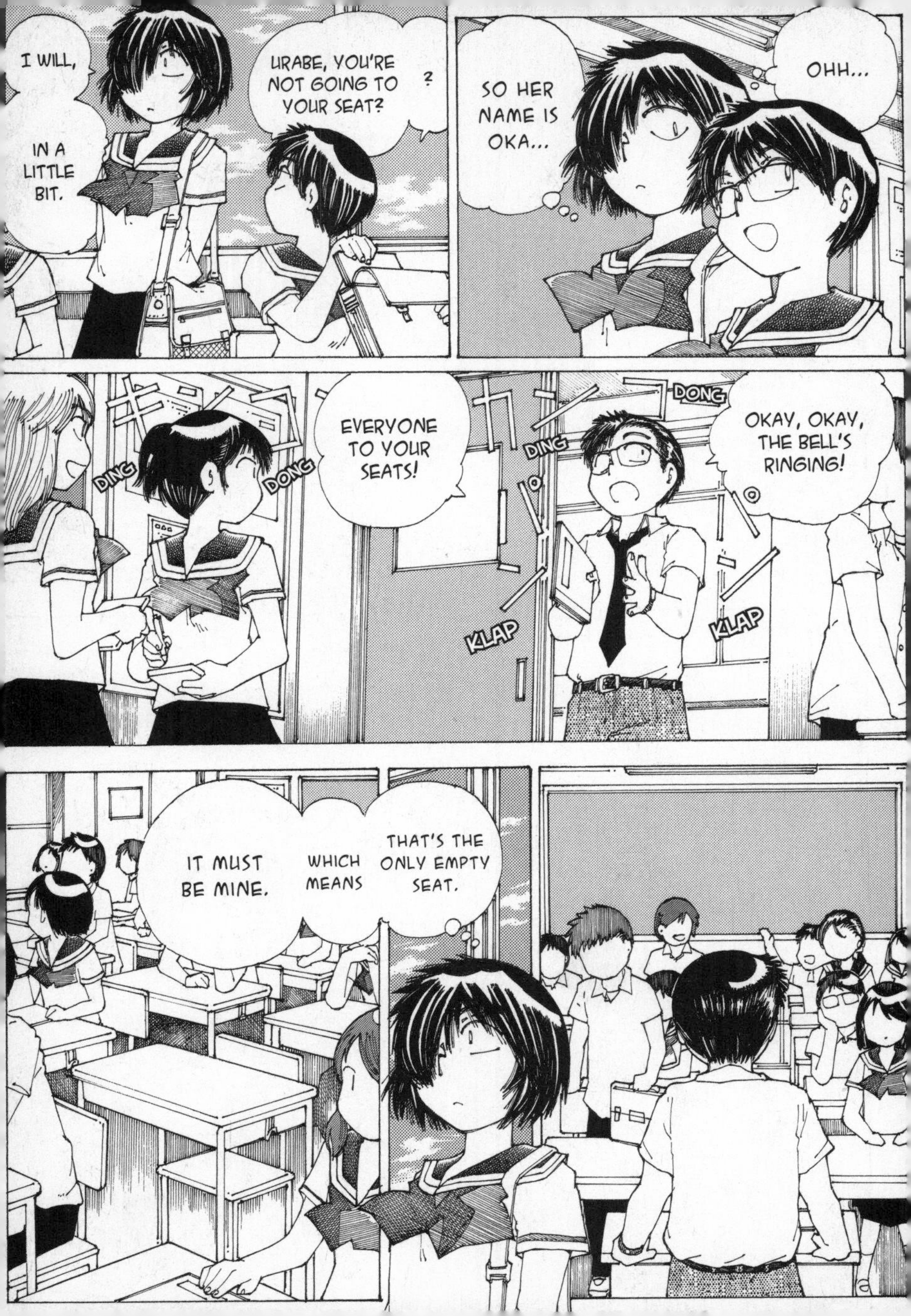
OHH...
SO HER NAME IS OKA...
URABE, YOU'RE NOT GOING TO YOUR SEAT?
?
I WILL,
IN A LITTLE BIT.
DONG
OKAY, OKAY, THE BELL'S RINGING!
DING
KLAP
KLAP
EVERYONE TO YOUR SEATS!
DONG
DING
THAT'S THE ONLY EMPTY SEAT.
WHICH MEANS
IT MUST BE MINE.

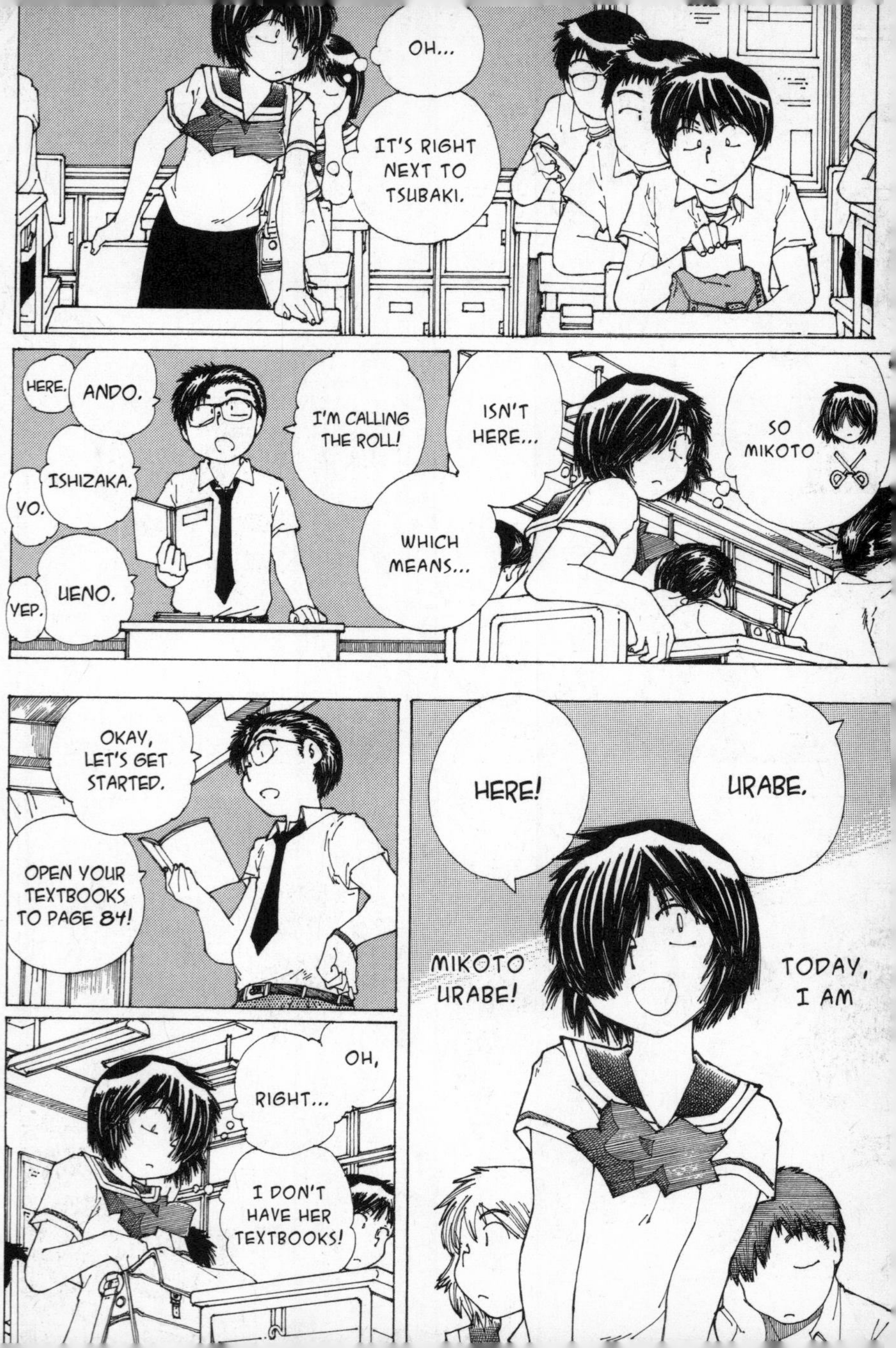
OH...
IT'S RIGHT NEXT TO TSUBAKI.
SO MIKOTO
ISN'T HERE...
WHICH MEANS...
I'M CALLING THE ROLL!
ANDO.
HERE.
ISHIZAKA.
YO.
UENO.
YEP.
URABE.
HERE!
TODAY, I AM
MIKOTO URABE!
OKAY, LET'S GET STARTED.
OPEN YOUR TEXTBOOKS TO PAGE 84!
OH, RIGHT...
I DON'T HAVE HER TEXTBOOKS!

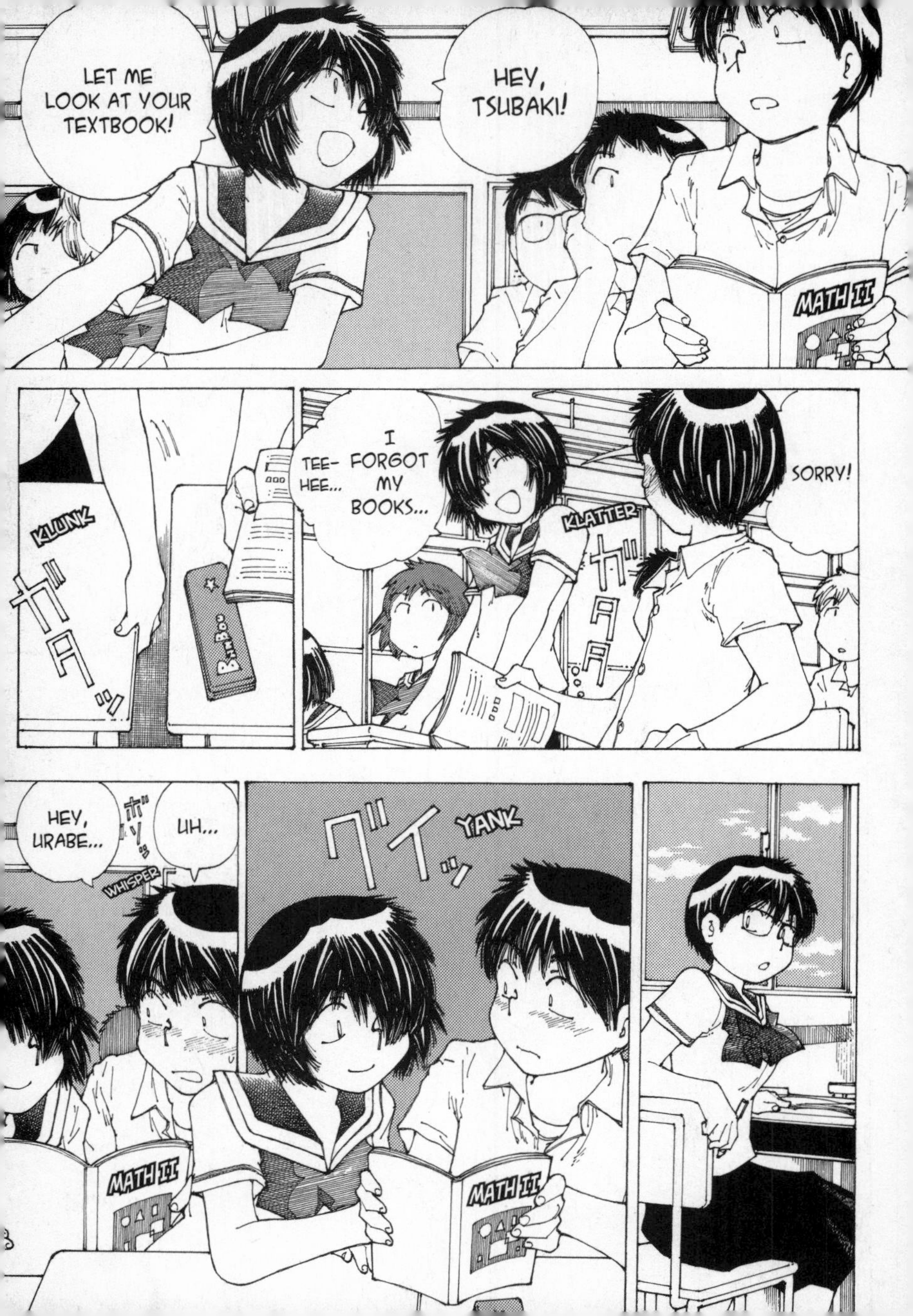
HEY, TSUBAKI!
LET ME LOOK AT YOUR TEXTBOOK!
MATH II
SORRY!
KLATTER
ガタタ
I FORGOT MY BOOKS...
TEE-HEE...
KLUNK
ガタッ
グイッ
YANK
UH...
ボソッ
WHISPER
HEY, URABE...
MATH II
MATH II

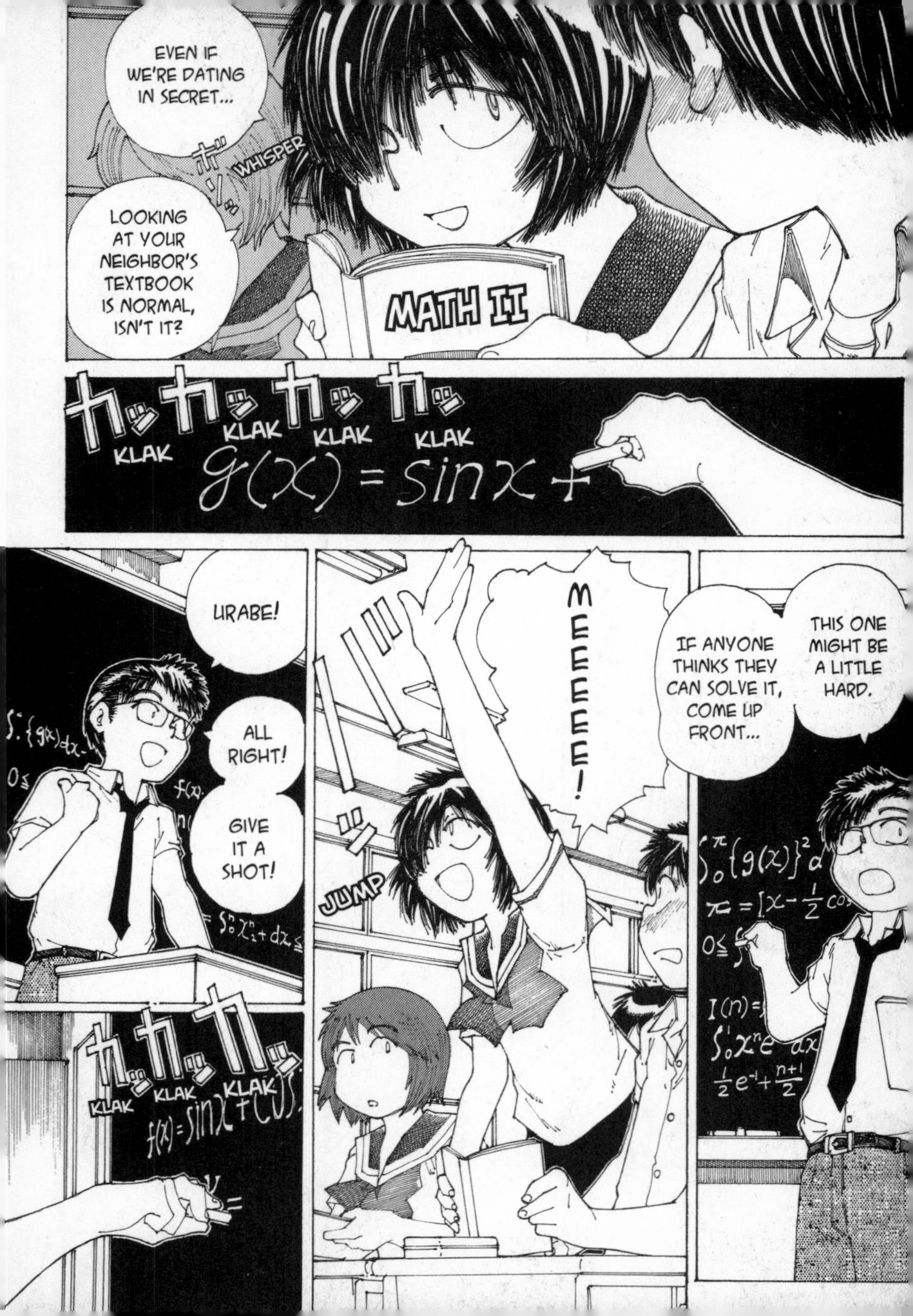
EVEN IF WE'RE DATING IN SECRET...
WHISPER
LOOKING AT YOUR NEIGHBOR'S TEXTBOOK IS NORMAL, ISN'T IT?
MATH II
KLAK
KLAK
KLAK
KLAK
g(x) = sin x +
THIS ONE MIGHT BE A LITTLE HARD.
IF ANYONE THINKS THEY CAN SOLVE IT, COME UP FRONT...
MEEEEEE!
JUMP
URABE!
ALL RIGHT!
GIVE IT A SHOT!
KLAK
KLAK
KLAK

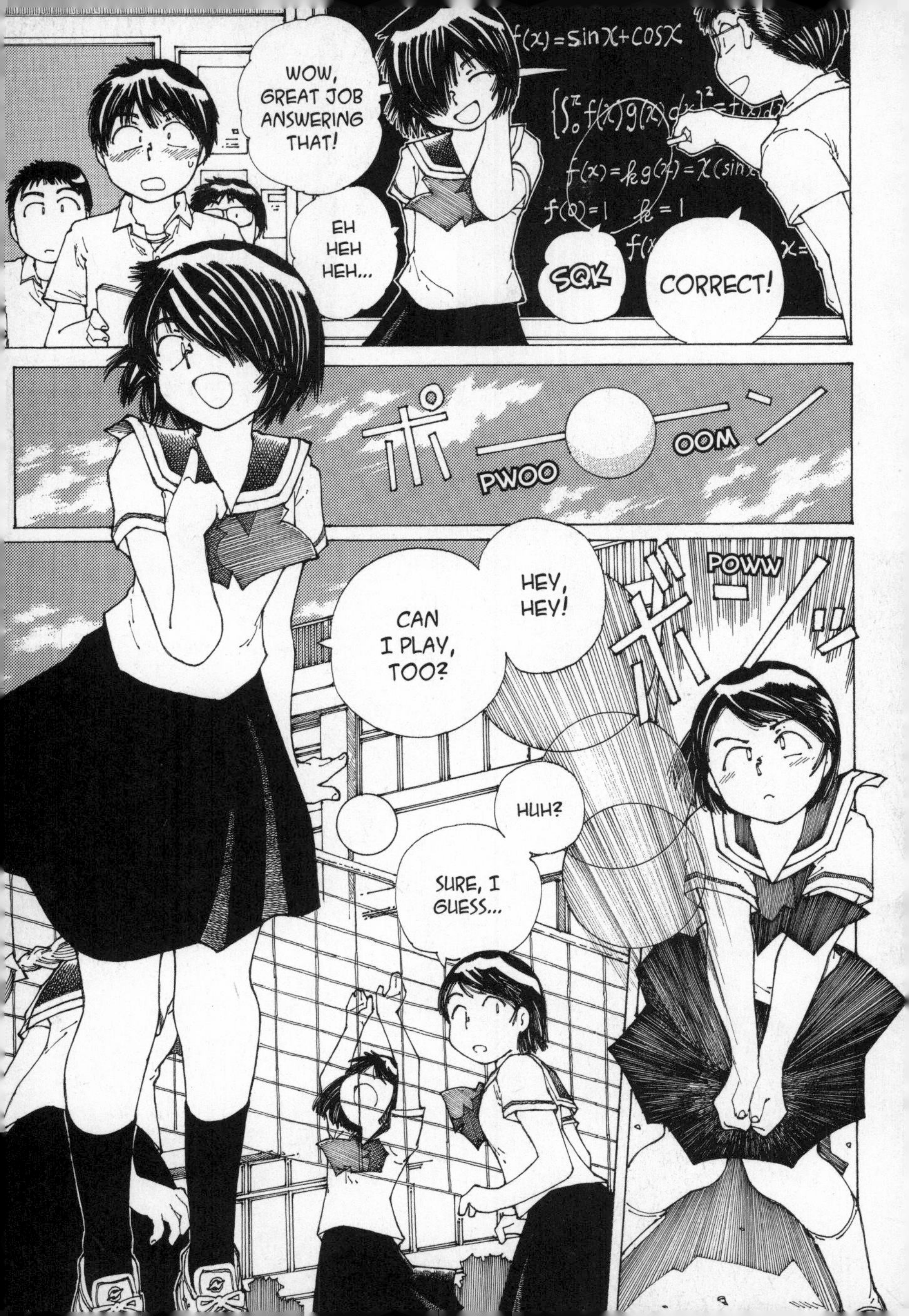
f(x)=sinx+cosx
CORRECT!
SQK
WOW, GREAT JOB ANSWERING THAT!
EH HEH HEH...
PWOO
OOM
POWW
HEY, HEY!
CAN I PLAY, TOO?
HUH?
SURE, I GUESS...

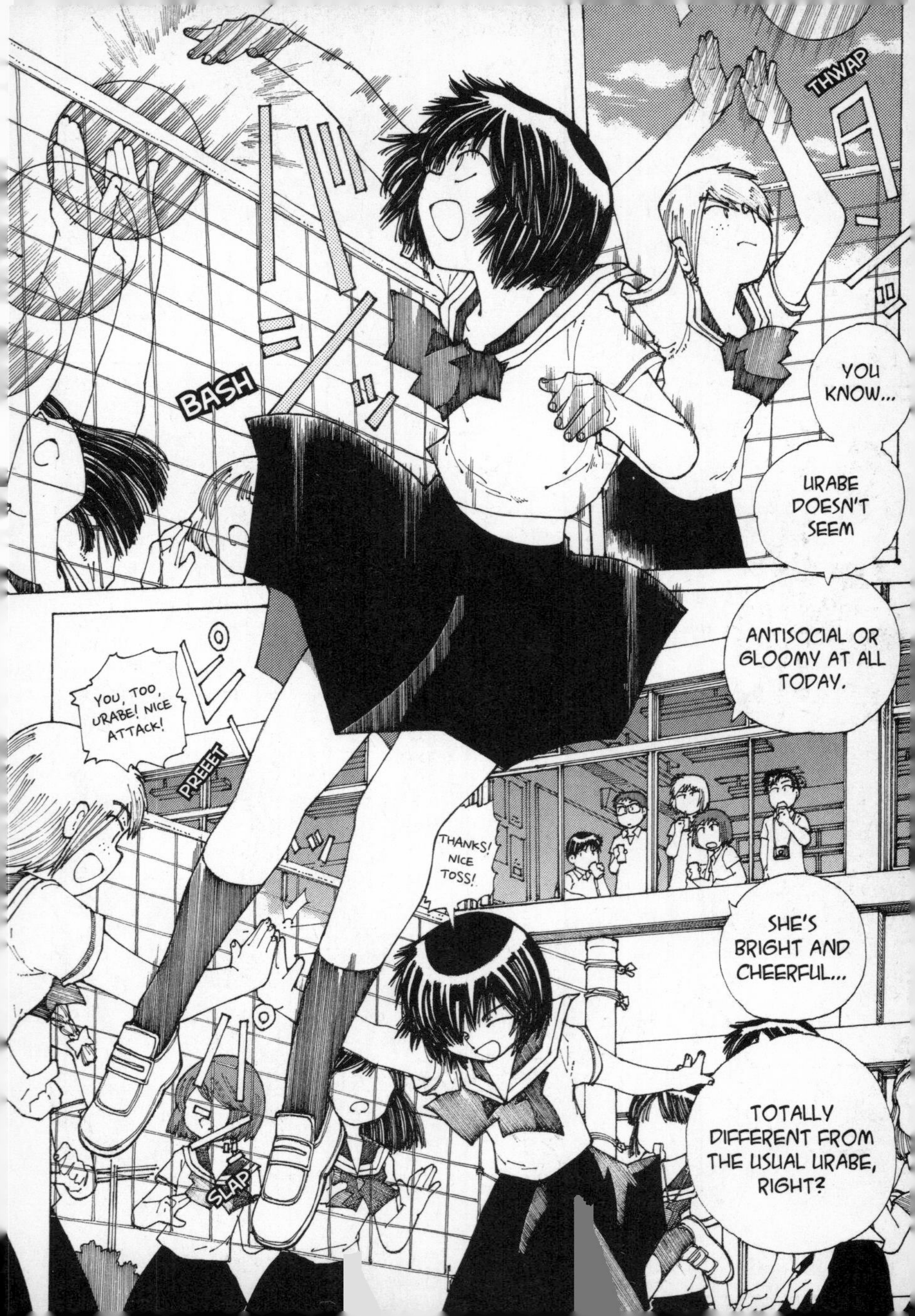
THWAP
YOU KNOW...
URABE DOESN'T SEEM
BASH
ANTISOCIAL OR GLOOMY AT ALL TODAY.
YOU, TOO, URABE! NICE ATTACK!
PREEET
THANKS! NICE TOSS!
SHE'S BRIGHT AND CHEERFUL...
TOTALLY DIFFERENT FROM THE USUAL URABE, RIGHT?
SLAP

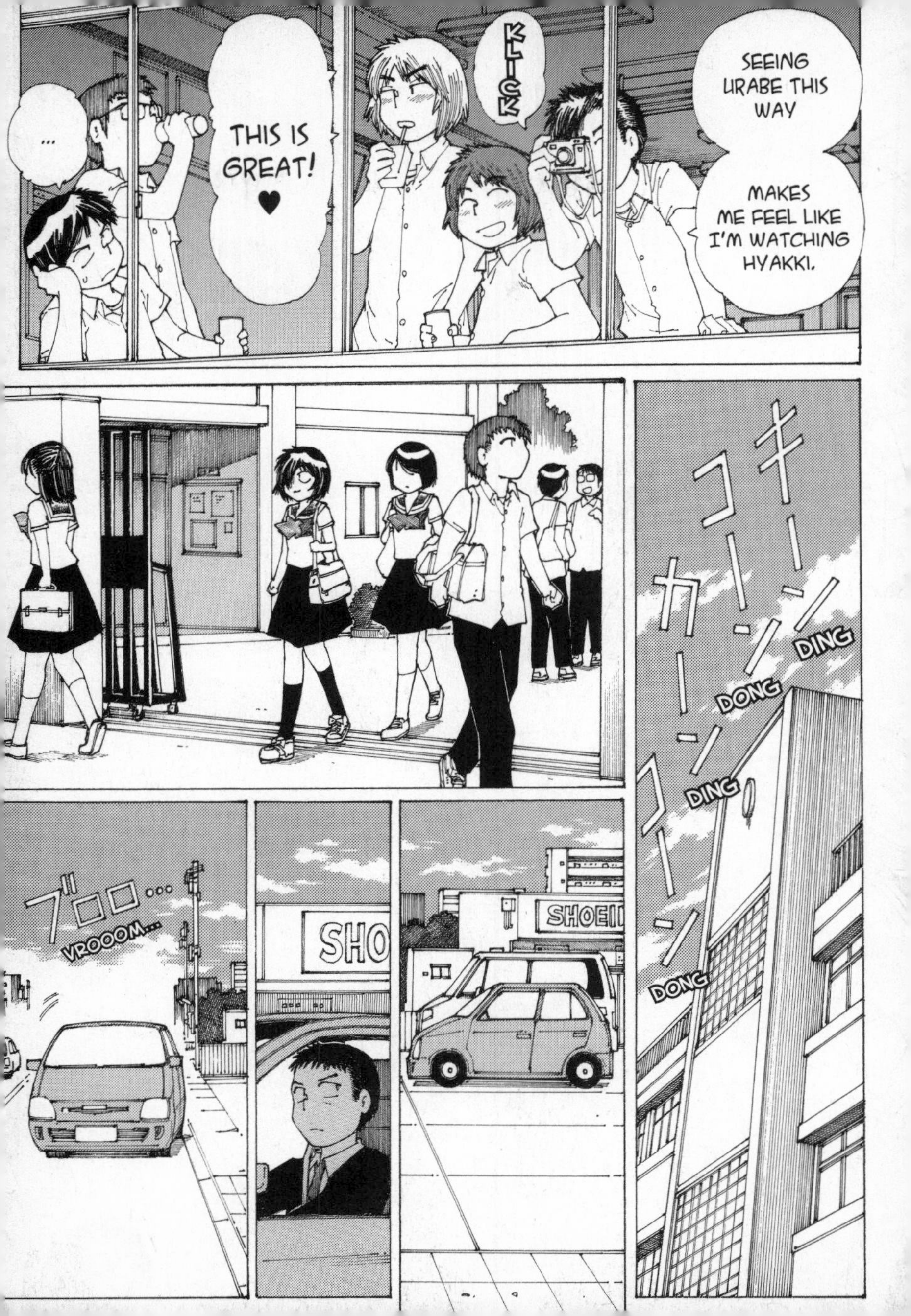
SEEING URABE THIS WAY
MAKES ME FEEL LIKE I'M WATCHING HYAKKI.
KLICK
THIS IS GREAT! ♥
...
キーンコーン
カーンコーン
DING
DONG
DING
DONG
SHOEI
SHO
ブロロ…
VROOOM...

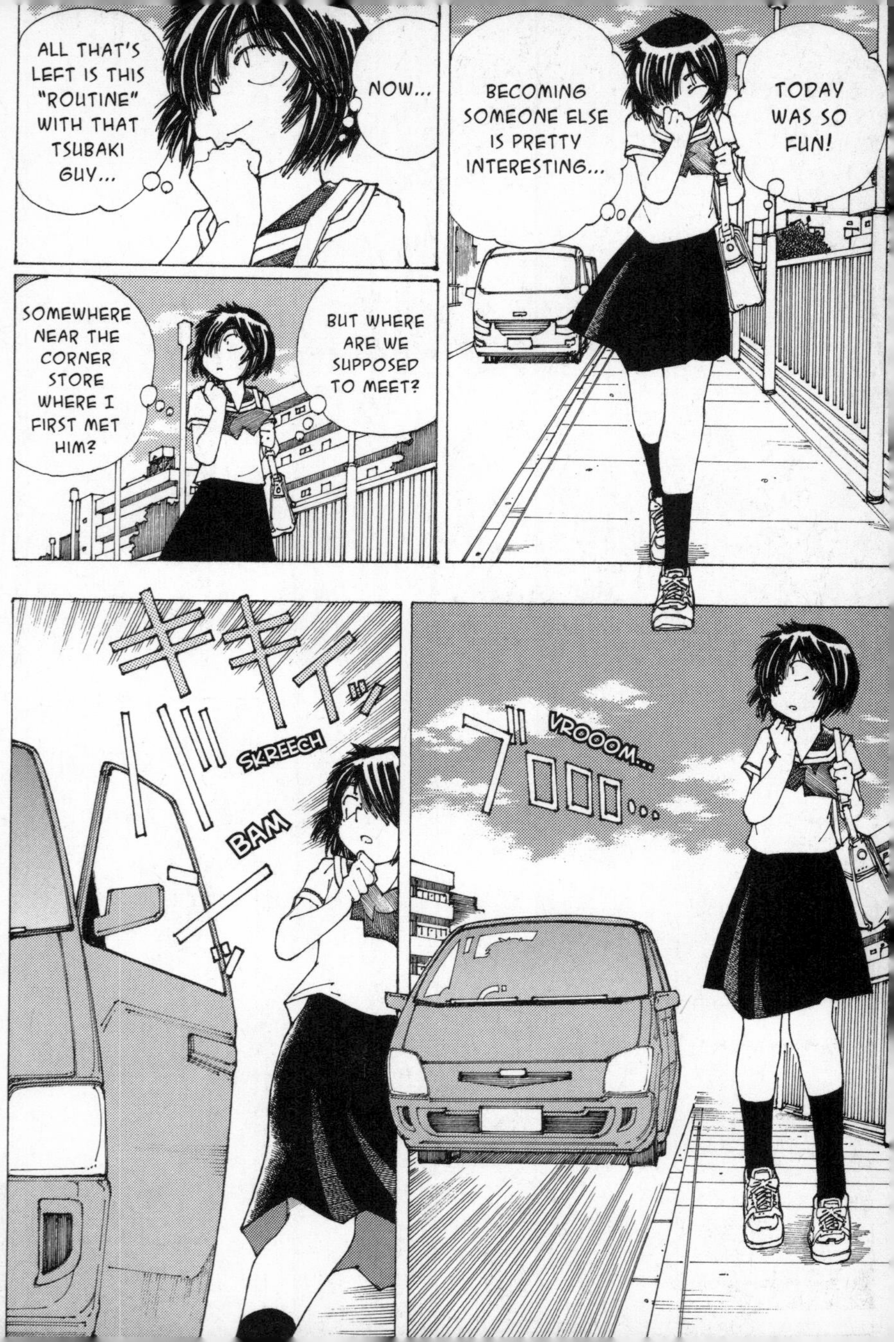

TODAY WAS SO FUN!
BECOMING SOMEONE ELSE IS PRETTY INTERESTING...
NOW...
ALL THAT'S LEFT IS THIS "ROUTINE" WITH THAT TSUBAKI GUY...
BUT WHERE ARE WE SUPPOSED TO MEET?
SOMEWHERE NEAR THE CORNER STORE WHERE I FIRST MET HIM?
VROOOM...
キキイッ
SKREECH
BAM

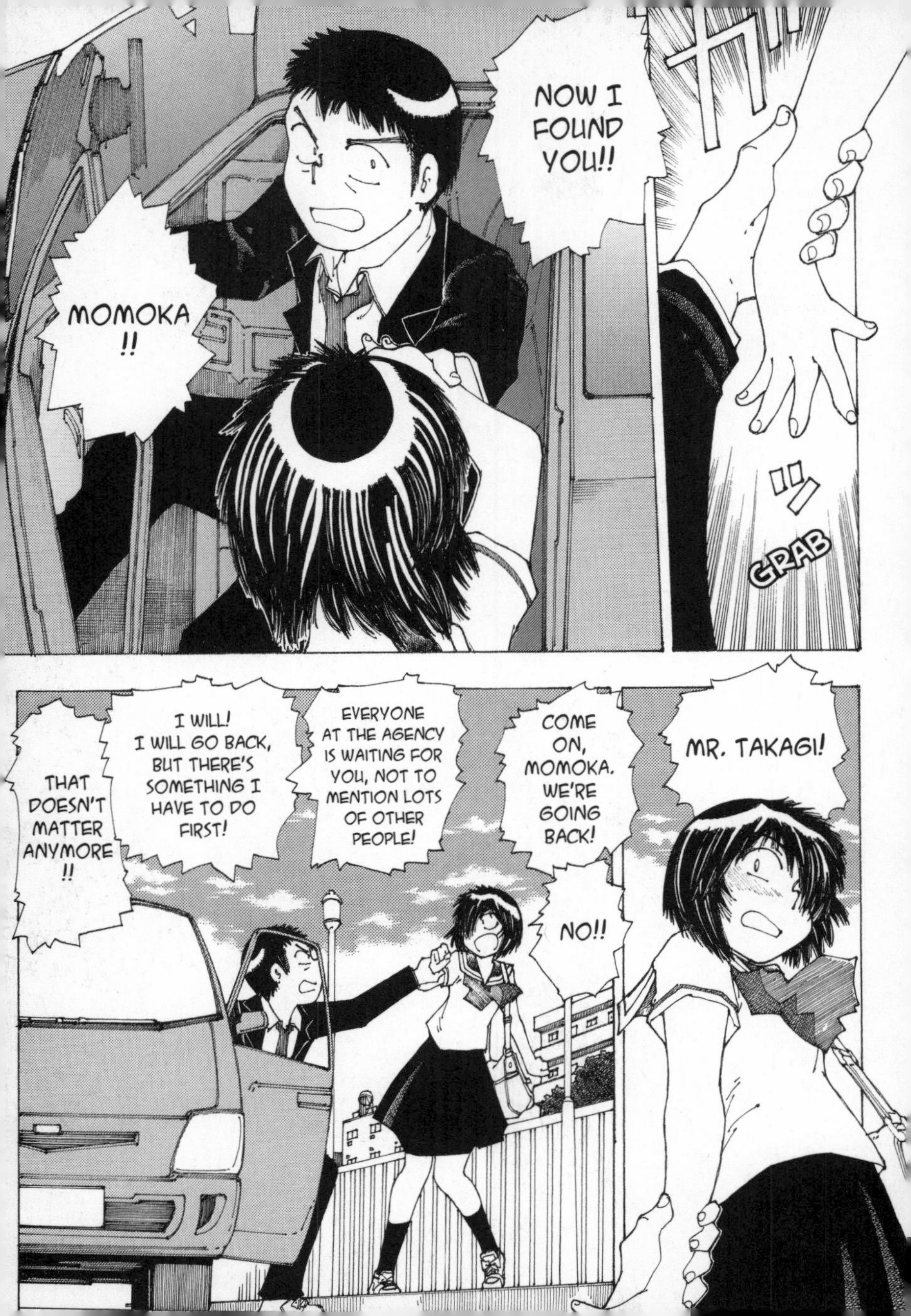
GRAB
NOW I FOUND YOU!!
MOMOKA!!
MR. TAKAGI!
COME ON, MOMOKA. WE'RE GOING BACK!
NO!!
EVERYONE AT THE AGENCY IS WAITING FOR YOU, NOT TO MENTION LOTS OF OTHER PEOPLE!
I WILL! I WILL GO BACK, BUT THERE'S SOMETHING I HAVE TO DO FIRST!
THAT DOESN'T MATTER ANYMORE!!

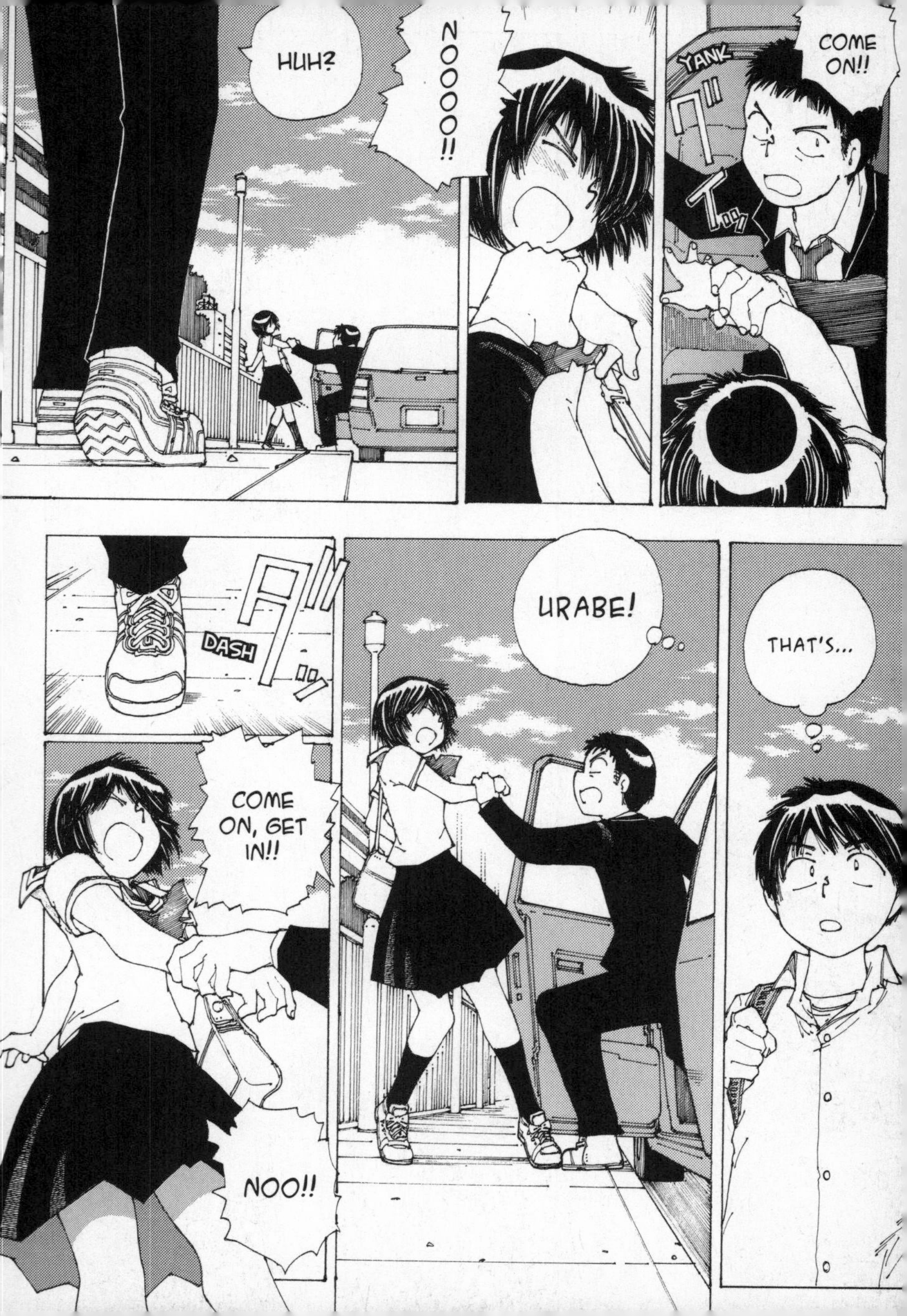
YANK
COME ON!!
NOOOOO!!
HUH?
THAT'S...
URABE!
DASH
COME ON, GET IN!!
NOO!!

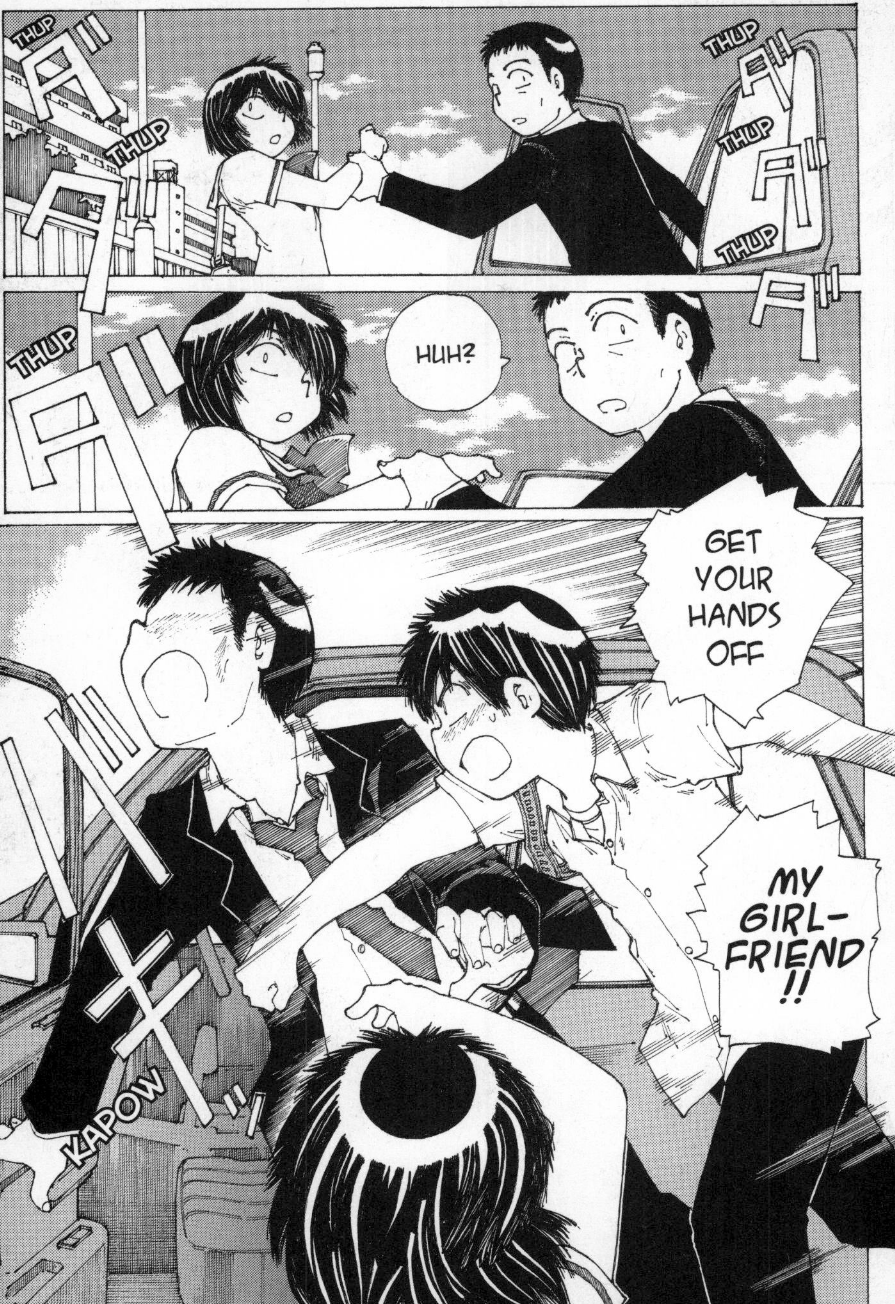
THUP
THUP
THUP
THUP
THUP
THUP
HUH?
GET YOUR HANDS OFF
MY GIRL-FRIEND!!
KAPOW

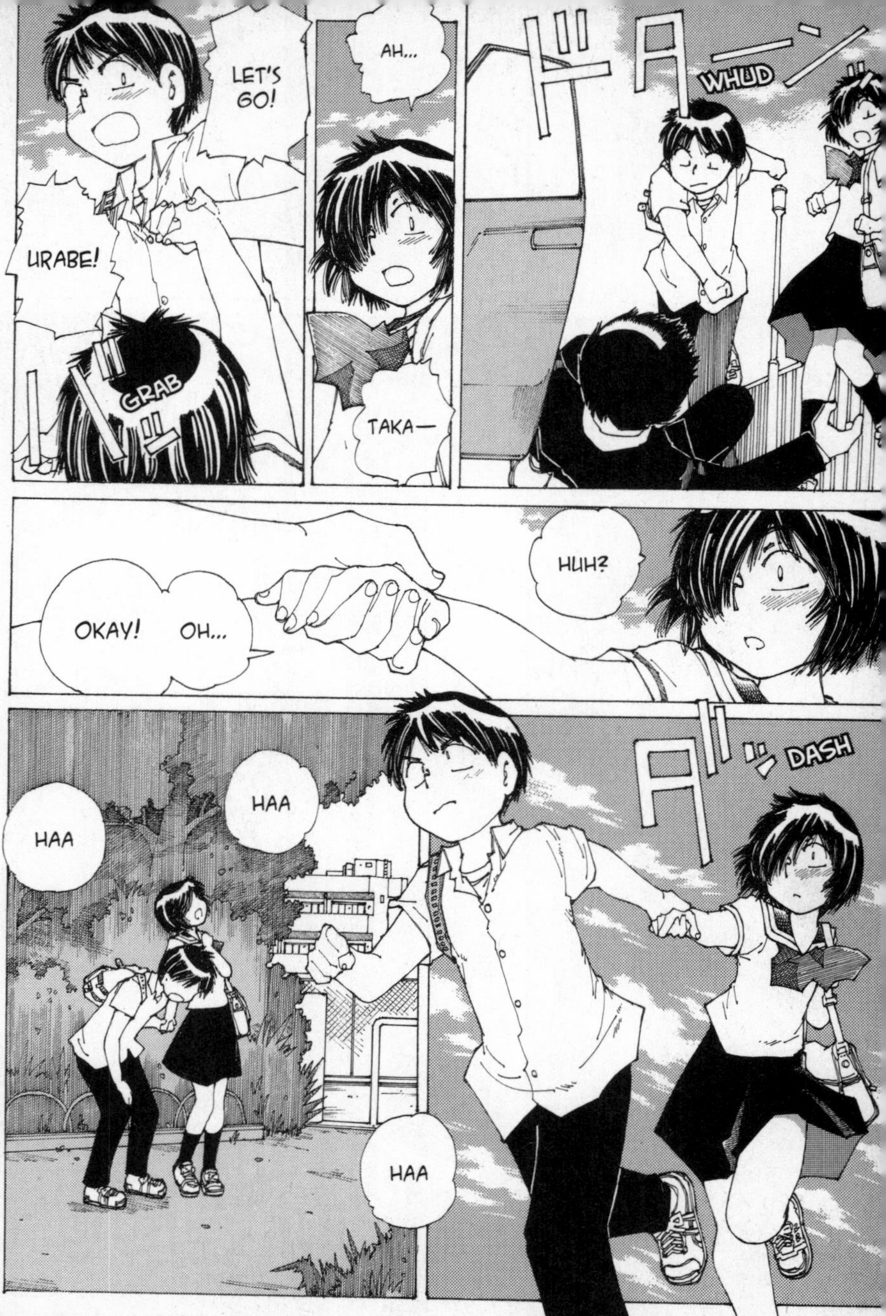
WHUD
AH...
TAKA—
LET'S GO!
URABE!
GRAB
HUH?
OKAY! OH...
DASH
HAA
HAA
HAA

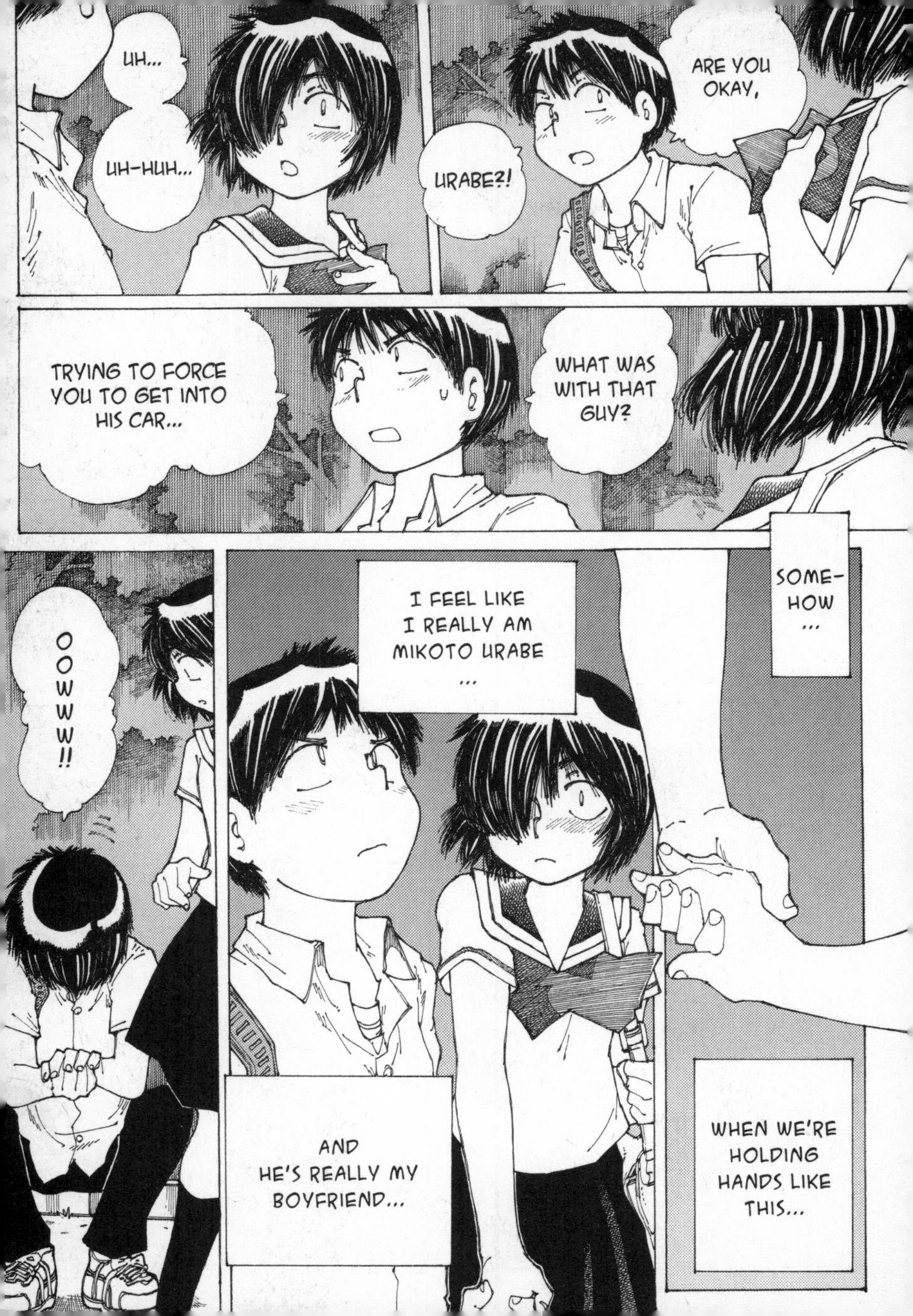
ARE YOU OKAY,
URABE?!
UH...
UH-HUH...
WHAT WAS WITH THAT GUY?
TRYING TO FORCE YOU TO GET INTO HIS CAR...
SOME-HOW ...
I FEEL LIKE I REALLY AM MIKOTO URABE ...
WHEN WE'RE HOLDING HANDS LIKE THIS...
AND HE'S REALLY MY BOYFRIEND...
OOWWW!!

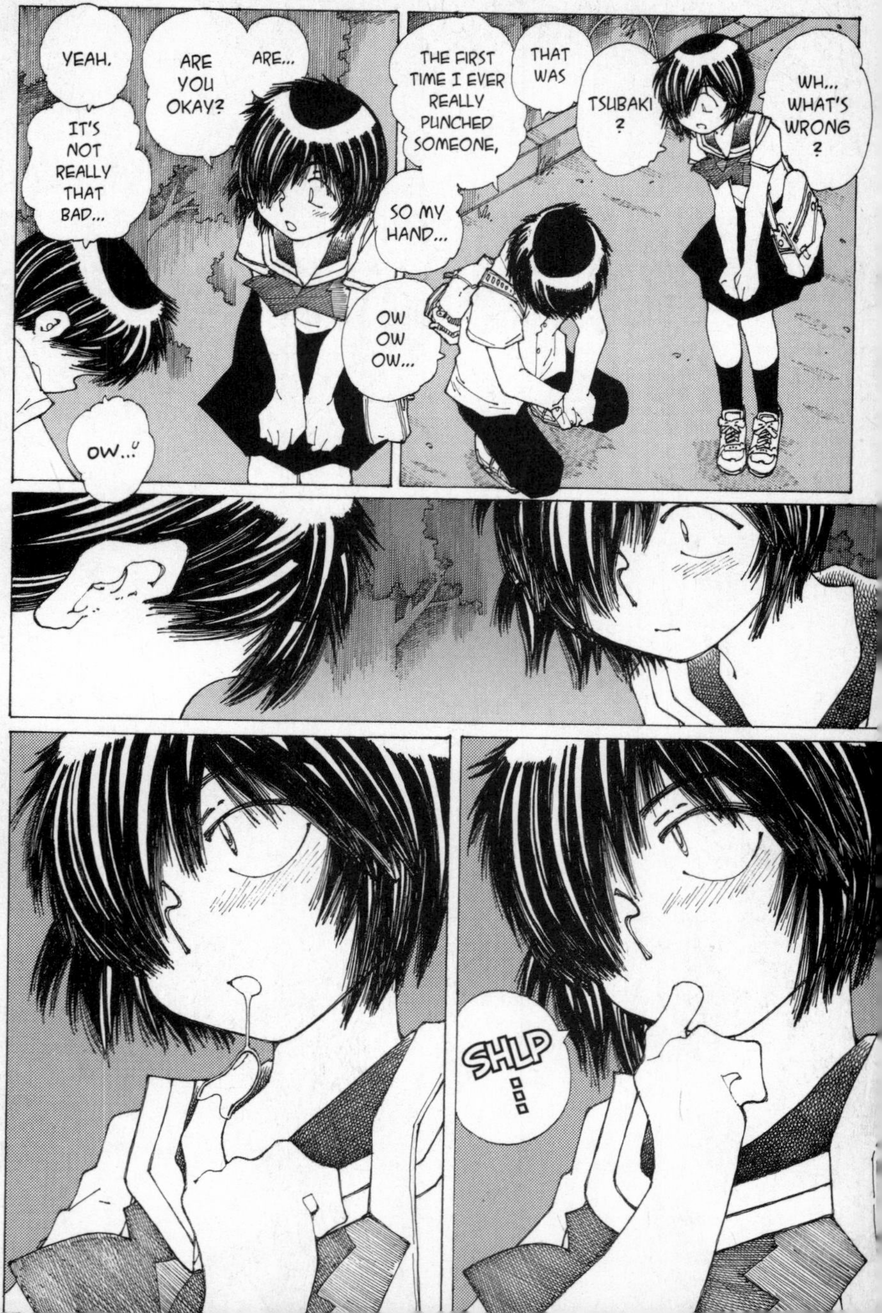
WH... WHAT'S WRONG?
TSUBAKI?
THAT WAS
THE FIRST TIME I EVER REALLY PUNCHED SOMEONE,
SO MY HAND...
OW OW OW...
ARE...
ARE YOU OKAY?
YEAH.
IT'S NOT REALLY THAT BAD...
OW...
SHLP...

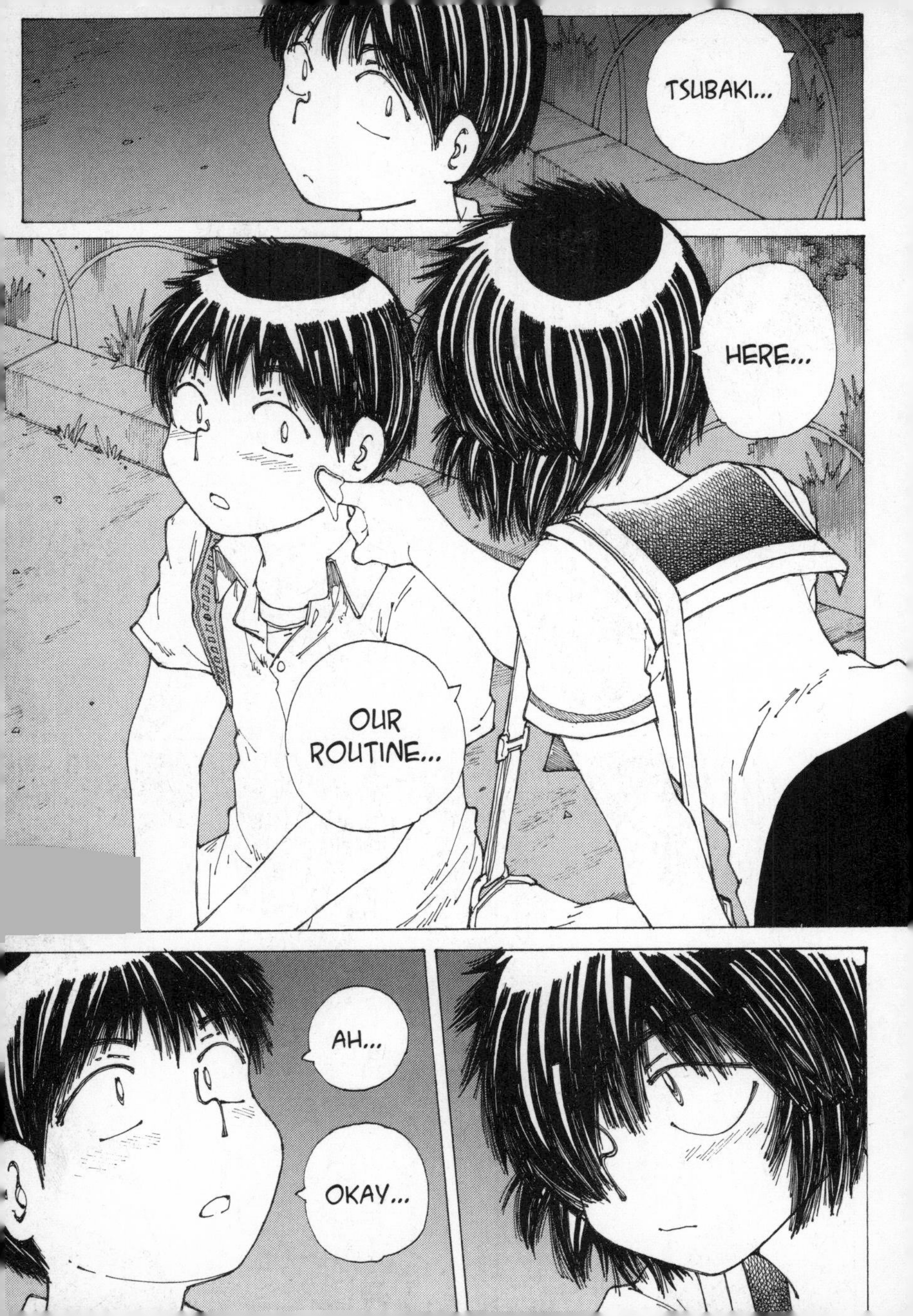
TSUBAKI...
HERE...
OUR ROUTINE...
AH...
OKAY...

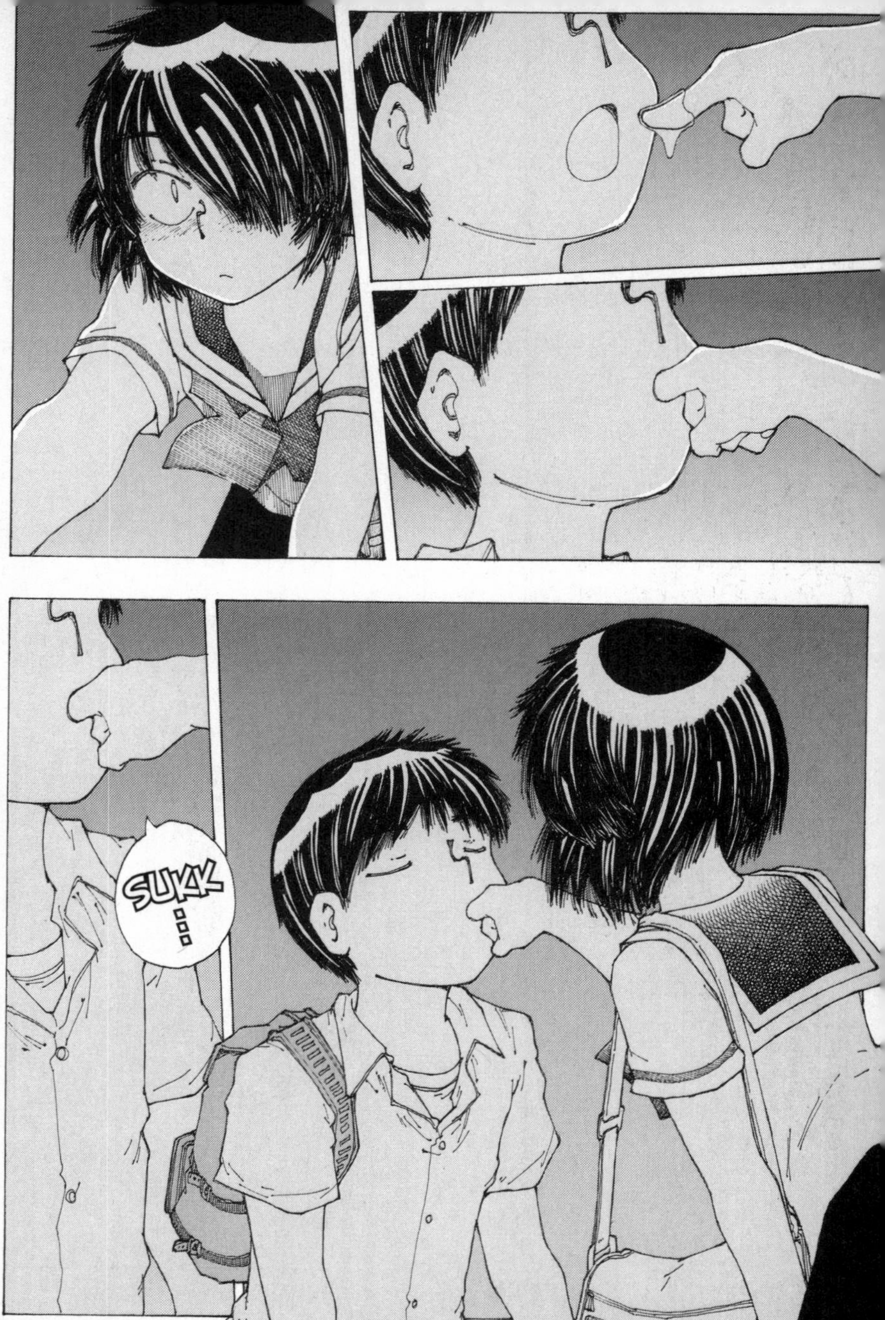
SUKK
...

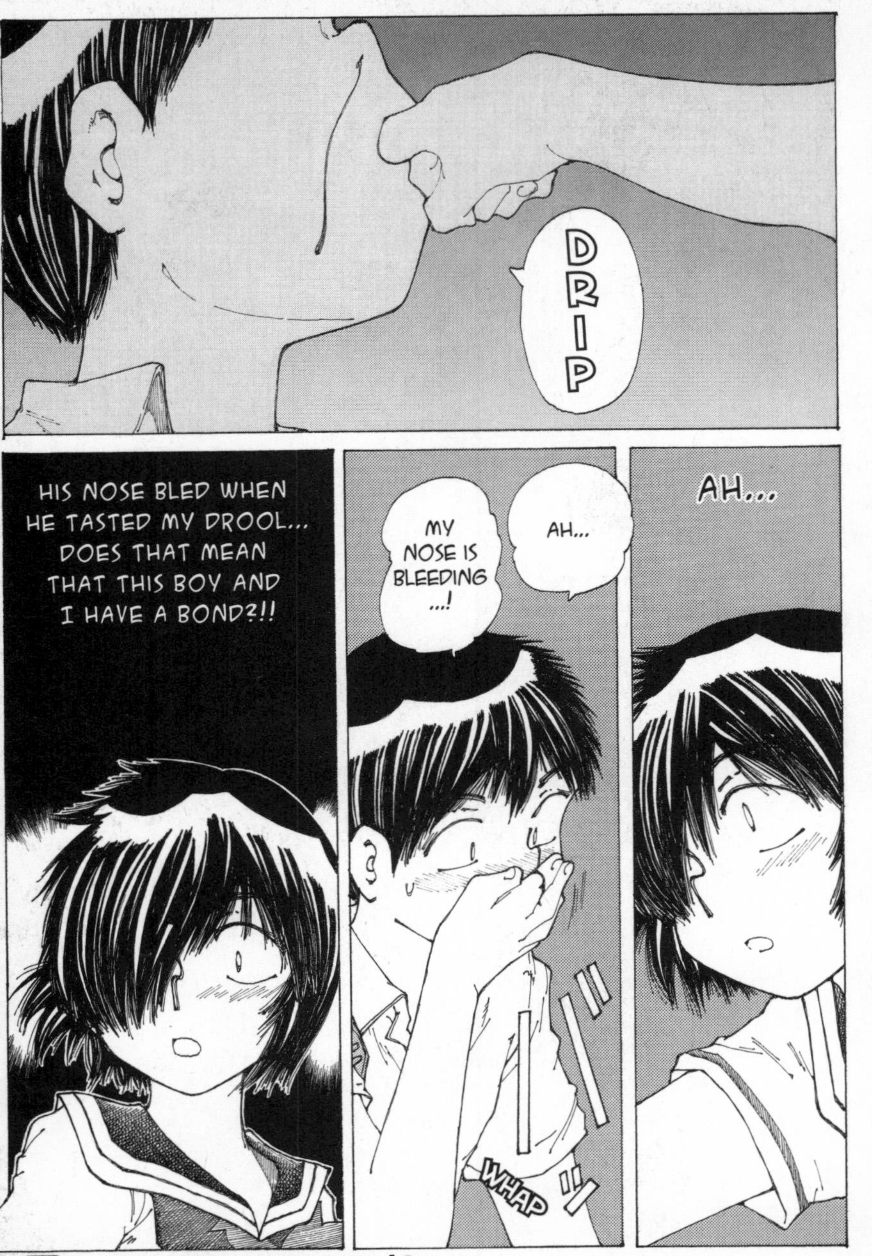
DRIP
AH...
AH...
MY NOSE IS BLEEDING ...!
WHAP
HIS NOSE BLED WHEN HE TASTED MY DROOL... DOES THAT MEAN THAT THIS BOY AND I HAVE A BOND?!!

END OF CHAPTER 42

MY IDOL: 3

YMO (YELLOW MAGIC ORCHESTRA)

HARUOMI HOSONO (1947-), RYUUICHI SAKAMOTO (1952-), YUKIHIRO TAKAHASHI (1952-)

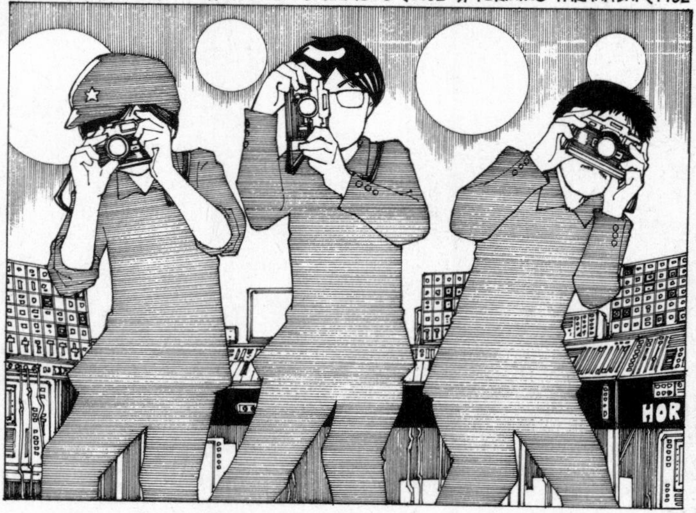
HOR

I've been listening to YMO since I was a teenager, and I still listen to them while I work! In the 80's, when I was in middle school, I'm sure there were many boys and girls throughout Japan, who, when asked who they'd want to reborn as, answered in all seriousness with Hosono, the "Professor," or Yukihiro.

They're definitely idols to me.

By the way, I've also been listening to Hatsune Miku's YMO cover album, "HMO→Hatsune Miku Orchestra," a lot lately. My favorite songs from that album are "Propaganda," "Behind the Mask," "La Femme Chinoise," and "Nice Age."

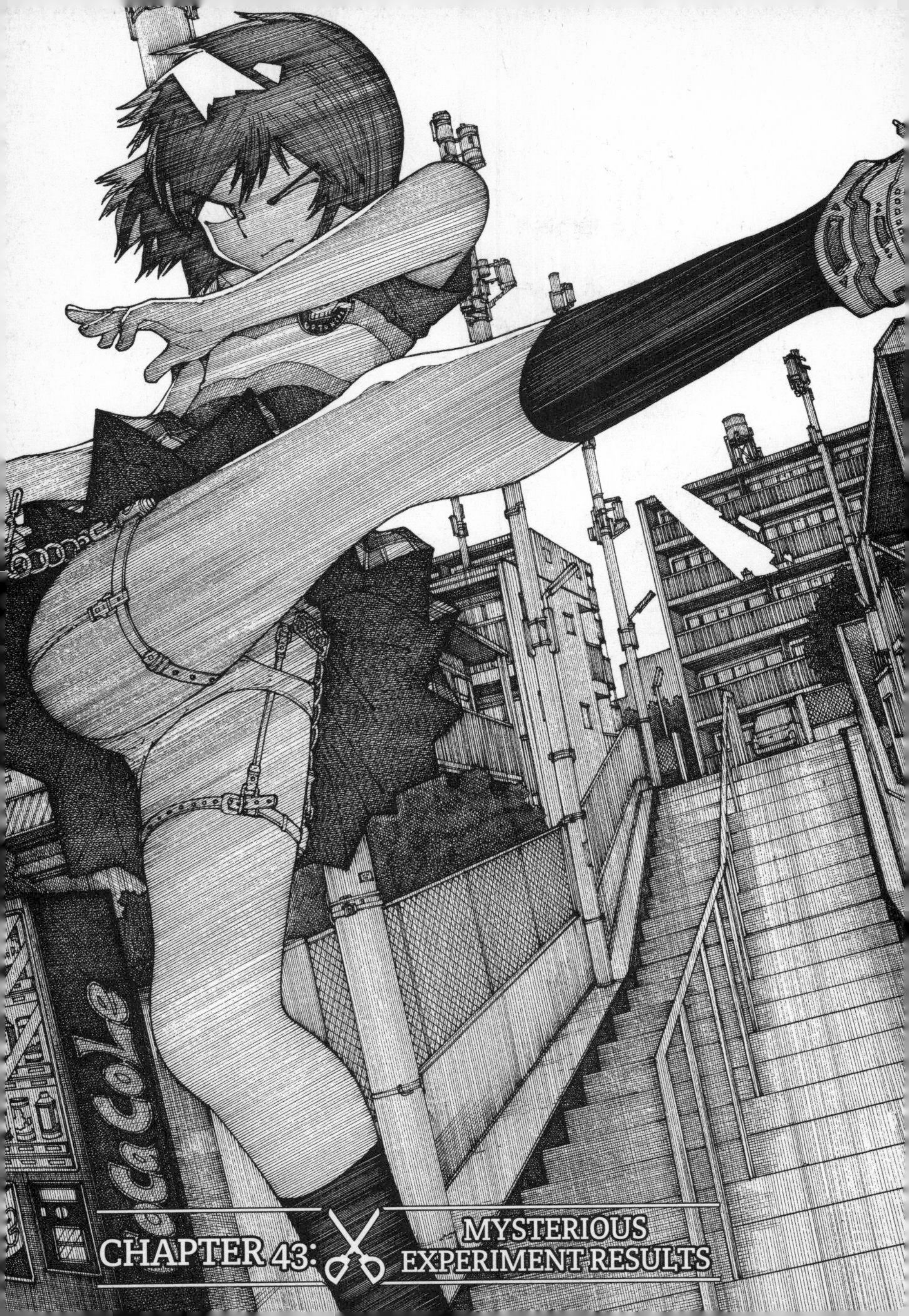

CHAPTER 43: MYSTERIOUS EXPERIMENT RESULTS

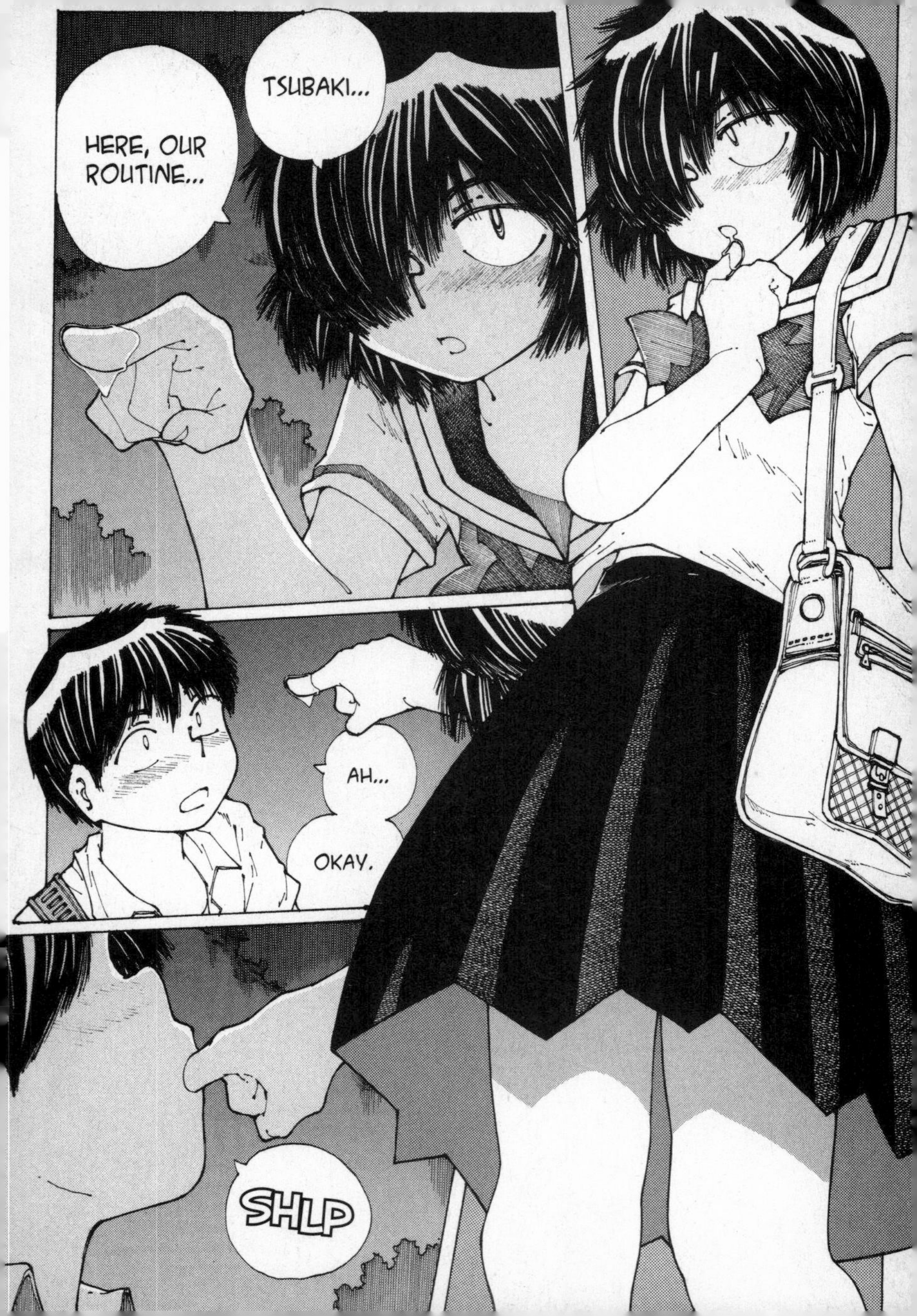
TSUBAKI...
HERE, OUR ROUTINE...
AH...
OKAY.
SHLP

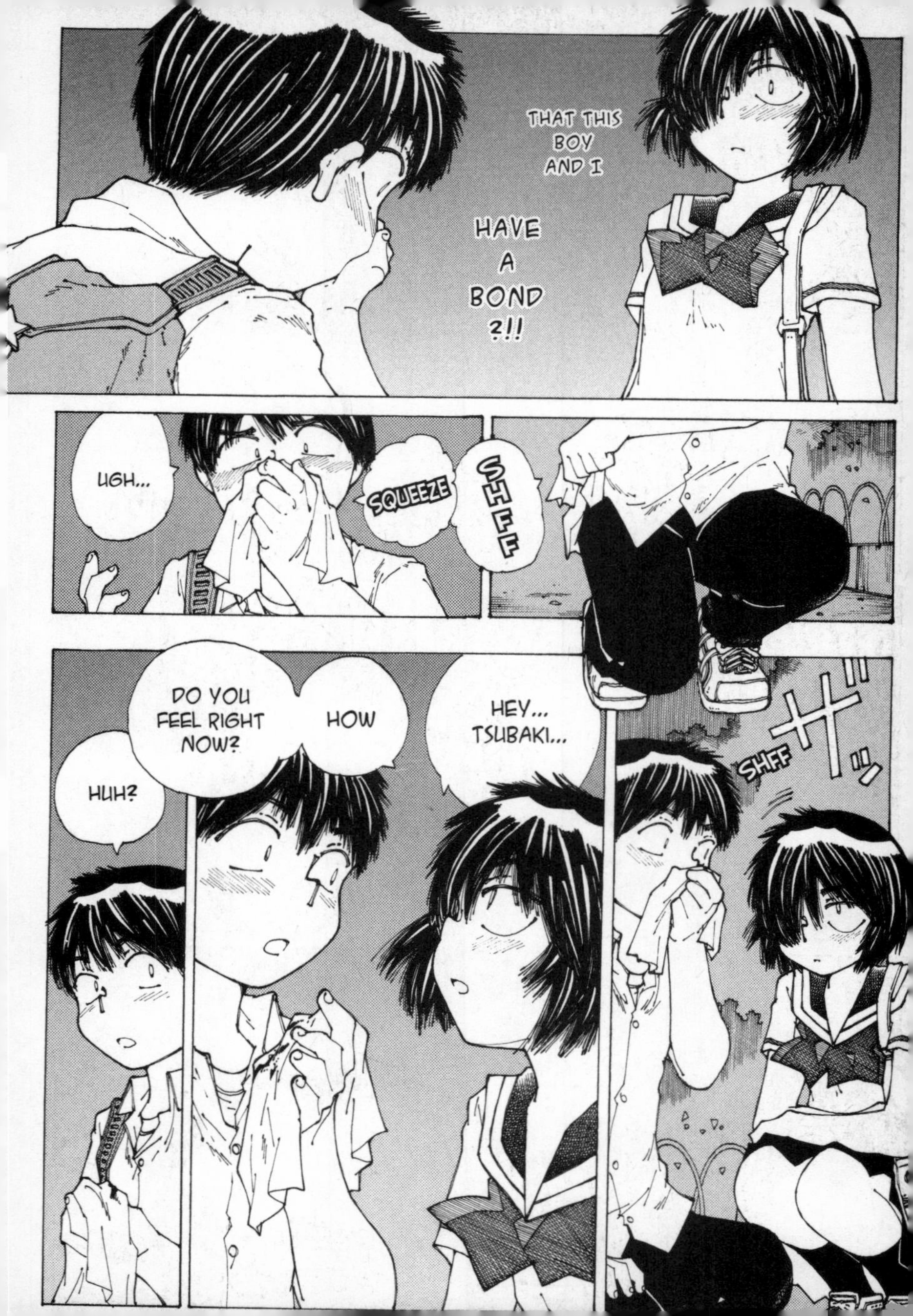
THAT THIS BOY AND I
HAVE A BOND ?!!
SHFF
SQUEEZE
UGH...
SHFF
HEY... TSUBAKI...
HOW
DO YOU FEEL RIGHT NOW?
HUH?

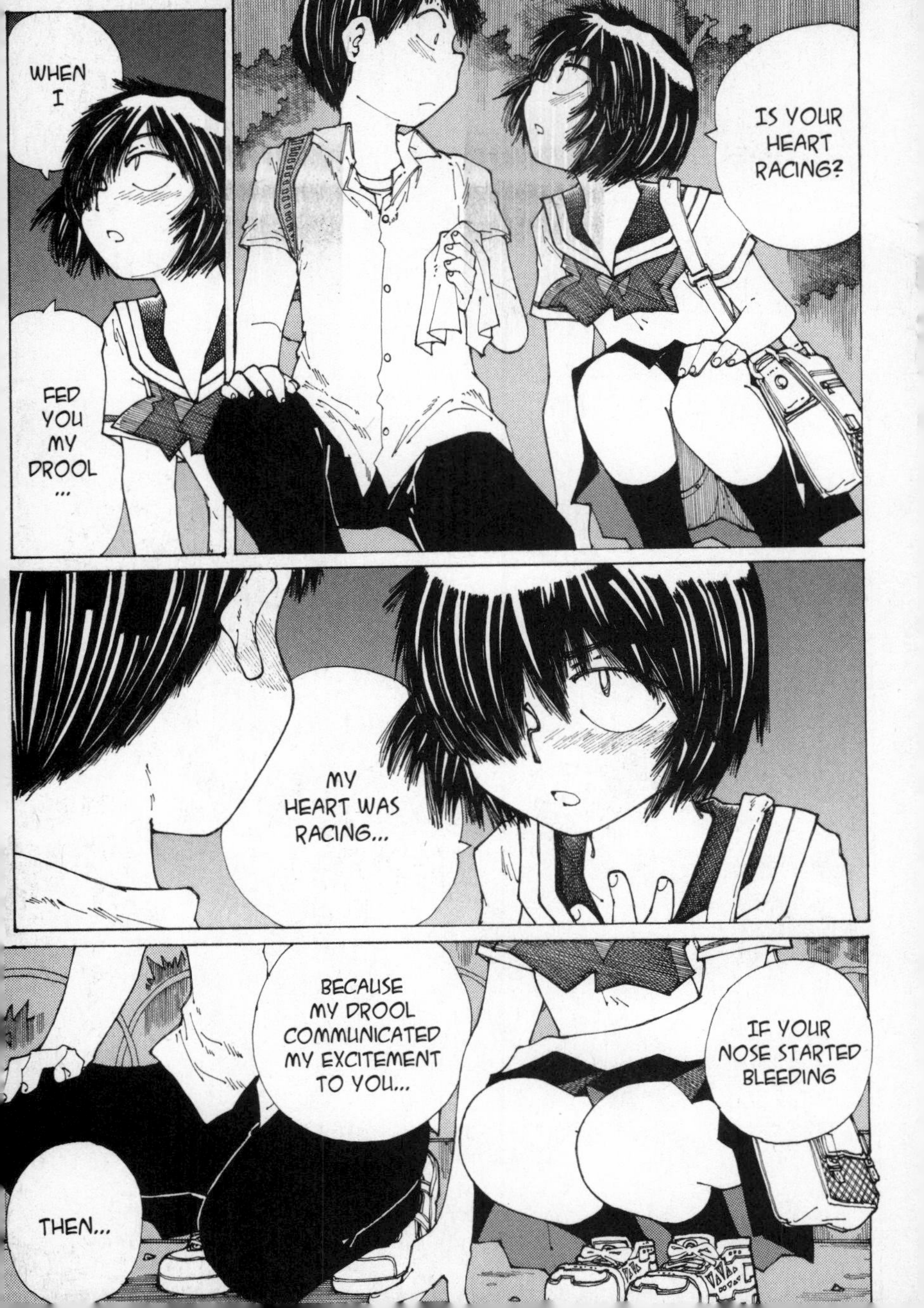
IS YOUR HEART RACING?
WHEN I
FED YOU MY DROOL ...
MY HEART WAS RACING...
IF YOUR NOSE STARTED BLEEDING
BECAUSE MY DROOL COMMUNICATED MY EXCITEMENT TO YOU...
THEN...

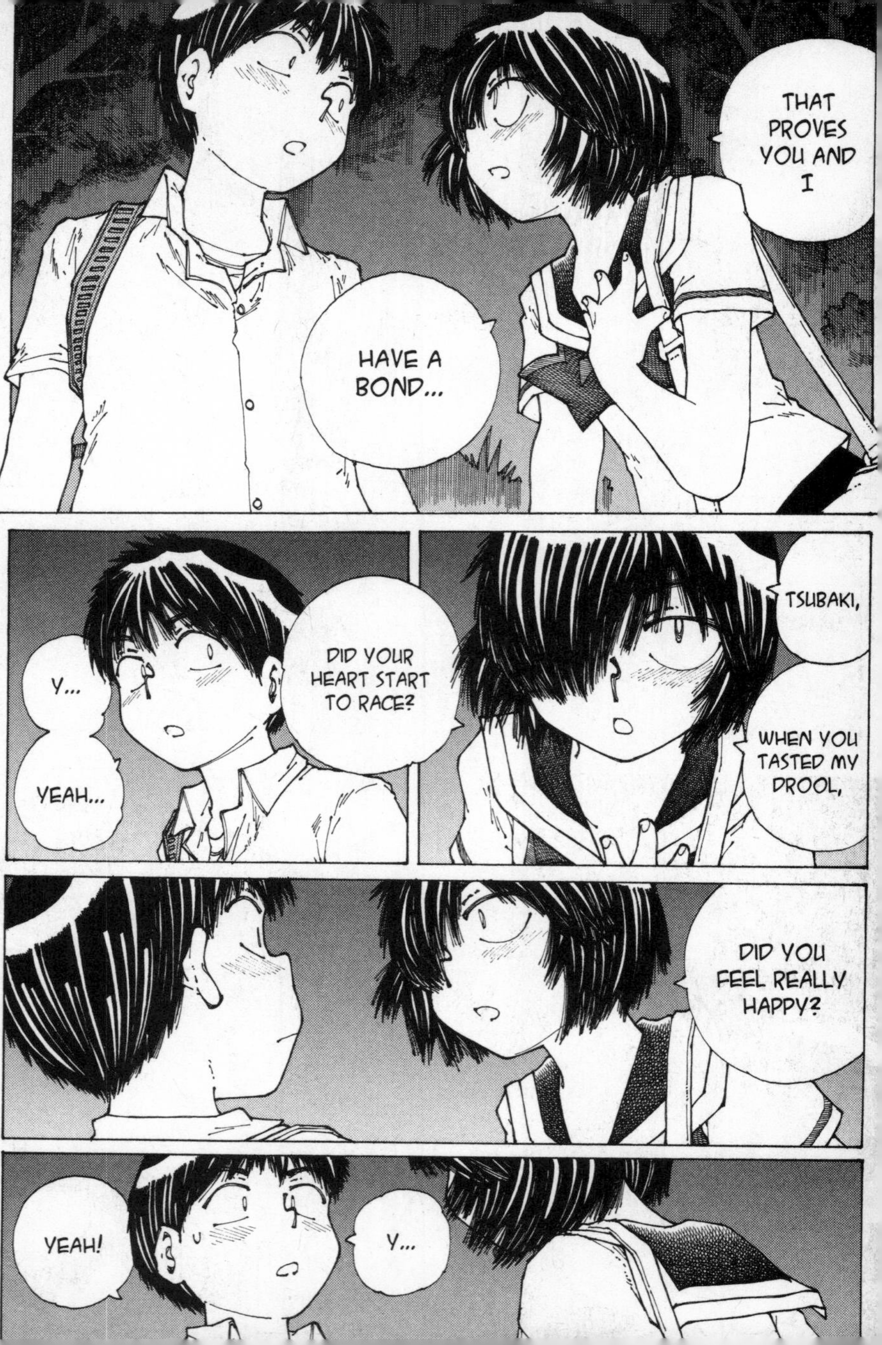
THAT PROVES YOU AND I
HAVE A BOND...
TSUBAKI,
WHEN YOU TASTED MY DROOL,
DID YOUR HEART START TO RACE?
Y...
YEAH...
DID YOU FEEL REALLY HAPPY?
Y...
YEAH!

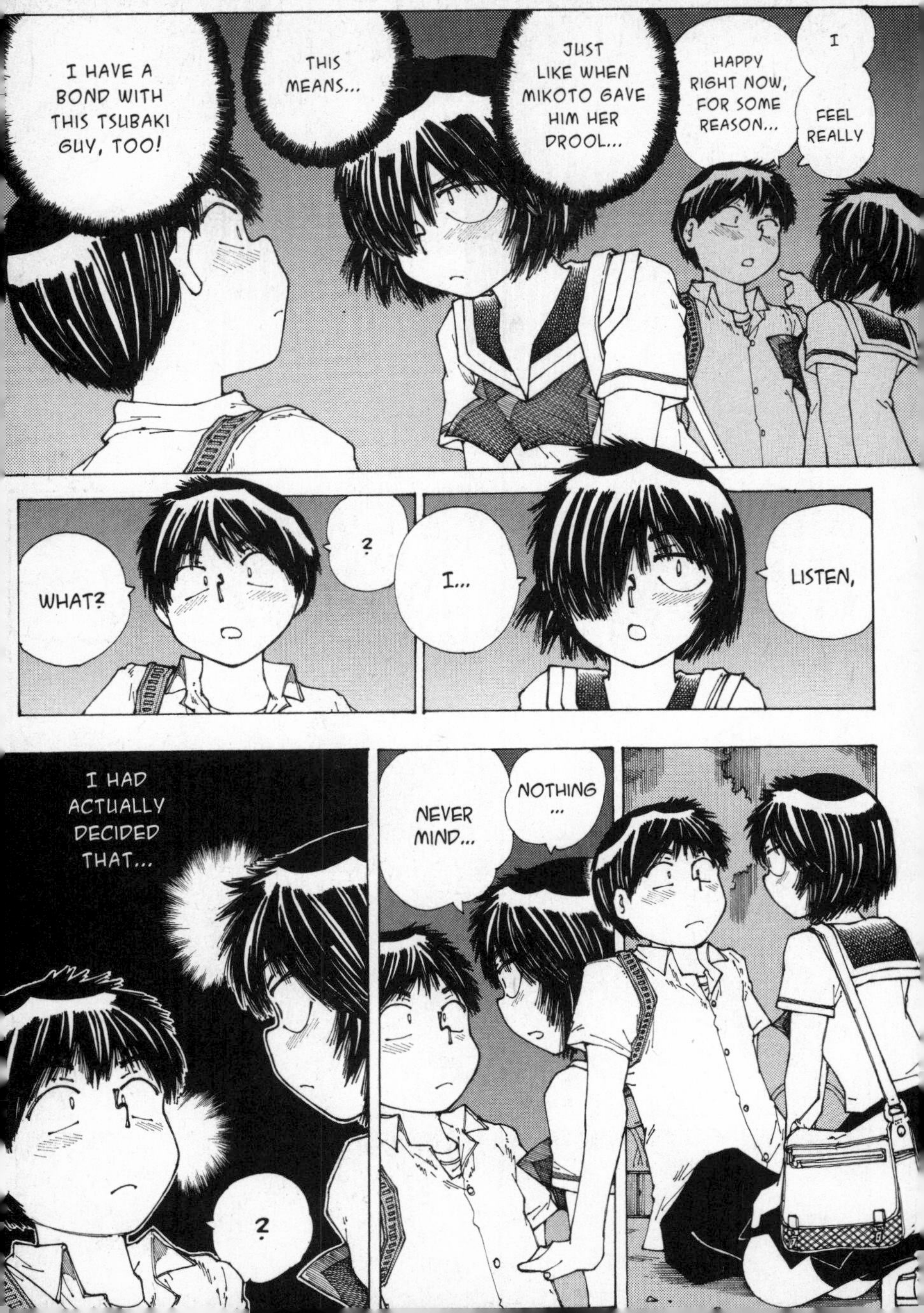
I FEEL REALLY
HAPPY RIGHT NOW, FOR SOME REASON...
JUST LIKE WHEN MIKOTO GAVE HIM HER DROOL...
THIS MEANS...
I HAVE A BOND WITH THIS TSUBAKI GUY, TOO!
LISTEN,
I...
?
WHAT?
NOTHING ...
NEVER MIND...
I HAD ACTUALLY DECIDED THAT...
?

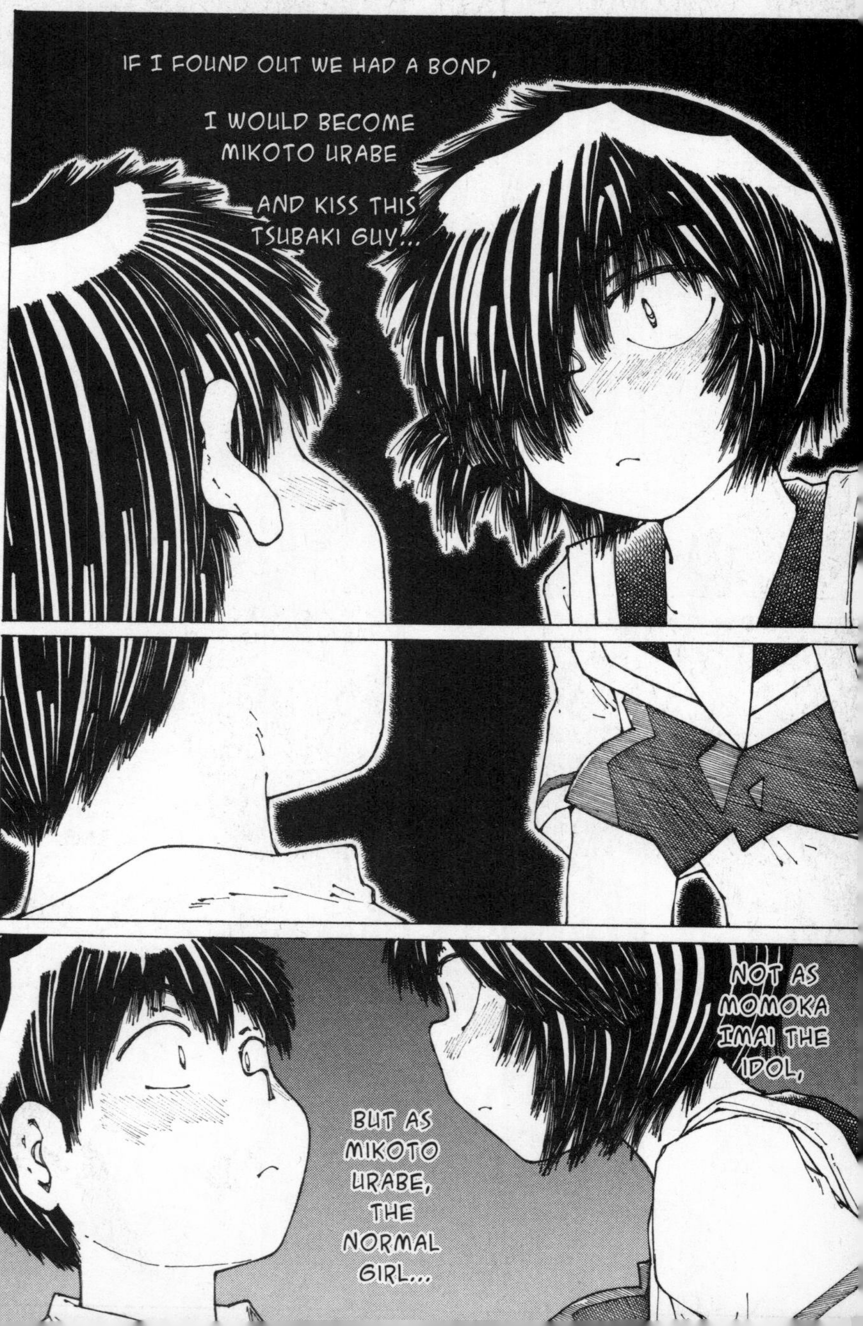
IF I FOUND OUT WE HAD A BOND,
I WOULD BECOME MIKOTO URABE
AND KISS THIS TSUBAKI GUY...
NOT AS MOMOKA IMAI THE IDOL,
BUT AS MIKOTO URABE, THE NORMAL GIRL...

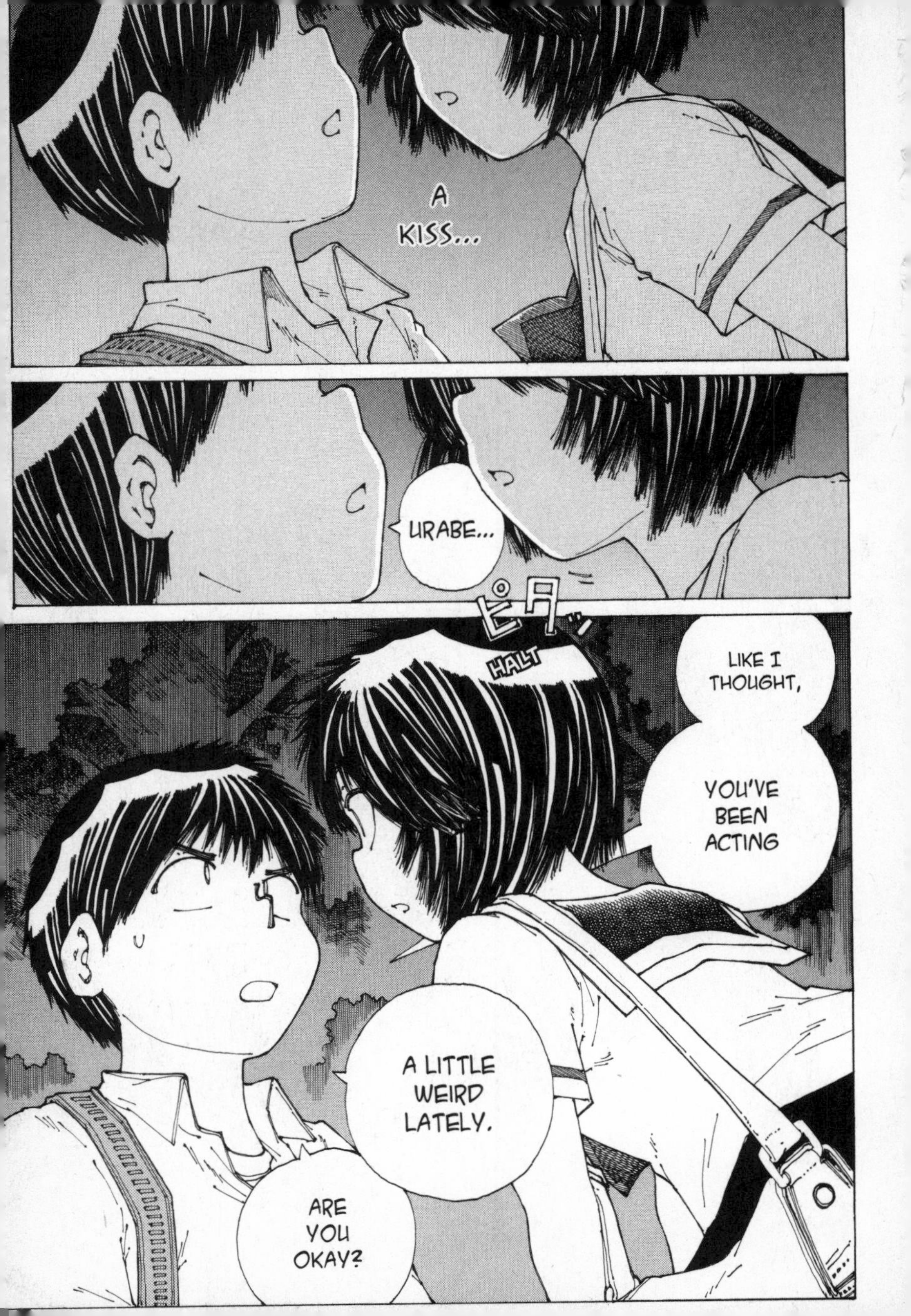
A KISS...
URABE...
ピタッ
HALT
LIKE I THOUGHT,
YOU'VE BEEN ACTING
A LITTLE WEIRD LATELY.
ARE YOU OKAY?

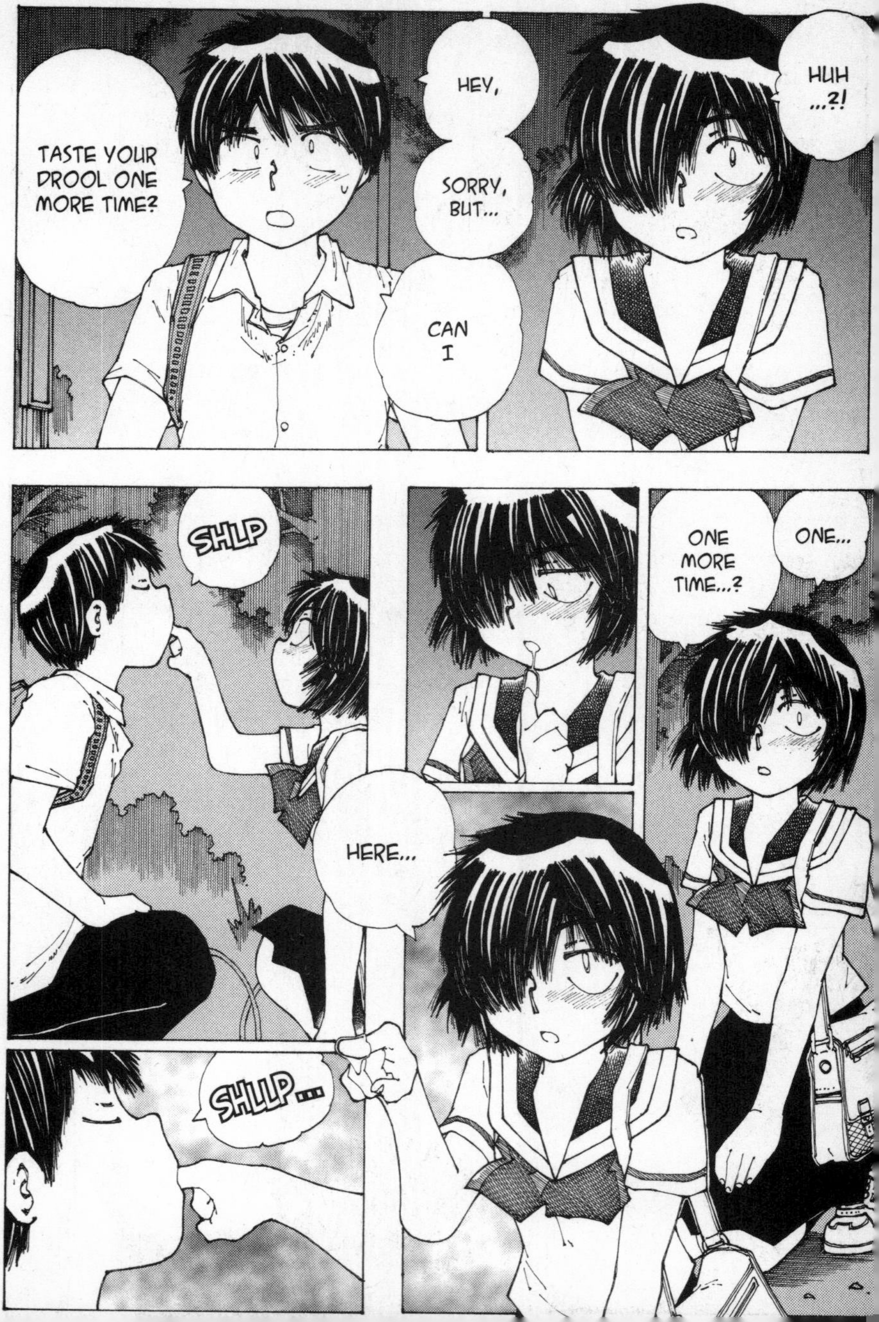
HUH ...?!
HEY,
SORRY, BUT...
CAN I
TASTE YOUR DROOL ONE MORE TIME?
ONE...
ONE MORE TIME...?
HERE...
SHLP
SHLLP...

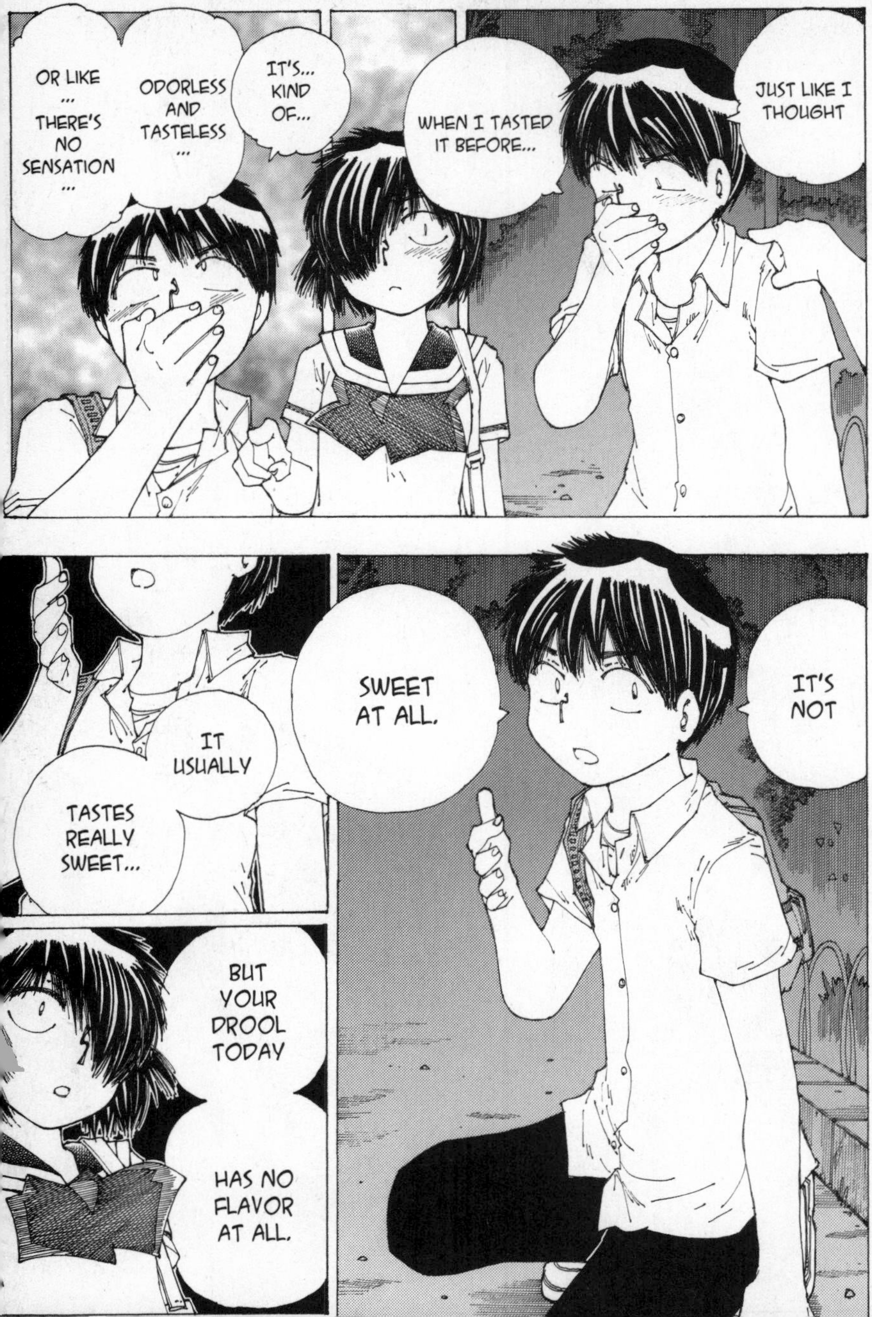
JUST LIKE I THOUGHT
WHEN I TASTED IT BEFORE...
IT'S... KIND OF...
ODORLESS AND TASTELESS ...
OR LIKE ... THERE'S NO SENSATION ...
IT'S NOT
SWEET AT ALL.
IT USUALLY
TASTES REALLY SWEET...
BUT YOUR DROOL TODAY
HAS NO FLAVOR AT ALL.

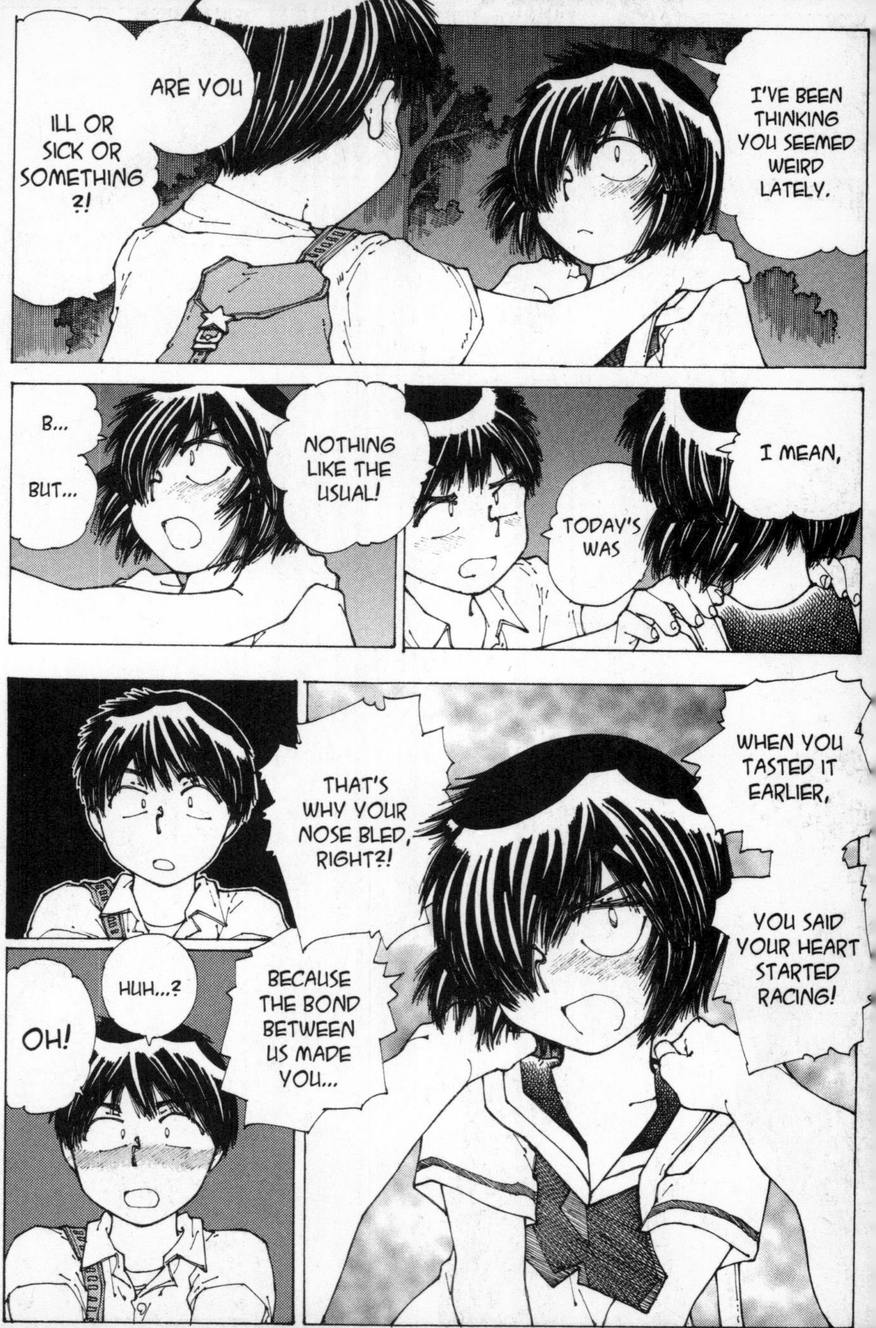
I'VE BEEN THINKING YOU SEEMED WEIRD LATELY.
ARE YOU ILL OR SICK OR SOMETHING?!
I MEAN,
TODAY'S WAS
NOTHING LIKE THE USUAL!
B... BUT...
WHEN YOU TASTED IT EARLIER,
YOU SAID YOUR HEART STARTED RACING!
THAT'S WHY YOUR NOSE BLED, RIGHT?!
BECAUSE THE BOND BETWEEN US MADE YOU...
HUH...?
OH!

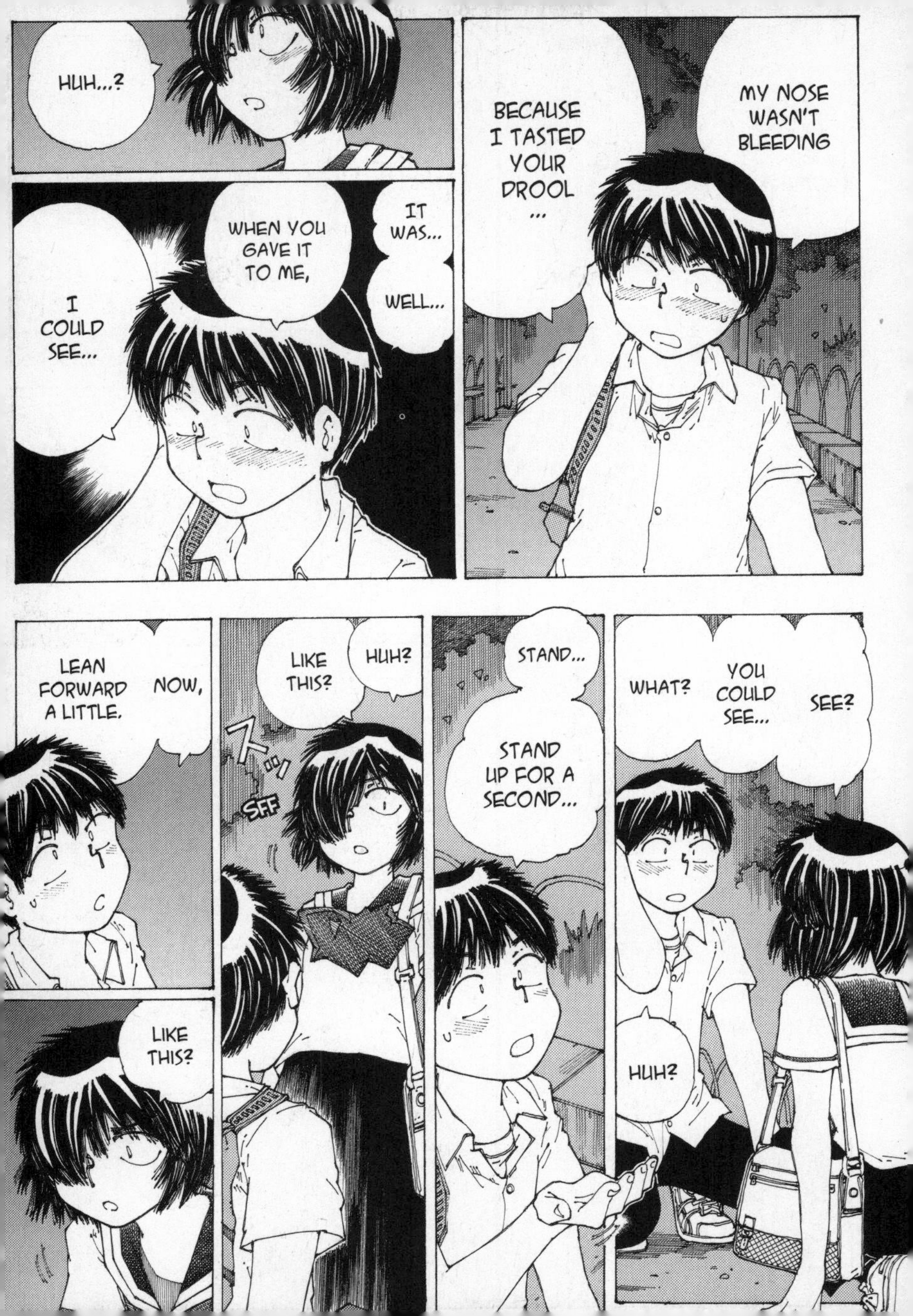
MY NOSE WASN'T BLEEDING
BECAUSE I TASTED YOUR DROOL ...
HUH...?
IT WAS...
WELL...
WHEN YOU GAVE IT TO ME,
I COULD SEE...
SEE?
YOU COULD SEE...
WHAT?
HUH?
STAND...
STAND UP FOR A SECOND...
HUH?
LIKE THIS?
SFF
NOW,
LEAN FORWARD A LITTLE.
LIKE THIS?

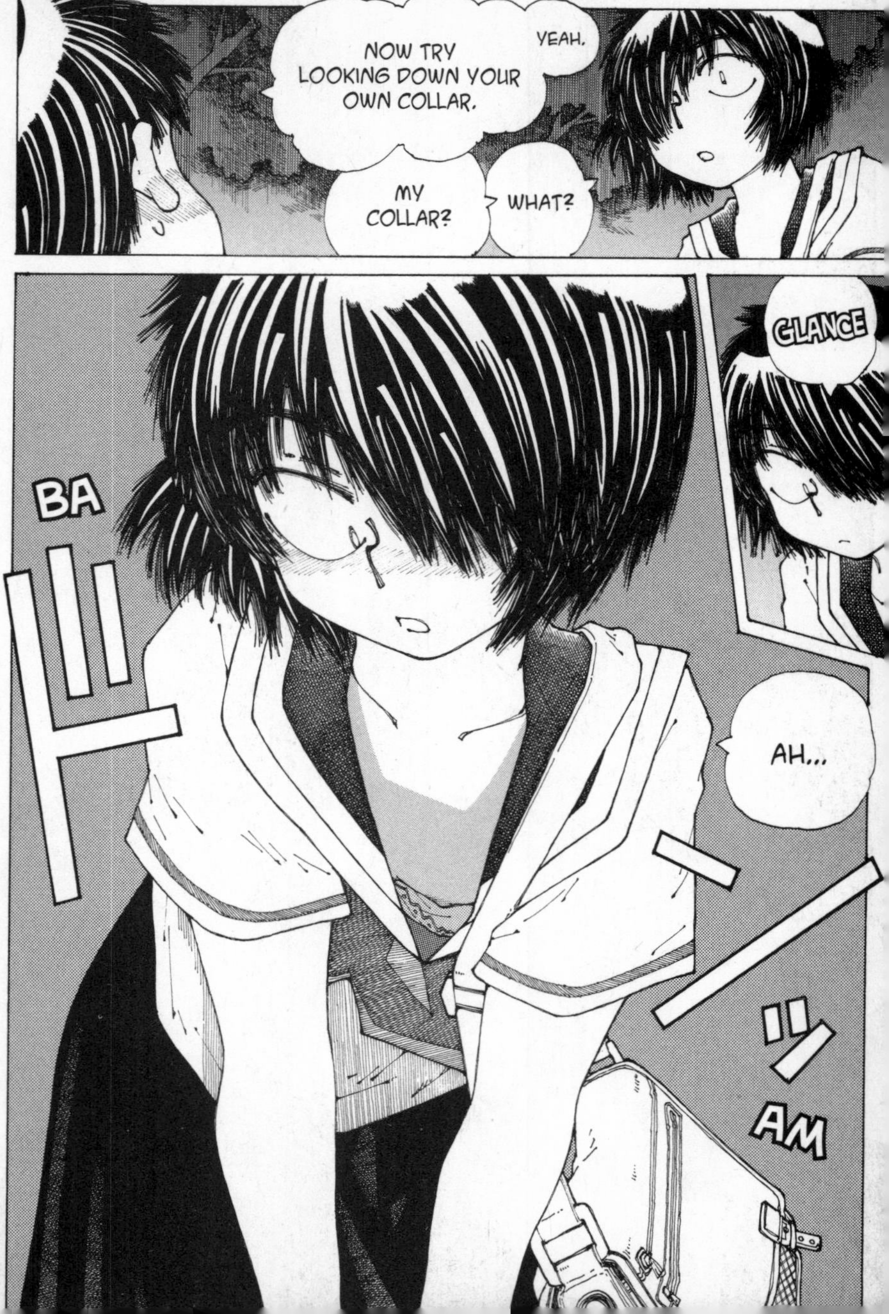
YEAH.
NOW TRY LOOKING DOWN YOUR OWN COLLAR.
WHAT?
MY COLLAR?
GLANCE
AH...
BA
AM

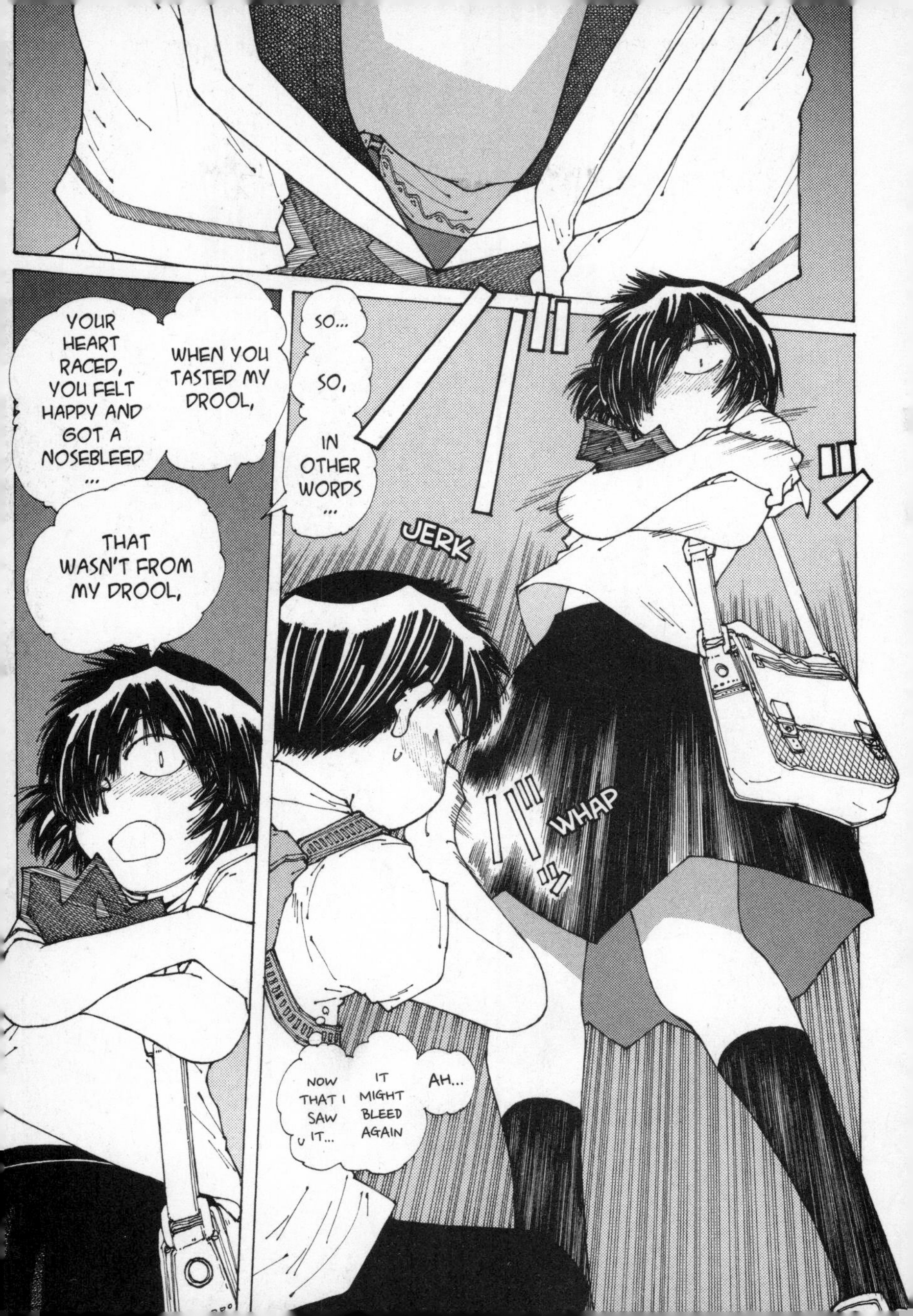
SO...
SO,
IN OTHER WORDS...
JERK
WHAP
AH...
IT MIGHT BLEED AGAIN
NOW THAT I SAW IT...
WHEN YOU TASTED MY DROOL,
YOUR HEART RACED, YOU FELT HAPPY AND GOT A NOSEBLEED...
THAT WASN'T FROM MY DROOL,

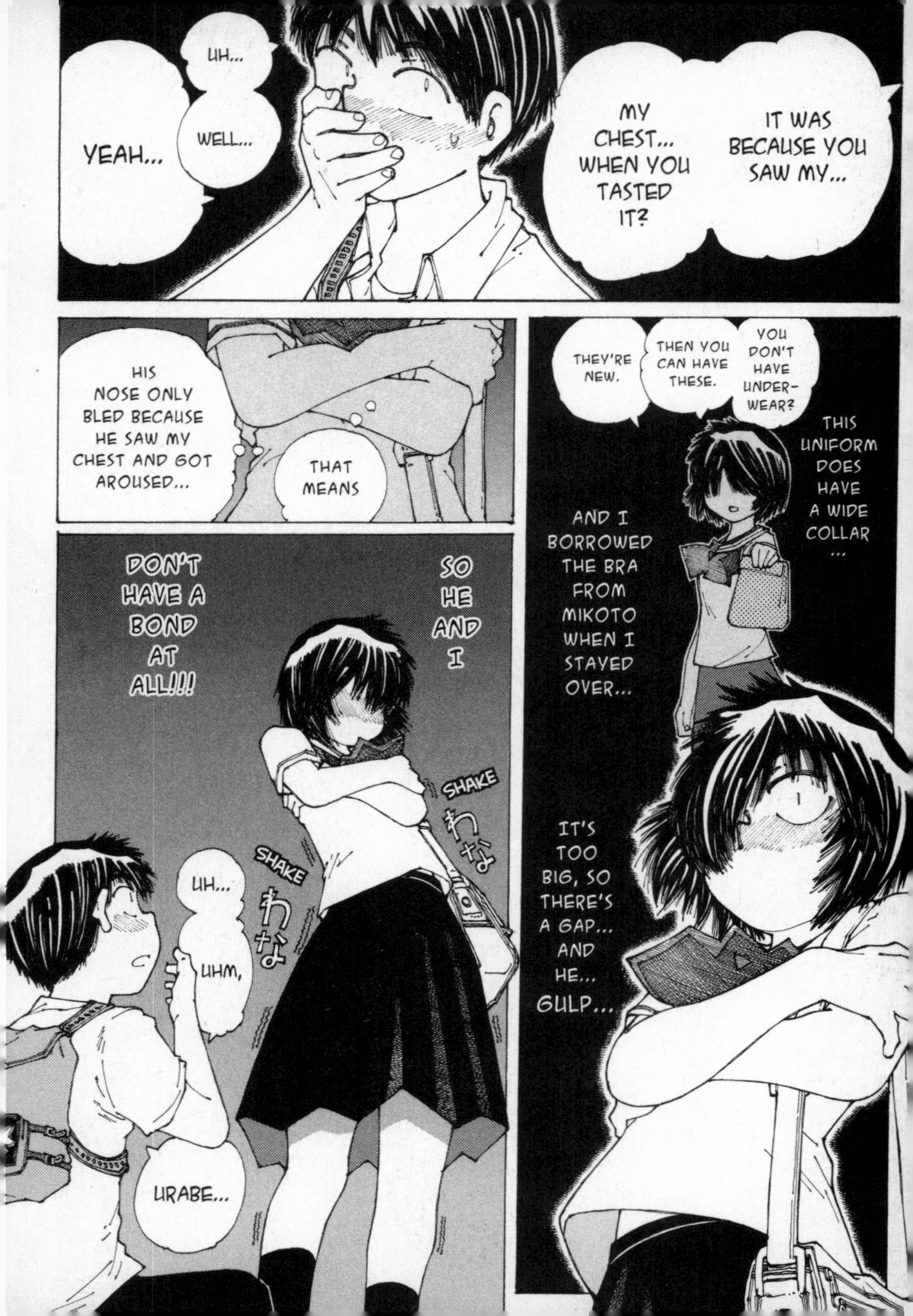
IT WAS BECAUSE YOU SAW MY...
MY CHEST... WHEN YOU TASTED IT?
UH...
WELL...
YEAH...
YOU DON'T HAVE UNDER-WEAR?
THEN YOU CAN HAVE THESE.
THEY'RE NEW.
THIS UNIFORM DOES HAVE A WIDE COLLAR...
AND I BORROWED THE BRA FROM MIKOTO WHEN I STAYED OVER...
IT'S TOO BIG, SO THERE'S A GAP... AND HE... GULP...
THAT MEANS
HIS NOSE ONLY BLED BECAUSE HE SAW MY CHEST AND GOT AROUSED...
SO HE AND I
DON'T HAVE A BOND AT ALL!!!
SHAKE
わな
SHAKE
わな
UH...
UHM,
URABE...

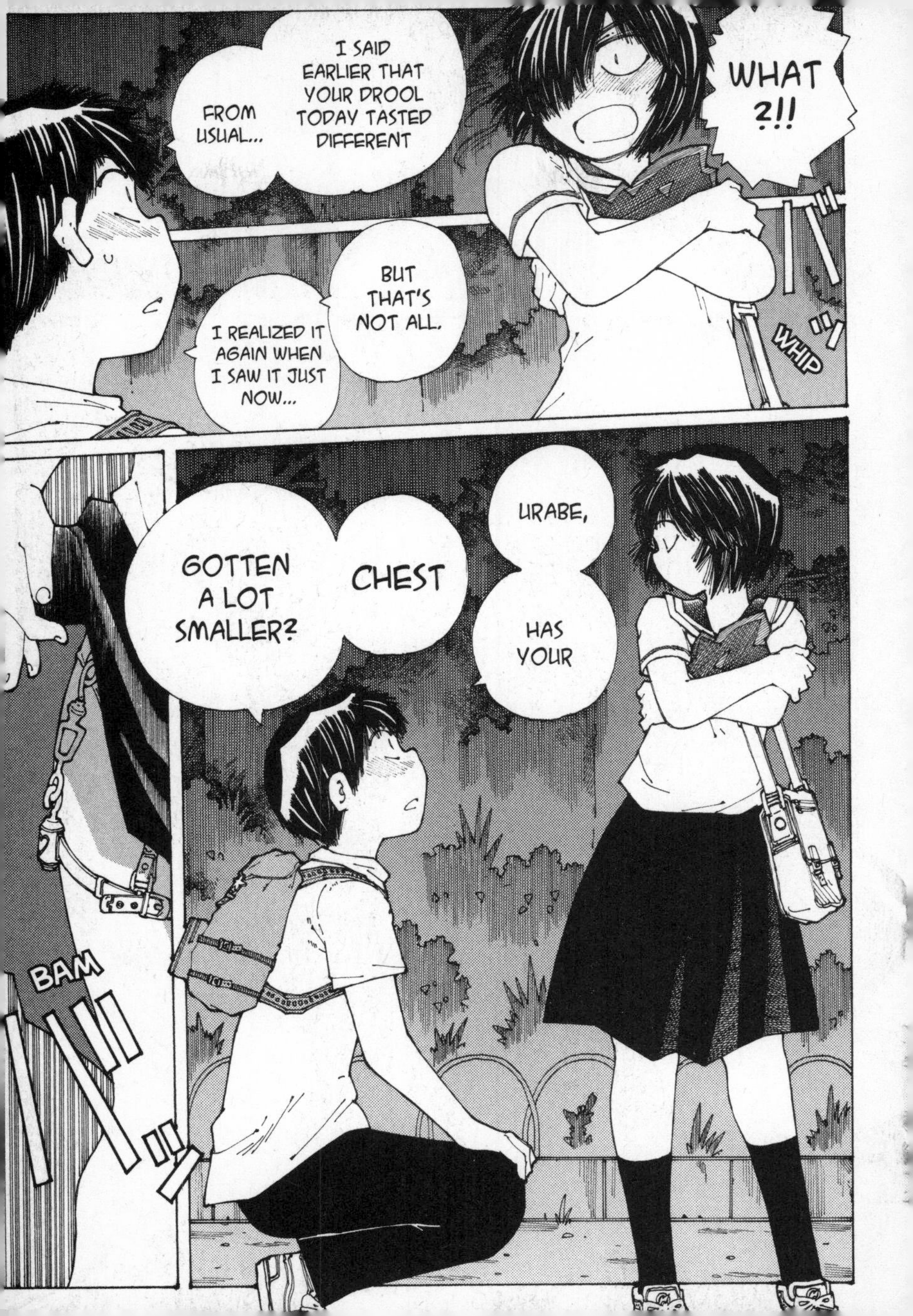
WHAT ?!!
WHIP
I SAID EARLIER THAT YOUR DROOL TODAY TASTED DIFFERENT
FROM USUAL...
BUT THAT'S NOT ALL.
I REALIZED IT AGAIN WHEN I SAW IT JUST NOW...
URABE,
HAS YOUR
CHEST
GOTTEN A LOT SMALLER?
BAM

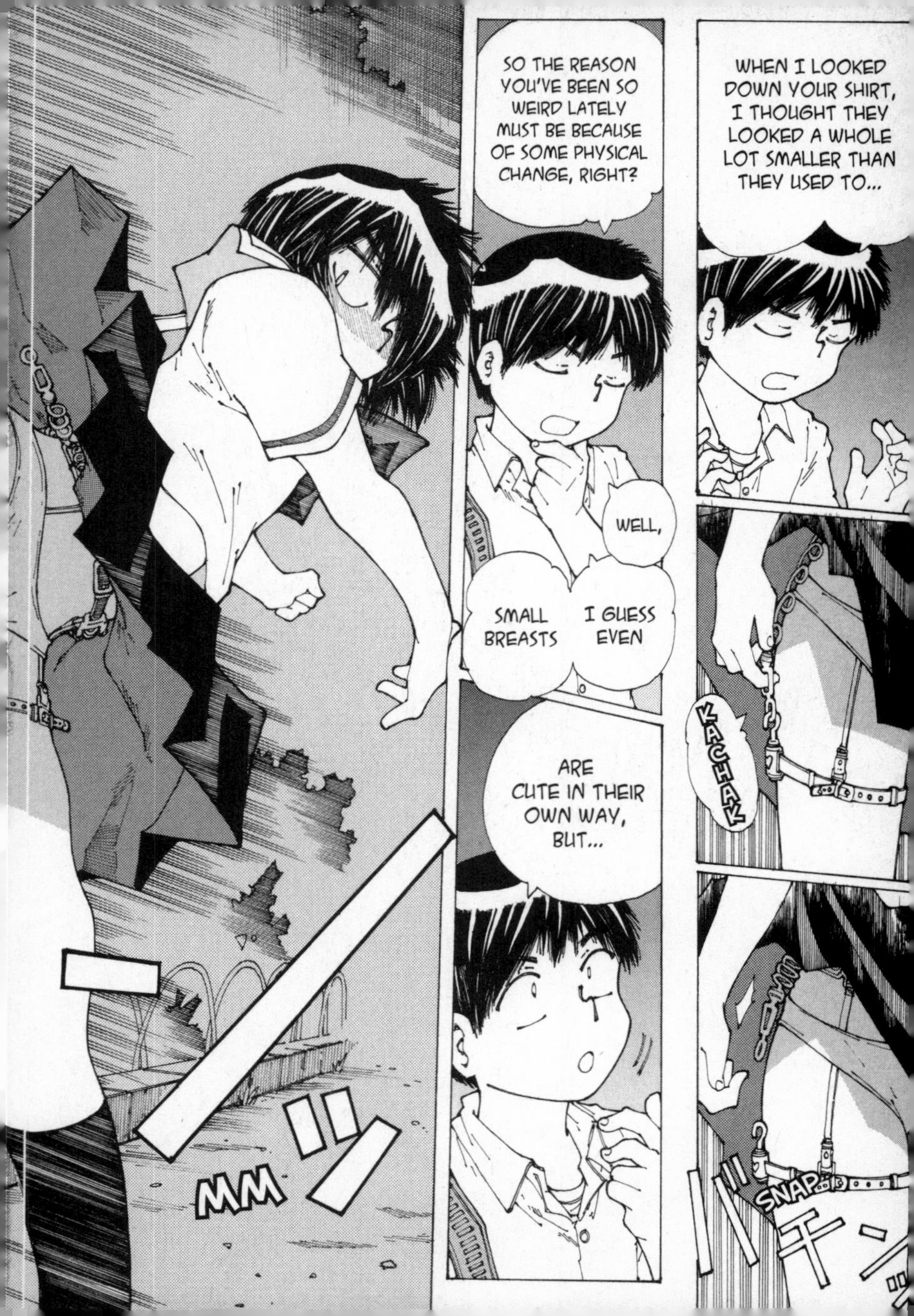
WHEN I LOOKED DOWN YOUR SHIRT, I THOUGHT THEY LOOKED A WHOLE LOT SMALLER THAN THEY USED TO...
KACHAK
SNAP
SO THE REASON YOU'VE BEEN SO WEIRD LATELY MUST BE BECAUSE OF SOME PHYSICAL CHANGE, RIGHT?
WELL,
I GUESS EVEN
SMALL BREASTS
ARE CUTE IN THEIR OWN WAY, BUT...
MM

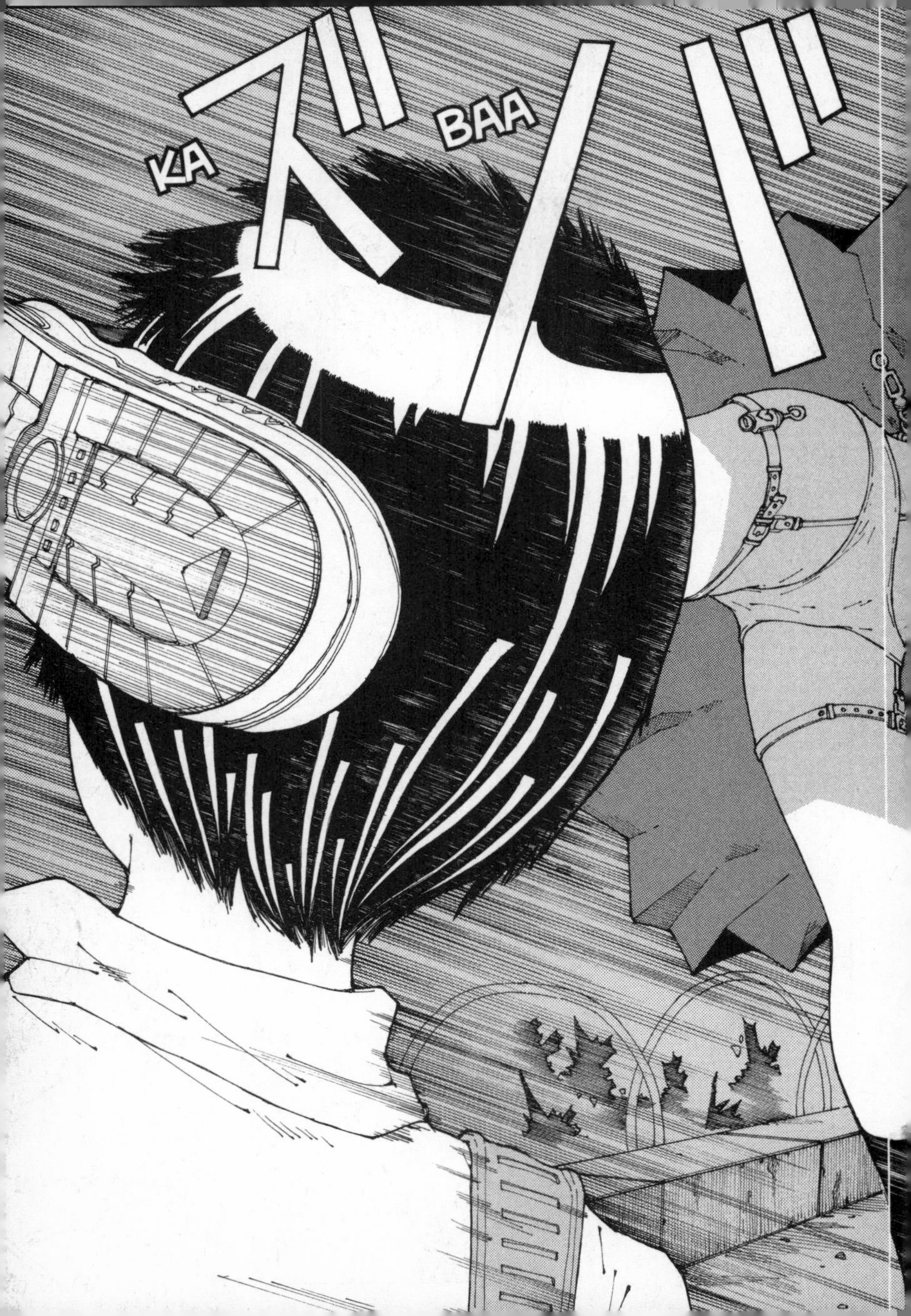
KA
BAA

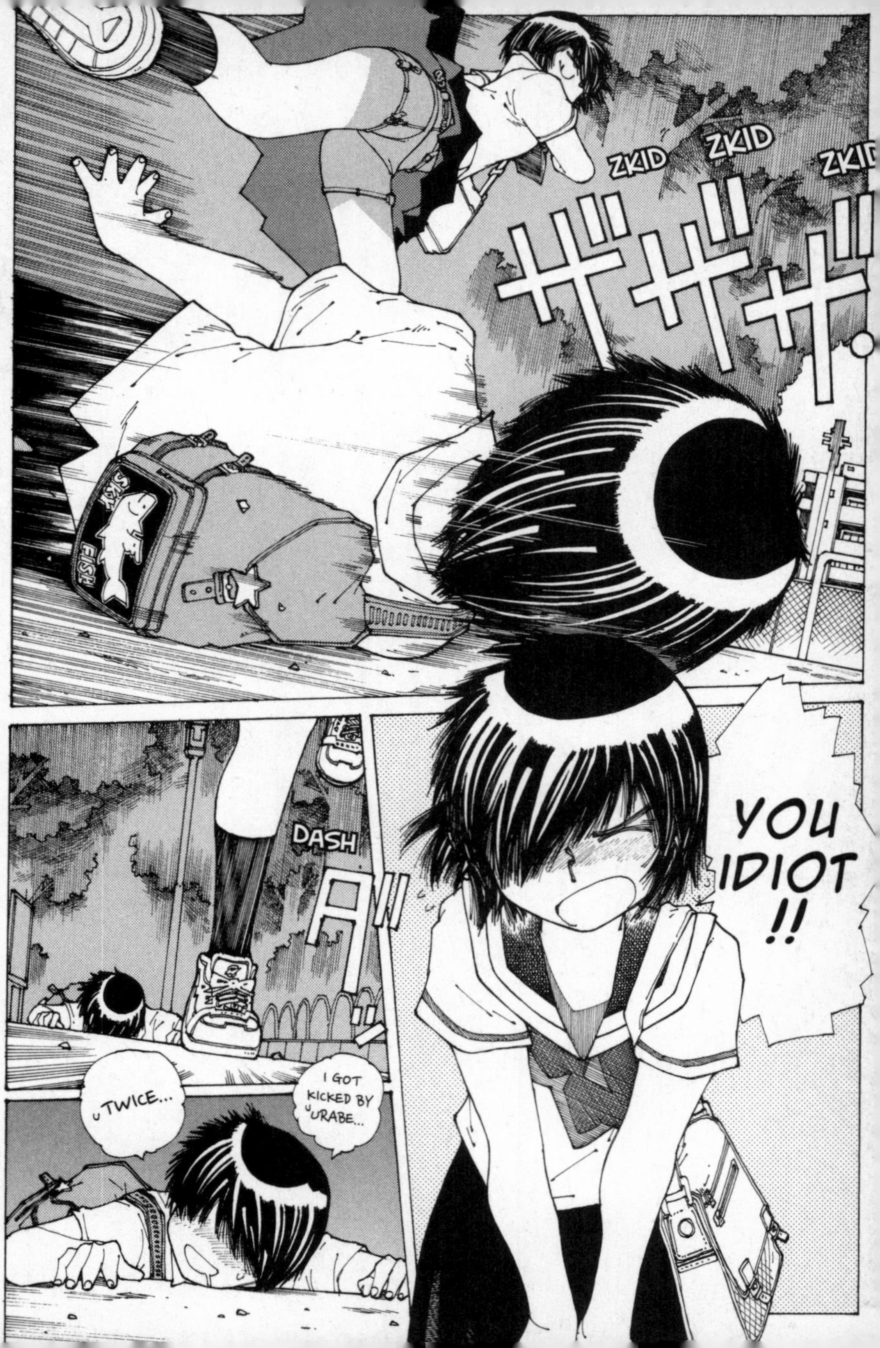
ZKID ZKID ZKID
ザザザ
YOU IDIOT !!
DASH
I GOT KICKED BY URABE...
TWICE...

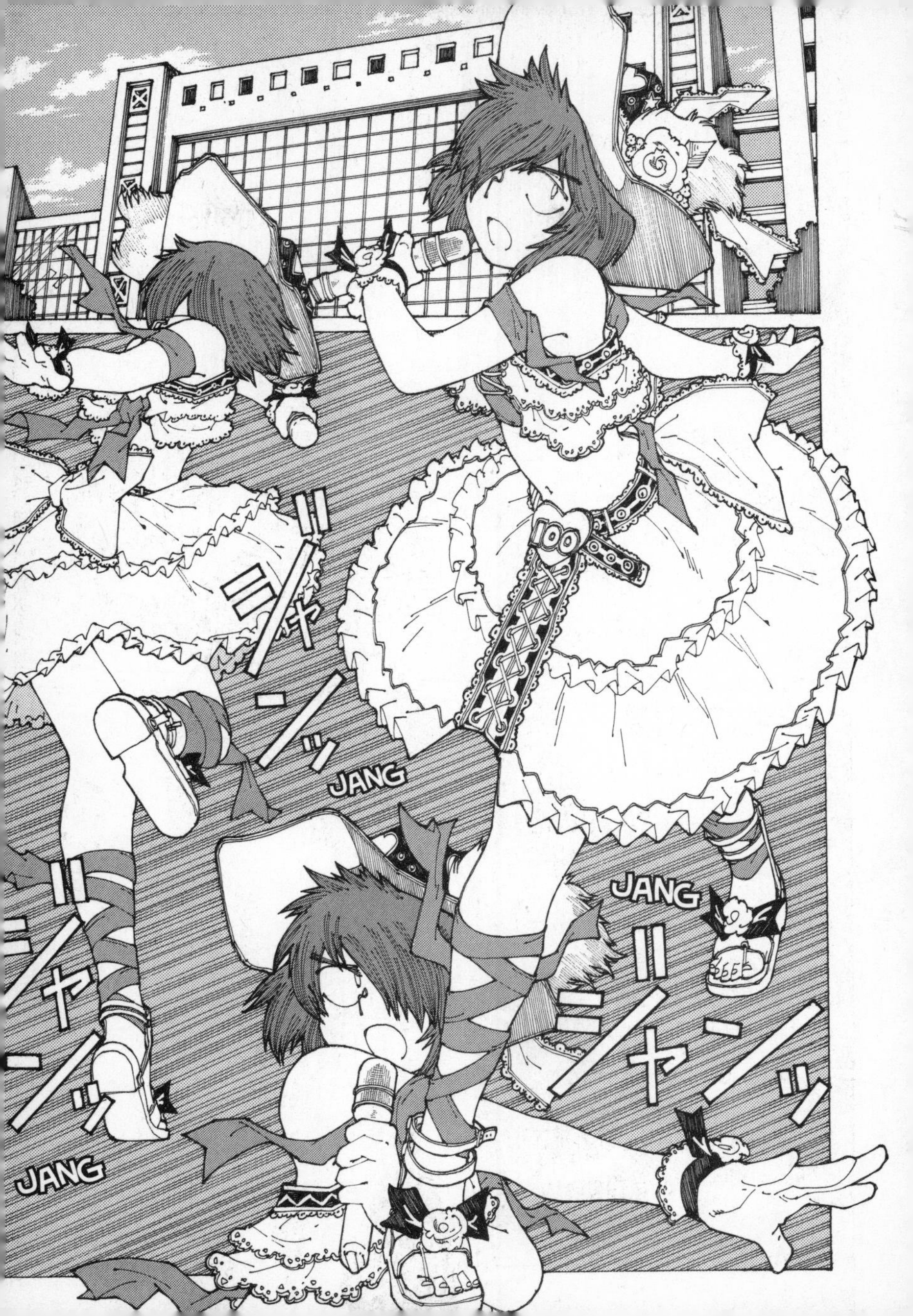
JANG
JANG
JANG

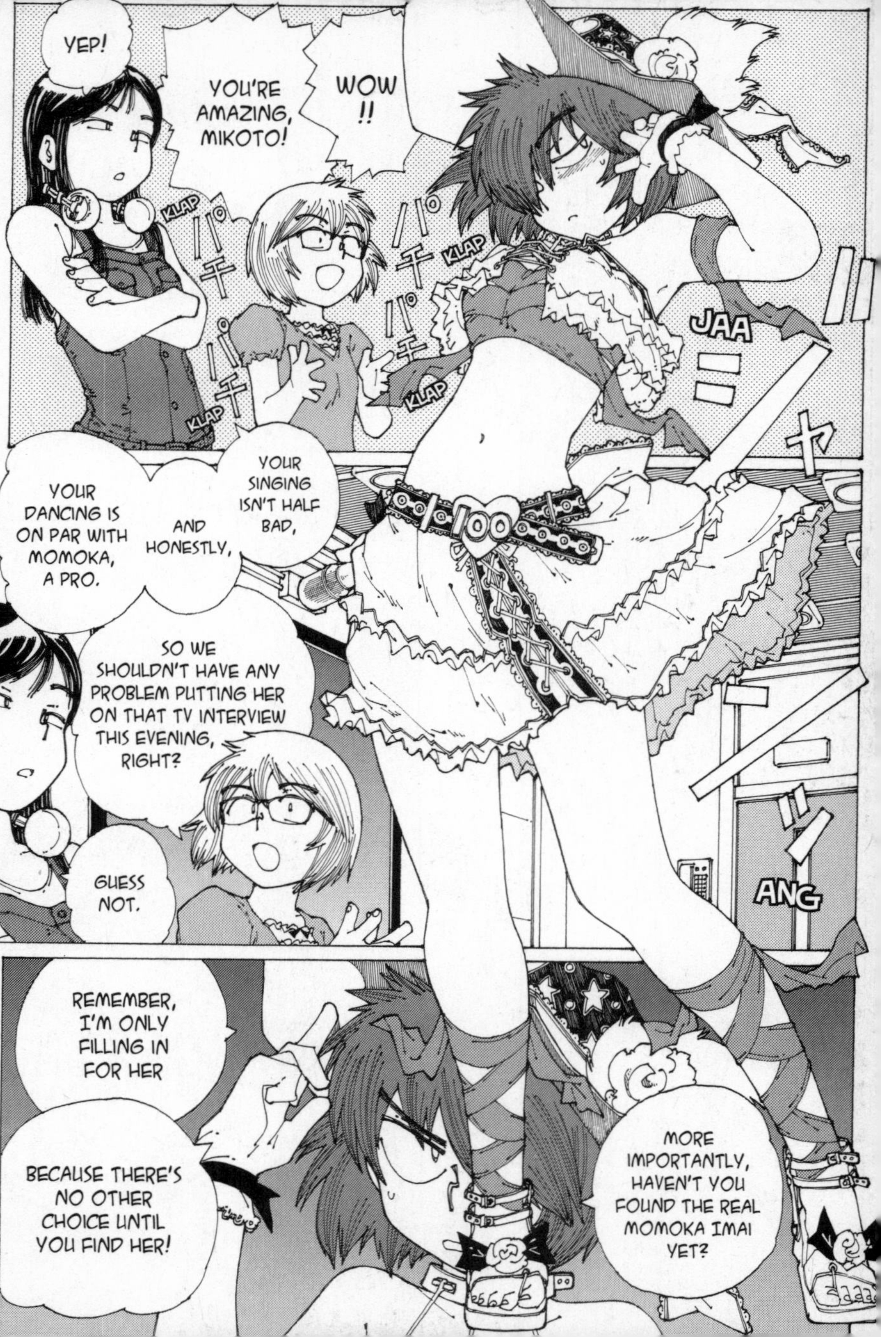
WOW !!
YOU'RE AMAZING, MIKOTO!
YEP!
KLAP
KLAP
KLAP
KLAP
JAA
ANG
YOUR SINGING ISN'T HALF BAD,
AND HONESTLY,
YOUR DANCING IS ON PAR WITH MOMOKA, A PRO.
SO WE SHOULDN'T HAVE ANY PROBLEM PUTTING HER ON THAT TV INTERVIEW THIS EVENING, RIGHT?
GUESS NOT.
MORE IMPORTANTLY, HAVEN'T YOU FOUND THE REAL MOMOKA IMAI YET?
REMEMBER, I'M ONLY FILLING IN FOR HER
BECAUSE THERE'S NO OTHER CHOICE UNTIL YOU FIND HER!

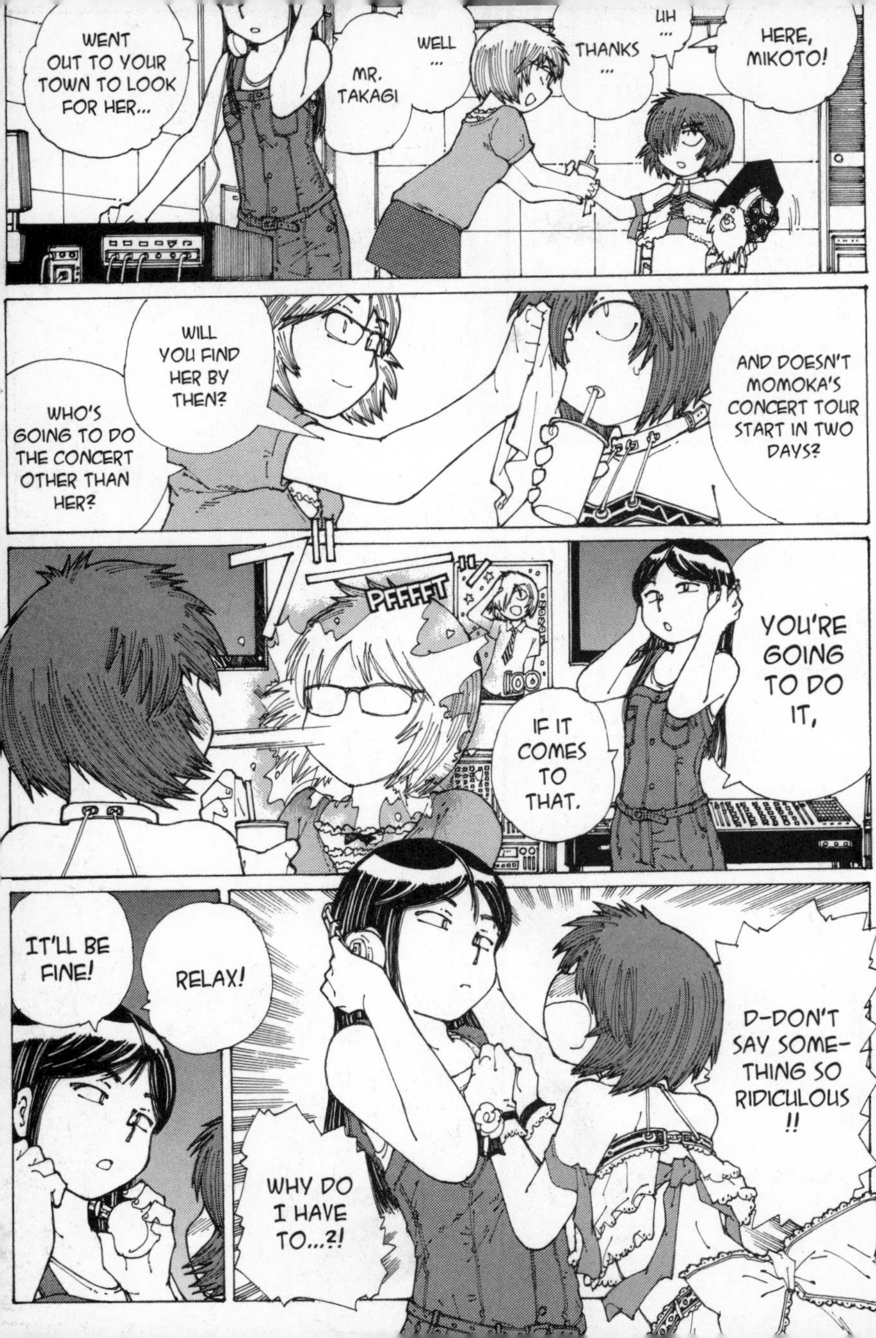
HERE, MIKOTO!
UH ...
THANKS ...
WELL ...
MR. TAKAGI
WENT OUT TO YOUR TOWN TO LOOK FOR HER...
AND DOESN'T MOMOKA'S CONCERT TOUR START IN TWO DAYS?
WILL YOU FIND HER BY THEN?
WHO'S GOING TO DO THE CONCERT OTHER THAN HER?
YOU'RE GOING TO DO IT,
PFFFFT
IF IT COMES TO THAT.
D-DON'T SAY SOME-THING SO RIDICULOUS !!
WHY DO I HAVE TO...?!
RELAX!
IT'LL BE FINE!

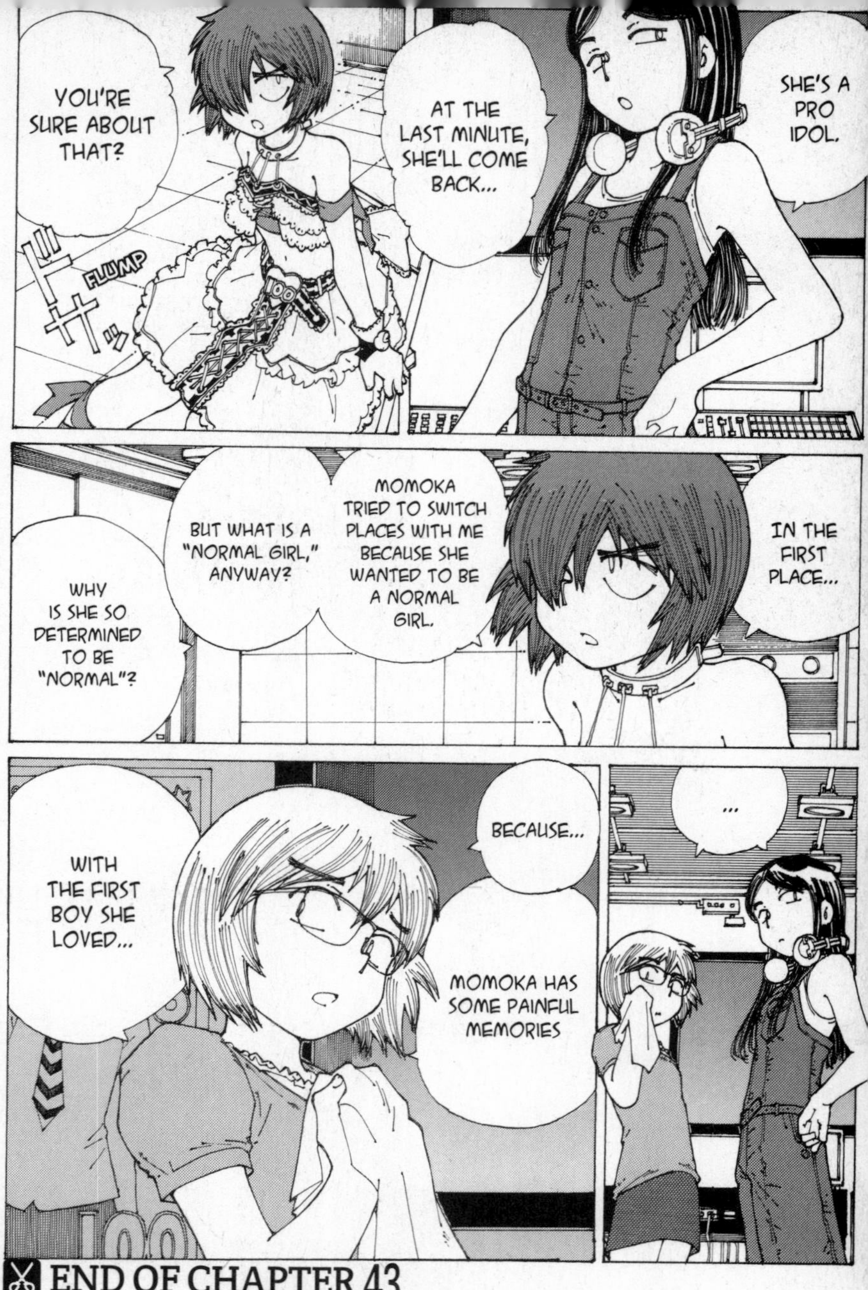
SHE'S A PRO IDOL.
AT THE LAST MINUTE, SHE'LL COME BACK...
YOU'RE SURE ABOUT THAT?
FLUMP
IN THE FIRST PLACE...
MOMOKA TRIED TO SWITCH PLACES WITH ME BECAUSE SHE WANTED TO BE A NORMAL GIRL.
BUT WHAT IS A "NORMAL GIRL," ANYWAY?
WHY IS SHE SO DETERMINED TO BE "NORMAL"?
...
BECAUSE...
MOMOKA HAS SOME PAINFUL MEMORIES
WITH THE FIRST BOY SHE LOVED...

END OF CHAPTER 43

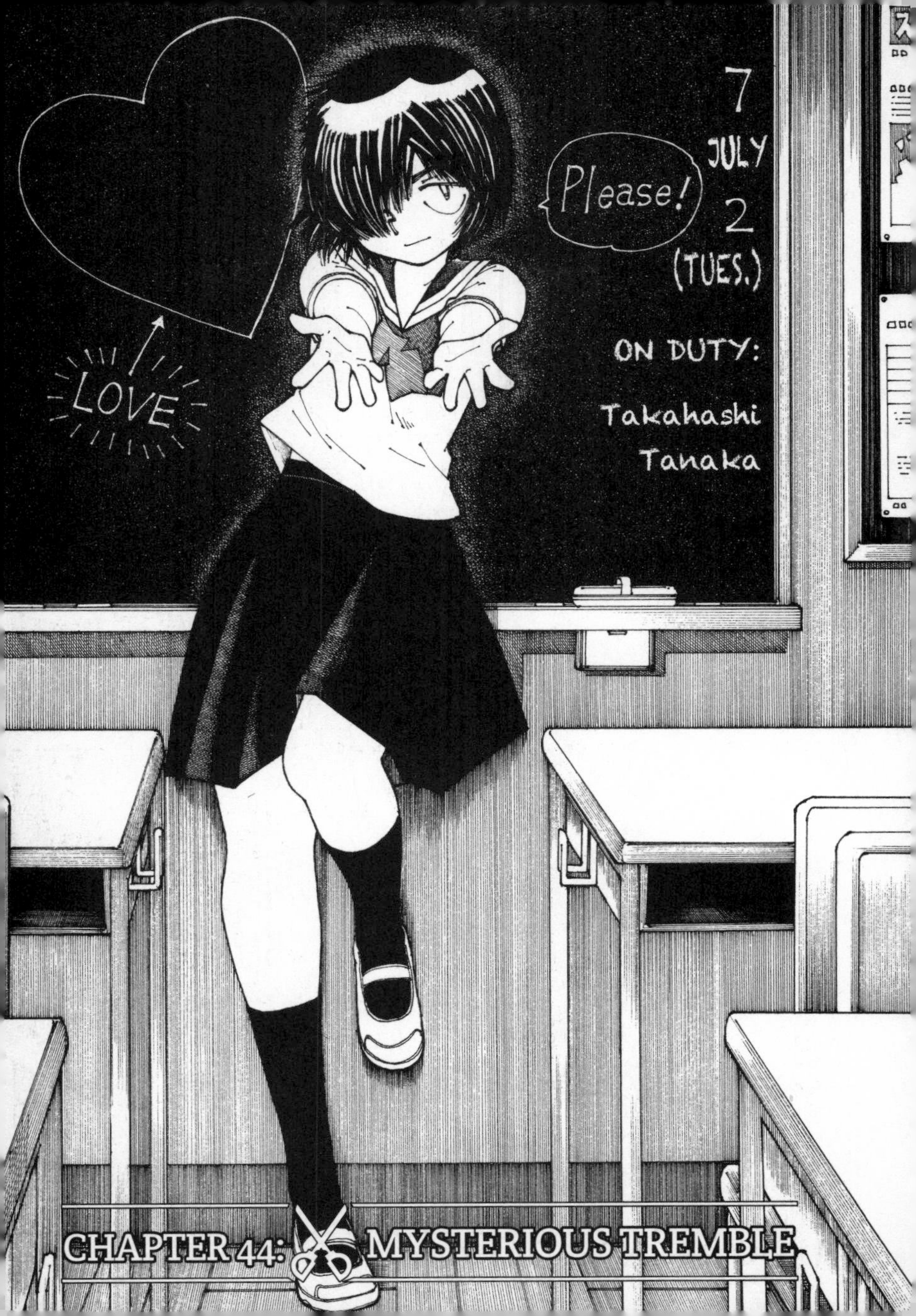
Please!
7
JULY
2
(TUES.)
ON DUTY:
Takahashi
Tanaka
LOVE
CHAPTER 44: MYSTERIOUS TREMBLE

BUT WHAT IS A "NORMAL GIRL," ANYWAY?

MOMOKA TRIED TO SWITCH PLACES WITH ME BECAUSE SHE WANTED TO BE A NORMAL GIRL.

IN THE FIRST PLACE...

WHY IS SHE SO DETERMINED TO BE "NORMAL"?

BEFORE MOMOKA

BECAME AN IDOL,

OR IN OTHER WORDS, WHEN SHE WAS A "NORMAL GIRL"...

MOMOKA HAS SOME PAINFUL MEMORIES

WITH THE FIRST BOY SHE LOVED...

BECAUSE...

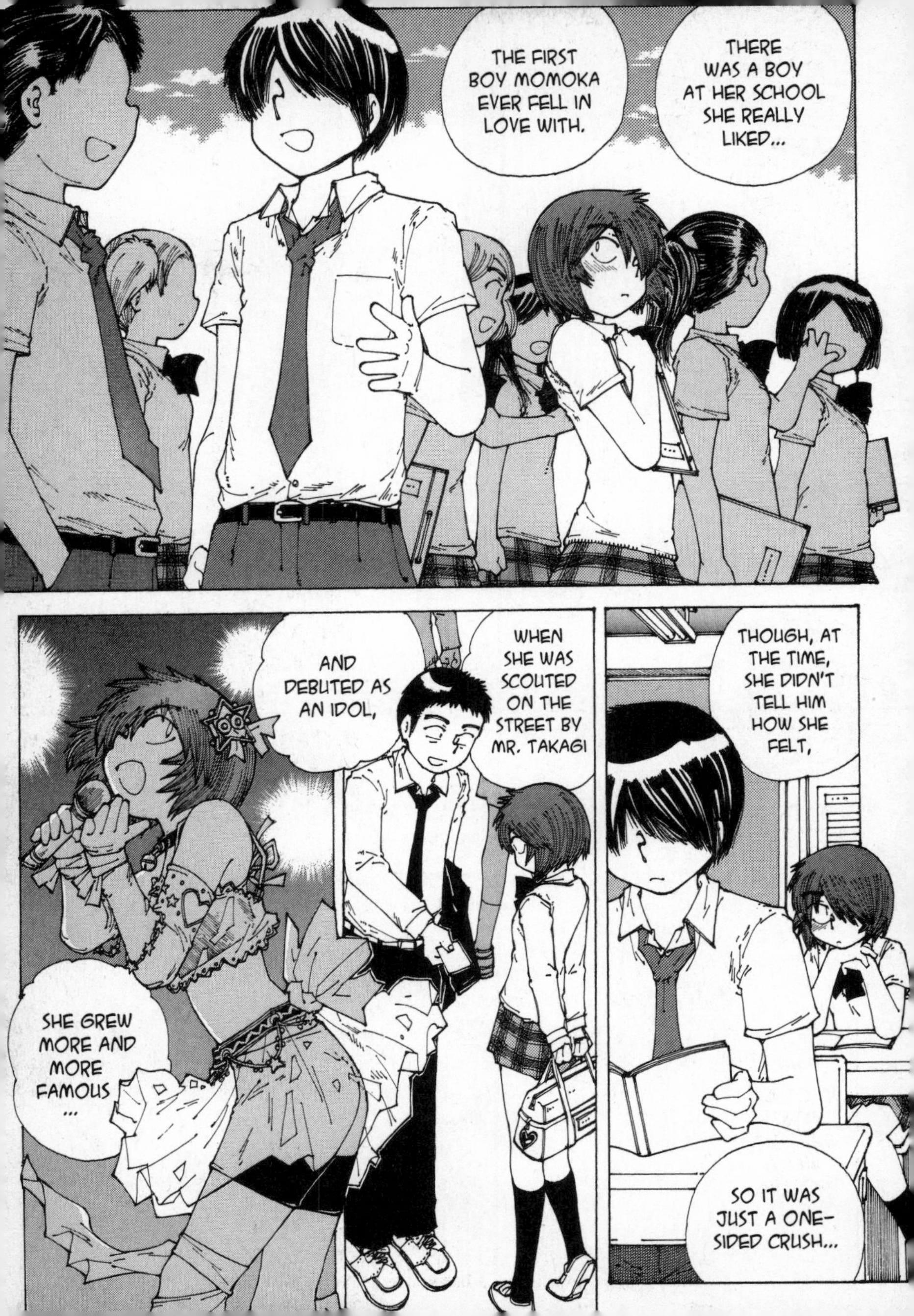
THERE WAS A BOY AT HER SCHOOL SHE REALLY LIKED...
THE FIRST BOY MOMOKA EVER FELL IN LOVE WITH.
THOUGH, AT THE TIME, SHE DIDN'T TELL HIM HOW SHE FELT,
SO IT WAS JUST A ONE-SIDED CRUSH...
WHEN SHE WAS SCOUTED ON THE STREET BY MR. TAKAGI
AND DEBUTED AS AN IDOL,
SHE GREW MORE AND MORE FAMOUS ...

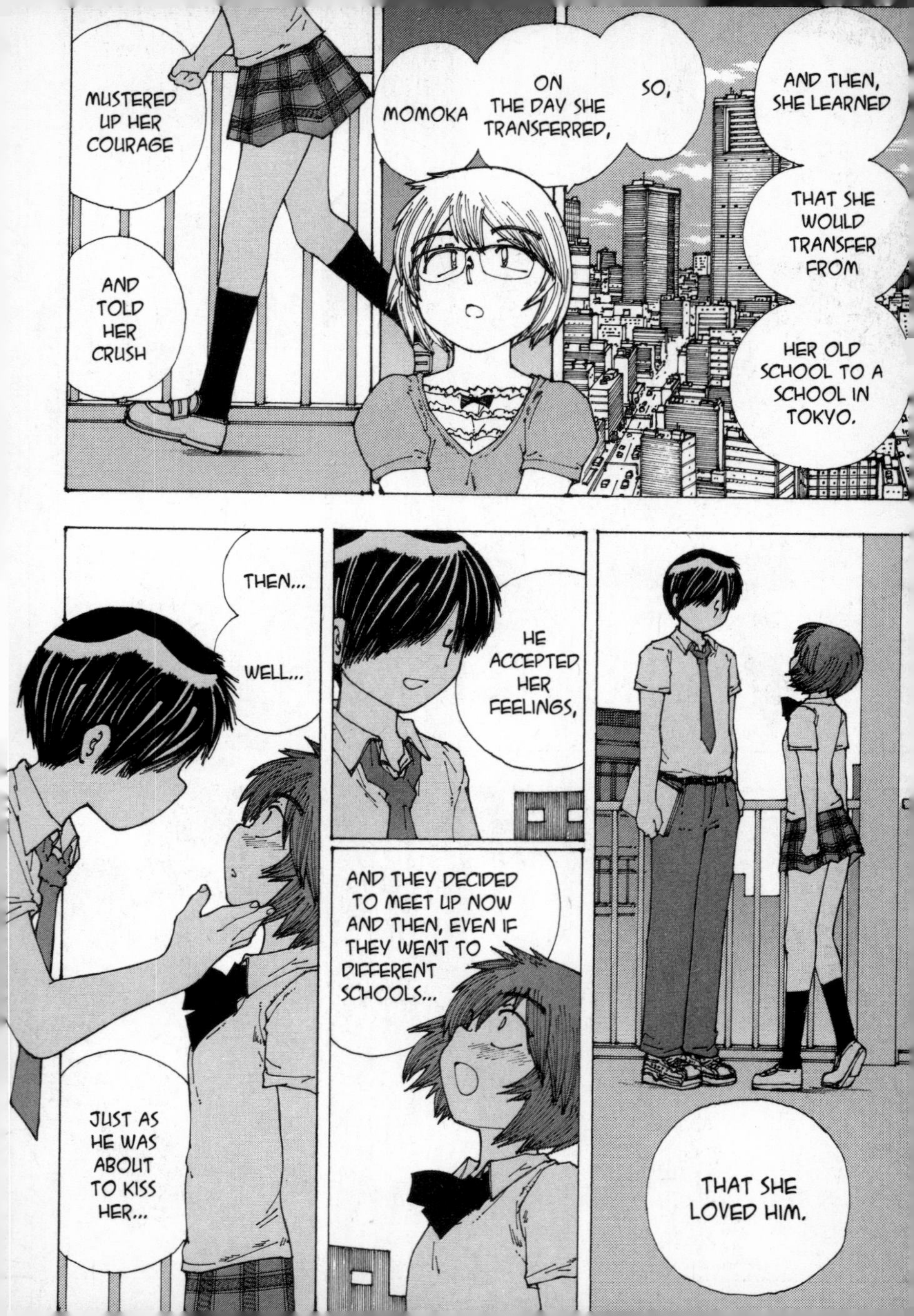
AND THEN, SHE LEARNED
THAT SHE WOULD TRANSFER FROM
HER OLD SCHOOL TO A SCHOOL IN TOKYO.
SO,
ON THE DAY SHE TRANSFERRED,
MOMOKA
MUSTERED UP HER COURAGE
AND TOLD HER CRUSH
THAT SHE LOVED HIM.
HE ACCEPTED HER FEELINGS,
AND THEY DECIDED TO MEET UP NOW AND THEN, EVEN IF THEY WENT TO DIFFERENT SCHOOLS...
THEN...
WELL...
JUST AS HE WAS ABOUT TO KISS HER...

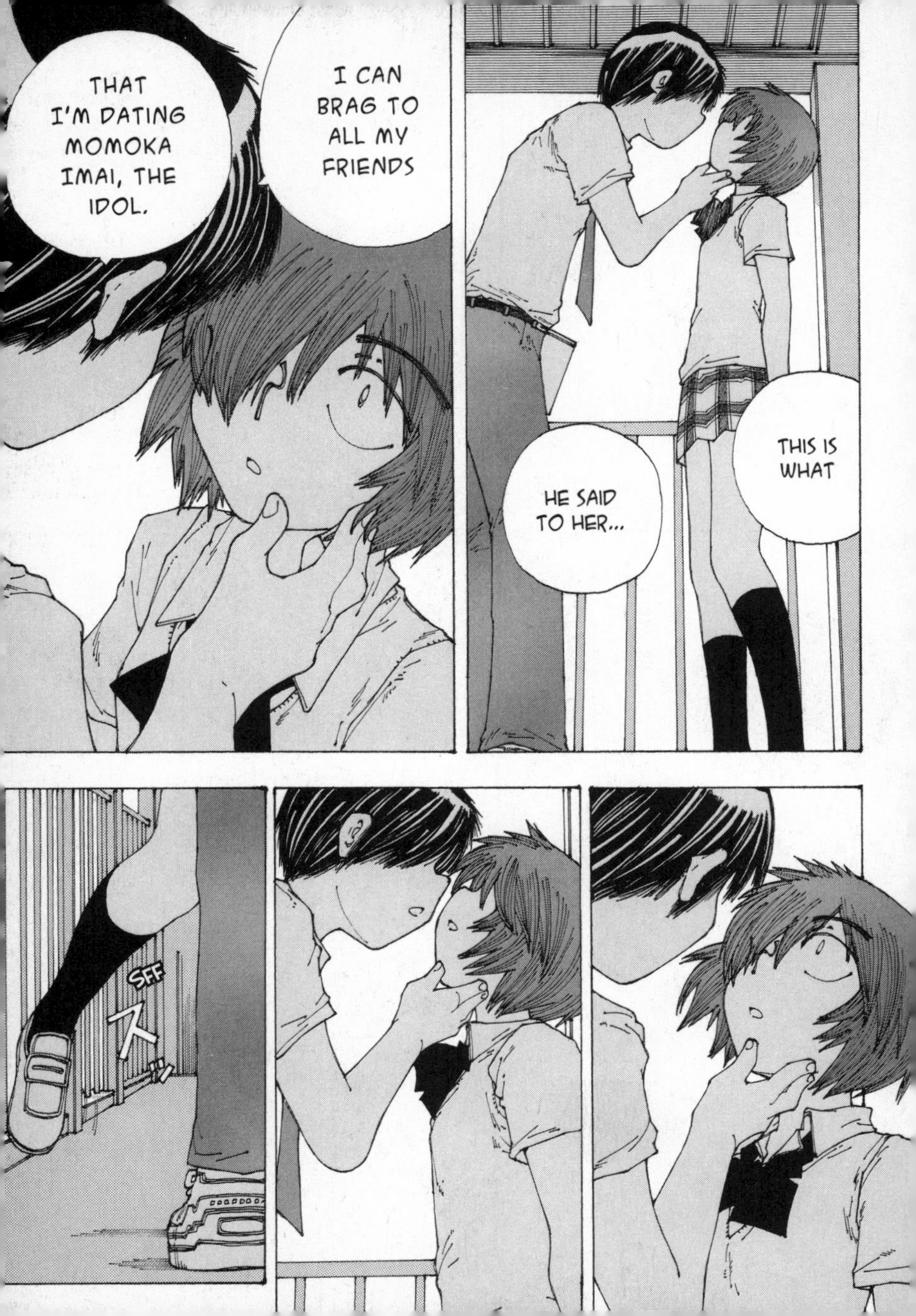
THIS IS WHAT
HE SAID TO HER...
I CAN BRAG TO ALL MY FRIENDS
THAT I'M DATING MOMOKA IMAI, THE IDOL.
SFF

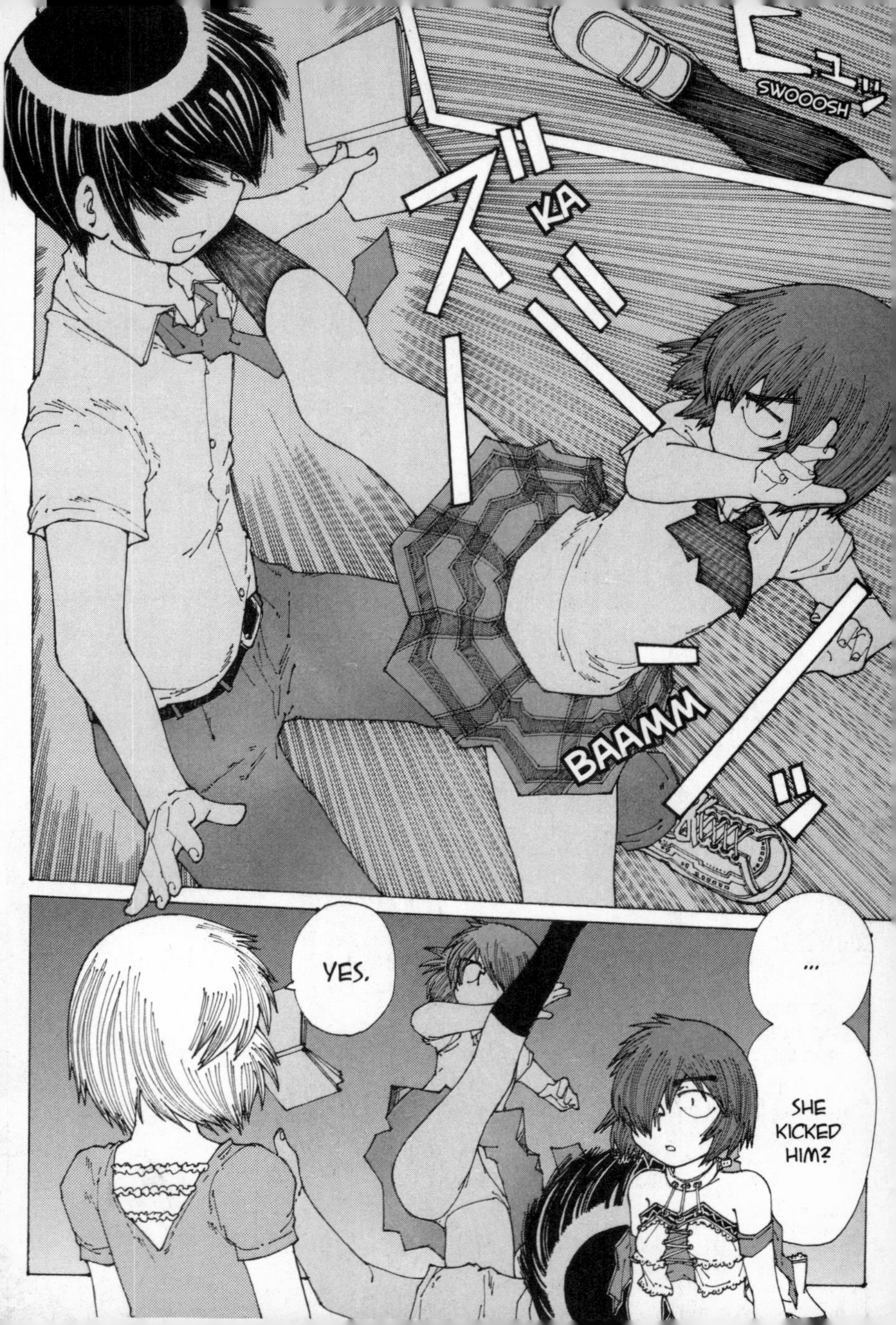
SWOOOSH
KA
BAAMM
...
SHE KICKED HIM?
YES.

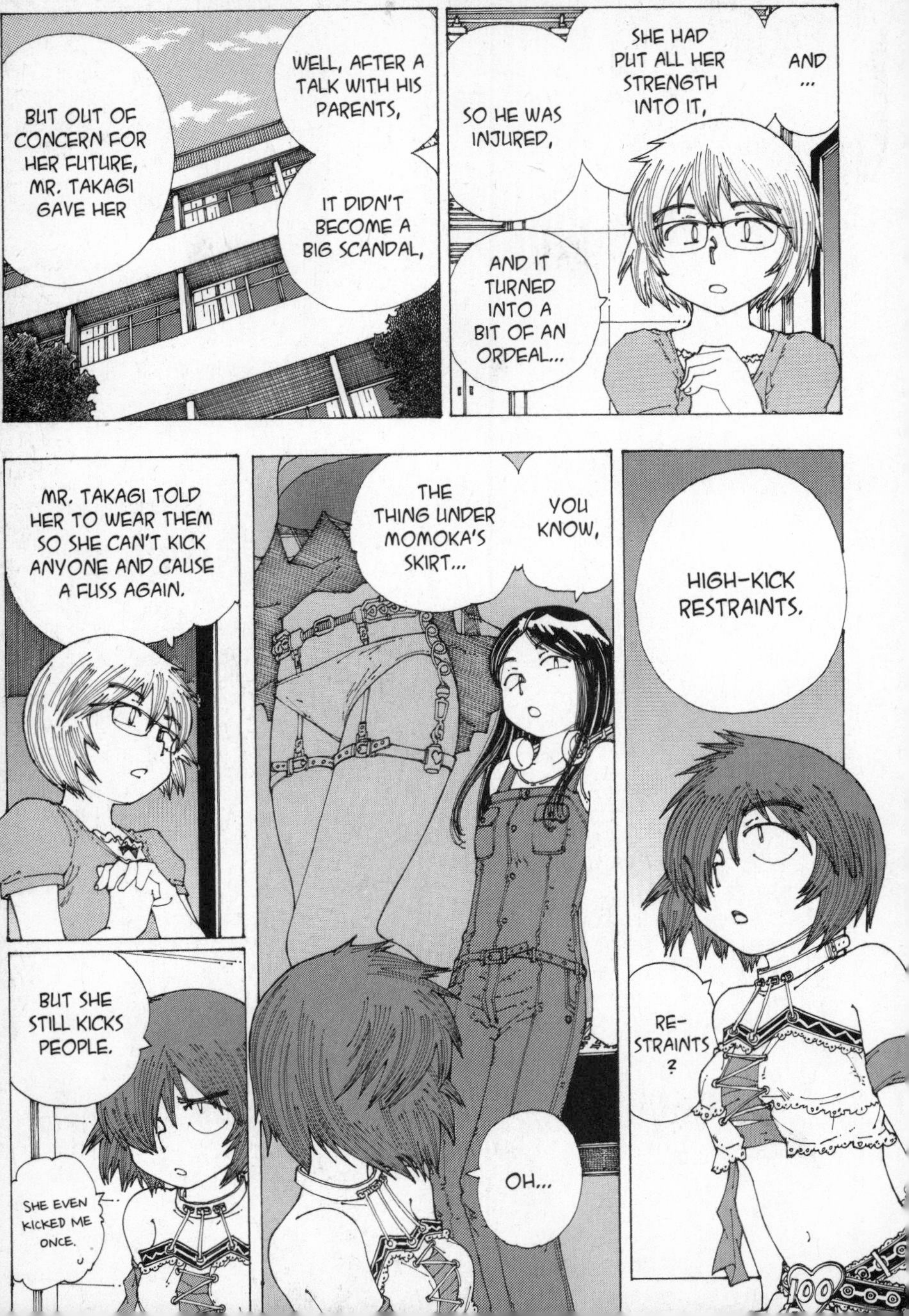
AND ...
SHE HAD PUT ALL HER STRENGTH INTO IT,
SO HE WAS INJURED,
AND IT TURNED INTO A BIT OF AN ORDEAL...
WELL, AFTER A TALK WITH HIS PARENTS,
IT DIDN'T BECOME A BIG SCANDAL,
BUT OUT OF CONCERN FOR HER FUTURE, MR. TAKAGI GAVE HER
HIGH-KICK RESTRAINTS.
RE-STRAINTS?
YOU KNOW,
THE THING UNDER MOMOKA'S SKIRT...
OH...
MR. TAKAGI TOLD HER TO WEAR THEM SO SHE CAN'T KICK ANYONE AND CAUSE A FUSS AGAIN.
BUT SHE STILL KICKS PEOPLE.
SHE EVEN KICKED ME ONCE.

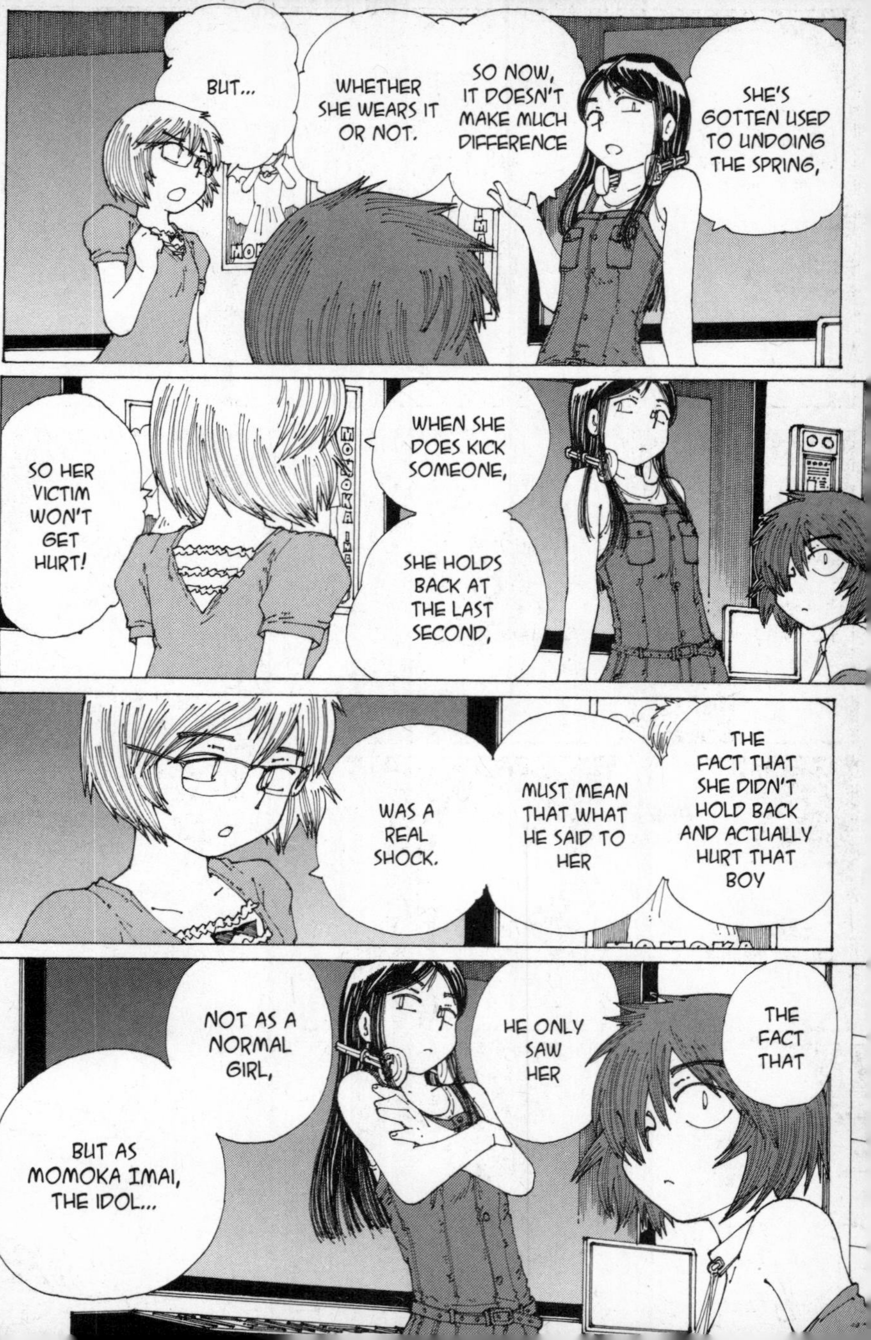
SHE'S GOTTEN USED TO UNDOING THE SPRING,
SO NOW, IT DOESN'T MAKE MUCH DIFFERENCE
WHETHER SHE WEARS IT OR NOT.
BUT...
WHEN SHE DOES KICK SOMEONE,
SHE HOLDS BACK AT THE LAST SECOND,
SO HER VICTIM WON'T GET HURT!
THE FACT THAT SHE DIDN'T HOLD BACK AND ACTUALLY HURT THAT BOY
MUST MEAN THAT WHAT HE SAID TO HER
WAS A REAL SHOCK.
THE FACT THAT
HE ONLY SAW HER
NOT AS A NORMAL GIRL,
BUT AS MOMOKA IMAI, THE IDOL...

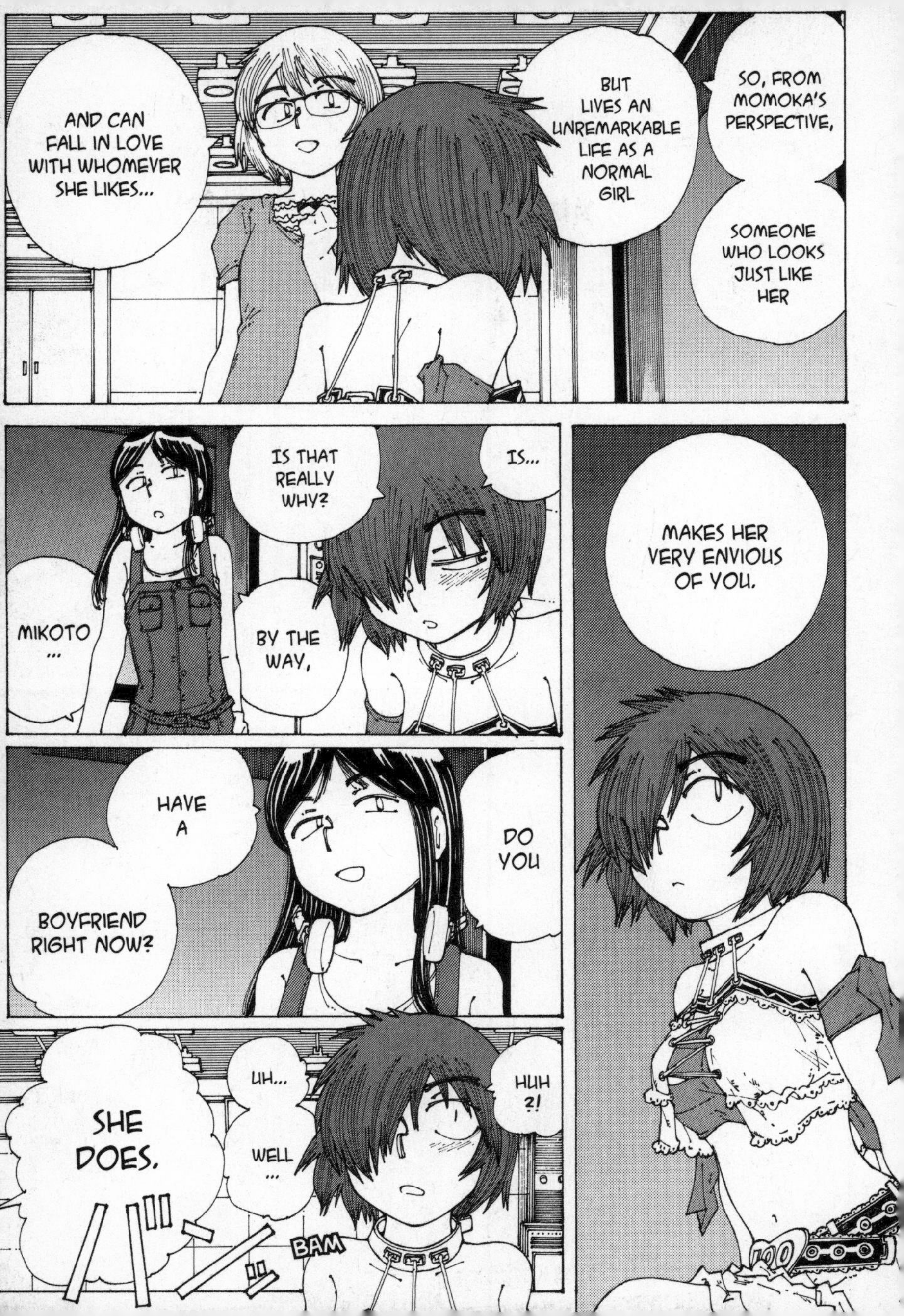
SO, FROM MOMOKA'S PERSPECTIVE,
SOMEONE WHO LOOKS JUST LIKE HER
BUT LIVES AN UNREMARKABLE LIFE AS A NORMAL GIRL
AND CAN FALL IN LOVE WITH WHOMEVER SHE LIKES...
MAKES HER VERY ENVIOUS OF YOU.
IS...
IS THAT REALLY WHY?
BY THE WAY,
MIKOTO ...
DO YOU
HAVE A
BOYFRIEND RIGHT NOW?
HUH ?!
UH...
WELL ...
SHE DOES.
BAM

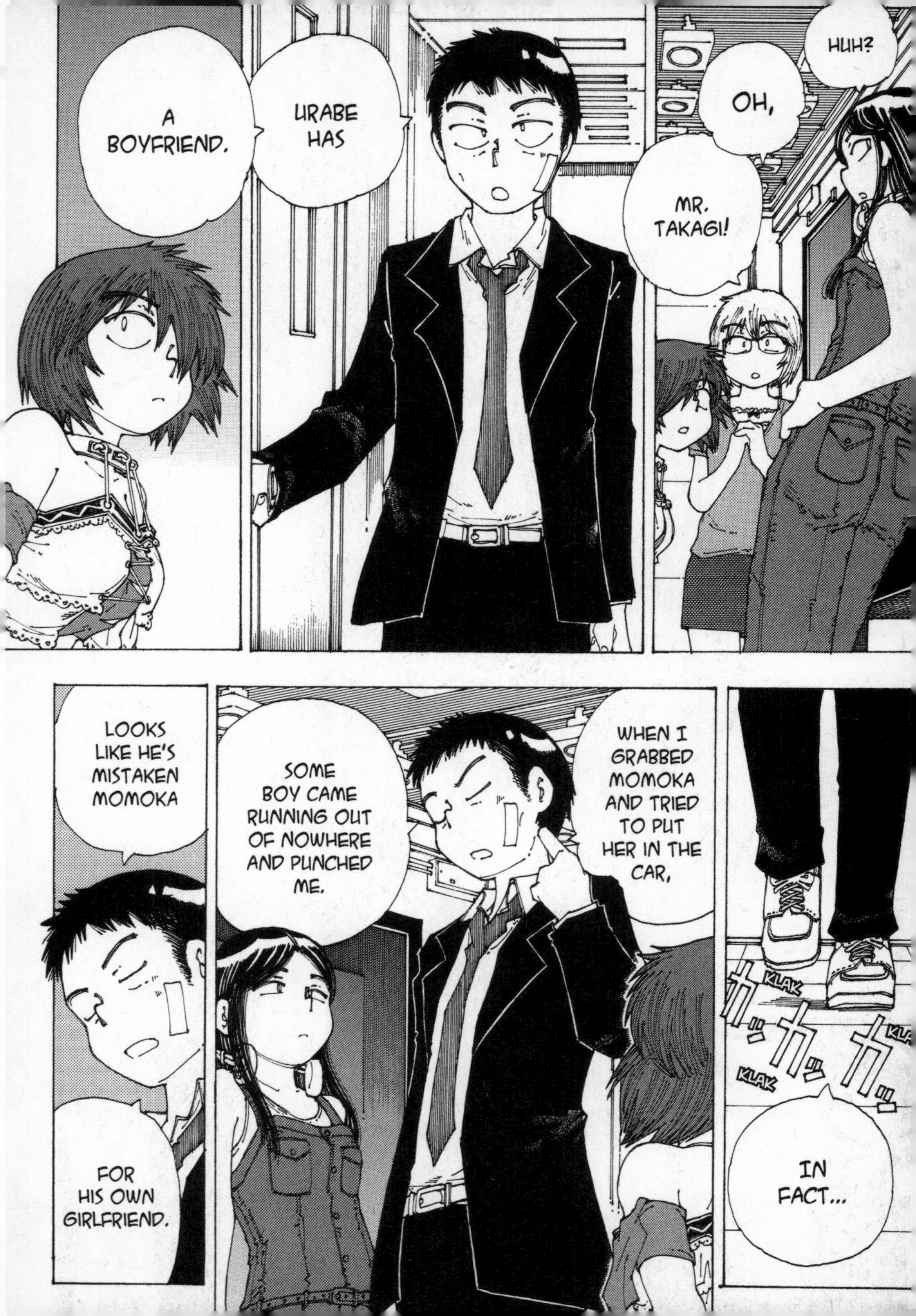
HUH?
OH,
MR. TAKAGI!
URABE HAS
A BOYFRIEND.
カッ
KLAK
カッ
KLAK
カッ
KLAK
IN FACT...
WHEN I GRABBED MOMOKA AND TRIED TO PUT HER IN THE CAR,
SOME BOY CAME RUNNING OUT OF NOWHERE AND PUNCHED ME.
LOOKS LIKE HE'S MISTAKEN MOMOKA
FOR HIS OWN GIRLFRIEND.

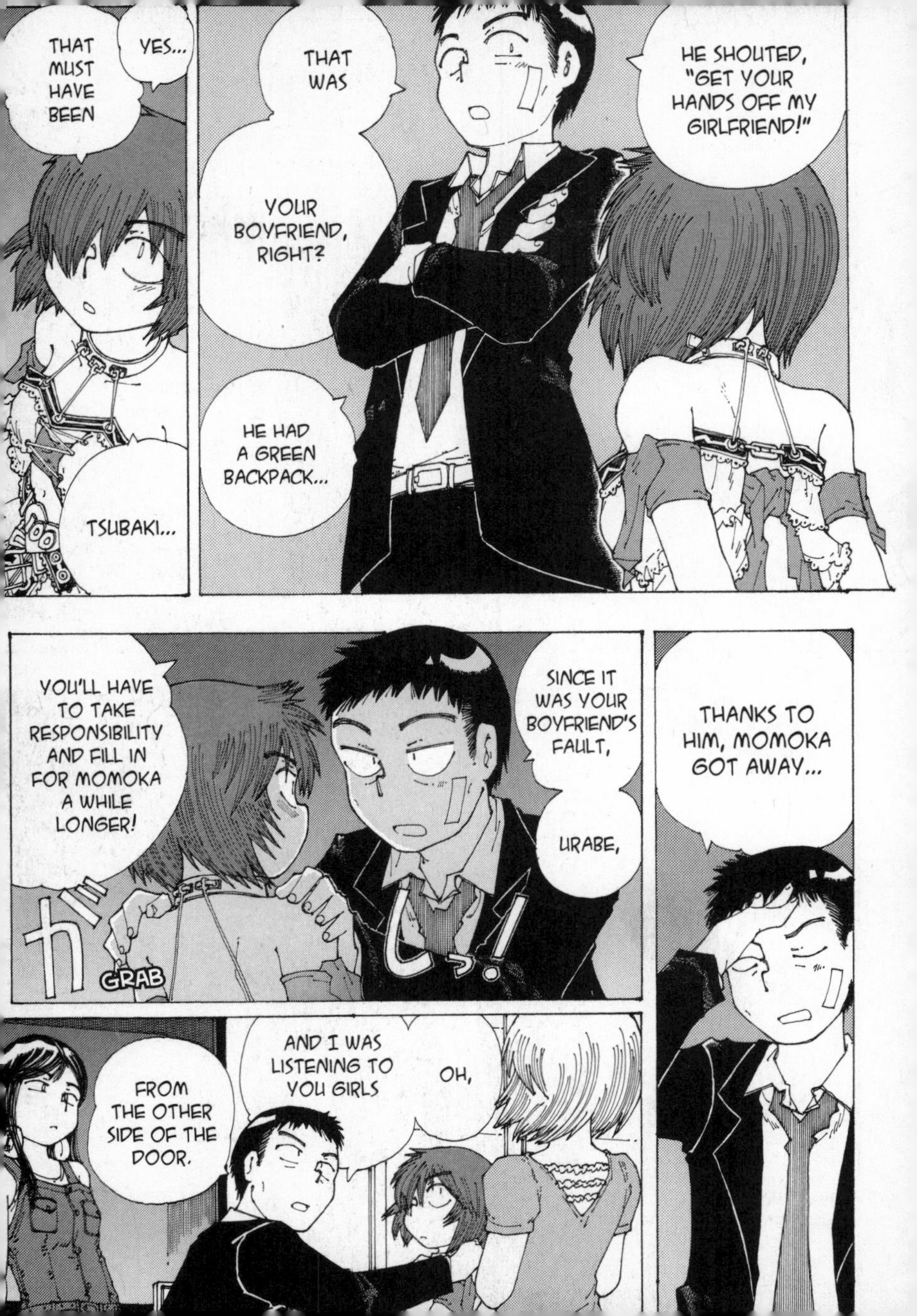
HE SHOUTED, "GET YOUR HANDS OFF MY GIRLFRIEND!"
THAT WAS
YOUR BOYFRIEND, RIGHT?
HE HAD A GREEN BACKPACK...
YES...
THAT MUST HAVE BEEN
TSUBAKI...
THANKS TO HIM, MOMOKA GOT AWAY...
SINCE IT WAS YOUR BOYFRIEND'S FAULT,
URABE,
YOU'LL HAVE TO TAKE RESPONSIBILITY AND FILL IN FOR MOMOKA A WHILE LONGER!
GRAB
OH,
AND I WAS LISTENING TO YOU GIRLS
FROM THE OTHER SIDE OF THE DOOR.

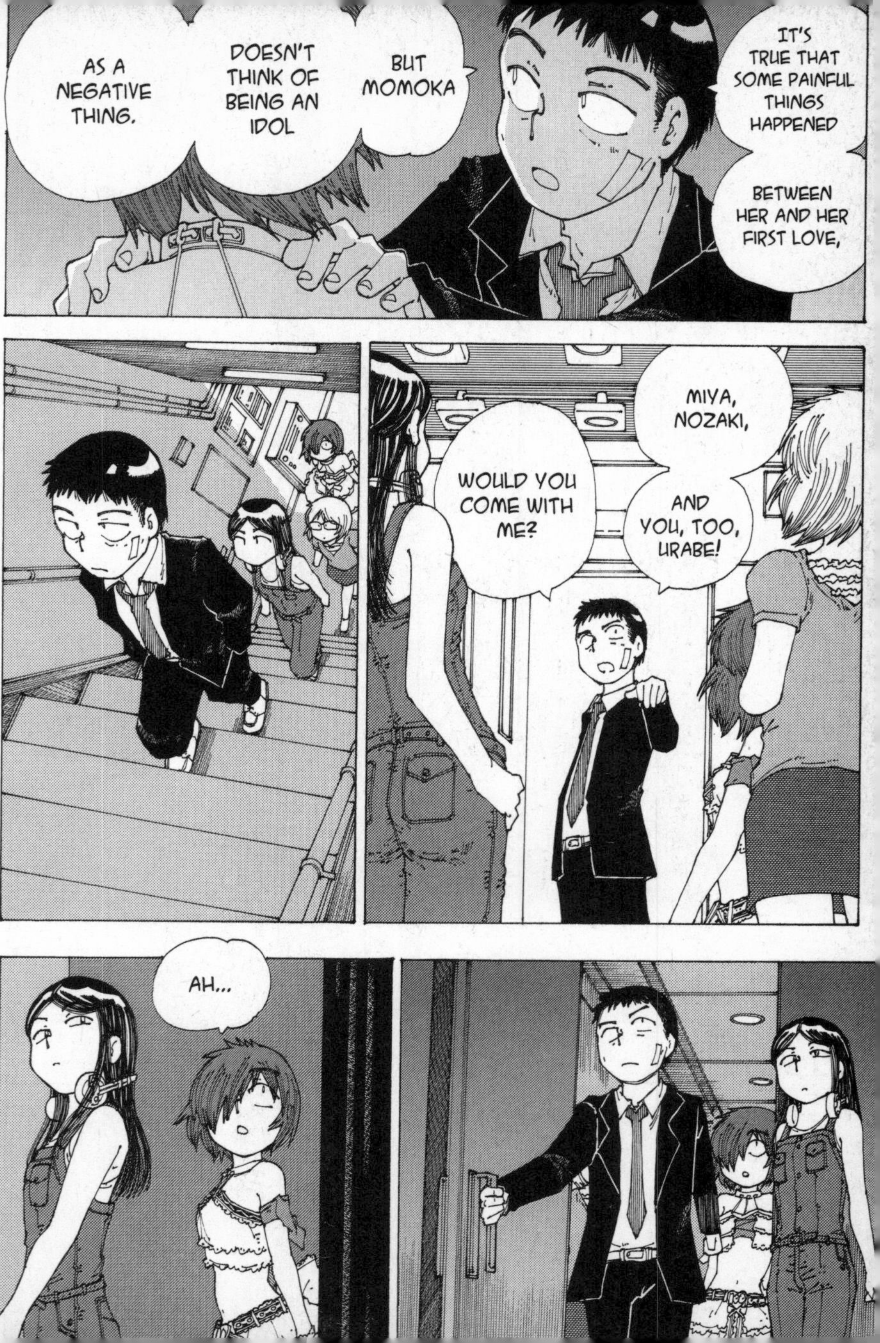
IT'S TRUE THAT SOME PAINFUL THINGS HAPPENED
BETWEEN HER AND HER FIRST LOVE,
BUT MOMOKA
DOESN'T THINK OF BEING AN IDOL
AS A NEGATIVE THING.
MIYA, NOZAKI,
AND YOU, TOO, URABE!
WOULD YOU COME WITH ME?
AH...

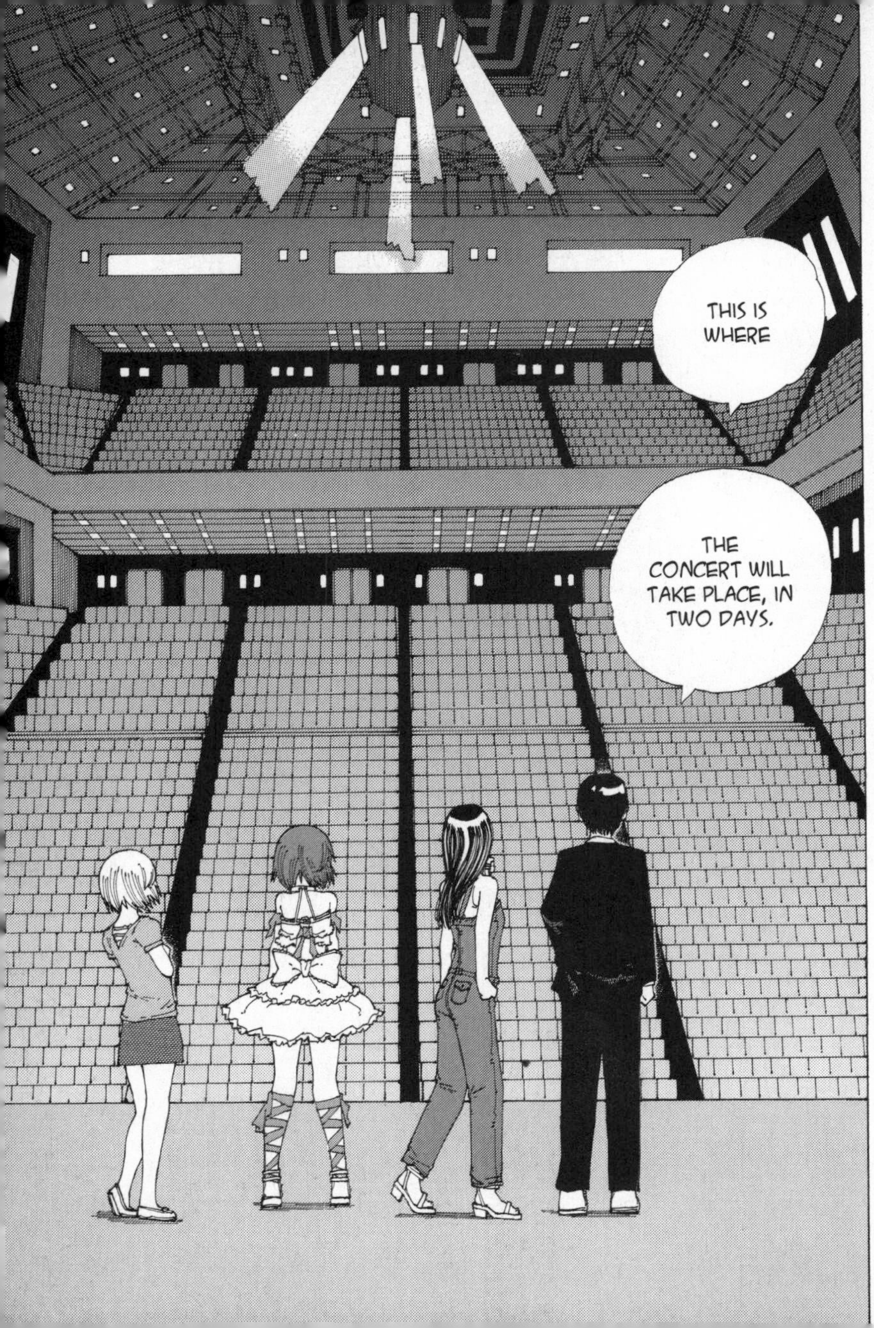
THIS IS WHERE
THE CONCERT WILL TAKE PLACE, IN TWO DAYS.

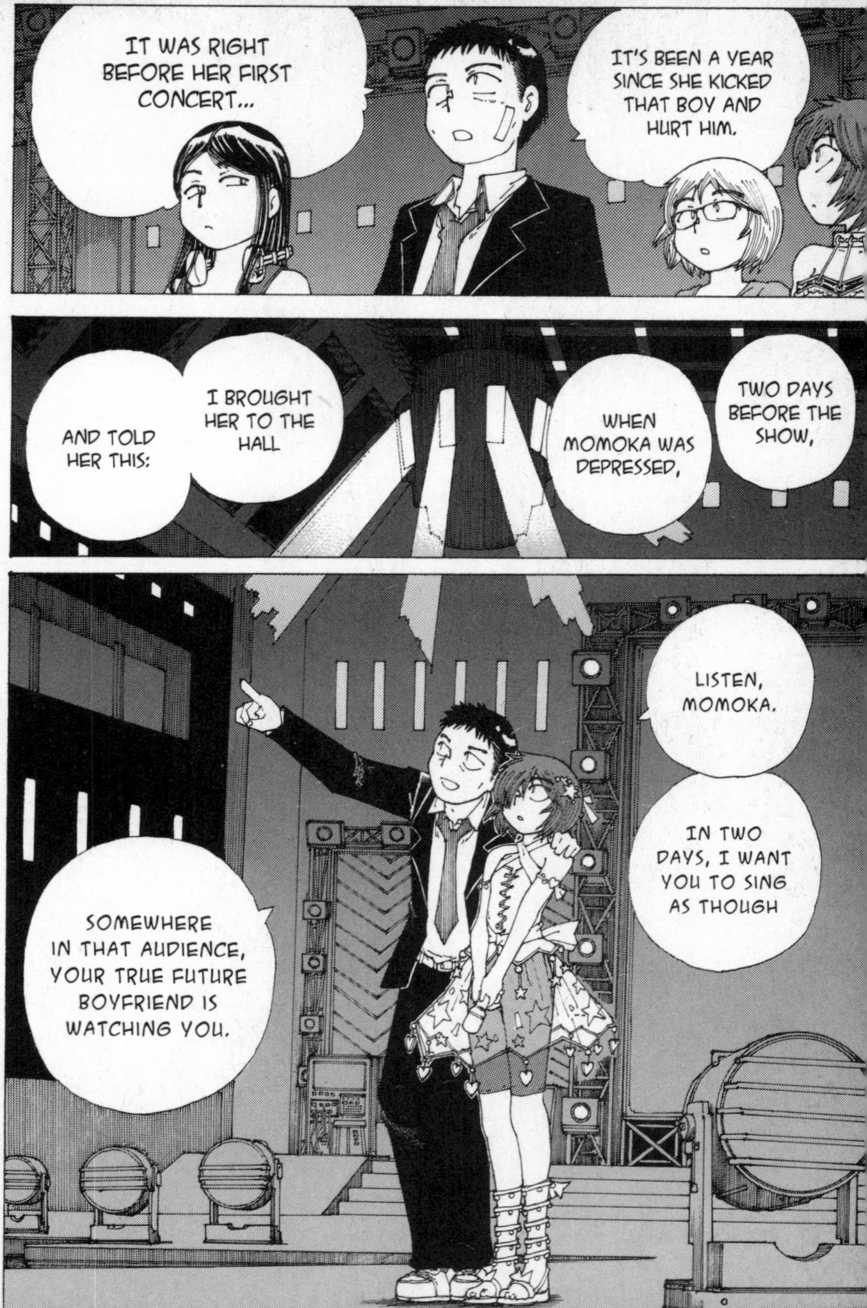
IT'S BEEN A YEAR SINCE SHE KICKED THAT BOY AND HURT HIM.
IT WAS RIGHT BEFORE HER FIRST CONCERT...
TWO DAYS BEFORE THE SHOW,
WHEN MOMOKA WAS DEPRESSED,
I BROUGHT HER TO THE HALL
AND TOLD HER THIS:
LISTEN, MOMOKA.
IN TWO DAYS, I WANT YOU TO SING AS THOUGH
SOMEWHERE IN THAT AUDIENCE, YOUR TRUE FUTURE BOYFRIEND IS WATCHING YOU.

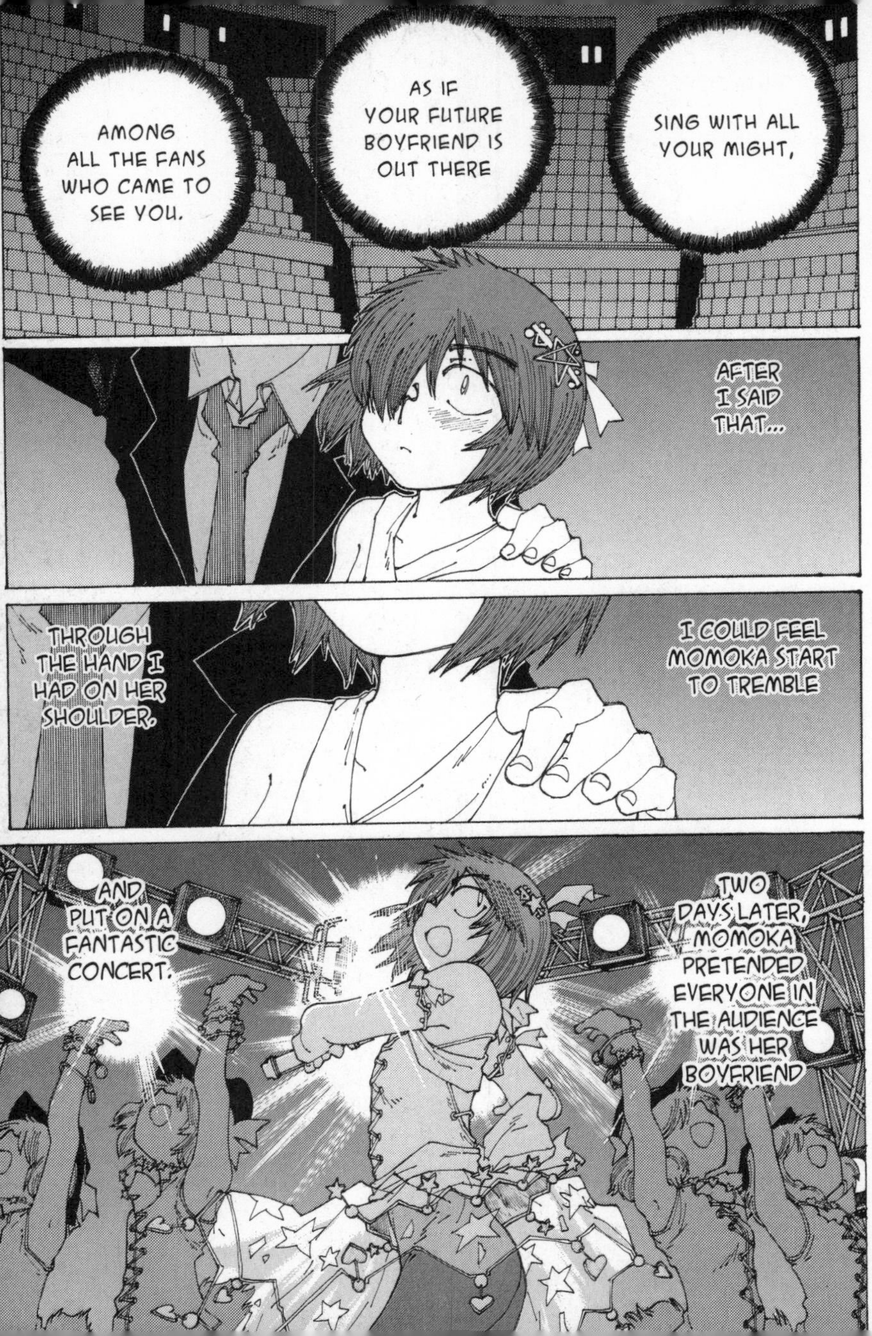
SING WITH ALL YOUR MIGHT,
AS IF YOUR FUTURE BOYFRIEND IS OUT THERE
AMONG ALL THE FANS WHO CAME TO SEE YOU.
AFTER I SAID THAT...
I COULD FEEL MOMOKA START TO TREMBLE
THROUGH THE HAND I HAD ON HER SHOULDER.
TWO DAYS LATER, MOMOKA PRETENDED EVERYONE IN THE AUDIENCE WAS HER BOYFRIEND
AND PUT ON A FANTASTIC CONCERT.

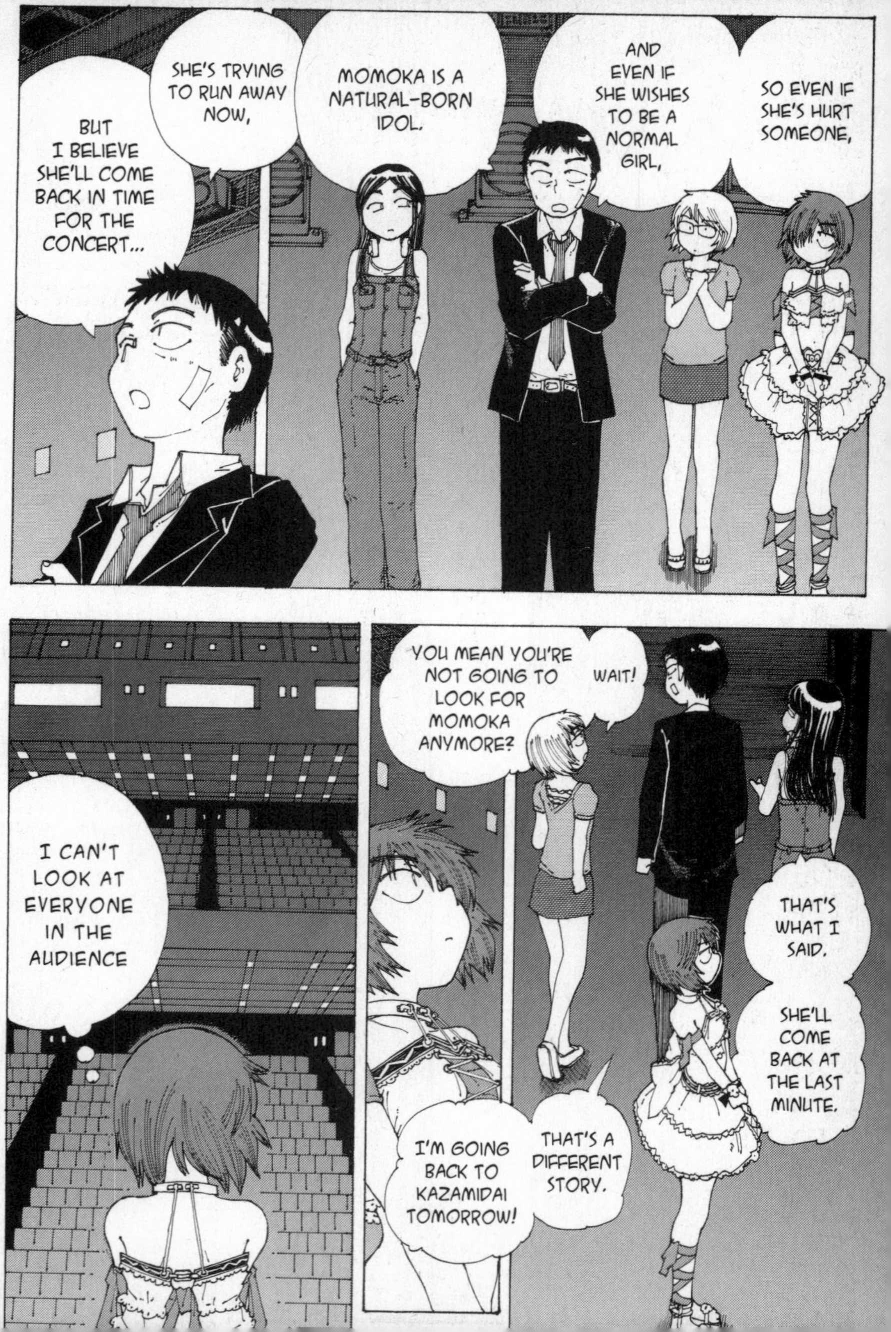
SO EVEN IF SHE'S HURT SOMEONE,
AND EVEN IF SHE WISHES TO BE A NORMAL GIRL,
MOMOKA IS A NATURAL-BORN IDOL.
SHE'S TRYING TO RUN AWAY NOW,
BUT I BELIEVE SHE'LL COME BACK IN TIME FOR THE CONCERT...
WAIT!
YOU MEAN YOU'RE NOT GOING TO LOOK FOR MOMOKA ANYMORE?
THAT'S WHAT I SAID.
SHE'LL COME BACK AT THE LAST MINUTE.
THAT'S A DIFFERENT STORY.
I'M GOING BACK TO KAZAMIDAI TOMORROW!
I CAN'T LOOK AT EVERYONE IN THE AUDIENCE

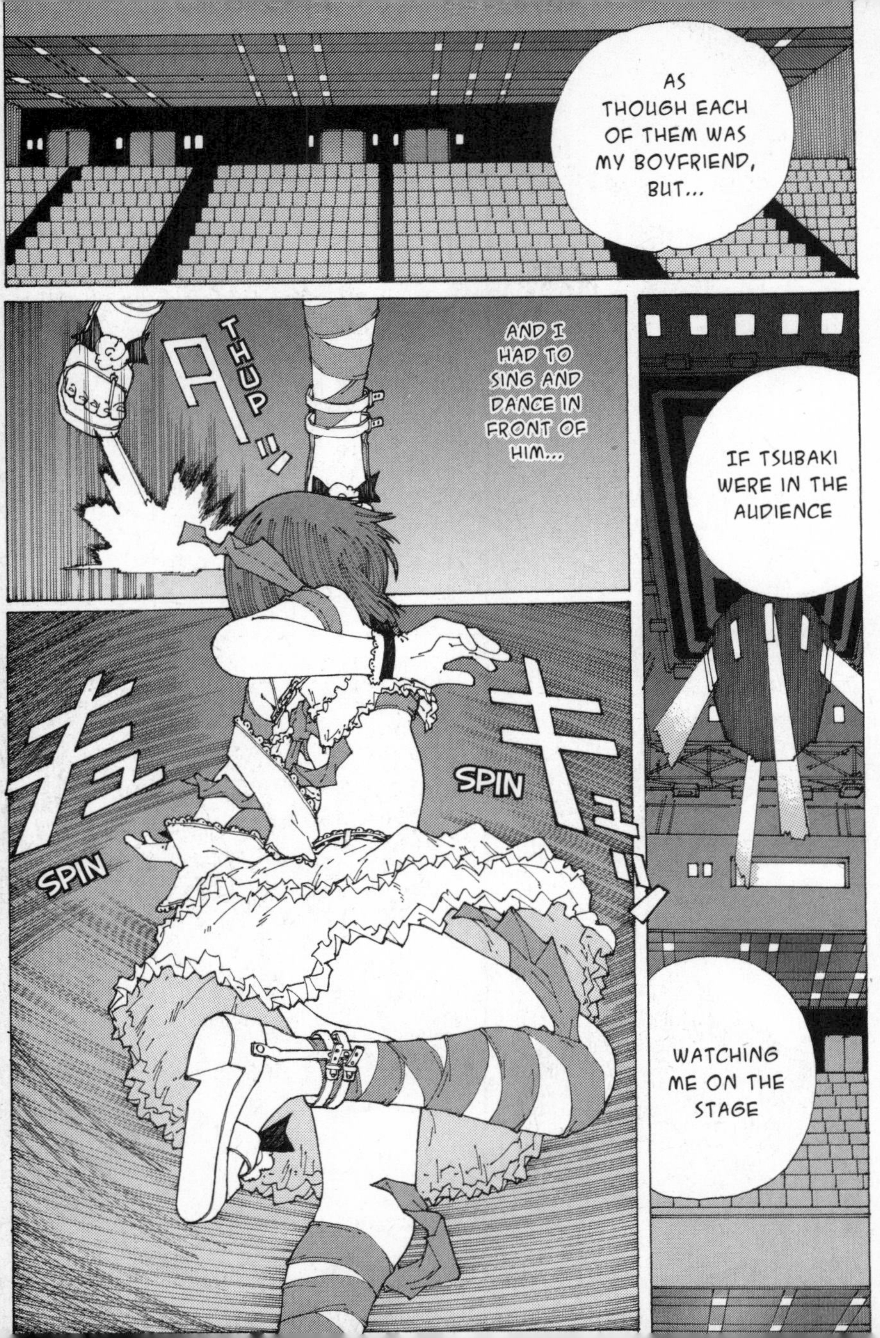
AS THOUGH EACH OF THEM WAS MY BOYFRIEND, BUT...
IF TSUBAKI WERE IN THE AUDIENCE
WATCHING ME ON THE STAGE
AND I HAD TO SING AND DANCE IN FRONT OF HIM...
THUP
キュッ
SPIN
キュ
SPIN

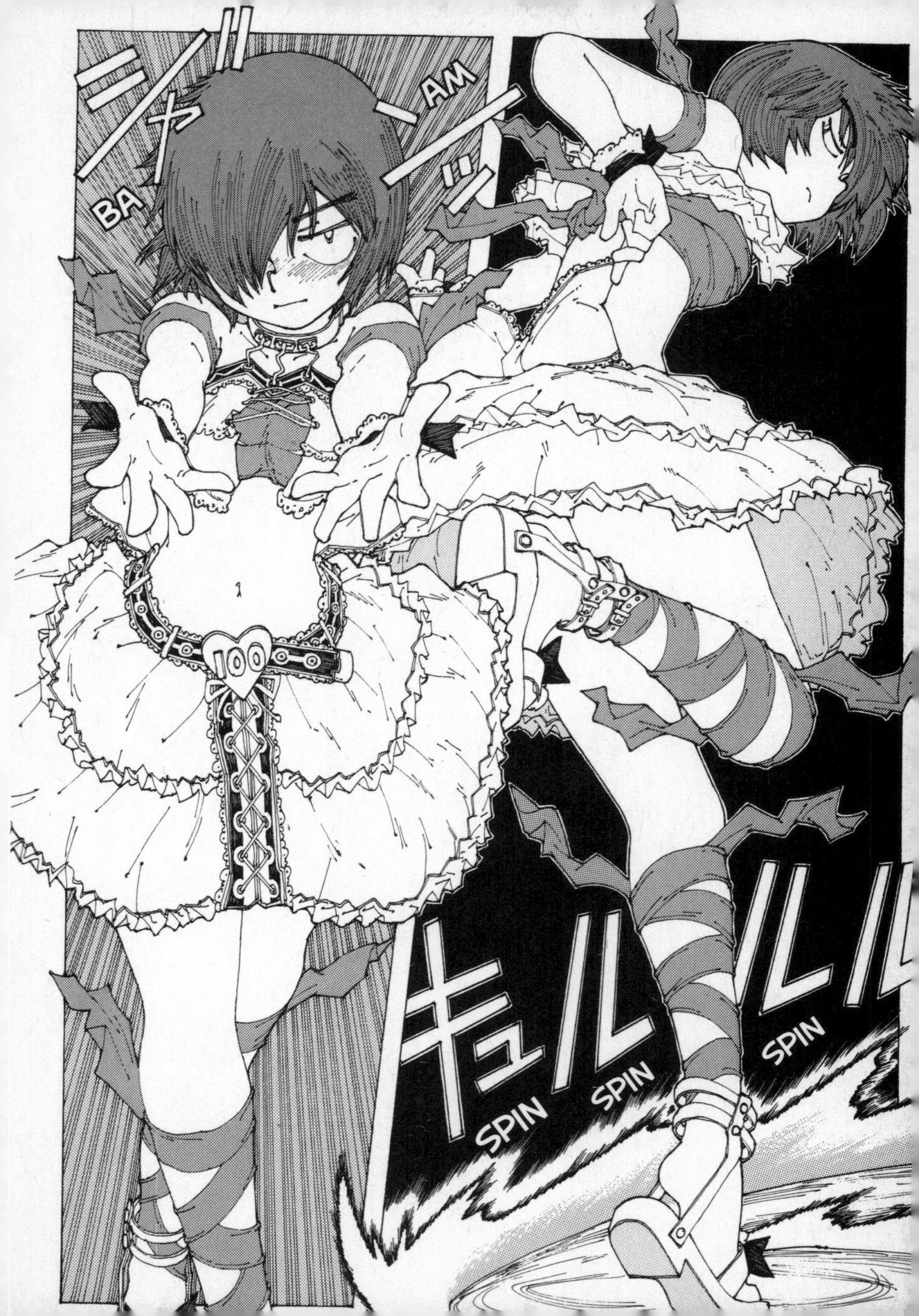
AM
BA
キュルルル
SPIN
SPIN
SPIN

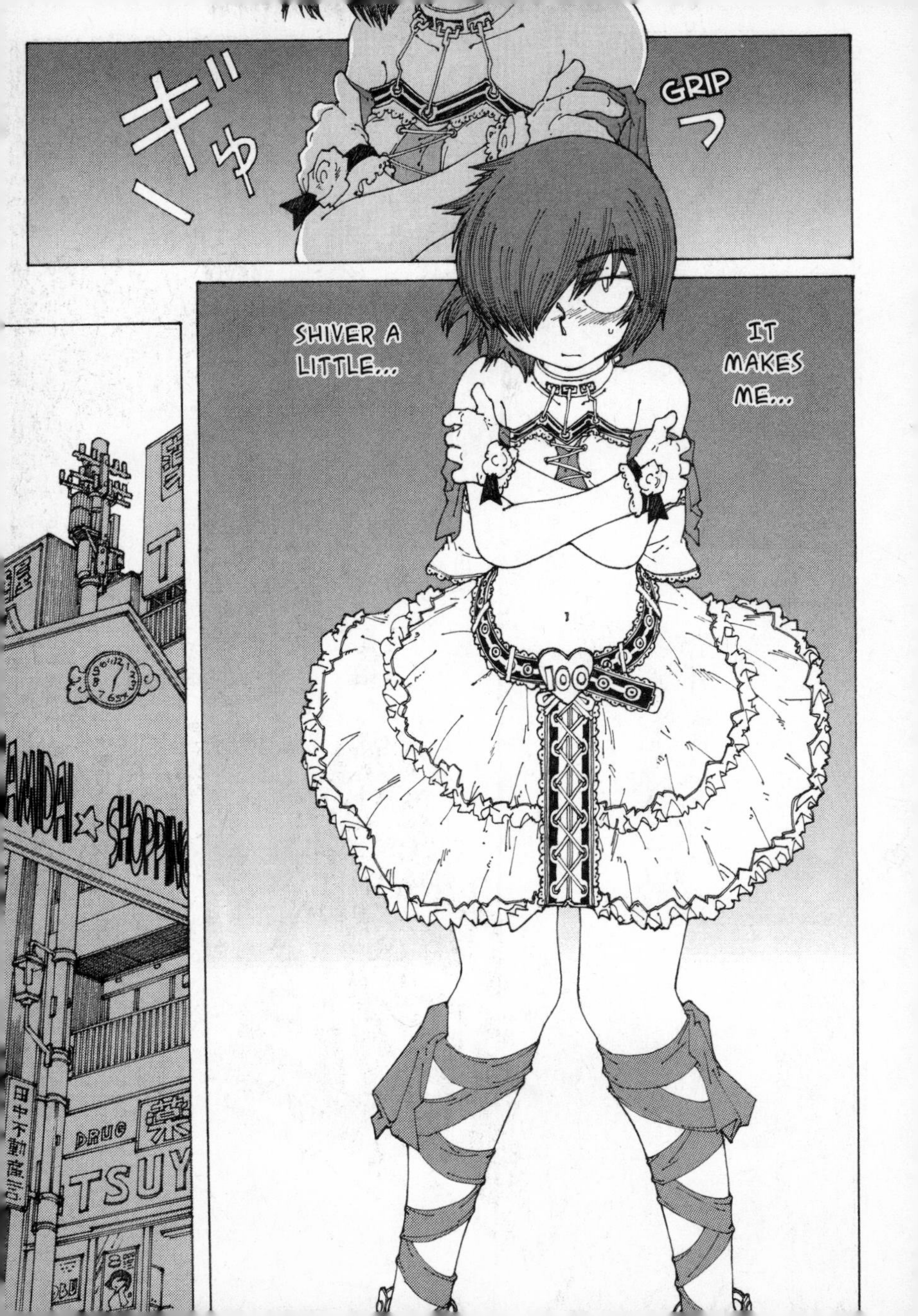
ギゅー
GRIP
っ
IT MAKES ME...
SHIVER A LITTLE...
田中不動産
DRUG

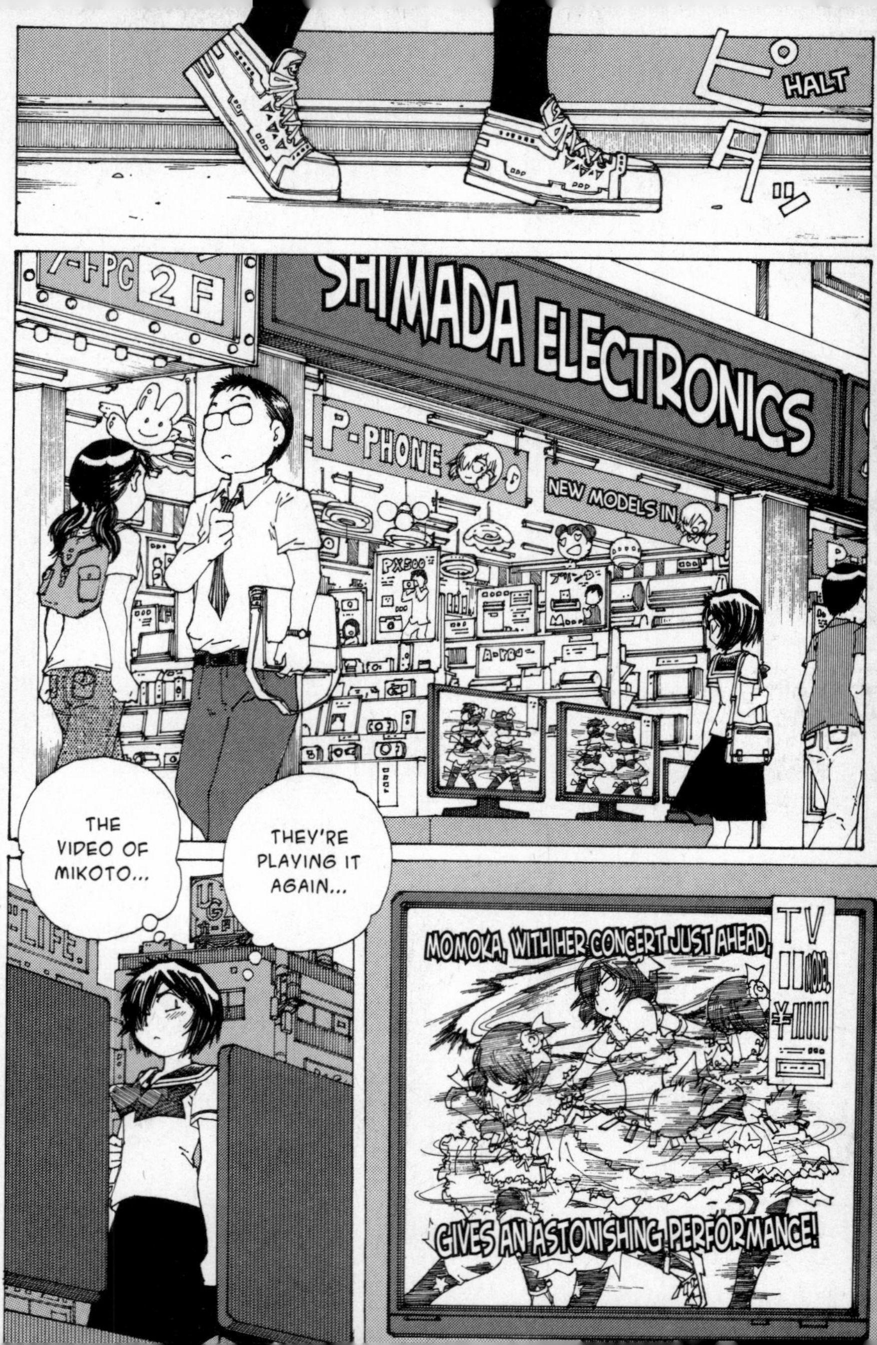
ピタッ
HALT
SHIMADA ELECTRONICS
2F
P-PHONE
NEW MODELS IN
PX500
MOMOKA, WITH HER CONCERT JUST AHEAD,
GIVES AN ASTONISHING PERFORMANCE!
TV
THEY'RE PLAYING IT AGAIN...
THE VIDEO OF MIKOTO...

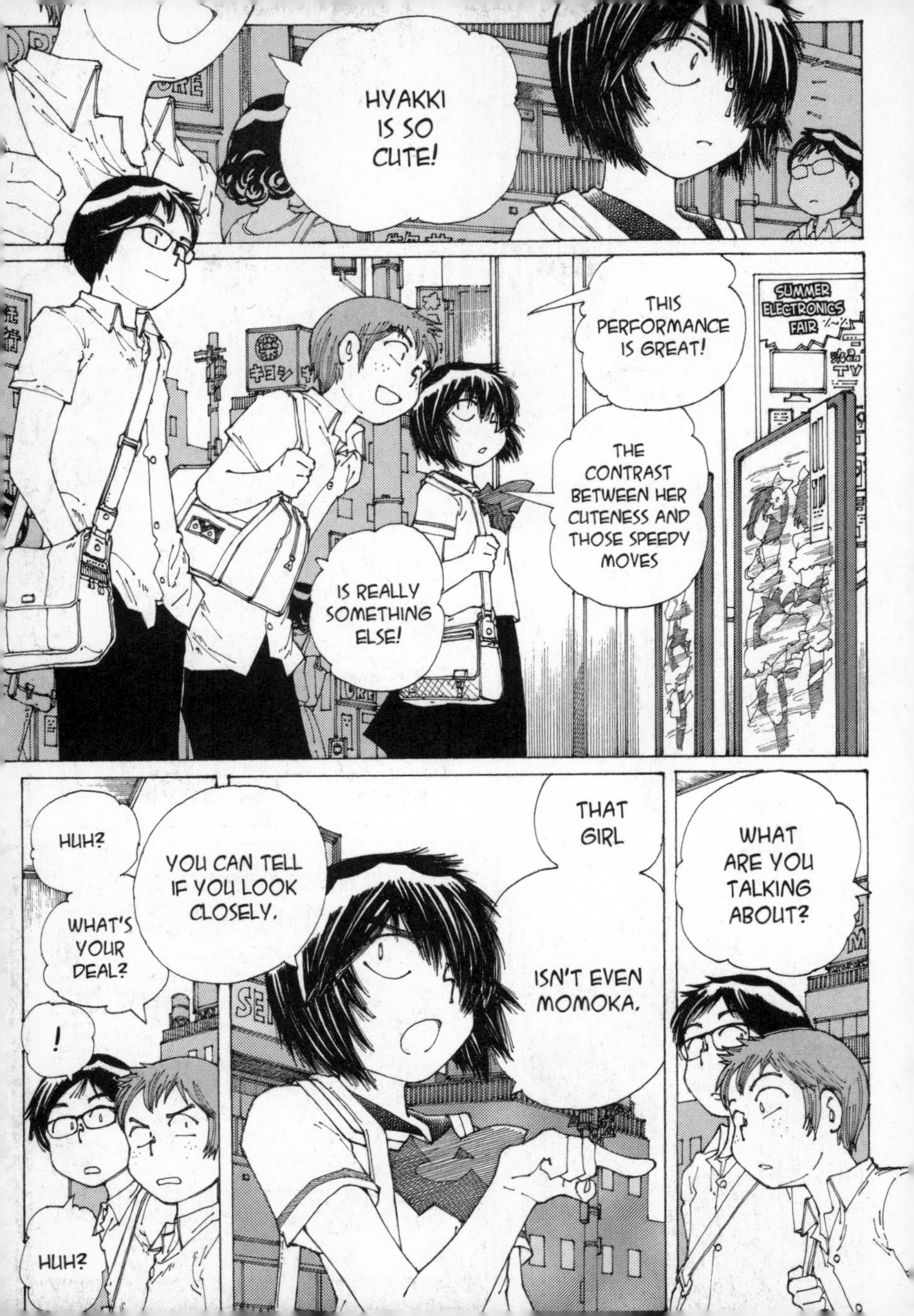
HYAKKI IS SO CUTE!
THIS PERFORMANCE IS GREAT!
SUMMER ELECTRONICS FAIR
TV
THE CONTRAST BETWEEN HER CUTENESS AND THOSE SPEEDY MOVES
IS REALLY SOMETHING ELSE!
WHAT ARE YOU TALKING ABOUT?
THAT GIRL
ISN'T EVEN MOMOKA.
YOU CAN TELL IF YOU LOOK CLOSELY.
HUH?
WHAT'S YOUR DEAL?
!
HUH?

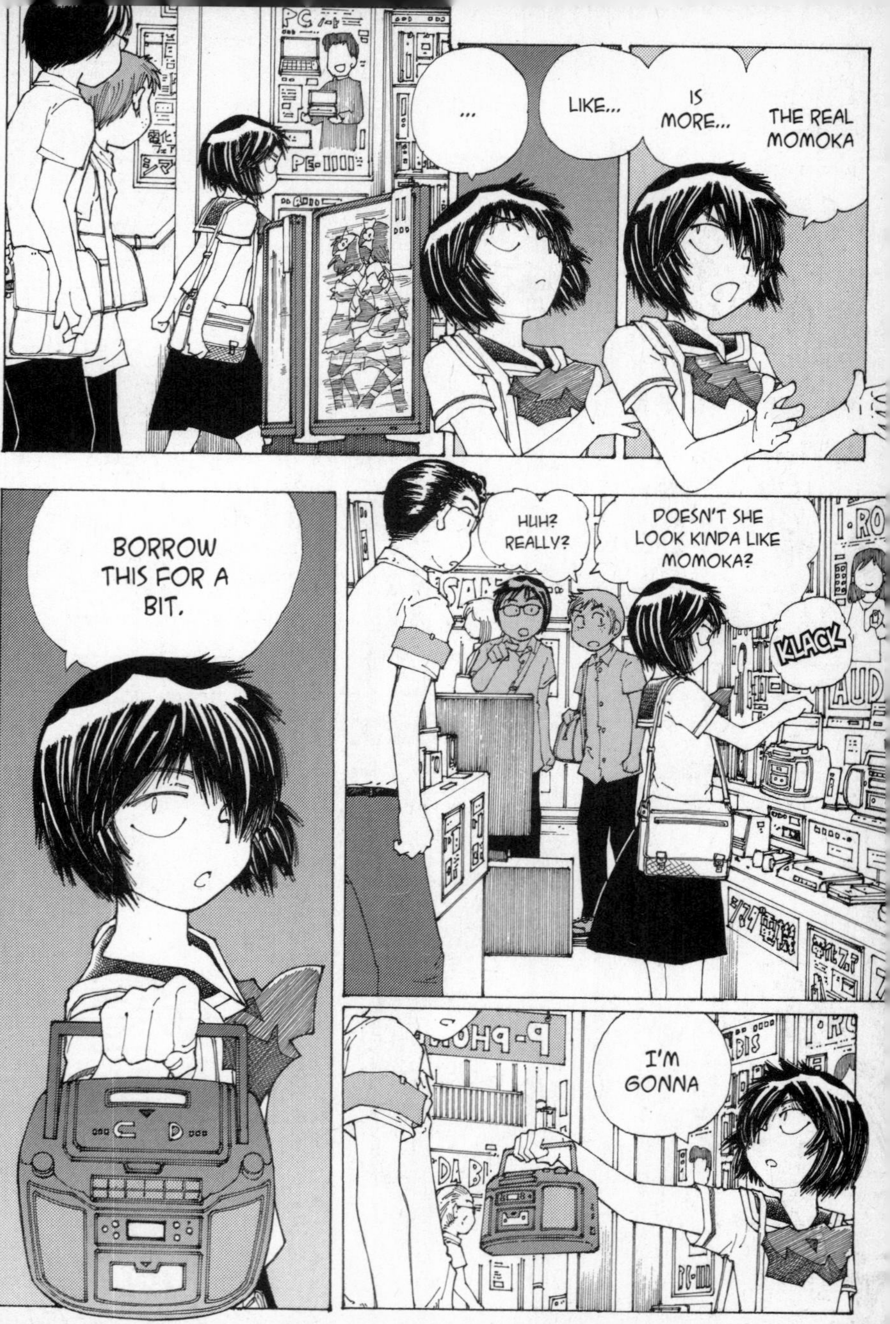
THE REAL MOMOKA
IS MORE...
LIKE...
...
DOESN'T SHE LOOK KINDA LIKE MOMOKA?
HUH? REALLY?
KLACK
I'M GONNA
BORROW THIS FOR A BIT.

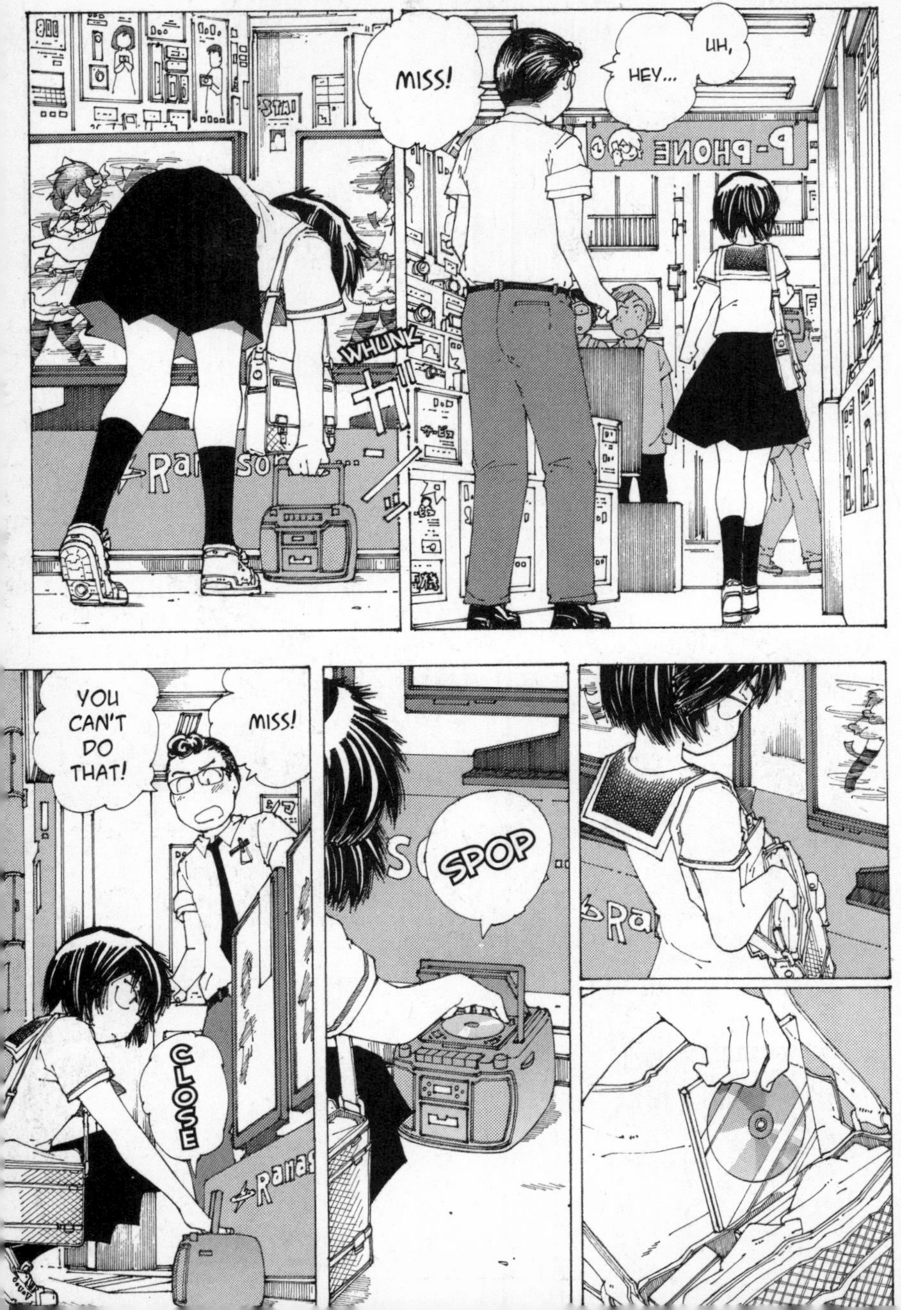
UH,
HEY...
MISS!
P-PHONE
WHUNK
SPOP
MISS!
YOU CAN'T DO THAT!
CLOSE

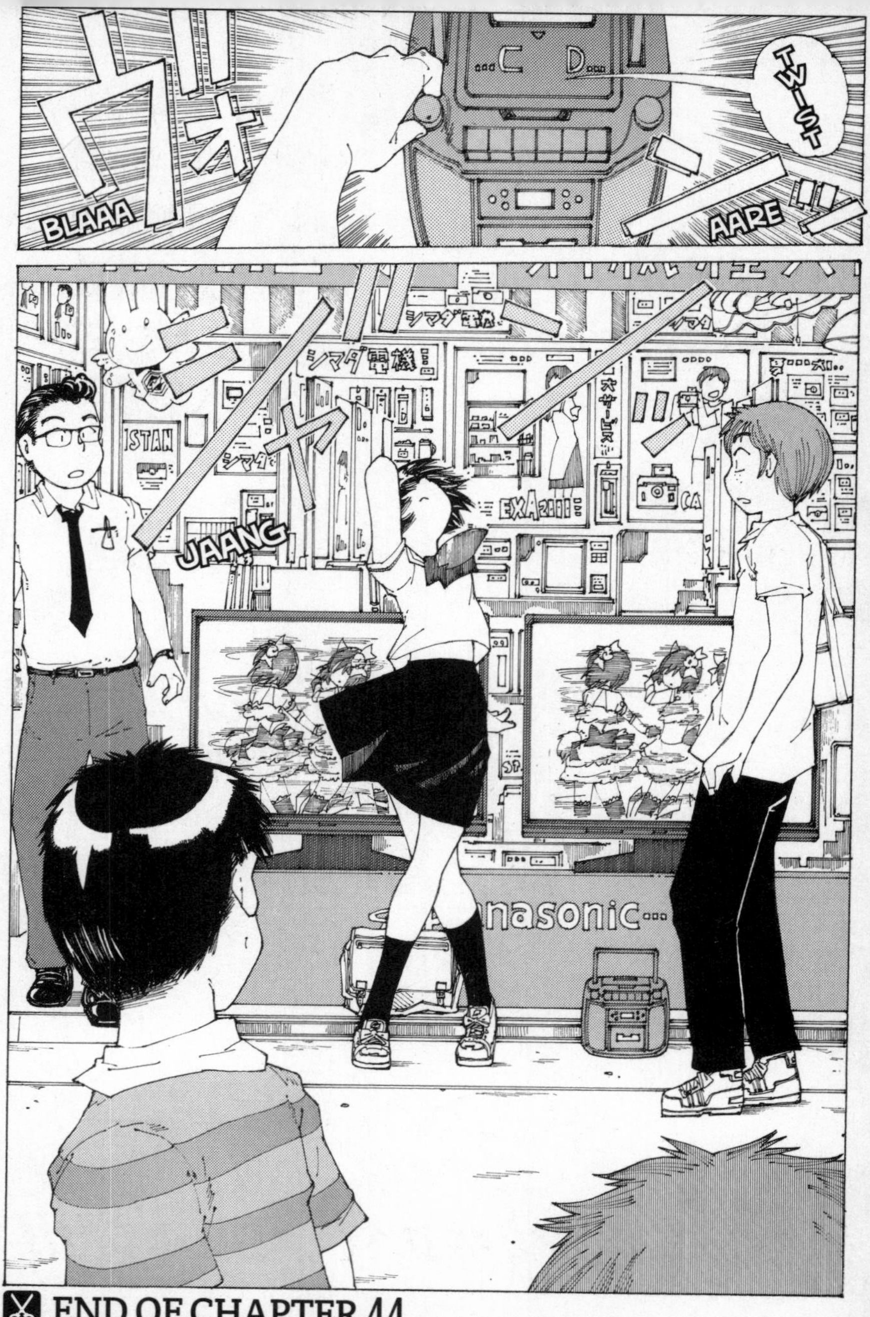
TWIST
AARE
BLAAA
JAANG
シマダ電機

END OF CHAPTER 44

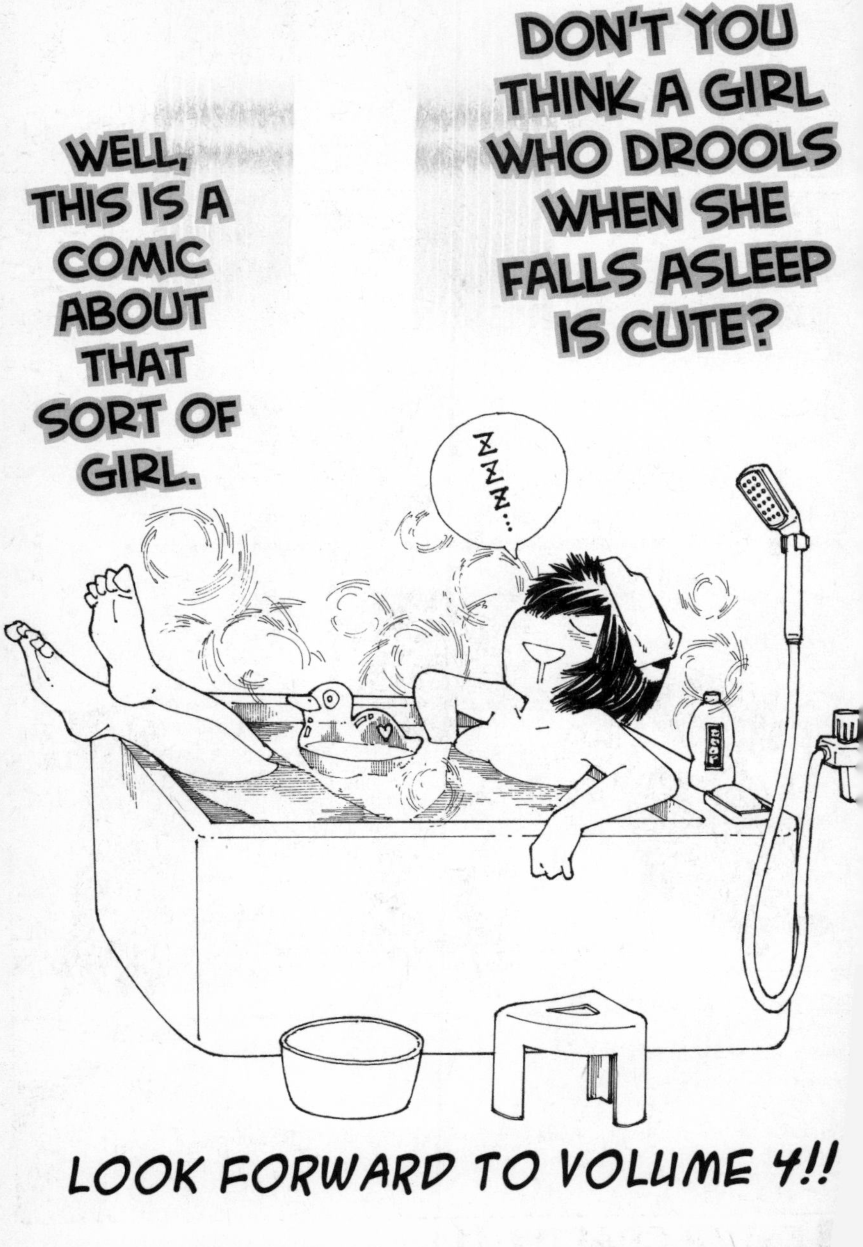
DON'T YOU THINK A GIRL WHO DROOLS WHEN SHE FALLS ASLEEP IS CUTE?
WELL, THIS IS A COMIC ABOUT THAT SORT OF GIRL.
ZZZ...
LOOK FORWARD TO VOLUME 4!!

MYSTERIOUS GIRLFRIEND X, VOLUME 3

A Vertical Comics Edition

Translation: Rebecca Cottrill
Production: Risa Cho
          Anthony Quintessenza

First published in Japan in 2009-10 by Kodansha, Ltd., Tokyo
Publication rights for this English edition arranged through Kodansha, Ltd., Tokyo
English language version produced by Vertical, Inc., New York

Published by Vertical, Inc., New York

Originally published in Japanese as *Nazo no Kanojo X 5 & 6* by Kodansha, Ltd., 2009-10
Nazo no Kanojo X first serialized in *Afternoon*, Kodansha, Ltd., 2004, 2006-2014

This is a work of fiction.

ISBN: 978-1-942993-70-4

Manufactured in Canada

First Edition

Vertical, Inc.
451 Park Avenue South
7th Floor
New York, NY 10016
www.vertical-comics.com

Vertical books are distributed through Penguin-Random House Publisher Services.